The Heroes We Needed

The B-29ers Who Ended World War II and My Fight to Save the Forgotten Stories of the Greatest Generation

---

Trevor B. McIntyre

Helion & Company

Helion & Company Limited
Unit 8 Amherst Business Centre
Budbrooke Road
Warwick
CV34 5WE
England
Tel. 01926 499 619
Email: info@helion.co.uk
Website: www.helion.co.uk
Twitter: @helionbooks
Visit our blog at blog.helion.co.uk

Published by Helion & Company 2024
Designed and typeset by Mach 3 Solutions (www.mach3solutions.co.uk)
Cover designed by Paul Hewitt, Battlefield Design (www.battlefield-design.co.uk)

Text © Trevor B. McIntyre 2024
Images © as individually credited
Maps drawn by George Anderson © Helion & Company Ltd 2024

ISBN 978-1-804511-65-7

British Library Cataloguing-in-Publication Data.
A catalogue record for this book is available from the British Library.

For details of other military history titles published by Helion & Company Limited contact the above address or visit our website: http://www.helion.co.uk.

We always welcome receipt of book proposals from prospective authors.

To the Missing in Action, I dedicate this book to you.

You are not forgotten.

The Veterans Crisis Line is a free and confidential 24-hour helpline staffed by councilors specially trained to help veterans in crisis. If you or a veteran you know is in distress, please reach out to the Veterans Crisis Line by dialing 988 and then press 1, or visit veteranscrisisline.net.

Contents

List of Photographs in Text | vi
List of Maps | vii
Prologue | xi

1 The Greatest Gamble of All | 17
2 The War of Production | 31
3 Tempting Fate | 39
4 We Are Going to Build It | 46
5 The Battle of Kansas | 55
6 The Global 20th | 66
7 Friends Through History | 78
8 The Beginning of the End | 99
9 Miracle Over Nagoya | 111
10 The Price of Freedom | 119
11 Thank God for the Marines | 135
12 Letters from Iwo Jima | 150
13 Japan's Invisible Ally | 157
14 The Night Tokyo Died | 168
15 It's All Ashes | 176
16 Voices from the Past | 182
17 Flying for Uncle Sam | 190
18 The Red, White and Blue | 201
19 Downfall | 226
20 Little Boy and Fat Man | 238
21 The Victory Boys | 248
22 A New Type of Bomb | 255
23 Evacuate Your Cities | 265
24 A New Gimmick | 268
25 The Sacred Decision | 279
26 The End | 298
Epilogue | 304
Postscript | 322

Acknowledgments | 325
Notes | 327
Bibliography | 358
Index | 371

List of Photographs in Text

The telegram informing Mrs. Bonne that her son is missing over Japan.   xv
"We Can Do It!" war production poster.   31
The major sub-assemblies of the B-29.   37
An early Wright R-3350 engine that powered the XB-29.   41
A warning that any B-29er who bailed out over Japan would be executed.   77
Sergeant Jim Krantz and the crewmates who saved his life.   115
A letter written to a B-29 gunner missing over Japan.   131
The Fourth Marine Division cemetery on Iwo Jima.   149
A thankful B-29 crew after crash landing on Iwo Jima.   156
Harold Brown interviews Ben Kuroki for *The Fighting AAF* radio show.   200
Lieutenant Raymond Shumway's B-29 crew.   209
The Trinity explosion.   226
"Heed this warning and evacuate these cities immediately" leaflet.   238
Armorers prepare to load the Little Boy atomic bomb.   247
The Fat Man atomic bomb.   264

See also Plate section containing additional photographs.

List of Maps

1   World War II B-29 Operations Against Japan.   x
2   The results of General LeMay's bombing campaign.   296

Warning: This book contains the wartime quotes of American service members and the slurs they used about the Japanese during World War II, all of which are considered to be highly offensive today. I do not believe in censoring history, no matter how offensive it may be. Therefore, I will not censor the history in this book. If you are offended by these words and the men who used them while fighting against a vicious and fanatical enemy, please do not read any further.

Respectfully,

Trevor B. McIntyre

We are in the midst of the most momentous war of modern times. A coalition of powerful and ruthless enemies seeks not only to overwhelm us, but to annihilate our institutions and our civilization. They have struck with suddenness and with all the force at their command and have shown that it is their aim to conquer swiftly and completely. Therefore, we must press them back behind their own borders and there defeat them so decisively that they can never again attempt to impose their wills and their ways of life on a people who cherish liberty above all things; a people always willing to lay down their lives to preserve their freedom.

The United States is now engaged in the greatest aircraft production program ever undertaken by any country. That program, however, can be translated into air supremacy only if we can muster the qualified man power to keep our planes flying. And the source of this man power lies in the youth of the land – they are the men who will "Keep 'em Flying!"

Youth alone has the physical fitness, the mental alertness, the personal daring to meet the acid test for air crews of high-powered military aircraft.

Our Nation's future depends upon command of the air. The future of freedom and liberty everywhere is in the hands of our youth.

U.S. Army Air Forces recruitment booklet, 1943

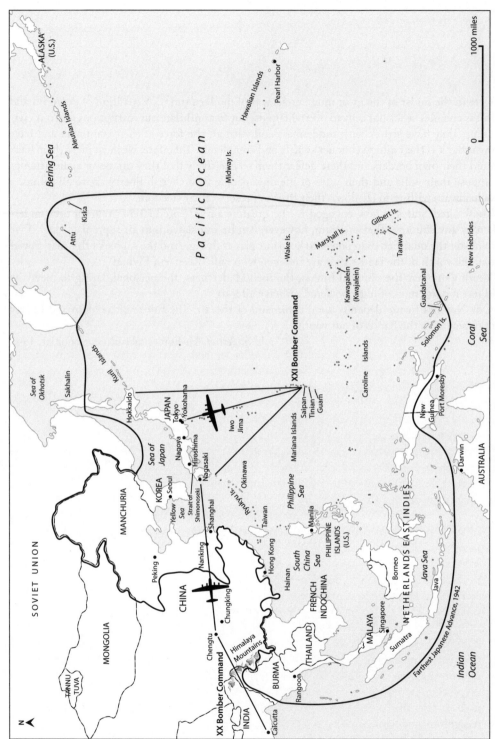

Map 1: World War II B-29 Operations Against Japan.

Prologue

If the mailman knew what he was delivering that day, he would have been much more careful with it. Don't get me wrong, the box wasn't *totally* destroyed during its journey across the country, but it was clearly kicked around without any concern for what was inside it. Why do they always do that? If they only knew what was passing through their hands, they all would have handled that box with the utmost care and respect.

It was the last Thursday in March, back in 2014, when I received that beat-up package in the mail from Seattle, Washington. After a miserable winter that will always be remembered here in North Georgia for the snowstorm that paralyzed Atlanta, I was looking forward to spring and warmer weather. What I wasn't looking forward to, in all honesty, is what was in that box from Seattle. Two whole days passed before I found the courage to open it.

When I sat down to write these words, I was exhausted because I couldn't sleep last night. The thought of what I was going to write about today had kept me up all night, and not in a good way. Even though years have since passed, I couldn't sleep because I kept thinking about what was in that box from Seattle, and the fact that I was going to have to look at it again. I knew this day would eventually come, but that didn't make it any easier.

You may have noticed that the subtitle of this book is *The B-29ers Who Ended World War II and My Fight to Save the Forgotten Stories of the Greatest Generation*. I know some of you will wonder why this generation deserves to be called the "Greatest Generation." The origins of the term date back to the 50th anniversary of D-Day, the Allied invasion of German-occupied France. During his coverage of the anniversary in 1994 for NBC News, Tom Brokaw looked out over a crowd of World War II Veterans and proclaimed: "I think this is the greatest generation any society has ever produced." It went on to become the title of Brokaw's best-selling book in 1998 that profiled the everyday Americans who came together to help defeat the Axis powers.

In the years that followed, many words were written as to why this generation of Americans, though far from infallible, are deserving of those accolades. But in all that has been written, I can find no better words to express why their generation is worthy of such a distinction than the following:

> This generation of Americans has come to realize, with a present and personal realization, that there is something larger and more important than the life of any individual or of any individual group – something for which a man will sacrifice, and gladly sacrifice, not only his pleasures, not only his goods, not only his associations with those he loves, but his life itself. In time of crisis when the future is in the balance, we come to understand, with full recognition and devotion, what this Nation is, and what we owe to it.

Those words were written by President Franklin D. Roosevelt two months after the Japanese attacked Pearl Harbor. While Americans were still coming to terms with their sudden entry into the largest war in the history of mankind, the President already knew how special this generation was, and the heavy price they would pay for freedom.

One of those men the President was referring to was Gerald Bonne. Jerry, as everyone called him, was just a boy when those words were written, but like most of his generation, boys would have to grow up very fast. When he was a junior in high school, Jerry took a part-time job at a shipyard to help with the war effort. He was only 17 years old then, but every day after school, Monday through Friday, Jerry worked a four-hour shift at the yard and helped build new ships for the U.S. Navy. On the weekends, when most teenagers had other things on their mind, Jerry was back at the shipyard working the 4 o'clock to midnight shift every Saturday. The local newspaper did a story once about Jerry and two other high school boys who had war jobs. The reporter said they were "boys studying books by day; men building ships and planes by night."

Three months after his 19th birthday, Jerry entered service with the U.S. Army Air Forces and left home for the first time. By the time he was 20, Jerry had earned his aerial gunner wings and a promotion to the rank of sergeant. He also began flying combat missions over Japan as a tail gunner on the most advanced bomber in the world, the Boeing B-29.

I wish I could tell you what Jerry was doing when he was 21, but Jerry never got to see his 21st birthday. On the evening of July 12, 1945, Jerry's crew took off from their base to bomb an oil refinery in Kawasaki, Japan. They never returned.

It's been nearly 80 years since Jerry and his crew disappeared, and to this day, no trace of their B-29 has ever been found. Jerry is still listed as Missing in Action by the Department of Defense. He is just one of the more than 72,000 American service members who are still missing from World War II alone.

Inside that beat-up package that arrived from Seattle on that last Thursday in March, back in 2014, there was an old scrapbook that was assembled decades before I was born. Jerry's mother put it together after he died. I didn't want to look at it though, because I knew what it would do to me. That's why it sat on my dining room table for two days before I opened it.

When I finally did open the box, the first thing I found in the scrapbook was the Purple Heart Certificate that was presented to Jerry's mother. It read in part:

> To Sergeant Gerald D. Bonne … for military merit and for wounds received in action resulting in his death July 13, 1945.

I wasn't able to serve in the military, but when I was a little boy, I already knew what the Purple Heart medal was for. My father was awarded the Purple Heart for the wounds he suffered in Vietnam. As I looked at Jerry's Purple Heart Certificate, I couldn't help but to think of my father's certificate and how similar they were, only Jerry's had four extra words printed on his: "resulting in his death." It reminded me of something you'll read about later in this book, but I'll share part of it with you now: "It's beyond us to understand the tragedies of war."

As I slowly looked through the rest of the scrapbook, I discovered everything from Jerry's birth certificate and baby pictures to his high school diploma. This was Jerry's entire life. Then I found the telegram from the War Department. It informed Jerry's mother that her son had gone missing somewhere over Japan. I couldn't imagine the anguish that small piece of paper must have caused her. On the next page, I found a letter to Jerry's mother from his commanding officer, written after Jerry and his crew disappeared. I'd heard about those kinds of letters before, but this was the first one I had ever seen. He didn't have any answers for her, though.

After a few minutes, I flipped back towards the beginning of the scrapbook to a large photo of Jerry and his crew standing in front of their B-29. I thought about that telegram again, and the letters from the War Department that came after it. They all looked so young.

This scrapbook was all that remained of Gerald Bonne's short life. And I had just bought it all on eBay for $266.25.

*   *   *

As I'm typing these words on my 1936 Underwood Champion typewriter, Jerry's scrapbook is sitting next to me on the kitchen counter. I got it out yesterday to prepare myself for what I'm writing now.

To be honest with you, I wasn't looking forward to this. I wasn't looking forward to the pain and the sorrow and the depression that I knew would return as soon as I looked at that scrapbook again. Before yesterday, I had not laid eyes on it since that day back in 2014. I know this is going to sound silly to you, and maybe I shouldn't even admit this, but I was afraid to look at it again. That's why it's been packed away this whole time. I knew what it would do to me the next time I saw it, and nobody wants to put themselves through something like that for no reason. No one *wants* to feel this way.

I tried, but I can't find the words to explain to you why it affects me so much. It just does. But now that it's sitting here next to me as I'm typing, it's hard not to look at it.

The words aren't coming so easy right now, so I just stare at the scrapbook and think about Jerry and his mother, and what his life could have been. And then it all starts to get to me, so I have to start typing again to distract myself. But it doesn't help.

*   *   *

You're probably wondering how a person could sell something like Jerry's scrapbook. As you embark upon this journey with me, you're going to ask yourself that question a lot. I won't always have the answers for you, though. (Jerry's scrapbook was found at an estate sale and resold for profit on eBay.)

You might also be wondering how I came to buy Jerry's scrapbook in the first place. That part of the story began when I was very young, after I discovered a book my father had about the Boeing B-29 Superfortress, the bomber that ended World War II. My father had lots of other books about other airplanes, but there was just something about the B-29 that I was drawn to. I'll never forget how I used to hide behind his chair in our family room and spend what felt like hours looking through that book. I was still too young to read then, but I was fascinated by all the pictures it had of these majestic bombers. Thanks to that book, my lifelong interest in the B-29 was born.

When I was 21 years old, my fascination turned into an obsession when I realized that I could actually own a piece of a B-29, if I looked hard enough. Up to that point in my life, I had only read about the B-29 in history books, but after some searching, I was soon holding an actual piece of B-29 history in my hands. I was hooked. From that moment on, I started buying all the B-29 parts I could find.

A short time later, my interests grew to include the remarkable stories of the men who flew on these bombers during the war. The B-29ers, as they were called, would fly some of the most harrowing missions of World War II, and the more I learned about them, the more I admired them. What troubled me, though, was that so many B-29ers and their fellow World War II Veterans were passing away now, and instead of being cherished as family heirlooms, I kept seeing their militaria from the war being sold off for easy cash. All of this history was for sale, and the clearinghouse was an internet auction site called eBay.

The numbers were shocking. Between 1941 and 1945, over 16 million Americans served in the military. When I first started collecting, the number of living American World War II Veterans was around five million. By the time this book is released, less than 100,000 of them will still be alive. It's heartbreaking to watch as the Greatest Generation slowly fades away. All too often, their stories are also fading with them. I found that there were a number of oral history projects already underway to record some of their stories before it was too late, but what about those who had already passed away? Who would record their stories?

I'm not a man of great means, but I felt obligated to do something about it. It soon dawned on me that some of these stories could be preserved through the militaria the veterans had left behind. By saving things like their old uniforms, photographs and souvenirs from the war, in a way, I could also save their stories. These veterans could no longer speak, but their militaria could.

From that day on, each and every night, I scoured eBay for B-29 parts and militaria that told a story. Usually, all I had to go with the items I found was the veteran's name, and then I'd research their service history to learn more about them. Some of the stories I discovered were astonishing.

I'm 42 years old now, and in the 20 years I've been collecting, I've found some incredible things. One night on eBay, I found a Boeing data plate that came from a B-29 named *Ding How* that flew on the first bombing mission to Japan. The seller didn't know what he had, and I only realized its significance after I looked up the B-29's serial number. I was amazed to learn that this little metal plate was actually there on that first historic mission to Japan. I had to buy it. Then I did some more research and discovered that most of its crew were killed six months later in another B-29. Those are the kind of stories that are easily forgotten, and that's exactly what I'm fighting to save, one piece at a time.

As you read this epic saga about the B-29ers and some of their stories that I've discovered, I hope that you will remember their names and their sacrifices. And I hope that you will share their stories with others. We have to remember men like Gerald Bonne, and what they sacrificed for us. Because if we don't, who will?

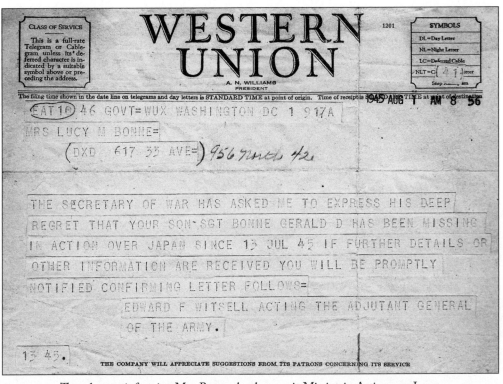

The telegram informing Mrs. Bonne that her son is Missing in Action over Japan.

1

The Greatest Gamble of All

On a warm autumn day in Washington, President Roosevelt looked up from his desk and smiled when his old friend Alexander Sachs walked into the Oval Office. Alex was known for always greeting the President with a joke, and today was no different. But what he came to talk about was no joking matter. After pouring his longtime advisor a glass of brandy, the two men toasted, and then the President listened intently as Alex briefed him on an urgent matter that sounded more like science fiction than fact.

"Alex, what you are after is to see that the Nazis don't blow us up," Roosevelt concluded, when Alex finished reading his report aloud.

"Precisely," he replied.

Recognizing the dire implications, Roosevelt summoned his trusted aide, General Edwin Watson, into the Oval Office and drew his attention to the file Alex had just presented to him: "This requires action."[1]

Inside the file that Alex gave to the President on October 11, 1939, was a two-page letter with an ominous warning:

> In the course of the last four months it has been made probable – through the work of Joliot in France as well as Fermi and Szilard in America – that it may become possible to set up a nuclear chain reaction in a large mass of uranium by which vast amounts of power and large quantities of new radium-like elements would be generated. Now it appears almost certain that this could be achieved in the immediate future.
>
> This new phenomenon would also lead to the construction of bombs, and it is conceivable – though much less certain – that extremely powerful bombs of a new type may thus be constructed. A single bomb of this type, carried by boat and exploded in a port, might very well destroy the whole port together with some of the surrounding territory.[2]

The letter was signed by Albert Einstein.

Having settled in the United States in 1933 after Adolf Hitler came to power in his native Germany, Einstein was now gravely concerned about the recent discoveries that could lead to the creation of a terrifying new type of bomb with a destructive power never before seen on earth. Nazi Germany had recently stopped all exports of uranium from its mines in Czechoslovakia as further research continued in Berlin, and acting together with fellow physicists Leo Szilard,

Edward Teller and Eugene Wigner, Einstein sought to forewarn the President about these troubling developments that could give Hitler the power to destroy entire cities with just a single bomb.

The Einstein-Szilard letter would spark the beginning of America's ultra-secret Manhattan Project that six years later produced the atomic bomb and propelled the world into the nuclear age, but there was another secret project soon to be underway whose size and cost would exceed even the development of the atomic bomb. It was often referred to as the "three-billion-dollar gamble," the largest and most expensive weapons program of World War II, and it would forever change the face of warfare.

1939

In the spring of 1939, 53-year-old Major General Henry H. "Hap" Arnold, the Chief of the U.S. Army Air Corps, was facing a serious problem. Arnold's long flying career began back in 1911 when he learned to fly at the Wright Brothers Flying School, which made him one of only two pilots in the entire U.S. Army. In the decades that followed, Arnold had watched the airplane advance from rickety wood and fabric flying machines into sleek warplanes that sped through the sky at hundreds of miles per hour. The problem was that those sleek warplanes were *not* American.[3]

Now less than a year into his new job as Chief of the Air Corps, with war clouds looming over Europe, Arnold found himself at the helm of an antiquated air force whose warplanes, with the exception of heavy bombers, were all outclassed by the latest German designs. The Air Corps had a lot of catching up to do, and Arnold began by convening a special advisory board led by Brigadier General Walter Kilner to make recommendations on what type of warplanes the Air Corps should develop in response to Nazi Germany and its highly advanced air force, the Luftwaffe.

Joining the Kilner Board that spring was legendary aviator Charles Lindbergh, the first pilot to fly solo across the Atlantic Ocean. During his visit to Germany less than a year earlier, Lindbergh's fame had gained him unprecedented access to German aircraft factories and the Luftwaffe's newest warplanes. The advances of the German aircraft industry, Lindbergh discovered, were staggering. The largest and best-equipped air force of the day, Lindbergh was thoroughly impressed by the Luftwaffe and later confided to Arnold that with an air force that powerful, he felt that Hitler held the destruction of any major city on the continent, or in Britain, in his hands.[4]

The rise of the Luftwaffe began after Adolf Hitler seized power in 1933 and undertook a massive rearmament program in direct violation of the Treaty of Versailles. As part of the peace terms that ended the First World War, the Treaty of Versailles imposed strict restrictions on the German military and forbid the country from possessing an air force, but the League of Nations did nothing to stop Hitler's rearmament as his lust for power grew. Nazi Germany was now openly violating the Treaty of Versailles with the mass production of new fighter, bomber and attack aircraft, among other rearmament programs, and the growing threat spurred a renewed urgency for the Air Corps to expand and develop better warplanes.

By the end of June, the Kilner Board had completed its report, and among its recommendations was the development of a new long-range heavy bomber. The design of heavy bombers was the only area in which the United States truly held an edge over the Luftwaffe. The Boeing B-17 Flying Fortress was the premier four-engine heavy bomber of its day, but the Air Corps only had 23 of them in service by September of 1939.[5]

The funding to procure more bombers and strengthen the Air Corps had long been stifled by both a short-sighted War Department, which believed airplanes were merely a support weapon for the infantry, and the isolationists in Congress, who could not conceive of a threat that would require an expenditure for heavy bombers, when the United States already had the battleships of the U.S. Navy and two oceans protecting it from the troubles of the world.[6]

In the interwar years, the former commander of American air units in France during the First World War, Brigadier General Billy Mitchell, fervently argued that air power would be a decisive factor in the next war, but his warnings were ignored by the Army and the Navy. To prove how vulnerable warships were to air attack, Mitchell's bombers sank the "unsinkable" First World War German battleship *Ostfriesland* during a bombing test in 1921 off Cape Hatteras, North Carolina. When the Joint Army and Navy Board issued its findings on the test, they stated that nothing conclusive had been proven with regard to air power, and that the battleship was still the "backbone of the fleet and the bulwark of the nation's sea defense."[7] General Mitchell continued to be an outspoken advocate for air power, and it eventually cost him his military career. Less than 20 years after sinking the *Ostfriesland*, his prophetic warnings were about to come true.

Faced with the rise of the Luftwaffe, the most powerful air force the world had yet seen, General Arnold was in a precarious position. By August of 1939, the Air Corps had a strength of just 26,526 men and 1,500 tactical aircraft. But of those warplanes, only 800 were first-line combat aircraft, and over 300 were light observation planes.[8] The standard fighter, attack and bombardment aircraft of the Air Corps were all woefully obsolete, which led President Roosevelt to accurately describe them as "antiquated weapons." Others were more blunt in their assessment, considering the Air Corps to be a "fifth rate air force" by the day's standards.[9]

The Air Corps' infrastructure was also severely lacking. To defend the entire 3.8 million square miles of the Continental United States, Arnold had just 17 air bases and a mere 2,000 pilots.[10] By comparison, the Luftwaffe had swelled to over half a million men and some 3,750 first-line aircraft, plus reserves. The number of men the Luftwaffe employed in maintenance and supply alone was almost three times greater than the entire Air Corps combined.[11]

The first program to strengthen the Air Corps and procure new warplanes was finally passed by Congress in April of 1939, but the $300 million plan was still barely underway by August. Arnold would have to work fast. In the predawn hours of September 1, 1939, war erupted in Europe. In the United States, Judy Garland was dazzling moviegoers in *The Wizard of Oz* as Hitler's forces invaded Poland.[12] World War II had begun.

France and Britain declared war on Germany two days later in defense of their ally, but they did little to help the Polish Army as it struggled against the German assault. On September 17, under a secret pact with Germany to divide Polish territory, the Soviet Union launched its own attack into Poland. By early October, crushed by an invasion on two fronts, all of Poland had fallen.

Emboldened by their victory in Poland, the Soviet Union invaded Finland on November 30. Despite being vastly outnumbered, the Finnish Army staged a masterful defense that ground the Red Army's advance to a halt.

1940

On the other side of the Atlantic, the recommendations of the Kilner Board were moving forward. The Air Corps released its performance specifications for a new "super-bomber" to aircraft manufactures in late January and invited submissions of preliminary designs for review. The Air Corps wanted a bomber that offered significantly greater range, speed and bomb capacity over the B-17. All of the proposals for the new bomber had to be submitted within 30 days, and among those responding to the challenge was the Boeing Aircraft Company of Seattle, Washington.[13]

As the design teams set to work on the new super-bomber, Hitler was already preparing for his next conquest in Europe. On April 9, Germany invaded Denmark and Norway to gain control of their ports and secure the iron ore shipments feeding Hitler's war machine. Denmark fell in a matter of hours; Norway held on for 62 days.

To keep pace with the new realities of war, the Air Corps was forced to drastically revise the specifications for their new super-bomber. All of the previous designs were rejected, and the Air Corps asked for greater bomb capacity, improved armor and self-sealing fuel tanks for better protection against battle damage, along with more defensive armament. The super-bomber was evolving from the air battles over Europe.

While the design teams worked feverishly to meet the Air Corps' new specifications, Hitler shocked the world with a massive invasion in May that consumed four more countries. Under the protective cover of the Luftwaffe, Hitler's forces swept into Luxembourg, Belgium, the Netherlands and France with frightening speed. The world was changing. On May 16, President Roosevelt addressed Congress:

> These are ominous days – days whose swift and shocking developments force every neutral nation to look to its defenses in the light of new factors. The brutal force of modern offensive war has been loosed in all its horror. New powers of destruction, incredibly swift and deadly, have been developed; and those who wield them are ruthless and daring.[14]

Nazi Germany seemed all but unstoppable in May of 1940. Luxembourg fell the first day of the invasion. The Netherlands held on for four days, while Belgium surrendered after 18 days. Even the mighty French Army was reeling and losing ground.

Back in the United States, just 24 hours after Hitler's offensive began, the Boeing Aircraft Company submitted their preliminary design plans to the Air Corps for a radically new bomber. Simply designated as the Model 345, it was a daring design that reflected all of the costly lessons learned in the skies over Europe.

Across the Atlantic in war-torn France, the fighting was not going well for the Allies. By the end of May, in what British Prime Minister Winston Churchill called a "colossal military disaster," the British Expeditionary Force was cut off by the Germans and nearly pushed back into the sea at the small French port of Dunkirk. The British launched an all-out effort to rescue the besieged force on May 26. After mustering a flotilla of every available vessel, including civilian pleasure craft, over 338,000 British and French troops were evacuated across the English Channel by June 4.

The "Miracle of Dunkirk" narrowly averted a disaster for the British Army, but the battle for the remainder of France raged on. A defiant Winston Churchill addressed the British people after the evacuation:

Even though large tracts of Europe and many old and famous States have fallen or may fall into the grip of the Gestapo and all the odious apparatus of Nazi rule, we shall not flag or fail. We shall go on to the end, we shall fight in France, we shall fight on the seas and oceans, we shall fight with growing confidence and growing strength in the air, we shall defend our Island, whatever the cost may be, we shall fight on the beaches, we shall fight on the landing grounds, we shall fight in the fields and in the streets, we shall fight in the hills; we shall never surrender.[15]

The total collapse of France loomed as Churchill spoke, and a German invasion of the British Isles now seemed imminent. But despite entire countries being overrun by Hitler, the U.S. Congress was still not forthcoming with new appropriations to further strengthen the Air Corps. As late as April of 1940, Congress had slashed an Air Corps request for 166 new warplanes down to 57, and refused to provide any funding for long-range bombers because they were "aggressive" weapons.[16]

Two months later, the Battle of France had changed everything. President Roosevelt was now calling for 50,000 new warplanes a year, and Congress was suddenly anxious to provide all of the money necessary for national defense. "In forty-five minutes I was given $1,500,000,000 and told to get an air force," General Arnold recalled. Arnold immediately set out to do just that.[17]

The Air Corps was so impressed with Boeing's plans for the Model 345 that an expenditure of $85,652 was quickly approved on June 14 for wind tunnel tests and further design data. Elsewhere in the world, the Allied resistance in France was crumbling, and Paris fell to the Germans the same day. Italy had also declared war on France and Britain four days earlier, and they would launch their own invasion into France on June 20. France was doomed.

Fearing an imminent Nazi invasion across the English Channel, and with nothing less than their very existence at stake, Churchill addressed his beleaguered countrymen about the battle ahead:

Upon this battle depends the survival of Christian civilization. Upon it depends our own British life, and the long continuity of our institutions and our Empire. The whole fury and might of the enemy must very soon be turned on us. Hitler knows that he will have to break us in this island or lose the war. If we can stand up to him, all Europe may be freed and the life of the world may move forward into broad, sunlit uplands. But if we fail, then the whole world, including the United States, including all that we have known and cared for, will sink into the abyss of a new Dark Age made more sinister, and perhaps more protracted, by the lights of perverted science. Let us therefore brace ourselves to our duties, and so bear ourselves that if the British Empire and its Commonwealth last for a thousand years, men will still say, "This was their finest hour."[18]

By the end of June, Germany had occupied the Channel Islands off the French coast of Normandy, while British colonies in Africa were under attack by Italian forces. The enemy was closing in.

On June 27, additional funds were approved for further design data on the Model 345, and construction began in Seattle on a full-scale wooden mock-up of the airframe. The Model 345 was now officially an Air Corps project and designated as the XB-29 (experimental bomber,

29th design).[19] The decision to move the XB-29 project forward came at a critical time. France had surrendered just days earlier, and while Hitler's advance was temporarily halted by the English Channel, that expanse of water, only 21 miles wide at its narrowest point, was now all that separated Britain from the German Army.

With the Battle of France having ended in disaster for the Allies, the Battle of Britain was about to begin. During June and July, the Luftwaffe began probing British defenses with small-scale bombing raids and attacks on supply convoys in the English Channel. By the middle of August, the Luftwaffe began their main assault to destroy the Royal Air Force in southern England, shifting their attacks to coastal radar stations and airfields. The fight for control of the skies was about to become one of the largest air battles in history. The 18th of August would go down as "The Hardest Day" of the Battle of Britain. The Luftwaffe was fighting to gain air superiority ahead of an invasion, while the RAF was fighting for survival. Hundreds of fighters and bombers dueled in the skies over southern England, making it the costliest single day for both air forces, but the RAF held the advantage and inflicted greater losses on the Luftwaffe.

Six days later, as the air battles continued to rage over Britain, the Air Corps signed a contract with Boeing to build two XB-29 prototypes for flight testing. A third XB-29 was ordered in November, along with a fourth example for destructive testing.

After failing to achieve air superiority over England, Hitler ordered the Luftwaffe to switch the focus of their attacks to British cities and industrial centers in September. Hitler was attempting to bomb the British into submission. London alone would be bombed for 57 straight nights.

On September 27, Germany, Italy and Japan signed the Tripartite Pact in Berlin, establishing the Axis powers. The three countries were now working together to establish a "new order" in Europe and Greater East Asia.[20] The need for the new super-bomber had never been greater.

With orders placed for four XB-29s, Boeing quickly went to work. The daunting task of turning lines on paper and wind tunnel models into a flying airplane fell to men like Wellwood Beall, Eddie Allen, George Schairer and Edward Wells. At 43 years old and Chief of Boeing Flight Test and Aerodynamics, Eddie Allen was the oldest member of the team and widely considered to be the greatest test pilot in the world. The rest of the men designing the B-29 were all in their late twenties and early thirties. Wellwood Beall, the Chief Engineer, was 33, and George Schairer, the Chief Aerodynamicist, was just 27 years old. From the talented minds of these young Americans would rise the most technologically advanced bomber in the world.

1941

From its inception, the B-29 was designed for one purpose: strategic bombing. The genesis of strategic bombing dated back to the First World War, long before the technology and aircraft existed to make it a feasible strategy, and work continued throughout the interwar years by men like General Billy Mitchell and others, who slowly advanced the concept until aircraft designs could make it a reality.

The early doctrine of strategic bombing was a radical concept that future wars could be fought and won through air power with a sustained bombing campaign that would systematically destroy the industrial heart of the enemy, deny it the ability to support its forces, and ultimately shatter its morale and determination to continue the war. In short, strategic bombing was a strategy to win wars by using air power to destroy the enemy's will and capability to continue fighting, without the need for the long and bloody land battles of the First World War.[21]

On paper, the XB-29 was a bomber that could potentially do just that, but actually building the new super-bomber presented a myriad of challenges to overcome. The first blueprints for the XB-29 were released in early May of 1941, and Boeing's Plant 1 in Seattle became a flurry of activity as construction began on the first prototype. It would still be another six months before all of the aerodynamic work was completed, and a full year before all of the blueprints would be available. In the meantime, the 50-man workforce on the plant floor, which would soon swell to 700, constructed the XB-29 in the order in which they received the drawings, leaving gaps in the airframe until the blueprints for those sections became available.[22]

Less than two weeks after construction began, the President of Boeing received a letter that changed everything:

> The War Department anticipates placing an order with you for approximately the following airplanes, funds for which in the amount of ten million dollars are available at this time: 250 B-29 type airplanes, 335 additional B-17 type airplanes.[23]

Hitler had launched two more invasions into Yugoslavia and Greece in April, and both countries were now firmly under Axis control. In North Africa, the Afrika Korps under General Erwin Rommel was advancing in Libya and pushing the British back into Egypt. The United States could not afford to wait any longer. The B-29 was ordered into mass production "off the drawing board," before the first prototype had been built, before all design and engineering work was completed, and before a B-29 had even been flown and tested.[24] These were ominous days.

The massive four-engine bomber that slowly began to take shape in Seattle was like nothing the world had seen before. The B-29's cylindrical fuselage stretched 99 feet long and featured pressurized crew cabins – a first for a military aircraft – and its two cavernous bomb bays could carry 10 tons of bombs. The top of the bomber's tail alone stood almost 30 feet above the ground. Without fuel or bombs, the B-29 weighed 36 tons empty.

The heart of the B-29 was Boeing's new "117" wing. Stretching 141 feet wide and developed after thousands of hours of research and testing, the "117" wing was the most efficient airfoil ever designed for a bomber of its day, and it would allow the B-29 to fly higher, farther and faster than any other bomber in the world.[25] The B-29 was so large that the Wright brothers' first powered flight at Kitty Hawk just 37 years earlier could have taken off and landed upon the bomber's wingspan with room to spare.

The futuristic design of the B-29 also featured other innovations, such as defensive gun turrets that were fired by remote control from inside the cabins, an advanced electrical system to operate everything from the wing flaps to machine guns, and dual turbosuperchargers for each of its four engines to boost high-altitude performance. Boeing even designed a long tunnel over the bomb bays to connect the forward and aft crew compartments, and four bunks were included in the aft cabin so the crew could rest during long missions. (The bunks were later deleted to make room for the radar observer's station.) Constructed with flush rivets and butt-jointed skin panels to further reduce aerodynamic drag, the B-29 was streamlined to such perfection that the drag created by just the extended landing gear was equal to that of the entire airframe with the gear retracted.[26]

"We simply undertook to produce an airplane that would have no more drag than the B-17, even though it was twice as big," recalled Wellwood Beall, the chief engineer. "In other words, an aerodynamically cleaner airplane."[27] George Schairer added that the "117" wing represented a refinement of all that was known in the science of aerodynamics, along with "a lot of darned hard work." The results were nothing less than stunning.[28]

While work was progressing on the B-29 at Seattle, a significant reorganization was happening within the U.S. Army. Based on the lessons learned in Europe, the Army Air Forces was established on June 20 to bring all aviation units of the U.S. Army under one command. The new Army Air Forces was still a subordinate division of the U.S. Army, but the restructuring gave General Arnold, now Chief of the Army Air Forces, greater autonomy and more flexibility as he continued the rapid expansion of American air power.[29]

Just two days after the Army Air Forces was established, Hitler launched Operation *Barbarossa* and invaded the Soviet Union. Spearheaded by the Luftwaffe and thousands of tanks, some three million German and Axis troops stormed across the Soviet border in what would be the largest military invasion in history. Thrusting hundreds of miles into Soviet territory with frightening speed, it was feared that the Soviet Union might totally collapse and allow Hitler to refocus all of his forces for a final assault on Britain.

Two weeks after the invasion began, President Roosevelt directed the Secretaries of War and the Navy to prepare an estimate of the "overall production requirements required to defeat our potential enemies" in the event that the United States entered the war. The planning for air requirements was given to the new Air War Plans Division, which had been created only weeks earlier with the establishment of the Army Air Forces.[30] By August, Air War Plan AWPD-1 was completed under the assumption that the United States might have to fight Germany and Japan simultaneously. In that event, the defeat of Germany would be given first priority, and AWPD-1 proposed to wage a strategic bombing campaign against Germany with B-29 raids from bases in Northern Ireland and Egypt, in addition to medium and heavy bombers from bases in Britain.[31]

Faced with the possible fall of both the Soviet Union and Britain to Hitler, the war planners also envisioned an intercontinental bomber even larger than the B-29 that could strike Europe from the Western Hemisphere. The contracts for such a bomber were awarded that October to Consolidated for two XB-36 prototypes, and to Northrop for a single XB-35 flying wing prototype. Both bombers would eventually fly in 1946, with the gigantic six-engine B-36 becoming the mainstay of the Strategic Air Command during the early days of the Cold War, but in 1941, the Army Air Forces had to prepare for any scenario.[32]

When AWPD-1 reached the Joint Army and Navy Board for review, the board took little notice of the plan and scoffed: "Air forces and naval forces can render valuable assistance, but it can be accepted as an almost invariable rule that only armies can win wars."[33] However, General George C. Marshall, the Army Chief of Staff, and Secretary of War Henry L. Stimson both liked the plan, and a date was set for it to be presented to the President. But before the President could be briefed on the plan, an event would take place that would change the course of history.

Far removed from the frozen battlefields of the Soviet Union, where fierce resistance and a harsh winter had halted Germany's advance on Moscow, the morning of December 7, 1941, was dawning bright in Oahu, Hawaii. At 7:55 a.m. on a tranquil Sunday morning, the first of more than 350 Imperial Japanese Navy warplanes from six aircraft carriers swarmed over Oahu and began attacking the American military forces on the island. The main attack was aimed at the powerful U.S. Pacific Fleet anchored at Pearl Harbor, whose destruction would eliminate the biggest threat to Japan's conquest of Southeast Asia. With the element of surprise on their side, the Japanese caught the United States completely off guard.

For the loss of only 29 aircraft during the two-hour attack, the Japanese sank or damaged 21 warships of the U.S. Pacific Fleet, and the airfields on Oahu were decimated with 188 aircraft destroyed, plus another 159 damaged. The attack left 2,403 Americans dead, and a further 1,178 were wounded.[34] The United States was at war.

While the fires were still raging at Pearl Harbor, the Japanese also attacked Hong Kong, Singapore, Guam, Midway and Wake Island, as well as launching invasions into the Philippines, Thailand and Malaya. Four days later, Germany and Italy followed Japan and declared war on the United States. On December 9, President Roosevelt spoke to a stunned nation about the long struggle that lay ahead:

> The true goal we seek is far above and beyond the ugly field of battle. When we resort to force, as now we must, we are determined that this force shall be directed toward ultimate good as well as against immediate evil. We Americans are not destroyers – we are builders.
>
> We are now in the midst of a war, not for conquest, not for vengeance, but for a world in which this Nation, and all that this Nation represents, will be safe for our children.
>
> We are going to win the war and we are going to win the peace that follows.
>
> And in the difficult hours of this day – through dark days that may be yet to come – we will know that the vast majority of the members of the human race are on our side. Many of them are fighting with us. All of them are praying for us. For in representing our cause, we represent theirs as well – our hope and their hope for liberty under God.[35]

The attack on Pearl Harbor was part of a larger Japanese offensive to expand its empire and seize control of badly needed natural resources, especially oil, after the United States imposed strict embargoes in response to Japan's hostile actions in the region. The Japanese had previously invaded Manchuria in 1931, China in 1937, French Indochina in 1940, and Korea was annexed by Japan in 1910. In the two months following Pearl Harbor, Japan would also invade the Dutch East Indies, Burma, New Guinea and the Solomon Islands, and Japanese warplanes began striking northern Australia with a devastating raid on Darwin in February that sank 11 ships, destroyed 30 aircraft, and killed 235 people.[36]

To the American people at home, the fighting still seemed thousands of miles away in the closing weeks of 1941, but the war was about to arrive on America's doorstep. Less than two weeks after Pearl Harbor, nine Japanese submarines had arrived off the West Coast of the United States. Armed with a powerful deck gun and up to 18 torpedoes each, the submarine commanders were eager to bring the war to the American homefront as they positioned themselves near key cities and ports including Los Angeles, San Francisco and San Diego.

In the predawn hours of December 18, the Japanese struck. While steaming south from Seattle near the mouth of the Columbia River, the captain of the oil tanker *L.P. St. Clair* noticed a sudden gun flash a few hundred yards away towards the open ocean. When a second flash occurred, the captain realized they were being fired upon by a submarine and immediately changed course for the safety of the Columbia River. The submarine fired eight more shells at the fleeing tanker, but the *L.P. St. Clair* escaped without any damage.[37]

A short time later, another Japanese submarine attacked the freighter *Samoa* 15 miles off California's Cape Mendocino. The submarine fired five shells and a torpedo at the freighter, and then closed to within 40 feet for a closer look. From his perch in the wheelhouse, the *Samoa's* captain watched helplessly as the submarine slowly approached.

"Hi ya!" yelled someone from the submarine.

"What do you want of us?" the captain shouted back.

No one answered as the submarine pulled away and disappeared into the night. Poor visibility and confusion had led the submarine's captain, Commander Kozo Nishino, to mistakenly believe the *Samoa* was sinking as the submarine departed. The next ship would not be so lucky.[38]

Two days later, around 1:30 p.m., Commander Nishino spotted the oil tanker *Emidio* off Cape Mendocino. Surfacing in broad daylight to attack, the submarine gave chase as the *Emidio* tried to escape, but the faster submarine overtook the slower tanker and opened fire with its deck gun. The *Emidio's* radio operator managed to send out a distress call that they were under attack just before a shell blast destroyed their radio antenna. After 10 minutes on the surface, the submarine quickly submerged just as two American bombers roared overhead. One of the bombers circled around and dropped a depth charge where the submarine went under, but it missed the target.

A few minutes later, some of the *Emidio's* crew, who were now in lifeboats, spotted the submarine's periscope rising above the surface. The *Emidio* was still afloat, so Commander Nishino fired a torpedo to finish it off. His torpedo struck the ship in the stern, killing two crewmen who stayed behind in the engine room, but the tanker still wouldn't sink. The bombers saw the torpedo hit and swooped down again to drop another depth charge, forcing Nishino to abandon any further attacks. Commander Nishino escaped that afternoon without any damage to his submarine, but his attack had killed five of the *Emidio's* crew, and the severely damaged tanker drifted for days until it finally ran aground 85 miles away.[39]

Only minutes after the *Emidio* was attacked, another Japanese submarine surfaced off Monterey Bay and attacked the oil tanker *Agiworld*. As the tanker fled for safety towards Santa Cruz, with the submarine in chase, several people on shore had unknowingly witnessed the attack as it unfolded. "Scores of golfers playing seaside courses reported today they had observed the tanker with huge clouds of smoke pouring from her funnel, fleeing toward Santa Cruz and zigzagging wildly," the local newspaper reported, "but most of them thought little more about it."[40]

The submarine attacks became even more brazen in the days that followed. One attack off Point Arguello, about 50 miles northwest of Santa Barbara, occurred less than two miles offshore and in plain view of stunned civilians.[41]

The sudden rash of submarine attacks led Lieutenant General John DeWitt, the commander of the Western Defense Area that included California, Oregon and Washington, to declare the West Coast a "theater of war" in the days before Christmas. No longer were the battles confined to Europe or far away in the Pacific; they were now being fought along America's coastline.[42]

1942

On January 12, the first shots between Nazi Germany and the United States were fired when U-boat Captain Reinhard Hardegen torpedoed and sank the oil tanker *Norness* off Long Island, New York. The attack marked the beginning of a long and deadly battle with German submarines as they attempted to cripple the war effort by devastating Allied shipping. The United States was woefully unprepared to counter the sudden onslaught of the U-boats, and many ships would be sunk within sight of American shores.[43]

One of the most stunning attacks occurred in April when Captain Hardegen, now on his second war patrol to America and having already sunk 12 ships, torpedoed the tanker *Gulfamerica* some four miles off Jacksonville, Florida, around 10:30 p.m. The massive explosion and fire immediately caught the attention of civilians on shore, who poured onto the beach to see what was happening.[44] As Captain Hardegen surfaced to finish off the *Gulfamerica* with his deck gun, he paused before opening fire. Looking to the nearby shore, Hardegen could see a brightly lit beachfront hotel, an amusement park and its Ferris wheel, and the headlights from cars that were stopping to watch the attack. From the position of his U-boat, Hardegen realized that a misplaced shot from his gun could land among the civilians on shore, so he maneuvered his submarine to a position between the beach and the *Gulfamerica*. With the *Gulfamerica* on fire, the U-boat was brilliantly silhouetted by the flames and clearly visible to the stunned beachgoers as Captain Hardegen opened fire with his deck gun. A few hours later, Hardegen's U-boat was badly damaged when it was attacked by an American destroyer, but the submarine managed to escape and sink three more ships before returning to its base in France.

By the middle of 1942, German U-boats would sink 397 ships along the U.S. East Coast and in the Gulf of Mexico and the Caribbean. The attacks killed 5,000 men in just six months. The submarine threat was so dire that author Ernest Hemingway would use his own personal fishing boat to hunt for U-boats in the Caribbean, but without success.[45]

Back on the West Coast, where rumors of Japanese subversion and even an invasion were running wild, the Army Air Forces ordered 500 more B-29s on January 31. This brought the total to 750 B-29s on order, plus $72.5 million in spare parts, before the first prototype had been fully built or flown.[46]

Three weeks later, as American and Filipino forces were fighting for their lives on the Bataan Peninsula in the Philippines, President Roosevelt addressed the American people on February 23 about fighting the Axis powers on a global scale:

> This war is a new kind of war. It is different from all other wars of the past, not only in its methods and weapons but also in its geography. It is warfare in terms of every continent, every island, every sea, every air lane in the world.
>
> The broad oceans which have been heralded in the past as our protection from attack have become endless battlefields on which we are constantly being challenged by our enemies.
>
> We must all understand and face the hard fact that our job now is to fight at distances which extend all the way around the globe. We fight at these vast distances because that is where our enemies are.[47]

At the precise moment President Roosevelt was speaking to the American people, a Japanese submarine was surfacing just off the California coast near Santa Barbara. Commander Kozo Nishino, who had landed the first shots against American shipping on the West Coast two months earlier, had returned with a fully rearmed submarine. The President was five minutes into his speech when Commander Nishino gave the order to commence firing. Lying just 2,500 yards off the beach, the submarine opened fire with its deck gun and would spend the next 20 minutes shelling the Ellwood Oil Field, 12 miles west of Santa Barbara.[48]

For Commander Nishino, the target that night was personal. According to legend, Nishino had visited the Ellwood Oil Field in the 1930s when he was the captain of a Japanese oil tanker. While walking up from the beach to a formal welcoming ceremony, Kozo slipped and fell into a cactus patch. The subsequent sight of the proud captain having cactus spines plucked from his butt caused a sensation with the nearby oil workers, who roared in laughter at the humiliating spectacle.[49] Perhaps Nishino had finally restored his honor after all those years, but his gunners failed to hit the refinery or any of the large storage tanks at the Ellwood complex.

While Nishino's attack did not inflict any significant damage, it did set the stage for one of the most bizarre incidents of the entire war. With fears of a Japanese invasion gripping the West Coast, nerves were running high the day after the Ellwood attack. At 7.00 p.m. that evening, naval intelligence in Los Angeles issued a warning that another Japanese attack could be expected within the next 10 hours. As darkness fell over Southern California, a large number of flares and blinking lights were reported near defense plants and oilfields. At 7:18 p.m., the California coast from Monterey to the Mexican border was placed on Yellow Alert and prepared for a possible attack.

Three hours later, when no attack came, the alert was lifted when it appeared the danger had passed. But then in the early morning hours of February 25, things suddenly began to happen.

At 1:44 a.m., a coastal radar station picked up an unidentified aerial target over the ocean. The target was quickly confirmed by two additional stations, and all three radars began tracking the target. By 2:00 a.m., the unidentified target was 120 miles west of Los Angeles and approaching the coast. Anti-aircraft batteries were put on Green Alert and readied to fire, and a blackout of Los Angeles and the surrounding area was ordered at 2:21 a.m. The radars continued tracking the target until it closed to within three miles of Los Angeles, and then it disappeared.

The target had mysteriously vanished from radar, but the skies suddenly came alive. At 2:43 a.m., a flight of unidentified airplanes were spotted near Long Beach and reported by a Coast Artillery Corps officer. A few minutes later, an Army colonel spotted about 25 planes flying over Los Angeles at 12,000 feet. At 3:06 a.m., what was described as a "balloon carrying a red flare" was spotted over Santa Monica, and four batteries of anti-aircraft guns opened fire on the object. The skies then "erupted like a volcano" as anti-aircraft guns all across the area began firing.

What followed for the next three hours would come to be known as the Battle of Los Angeles.

As searchlights frantically swept the skies for enemy raiders, reports of unidentified aircraft began streaming in as exploding anti-aircraft shells rained shrapnel down on the city. Ground observers reported seeing single, multiple, and even "swarms" of airplanes that paraded across the skies at speeds varying from "very slow" to over 200 miles per hour amid the shell bursts. A large dirigible and balloons were also spotted and fired upon, but none of the objects or aircraft could be picked up on radar.

The anti-aircraft battery at the Douglas Aircraft plant in Long Beach reported a flight of 25–30 bombers over the plant at 3:28 a.m. At 4:03 a.m., the battery spotted another flight of 15 airplanes flying over the plant. This flight flew away and then returned back over the plant two more times by 4:13 a.m. but were too high for the battery to engage with their 37mm anti-aircraft guns.

At 3:33 a.m., 15 airplanes were spotted flying over Artesia. Eight batteries of anti-aircraft guns fired 581 rounds of 3-inch shells at the aircraft before they passed out to sea over Long Beach. At 3:55 a.m., two batteries fired 100 rounds of 3-inch shells at a "balloon" over Santa

Monica. At 4:05 a.m., three batteries opened fire on another target over Long Beach and fired 246 rounds of 3-inch shells before the target passed out to sea.

The sightings and firing continued, but by dawn the skies were quiet again. Over 1,400 rounds of high-explosive shells had been fired during the battle, and despite some initial reports that proved to be wrong, not a single aircraft was shot down, nor had a single bomb been dropped from the mysterious aircraft. The battle was not without casualties, though. The pandemonium had left five people dead from heart attacks and traffic accidents.[50]

The official explanation of the incident offered no clear answers for the residents of Southern California. The Secretary of the Navy declared it a false alarm and stated that no aircraft were over the area. No American planes had left the ground that night, either. The Army's investigation, however, would come to a different finding. As announced by Secretary of War Stimson, the Army concluded that there were between one and five unidentified aircraft over the city that night.

After the war, it was determined that the Japanese had not launched any aircraft in the area that night. However, meteorological balloons were known to have been released over Los Angeles, and it is theorized that those balloons may have caused the initial alarm.[51]

It remains a mystery to this day who, or what, was in the skies over Los Angeles that night.

Had a real attack occurred, the United States would have been hard pressed to defend against it. By the end of 1941, only 45 fighters, 75 medium bombers, and 10 heavy bombers were available to defend the entire West Coast of the United States.[52]

Despite the bolstering of air defenses in the months following Pearl Harbor, the Air War Plans Division informed General Arnold in February of 1942 that there was "little probability that the air force units as now constituted could defend the vital targets against a determined carrier based attack" on the West Coast.[53] The Army Air Forces were stretched so thin that the newly formed Civil Air Patrol, a volunteer force of civilian pilots and airplanes, began flying patrols in March to spot enemy submarines. The United States was so unprepared for anti-submarine warfare that civilians in light aircraft were now an integral part in defending the American homefront.[54] To supplement the radar net along the coasts, a civilian Ground Observer Corps was also formed to report the movement of all aircraft over land. By February, the 2,400 posts established along the West Coast alone would even be staffed by inmates at Folsom Prison.[55]

On March 4, almost three months to the day after the sneak attack that thrust the United States into the war, the Japanese launched a second attack against Pearl Harbor. Using a pair of giant four-engine Kawanishi H8K flying boats, the plan for Operation *K* called for the flying boats to fly almost 2,000 miles from the Marshall Islands to the French Frigate Shoals, about 550 miles northwest of Oahu, where they would land and rendezvous with a Japanese submarine to refuel under the cover of darkness. The flying boats would then continue on to Oahu to conduct a reconnaissance of Pearl Harbor and bomb the ongoing salvage and repair operations. Operation *K* was a bold plan that ultimately ended in failure when heavy clouds and blackout conditions on Oahu prevented the crews from finding their target, and the only damage from the bombing was some broken windows in a nearby high school.

The United States took the war home to Japan on April 18 when Lieutenant Colonel Jimmy Doolittle led 16 B-25 medium bombers off the deck of the aircraft carrier *Hornet* and bombed targets in Tokyo and other Japanese cities before proceeding on to China. While the daring raid only caused minor damage, it was a huge psychological victory for the United States and greatly boosted morale after the fall of Bataan in the Philippines nine days earlier.

The Japanese struck back on June 3 when two aircraft carriers launched their warplanes and attacked Dutch Harbor in Alaska. The Japanese targeted Dutch Harbor again the following day, and by June 7 they had also invaded the islands of Kiska and Attu, part of Alaska's Aleutian Islands. The Japanese now occupied American soil.

While the attacks in the Aleutians were ongoing, the U.S. Navy dealt Japan a stunning defeat during the Battle of Midway in the North Pacific. The three-day battle in the waters surrounding the tiny Midway Atoll, plus the Battle of the Coral Sea a month earlier, resulted in the sinking of five Japanese aircraft carriers, four of which had participated in the Pearl Harbor attack, for the loss of just two American aircraft carriers. The Japanese Navy would never recover from the loss of so many of its valuable aircraft carriers.

On the East Coast of the United States, the submarine threat escalated in June when German U-boats landed two teams of saboteurs on Long Island, New York, and Ponte Vedra Beach near Jacksonville, Florida. Armed with enough cash, explosives and other specialized equipment to support a two-year campaign of terror, their mission was to spread fear and disrupt American war production by sabotaging industrial plants, transportation facilities and other targets. Germany hoped to repeat the success of a similar campaign during the First World War, when its agents blew up two million pounds of munitions that were stored at Black Tom Island in New York Harbor in July of 1916. The massive explosion caused an estimated $20 million in damages, and shrapnel from the blast even damaged the Statue of Liberty. Fortunately, all eight saboteurs would be captured by June 27 before they could carry out any attacks.

While the FBI hunted for Nazi saboteurs, the Japanese were still lurking off the West Coast. On June 20, a Japanese submarine shelled the Estevan Point lighthouse on Vancouver Island, but the only damage was some broken windows. The following night, another submarine surfaced off the mouth of the Columbia River in Oregon and fired 17 high-explosive shells at Fort Stevens, but they failed to hit the intended target. The damage from both attacks was minor, but it reaffirmed just how vulnerable the coastal regions were to submarine attack.

On August 7, the United States began the first major offensive against the Japanese when American forces invaded the island of Guadalcanal in the Solomon Islands, about 1,000 miles northeast of Australia. The brutal fighting that followed would be a harbinger of battles to come.

While the U.S. Marines were fighting it out on Guadalcanal, a Japanese submarine surfaced off the coast of Oregon on September 9 and launched a seaplane piloted by Warrant Officer Nobuo Fujita. Armed with a pair of incendiary bombs, Fujita's mission was to start a large forest fire that would spread and destroy the neighboring towns. The Japanese believed this attack would cause Americans to panic once they knew that Japan could "reach out and bomb their factories and homes from 5,000 miles away."[56]

Taking off before dawn, Fujita crossed over the Oregon coast near Brookings and flew inland before releasing his bombs, making him the first and only enemy pilot to ever bomb the Contiguous United States. However, soggy ground and the quick actions of two Forest Service employees prevented the fires from spreading. Fujita bombed the Oregon forest again three weeks later, but with the same results. While neither attack had caused any damage, the troubling fact still remained: nine months after Pearl Harbor was attacked, the Japanese were now bombing and occupying American soil. These were ominous days.

2

The War of Production

(National Archives 535413)

On the evening of February 23, 1942, the day after George Washington's birthday, more than 61 million Americans gathered around their radios to hear President Roosevelt's speech about the progress of the war. In the days leading up to his address, the President asked the listeners to have a world map in front of them so they could follow along as he talked about the "world-encircling battle lines" and the magnitude of the war effort, a struggle which he likened to the early years of the Revolutionary War and the overwhelming odds facing General Washington and the Continental Army. The 36-minute address that followed would be hailed as one of Roosevelt's greatest speeches:

> My fellow Americans:
> Washington's birthday is a most appropriate occasion for us to talk with each other about things as they are today and things as we know they shall be in the future.
> For eight years, General Washington and his Continental Army were faced continually with formidable odds and recurring defeats. Supplies and equipment were lacking. In a sense, every winter was a Valley Forge. Throughout the thirteen states there existed fifth columnists – and selfish men, jealous men, fearful men, who proclaimed that Washington's cause was hopeless, and that he should ask for a negotiated peace.
> Washington's conduct in those hard times has provided the model for all Americans ever since – a model of moral stamina. He held to his course, as it had been charted in the Declaration of Independence. He and the brave men who served with him knew that no man's life or fortune was secure, without freedom and free institutions.
> The present great struggle has taught us increasingly that freedom of person and security of property anywhere in the world depend upon the security of the rights and obligations of liberty and justice everywhere in the world.
> This war is a new kind of war. It is different from all other wars of the past, not only in its methods and weapons but also in its geography. It is warfare in terms of every continent, every island, every sea, every air lane in the world.[1]

Continuing in his direct and plain-spoken style, Roosevelt made it clear that every American would have to make sacrifices in this war; every American would share in the struggle to defeat the Axis powers. Those sacrifices were already being felt on the American homefront. As his address came to a close that night, with the country fully aware of the struggle that lay ahead, Roosevelt evoked the words of one of America's Founding Fathers, Thomas Paine, to inspire the American people:

> The task that we Americans now face will test us to the uttermost. Never before have we been called upon for such a prodigious effort. Never before have we had so little time in which to do so much.
> "These are the times that try men's souls." Tom Paine wrote those words on a drumhead, by the light of a campfire. That was when Washington's little army of ragged, rugged men was retreating across New Jersey, having tasted nothing but defeat.
> And General Washington ordered that these great words written by Tom Paine be read to the men of every regiment in the Continental Army, and this was the assurance given to the first American armed forces:
> "The summer soldier and the sunshine patriot will, in this crisis, shrink from the service of their country; but he that stands it now, deserves the love and thanks of man and woman.

Tyranny, like hell, is not easily conquered; yet we have this consolation with us, that the harder the sacrifice, the more glorious the triumph."

So spoke Americans in the year 1776.

So speak Americans today![2]

The war quickly consumed every facet of American life. As families gathered around their radios each evening, a constant stream of war news, dramas and patriotic songs flowed over the airwaves and into their homes. Newspapers and magazines were filled with stories from battlefields across the world, and Hollywood produced a surge of war movies to boost morale and inspire audiences.

As scores of Americans entered military service and swelled the ranks of the armed forces to more than 16 million strong, another kind of war was also being fought across the United States. Upon these battlefields of the Third Front, with the help of "America's Junior Army" of schoolchildren, Americans scoured their neighborhoods for scrap metal, discarded tires, and other crucial materials needed for the war effort. "The Third Front includes every man, woman, and child in the United States, whose chief duty is to comb the entire Nation for the scrap materials that are absolutely necessary to keep our factories running – absolutely necessary for Victory," said the War Production Board in 1942.[3]

The industrial might of the United States was rapidly converting to war production, and the scrap gathered on the Third Front was vital for producing everything from rifles and tanks to airplanes and battleships. The steel reclaimed from just one set of golf clubs could make a machine gun. The rubber from one used tire could produce 12 gas masks. An old copper kettle contained enough copper for 84 rounds of rifle ammunition.[4]

To defeat the Axis powers, the United States would first have to win the war of production.

The demands of the war effort were felt almost immediately on store shelves. Certain groceries and household items were suddenly in short supply, or not available at all. The shortages even affected bubble gum, whose main ingredient, chicle, was no longer available. A synthetic rubber was substituted in its place, which gave the gum a grainy texture. To keep store prices from soaring, the Office of Price Administration created a rationing system to control certain goods and limit the amount that people could buy. Everyday items like gasoline, meats, sugar, cheese, butter, coffee, and even shoes, were now rationed and strictly controlled. To purchase a rationed item required more than just money. Ration books with special stamps were issued to every man, woman and child in America, which authorized the type and the amount of goods they were allowed to buy. Without the required number of ration stamps, those items could not be purchased.

The production of most consumer products using critical metals was also halted. Bicycles and household goods like toasters, refrigerators and bathroom fixtures were not available for purchase after the existing stocks were depleted. To save copper that was needed to make ammunition, the U.S. Mint studied different metals that could be substituted for the penny. In 1943, new pennies were minted from zinc-plated steel.

Companies that had never made anything for the military before were now converting their factories for war production. IBM and Underwood Typewriter retooled to manufacture rifles. The Anheuser-Busch Brewing Company, famous for its beer, started building wing panels for Army gliders. The Kimberly-Clark Corporation, known for Kleenex and other consumer products, began manufacturing machine-gun mounts.

As the great automobile factories of Detroit were being converted to build tanks, jeeps and airplanes, *Life* magazine ran pictures of the old assembly lines being dismantled with cutting torches and the machinery moved outside into the snow to make way for the new tooling. The last civilian automobile drove off the assembly line in February 1942. New cars would not be made again until the war was won, *Life* magazine reported.[5]

The rapid conversion of American industry to war production came with a substantial price. At a time when the federal minimum wage was $0.30 an hour, President Roosevelt told the American people in April of 1942 that the government was spending almost $100 million a day solely for war purposes, and by the end of the year, that amount would double. "All of this money has to be spent – and spent quickly – if we are to produce within the time now available the enormous quantities of weapons of war which we need," Roosevelt said.[6]

To out-produce the Axis powers, billions of dollars were now being spent to build new factories, hire workers and equip the armed forces. To help pay for the war effort, Americans were asked to spare all the money they could to buy war bonds. "All of us are used to spending money for things that we want, things, however, which are not absolutely essential," Roosevelt said. "We will all have to forego that kind of spending. Because we must put every dime and every dollar we can possibly spare out of our earnings into war bonds and stamps."[7]

Promoted as a way for the public to directly help with the war effort, war bonds were sold for as little as $18.75, and could be redeemed for $25 in 10 years. War saving stamps could also be purchased with spare change and were popular with children, who pasted them into booklets until they added up to $18.75 and were then exchanged for a bond.[8] Spurred by free ad space donated by magazines and newspapers, advertisements appeared across the country urging Americans to buy war bonds with slogans like "Back the Attack!" and "For Freedom's Sake – BUY WAR BONDS." With the help of movie stars, singers, and even clowns at the Barnum and Bailey Circus, the first war bond drive was held in 1942 and raised nearly $13 billion in 23 days for the war effort.[9]

To illustrate the price that would be paid in the long war ahead, a war bond poster appeared in 1942 that portrayed a widowed mother with two small children and the words: "I gave a man! Will you give at least 10% of your pay in war bonds?"[10] To win the war, every American would be asked to share the cost.

*   *   *

While Americans were learning to cope with life under the strains of war, Boeing was working to complete the first XB-29 prototype in Seattle and preparing for mass production. The tremendous amount of new tooling required to build the B-29, along with a myriad of specialized jigs, dies and master gauges, all had to be designed and built from scratch. Every component of the bomber had to be designed and approved before proceeding with construction of both the part, and the tooling needed to make the part. For this monumental undertaking, Boeing assigned 60 designers and 1,500 workers for the B-29's tooling alone.[11]

As part of the tooling process, Boeing created master layout drawings of all the B-29's components. These drawings were duplicated on thin steel sheets that ranged in size from four square feet to hundreds of square feet and would be used as templates for mass-producing the parts. Creating these life-size templates, a process called lofting, and then supplying the photo templates to the other factories, would ensure that all of the B-29's parts were interchangeable, no matter where they were produced.[12]

Thousands of people were now working around the clock to prepare the B-29 for mass production, but another challenge was looming: where would the B-29s be built, and who would build them? The existing aircraft factories were already overflowing with orders and could not be converted for the B-29. Boeing itself was also increasing production of the B-17 and had to form a consortium with two other manufacturers just to keep up with demand. After months of planning, changes and delays, it was concluded that four giant new factories would be needed to produce the sheer number of B-29s required by the Army Air Forces. None of these factories existed when Boeing received the contract to build the XB-29 prototypes. To meet the production demands, Boeing would manufacture the B-29 at factories in Wichita, Kansas, and Renton, Washington, and Bell Aircraft in Marietta, Georgia, and the Glenn L. Martin Company in Omaha, Nebraska, would also produce the B-29.[13]

Finding enough workers to staff the new factories would also be problematic. The influx of men into the armed forces after Pearl Harbor, together with the rapid industrial mobilization for the war effort, had left America's factories with a critical shortage of workers. There was only one untapped labor source remaining that could fill the vacuum, and they would be America's secret weapon to win the war of production.

On December 24, 1941, a short film entitled *Women in Defense* premiered in theaters across the United States. Written by First Lady Eleanor Roosevelt and narrated by Hollywood actress Katherine Hepburn, the documentary featured women performing war-related jobs that traditionally were only held by men, and lauded them as modern pioneers working in defense of their country. The film declared:

> Our history is full of the inspiration which our pioneer women left us as a proud heritage, and again today American women are stirred by that heritage. Serving their country in the laboratory, on defense production lines, in the civilian defense services, and in the home, which is after all the first line of defense. Women have always been the guardians of the home and the children, the future of our country, and they are determined that our democracy shall survive and that our precious freedoms shall be preserved.[14]

The social barriers of the era had left women with few options outside of a housewife, and those who did work only found employment in what were considered to be gender-appropriate jobs like secretaries and store clerks, but the war changed everything. Through a national campaign to recruit female workers, women were urgently called upon to enter the workforce and fight *with* their husbands by providing them with the tools for victory.

As more men entered military service, the Bureau of Labor Statistics predicted a shortage of six million defense-related workers by late 1943, which would have a crippling effect on the war effort. To keep up with production schedules and meet the industrial demands of the war, women would have to bridge the shortfall, and they were needed by the millions.[15]

"The more WOMEN at work the sooner we will WIN," declared one recruiting poster.[16]

The women of America answered the call and began reporting in droves to work in the factories, shipyards and steel mills across the United States. Women were hired and trained for every kind of job imaginable. They became welders, fabricators, riveters, crane operators and truck drivers. As the ranks of the armed forces swelled with manpower, the factories of America surged with *womanpower*. Millions of women also volunteered with the Red Cross and Civil Defense, and hundreds of thousands joined the armed forces. A shortage of pilots led to the creation of the Women Airforce Service Pilots. The WASPs delivered warplanes from factories to air bases across the United States and performed other training and non-combat missions.

A remarkable transformation of the workplace, and America, was occurring. Despite the reservations of their male counterparts, women were now performing jobs once only reserved for men, and they were excelling at them. A song entitled "Rosie the Riveter" was released in 1942 and became a rallying cry for the women "working for victory" in the factories across America. The song was a national hit.[17]

In 1943, the year that nearly three million new women entered the workforce, the spirit of the American working woman was immortalized by Norman Rockwell when his painting "Rosie the Riveter" appeared on the cover of the *Saturday Evening Post*, and it quickly became a symbol of social change. A cultural icon was born.[18]

With the new opportunities available to women, as well as men who were ineligible for military service, a great migration began to take place as eager workers swarmed to the cities and industrial centers for jobs in the war effort. The population of Seattle, Washington, increased by more than 110,000 in just two years. Mobile, Alabama, saw 80,000 new workers arrive in 1942 alone, and the shipyards and aircraft factories of California drew 1.4 million people. So many workers were needed that child-labor laws were relaxed, and millions of teenagers also joined the workforce.[19]

Of all the women who entered the workforce for the first time during the war, 60 percent were over the age of 35. The number of married women with jobs doubled, and between 1940 and 1944, the total employment of women increased by 6.2 million. Among the "Rosies" employed in the war effort was a young woman at the Radioplane Corporation plant in California. In later years, she would be known to the world as Marilyn Monroe.[20]

Faced with its own shortage of workers, Boeing actively recruited women to help build the B-29. One recruiting booklet emphasized the ease of training:

> Women find Boeing equipment is simple to operate … The Boeing production system reduces building an airplane to simple units. No previous training is necessary. It's only a short step from operating an egg beater to a drill or rivet gun.[21]

Boeing's recruiting campaign even reached as far as a storefront window display in downtown Seattle, which featured women actually assembling wiring harnesses for the B-29 as passersby looked on. A large "Women At Work" sign hung on the wall behind them as they worked. "Here on forming boards, wire assemblies are made ready to fit into the plane," a sign next to the women read. "Nearly all the wiring assemblies are prepared by women."[22] Women responded to Boeing's campaign in overwhelming numbers. For many women, building the B-29 would be their first job.

While the industries of the United States were mobilizing for the war effort, Boeing and the government planners moved forward with the monumental task of getting the B-29 into full-scale production. The B-29 would be the most complicated thing America ever attempted to mass-produce. By the spring of 1942, while the first XB-29 was still under construction in Seattle, the Army Air Forces had increased its order to 1,664 B-29s, plus spare parts. Creating the infrastructure to mass-produce an aircraft as large and complex as the B-29 on such a wide scale was a daunting challenge. To supply the assembly lines with parts, hundreds of subcontractors would manufacture everything from tires to fuel tanks for the B-29. This vast network of suppliers had to be set up from scratch.[23] Most of the new subcontractors had never produced anything aviation-related before. The Frigidaire Refrigerator Company, a division of General Motors, signed a $40 million contract to make the propeller blades for the B-29.[24]

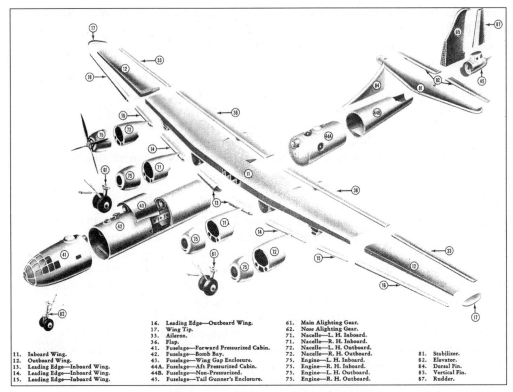

16. Leading Edge—Outboard Wing.	61. Main Alighting Gear.	
17. Wing Tip.	62. Nose Alighting Gear.	
53. Aileron.	71. Nacelle—L. H. Inboard.	
36. Flap.	71. Nacelle—R. H. Inboard.	
41. Fuselage—Forward Pressurized Cabin.	72. Nacelle—L. H. Outboard.	
42. Fuselage—Bomb Bay.	72. Nacelle—R. H. Outboard.	81. Stabilizer.
43. Fuselage—Wing Gap Enclosure.	75. Engine—L. H. Inboard.	82. Elevator.
44A. Fuselage—Aft Pressurized Cabin.	75. Engine—R. H. Inboard.	84. Dorsal Fin.
44B. Fuselage—Non-Pressurized.	75. Engine—L. H. Outboard.	85. Vertical Fin.
45. Fuselage—Tail Gunner's Enclosure.	75. Engine—R. H. Outboard.	87. Rudder.

11. Inboard Wing.
12. Outboard Wing.
13. Leading Edge—Inboard Wing.
14. Leading Edge—Inboard Wing.
15. Leading Edge—Inboard Wing.

The major sub-assemblies of the B-29. (USAAF)

The resources needed to build just a single B-29 were staggering. Each B-29 contained 40,540 different parts, not including duplicates, such as 3,461 lock nuts of just one size alone, and the airframe was constructed with more than a million rivets. Over 10 miles of wiring snaked through the bomber, connecting 150 different electric motors and seven generators. Some two miles of hose and tubing were spread throughout the wings and fuselage, and the rubber used for the B-29's tires and tubes alone weighed nearly 1,200 pounds. When measured by weight, the materials required to build just one B-29 equaled the requirements to build 11 P-51 Mustang fighters.[25]

To manufacture the B-29 as efficiently as possible, Boeing would use the innovative multiline assembly system that was originally developed to mass-produce the B-17. The B-29's fuselage would be constructed in five different sections, which were then simply bolted together along with the wings during final assembly to form a complete airplane. This system allowed the B-29 to be kept as small as possible until final assembly, saving valuable time and space on the factory floor.[26]

To enable unskilled workers to quickly become skilled in its manufacture, the B-29's parts were reduced to their simplest forms during production. Few who built the B-29 had any previous experience or training in aircraft manufacturing. Most of the workers had never even been near an airplane before, let alone attempted to build one. The layout of the factories were also studied to maximize speed and efficiency as parts flowed in from subcontractors all across the country, some as far away as Canada, to construct the bombers. The B-29 would truly be built by the entire nation, for practically every state in America would contribute in some way to the B-29 program.

Hundreds of thousands of Americans would be directly involved in manufacturing the B-29, and women would account for a substantial portion of the workforce. Nearly 60 percent of the workers at the Bell Aircraft factory in Marietta were female, and at Boeing's Renton plant, 54 percent of the workforce were women. But beyond breaking the gender barrier, the B-29 program also provided opportunities to other groups that had difficulty finding meaningful work before the war. The deaf and blind found jobs that were uniquely suited for them on the production lines, and little people performed interior inspections of the wings before final assembly.[27] Regardless of gender or handicap, no skill was overlooked in building the B-29.

*   *   *

By September of 1942, just 16 months after construction began, the first XB-29 prototype was completed and moving under its own power in Seattle. The feat was a huge triumph for Boeing, but the B-29 now had to prove itself in the air. So much was riding on the first flight, with billions of dollars having already been spent on the B-29 program. Hundreds of factories and thousands of workers across the country were starting to build parts for the B-29, and war plans for the bombers were already being drawn.[28] The gamble had to work.

Late in the afternoon of September 21, with Eddie Allen at the controls, the first XB-29 roared down the runway at Boeing Field and climbed into the sky for its first test flight. Back on the ground, after years of work and more than 1.4 million engineering work-hours, a crowd of Boeing executives, engineers and mechanics anxiously waited. It was all out of their hands now.

After a long hour and 15 minutes, the XB-29 gracefully swept over the field and landed. The crowd quickly swarmed the bomber as the crew climbed down from the cockpit, but Eddie Allen remained coy as the men gathered around him. Finally, Allen could contain himself no more. "She flies!" he proclaimed with a broad smile.[29]

Within 30 minutes of landing, Wellwood Beall dispatched the eagerly awaited news to Washington: "Eddie Allen reports that we have an excellent airplane."[30] The results of the first flight had exceeded all expectations. The basic design of the B-29 was so sound that no significant aerodynamic changes had to be made. For such a massive aircraft, it was quite an accomplishment for Boeing's engineers. "It's the first ship which, after the first flight, permits me to go home and have damn little to do," said George Schairer, Boeing's Chief Aerodynamicist.[31]

The XB-29 took to the skies again the following day with Colonel Donald Putt, the XB-29's Army Air Forces project officer, to further explore the bomber's flight characteristics. Colonel Putt later recalled:

> The next day, after a final check-out, I made a second flight in our new XB-29. After a short hop, I jotted down some notes: unbelievable for such large plane to be so easy on controls … easier to fly than B-17 … faster than any previous heavy bomber … control forces very light … stall characteristics remarkable for heavy plane.[32]

There was still a lot of work left to do, but the B-29 was on its way. The gamble had paid off.

3

Tempting Fate

Following its successful first flight, the XB-29 was ready to begin the greatest flight test program of its day. To make the B-29 combat-ready as quickly as possible, an unprecedented testing program would be undertaken to evaluate all of the bomber's systems and its flight performance under every condition imaginable. The first B-29s were already under construction in Wichita and would begin rolling off the assembly lines in seven months, while factories across the United States were producing parts for the B-29 that had to be proven in flight. There was no time to waste.

The man tasked with leading the XB-29 flight test program was Edmund T. "Eddie" Allen, Boeing's director of flight and aerodynamics. Hailed as the world's greatest test pilot, Allen had worked for most of the major aircraft manufactures over the years and had conducted the first test flights of over 30 different aircraft, but he was not the flamboyant daredevil that Hollywood portrayed test pilots to be. Standing 5 feet 8 inches tall, with a very thin build and unassuming demeanor, a fellow test pilot once described Allen as better fitting the image of a "naturally friendly, soft spoken, mild mannered midwestern farmer" than a world-renowned test pilot.[1]

Unlike the movies, Eddie Allen was a conservative test pilot and was not prone to taking chances. In the cockpit, he believed that fear was healthy, but panic was debilitating. During a test flight in 1931, his ability to remain calm in life-threatening situations was dramatically displayed when he miraculously landed a Northrop Beta 3 prototype with jammed aileron controls out of a barrel role. Allen had a reputation for staying cool under pressure and always bringing the airplane back in one piece. His abilities as a test pilot were held in such high esteem that for some insurance companies, Allen's involvement with testing a new airplane was a prerequisite to insuring it.[2]

Through his years of extensive work both in flight and in the wind tunnel evaluating new designs, Allen had become the foremost authority on the control and stability of large aircraft, and his leadership would be crucial to getting the B-29 combat-ready as soon as possible.[3]

Eddie Allen's rise to prominence had all the makings of a great American success story. Born in Chicago in 1896, he had shown no great promise in school as a child, but after his father died when he was 17, Allen went to work on a dairy farm to support his family, and it was there that his interest in science and engineering began to grow. When the United States entered the First World War in 1917, Allen enlisted in the Army, learned to fly, and at just 21 years old – after logging only 15 solo flying hours – he became a flight instructor and taught new pilots how to fly.

Flying opened up an exciting new world of opportunities for young Eddie Allen. Recognizing his skills as a pilot, the Army sent Allen to England to study British flight-testing techniques, and he returned home in 1918 to apply his new experience at the Army's flight test center at McCook Field in Dayton, Ohio. After the war was over, Allen became the first test pilot for the National Advisory Committee for Aeronautics, the forerunner of NASA, and he completed a second year of college at the University of Illinois before going on to study aeronautical engineering at MIT, where he designed and built his own glider for competitions in Europe.

In the years that followed, Allen continued working as a freelance test pilot and aeronautical engineer consultant, and in his spare time he built eight airplanes in his basement to test his aerodynamic theories. Allen also flew air mail for the U.S. Post Office and Boeing Air Transport, an affiliate of the Boeing Airplane Company, which later became United Airlines.

His reputation as a safe and competent test pilot placed his services in high demand, and Allen found himself conducting more test flights, particularly for Boeing. In 1939, Allen joined Boeing full time as its director of flight and aerodynamics, a department that he created to combine ground and flight research for designing new airplanes. The ideas that Eddie Allen brought to Boeing would become the roots of modern-day aeronautical research.[4]

Eddie Allen was an exceptional test pilot because he approached aircraft design and testing as a science. To Allen, the practice of calling in a test pilot after a new design had been built was the wrong approach. What was really needed in aviation, he felt, was exhaustive scientific research to gather accurate data – both on the ground in laboratories and wind tunnels, and in flight with sophisticated instruments and specially trained crews – that could then be applied during the design process.[5] Allen believed that new aircraft designs should be subjected to extensive testing while still in the early stages of development, long before an actual prototype was built, to ensure the design was aerodynamically sound before proceeding with construction. This would avoid costly delays and changes after the prototype was flown. Allen's vision was to form a collaboration between the designer, engineer and test pilot that would bring all this data together to influence new designs, and that's exactly what he created at Boeing with his new department.[6]

The exhaustive work of Allen and his staff was the reason why the B-29's basic design, after nearly 9,000 hours of wind tunnel testing, did not require any major aerodynamic changes after the prototype was first flown.[7]

While the aerodynamics of the B-29 had already been solved before the first flight, the rest of the airframe and all of its systems still needed considerable testing. Allen estimated that the XB-29 would require 252 flight hours to fully test the bomber, and all of this testing would be compressed into a period of four to five months.[8] "The XB-29 test program will be the greatest ever conducted on any airplane," Allen declared as the program got underway.[9]

Such an extensive test program had never been attempted so quickly before, but there was no time to waste: Americans were dying on battlefields across the world. The faster the B-29 could be used in combat, the sooner the war would be over, and more American lives would be saved. But the problems that soon befell the test program were far beyond the control of even Eddie Allen.

*   *   *

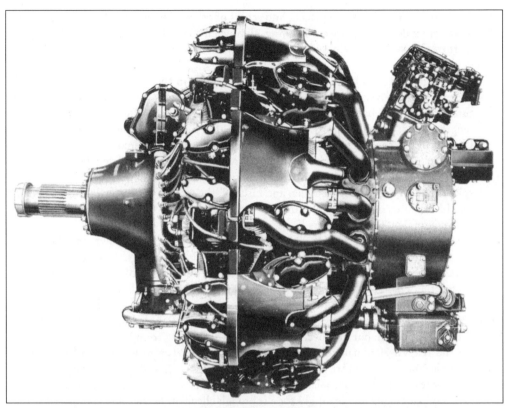

An early production Wright R-3350 engine that powered the XB-29. (USAAF)

The B-29 program was a "three-billion-dollar gamble" because it relied upon so many new and unproven elements to succeed. After the design of the airframe itself, no other component would be more critical to the success of the B-29 than its engines.

The engine selected to power the B-29 was the Wright R-3350, a massive 18-cylinder radial engine that produced 2,200 horsepower, but it was still an experimental engine when Boeing submitted the Model 345 design to the Air Corps in 1940. In a normal course of development during peacetime, the B-29 would not have been ready for service before 1946, but the demands of the war changed everything. Out of necessity, the time normally required to fully develop and test the B-29 and its engines had to be significantly reduced to get the bomber into service as quickly as possible.[10]

The Wright Aeronautical Corporation had been working on the R-3350 engine since 1936, but serious problems with the design continued to hinder their progress. When the Air Corps placed its first production order for the R-3350 in 1941, less than 15 of the engines had been produced since 1938, and testing had shown that the engines were still plagued by a host of mechanical failures.[11] By the time the XB-29 was ready for its maiden flight on September 21, 1942, the R-3350 was still far from being a safe and reliable engine, but flight testing had to proceed.

Nine days after the XB-29 first roared into the sky, with so much riding on the test program, its engines began failing after running for just seven hours. Flight testing was suspended for

10 days while the engines were replaced, and scores of other adjustments were made while the XB-29 was grounded.[12] Hopes were running high when the XB-29 returned to the air in the latter part of October, but were quickly dashed when another engine failed, and testing was suspended again.

Sporadic flights plagued by additional failures continued in the weeks that followed, but by early December, the XB-29 was successfully flown to 25,000 feet. The first high-altitude flight was cause for optimism, but a test on December 28 had to be halted after 26 minutes when the No. 1 engine failed, and an inspection later revealed that the No. 2 engine was about to fail as well. (Sitting in the cockpit facing forward, the engines were numbered, left to right, one to four.) The two engines were quickly replaced, but another engine failed later the same week.[13] The XB-29 was grounded again pending new engines and other changes.

Despite the best efforts of Eddie Allen and his staff, the test program was falling way behind schedule. In the three months since it first left the ground, the XB-29 had only managed to fly 23 times for a total of 27 flying hours.[14]

In terms of aerodynamics, the XB-29 was superb at any altitude it was flown, but the engines were wreaking havoc with the test program. By the end of the year, 16 engines had been changed, 22 carburetors were replaced, and 19 revisions were made to the exhaust system, in addition to other changes and adjustments. The average test flight had only lasted for an hour and 10 minutes, which made it nearly impossible to gather any meaningful data, with most of the flight time being spent fighting problems and getting back to the field. More reliable engines were desperately needed, but improvements were slow in coming from Wright.[15]

While the first XB-29 remained grounded, the second XB-29 prototype was finally completed and rolled out in late December. The weather on the day of its first flight was marginal at best for flying, but testing had to continue. With Eddie Allen at the controls, the second XB-29 took to the gloomy skies on its maiden flight for a thorough check of the airplane and its test instruments. The checks were proceeding normally until the No. 4 propeller refused to feather and its governor began malfunctioning. Allen terminated the test flight and immediately headed back to Boeing Field for landing. The weather was deteriorating rapidly.

Six minutes out from landing, without warning, flames suddenly burst from the No. 4 engine. As fire streamed from the engine, the propeller governor that controlled the pitch of the blades and maintained the desired engine speed also failed, causing the propeller to dangerously overspeed the already burning engine. The pilots tried to feather the propeller again, which would rotate the blades knife-edge into the wind to stop the propeller from windmilling and reduce drag, but it still would not feather.

While Allen fought with the propeller, the flight engineer shut off fuel to the engine and discharged its fire extinguisher to smother the flames, but the extinguisher was ineffective. The fire was getting worse. Two minutes away from landing, heavy smoke and flames were pouring from the engine nacelle and trailing behind the wing. Inside the forward cabin, the cockpit filled with smoke as the fire raged out of control. As the XB-29 approached the field, the crew were choking and nearly blinded by all the smoke, but in a remarkable feat of airmanship, Eddie Allen managed to safely land the bomber and the fire was finally put out by ground crews.

When the smoke eventually cleared, the crews discovered that a fire had also started in the No. 1 engine, and the No. 3 engine was close to failure as well. The engines had run for less than three hours before they failed.[16]

1943

As winter took hold of Seattle, work began in earnest on the fire-damaged XB-29. To complete the repairs as quickly as possible, engines and other parts were cannibalized from the first XB-29 while it was undergoing some modifications, but the bitter cold made it difficult, and at times impossible, to work on the airplane. With no hangars available that were large enough to house the XB-29, the workers had to make do with a small hangar that left half of the airplane exposed to the freezing elements. A large icicle added to their difficulties when it fell and damaged the right aileron, requiring even more repairs.[17]

After working around the clock for a month, the second XB-29 took to the skies again on January 29. Two days later, during a high-altitude test at 20,000 feet, another engine failed, and Eddie Allen was forced to bring the XB-29 back for yet another emergency landing. The engines were putting the entire test program in jeopardy.

By the middle of February, five months after the first XB-29's maiden flight, both prototypes combined had only flown 31 times for a total of 34 hours and 27 minutes in the air. The program was a long way from reaching the 252 hours needed to fully test the XB-29.[18]

Eddie Allen was now faced with a serious dilemma. In peacetime, grounding the XB-29 until improvements could be made to the engines would be the normal thing to do, but these were not normal times. The faulty engines had made the XB-29 a very dangerous airplane to fly, but more delays in the program meant that more American lives would be lost. Allen's concerns came to a head during a test flight on February 17, when the second XB-29 developed a fuel leak from the No. 4 fuel filler cap on the right wing during the climb-out after takeoff. The leak increased as the XB-29 leveled off and left a heavy stream of fuel vapor trailing behind the airplane. A strong odor of fuel was also noted in the bomb bay.[19]

Later that afternoon, while walking to a post-flight conference with one of his engineers, Allen expressed his reservations about continuing the test flights until the more serious problems could be fixed. But weighing heavily on Allen was the fact that the B-29 was already committed to mass production. The first of the 1,664 B-29s ordered would begin rolling off the assembly lines in two months, and answers were quickly needed to a multitude of questions that could only be solved by flight testing. To minimize disruptions in production, which now involved hundreds of factories across the United States, those answers were needed now.[20]

Despite his grave concerns, the flight tests must go on, Allen concluded. The risks were high, but the risk of more delays was even higher. Flight testing had to continue.

*   *   *

The morning of February 18 was cold and overcast as Eddie Allen and his crew boarded the XB-29 at 10:40 a.m. to begin their pre-flight checks. Their mission for the day was to collect flight performance and engine cooling data under various operating conditions at altitudes up to 25,000 feet. As part of the tests, the XB-29 would take off with over 5,000 gallons of fuel on board. With the heavy fuel load, the XB-29 weighed 105,000 pounds, more than the combined weight of three empty B-17 bombers.

At 12:09 p.m., Allen lifted the XB-29 into the grey sky to begin the day's tests. Just eight minutes after takeoff, while climbing at an altitude of 5,000 feet, a fire suddenly broke out in the

No. 1 engine. The propeller was immediately feathered while the flight engineer, Fritz Mohn, shut off the fuel to the engine, closed the cowl flaps, and discharged the fire extinguisher to smother the flames. As Mohn brought the fire under control, Allen turned the XB-29 around to return to Boeing Field for yet another emergency landing. The flight had not lasted 10 minutes before the engine failed. Another valuable day of testing was gone.

Back at Boeing Field, the flight was being monitored by Boeing Radio when Harry Ralston, the XB-29's radio operator, reported the engine fire: "Fire in No. 1 engine. Coming in. Had fire in engine and used one CO2 bottle and think we have it under control."

"Tell us if at any time you think you need fire equipment," Boeing Radio replied.

Three minutes later, Ralston radioed the control tower at Boeing Field: "Army 1003 to Seattle Tower. Renton, 2,400 feet descending. Request immediate landing clearance. No. 1 engine on fire. Propeller feathered and trouble not serious. Order crash equipment to stand by."

The tower replied: "Army 1003 from Seattle Tower. Roger Wilco. Cleared to land. Wind south 10, runway 13." Fire trucks were alerted and standing by.

Two minutes later, Ralston reported their position to Boeing Radio: "Lake Washington bridge, 2,500 feet; correction, 1,500 feet." Ralston then switched back to Seattle Tower. "Army 1003 to Seattle Tower …" Ralston radioed, but his transmission was cut off by other airplanes transmitting on the same frequency.

"Army 1003 from Seattle Tower, unable to read you. Continue on your approach," the tower replied. Seconds later, about five miles away from the field, a loud explosion was heard as the bomber passed over the city. Debris rained down from the XB-29 as smoke and flames began pouring from the No. 2 engine.

Looking skyward, witnesses could clearly see that the leading edge of the left wing had been blown away between the No. 1 and No. 2 engines. In an instant, a massive fuel leak erupted and became an inferno. Smoldering pieces of instrument tubing, hose clamps and a deicer valve tumbled to the ground. The XB-29 was burning.

"Have fire equipment ready," Ralston radioed. "Am coming in with wing on fire."

Four miles away from the field, the tower overheard Ralston talking to Eddie Allen: "Allen, better get this thing down in a hurry. The wing spar is burning badly."[21]

Trailing heavy smoke and flames, the XB-29 continued in a left turn over the south side of Seattle onto its final approach to Boeing Field. Witnesses on the ground reported that the engines were sputtering and back-firing as the crippled bomber rapidly lost altitude. Smoke was now seen trailing from the No. 3 and No. 4 engines as well.

Eddie Allen and his 27-year-old co-pilot, Bob Dansfield, struggled to maintain control as the bomber's altitude sank below 250 feet. Fed by raw gasoline streaming from the wing, the XB-29 was being devoured by fire.

To escape the horror of burning alive, the crew in the forward cabin began to bail out. Allen and Dansfield stayed at the controls, fighting to save the XB-29. Fritz Mohn's flight data sheet fluttered to the ground as the men frantically scrambled to get out. It was later found along the flight path with other debris from the bomber.

Charles Blaine, a 26-year-old flight test engineer, was the first man to jump, but the XB-29 was too low for his parachute to open. Harry Ralston followed Blaine out. His body crashed into high-voltage power lines with a sickening flash. Both men were killed instantly.

The XB-29 continued on, its left wing dipping and slicing through the power lines. At Boeing Field, the lights flickered and then went out as power was lost. The control tower was knocked off the air, but Boeing Radio quickly switched to backup power and tried to re-establish contact with the bomber. The XB-29 was not responding to their calls.

Three miles away from the field, and flying at building-top level, Eddie Allen and Bob Dansfield pulled back on the controls in a desperate attempt to gain altitude. Flames could be seen in the cockpit from the ground.

Ed Wersebe, a 28-year-old flight test engineer, was the next to jump from the burning airplane, but he was far too low for his parachute to open before he hit the ground. There was no hope.

Seconds later, the XB-29 slammed into the five-story Frye Meat Packing Plant and exploded in a massive fireball. The XB-29 and its entire 11-man crew were gone. [22]

4

We Are Going to Build It

The Boeing Aircraft Company and all its employees deeply feel the loss of their associates, and regret equally the loss of life and injuries to the personnel of the Frye and Company packing plant, and to the fireman who died in the line of duty. Boeing extends its heartfelt sympathy to the families of these unfortunate victims.

The accident resulted from a fire which developed in an engine in the course of a regular test flight. The fire, although extinguished temporarily by automatic carbon dioxide equipment, according to the plane's radio report, resumed and apparently spread over one wing while the crew was making an approach to Boeing Field for an emergency landing. It was at this time that the plane struck light wires and the Frye and Company packing plant.

The eleven men of the flight crew all were outstanding in their field. They died in line of duty in their work of constantly improving the fighting planes with which America is combating the Axis.

To Edmund T. Allen, often called the world's greatest test pilot, the Boeing company pays everlasting tribute. With his death America has lost not only a pioneer airman and the country's outstanding test pilot of large airplanes, but also a great figure in the aircraft sciences. It has been the efforts of men like Allen and his crew, who even at the time of their death were engaged in aeronautical research, that have helped make American planes, military and commercial, the best in the world.

Boeing crash statement, February 1943[1]

(The type of bomber that crashed was not publicly disclosed for security reasons.)

*   *   *

The disaster of February 18, 1943, was a stunning setback for the B-29 program. With the loss of Eddie Allen, his crew of highly trained engineers, and the only flyable XB-29, the future of the entire program was now in question. For Boeing, the loss of so many men decimated their flight test department, and morale plummeted after the crash. "Walking down the halls of [Boeing] company buildings you could feel the hush," recalled Thomas Collison, who was documenting the B-29's development for a book. "You saw in the faces of men you know – strong men who also had lived in the presence of death – the quality of their grief."[2]

One of Boeing's test pilots, Al Reed, was so distraught that he left Boeing a few weeks after the crash and dropped from sight. Reed never flew again.[3]

The last seven years had been filled with tragedy for Boeing. In 1935, the first B-17 prototype crashed when Army Air Corps test pilots took off with the control surfaces locked. The crash destroyed the Model 299, and Boeing's chief test pilot, Les Towers, who was on board as an observer, died of his injuries. (The co-pilot was Lieutenant Donald Putt, who went on to become the XB-29 project officer.) Three-and-a-half years later, chief test pilot Julius Barr and a number of Boeing engineers and airline representatives were killed when the first Boeing 307 Stratoliner crashed during a performance demonstration. And now, with the loss of Eddie Allen and his crew, tragedy had befallen the company again.[4]

General Arnold was shocked by the news of the crash and immediately ordered an investigation. With a track record of failures that had culminated in the deaths of 31 people in Seattle, Arnold grounded all R-3350 engines until the investigation was completed. Senator Harry Truman's investigating committee also launched its own probe into the troubled engines. Both investigations ultimately found that Wright had produced a lot of defective engines due to gross mismanagement and a poorly trained workforce and concluded that the R-3350 needed engineering changes and better quality control. With orders for 30,000 engines, quality had been sacrificed for quantity. The Army Air Forces was also admonished for pressuring Wright to accelerate R-3350 production.[5]

While the crash investigation was ongoing and all flight testing suspended, the B-29 project quickly lost momentum. "It can truly be said that the Boeing Company never did lose faith in its baby, but it was a discouraging period after the deaths of Allen and his men who nursed the B-29 from the drawing board," recalled Lieutenant General William Knudsen, the former president of General Motors, who was brought in to consult on B-29 production.[6] The discouragement reached as far as some Army Air Force officers who now openly doubted that the B-29 project would succeed. Brigadier General Kenneth B. Wolfe, who was then the chairman of the B-29 Liaison Committee that coordinated production matters, recalled after the war that "within the Air Force itself there were certain people who didn't think that we should spend our time and effort on a bomber that far advanced."[7]

Despite the misgivings of some, General Arnold never wavered in his support for the B-29. To the critics who questioned the project, Arnold was resolute: "We are going to build it."[8]

However, to move the project forward would take all of Arnold's determination and some major changes to the program. The impetus for those changes would be found with a 36-year-old colonel at Wright Field in Dayton, Ohio. Colonel Leonard F. "Jake" Harman had a close connection to the B-29. As Chief of the Bombardment Branch, Production Division, at Wright Field, Harman was involved with the project early on, and had actually flown with Eddie Allen and his crew. Harman also shared Arnold's belief that the B-29 was the future of air power, recognizing that it was the only bomber capable of striking the Japanese homeland. But the investigation into the XB-29 crash had stalled the program's momentum, and if the B-29 stood any chance of striking Japan by 1944, something drastic had to be done. Harman had an idea that would reshape the entire B-29 program and get it back on track:

> I told K.B. Wolfe, my boss, we ought to package a whole deal … a special project on the B-29, to consist of flight test, production, training the crews. So K.B. said, "Well, write it down and we'll go in to show the Old Man." I made about a half a page letter saying,

"a special project is hereby formed to have complete control over the B-29 consisting of control over production, flight tests, training ... to get this airplane in combat with the least possible delay." And I put down at the bottom a place for, typed in, "H.H. Arnold."[9]

Harman and Wolfe then traveled to Washington to see their boss, Major General Oliver Echols. "I suppose you know what you're getting into," Echols said, after reading the letter. Harman continued:

So we went down the hall to see General Arnold. He came out and I told him, "Good morning" and I tossed this letter on his desk, and he read it, slapped the desk, and said, "That's fine. Why doesn't somebody else do something for me once in a while?" So I passed him a pen and he signed it.[10]

Arnold asked Harman where he was staying in Washington, and then cautioned: "Not a word of this to anybody." Harman later learned that Arnold went to see General Marshall, the Army Chief of Staff, and then both men went to see the President. Later that afternoon, Harman received a phone call at his hotel. No names were mentioned, but he recognized the voice. "Be careful what you say," Arnold said. "Approved."[11]

The B-29 Special Project was born. With his intimate knowledge of the B-29, General Wolfe was placed in charge of the project, and Colonel Harman was appointed as his deputy. The future of the super-bomber was now in their hands.

*   *   *

From the dawn of aviation, engine weight had been a problem since the first powered flight in 1903, when the Wright Brothers conquered the air with a 12-horsepower engine that weighed 180 pounds. By 1932, advancements in aircraft engine designs and materials had seen the power-to-weight ratio increase to one horsepower for every 1½ pound of engine weight. A promising new magnesium alloy was expected to further reduce engine weight in the coming years, with the ultimate goal being an engine that could produce one horsepower per pound of engine weight.[12]

The new R-3350 came very close to achieving that goal. Wright's engineers had developed an engine that produced 2,200 horsepower and weighed 2,668 pounds. But the price for their breakthrough would be deadly.[13]

When work began on the R-3350 in 1936, Wright Aeronautical was one of the largest aircraft engine manufacturers in the world. Part of their success was due to the popular Wright Cyclone 9 engine. The R-1820, the Cyclone 9's designation for military service, was a nine-cylinder radial engine that produced 1,200 horsepower and was used on a variety of aircraft, including the Boeing B-17. Wright hoped to carry that success over to their new engine by borrowing from the proven R-1820 design, but serious problems were encountered almost immediately. To create the R-3350, the design grew to include a second row of nine cylinders that were added to a lengthened crankcase, which increased the overall length of the engine. But while the number of cylinders had grown from 9 to 18, the frontal area of both engines remained the same: 55 inches in diameter. This meant that Wright would attempt to cool an engine twice as powerful as the R-1820 with the same volume of air.

All radial engines depend upon a constant stream of air to cool the cylinders during operation, but a large air intake on the cowling that encloses the engine creates drag and was not practical for the B-29. The cowling that Boeing designed for the R-3350 greatly reduced drag, but while the aerodynamics of the cowling was excellent at high altitude, its design constricted airflow during ground operations and takeoff. For an engine that measured 4½ feet in diameter, the air intake on the B-29's cowling was reduced down to just 38 inches. By comparison, the air intake on the B-17's cowling was 41 inches in diameter. The B-29's cowling restricted airflow to such an extent that even less air was now available to cool the R-3350 than the R-1820.

The R-3350 was touted as an engine that produced the power of a freight locomotive, but weighed no more than the locomotive's wheels, and was compressed into less space than the locomotive's cab. A significant amount of those weight savings came from the materials used to construct the engine. As the early design of the R-3350 was taking shape, the engineers continued to explore ways to decrease the engine's weight while increasing horsepower. One of the solutions they found was magnesium. In place of heavier steel and aluminum components, engine manufactures began using a magnesium alloy for parts that were not subjected to high operating temperatures to further reduce weight.[14]

The use of magnesium had many advantages: it was strong and lightweight. But the problem with magnesium is that it burns intensely if it's heated to the point of combustion, and once magnesium starts burning, there isn't much that can be done about it. A booklet later distributed to B-29 combat crews warned about the dangers of magnesium fires:

> The most hazardous fire in an aircraft is a magnesium fire. An aircraft engine, to achieve the desired light weight, is constructed with considerable magnesium alloy. Enough, in fact, to provide fuel to support a large fire for a long time. Magnesium is a combustible substance which has the property of readily oxidizing and producing terrific heat accompanied by a piercing white light. A magnesium fire is extremely dangerous and almost impossible to extinguish.[15]

Together with the cooling and other design problems that had plagued the R-3350 since its inception, a perfect storm was now brewing for the B-29 and its crews.

*   *   *

The Army Air Forces' report on the XB-29 crash was completed on April 27, 1943, but after a thorough investigation, a definitive cause for all of the events leading up to the crash could not be determined. In light of a previous engine fire that had occurred on December 30, which was so severe that the entire No. 4 engine nacelle had to be replaced, the investigation began with a focus on the engines. While the wreckage was being recovered from the crash site, a committee of engine specialists was formed to examine the XB-29's engines for any signs of a failure that could have caused the crash. Multiple pieces of debris were also recovered along the flight path and sent to the University of Washington for analysis. All of the samples bore evidence of a magnesium fire.[16]

As the crash investigation got underway, important clues were provided by witnesses who observed the XB-29 as it overflew the south side of Seattle. With the assistance of the FBI, some 200 witnesses from along the flight path, ranging from housewives to pilots, were interviewed to establish a chronology of events leading up to the crash. A number of witnesses reported that the engines were "sputtering constantly" and "continuously back-firing" just prior to the crash. Others had observed trails of smoke coming from the No. 3 and No. 4 engines on the right wing, in addition to flames and smoke from the No. 1 and No. 2 engines on the left wing.[17]

One of the closest witnesses to the crash was Les Larson, who was in a car traveling on Airport Way just east of the Frye plant. Larson was so close to the crash that fuel expelled from the impact actually struck his clothing. His terrifying account was recorded in the Army Air Forces' report:

> He [Larson] stated that just before the crash there was only one engine running, the No. 4 engine, and that the No. 1 engine exploded in the air, either the propeller flew apart or part of the motor. There seemed to be lots of parts in the air. Immediately following the crash a large umbrella of flame covered the entire area and gasoline showered over the street striking the car in which the witness had been riding and on his clothing.[18]

Together with the radio reports from the XB-29 before the crash, all signs seemed to be pointing to a catastrophic engine failure. But upon examination of the engines, the inspectors were left with more questions than answers. The No. 1 and No. 2 engines were so badly damaged that all possible evidence of an internal failure was destroyed by fire. Despite witnesses reporting smoke trailing from the No. 3 and No. 4 engines, no evidence of an internal failure could be found in either engine. However, the inspection did find that the reduction gear pinions and bearings had circular grooves cut into them and were discolored due to friction. The inspector noted in his report: "I would state their condition as questionable as to the length of serviceability." It was only a matter of time before the No. 3 and No. 4 engines failed.[19]

With no evidence of an internal failure to be found, the investigators began exploring the possibility that an engine backfire could have caused the events that led to the crash. The R-3350's fuel induction system had never functioned satisfactorily and was the source of many problems for Boeing's mechanics. In an effort to improve the system, 22 carburetors had been changed within the first three months of flight testing alone, in addition to other adjustments, but the troubles continued.[20]

The seriousness of the problems came to a head during the first test flight of the second XB-29 on December 30, when an uncontrollable fire suddenly broke out in the No. 4 engine. It was later determined that the fire was caused by a severe backfire that ignited the engine's magnesium blower case and eventually gutted the entire nacelle.[21] A similar backfire had occurred just days earlier on another R-3350 that was undergoing testing at the Wright factory. In that case, the backfire was so violent that 17 of the 18 intake pipes, which supply the fuel-air mixture to the cylinders, began leaking or were blown loose at the cylinder heads and immediately resulted in a fire. An Army officer present for the test further stated that he had witnessed several other backfires during testing that had also loosened the intake pipes and resulted in fires.[22]

The induction system of the XB-29's four engines were carefully examined for any signs of a backfire, but nothing conclusive could be found. The No. 2 engine was immediately suspect as a new carburetor had been installed since its last flight, but the intense fire had destroyed the engine along with any possible evidence of a backfire. The inspectors noted in their report that the induction system and the rear case of all four engines were destroyed by fire, with each exhibiting the "same degree and pattern of fire," but no evidence of a fire originating in these sections could be found.[23] With no clear evidence of an engine failure or backfire, the investigation turned to other possibilities that could explain the fires reported by the crew. An important piece of evidence were the witnesses who reported hearing an explosion and then observed damage to the leading edge of the left wing as the XB-29 flew overhead.

Within a matter of weeks, a likely scenario that could explain the events leading up to the crash had been formed, but little could be proved with absolute certainty. The official cause of the XB-29 crash was listed as "Power Plant – Undetermined," and the crash report stated:

> Fire in No. 1 engine nacelle was followed by fire and gasoline explosion in entire left wing. This resulted not only in loss of power in both No. 1 and No. 2 engine but also fire, smoke and flame in control cabin which in turn resulted in pilot's inability to prevent crash.[24]

After a nine-week investigation, the available evidence suggested that the disaster of February 18, 1943, was caused by a fuel leak. A cascade of events that followed would doom the XB-29.

The investigation concluded that the source of the fuel leaks were the fuel filler neck assemblies that were located inside the leading edge of the wing on the forward wing spar. It was believed that after takeoff, when the XB-29 leveled off at 5,000 feet and reduced power, this caused the fuel in the tanks to level out and possibly surge forward. Situated in the leading edge of the wing, the filler neck assemblies were in an area of greatly reduced air pressure, suction that equaled approximately one pound per square inch. Together with the leveling off and possible surge in the fuel tanks, this suction effect caused the filler necks to fill with fuel, which then leaked out through the fuel cap and into the filler neck wells. The filler neck wells had drains that extended to the bottom of the leading edge of the wing, but this was an area of high air pressure, and the fuel would have instead been drawn back into the leading edge itself and out over the top of the wing. It was believed that this scenario was also the cause of the in-flight fuel leak observed the day before the crash, but the report failed to explain why a leak of this nature had not been encountered during previous flights.

As the XB-29 continued on in level flight, fuel started building up in the No. 1 and No. 2 filler neck wells, and being unable to properly drain, the fuel began to seep into the leading edge of the wing. After three minutes, enough fuel had entered the leading edge to flow along the forward wing spar through seams and joints and into the No. 1 engine nacelle. To test this theory, the investigators conducted a test on the first XB-29, in which water was poured on the front edge of the spar in the vicinity of the filler neck. The test showed that the water would flow along the spar and into the No. 1 engine nacelle, where it collected in pockets near two small nacelle vents that were located in close proximity to the engine exhaust outlet, and near one of the supercharger regulators. It was believed that this accumulation of fuel could have ignited after contacting the hot engine exhaust, or through the operation of electrical equipment, and caused the first fire in the No. 1 engine nacelle.[25]

Based on the radio reports received from the XB-29, the crew believed they had extinguished the fire and began their return to Boeing Field with no undue alarm. What Eddie Allen did not know, as the investigation later determined, was that the fire had found its way into the leading edge of the wing and, due to a lack of oxygen, continued to burn very slowly. Once inside the leading edge, the fire progressed undetected towards the No. 2 engine nacelle and consumed a magnesium deicer valve that was mounted next to the No. 2 filler neck on the forward wing spar. The burning magnesium then melted its way through the aluminum skin of the leading edge and permitted a surge of air to enter the leading edge of the wing. The sudden addition of this oxygen instantly produced an explosion within the leading edge of the wing and was the first indication to the crew that the fire was out of control. The force of the explosion was so violent that a section of the leading edge was blown away and the No. 2 filler neck was torn loose, which released a huge quantity of fuel that quickly ignited and consumed the left wing. The remains of the deicer valve and other debris recovered along the flight path confirmed this scenario.[26]

The status of the three functioning engines after the explosion was not immediately clear, and the witness observations varied. Some stated that the No. 1 and No. 2 engines were not functioning, while others reported that none of the engines appeared to be under power. It was believed that the intense fire following the leading edge explosion probably caused the No. 2 engine to fail, but no evidence remained to prove this conclusively. The inspection of the No. 3 and No. 4 engines revealed that both had damage that was consistent with the engines "revving up" just prior to impact, and a witness also stated that it appeared power was applied to these engines after the XB-29 struck the power lines on Holgate Street.[27] Curiously, a Boeing investigation found that the XB-29's rate of descent in the final moments before the crash was greater than could be accounted for, even with two engines out and the increased drag of the lowered landing gear. No explanation for this was ever given, but it was theorized that the XB-29 was out of control just before impact due to smoke and flames in the cockpit.[28]

The status of the No. 3 and No. 4 engines in the moments leading up to the crash will never be known with any certainty, but what was clear was that the fire had spread into the cockpit just before the crash. This was evident from the burns found on the body of Ed Wersebe, the last man to jump from the XB-29.[29]

To aid the investigation, a timeline of the flight was established based on radio reports and witness testimony, and a B-17 was then flown along the flight path to simulate the final moments before the crash. From all of this data, it was determined that after the explosion in the leading edge of the wing, Eddie Allen and his crew had less than a minute to react before the crash. The fire went from undetected to fatal in just 45 seconds.[30]

*　　*　　*

After the devastating loss of Eddie Allen and his crew, resuming the XB-29 flight test program would be no easy task. All of the XB-29's pre-crash problems still remained, and now there were a lot of new ones as well. All of these issues would have to be fixed before another B-29 flew again.

"Naturally, the crash retarded the program," recalled Colonel Donald Putt, the XB-29 project officer. "Causes were indefinite according to the investigation report of the crash board. Steps immediately were taken to reduce all fire hazards in the airplane and, until these changes were made, flight operations were suspended."[31]

Based on the recommendations of the accident committee, the changes ranged from installing fire stops and providing proper ventilation in the leading edge of the wings and engine nacelles, to relocating the fuel filler necks and redesigning the fuel caps so they would not leak even under internal pressure. Until all of these changes could be made on the two remaining XB-29s and incorporated into the production line, no B-29 would be permitted to fly.[32]

By the end of May, three months after the crash, flight testing was ready to resume. The first XB-29 prototype was still undergoing work, but on May 29, the third XB-29 was completed and released to Colonel Harman and his Army flight crew, who would be taking over the test flights. The brand-new XB-29 had not yet been cleared to fly by Boeing, but Harman planned to make a high-speed taxi test down the runway and approach flying speed to test the bomber's handling characteristics. At the north end of Boeing Field, Harman lined the XB-29 up on the runway centerline and advanced the throttles for the first run. Scattered groups of Boeing and Army personnel watched as the gleaming XB-29 surged and picked up speed.

Roaring down the runway, the XB-29 was just beginning to lift into the air when Harman suddenly realized that something was dreadfully wrong. "Next thing I knew, we were in flight," Harman recalled. "And then it was just like going down the highway at sixty miles an hour and turning the wheel to the left and the airplane went right instead. Next thing I knew the wingtip was dragging on the runway. I was in a vertical bank."[33]

For those watching the taxi run, no one could believe what they were seeing. For eight terrifying seconds, the XB-29 flew above the runway in a precariously steep bank, dragging its right wingtip on the ground and kicking up a plume of debris as the No. 4 propeller blades slammed into the concrete. Harman tried to level the wings, but his control inputs only made the bank steeper. The XB-29 was going out of control and about to crash. Harman had to act fast.

"So I gave it full power on the starboard engines and throttled the left-hand engines," Harman continued. "The wing gradually came up and kind of went over and we landed on a taxi strip parallel to the runway." By using differential engine power, Harman was able to level the wings and bring the XB-29 to a skidding stop next to the runway. "I had the hell scared out of me," Harman said, but his quick thinking had averted another disaster.[34]

The entire incident was captured on film by Boeing employees who were stationed along the runway to record the test. One cameraman was sent running for his life when the XB-29 suddenly veered in his direction. The final dramatic seconds of his footage captured the XB-29 skidding sideways out of control and heading straight for his camera. General Wolfe, who happened to be watching the test from a nearby office window, recalled thinking "My God, we're going to lose the second one!" as the XB-29 went out of control. Wolfe and Harman "didn't dare" tell General Arnold about the incident, who only found out about it long afterward.[35]

An examination of the XB-29 after the incident revealed that the aileron control cables had been improperly installed in the control columns, which resulted in a reversal of the pilot's control inputs. When Harman attempted to raise the right wing, the crossed cables had the opposite effect and lowered it instead. The oversight had nearly resulted in the loss of another prototype, but there was plenty of blame to go around: no one had cycled the control surfaces and visually confirmed their function before the test.[36]

Eight days later, with the aileron cables properly rigged, Harman took the XB-29 up for its maiden flight. The ensuing 46-minute flight made quite an impression on Harman: "Boy, I put it through the paces and found out we had a hell of a good airplane, just a tremendous airplane."[37]

On June 27, Harman flew the XB-29 to Wichita, Kansas, on its first long-distance flight. After arriving over Wichita in record time, an invigorated Harman buzzed the massive Boeing-Wichita factory, which was just starting to produce B-29s, and then crisscrossed the town in a spirited display of the new super-bomber. The B-29 was still a military secret, but it was said that Harman's aerial display was so spectacular that news of the bomber's arrival leaked out over the local airwaves.[38] Later that evening, and still animated from the day's flight, Harman sent a cable to General Wolfe stating that the XB-29 was the greatest airplane he'd ever flown.[39]

The B-29 program was finally moving forward again, but serious problems with the engines still remained. In an effort to improve its reliability and performance, over 2,000 design changes were made to the R-3350 engine in 1943 alone. By the end of the war, that number would grow to a staggering 6,274 design changes, which resulted in 48,500 engineering releases and change notices for the engine. The engineers would try to perfect the R-3350 while the combat crews fought a war with it.[40]

5

The Battle of Kansas

Now all the city is black. Suddenly in the north we heard the sound of plane engines. The orders were flashed everywhere and all the sounds on the street stilled. The propeller noise of the enemy planes spread over the whole sky. Minute by minute the noise approached. At this moment there was a shot, like a skyrocket, into the air. Several tons of shots. I could see clearly the figures of the enemy planes. At once anti-aircraft began to shoot. The guns shouted like lightning. But the hateful enemy planes flew on. Suddenly fire dropped from them – one, two, three. These were the flares. The whole city could be clearly seen in reddish light. Then came big black things from the white bodies of the planes. Bombs! And boom! boom! boom! The devils, the beasts! Again boom! boom! boom!

Japanese newspaper account of the first B-29 bombing raid against Japan[1]

Half a day earlier, the briefing room packed with eager B-29 crews became hushed when the large target map was finally revealed. After years in the making, through painful delays, challenges and tragedies, this was the moment everyone had been waiting for.

"We are going to hit the biggest steel mills in the Japanese Empire," Colonel Harman announced, as he highlighted the Japanese city of Yawata – the Pittsburgh of Japan – with a red crayon. "And if you put your cookies on the target it will be at least 14 months before the Japs can replace the loss." Harman paused, then added: "If there ever was a juicy target, this is it."[2]

For the men of the 58th Bomb Wing, the pioneers of the B-29, it had been a long and arduous journey, but the moment had finally arrived. The B-29 was going to war.

* * *

The journey of the 58th Bomb Wing, the first combat unit to be equipped with the B-29, began a year earlier in the middle of a hot Georgia summer. With only a handful of B-29s beginning to roll off the production lines, the 58th Bomb Wing established its first headquarters in June of 1943 on an old Southern estate at the Cobb County Army Airfield in Marietta, Georgia.

Resting in the shadow of Kennesaw Mountain, the site of a fierce battle during the Civil War, upon this old battlefield had risen a colossal factory to build B-29s. But the new headquarters of the 58th Bomb Wing and the Bell Bomber Plant had another connection to the Civil War besides the red Georgia clay they called home. Among the thousands of women who would be employed on the B-29 production lines at Bell was Helen Longstreet, the widow of Civil War Confederate General James Longstreet, who was one of Robert E. Lee's most trusted generals.

At 80 years old, Helen Longstreet had been waiting by the front gates the first day the factory opened and was quickly hired to be a riveter, even though she had never even seen a rivet gun before. "I was head of the class in riveting school," Mrs. Longstreet liked to say. "In fact, I was the only one in it." With a feisty personality and a tireless work ethic, Helen Longstreet was an inspiration to her co-workers, and she never missed a day of work for the duration of the war. (General Longstreet died in 1904 at the age of 82, but as late as 1938, there were still some 8,000 Civil War veterans living. The last Civil War veteran died in 1956.)[3]

The man tasked with organizing the 58th Bomb Wing and leading the first B-29s into combat, arguably the most coveted command in the Army Air Forces, was 46-year-old Brigadier General K.B. Wolfe. Despite having no combat experience, Wolfe was a logical choice for the job, and he quickly seized the reins of his new command with the "hard hitting, but soft spoken" fervor he was known for. But as had been painfully learned during the XB-29 flight testing, nothing would be easy with the new B-29s.[4] "We started from scratch," Wolfe remembered. "We began with what was still, by military necessity, an incompletely designed, experimental airplane – more complicated than any ever before used in aerial warfare. When the 58th Bombardment Wing was activated on June 1, 1943, we had no personnel, no planes, no precedents."[5]

The directive from General Arnold for Wolfe and the 58th Bomb Wing was simple: commit the B-29 to combat without delay. Carrying out those orders would not be so easy.[6]

To accelerate the next phase of B-29 testing, Wolfe moved Colonel Abram Olson and his test branch from Wright Field to Smoky Hill Army Airfield in Kansas to begin the service testing of the B-29. Olson's program would test the B-29 under operational conditions, but just like the XB-29 flight tests, severe problems would be encountered almost immediately. The R-3350 engines were still failing, and compounding the maintenance problems was the fact that Olson's mechanics had never worked on a B-29 before. "In the area of maintenance, most things had to be learned as we went along and some frustrating problems proved to be very simple – once we learned the tricks," recalled John Mitchell, a mechanic assigned to Olson's test branch. Performing maintenance on the B-29s was challenging because the maintenance manuals had not yet been written. The first engine change at Smoky Hill took two weeks to complete because there were no instructions on how to do it.[7]

The need for basic information about the B-29 was so great that in July, the 58th Bomb Wing published its own operating manual. The *B-29 Familiarization File* contained general information about the B-29 and outlined the first operating procedures that were established by trial and error. To aid the new crews, the manual included step-by-step instructions that ranged from starting the engines to how to land a B-29. The fact that there were so many unknowns about operating the B-29 was reaffirmed on the second page of the manual, where the authors openly invited suggestions and revisions to their techniques.[8] By the time the first comprehensive maintenance manual was released that August, it still contained many blank pages that simply stated: "To be furnished when available."[9]

Some of the most extensive technical manuals of the war would eventually be created for the B-29, but the complexity of the bomber presented a unique challenge. With nearly 300,000 aircraft mechanics graduating from technical schools in 1943 alone, the demands of the war had created a surge of new mechanics who would have to quickly learn how to maintain the most technologically advanced bombers in the world.[10] Many of the new graduates had no prior mechanical experience before joining the service. To now train these men as quickly as possible would take some creative approaches to teaching, which included extensive use of training films. With the help of the First Motion Picture Unit and its staff of movie professionals from Hollywood, a variety of training films were produced about the B-29. Future President Ronald Reagan, who was one of the movie stars assigned to the unit, narrated a flight engineer training film, and he also starred in a film about how to identify a Japanese Zero fighter in flight.

The B-29's massive technical manuals were also written in such a way that a person with no mechanical background could easily understand them. Some topics were even presented in comic book fashion, including a manual filled with step-by-step illustrations for changing an engine. However, not everyone agreed that the new manuals were worth all of the trouble. A gentleman's disagreement had been brewing for weeks between General William Knudsen and Colonel Howard Couch, chief of the B-29 project technical staff, over how much time and money was being spent on the manuals. Knudsen had been arguing that the manuals were too elaborate and filled with "pretty pictures," but their value was demonstrated one day when Knudsen and Couch were together on the Boeing flight line.

To prove how effective the manuals were, Couch approached a civilian worker who had never been inside an airplane before, handed him a flight manual, and told him to read it for five minutes. He was then to climb inside a nearby B-29 and start the engines by following the instructions in the manual. Within 18 minutes, the ex-farmer, whose only mechanical experience had been operating a tractor, had all four engines running smoothly. Knudsen's criticisms abruptly ceased.[11]

*   *   *

The 58th Bomb Wing began forming its bomb groups at four massive new airfields in Kansas at Great Bend, Pratt, Walker and Smoky Hill, which became the wing's new headquarters in September of 1943. The plan was to train four bomb groups for combat, while a fifth would stay behind as a training unit when the wing deployed overseas.

A great migration of men from all across the Unites States began pouring into Kansas to begin training, but the fledgling bomb groups were missing one very important thing: B-29s. By the end of September, only 26 B-29s had rolled off the production lines, and most were awaiting modifications before being delivered to the groups.[12] "Occasionally they saw a B-29," General Wolfe said of the men in the bomb groups, "but most of them spent many months with synthetic training devices, in high altitude pressure chambers, on firing ranges and in other types of planes before they set foot in a Superfortress."[13]

While the bomb groups waited for more B-29s to arrive, the flight training proceeded with B-26 and B-17 bombers, and the gunners used mock-ups to familiarize themselves with the B-29's complex gunnery system. The ground crews also required additional training, so a special B-29 school was organized in Seattle by Boeing and the Army Air Forces to train mechanics how to work on the new bombers. The B-29 school was modeled after a similar program that trained B-17 mechanics, but the school was set up so quickly that the graduates received diplomas that were still marked "Boeing Flying Fortress School." No one had time to make new diplomas.

With its wide-open spaces, Kansas was an ideal place for the 58th Bomb Wing to begin training, but the men forming the bomb groups had a different take on it. Lieutenant Philip Oliver of the 462nd Bomb Group recalled those early days in Kansas:

> Our first impressions of our Kansas home were not too favorable. Nothing in sight for miles but the famous "bread basket of the nation" … no nearby town except Walker, whose farmer inhabitants were not quite prepared to absorb the social attentions of the thousands of G.I.s … Training was the key activity of those days with a lot of flying and maintenance work, not to mention the many days of trotting from one classroom to another – aircraft identification, gunnery, radio and radar procedure, ditching and first aid, operational procedure, photography, etc. … After a summer of Kansas heat, a short period of fairly comfortable weather arrived with fall. This relief from the dog days was accompanied by the arrival of the first few of our authorized B-29s to replace the B-17s and B-26s the boys had been flying … Many of us will never forget our first awed impression of the Superfort when the first touched down on our runway – it seemed just too damn big to fly.[14]

When the first B-29s began trickling in to the bomb groups, the bombers brought with them a whole new set of problems. One of the many challenges would be training the pilots how to fly an aircraft that was so vastly different from the smaller bombers they had been flying. Surrounded by plexiglass panels that made the cockpit look like a greenhouse, one instructor said transitioning to the B-29 felt like "sitting on the front porch facing the street and practicing flying the house."[15] (The B-29's cockpit was so unique that it later inspired George Lucas when his team created the cockpit of the *Millennium Falcon* for *Star Wars*.)

Engine failures continued to plague the new bombers, and the problems were only getting worse as the groups tried to keep pace with their training schedules. "Each flight was a thrill in itself," recalled Colonel Alva Harvey, a B-29 project officer who later commanded the 444th Bomb Group. "If we returned to base with three of the four engines running, that was considered par for the course."[16] A range of new modifications that would improve the B-29 were already underway, but no real solution had been found yet for the engine failures. As one mechanic noted, it appeared that the aircrews would have to live – or die – with the engine problems.[17]

By the end of 1943, due to ongoing delays, modifications and mechanical problems, only 67 pilots had been checked out in the B-29. The average 58th Bomb Wing crew had only flown 18 hours in a B-29, and only a single B-29 had flown a long-range practice mission. The mechanical problems were so bad that the B-29s were only flying an average of two hours out of every 24. The cost for so little progress had been high: five B-29s were involved in serious accidents that killed 46 men.[18] The growing number of crashes led to the creation of a booklet entitled *How Not to Fly the B-29*, which examined various training accidents and highlighted what the pilots did wrong. Over 17,000 copies of the booklet would be distributed to B-29 crews during the war.[19]

The training accidents were not just limited to the B-29, however. With aircraft production surging and the need for new pilots greater than ever, 1943 would go down as the deadliest training year for the Army Air Forces. By the end of the year, with almost 248,000 pilots and aircrew undergoing training in the fourth quarter alone, a staggering 20,390 aircraft had been involved in accidents within the Continental United States, which resulted in 5,603 fatalities.[20] Averaged over the entire year, the accident rate equated to 56 crashes and 15 fatalities per day.

When all of the accidents were tallied after the war, over 52,000 aircraft had crashed in training accidents. The human toll for training the Army Air Forces would cost almost 15,000 lives.[21]

1944

"Two years after Pearl Harbor we have reached the moment when the basic change in our strategic position has become apparent to all," General Arnold reported to the Secretary of War on January 4, 1944. "It is now plain that for us the beginning has ended; for our enemies, the end has begun."[22]

After a period of setbacks following the Pearl Harbor attack, on the same day that Arnold released his report to the Secretary of War, the Army Air Forces were now fully engaged in aerial warfare across the globe. On that January day, a force numbering over 500 B-17 and B-24 bombers struck targets inside Germany, and another 253 B-26 bombers attacked German targets across France. Elsewhere in Europe, more than 100 B-17s bombed German targets in Bulgaria, B-25 bombers struck targets in Yugoslavia, and P-40 fighters attacked bridges and Axis supply trains in Italy.[23] In the Pacific, hundreds of fighters and bombers attacked Japanese targets stretching from New Guinea to the Solomon Islands, and a force of 18 B-24 bombers staging through Tarawa – an island that had been captured from the Japanese just six weeks before after a bloody 76-hour battle that cost the lives of over 1,000 Marines and sailors – bombed Japanese targets in the Marshall Islands.[24]

From a force of just 354,000 men and 4,400 combat aircraft when Pearl Harbor was attacked, the Army Air Forces had now swelled to over 2.4 million personnel and 67,000 aircraft.[25] In the rapidly expanding battle to crush the Axis powers, nearly 800,000 Army Air Forces personnel were already serving overseas by January of 1944, and more were arriving each day. By the end of the year, over 1.6 million men would be serving abroad.[26]

At home, the volume of new trainees continued to grow exponentially. The first quarter of 1944 alone saw more than 103,000 pilots, 4,500 bombardiers, 35,500 gunners, and 48,000 aircraft mechanics graduate from training. The war of production had also surged to more than 9,200 new airplanes and 22,600 aircraft engines produced in January alone.[27] The tide was turning.

While the Army Air Forces were fighting on a global scale, its newest bombers were still far from combat-ready in January of 1944. For the 58th Bomb Wing, the new year brought nothing but old problems and new delays. Of the 97 B-29s that had been produced by January, due to ongoing modifications, only 16 were actually flyable, and none were ready for combat.[28] The 40th Bomb Group at Pratt only had six B-29s and one pre-production YB-29 assigned to the entire group and its four squadrons. Their full strength was supposed to be 38 B-29s. Of the seven B-29s they did have, when they weren't grounded for maintenance or lack of spare parts, their flying was hampered by the fact that 14 engines had failed in January alone.[29]

When the B-29s were flying, the crews began to discover some concerning issues with the new bombers, such as the tendency for the gunner's plexiglass sighting blisters to suddenly blow out in flight when the cabins were pressurized. During one crew's first high-altitude flight in December, gasoline fumes began filling the cabin as they climbed through 20,000 feet over Texas. As the pilot ordered the crew to return to their stations and put on their parachutes, the fumes seemed to slowly dissipate. Back in the gunner's compartment, Sergeant George Olson, the right gunner, was sitting at his station when his sighting blister suddenly blew out. The force of the explosive decompression was so violent that it sucked Olson out of the hole in the fuselage where the blister had been and sent him free falling at 20,000 feet.

Up in the cockpit, the B-29 jolted and filled with fog as it decompressed, but no one knew what happened. After donning oxygen masks, the pilot asked each crew member to report in with their status over the interphone. When the pilot asked Sergeant Olson to report, there was no reply. The pilot called to Olson a second time, but again there was only silence. The pilot then asked the left gunner, Sergeant Carnes, to check on Olson and find out why he wasn't responding:

> Pilot: "Sergeant Carnes, check with Sergeant Olson and find out why he's not reporting."
> Gunner: "Sergeant Olson isn't here, sir."
> Pilot: "Where is Sergeant Olson?"
> Gunner: "He's gone, sir."
> Pilot: "What you mean, he's gone?"
> Gunner: "He's gone, sir. The blister is gone. Everything at his position went right out the side."[30]

The crew immediately informed Pratt of what happened, and then, believing that Olson was dead, began a very somber flight back to Kansas. A few hours later, just as the B-29 was landing, the base received a phone call from a small town in Texas. Olson had managed to pull the ripcord of his parachute just before he passed out from a lack of oxygen and miraculously landed on a remote ranch without a scratch. After he came to and landed, Olson was collecting his parachute and trying to figure out where he was when the confused ranch owner drove up.

"Where in hell did you come from?" the shocked rancher asked.

"Oh, I fell out of an airplane," Olson casually replied.

The B-29 was still a military secret, and Olson couldn't divulge what really happened. A B-26 was soon dispatched from Pratt and flew Olson back to base, where the crew held a "blister party" in his honor.[31] As a result of this and other incidents, the sighting blisters would have to be redesigned and strengthened, and that meant even more delays. In the meantime, metal cages were temporarily installed inside the blisters to prevent a gunner from being sucked out again.

Despite the fact that not a single B-29 was ready for combat, halfway around the world, the groundwork for a new air offensive against Japan was already well underway. On January 13, General Wolfe arrived in India to oversee the construction of new airbases and set up his XX (20th) Bomber Command to lead the B-29s into combat. Wolfe had been promoted to organize and lead the command just six weeks earlier, and he wasted no time in getting things moving.

The question of where the B-29s would be based had been the subject of much debate, with locations ranging from Australia to Alaska's Aleutian Islands being considered, but in the end, Operation *Matterhorn* was chosen as the beginning of the strategic bombing campaign against the Japanese homeland. The plan called for the B-29s to be based in India, fly to forward bases in China, overnight and refuel, and then fly on to their targets in Japan. After striking their targets, the B-29s would return to China, overnight and refuel, and then continue back to

India. All of this flying would span thousands of miles over some of the most hostile terrain in the world.

The challenge that General Wolfe now faced with implementing Operation *Matterhorn* was monumental. His first task would be overseeing the construction of new airbases in two very different parts of the world. The four bases selected in India were spread out west of Calcutta, but they were originally built by the British for B-24 bombers and would need considerable improvements to handle the B-29s. The forward bases in China presented the greatest challenge of all. Unlike the bases in India, which had good rail and road access for supplies, the China bases were completely cut off from Allied forces by the Himalayas, the highest mountain range in the world. Everything that was needed to sustain the bases and the bombers would have to be flown in from India over the "Hump," as the airmen referred to the Himalayas, some 1,200 miles away.

It was already clear that Operation *Matterhorn* would be a logistical nightmare, but it was the only option for the B-29s to strike Japan by early 1944.

The construction of the forward bases located in the Chengtu region of southwest China seemed like an impossible task. Since no heavy equipment could be brought in, the four B-29 airbases, each with a 1½-mile-long runway, plus additional fighter, transport and emergency strips, would have to be constructed entirely by hand. But what China lacked in modern equipment was made up for in sheer manpower. Hundreds of thousands of Chinese laborers – men, women and children – were drawn from the countryside and descended upon the rice paddies to begin a herculean undertaking. The construction of the bases would be overseen by just 26 American engineers, along with a large corps of Chinese engineers and officials. Some Americans would have up to 23,000 men working under them at a time.[32]

A great transformation began to take place as work got underway in China. First the rice paddies were drained and then the mud, up to nine feet deep in places, was carried away in shoulder-borne tandem baskets. Tons of stones were then carried from riverbeds in the same baskets and individually hand-fitted to form a solid foundation for the runways. Since no concrete was available, larger stones and boulders were crushed by hand to make gravel and then mixed with dirt to build up the runways. Massive 10-ton rollers carved out of sandstone were then pulled by teams of hundreds of men to compact the runway surface. The rollers were so heavy that they could not be stopped quickly, and some 25 men were crushed to death when they fell in the path of one. To finish the surface of the runways, tung oil was used to bind the dirt and gravel together.[33]

While the Chinese were building airbases for the new super-bombers, back on the other side of the world, a B-29 crew from the 40th Bomb Group was dispatched from Pratt on a very special mission. On February 21, a limousine escorted by a small convoy of vehicles approached a brand new B-29 parked at Bolling Field in Washington, D.C. The crew had been personally briefed by General Arnold the day before, and as the limousine slowly came to a stop in front of them, they were all keenly aware of just how important this moment would be. Surrounded by heavy security, the door of the limo opened. Sitting inside was President Franklin Roosevelt, his daughter, two grandchildren, and the President's dog, Fala. Roosevelt had been personally following the B-29's progress since the beginning, and with the new bombers set to start moving overseas to India in a matter of weeks, today would be the first time the President would get to see the "three-billion-dollar gamble" in person. He would not be disappointed.

After the President cheerfully talked with each member of the crew, who described their duties on the bomber, his limo slowly circled around the B-29 so Roosevelt could view it from all sides. (Due to polio which left him paralyzed from the waist down, Roosevelt did not leave the limo to look inside the B-29.) The President was very interested in the tail turret and had asked the tail gunner, Bill Mackey, to show him how it worked. Mackey climbed into the tail compartment and as the limo pulled around, he proceeded to demonstrate the tail turret by pointing his guns directly at the President. "I still say I am the only person on earth who has had two .50 caliber machine guns and a 20mm cannon trained on the President and his limo," Mackey recalled years later. "I made sure there was no ammo in that turret."[34]

While the Secret Service was not amused, Roosevelt was thrilled by the demonstration and felt very confident about the B-29 and its prospects for crippling Japan. But back in Kansas, with the delays mounting, confidence was quickly giving way to chaos.

*   *   *

"This is the plane I want," General Arnold said, pointing to a B-29 fuselage under construction at the Boeing-Wichita factory. "I want it before the first of March." To implement Operation *Matterhorn*, the 58th Bomb Wing needed 150 B-29s ready by early March, and this fuselage would become the final B-29 to reach that goal.[35] Pleased with the progress he saw at Wichita, Arnold inscribed a message below the co-pilot's window: "The end of a good job splendidly done. Thanx from the AAF." From that moment on, the B-29 would be known as the *Gen. H.H. Arnold Special*, and it was delivered to the 468th Bomb Group at Smokey Hill right on schedule.[36]

New B-29s were also beginning to roll off the production lines at Marietta and Omaha, and Renton would produce its first B-29 in just a matter of weeks. After a nationwide industrial mobilization, B-29s would soon be streaming out of four factories at a rapidly increasing pace.

To get Operation *Matterhorn* underway, in February the 58th Bomb Wing began the massive undertaking of moving from Kansas to India. The first to leave were the ground personnel, who were crammed into troopships packed with thousands of men. "Our quarters were very close – 450 men in a space no larger than twice the size of a four-room compartment," recalled Morton Roth, a B-29 mechanic. In order to fit so many men in such confined spaces, the sleeping cots on the ships had to be suspended on poles and stacked up to six cots high, floor to ceiling.[37]

The voyage to India would take over two months for some of the ships, and adding to the misery were the severe storms, seasickness, bad food, and the threat of enemy submarines. The final leg of the journey was a miserable cross-country trip by Indian railroad before finally reaching the airbases. For the men who had been traveling for months over sea and land, it felt like they had reached the end of the earth.

Following the ground personnel, the first B-29s were scheduled to begin leaving for India on March 10. The previous day, General Arnold arrived in Kansas to see off the first bombers, but when he asked how many B-29s would be leaving the next day, he was shocked by the answer: none.[38] With so much riding on the B-29, and the eyes of the President and other Allied leaders watching, General Arnold immediately demanded answers. What he found left him seething. Arnold quickly discovered that the entire modification program, whose sole purpose was to get the B-29s ready for combat, was "void of organization, management and leadership," and fumed that the entire situation was a "disgrace to the Army Air Forces."[39]

No one seemed to know what the status of each B-29 was, or when the missing parts needed for a slew of modifications would even arrive. Arnold was incensed by this revelation and demanded a detailed assessment of the work yet to be completed. Later that night, a chart was prepared that revealed the startling truth: not a single B-29 was ready for war.[40]

How the 58th Bomb Wing found itself in such a precarious state could be traced directly to the accelerated program to get the B-29 into production as quickly as possible. A new airplane would typically undergo years of testing before the final design entered mass production, but in the case of the B-29, the need for the new bomber was so great that production had to begin while design changes were still being made. All of these changes would now have to be made without slowing down the production lines, and there were literally hundreds of them.

"Between the time the XB-29 design was approved and the day it made its first test flight, 900 changes were incorporated to improve the plane; 240 more were made before the first production model was completed," explained Colonel Donald Putt in a 1944 article. "Hundreds more have been made since production started."[41]

The design changes were coming so fast that the factories could not possibly keep up with them. Now faced with even more delays, it was decided to freeze the design of the B-29 in order to keep the production lines moving, and the changes would then be completed at modification centers. The problem was that so many changes were being made that by the end of 1943, each B-29 needed almost 25,000 worker hours just to complete the modifications alone.[42] The modification centers were quickly overwhelmed and fell behind schedule.

With Arnold's March deadline approaching, and with rows of B-29s sitting idle at modification centers across the country, action had to be taken. Major Victor Agather, who was assigned to help speed the work at Pratt, recalled:

> As the modification centers dropped behind schedule and the combat crews did not have B-29 aircraft for training purposes, the decision was made to switch the modification from the modification centers to the four bases in Kansas ... and in so doing, the crews could become familiar with the aircraft and its modifications ... within a short period of time, there was not a flyable B-29 in Kansas and utter confusion reigned ... the B-29 ground crews had already left for India and there were no adequate ground crews at the Kansas bases to accomplish the modifications, provided anybody knew what modifications had to be made on any given aircraft.[43]

When the B-29s were delivered to the bomb groups in Kansas to complete the modifications, they arrived with non-standard equipment and incomplete work logs. As a result, no one knew which B-29 needed what modifications, or where the missing parts for those modifications were. It didn't take long for the program to descend into total chaos.

There were also some confusing changes made to the bombers. One day, a sergeant was inspecting a newly arrived B-29 when he noticed that something very important was missing. "Where the hell did they put the toilet?" the confused sergeant yelled. It was later explained to him that the toilet had been moved to another part of the cabin for reasons of weight and balance.[44]

The chaos wrought by all of these changes was now threatening to derail the entire 58th Bomb Wing and Operation *Matterhorn*.

The B-29 program had once again found itself teetering on the brink of disaster. But just as before, men would always rise to pull it back from the brink. This time Arnold called upon

Major General Bennett Meyers, a top troubleshooter from Wright Field, and he would have the full resources of the Army Air Forces behind him. To get the B-29s ready for combat, the modification program was now given top priority over everything, and Meyers, who Arnold described as a "go-getter, a pusher" who "got things done," was given full authority to act on Arnold's behalf.[45]

"I told Meyers he had to get those airplanes out on time, and the crews must be ready to go with them," Arnold recalled. "He was to send special airplanes for the parts, if necessary, so they could be installed on the B-29s with the least possible delay."[46]

Meyers set up his headquarters in the base hospital at Salina, and phones quickly began ringing across the country in a rush to get the missing parts to Kansas. Meanwhile, an army of mechanics and technicians were mobilized and rushed to Kansas. Their orders were simple: there would be no paperwork except for short notes about the work completed; the hours would be as long as a man could stand on his feet; and the last B-29 must be ready to leave by April 15.[47]

The epic struggle that followed would become known as the Battle of Kansas. In just a matter of weeks, all 150 B-29s of the 58th Bomb Wing would need every modification completed and be ready to leave for India. In most cases, each B-29 needed well over 50 different modifications to prepare it for combat.[48] The list of work for just the 40th Bomb Group alone was staggering: 100 propeller assemblies and 124 cowl flaps had to be removed and modified; 100 sets of engine exhaust collector rings had to be changed; 144 tires, 22 rudders, and 24 turbosuperchargers had to be replaced; and 36 APQ-13 radar sets had to be installed by men who had never installed that type of radar before. The list went on and on.[49]

The most critical job would be replacing all four of the B-29's R-3350 engines with an updated "war" version that had all the latest changes to improve cooling and reliability. For just the 40th Bomb Group, that meant that 116 engines had to be changed.[50]

Just as the Battle of Kansas was getting underway, a blizzard swept across the plains and blanketed the airfields with snow, ferocious winds and sub-zero temperatures. Since there were very few hangars available, practically all the work had to be completed outside in the weather. At times it was so cold that the men could only work for 20 minutes before retreating indoors, but no matter how bad the weather became, the work had to continue around the clock.

"Most of us were spending a solid 18 hours daily on the flight line, seven days per week," recalled Ira Mathers, a pilot with the 40th Bomb Group. "The weather was atrocious with surface temperatures below zero, driving north winds and giant snow drifts across the parking ramp."[51]

The long hours and lack of sleep made tempers short, and at times tensions flared between the Army crews and some of the civilian technicians, who were accused of not working as long or as hard as they should have been. The grievances were quickly settled, and work continued.

"We worked as many hours as we could stand up, then took over someone else's bed in one of the two tiny hotels in the near-by town," recalled one technician from General Electric. "Each bed had a different occupant for two or three shifts a day, and every so often an open army reconnaissance car delivered a group in town and took another out."[52]

Despite the horrendous weather, thousands of men were now working on the frozen Kansas plains in an all-out effort to prepare the B-29s for combat. To reinforce the Army crews and civilian technicians, Boeing pulled 600 of its mechanics off the production lines at Wichita, and other specialists were flown in from across the country. Many didn't even have time to go home and pack before they were rushed to a waiting plane and whisked away to Kansas.[53]

Most of the men arriving at the airbases were not prepared for the weather that greeted them. At one point during the battle, two B-29 gunners were trying to figure out how to install a new gun turret when a B-17 landed and a group of men wearing summer uniforms piled out into the snow and howling winds. As the shivering men ran past the gunners into the hangar, one of them turned and asked: "My God, does the wind blow this way all the time in Kansas?" Without hesitation, one of the gunners answered in a slow Kansas drawl: "No, sometimes it turns around and blows the other way."[54]

6

The Global 20th

In the early hours of March 25, 1944, beneath the dull silver sheen of a lone B-29, shadowy figures stirred about in the frigid Kansas air. It had been less than three weeks since the Battle of Kansas began, but on this morning, after so many hectic days and nights of exhausting work, an anxious crew finally settled into their seats to begin the pre-flight checks. A mountain of flight gear, clothing and equipment was stuffed inside the bomber. The crew's vaccination shots for smallpox, yellow fever and other diseases were all up to date, and their life insurance policies and wills were signed. The last letters had been mailed. The final goodbyes were bid.

Then came the signal from the pilot, and the whine as the first engine coughed to life, followed by another, and another, until all four of the super-bomber's engines filled the air with a thunderous roar. With Colonel Jake Harman at the controls, the first B-29 rumbled down the runway and slowly faded into the dark sky. The 58th Bomb Wing was on its way.

Following behind Harman, and crammed full of equipment, extra parts, emergency repair kits, and a spare engine loaded in the forward bomb bay, more B-29s began leaving Kansas each day. But due to all of the delays and engine problems that had prevented the B-29s from flying with any regularity, most of the crews were still far behind in their training. "I doubt if there was a pilot in our group that had more than 50 or 75 hours in the big bird when we took off for India," recalled James Edmundson, the commander of the 468th Bomb Group.[1]

The long journey to India, which Lieutenant Philip Oliver described as an "11,000-mile round-the-world flight by crews with only a few weeks actual training in the B-29," would be flown in five legs with stops in Newfoundland, French Morocco, Cairo and Karachi before reaching the bases near Calcutta. For security reasons, the final destination of the B-29s remained a secret and the crews were only briefed on the next leg of their flight, not the entire route. At Gander Lake, Newfoundland – a base overflowing with bombers headed to Europe – any speculation that the B-29s might be going to England ended when the crews received orders for the next leg of their trip: Marrakech, French Morocco.[2]

The thought of a 2,700-mile flight over the Atlantic Ocean was cause for apprehension. "By now all the B-29s had about ten hours on their four new engines," recalled Hibbard Smith, a bombardier with the 40th Bomb Group. "Since no B-29 had ever gone much over ten hours without losing an engine, we started out for Africa with a certain amount of concern."[3] The average flight time across the Atlantic was 10½ hours, but fortunately all of the bombers made the crossing without incident.

On a sweltering afternoon in Chakulia, India, only eight days after leaving the snowy plains of Kansas, a silver giant appeared in the distance to the west. As the first B-29 to reach its base in India, Colonel Harman made a low pass over the field in celebration, and then he swung around and brought the bomber in for a perfect landing. Just 18 months after Eddie Allen lifted the first prototype into the air, and only six months after the first production model rolled out of the factory at Wichita, the B-29 was now in a theater of war.

Four days later, a second B-29 touched down in India after completing a very special mission. The bomber was actually a pre-production YB-29 built for service testing, and Colonel Frank Cook had just flown it in from England, where he'd spent the last two weeks showing off the bomber in an elaborate ruse. "We hoped to give the Germans the idea the B-29s were going to be used to supplement the B-17s and B-24s in our offensive against them, and thus to keep the Japanese from anticipating our real plans for sending the B-29s to India," General Arnold explained after the war. The ploy was effective, and no Axis fighters intercepted the B-29s as they moved overseas.[4]

The arrival of the first two bombers in India marked a high point after months of delays, but there was still much work to be done before the B-29s could strike Japan. Harman had made the journey from Kansas in eight days, but the B-29s following behind him were hampered by bad weather and mechanical problems. The engines were not faring well in the heat of Africa, and the temperatures would only become more extreme as the bombers neared India.

On April 13, with only 20 B-29s having reached India so far, disaster struck when one of the bombers crashed at Marrakech. In the days that followed, a string of crashes that resulted in the total loss of several B-29s forced Wolfe to temporarily ground the bombers while the engine failures were investigated. Wolfe quickly advised Arnold that it was "imperative that improved engine cooling be obtained immediately," and that meant more modifications would now be needed. The new "war" engines, which had been installed with so much difficulty during the Battle of Kansas to improve reliability, appeared to have changed nothing.[5]

While the engine cooling issues were being studied back in the States, the B-29s resumed their flights and by May 8, 130 bombers had reached their bases in India.[6] James O'Keefe, a bombardier with the 40th Bomb Group, recalled his first impressions of their new home at Chakulia:

> From the air we saw the entire layout – the red dirt runway, parked alongside of it the few B-29s of the earlier arrivals, a cluster of thatch-roofed buildings, and a scattering of tents. It looked dusty, sun-baked, and forlorn, as if someone had begun the building of it, and halfway through the job they had gone away and forgotten all about coming back. In all directions stretched a gentle plain, most of it covered with a sparse scrub forest. Villages surrounded by tiny, cultivated fields were scattered across the plain. Anything moving on that landscape raised a cloud of red dust.[7]

For the crews who had been struggling with blizzards only weeks before, India was a totally foreign world. During the day, temperatures could soar to a blistering 120 degrees, and the winds filled the air with a thick red dust that clung to everything. Practically everyone came down with a severe case of diarrhea within their first week in India, and for many it would be a reoccurring problem.

The bases were still far from completed when the crews arrived and offered no escape from the sweltering heat. At Chakulia, an airfield originally built by the British for B-24 bombers, the size of the arriving B-29s rendered the existing taxiways and parking revetments unusable. Until improvements could be made, the B-29s had to be parked in long rows along either side of the runway, which made for an inviting target.

If the conditions weren't challenging enough for the newly arrived crews, veterans often quipped that the CBI Theater (China-Burma-India) was "the only theater of war where you could be shot by a Japanese infiltrator, bitten by a cobra, or eaten by a tiger; all just while walking to and from the latrine." Sometimes the wildlife even stopped the war. One night, a supply train had to be halted when a tiger was discovered eating a cow on the railroad tracks. A brave GI pulled his pistol and began to approach, but quickly concluded that his firepower was insufficient. The entire supply train sat idle for over half an hour until the tiger finished its meal and wandered away. It was a strange war in the CBI.[8]

Despite the unbearable heat, work continued on the bases as the B-29s were readied for combat. But as the crews would soon learn, even the simplest tasks were a challenge in their new environment. "As operations and construction continued, the weather grew hotter and hotter until it became a problem to work as well as to sleep," recalled Lieutenant Philip Oliver. The extreme heat turned the B-29s into virtual ovens and made working inside the bombers nearly impossible during the afternoon hours. "The planes would get so hot we couldn't crawl inside for more than five minutes at a time," Oliver said, "and to touch the metal would produce second degree burns."[9]

Due to the heat, maintenance could only be performed in the morning and evening, which made it difficult to accomplish much of anything. Generators and portable lighting soon allowed the mechanics to work through the night, but the lights attracted swarms of insects. All of the discomforts aside, the crews tirelessly carried on with their mission. "We put in some long hours in the 'Land of Romance,' but what the heck!" Oliver recalled. "Where we were there wasn't any place to go and no romance to be had."[10]

While the crews were struggling to adjust to the extremes of India, the heat was also proving to have an adverse effect on the B-29s, and the biggest issue continued to be the R-3350 engines. After Wolfe pleaded to Arnold for a solution that would improve engine cooling, the engineers studied the problem and determined that the engines were failing due to insufficient airflow to cool the rear cylinders, and a lack of lubrication to the exhaust valves. This resulted in the exhaust valves becoming so hot that the valve stem would snap, and the valve head would then be sucked down into the combustion chamber of the cylinder. When a "swallowed valve" occurred, the moving piston would violently smash the valve head into the top of the combustion chamber, which quickly destroyed the piston and the cylinder. This rapid destruction would cause the engine to fail and usually resulted in a fire.

A number of new modifications were soon implemented to alleviate the cooling issues, but the ground temperatures in India were so hot that the improvements were only marginal at best. The lack of oil reaching the exhaust valves was not a new problem, having first become apparent during the hot summer in Kansas. Wright had already tried increasing the oil pressure to get more lubrication to the valves, but there still wasn't enough oil reaching these critical parts.

Before the 58th Bomb Wing left Kansas, a number of crew chiefs who battled with the problem during the summer resorted to some drastic measures in an attempt to lubricate the valves. First they removed all of the rocker box covers on the cylinders, which exposed the rocker arms that open the valves, and then they filled the surrounding cavity with oil. For the lower cylinders, small buckets of oil were sprayed with CO_2 fire extinguishers to solidify the oil into a gooey, tar-like consistency, which was then stuffed into the rocker boxes. Despite a lot of extra work, most of the oil was lost as soon as the engines were started, but the mechanics were willing to try anything to improve the reliability of the engines.[11]

As the B-29s began operating in India, the crews discovered that precautions had to be taken just to taxi out to the runway. If the B-29 was taxied too fast, the engines would already be overheated by the time they reached the runway. The engines would then have to be shut down and allowed to cool before a takeoff could be attempted.

Once a B-29 was in the air, the cooling problems were still not over. It was discovered that climbing a B-29 too fast after takeoff would also cause the engines to overheat, so a new takeoff procedure had to be developed. There was even a special landing procedure that had to be followed, or else the engines would overheat before the B-29 touched down on the runway.

The streamlined design of the B-29's engine cowling, coupled with the troubled R-3350 and a sweltering climate, had resulted in a very dangerous combination that could quickly lead to an engine failure and a severe fire in just a matter of seconds. The problem was so bad that in the first half of 1944, fires started seven out of ten times a B-29 had an engine failure in flight.[12]

"The engine fire stories were not overdone and if anything they were underplayed," recalled Jack Ladd, a 58th Bomb Wing pilot. "I had more two and three engine time on the B-29 than I had with all four engines running. It got so I'd tell my flight engineer to keep his mouth shut about how hot they were running. I said I didn't want to know."[13]

If an engine fire wasn't quickly brought under control, the R-3350's weight-saving innovation would now come back to haunt the crews. Of the five major sections that formed the engine case, only the crankcase was forged from steel. The rest were magnesium.[14]

As the war progressed, there were even cases where fires that spread into the nacelle caused the entire engine to fall off the wing in flight. "Several instances have been reported where engine mounts under intense heat of an uncontrollable nacelle fire have failed and allowed the engine and part of the nacelle to drop from the wing," cautioned one report distributed to B-29 flight engineers.[15] One of these incidents occurred during a routine test flight in India when an engine suddenly burst into flames. Before the pilots could land, the burning engine "dropped off the wing" and tumbled to the ground.[16]

Another incident occurred later on Saipan when a B-29 landed with an engine consumed in flames. The ground crews and firefighters quickly sprang into action and smothered the engine with foam from five different hoses, but the magnesium continued to burn out of control. As a last resort, the ground crews wrapped a cable around the engine and literally ripped it off the wing with a tractor to save the B-29 from further damage.[17]

If an in-flight engine fire could not be brought under control, the emergency procedure was blunt: "If the fire is out of control, open the bomb bay doors, and abandon the airplane."[18]

* * *

On April 4, 1944, the dreams of General Billy Mitchell came one step closer to reality with the creation of an independent command structure for the B-29s: the 20th Air Force. Instead of being assigned to a theater commander, the 20th Air Force would be headquartered in Washington under the centralized control of the Joint Chiefs of Staff, with a single commander, General Arnold, directing B-29 operations throughout the world.

"The power of these new bombers is so great that the Joint Chiefs of Staff felt that it would be uneconomical to confine the Superfortress organization to a single theater," General George C. Marshall explained in 1944. "The planes will be treated as major task forces, in the same manner as naval task forces are directed against specific objectives."[19]

This unique command structure did not go over well with the theater commanders or the U.S. Navy, but it would allow the B-29s to wage a strategic bombing campaign directly against the Japanese homeland, as opposed to tactical bombing operations along a theater commander's front lines. If the 20th Air Force succeeded in its mission, it could be the catalyst for a new post-war Air Force independent from the Army, just like General Mitchell and so many others had dreamed.

On April 24, a pair of B-29s made the first journey across the Hump and landed in China. The conditions over the Himalayas were notoriously dangerous, but for the pilots of the first two B-29s to cross over the treacherous mountains – Colonel Jake Harman and Brigadier General LaVerne "Blondie" Saunders, the commander of the 58th Bomb Wing – the weather was absolutely perfect and afforded stunning views of the ruggedly beautiful terrain. Captain William O'Malley, the navigator of the B-29 flown by General Saunders, recalled that first flight over the Hump into China:

> On the way up we flew directly over the Japanese lines in the vicinity of the Kohim Road and the Imphal Plain, without incident. The flight over the Hump was by-God amazing; perfect weather, incredible mountain valleys and gorges, tiny villages on the lesser mountains. We sighted three huge peaks about 200 miles distant. An ATC [Air Transport Command] safety pilot told us nobody knew how high they were.
>
> After finally getting over the Hump, we flew above an overcast through which we let down into the Yangtze Valley. And there was China! A most amazing landscape of thousands of cultivated rice paddies. For the first time in my life I had the feeling of being in a different world – one that could not be described with a "Well, this looks like Texas," or "This looks like Iowa."
>
> The airfield at Kwanghan looked wonderful from the air. The landing was apparently quite an event. Thousands of coolies lined each side of the runway. After getting out of the plane, we lined up and motion and still pictures were taken. General Chennault and his staff greeted us, as well as Chinese officials and American engineers. Everywhere the Chinese would smile and yell "Ding Hao" – which means "very best."[20]

With the arrival of the first B-29s in China, the challenge now facing the XX Bomber Command would be stockpiling enough fuel and supplies at the forward bases, which were some 1,200 miles away from India and only accessible by air, to begin bombing operations against Japan. For planning purposes, General Wolfe estimated that 23 tons of fuel and supplies would have to be flown into China to send a single B-29 to Japan and back.[21]

The planning behind Operation *Matterhorn* relied heavily upon the B-29s to supply themselves by flying all of their supplies to the forward bases, but this was not an efficient means of transportation. When the cargo flights began, it was discovered that the B-29s were consuming 7 gallons of fuel for every gallon they delivered to China. To improve fuel consumption, the bomb groups began converting some of their B-29s into "tankers" to transport the valuable fuel to China. With additional fuel tanks installed in the bomb bays and stripped of all non-essential equipment, the B-29 tankers improved the situation by consuming 2¼ gallons for every gallon delivered.[22]

All of the difficulties associated with moving so much fuel and cargo over such a vast distance only served to prove that Operation *Matterhorn* would be the logistical nightmare that many had predicted, even with the addition of converted B-24 bombers and C-46 transports to help move the supplies, but the plan was approved and the XX Bomber Command was already committed. It was too late to stop now.

For the B-29ers, May would be remembered as a hectic month of cargo flights, practice missions, maintenance problems, and the ever present "searing, disabling heat." All of the flying was taking a toll on the B-29s, and many had to be grounded for extended periods of time due to a lack of spare parts.[23] Captain Clarence Lowman of the 40th Bomb Group recalled those hectic days:

> Flying the "Hump" was hard on the airplanes. Bad weather was frequent and the long hours of making a round trip to China was putting time on the engines and creating a demand for spare parts. The B-29 was an expensive piece of equipment, designed for combat, and yet it was being used to haul gasoline, which in contrast to the anticipated flood amount to be needed seemed to only amount to a trickle … Yet, as each mission and each hour of flying was completed, much was being learned about the B-29 that had been impossible to learn at training stations in the States due to lack of planes, and flying time.[24]

To keep the B-29s flying, the 40th Bomb Group found that on average, over 61 man-hours of maintenance was being performed on each aircraft per day. The difficult job of the ground crews was made even more miserable by the unbelievable heat, with temperatures that were estimated to have reached up to 130 degrees on the runways, and were even higher inside the B-29s.[25]

When the B-29s were flying, the aircrews focused on training missions, including dropping bombs by radar, which no one had done before, and moving supplies to China. Depending on the unpredictable weather, the Hump cargo missions would typically last five to six hours one way and would exact a heavy price. So many aircraft were being lost over the dangerous supply route that it was dubbed "The Aluminum Trail." By the end of the war, over 450 aircraft were lost along the route. Many simply vanished without a trace.[26]

Colonel Howard Couch, who had the gentleman's disagreement with General William Knudsen over the B-29's manuals, disappeared when his B-24 went down somewhere over the Hump in 1944. Colonel Couch is still listed as Missing in Action to this day.

*   *   *

On June 4, after a grueling month of flying supplies to China, a briefing was scheduled for all combat crews of the 58th Bomb Wing. As the crews worked around the clock to prepare every available B-29, speculation was running wild that this might be the moment everyone had been waiting for. They would soon have their answer. At the briefing that Sunday, it was announced that the B-29 was about to embark upon its first combat mission. The target, which was not revealed until the final briefing the next morning, would be the Makasan railway shops in Bangkok.

It was stressed at the briefing that this would be a shakedown mission, the first real operational test of the B-29 and its crews, before a strike against the Japanese homeland. Bangkok was an excellent choice for the B-29's first combat test. The mission could be launched from India, which would not affect the precious fuel stockpiled in China, and the 2,000-mile flight would give the crews valuable experience for the coming strikes against Japan.

The last man to address the crews at the briefing was General Saunders, whose exploits battling the Japanese went all the way back to Pearl Harbor. As Saunders stood to address his men, his words were short and to the point: "Hit those Jap Bastards hard, for they are Bastards." The briefing room went wild in agreement.[27]

Just before 6:00 a.m. on June 5, rumbling down the runways at one-minute intervals, 100 B-29s began taking to the early morning sky. Groups of men, many who'd worked all night preparing the bombers for the mission, gathered along the runways at the four bases to watch the B-29s depart.

At Chakulia, Father Bartholomew Adler, a Catholic priest, stood near the end of the runway and said a prayer as each B-29 lifted off. "As the planes one by one rumbled by and the pilots squeezed aloft, he would chant aloud from his prayer book as if trying to give the wings just an extra bit of lift in Christ's name, amen," recalled Theodore White, a reporter for *Time* magazine.[28]

Most of the bombers had already taken off when Father Adler recognized the B-29 piloted by his friend, Major John Keller, was now gaining speed down the runway. Father Adler recalled what happened next:

> So far the planes are taking off at the rate of one a minute, and this is good, very good … And then it happens. Maybe John figures because of the cloud of dust at the end of the runway that the plane ahead of him hasn't cleared the runway so he is trying to lift his plane as early as possible. The plane doesn't respond. Instead, her tail skid drags the concrete, causing bluish flames to leap up from it. John puts her nose down again, but by dragging the skid the plane has lost precious speed. The end of the runway is coming up fast; he will have to raise her now. Again John tries to lift her off the concrete, she rises slowly and is airborne.
>
> Johnny is away. He got out of that one nicely. But no, he isn't out of trouble yet. He rises to about 150 feet, and the plane is slipping toward the left. Johnny's left wing is down.
>
> "Bring her up, Johnny, bring up your left wing or you will crash. Dear Mother of God help him," you murmur. And then as the plane slips down behind the trees that lie west of the runway, you raise your hand in Absolution, "*Ego vos absolvo … in nomine patris, et Filii, et Spiritus Sancti …*"
>
> The words are hardly out of your mouth when a huge column of flame shoots into the sky, and then over the sound of your racing car you hear the dull thud of the explosion as the plane blows up. Frantically you drive down the road toward the wreck, over fields, and across streams. As you draw close you hear the ammunition popping off, set off by the terrific heat.
>
> You drive as close as you can, and then you run across the field that lies between. Suddenly you are thrown on your face by the impact of a bomb which "cooks off." Bullets whistle overhead. For a minute or so you hug the ground. Finally you circle and come up to the wreck from another direction.
>
> It is a gruesome scene. Sadly you make out various forms among the scattered, burning debris. John is there, and Willie. You scarcely recognize them. Willie will never bounce

into your office again to tell you about Junior. He won't ever ask you again to buy him something to send home to the "kid" … And Johnny has received his last Holy Communion from you.

As you have difficulty recognizing them so you bend down to look at their identification tags. They are Burt and Al, co-pilot and flight engineer. Burt is still strapped to his seat. He was thrown clear by the explosion, with his safety belt still fastened. His legs are broken, and he has a deep gash over his eyes, but he is still breathing. You look a little more closely at Al. You can tell that he hasn't much of a chance. But he is still living.

In no time at all, the doctor and his assistants are giving both men morphine and injecting plasma. Frantically they work over them, even while the stretcher-bearers carry them tenderly to the ambulance; a slim chance. All the rest have gone.

Having paid the price of freedom, they have gone to the reward promised to men who lay down their lives for their friends.[29]

Lieutenant Burt Elsner, the co-pilot, was found near the first point of impact. Elsner could be heard murmuring "the No. 2 engine failed" as the medics worked on him.[30] Miraculously, he somehow survived the crash. Decades later, Elsner recalled that the engine had failed just before they lifted off, leaving Major Keller fighting to keep the B-29 under control. "The next thing and the last thing I remember was seeing the ground coming up at a very steep angle," Elsner said. "I was told later they found me where the plane first hit the ground. I was still strapped in my seat." Elsner would spend the next 10 months recovering from his injuries. He was the only survivor.[31]

The loss of Major Keller's B-29 would be the first in a string of misfortunes that befell the mission. Bad weather hopelessly scattered the bombers en route to the target, and 14 B-29s had to abort the mission altogether due to mechanical problems. As the remaining bombers approached Bangkok, the target area was found to be obscured by heavy cloud cover and most were forced to drop their bombs by radar, with poor results. On the way back to India, the B-29s encountered a typhoon that further scattered the bombers. In the end, five B-29s were lost due to operational causes and 17 men were dead. It was an expensive price to pay for a shakedown mission.

*   *   *

On the morning of June 15, the combat crews of the 58th Bomb Wing anxiously gathered in the briefing rooms at their bases in China. The crews had all flown in from India over the last two days, and after preparing their B-29s for something big, they were about to learn what their next mission would be. At Hsingching, the forward base of the 40th Bomb Group, Colonel Jake Harman began the briefing with a talk about security and asked that everyone look around to make sure there were no strangers present. Satisfied that the briefing could begin, General Wolfe rose and wished every man "good luck and happy hunting." Japan would be the target.[32]

The Imperial Iron and Steel Works at Yawata, the largest steel producer in Japan, was chosen for the first B-29 raid on the Japanese homeland. Its destruction would have a crippling effect on Japan's war industry, and in the words of one intelligence officer at the briefing: "This was the best target Japan had to offer."[33] Bloated with bombs and extra fuel, the B-29s would proceed individually to Yawata in a long bomber stream that would arrive over the target area under the cover of darkness. No one really knew what to expect in the way of Japanese opposition. (Tokyo was the target everyone wanted, but even with the B-29's long range, it was still too far to reach from the forward bases in China.)

With no less than 11 generals and scores of war correspondents looking on, the first of 68 B-29s lifted off just after 4:00 p.m. and began the grueling 14-hour, 3,200-mile round-trip to Japan. The moment everyone had been waiting for had finally arrived.

Sergeant Lou Stoumen, a correspondent for *Yank* magazine, managed to get in on the mission with Captain Ronald Harte's crew from the 40th Bomb Group after winning a coin toss with another reporter. His account of the mission was published a month later:

> The B-29 needs a longer runway for take-off than any other plane. I stood on my knees during the take-off and looked out of a side [gunner's] blister as the ship, the world's heaviest aircraft, pounded and blasted her way down the runway. The strip unfolded like a never-ending drive belt of a factory motor, going by in slow motion until it seemed we had been roaring along for a full 10 minutes and were still not airborne. Then there was the green end of the runway, and we were skimming a few feet above trees and rice paddies.
>
> During the take-off I also watched [the other crew members] … They held on tight. When we were airborne, their faces cracked in smiles and their bodies eased. "She's a good ship," said Johnson as he wiped a wet hand across his face. "But some good guys get killed in take-offs."
>
> That was the first of several sweating outs. A few miles out and a few hundred feet up, someone noticed the No. 2 engine smoking and reported it over the interphone to Captain Harte. "Probably the fuel mixture's too rich," said Lieutenant Tash. And that's what it turned out to be; the smoking soon stopped. But the men sweated it out anyway. They were afraid the ship might have to turn back. As anxious as they were to return home safely, the dangers of the mission evidently meant much less to them than the danger of missing out on bombing Japan.
>
> One ship did have to turn back, we learned later. The men returned only four hours after takeoff, both GIs and officers with tears in their eyes, some of them openly crying and all of them cursing. The pilot kept repeating, over and over: "God damn the engines! God damn the engines! God damn the engines!"
>
> After getting the plane commander's okay over the interphone, I followed Lieutenant Tash forward on hands and knees through the long padded tunnel over the bomb bay. Lieutenant Tash took his position in the greenhouse nose, and I kneeled over the hatch cover behind the pilot and next to the [flight] engineer, Second Lieutenant G.I. Appignani of New York, New York. The engineer sits before a four-foot panel of dials, flashing lights, switches and control levers. He handles the main throttles for the four engines, controls the fuel supply and mixture, regulates the ship's electrical system and operates the pressure cabin's mechanism.
>
> There was still light in the sky as we crossed the border of Free China into Occupied China, flying higher now, and began our next sweating out – waiting for interception by enemy fighters. There was a large force of B-29s on the mission, but we saw only an occasional plane ahead of us through the clouds or above and to the left of us.
>
> Still no Jap fighters. It was dark now, and we were approaching the coast of China. Each man was wearing a Mae West [life preserver] over his parachute. The plane groaned on at terrific speed. There was practically no vibration inside and very little noise. In the cabin,

the ride was as comfortable as a Pullman – a design for airliners of the future. But the Jap fighters – where were they?

"We are four and a half hours from Japan," said Second Lieutenant E.K. Johnson of Portland, Oregon, over the interphone. Then came the voice of Matulis: "No. 3 engine throwing a lot of sparks." The engineer, Lieutenant Appignani, looked out his window and confirmed this. No. 3 engine kept throwing sparks most of the way out and back. That was something else to sweat out.

The radio operator, Sergeant E.A. Gisburne of Norway, Maine, broke open a carton of rations and handed a candy bar to each man in the forward compartment. We were one short, and the engineer shared his bar with me. Candy never tasted so good. We downed it with long swigs of water from canteens. The engineer and the navigator also took benze-drine tablets, the same drug I remembered using back in school to keep awake for my final exams. By this time I was comfortably stretched out on the hatch cover in back of the pilots, using my parachute and jungle kit as a bed. We were flying over the Yellow Sea toward Japan, but the sea was not visible; the weather was too dark and too cloudy.

At last a voice came over the interphone: "We are approaching the target." Everyone began to struggle into his heavy flak suit, putting it on over the parachute, strapping it securely at the sides and pulling the bottom flap down over the thighs like a baseball catcher's chest protector.

We were over Japan now. Through breaks in the clouds I could see the ground below. The Japanese blackout was perfect. Then dead ahead, a faint white globe – Jap searchlights over Yawata, the target city.

The sharp voice of Matulis, the chief gunner, came over the interphone: "Tracers. They are coming right past the ship." There was a pause, then someone said: "Tracers, hell. It's only No. 3 engine throwing sparks again." He was right. Over the interphone came a chorus of wry laughs.

The searchlights were brighter now, but their dangerous pointing fingers were diffused through the undercast of clouds. The tail gunner, Staff Sergeant F.G. Hodgen, said our tail was caught several times by lights. Apparently we were not seen through the clouds, and the lights moved on. Still no Jap fighters.

The target was just ahead. There was no fiery glow through the clouds to show it had already been hit. We had been the fourth plane to take off from the field and were evidently one of the first over the target.

Flak! The gunners said the sky was full of exploding ack-ack shells, some close, most of them beneath us. Intelligence reports confirmed this later, calling the ack-ack "moderate to intense." But I saw no flak.

Our bomb bay doors were swinging open now, without noise and without making the rest of the ship vibrate. The bombs dropped, one by one, one by one. Then, over the inter-phone: "Bombs away!" The doors closed.

The B-29 seemed to sprout an extra set of engines and props. At a terrifically increased speed, she made a sharp left turn and headed back toward the Yellow Sea. Over the inter-phone, tail gunner Hodgen yelled: "I can't see very much through the clouds, but there's a big glow over the target."

The clouds were still below us. B-29s that came in later could see, from 50 miles away, columns of smoke and fire rising 5,000 feet into the air. Yawata, the Pittsburgh of Japan, had been hit hard. This was no token raid but, as Brigadier General Wolfe put it, "the beginning of the organized destruction of the Japanese industrial empire."

We were still tense after the bomb run. The Jap fighters had not come up to meet us yet, and the sweating out continued. We left Japan without interception and flew out over the Yellow Sea.

An hour out and radio operator Gisburne broke into the ration box. For each man there was a large can of grapefruit juice, which we opened with jungle knives, and chicken sandwiches, not too expertly made. The bread was too thick. Good, though. We chewed gum and smoked.

Over the China coast – Occupied China – not a single fighter came up.

Time marched on like a crippled snail. We had been flying almost half a day. With the flak suits off again, we were more comfortable. The No. 3 engine was behaving well enough. My parachute bed was soft. I slept.

Dawn over Free China: a wild, gray sky of tumultuous clouds, empty of aircraft. I crawled back through the tunnel and batted the breeze with the gunners for a while. Then I returned to the forward compartment. Captain Harte and Lieutenant Haddow looked plenty different from the eager beavers who had coaxed the B-29 off the ground so many hours ago. Now their bloodshot eyes hung heavily over pouches that looked like squashed prunes. You'd have thought that someone had been beating them about the head with a rubber hose, judging by their appearance toward the end of this longest bombing mission in history.

"Fighters!" exclaimed Lieutenant Tash. He put his binoculars on them. They were ours – fast, high-altitude American fighters flying top cover over the B-29 fields.

At last, at the dead center of our course, the home field came into sight. It looked miles long, even from our altitude.

Loud flopping, banging noises came from the No. 3 engine. "Engineer to pilot," said a voice over the interphone, "don't count on No. 3 engine for landing" … There was a burst of sparks from No. 3's exhaust, and the engineer said he was afraid the engine would catch fire.

We made a long, sharp bank and approached for the landing. No. 3 continued to bang and throw sparks, but it didn't get any worse. We came in fast, about 20 feet above the end of the runway. Gently Captain Harte set her down, like a mother placing a child in a crib. We rolled a great distance, about the speed of a fast car on a U.S. highway. Then slower, without stopping, we turned and taxied to a parking strip. The crew piled out through the bottom hatches, limp and happy. Ground crewmen and intelligence officers were there to greet them.

While the handshaking and congratulations were still going on, Master Sergeant Herb Coggins of Nashville, Tennessee, chief of the B-29's ground crew, was already walking around the ship with Lieutenant Appignani, the engineer, looking for flak holes.

Later, in the interrogation room, A-2 [intelligence] officers gave each man some egg sandwiches, coffee and suitable refreshments. Then the questioning began [for intelligence about the mission].

Back in the barracks, still sweating out their unreported buddies, the weary flight crews turned to their sacks. From beneath the mosquito-net cover on a bed came a last crack:

"Somebody tell me a spooky story. I love to hear a spooky story before I go to sleep."[34]

(Captain Harte and most of the men you just read about were killed 11 months later when their B-29 was shot down over Tokyo.)

*   *   *

When news of the raid hit American shores, it caused a sensation. Newspapers across the country were splashed with pictures of the B-29 and the headline: "JAPAN BOMBED!" Two-and-a-half years after the attack on Pearl Harbor, the B-29s had finally brought the war home to Japan.[35]

DEATH TO FLIERS, JAPANESE WARN

"Those who bailed out met with the same fate meted out to the raiders of Tokyo some two years ago. Any Allied airman who falls or bails out over Japan will be executed. This is the Order of the Day."

With these words, radiocast from Singapore to American forces in the Southwest Pacific, the Japanese suggested the execution of U.S. airmen who fell into their hands in the B-29 attack upon Yawata from the CBI Theater, June 15.

After the Yawata raid, the Japanese warned that any B-29er who bailed out over Japan would be executed. (Thurman Sallade collection)

7

Friends Through History

The 58th Bomb Wing began its long journey with the B-29 in the summer of 1943, but my personal journey with the B-29 would start almost 60 years later in 2002, when I watched a documentary on the History Channel called *Stealing the Superfortress*. My life would never be the same again.

Stealing the Superfortress told the story of how the Soviet Union reverse-engineered three B-29s that made emergency landings in Russia during World War II to make a new strategic bomber, the Tupolev Tu-4, that was nearly an exact copy of the B-29. The documentary also followed the B-29's development and its early missions against Japan. I was only 21 years old at the time, and I was surprised by all the people in the footage from the war who looked younger than me.

Near the end of the documentary, a retired Russian engineer showed off one of his most prized possessions: a B-29 pilot's control yoke cap. The round plastic cap, which had the Boeing logo and "B-29" embossed on it, had been discovered hidden under a seat in the *Gen. H.H. Arnold Special*, the very same B-29 that Hap Arnold singled out on the production line at Wichita. After making an emergency landing in Vladivostok, Russia, the Soviets had completely disassembled the bomber to study each part for replication. Nearly 60 years later, that control yoke cap was now the only known surviving piece of the *Gen. H.H. Arnold Special*. And I had to have one just like it.

A few months later, after a lot of searching, I found my first B-29 control yoke cap. I remember thinking to myself how incredible it was to be holding an actual piece of a B-29 in my hands for the first time. This was a real piece of history, not some picture in a book. I couldn't help but wonder about the B-29 it came from. Did it fly missions over Japan? Unfortunately, I'd never know. The stories behind this control yoke cap were lost for good. But I knew one thing for sure: I wanted to hold more history in my hands. In the weeks that followed, I bought a silk escape map that was issued to B-29 crews in the Pacific, and then I bought a B-29 cowl flap. I was hooked.

My B-29 collection was off to a good start, but I still didn't have anything that actually told a story. That all changed one January night in 2005, when I found something on eBay that was so extraordinary that I almost couldn't believe what I was seeing. The auction picture showed a large section of white silk that was cut from a parachute, but what made it so incredible was the story that was written on it:

This is part of panel 13 from the Switlik chute used by S/Sgt B.K. Baldwin, left gunner, to bail out from AC #26273, B-29 'Old Bitch U Airy Bess' on Oct. 14, 1944 in Szechwan Province of China.

Also bailing out and safely returning the next week were:

S/Sgts G. Golden – Right Gunner
L.N. DeCory – Radar Operator
W.W. Sheffield – Senior Gunner
L. J. Arents – Tail Gunner[1]

I was looking at an actual piece of a parachute that was used to bail out of a B-29 during a combat mission in World War II. The fact that it even survived the war and still existed six decades later was astonishing, and someone had just listed it for sale on eBay. I didn't know it at the time, but that parachute was about to change my life.

* * *

He told me that I'd hit pay dirt, but I didn't understand what he meant at first. I had to read a few more lines into his e-mail before I realized what he was talking about. Looking back on it now, he was right in so many ways. But before I go any further, I should back up a bit.

It's been so long now that I don't remember what I paid for that parachute, but I want to say it was around $25.00. I was ready to spend a lot more, though. For some odd reason, very few people were interested in it. Maybe they just didn't realize what a piece of history it was, and that's why it sold for so little. Or maybe, as I've since come to believe, I was just meant to have it. By the time you reach the end of this chapter, I think you'll understand why.

Since the parachute was the first piece in my collection that had an actual story behind it, I just had to learn more about it. As it turned out, the story behind the story was pretty interesting, too. The person who listed the parachute, Richard, taught an eBay class for senior citizens in Upstate New York, and one of his students had asked him to sell the parachute for them. That student was a World War II Veteran named Charles Trabold. Mr. Trabold was an 81-year-old "ball of fire," Richard said. He loved talking to people, and he *really* loved talking to people who knew something about B-29s. He sounded like just the man I needed to talk to! Richard was kind enough to give me Mr. Trabold's e-mail address, so I wrote him a short note to introduce myself. I wasn't really sure what to expect as I pressed "send."[2]

The next morning, I received a reply from Mr. Trabold. He began by saying: "Trevor, you have hit pay dirt in a lot of ways. You will soon understand why."[3] Mr. Trabold explained that he was a Senior Gunner, Central Fire Control (CFC) Specialist, on B-29s during World War II. He began his training in 1943 to be a gunner on a Northrop P-61, a twin-engine night fighter, but two weeks into the class, the students were told they would now be training for the B-29. Since there were no B-29s available yet, their first task was to build a full-size mock-up of a B-29's aft fuselage and install all of the gun turrets, wiring and associated equipment so they could begin training.[4]

From those early days at the CFC school where no one had actually seen a B-29 before, Mr. Trabold would go on to serve an incredible 15 months overseas in combat with the 462nd Bomb Group, the "Hellbirds," one of the four bomb groups of the 58th Bomb Wing. To be able to talk to someone like Mr. Trabold was a dream come true. Everything that I ever wanted to know about the B-29, especially about the B-29 in combat, was now just a short e-mail away. As you can imagine, we really hit it off![5]

Mr. Trabold's involvement with the B-29 stretched all the way back to before his bomb group even had a B-29 to train with, and I found those stories really fascinating. In those days, all of their training missions were flown in B-17s while they waited for the first B-29s to arrive.[6] To my delight, he also shared many stories about the pre-production YB-29s and how troublesome they were. Mr. Trabold was the only person I've ever talked to who actually flew on a YB-29, and I couldn't get enough of those stories. He explained that the YB-29s were a real worry because you never knew what might happen during the flight.[7] The first production B-29s that filtered out to the 58th Bomb Wing were also just as troublesome. Mr. Trabold summed it all up this way:

> The fact that we were the first Wing flying in the first B-29s meant that there was very little that anyone really knew about the plane and organization, as it was pushed into combat as fast as possible … The bottom line is that we had no idea as just how much we were to be guinea pigs in the whole scheme of things. There was not the slightest idea that those of us who survived would be in combat for fifteen straight months![8]

That last sentence really struck me: "those of us who survived."

On April 6, 1944, as the Battle of Kansas was nearing its end, Mr. Trabold and his crew climbed into their brand-new B-29 and took off for India. After 11 days and five legs totaling 48 flying hours, they arrived at their new home in Piardoba. Mr. Trabold would spend the next year and three months in combat, and he shared endless stories with me about those experiences. I couldn't believe how lucky I was.[9]

Soon after they arrived in India, his crew gave their B-29 a very unique name: *Old-Bitch-U-Airy Bess*. They figured that, be it the enemy or themselves, their B-29 would contribute to the obituary column one way or another. Bess was the name of a bulldog that the radio operator, Seymour "Sandy" Sandhofer, had as a boy, and the two names just seemed to go together. The bombardier, Thurman Sallade, came up with the unique spelling, and the tail gunner, LeRoy "Big Red" Arents, painted it on the fuselage.[10]

By this time my collection had grown to include an actual B-29 gun turret, and since I was really interested in the B-29's gunnery system, and Mr. Trabold was one of the first CFC gunners, we talked a lot about its use during the war. Even though he was in his 80s by then, Mr. Trabold said he remembered the operation of the electrical circuits like it was yesterday, and he thought he could still troubleshoot the entire system. He went on to explain how everything worked in detail, which left no doubt in my mind that he could still operate the gunnery system after all those years!

As the CFC gunner, Mr. Trabold sat in the "barbers chair" in the aft compartment, which got its name because the seat was mounted on a pedestal to allow the gunner to look through his sighting blister on the top of the fuselage. This unique seating gave the CFC gunner a spectacular 360-degree view over the B-29. Mr. Trabold said it was the best seat in the house because he could see everything that was going on around them.[11] During a mission to Singapore, his seat afforded him a spectacular view of a very close call. As they flew in a tight formation through a flak barrage over the target area, the B-29 next to him took a direct hit in the outer left wing. Miraculously, the shell went right through the wing and left a big hole without exploding. The B-29 was only about 150 feet away from where he was sitting, and Mr. Trabold vividly recalled watching as it happened. If that shell had exploded, the B-29 would have rolled over and collided with *Old-Bitch-U-Airy Bess*, and I would not be talking to Mr. Trabold about it all these years later.[12]

Mr. Trabold shared another story with me about the time his squadron commander's B-29 took a direct hit. The shell came up through the bottom of the fuselage and smashed clean through the radar observer's table and his radar scope without exploding. Talk about a close call. Mr. Trabold went on to say that he never got used to the flak, and he'd flown through tons of it.[13]

During another discussion about his experiences, Mr. Trabold told me the story about the first Japanese fighter he shot down. He began by saying that it was actually very simple, and not like what you see in the movies. Somewhere over Singapore, he spotted a lone fighter flying in the opposite direction of his B-29. The pilot must have thought he was out of range, because he never fired a shot at them. As the fighter came within range, Mr. Trabold opened up with the two .50 caliber machine guns in his gun turret. He immediately scored hits, and continued pouring fire into the fighter. The hail of .50 caliber bullets were devastating and the fighter quickly broke apart in midair. The tail gunner watched as the wreckage fell through the clouds and confirmed the kill. From start to finish, the whole encounter was over in less than 10 seconds, he said.[14]

From what I knew of the CFC gunnery system, I was already impressed by how advanced it was for its day and how all of the gun turrets were operated by remote control, but I was even more amazed when Mr. Trabold told me how reliable it was. They had a lot of problems with the early B-29s that persisted for a long time, he explained, but the CFC system worked flawlessly. In the 15 months that he was in combat, the CFC system did not suffer a single failure during any of his missions.[15] The only time Mr. Trabold ever had a problem was during one mission when they encountered a lot of fighters and used up most of their ammo. One of the machine guns in the lower aft turret had suddenly stopped firing, and when they examined the gun after landing, they made an interesting discovery. A paper tag from the can the ammo came in had somehow ended up inside the turret, and as the ammo belt was feeding into the gun, the paper tag caused the gun to jam. That was the only malfunction Mr. Trabold ever had with the entire gunnery system.[16]

It's hard for me to express what it was like hearing all of these stories from Mr. Trabold. He had so much first-hand knowledge about the B-29 that it was almost like talking to an encyclopedia, but it was even better because I could ask him questions. I relished every minute of it. As we delved deeper into his experiences, even a simple question about the kind of food they ate would evoke a fascinating story. And their food, by the way, wasn't very good. In fact, it was so bad that the crew of *Old-Bitch-U-Airy Bess* came up with an ingenious way to cook their own meals.

One of the traits I've noticed about the Greatest Generation is how frugal they are. I think it goes back to when they were growing up during the Great Depression and how nothing went to waste. That frugality carried over to the war zone and led to a fascinating story Mr. Trabold shared with me about the food they ate. The aft compartment of the B-29, where the gunners and radar observer sat, was divided by a wall of armor plating that included a door to allow access between the gunner and radar stations. When it became apparent that the door could jam and prevent the gunners from escaping aft in an emergency, the doors were all removed, but Mr. Trabold's crew didn't throw theirs away. They took the door, which was just a large steel plate, and carefully sanded down one side to make it as smooth as possible. Then they mounted it flat above the ground, and with two blow torches for heat, they now had a perfect griddle to cook on. With bread from the mess hall and cheese they bought from Australia with their own money, they used the armor plate to make toasted cheese sandwiches. The armor plate was such a good griddle that they used it all the time in India, and they even carried it back and forth over the Hump to cook with in China.[17] Of all the stories Mr. Trabold shared with me, the armor plate griddle was one of my favorites.

The toasted cheese sandwiches reminded me of another story I'd read about in an old magazine from 1945. It almost seemed too tall of a tale to be true, but after Mr. Trabold mentioned how bad their food was, I decided to do some research and get to the bottom of it. Much to my surprise, the story I read about actually happened.

During a mission to Manchuria, two cannon shells from a Japanese fighter tore through the nose of a B-29 only inches from where James O'Keefe, the bombardier, was sitting. O'Keefe narrowly escaped injury in the attack, but the explosions destroyed his sighting station (gunsight) and peppered the windows in front of him with holes. O'Keefe began stuffing rags in the holes to try to maintain the cabin pressurization, but they continued to lose pressure. After some searching, he found the two holes where the cannon shells had punched through the fuselage, but he didn't have any rags left to plug them with. That's when the flight engineer had an idea.

For their in-flight meal, the crew were carrying an assortment of K-rations, which were small, individually boxed meals for use in combat. The K-rations came in three varieties for each meal of the day, but the dinner rations had something that the others didn't: a 4-ounce can of processed cheese. With nothing to lose except for part of their dinner, two of the cans were opened, and the flight engineer began stuffing the rubbery cheese into the holes. Not only did the cabin pressure stabilize, but the cheese held the pressure steady all the way back to base.[18]

That was probably the first and only time in history that combat repairs were made using cheese!

* * *

Throughout his 15 months in combat, Mr. Trabold would experience his share of triumphs and tragedies. One of his many close calls came during a mission to strike the Japanese-held oil refineries at Palembang in Indonesia. While the 58th Bomb Wing was hitting the refineries, the 462nd Bomb Group had been selected for a special mission to mine the Moesi River Channel and prevent the oil tankers from reaching Japan. The round-trip flight to Palembang spanned nearly 4,000 miles and would be one the longest bombing missions attempted during the war. To reach the target, the B-29s first had to fly six hours to a British air base in Ceylon (modern-day Sri Lanka) and stage for the mission the next day.[19]

In *Old-Bitch-U-Airy Bess*, it was a long but routine flight to the target area for Mr. Trabold and his crew. Guided by a full moon, the Hellbirds began their run at the mouth of the Moesi River in the South China Sea by dropping down to 1,000 feet above the water and snaking along the river for upwards of 35 miles to their drop areas. As the Hellbirds flew upstream, some of the gunners unleashed their machine guns on the Japanese vessels in the river. In the lead B-29, a large tanker was sighted in the channel as they reached their drop point. After the bombardier dropped his first mine in front of the tanker, he raked the ship with machine-gun fire as they flew over it at 350 feet, and then he dropped his second mine behind it.[20] While the

Hellbirds were completing their drops, they witnessed a spectacular fireworks show as the rest of the 58th Bomb Wing began bombing the nearby oil refinery.

After successfully dropping their mines, *Old-Bitch-U-Airy Bess* turned for home and began the long flight back to Ceylon. Everything was going as planned until 15 hours into the mission, when a problem was discovered with the fuel system. The flight engineer, Master Sergeant Vaughan Plevan, had been carefully transferring fuel between the tanks to give the B-29 the best flying balance, but something had gone wrong. For some reason, fuel could not be transferred from one of the rear bomb bay tanks. The tank would not jettison, either, when they tried to salvo it. The crew was now stuck with all of this additional weight they couldn't get rid of, and the aircraft became increasingly unbalanced as the fuel in the other tanks was used up.

Three hours later, *Old-Bitch-U-Airy Bess* was in serious trouble. The crew had surpassed their original flight plan and were convinced they would run out of fuel and have to ditch in the ocean. To make matters worse, the B-29 had become so unbalanced that the pilot, Major K.D. Thompson, had to move the entire 11-man crew into the forward cabin to keep from going out of control. The only thing *Old-Bitch-U-Airy Bess* had going for it was the skill of its crew. With Thompson's flying abilities and Plevan's masterful handling of the engines to burn as little fuel as possible, they had just enough fuel to make it back to base. As they taxied off the runway after a heart-stopping landing, the engines began to sputter as they ran out of fuel. You couldn't cut it any closer than that. They had been in the air for exactly 19 hours straight.[21]

Two months later, *Old-Bitch-U-Airy Bess* lifted off from China to bomb Formosa (modern-day Taiwan), but as fate would have it, Mr. Trabold wasn't on board. The night before the mission, he suffered an appendicitis and had to be taken to the hospital. A replacement gunner was quickly found and the crew took off for Formosa as planned. About 400 miles from base, something went terribly wrong. Without warning, the No. 4 engine suddenly burst into flames. The flight engineer, Plevan, tried to bring the fire under control by cutting off the fuel and discharging the engine's fire extinguisher, but it didn't have any effect. The fire was getting worse.

Fearing that the flames would spread and trap part of the crew in the aft compartment, the pilot ordered the gunners and the radar observer to bail out before it was too late. As the five parachutes blossomed behind *Old-Bitch-U-Airy Bess*, Plevan was still fighting to put the fire out. He tried the fire extinguisher again, which only had one shot left. If it didn't work, the rest of the crew would be forced to bail out. As their last hope, Plevan pulled the red fire handle on his panel. The flames began to smother as the extinguisher discharged, and then the fire died out. Plevan had done it. *Old-Bitch-U-Airy Bess* was saved, and the remaining crew limped back to base on three engines.[22]

One of the men who bailed out of *Old-Bitch-U-Airy Bess* that day was Staff Sergeant Burton Baldwin, the left gunner. After he landed, Baldwin cut out a section of his parachute to keep as a souvenir. In 2005, 60 years after he bailed out, I became the new caretaker of Baldwin's parachute.

In the decades following the war, Mr. Trabold had made it a point to keep in touch with his fellow Hellbirds, and many of their souvenirs from the war gravitated to him. He would either send those souvenirs to a museum, or sell them for the owners. Baldwin had sent his parachute to Mr. Trabold for him to sell, and that's how it ended up on eBay.

Baldwin's parachute will always be special to me because it was the first piece in my collection that actually told a story, and it introduced me to Mr. Trabold and led to our friendship. I'll cherish it for the rest of my life.

To go with the parachute, Mr. Trabold later sent me a copy of Baldwin's logbook from the war. Each time Baldwin flew, he entered the details of the flight in this book. Before he mailed it to me, Mr. Trabold went through the pages and marked all of the missions that were significant. For a historian, it was a treasure trove of information about *Old-Bitch-U-Airy Bess* and the missions they flew. One of the most surprising things I learned from the logbook was that Mr. Trabold's crew only flew one gunnery training mission before they went overseas. When I added up his flight time, I was stunned to discover that Baldwin had flown less than 29 hours in B-29s before leaving for India. It was startling to see how little training the 58th Bomb Wing had before they left for war.[23]

Baldwin's logbook brought back a lot of memories that Mr. Trabold shared with me, but there was one story that we never really talked about. He only mentioned it a few times, always in passing, and I could never bring myself to ask him about it. Deep down, I knew that if he really wanted to talk about the events of that day, he would. But aside from those few times when he alluded to it, we never discussed it. I later did some research of my own and discovered the whole story.

It happened on December 7, 1944, during a mission to Mukden, Manchuria, when *Old-Bitch-U-Airy Bess* came under heavy fighter attack and was badly shot up. It was during one of those attacks that an incendiary shell from a Japanese fighter sliced through the cockpit. The flight engineer, Master Sergeant Vaughan Plevan, was hit as he sat at his station monitoring the engines.[24]

Plevan was killed almost instantly.

I was starting to understand why Mr. Trabold didn't talk about it.

I later looked up that mission in Baldwin's logbook. After they lifted Plevan out of his seat, Baldwin took over for the remainder of the flight. Plevan had been training him to be the assistant flight engineer. In his logbook, Baldwin simply wrote: "Bombed Mukden. Plevan was killed."[25]

The next day, *Old-Bitch-U-Airy Bess* flew back across the Hump to India. Baldwin was the acting flight engineer and took his place in Plevan's seat. According to his logbook, the flight lasted for six hours and 30 minutes. I couldn't imagine what those six-and-a-half hours must have been like.

Within a week, the crew was back flying missions again with a new flight engineer, but *Old-Bitch-U-Airy Bess* was done. The venerable B-29 that had been with the crew for eight months and had taken them to the far side of the world would never fly another combat mission. Less than a month after Plevan was killed, *Old-Bitch-U-Airy Bess* was declared "war weary" and returned home to the United States. I don't know what happened to her after that, but she probably helped train new crews until being placed in storage with other war-weary B-29s.[26]

A few days before Christmas in 1949, on the lonely plains of West Texas near Pyote, *Old-Bitch-U-Airy Bess* finally met her end. The beloved B-29 that always brought her crew home was dismembered by men with cutting torches and scrapped for her aluminum.[27] *Old-Bitch-U-Airy Bess* was gone, but not forgotten. She continued to live on in the hearts of her crew, and now she will live on through the words on these pages. I think the crew would have liked that.

*   *   *

One of the most incredible stories that Mr. Trabold ever shared with me involved the B-29 that replaced *Old-Bitch-U-Airy Bess*. The crew referred to their new B-29 by the last three digits of its serial number, '728, and never gave her an official name. In the spring of 1945, there was an incident with '728 that Mr. Trabold never would have believed, as he put it, if he hadn't been there.

On the morning of April 28, Mr. Trabold and his crew prepared to take off from India for the last time. After a year of operations, the 58th Bomb Wing was moving thousands of miles away to Tinian, where it would join the other bomb wings operating from the Mariana Islands. The journey to Tinian would be flown in two legs, with a refueling stop in Luliang, China, before proceeding on the long 12-hour flight to their new home. In addition to its crew, '728 would also be carrying seven passengers and their baggage, plus extra gear stowed on pallets in the bomb bays. With 18 men crammed inside the bomber, it was not going to be a comfortable flight.[28]

As they left India behind, the notoriously bad weather over the Hump gave way to beautiful sunny skies and spectacular views as '728 soared high above the rugged Himalayas. After making 30 crossings in the past 12 months, today would be the last time the crew would ever look down upon the treacherous mountains that had taken so many lives.[29] Five hours later, '728 touched down in Luliang, China, to refuel. For the crew and passengers, it felt good to get out of the cramped bomber and stretch their legs. After refueling, everyone piled back in the B-29 and readied themselves for the long flight to Tinian. As the flight engineer was running up the engines and doing his checks before takeoff, a loud noise was heard from one of the engines that sounded like a blown exhaust collector ring. The flight was not going to proceed with a problem like that, Mr. Trabold explained, because "you very soon will have one helluva fire."[30]

The engines were quickly shut down and the crew climbed out to investigate. To everyone's surprise, the cause of the noise wasn't a blown exhaust, but a large hole in one of the propeller blades. All anyone could figure was that the prop had sucked up a rock while the engine was being run up, and it left a ragged hole in the blade that was about the size of a 20mm shell. After carefully examining the damage, the crew concluded that the hole wouldn't affect the balance or aerodynamics of the blade, and they set to work pounding and filing the ragged edges smooth. When the engine was started again, aside from a slight whistle, the loud noise was gone. Everyone climbed aboard and got ready for takeoff.

Because of the time it took to dress the hole, the pilots would now be taking off at night. With the pre-flight checks complete, the throttles were advanced and '728 surged down the long runway that was nestled between two mountains. Seconds after they left the ground, Mr. Trabold realized they were in serious trouble. For reasons unknown, the bomb bay doors shot open just after they lifted off the runway. At that low airspeed, the sudden aerodynamic drag from the doors caused the B-29 to start mushing through the air on the verge of a stall. As the pilots fought to control the bomber, '728 began sinking down into the dark valley off the end of the runway.

In the back of the B-29, no one knew what was going on or why they were dropping. They couldn't see what was happening, either, but everyone knew something had gone horribly wrong. As the bomber continued to sink into the darkness beyond the runway, the crew suddenly heard the terrifying crash of something hitting the airframe that sounded like trees. Mr. Trabold thought it was all over for them. With the engines roaring at full emergency power, the impacts abruptly stopped as the pilots regained control and slowly began climbing out of the valley. They quickly brought '728 back around and landed.

When the crew got out and began to look the bomber over, they realized just how close they came to death. What they found left them terribly shaken. No one could believe how badly damaged the B-29 was. Whatever they hit, it had ripped the bomb bay doors completely off the fuselage. As they looked closer, they discovered a big groove running down the left side of the fuselage below the blister where Baldwin had been sitting, and another groove under the left wing behind the No. 2 engine. A big chunk of the left flap was also gone.

The next morning, the crew got a jeep and drove down into the valley to see what they hit. They were shocked to find a row of eight telephone poles that were all knocked down. But what made it even more incredible was when they took into account the groove under the left wing behind the No. 2 engine and that missing section of flap. The only way that damage could have happened, they concluded, was if the telephone pole had synced perfectly through the propeller arc *between* the turning blades. Looking back on it decades later, Mr. Trabold said if the propeller blades had hit that pole, that would have been the end for them. Now I knew what he meant when he said that he never would have believed it if he hadn't been there.[31]

A week after their close call, '728 was patched up enough for the crew to continue on to Tinian, but the bomber still needed major repairs before it could return to combat. While the repairs were underway, Mr. Trabold painted eight telephone poles on the nose to go with all the bombs and camels of their previous missions – the bombs represented bombing missions and the camels were flights over the Hump. As the story got around Tinian, the unique nose art became a magnet for people to have their picture taken with, and '728 was now the stuff of legends. I don't think I would have believed it either, if Mr. Trabold wasn't there.

*   *   *

I've always had good luck in finding rare and unique B-29 items while searching through eBay, but over the years that I've known him, I've stumbled upon a number of things on eBay that incredibly had a connection to Mr. Trabold. The first was a 20th Air Force award roster that belonged to a bombardier who served in Mr. Trabold's bomb group. After the veteran passed away, someone had taken all of his effects from the war and was selling them on eBay, piece-by-piece. I was hoping to keep some of the grouping together, but most things sold for more than I could afford.

I did manage to win a couple of the auctions, and one of them was a 15-page award roster. I think I only paid a few dollars for it, and I'm not even sure why I bought it in the first place. After it arrived in the mail, I was looking through all the names on the roster when I turned over to the second page, and whose name did I find? Staff Sergeant Charles Trabold! As I looked closer, I recognized some other names that were also members of his crew. I couldn't wait to tell Mr. Trabold and send him some copies of my find. It turned out there were a lot of names on that roster that he fondly remembered, and he shared some of their stories with me. I was amazed by all the memories that were evoked by those old sheets of paper.

During another night of browsing eBay for all things B-29, I came across an old magazine article from the war. Vintage magazines are apparently worth a lot more money if you cut all the pages out and sell the advertisements for collectors to frame, and this person was also selling the articles, one of which was about B-29s. You can imagine my surprise when I noticed the article featured a picture of *Old-Bitch-U-Airy Bess* in all her glory. I glanced at the title again, "B-29 Superforts Bomb Japanese Mainland," and then it dawned on me that I was looking at the July

10, 1944, issue of *Life* magazine that Mr. Trabold had told me about, which featured pictures from their first mission to Japan. I won the auction for only $4.00. Mr. Trabold was thrilled that I'd found a copy of it.

Throughout our discussions, Mr. Trabold frequently mentioned a book that contained the entire wartime history of the 462nd Bomb Group, the *Hellbird War Book*. What really interested me about the book, aside from the great photographs, was that it contained a personnel roster of the entire bomb group. That roster would be a tremendous tool for my research, and instead of sending names to Mr. Trabold to look up for me, I concluded that I needed to find my own copy of the book. The only problem was that the book was published shortly after the war ended and was now very rare. I'd never even seen one for sale before. But then a few days later, a beautiful copy appeared on eBay out of nowhere. I was so excited that I e-mailed Mr. Trabold that night to tell him what I found. When the auction later ended, I was the proud new owner of a *Hellbird War Book*. It cost me over $200, but I didn't care; to me, the book was priceless.

The best part of the book was the photo of Mr. Trabold and his crew standing in front of *Old-Bitch-U-Airy Bess*. He often talked about that photo, and I'll never forget the first time I opened up the book and saw it. After hearing so many stories about these men, it was quite a moment when I could finally put faces to all of their names. It might be hard for you to understand, but for me, that one photo was worth the price of the entire book.

Old-Bitch-U-Airy Bess was such a uniquely named B-29 that it's no surprise a lot of people took photographs of her. I found one of those photos on eBay one night, but it was odd because there was a large tarp draped over its nose. I sent Mr. Trabold a copy to see if he might know where it was taken and what the tarp was for. The photo was definitely taken in India, he said, because that was the only place where they had to put tarps over their B-29s to cover up the cockpit glass. He explained that the weather was so hot that if the nose wasn't covered up and the pilot windows left open for ventilation, the heat that built up inside the cockpit would cause a lot of problems.[32]

About a month later, I discovered another photograph of *Old-Bitch-U-Airy Bess* on eBay, but I almost missed it. The photo was of a man squatting down to pose for the camera, and in the background sat *Old-Bitch-U-Airy Bess*. I would have missed it if I hadn't looked closely and saw the name painted on the nose of the B-29. On the back of the photo, someone had written: "Get a gander at the B-29 (and name) in the background. Some of the names are hum-dingers."

I was excited that I'd found another photo of *Old-Bitch-U-Airy Bess*, so I sent a copy of it to Mr. Trabold right away. I couldn't believe it, but he actually recognized the man in the photo! Even though the photo had been taken almost 70 years ago at that point, Mr. Trabold clearly remembered who the man was, and that he was on the ground crew of another B-29 in his squadron. I hope my memory is still that good when I'm half his age.[33]

In the background of the photo, there was also a large hoist that was used to change engines. Mr. Trabold noticed it right away, and he said the photo must have been taken in India during one of their many engine changes. He then mentioned, rather casually, that they had flown five missions in *Old-Bitch-U-Airy Bess* before they finally came back with all four engines still running![34]

As popular as *Old-Bitch-U-Airy Bess* was for photographers, Mr. Trabold's second B-29, '728, would also capture a lot of attention because of its nose art. One day I was flipping through a July 1945 issue of *Brief* magazine, a publication about the Army Air Forces in the Pacific, when I noticed a photo of a B-29 that had something very unique painted on its nose. I did a double take, and then I realized that I was looking at a photo of '728. And there were the eight telephone poles Mr. Trabold had painted on its nose, just like he said.[35]

* * *

I've always thought it was uncanny how often I find things that have a connection to Mr. Trabold. I don't know how to explain it, but it's happened so often over the years that it's almost routine now. In fact, would you believe that as I was writing this chapter, I found something else on eBay that was connected to him?

While talking about his experiences, there were a few occasions when Mr. Trabold mentioned his best friend during the war, David McNeley. It was always out of the blue, and I think he just wanted to talk about him. They first became friends when they were classmates at the CFC school, and their friendship continued into combat when they were both assigned to the 462nd Bomb Group. What I found on eBay while writing this chapter was an old photograph of McNeley's B-29, but I didn't know that at first. The photo only showed the giant tail of a B-29, along with a smiling tail gunner waving from his compartment. I could tell that it was a very early B-29 by its olive drab paint job, so I looked up its serial number to see if it had any combat history. That's when I discovered it was McNeley's B-29, so I just had to buy the photo to show Mr. Trabold.

There's a lot of truth behind the old saying that a picture is worth a thousand words, because there was quite a story behind this B-29 and David McNeley. I soon discovered that the B-29 in the photo would later crash in India when an engine failed just after takeoff, but McNeley wasn't on board. At the time of the crash, which killed four of the crew, he was flying with another crew on a supply mission to China. McNeley was lucky that he wasn't with his regular crew that day, but in a strange twist of fate, later that same afternoon, he was forced to bail out when his B-29 ran out of fuel while crossing back over the Hump. McNeley parachuted to safety and returned to base two days later, but the gunner who took his place that day with his regular crew was not so lucky: he was killed in the crash.[36]

The young CFC gunner from Iowa would go on to have many more close calls, but his luck almost ran out a year later on June 5, 1945, when his B-29 was shot down after striking Kobe, Japan. After flak and fighter attacks left their B-29 severely damaged and on fire, McNeley's crew began to bail out just before their bomber exploded over Osaka Bay, but only five survivors, including McNeley, were found and taken prisoner by the Japanese.[37]

There weren't many people who bailed out of a B-29 twice and lived to tell about it. At 20 years old, David McNeley had just done it. It was a miracle he survived.

Two months after he was captured, and only days before the war ended, David McNeley and 13 other B-29ers were suddenly pulled out of their prison cells and tied up by the Kempeitai, the brutal Japanese military police. A witness later said that the Kempeitai had been taking the Americans out of their cells every day to question and beat them, but this time the Americans would not be coming back.[38]

After they were bound and blindfolded, the Americans were separated into two groups and taken to a nearby firing range. The first group of Americans were made to sit in a row along the edge of a freshly dug pit. They were still bound and blindfolded and couldn't see the Kempeitai lining up in front of them with pistols, but they probably knew what was coming.

Then the death sentence for the crime of "indiscriminate bombing" was read aloud by the Kempeitai commander, even though the Americans were given no trial. Another Kempeitai translated the death sentence into English. The Americans just sat there along the edge of the pit, too weak from the beatings and starvation to resist. Then the commander gave the order to fire.

Using captured American .45 caliber pistols, which may have been taken from the very Americans who were now sitting bound and blindfolded before them, the Kempeitai executed the Americans by shooting them all in the forehead.

Then the second group of Americans, bound and blindfolded, were brought over and made to sit in a row along the edge of the same pit. And then the same Kempeitai lined up in front of them with pistols. And then the death sentence was read aloud. And then the order was given to fire. And then the Kempeitai shot them all in the head.[39]

After all he had been through, David McNeley was murdered just as the war was ending.

To cover up the war crime, the Japanese dumped the 14 bodies into the pit and carefully concealed its location so that it would not be found. It wasn't until a witness later came forward with information about the murders that the mass grave was finally discovered after the war.[40]

In 1952, David McNeley's remains were returned home and laid to rest in Des Moines, Iowa.

Mr. Trabold never came out and said it, but reading between the lines, I could tell that what happened to his best friend still bothered him. And to be honest with you, as I was researching all of this, it bothered me too, just thinking about what happened to David and those 13 other defenseless prisoners. I think it helped Mr. Trabold to talk about it, though.

*   *   *

Of all the things I've found on eBay that were connected to Mr. Trabold, none were more significant than the discovery I made in August of 2010. The auction was simply titled "WW2 USAAF Bombardier Wing Badge-Luxenberg-Sterling-Id'd." Looking back on it now, I'm not even sure why I clicked on that auction to begin with. But when I did, my jaw dropped.

The auction included a heap of old papers and such from the war, but what grabbed my attention was the large photograph of Mr. Trabold and his crew standing in front of *Old-Bitch-U-Airy Bess*. I instantly recognized it as the same photo from the *Hellbird War Book*, but what was it doing there? Searching for an answer, I found a name as I scanned the auction pictures for clues. All of this material, and there was a lot of it, had belonged to a Lieutenant Thurman Sallade. That name sounded very familiar, so I ran upstairs and grabbed my copy of the *Hellbird War Book*. I quickly flipped through the pages until I found the picture of Mr. Trabold's crew, and then I turned to the roster in the back of the book. I ran through the names until I came upon a Thurman Sallade. Was this really happening?

Thurman Sallade was the bombardier on *Old-Bitch-U-Airy Bess*. He was an actual member of Mr. Trabold's crew. And someone had just listed all of his belongings from the war on eBay.

I ran back downstairs and looked at the auction pictures again. It was now very late at night, and I'd had a long day at work. As I stared at the pictures in disbelief, I remember saying to myself: *is this real?* But there was no one here to assure me that I wasn't dreaming. I just couldn't believe what I was seeing. What were the chances of finding something like this?

Once I got over the shock, I became determined to save this grouping at any cost. The first thing I had to do, above all else, was share my discovery with Mr. Trabold. It was almost 3:00 a.m. when I sent him a very excited e-mail. I began by saying that he wasn't going to believe what I just found on eBay, and then I dropped the bombshell news. I could just imagine the expression on his face later that morning when he checked his e-mail. I went on to say that I was going to do everything I could to save the grouping and preserve it for display with Baldwin's parachute. If need be, I was prepared to spend every last penny I had. My only focus in life now was to save Thurman Sallade's belongings at any cost.

When I finally went to bed, I couldn't sleep at all that night. And it wasn't necessarily because I was so excited about what I found, which I was, but I was more worried than anything. When I told Mr. Trabold that I would throw every last penny I had towards saving the grouping, it wasn't just a figure of speech. To have any real chance of winning the auction, it was going to come down to me literally counting pennies. Even though the grouping mainly consisted of documents, I already knew that it was going to sell for a lot of money – probably more money than I had. What made this grouping stand out, and the reason it was so valuable, was the crown jewel of the collection: Thurman Sallade's silver Luxenberg bombardier wings.

The Luxenberg wings were top of the line in their day. With exquisite detailing that set them far above other makers, they were the finest wings you could buy during the war and were now highly sought after by collectors. What made Sallade's wings even more valuable was that they were the very rare first pattern Luxenberg wings. The seller knew those Luxenberg wings were something special. To entice bidders, he proudly showed them off in the auction pictures. I have to admit, they were absolutely stunning.

It was hard to say what the grouping might sell for, but I knew those wings alone were worth many hundreds of dollars. And to the right person, whose collection was missing them, who knows what they'd be willing to pay for a Luxenberg with such fantastic provenance. You could even see Sallade wearing those wings on his uniform in the crew photo, and that upped their value even more. As I tossed in bed that night, I kept asking myself how was I going to pay for it all? I didn't have an answer.

The next morning, after a few hours of restless sleep, I woke up to find a reply from Mr. Trabold. He was astounded by what I found. Sally, as he was known to everyone on the crew, had been a very special friend, and they'd kept in touch until he passed away in 1980. Mr. Trabold still thought of him often, and he was thrilled that his things might be part of my display with Baldwin's parachute. Mr. Trabold also mentioned that he kept in touch with the families of the pilot and navigator from *Old-Bitch-U-Airy Bess*, and he would inform them of my discovery and plans to save the grouping. The pressure was definitely on now.[41]

The money issue dominated my thoughts as I left for work that day, but there was something else that was also bothering me: how did the seller end up with all of Sally's things? The answer to that question, as I soon learned, was one I'd heard many times before. But that didn't make it any easier to stomach.

Over 30 years ago, the seller was invited to attend an estate sale in Pennsylvania with a friend who was a book dealer. His friend was looking for old books, but everything else in the house was fair game. While searching the basement, where practically everything had suffered water damage to some degree, he found all of Sally's things from the war. The woman who owned the house was cleaning it out and possibly moving, but he didn't know who she was in relation to Sally. Thinking back on it, he thought she might have been Sally's second wife, and added that he'd gotten so much stuff from second wives over the years because the attachment just isn't there. (Mr. Trabold later told me that Sally's first wife died of cancer.)

After all these years, he finally decided to sell everything he bought that day and listed it all on eBay. I never asked what he paid for it all, but I'm sure it wasn't much. To give you an idea of how much stuff he pulled out of that basement, the entire grouping weighed 12 pounds.

The more I looked at the auction pictures, the more nervous I became. This grouping was going to sell for a lot of money, and now I had to figure out how I was going to come up with enough cash to buy it. By the time the auction ended, I'd have two paychecks in the bank from my job as a line cook at a small Italian restaurant, plus any other cash I could come up with. I didn't have any real savings to speak of, but I was prepared to spend everything I had to save Sally's things.

I had been trying to save up some money recently, but the last couple of weeks were pretty rough. First I had to buy two new tires for my Ford Explorer, and with an oil change thrown in, the bill came to nearly $300. Then the battery died while I was at the grocery store the very next week, and there went another $100. To top it all off, only days before Sally's things appeared on eBay, I made a deal for a large collection of target maps that were used on B-29s during the war. I really didn't want to spend the money, but it was such a great collection and I knew I'd never find so many of those maps together again, so I had to buy them. That was another $450 gone.

All of this together, for someone like me, was an awful lot of money out the door. But I didn't have time to fret over money that was already gone, so I got busy and scoured the house for any loose change and misplaced cash that I could find. While I was tearing the house apart, Mr. Trabold surprised me with something I never expected: an offer to loan me money. He knew things were pretty tight for me, and he wanted to do everything he could to help me save Sally's things. What an amazing friend.[42] He was also keeping the son of the pilot of *Old-Bitch-U-Airy Bess* abreast of the situation, and he offered to loan me some money too.

I was deeply moved by their generosity, especially the pilot's son, whom I'd never met or spoken to before, but I was just too proud to accept their offers. This was something that I had to do on my own. I'd find a way, even if it came down to my last penny.[43]

After desperately searching my house for money, I moved on to the garage. I'd been filling my Explorer up with gas twice a week for years now, and I'd always throw the change in the center console and forget about it. After a few years of accumulation, the console was literally overflowing with change. About two weeks before Sally's things appeared on eBay, I finally had to empty it out when the lid wouldn't shut anymore. I never gave all that change much thought before, but now it might just be enough to ensure I could save Sally's things.

With five days left on the auction, I started counting everything I had. I went through the paper money first that was buried in my center console, and I found $115 in dollar bills. The bank teller would probably question my line of work if I walked in with all those singles, so I convinced my boss at the restaurant to exchange them for me. I moved on to the coins next, which I had in two big plastic bags. Out of curiosity, I'd already weighed them and was amazed to learn that I'd been driving around with 30 pounds of change in my truck. I dumped all the change out on my coffee table and began counting the quarters first. In what seemed like no time at all, I had $200 in quarters, and there were still a lot left in the pile. I was starting to feel giddy.

I kept on counting, not believing how much money was there, until I came to the last quarter in the pile that would make an even $300. I noticed it was a state quarter, and I remember saying to myself that if it was a Georgia quarter, my home state, that would be a sign of good luck. I turned the quarter over, and there was the Georgia peach on the back. (I kept it for good luck.)

Before I counted the rest of the change, I took a break and thought about the man whose legacy I was trying to save. I'd been e-mailing Mr. Trabold with updates practically every day, and he in turn had been sharing so many wonderful memories with me about Sally. It was heartwarming to hear how good a person Thurman Sallade was. During the war, there was no distinction between an officer and an enlisted man in his eyes, Mr. Trabold said, and he treated everyone as equals. I could tell that he deeply missed his friend. I had to win this auction for him.[44]

Time to start counting again. I sorted through the dimes, nickels and pennies next. I stopped when I reached another $100 in change. There were still a lot of coins left on the table, but it didn't look like I'd need them. With a total of $515 in change and dollar bills from my Explorer, plus some extra cash I found around the house, and what I could spare from my two paychecks, I'd somehow scraped together over $1,000 in just six days. I felt more confident now than ever before.

After a hectic week, it was now the night before the auction ended. With 17 hours left, the bidding was already up to $205.50, and it was going to go up a lot higher before it was all over with. I sent Mr. Trabold another update before I went to bed. It felt good to tell him that I had over a grand to spend, and that I was going to risk it all on the auction. I know that probably sounds crazy to you, but I knew what this grouping would mean to Mr. Trabold and the family members of his crew. For all of us, it was worth something far more valuable than money.

I went to bed that night feeling pretty good about things, but part of me was still nervous. For the past week, I'd been losing sleep worrying about the auction and trying to find enough money to bid on it. Now as the final hours ticked away, I'd have no regrets if I had to spend everything I had to save Sally's things, but I was afraid there might be someone out there who would bid more than I could afford. I figured the grouping should sell for somewhere between $400 and $500, but with eBay, you never really know what something is going to go for. All of these scenarios were playing out in my mind when I went to bed that night. I didn't get much sleep.

I woke up the next day feeling exhausted, but then again, I'd woken up for the past six days feeling like that. The auction was set to end at 9 o'clock that evening, and that was a bad thing. I had to work that night, which meant that I'd have to bid hours before the auction ended. I'd learned in the past that it was best to wait until the last few seconds to bid, otherwise someone could keep bidding against me. But there was nothing I could do, so I tried not to worry about it.

Before I left for work, I checked my e-mail and found a reply from Mr. Trabold. He was very excited about the end of the auction and was going to stay up past midnight, if need be, waiting to hear from me. I didn't have time to send a reply, but I was going to win this auction for him no matter what. I couldn't wait to get home that night and let him know that we'd won.

With a little over seven hours to go, I placed my bid, and then I left for work. It was all out of my hands now. My drive to work took about half an hour, and I usually spent that time listening to loud music to motivate myself. But on this day, I took some time to quietly reflect on every-thing as I drove. It was hard to believe how I'd gotten here. In a way, it still didn't seem real.

A few days earlier, as I was writing another update to Mr. Trabold, my curiosity got the better of me, and I began to wonder if there was something going on here that went beyond a coin-cidence. It just seemed odd how we first met through Baldwin's parachute, and then stayed in touch over the years as I kept finding all of these other things that were connected to him. And now to top it all off, the belongings of his dear friend and crewmate suddenly appeared on eBay. I wrote to Mr. Trabold that I've always believed in fate, and that some things are just meant to be. I wondered if fate could explain all of this?

For his part, Mr. Trabold was much more pragmatic. I think it was the engineer in him. He didn't really believe in fate, and he chalked it up to statistics and the billions of occurrences each day. I could see his point of view – but still, I wondered.[45]

As the hours slowly ticked by at work, I kept thinking about all the things that could be in Sally's grouping. The seller still hadn't looked through everything, despite owning it all for 30 years, so there was no telling what all was there. For the auction pictures, he did pull out a few interesting things. One was a really nice photo of Sally in uniform that I could tell was taken in India by the unique theater-made patches. In another picture, I could see a bombardier's checklist in the background. That really got me excited, because Sally would've used that during his missions. There was also a large folder that was bursting with newspaper clippings about the B-29 that Sally's wife had saved during the war. I've always been fascinated by old newspapers, and those clippings were like little snapshots of history. I couldn't wait to look through them all.

Below the clippings, there was a stack of other folders and binders that were also overflowing with documents. I couldn't tell what they were, but I did see part of a flight log sticking out of the pile. Mr. Trabold really got excited when I told him about that. Sally was so skilled behind the bombsight that he was promoted to a lead bombardier and began flying with other crews. Mr. Trabold never got the whole story of where he went after that, and those logs could fill in the blanks for him. Just the flight logs alone would be quite a find, Mr. Trabold said, and he offered to pay me for copies of them, but I could never accept any money from him. I'd happily make copies for him all day. Along with everything else in the grouping, they could answer a lot of questions that he never thought to ask before Sally died.[46]

I could tell by the animated tone of his e-mails that the thought of all this had awakened something inside him. It truly warmed my heart to see Mr. Trabold, at 86 years old, so full of excitement, and it was definitely rubbing off on me. I couldn't wait to get home that night.

*   *   *

As I look back on it now, some parts of that night are a total blur. I recall being at work and how my thoughts were consumed with the auction, but that's all I remember. I went back and checked, and I sent Mr. Trabold an e-mail at 9:32 p.m. that evening, about half an hour after the auction ended. It must have been a slow night at the restaurant, because I usually didn't get home until much later. Strangely, I have absolutely no recollection of that. Maybe I was just too excited about the auction to allow another boring shift behind the line to become a lasting memory of that day.

But what I do remember, ever so vividly, is how I felt when I got home that night. Instead of trying to put it all into words now, I'll just quote from the e-mail I sent Mr. Trabold: "I just can't believe it, but I didn't win! I'm literally stunned right now."[47]

Stunned was an understatement. My whole world had just come crashing down. I had to walk away and collect myself. After it all sank in, I came back and looked at the bidding to see what went wrong. My bid of $1,126.99 was everything I had. The next bid below mine was $450, and that was right in the ballpark of what I expected the grouping to sell for. Then just before the auction ended, someone outbid me, and it sold for an incredible $1,151.99.

Who would spend over $1,100 on a grouping like that? It just didn't make any sense.

The message I had to send to Mr. Trabold that night broke my heart. After everything it took to get here, and all the memories that were roused along the way, to now inform him that it was all for nothing was very hard to swallow. I'd let him down, and that's what hurt the most. I couldn't understand how this had happened.

Maybe it was the eternal optimist in me, but I told Mr. Trabold that I'd reach out to the seller and see if he could put me in touch with the buyer. After I explained their importance, the new owner might be willing to make some copies of the documents for us, and maybe he'd be open to an offer for everything. I'd have another paycheck in the bank by then, and he might be interested in a quick flip. All I knew was that I had to try something. I wasn't going to give up hope yet.

I heard back from Mr. Trabold just before midnight. He'd stayed up late waiting for news about the auction. I could tell that he was disappointed, but he wrote that I'd given it my best shot and thanked me for all the energy I put into it. He added that he felt bad because he could've sent me an extra $500 to help save Sally's things.[48] That broke my heart even more, him feeling bad. I didn't want Mr. Trabold to feel like any of this was his fault. There was no one to blame but myself.

I waited two more sleepless nights before I got back in touch with the seller. I wasn't sure what to say at first, but with hopes of salvaging something from this stunning loss, I asked if he could put me in touch with the buyer. I heard back from him a few hours later. He was disappointed that I didn't get the grouping, but admittedly, he wasn't displeased with what it all sold for. The seller was a really nice guy, though, and he was more than happy to approach the buyer for us as soon as he heard from him. I perked up when I read that last part. By that time, it had already been two days since the auction ended, and it was very unusual to have not heard from the buyer yet. It was a long shot, but with that revelation, we might have a chance to get much more than just copies.

The thought first entered my mind in the hours after the auction ended. I was looking at the bidding and I noticed that the winner only had a feedback score of 32. That meant they were very new to eBay. I'd seen new people get carried away before by bidding more than they could spend, and that could explain why the grouping sold for what it did. The longer the buyer went without contacting the seller, the more likely they would back out of the sale. The terms of the auction stated that payment had to be made within 10 days, and that meant the buyer now had eight days left to follow through.

I sent Mr. Trabold another update and told him to keep his fingers crossed, because this could all work out for us in the end. After such a heartbreaking loss, I was starting to feel the life flow through my veins again. Mr. Trabold was getting excited again, too. His optimism was infectious. Eight days for the buyer to act, and I was losing sleep all over again. At this rate, it was going to be a very long week.

The seller was going to let me know as soon as he heard from the buyer, but after another two days passed without word, I contacted him again. Was there any news? Had the buyer paid yet? He didn't answer. The loss of sleep continued. Two more agonizing days went by. No news.

It was now Monday, and the buyer had four days left to pay. At 9:38 p.m. that evening, I finally received a message from the seller. With everything that was on the line, I felt a surge of both excitement and trepidation as I clicked to open it. One way or another, this could be the end.

"Looks like the lady has folded," he wrote. "This suits me as I wanted this to go to a good home." Even though this was the moment that I'd been hoping and praying for, it still didn't seem real. But I guess dreams never do.[49]

A part of me wanted to jump out of my seat in joy, but before I allowed myself to celebrate, I offered the seller $550 for everything. I was not going to lose this grouping again. While I waited to hear back from him, I sent Mr. Trabold the greatest e-mail I've ever written. The subject line said it all: "VICTORY!!"[50]

Less than eight hours later, it was a done deal. The seller happily accepted my offer.

After the highs and lows and loss of sleep over the past two weeks, it felt good to look in the mirror again. It felt good to know we'd won. Maybe there was something to fate, after all.

* * *

As I'm writing this now, it's been seven years since that night in September when I came home from work and found the box of Sally's things waiting for me. A lot has happened since then, and with life getting in the way – as it always does – it had been a long time since I looked through it all. But tonight, before I sat down to write this, I went back in time. As I slowly flipped through his papers again, careful not to tear any of the fragile pages, that old paper smell brought back a flood of memories from those two weeks in the waning days of summer. Even now, all these years later, there was still something magical about it all.

I'll never forget the excitement when I opened the package that night. The first thing I did was spread everything out on my kitchen counter so I could take a picture for Mr. Trabold. When the seller said there were 12 pounds of material here, he wasn't lying. The grouping practically covered the entire counter. I wanted to go through it all that first night, but I was totally exhausted from work. I quickly skimmed through what I could, but there was just so much material that it was overwhelming. I was working six days a week then, so I'd have to wait until Sunday before I could go through it all, but it was worth the wait.

When I went back and looked through it all again just now, I rediscovered so many things I'd forgotten about. It felt like I was reliving that September night all over again.

One of the things I rediscovered was a memo entitled "Bombing Equipment in B-29 Airplane," which contained the "latest information available" on the B-29's bombing equipment. There was one passage that really caught my eye: "It must be remembered that we are dealing with a new airplane, and it is the responsibility of everyone concerned to learn as much about it as possible, even though some information is lacking at the present time."[51] What struck me about that memo is that it was dated just two months before *Old-Bitch-U-Airy Bess* left for India. With all the problems they had with the early bombers, including a lack of basic information, as pointed out in the memo, the fact that the B-29s were able to deploy overseas and drop bombs on Japan when they did is truly a testament to the men of the 58th Bomb Wing.

I knew from the moment I first saw the auction that Sally's papers would give me an incredible insight into his life during the war, but in reality, not all of those insights were pleasant. I was just reminded of that a few moments ago, when I rediscovered his Last Will and Testament. It was signed five days after the memo about the bombing equipment. I also found his life insurance policy for $10,000 that was signed four weeks before he left for war. In today's money, that was about $174,000 to take care of his wife and baby girl. Looking at those papers, it made me think of Plevan and McNeley.

As I dug deeper, searching for something to rid the visions of their deaths from my mind, I rediscovered a glowing letter of commendation from the deputy commander of Sally's bomb group. I thought I'd share part of it with you:

4 March 1945
To: First Lieutenant Thurman W. Sallade,

Your service as a Bombardier-Navigator in the 462nd Bombardment Group, an original B-29 Group operating under extreme difficulties out of bases in China and India against numerous targets extending from the Japanese mainland to Mukden to Singapore, has been singularly outstanding. Without your own individual effort the great record of this organization could not have been attained.

Your return to the United States has been based in its entirety upon your superior achievements in this combat theater of operations. If ever, it will be a considerable length of time before your loss to this organization can be erased.[52]

Like the commendation, I rediscovered a lot of papers tonight that I'd forgotten about, but I also found some other things that I remembered quite well. I'll always be fond of the bombardier's checklist I first saw buried beneath a pile of documents in the auction pictures. When I opened the box that September night, it was one of the first things I looked for. It was also the first thing I looked for tonight. For me, to actually hold the checklist Sally used in combat is beyond words.

The flight log I spotted in the auction pictures will always be special to me as well, but I didn't know at the time how truly significant it was. What I saw in the pictures was actually the flight log when Sally came home from the war. I never expected to find something like that. Sally's achievements as a lead bombardier had earned him an early ticket home aboard a war-weary B-29, and he assumed the duties of the navigator during the two-week journey back to the United States. In this six-page flight log, Sally recorded his entire journey home. The first entry was his final takeoff from India. You can imagine how happy those men were to be going home. I grinned at the note Sally made about the pilots buzzing the runway 100 feet off the ground in celebration. What a sight that must have been. I think I know why that flight log was so special to him, and why he held on to it after the war.

Next to the flight log was something else that I was shocked to discover all those years ago. It was the original orders from April of 1944 that sent the crew of *Old-Bitch-U-Airy Bess* overseas and off to war. I couldn't believe Sally had kept them. I'd always heard that the crews didn't know where they were going when they left Kansas, and sure enough, these orders didn't include a destination, only that it was an "overseas destination to be designated by Commanding General, Air Transport Command."[53]

When I held them next to each other tonight and thought about everything that happened in between those orders and the flight log, it made for quite a sight. These were the bookends of that defining period in Thurman Sallade's life. And to think, were it not for a book dealer and his friend over 30 years ago, they would have been lost forever in that damp Pennsylvania basement.

Within five days of it all arriving here back in 2010, I mailed Mr. Trabold a big package of all the copies I'd made. There were so many fascinating things in Sally's papers that it was hard not to copy all 12 pounds of it. It seemed like every page revealed another piece of his wartime story, and I didn't want to miss any of it. By the time I got it all in the mail, Mr. Trabold was getting ready to leave for the 58th Bomb Wing's reunion at the New England Air Museum in Connecticut. I was hoping he'd get it before the reunion so he could share the copies with everyone, but the package didn't quite get there in time.

Beyond everything going on with Sally's things, the reunion that year had some extra significance for Mr. Trabold. At that time, the New England Air Museum was in the final stages of restoring a B-29 that was the centerpiece of the new 58th Bomb Wing Memorial at the museum. The volunteers had done an amazing job restoring the B-29, but they were missing an important piece: the wooden footrest for the CFC gunner's chair. He was always modest about it, but Mr. Trabold was a very talented woodworker and had won many awards at the New York State Fair. When he found out about the missing footrest, he put his skills to work and built one from scratch in his workshop for the museum. (He also made a footrest for the B-29 at the Seattle Museum of Flight.)

Even though it had been well over six decades since he last flew a mission, I thought it was pretty neat that Mr. Trabold was still working on his beloved B-29s.

The museum always opens up their B-29 for the veterans to get inside during the reunions, and Mr. Trabold was looking forward to climbing up into his old seat again, complete with the footrest he made. It would be the first time he saw it installed. He was also going to try to crawl through the bomb bay tunnel again, like he'd done so many times in his youth. His drive was truly inspiring.

I heard from Mr. Trabold about a week later, after he got home from the reunion and opened the package with Sally's papers. You can imagine what it must have been like for him to see everything. And if you were wondering, Mr. Trabold did indeed climb up into his old seat again in the B-29, and at 86 years old, he easily crawled on his hands and knees all the way through the 35-foot-long bomb bay tunnel, just like he said he would.[54]

Before I sat down to write this, I also looked at Sally's Luxenberg wings again, and the large crew photo of *Old-Bitch-U-Airy Bess* that was in with his papers. It's funny how worried I was about those wings and what they were worth. When I was going through his papers that September night, I actually found the original receipt from when Sally bought the wings during the war. They cost him $17.50. I know my fellow collectors will get a kick out of that.

When it came time to think about a cover for this book, there was never any question in my mind that the crew of *Old-Bitch-U-Airy Bess* would be on it. The photo we used is the very same one from Sally's papers. If you turn to the cover, Sally is standing in the back row, third on the left. If you look closely, you can see those Luxenberg wings on his shirt. In the front row, Baldwin is kneeling second on the left. Mr. Trabold is kneeling second on the right, and kneeling next to him on the end is Plevan; the photo was taken about five months before he was killed.

A few weeks after Sally's things arrived here back in 2010, Mr. Trabold said that he never could have guessed all the wonderful things that would happen after he put Baldwin's parachute on eBay. He still wasn't convinced of fate, like I was, but he recognized how truly remarkable it all was.[55]

Mr. Trabold was a living connection to all of this history, and he told me to make use of it. He was sure that I would. I hope the words on these pages have lived up to his expectations.

*   *   *

It's hard to believe that it has been well over a decade since I opened that first e-mail from Mr. Trabold. I sometimes wonder how different things would have been if we'd never connected through Baldwin's parachute. I know this chapter would not exist were it not for that piece of silk, and the events surrounding it all those years ago. It's funny how things work out like that.

Mr. Trabold is in his 90s now, and he's the last surviving member of the *Old-Bitch-U-Airy Bess* crew. He's slowed down a lot with age, but to me, he'll always be that "ball of fire" from when we first connected all those years ago.

As I look back on it all, I still can't believe my good fortune the night I discovered that parachute on eBay, and all that would come about because of it. But most of all, for someone of my generation, I still can't believe that I'm fortunate enough to call Mr. Trabold a friend. And every time I hear from him, it feels like I've hit pay dirt all over again.

8

The Beginning of the End

While the B-29s were bombing Yawata on June 15, 1944, bombs were also falling 1,500 miles away in the Mariana Islands. After a bloody island-hopping campaign that began with the Battle of Tarawa in 1943 and steadily advanced across thousands of miles in the Central Pacific towards Japan, it all came down to this. The invasion of Saipan had begun.

With the massive new airbases that would be carved out of the coral and jungles after the capture of Saipan and the neighboring islands of Tinian and Guam, all of Japan's industrial centers – including Tokyo – would finally be within range of the B-29s. Taking the Marianas would not be easy, however. As was painfully learned in previous battles like Tarawa, where practically the entire garrison of 4,500 men had fought to the death, the Japanese would put up a fanatical fight to hold the Marianas. On June 15, the first of more than 70,000 Americans poured onto the beaches of Saipan. The fighting that followed would be some of the most brutal yet seen in the Pacific.

In an attempt to win a decisive battle against the Americans, the Japanese Navy launched a counterattack in defense of the Marianas on June 19 that included nine aircraft carriers and five battleships. Facing off against the 15 aircraft carriers of the U.S. Navy's Task Force 58, the ensuing Battle of the Philippine Sea became the largest aircraft carrier battle in history and resulted in a stunning defeat for Japan, who lost three aircraft carriers and nearly 600 airplanes. The American fighter pilots shot down so many Japanese aircraft that they dubbed it "The Great Marianas Turkey Shoot." Together with the catastrophic losses suffered four months later during the Battle of Leyte Gulf, Japan's once-mighty surface navy was effectively neutralized.

Three weeks after the Battle of Saipan began, the remaining Japanese forces under the command of General Yoshitsugu Saito had been pushed back to the northern part of the island. With nowhere left to retreat, and no hope of support after the disastrous Battle of the Philippine Sea, Saito ordered a final Banzai charge. "We will advance to attack the American forces and will all die an honorable death," Saito said to his men. "Each man will kill ten Americans."[1]

On the morning of July 7, well over 4,000 Japanese soldiers, sailors and civilians, some armed only with sticks, charged the American lines. About 50 yards behind the front lines held by the 2nd Battalion of the U.S. Army's 105th Infantry Regiment, Captain Ben Salomon had set up his aid station in a small tent to treat wounded soldiers. Captain Salomon was actually the regimental dentist, but after the battalion's surgeon was wounded during a mortar attack two weeks earlier, Salomon volunteered as his replacement.[2]

Within the first minutes of the attack, Salomon's aid station was overwhelmed with more than 30 wounded soldiers. As the Japanese charged and broke through the American lines, they quickly reached the small aid station. Salomon was busy working on the wounded when he saw a Japanese soldier bayonet one of the wounded Americans lying on a stretcher near the tent. Picking up a rifle, Salomon shot and killed the attacker. As he turned his attention back to the wounded, two more Japanese charged through the entrance of the tent. Salomon clubbed both men with his rifle, then shot one and bayoneted the other. Just then, four more Japanese crawled under the sides of the tent. Salomon charged into them, kicking, shooting, bayoneting and head butting. With seven dead Japanese soldiers lying around him, Salomon ran out of the tent to find help to defend his aid station, but he quickly realized the situation was hopeless. The Japanese had completely overrun the regiment's two understrength battalions.

Salomon returned to the tent and told the wounded to make their way back to the regimental aid station while he attempted to hold off the Japanese. He then rushed out of the tent with rifle in hand and joined the few Americans who were still alive and fighting inside the perimeter, eventually taking over a machine gun after its crew was killed. Salomon continued fighting by himself as wave after wave of Japanese soldiers charged his position. That was the last time anyone saw Captain Ben Salomon alive.

The next morning, after fierce counterattacks, American forces finally retook the positions originally held by the two battalions. When the Japanese began their attack, the 1st and 2nd Battalions of the 105th Infantry Regiment had a strength of 1,108 men. When the battle was over, only 189 remained fit for duty; the other 919 men were either dead, wounded or missing.[3]

Captain Edmund Love recalled when they found Salomon slumped over a machine gun after the battle:

> There were 98 Japanese bodies piled up in front of that gun position. Salomon had killed so many men that he had been forced to move the gun four different times in order to get a clear field of fire. There was something else that we noted, too. There were 76 bullet holes in Salomon's body. When we called a doctor over to examine him, we were told that 24 of the wounds had been suffered before Salomon died. There were no witnesses, but it wasn't hard to put the story together. One could easily visualize Ben Salomon, wounded and bleeding, trying to drag that gun a few more feet so that he would have a new field of fire. The blood was on the ground, and the marks plainly indicated how hard it must have been for him, especially in that last move.[4]

On May 1, 2002, almost 58 years after he died defending his wounded comrades, Captain Ben Salomon was posthumously awarded the Medal of Honor for his actions that morning on Saipan. The delay had been due to a technicality in the rules of the Geneva Convention, which forbid medical officers from bearing arms against the enemy. A review later determined that medical personnel were in fact permitted to bear arms in self-defense, or in defense of the wounded.[5]

When the island was finally declared secure on July 9, the human toll of the battle was incomprehensible. The Japanese had fought to the death. In just 24 days, almost the entire 30,000-man garrison on Saipan had been killed. Only 921 Japanese soldiers and sailors were captured alive.[6] Of the more than 71,000 Americans who landed on Saipan, 3,426 were dead or missing, and 10,685 were wounded. After the brutal fighting and the battles for neighboring Tinian and

Guam, there could be no doubt of Japan's resolve. As American forces closed in on the home islands, the Japanese would fight to the last man.[7]

Even though Saipan was declared secure on July 9, there were still thousands of Japanese left on the island. In the days that followed, a tragedy began to unfold on the northern tip of the island. Saipan was the first battle in which Japanese civilians were encountered in large numbers. Before the invasion, some 20,000 Japanese civilians called Saipan home. Over 10,000 had surrendered in the weeks following the battle, but many chose to commit suicide rather than surrender to the Americans, who they had been indoctrinated to believe would rape, torture and murder them.[8]

Robert Sherrod was a war correspondent for *Time* and *Life* magazines and covered the battle with the Marines. A veteran of the Attu and Tarawa invasions, Sherrod was not prepared for what he encountered on Saipan. Near the high cliffs above Marpi Point on the northern tip of the island, Sherrod listened as a Marine described what he had witnessed over the past days:

> You wouldn't believe it unless you saw it. Yesterday and the day before there were hundreds of Jap civilians – men, women and children – up here on this cliff. In the most routine way, they would jump off the cliff and smash themselves on the rocks or would climb down and wade into the sea. I saw a father throw his three children off, then jump down himself. Sometimes the parents cut their children's throats before they threw them off the cliff. Those coral pockets down there under the cliff are full of Jap suicides.[9]

As Sherrod stood with the shocked Marines, he saw a Japanese boy, about 15 years old, pacing back and forth on the rocks below. The boy hesitated, paced some more, and then eased into the water. He then swam out and drowned himself. Looking down from the cliffs, Sherrod counted the bodies of seven others floating in the surf who had killed themselves. Close to shore was the body of a child, about 5 years old, bobbing in the water. "This is nothing," the Marine said, as Sherrod turned to go. "Half a mile down, on the west side, you can see hundreds of them."[10]

Sherrod later talked to a U.S. Navy officer from a minesweeper operating on the west side of the island who said the waters were so full of bodies – "hundreds and hundreds" of bodies – that they couldn't avoid hitting them:

> Part of the area is so congested with floating bodies we simply can't avoid running them down. I remember one woman in khaki trousers and a white polka dot blouse, with her black hair streaming in the water. I'm afraid every time I see that kind of blouse, I'll think of that girl. There was another one, nude, who had drowned herself while giving birth to a baby. The baby's head had entered this world, but that was all of him. A small boy of four or five had drowned with his arm firmly clenched around the neck of a Jap soldier; the two bodies rocked crazily in the waves.[11]

Entire families had jumped off the cliffs at Marpi Point, drowned themselves in the sea, or huddled together around grenades and pulled the pins. Sherrod described another incident when 100 Japanese civilians were spotted on the rocks below Marpi Point. The group suddenly bowed to the Marines watching above from the cliff, stripped off their clothes, and bathed in the sea. Then they returned to shore, put on new clothes, and spread a large Japanese flag on the rocks. The leader then distributed hand grenades to the group. One by one, the Japanese pulled the pins and blew themselves up. The gruesome scene left even the battle-hardened Marines aghast.[12]

Reports of the mass suicides on Saipan were soon picked up in Japan from American news stories and were used to spin propaganda to the Japanese people. Robert Sherrod's own words were lifted from his *Time* magazine article, "The Nature of the Enemy," and were widely reprinted in the Japanese press – except for the parts that conflicted with the Government's narrative that all Japanese civilians had willingly died rather than surrender.[13] One Japanese newspaper reported:

> It has been reported that noncombatants, women, and children have chosen death rather than to be captured alive and shamed by the demonlike American forces. The world has been astounded by the strength of the fighting spirit and patriotism of the entire people of Japan.[14]

The stories in Japan all ignored certain aspects of Sherrod's reporting, like a couple who were shot dead by a Japanese sniper while leading their children back from the edge of the sea to safety.[15]

The true number of Japanese civilians who committed suicide rather than surrender will never be known. At the time and in the decades that followed, it was thought that upwards of 10,000 civilians had killed themselves, but subsequent research has concluded that the actual number was probably around 1,000.[16] Whatever the real number was, the horrific scenes witnessed on Saipan would be a prelude of things to come as American forces closed in on the Japanese home islands.

*   *   *

I recognized the signature right away when I saw it on eBay, and the B-29 in the old black and white photo it was signed on, but it almost seemed too good to be true. The photograph had captured a moment in history that was years in the making and marked a turning point in the air war against Japan. Nothing would be the same after that day. But what I really couldn't believe was when I won the auction a few days later. The old photo had only cost me $7.90. Was nobody paying attention on eBay?

On October 12, 1944, just three months after the Battle of Saipan ended, Brigadier General Haywood S. "Possum" Hansell Jr., the Commanding General of the new XXI Bomber Command, landed the first B-29 on Saipan. Climbing down from the gleaming B-29 named *Joltin' Josie, The Pacific Pioneer*, Hansell briefly spoke to the huge crowd that surrounded the bomber. "The first element of the 21st Bomber Command has arrived," Hansell proclaimed to the cameras. "When we've done some more fighting, we'll do some more talking!"[17]

A veteran of the air war against Germany, 41-year-old Hansell was a staunch believer in the doctrine of strategic bombing and had helped draft Air War Plan AWPD-1 in 1941 before America's entry into the war. Hansell went on to lead the 8th Air Force's 1st Bomb Wing in 1943, and after returning from England, he developed plans for the coming air war against Japan. By April of 1944, Hansell was promoted to Chief of Staff of the 20th Air Force in Washington and was involved in all aspects of the new global bomber force.[18] A solid tactician and a proven combat leader, Hansell was now at the helm of the XXI Bomber Command in the Marianas. A new front in the air war against Japan was about to be opened.

The B-29s under the XXI Bomber Command would quickly grow to three bomb wings over the next four months, but on that October day in 1944, there was only a single B-29 in the entire Marianas. In the photo I found on eBay for $7.90, it captured the moment *Joltin' Josie* taxied in after landing that day. And the person who autographed the photo? It was General Hansell himself. I couldn't believe it, but this photo was actually signed by Hansell on Saipan during the war. The seller had no idea what he had, and I was so lucky to find it. (I've included the photo in this book.)

Following eight days behind *Joltin' Josie*, the second B-29 piloted by 38-year-old Brigadier General Emmett E. "Rosie" O'Donnell, the commander of the 73rd Bomb Wing, touched down on Saipan. O'Donnell was a highly experienced veteran who led some of the first strikes against Japanese forces from the Philippines in the chaotic days after Pearl Harbor. Before the war was barely two days old, O'Donnell had earned a Distinguished Flying Cross for attacking a Japanese heavy cruiser and its destroyer escort in a lone B-17. Due to malfunctioning bomb racks, O'Donnell made five bomb runs over the ships through heavy flak and fighters in what was only the beginning of his epic battle against the Japanese. After his bombers were all destroyed, O'Donnell continued fighting with the infantry on Bataan before later escaping to Australia in a patched-up B-18.[19]

From the first days of the war leading a squadron of B-17s against impossible odds as the Japanese swept across the Pacific, O'Donnell had now returned to lead the 73rd Bomb Wing against his old foes. The vanguard of the XXI Bomber Command had arrived.

With the capture of the Marianas, the heart of the Japanese Empire was now within range of American bombers. A steady flow of men and B-29s would be arriving in the weeks that followed in preparation for the first strike against Tokyo, but Hansell didn't find much waiting for him when he landed on Saipan. Hansell later recalled:

> A survey of conditions on Saipan caused dismay. Of the two bases under construction on Saipan, one could not be used at all by B-29s, and the other had one runway 7,000 feet long (5,000 feet of it paved), a taxiway at one end only, about 40 hardstands, and no other facilities whatever except for a bomb dump and a vehicle park with gasoline truck trailers. It was hardly ready to receive the 12,000 men and 180 aircraft of the 73rd Wing.[20]

The living conditions for the 73rd Bomb Wing were primitive to say the least when its men began arriving on Saipan. After clearing away debris left over from the battle, the headquarters area and the encampments all had to be built from scratch by the men themselves in old sugar cane fields that quickly turned to mud when it rained. For sanitation, the only facilities were makeshift latrines that consisted of a barrel with a seat on top. Until proper showers could be built, washing was accomplished with a helmet full of water, or by gathering behind a water truck while a man sprayed you down with a hose. You could also bathe in the ocean. The lingering smell of rotting corpses were a constant reminder of the battle as the men built their encampments, as were the Japanese stragglers still roaming the area, but at least the insects wouldn't be a problem. The entire island had been sprayed from the air with DDT.

"For the first month or two you couldn't tell the officers from the men," recalled Colonel Lyman Phillips, commander of the 330th Air Service Group. "If a man knew how to use a hammer or a saw, he went to work and used it. If he didn't, he used a shovel, regardless of what kind of brass he had on his collar. There was too much work to do for anybody to wear a shirt, anyhow."[21]

Much like the 58th Bomb Wing in India and China, a lack of facilities seemed to welcome the B-29ers wherever they went, but at least there was optimism to be seen in the new bases in the Marianas. The U.S. Navy could now deliver all the fuel and supplies right to their doorstep. A turning point in the air war had been reached.

As the 73rd Bomb Wing established itself on Saipan, the XXI Bomber Command turned its attention north across some 1,500 miles of ocean towards Tokyo. But before Hansell could launch his first strike, he first had to find the targets. The Japanese were very secretive about their industrial buildup in the years leading up to the war, and very little was known about their strengths and whereabouts. Hansell was tasked with destroying Japan's industrial centers, with the top priority being its aircraft industry, but no one knew exactly where those factories were located. Back in Washington, intelligence was being culled from every available source, including old pictures taken by tourists, but so many questions remained unanswered.[22]

The only way to locate and photograph the targets would be to send a lone B-29 over Tokyo to find them. And that story would begin 6,000 miles away in a bar in Kansas.

*   *   *

If I told you what was sitting next to me on my desk as I'm typing this, you probably wouldn't believe me. I almost didn't believe it, either, when I discovered it on eBay that night.

A week after General Hansell landed on Saipan, 24-year-old Captain Ralph Steakley was enjoying a drink at the officers' club in Salina, Kansas, when he received some shocking news: he and his crew would be going overseas the next day. Steakley was the commander of a very special B-29. Instead of carrying bombs, the B-29s of the 3rd Photo Reconnaissance Squadron were extensively modified to carry an array of sophisticated cameras to photograph enemy installations. The XXI Bomber Command needed targets, and Steakley's crew would be the ones to find them. It would take them 10 days to reach Saipan from Kansas.

Only two days after arriving on Saipan, Steakley and his crew took off in the early morning of November 1, bound for Tokyo. They would be the first Americans over the capital since the Doolittle Raiders in 1942. On the way up, the crew passed the time by debating what they should name their B-29. Everyone agreed that it should be a girl's name, but the discussion ended as they neared Japan and the men got down to business.

"We didn't know what we'd find when we got there – if we got there," recalled Lieutenant Charles Hart, the photo navigator. "The trip was uneventful and luckily the sky over Honshu [Japan's main island] was clear as a bell – not a cloud in sight."[23]

Arriving over Tokyo on a rare sunny afternoon, Captain Steakley's astonished crew found themselves looking down upon a bustling city, as if the war was thousands of miles away. Sitting in the nose with an unobstructed view, Lieutenant Hart could see a sprawling metropolis below. Industrial and urban areas were buzzing with activity, and the streets were crowded with Japanese oblivious to the lone intruder above.

"We were way to hell up, above 32,000 feet, barreling along with a wind of almost 100 knots," Hart recalled. "The Japs were caught by surprise, of course; after all, it was the first enemy plane over their capital in more than two years."

But with air raid sirens beginning to wail across the city, the Japanese would not remain oblivious for long. As anti-aircraft guns opened fire, the residents of Tokyo looked up in awe at the massive B-29 flying high over their city. No one had ever seen an airplane like this before.[24]

Among those mesmerized by the sun glinting off the B-29's aluminum skin high above were hundreds of American and Allied prisoners held at the Omori Prisoner of War Camp on a manmade island in Tokyo Bay. One of the prisoners gazing skyward was a former Olympic track star turned bombardier named Louis Zamperini, whose experiences were later published in the bestselling book *Unbroken*. For Lieutenant Zamperini and all of the prisoners that day, the lone B-29 would have a profound effect on their morale. Zamperini vividly recalled looking up at the high-flying B-29, the largest aircraft he had ever seen, through a narrow window and watching as it left vapor trails like some sort of a white angel. "I knew it was a messenger from home, a harbinger of imminent revenge," Zamperini recalled. "It took my breath away."[25]

Also watching the B-29 soaring six miles high over Omori was Lieutenant Robert Martindale, a B-24 co-pilot who had been shot down and captured almost two years earlier. "The Japanese were pointing toward an unmistakable silhouette as they spoke its name in awe, *B-Niju Ku*," Martindale recalled. "Their words were echoed by shouts of jubilation from the POWs, 'B-29!' … Our spirits soared to its heights as the aircraft passed from sight, for we knew its presence marked the beginning of the end. The war had come to the heart of the Rising Sun."[26]

Defending the skies above Tokyo that day was the 47th Sentai (Air Group) of the Japanese Army Air Force, who were also caught off guard by the B-29's sudden appearance. Armed with Nakajima Ki-44 fighters, the 47th Sentai's three squadrons were quickly scrambled in pursuit of the Americans. Leading the fighters off the ground was Captain Jun Shimizu, commander of the 1st Squadron. Struggling in the thin air and high winds, the Japanese pilots fought in vain to reach the lone B-29 in fighters that were never designed for such high altitudes.[27]

"We counted 19 fighters climbing belatedly after us, but they never had a chance to catch us," Lieutenant Hart said. Shimizu fired a few short bursts in frustration as the B-29 easily slipped away from his fighters, having never come within range. "They just buzzed around underneath us," added Lieutenant Claude Stambaugh, the navigator. "They made passes at us, but they couldn't seem to get up enough speed to catch us at that altitude."[28]

Scattered flak bursts also added to the crew's excitement, but the B-29 did not suffer a single hit during the 35 minutes it spent photographing the heart of the Japanese Empire. "We got our pictures and tailed for home," Lieutenant Hart said after the mission. "It was all pretty tame considering how scared we were when we started."[29]

As they left Japan behind, the crew began shouting congratulations to each other over the interphone, and they wondered what Tokyo Rose, the English-speaking Japanese radio propagandist, was saying to her audience at that moment. Then it suddenly dawned on them: that was the perfect name for their B-29. From that moment on, the first B-29 over Tokyo would be known as *Tokyo Rose*.[30]

Almost 66 years after that first historic mission over Tokyo, I discovered an old U.S. Army Air Forces data plate on eBay that was removed from an F-13 after the war. The aluminum plate was about three-quarters the size of a playing card and was stamped with the aircraft type, serial number and order number, and was then riveted inside the cockpit to signify the acceptance of the aircraft by the Army Air Forces. I'm not sure how many people realized what they were looking at when this data plate appeared on eBay, but I knew right away that it was something special. The plate was stamped F-13A, which was the designation given to the highly modified photo reconnaissance version of the B-29. I became very excited just on that alone, because I had never seen a data plate from an F-13 before. But when I looked up the serial number of this F-13, 42-93852, I was in for one of the biggest shocks of my life. This data plate came from none other than *Tokyo Rose*, the first B-29 over Tokyo. It was actually there in the cockpit during that first historic mission.

I won the auction a few days later, and the data plate was soon safe in my collection. As a collector of all things B-29, it was one of my greatest finds ever.

The data plate from *Tokyo Rose* is sitting in front of me now as I'm typing this. I just picked it up and tried to imagine all the places it has been, and then I sat it down on the corner of my laptop. It's mind-blowing to think about all the history it witnessed. And there it is, right in front of me.

Tokyo Rose would go on to photograph a lot more of Japan during the war, but in the summer of 1949, having long fulfilled her duties, she was scrapped in Tucson, Arizona. This data plate is now the only known surviving piece of the first B-29 over Tokyo. I'll tell you more about how it survived and ended up on eBay later, but the fact that it still exists, and that it was sitting here with me as I wrote about her first mission, is truly extraordinary.[31]

Back on Saipan, almost 14 hours after they took off, *Tokyo Rose* touched down at 6:35 p.m. with its precious cargo of film. As they taxied in, the crew found a big celebration waiting for them. Drenched in rain, crowds of men were gathered around their hardstand and began cheering as *Tokyo Rose* pulled to a stop. General Hansell himself was even there and congratulated the crew with a bottle of Scotch.[32]

With the safe return of *Tokyo Rose*, the XXI Bomber Command was now set to get its first look at the heart of the Japanese Empire. The task of developing the 7,000 photographs *Tokyo Rose* delivered that evening would fall to the 3rd Photo Recon Squadron's hastily assembled photo lab. "On one occasion we had two Generals, six full Colonels and about a dozen Lt. Colonels pacing the floor waiting for the results, like twenty expectant fathers – but twice as anxious," recalled Lieutenant Elmer Dixson of the photo lab.[33]

But the wait had been worth it. The results of the mission exceeded everyone's wildest dreams. Even the sacred grounds of the Imperial Palace, the home of Emperor Hirohito, were clearly visible as the technicians feverishly developed the photographs. More reconnaissance missions would be flown in the days that followed as the shroud of secrecy was lifted from Japan's war industries. By November 13, after working around the clock seven days a week on two 12-hour shifts, the photo lab had processed an incredible 16,890 photographs of Japan's industrial centers.[34]

With so many of Japan's secrets finally revealed, General Hansell proudly boasted: "We have learned more about the industrial installations of Japan in 10 days, than we had learned in 10 years."[35] Hansell finally had his targets. The stage was now set for the mission everyone had been dreaming of since Pearl Harbor.

* * *

As the rain poured down on Saipan, over 100 B-29s sat ready and loaded with 8,000 gallons of fuel and 2.5 tons of bombs apiece. Under the wings and bomb bays, the anxious crews chatted as they looked up at the gloomy sky and waited. To eliminate any chance of interference with the coming mission, the Marines conducted a final sweep around the airbase and killed 240 Japanese soldiers, while another 47 were taken prisoner. It was all just a question of the weather now.[36]

The mission had to be canceled twice because of the storms, but then the weather finally broke. *San Antonio 1*, the code name for the first mission to Tokyo, was on. The target would be the massive Nakajima Musashino aircraft plant on the west side of Tokyo, about 10 miles from the Emperor's Palace. Later that evening in the packed briefing room, General O'Donnell stood to address his men:

> We've been together for eight months of training. We've become closely-knit, hard-hitting, smart pilots. This mission won't be any pushover. We face an enemy who is fanatically resolute. This first show won't be a knockout punch, but we will be throwing the first punch. Let's get some sleep and get ready to go to war in the morning.[37]

How much sleep would be gained that night was questionable, for the coming mission was enough to keep even the veterans tossing in their cots. In Europe, London to Berlin and back was 1,000 miles. But Saipan to Tokyo and back was over 3,000 miles, and there was nowhere to land in case of an emergency. Then there was the question of fighters and flak over Japan, plus the ever-present uncertainty of the R-3350 engines. The Japanese had also warned in radio broadcasts that "any Allied airman who falls or bails out over Japan will be executed." All of this weighed heavily on the crews as they tried to get a few hours of sleep.[38]

In the predawn hours of November 24, Saipan came alive. Thousands of men moved about the airfield making their final checks and preparations for the mission everyone had been waiting for. As takeoff time approached that morning, clouds of white smoke and dust rolled over the hardstands as hundreds of engines coughed to life and warmed up. Then the bombers slowly began moving along the taxiways in a long procession to the runway. "Out along the runways parked jeeps formed grandstands for the biggest show of the year," one GI later recalled. "Scattered among them were crash trucks, ambulances and heavy equipment. Crews were equipped with aluminum cutters and other emergency gear to be used to clear the runway in case of a crash which would interrupt the steady flow of bombers from the ground to the air."[39]

Behind the controls of the first B-29 to take the runway was 26-year-old Major Robert K. Morgan, the pilot of the 8th Air Force's famed B-17 *Memphis Belle*. After completing 25 missions over Europe in 1943, Morgan was back in the war again and taking the fight to the Japanese in his B-29 *Dauntless Dotty*, named in honor of his wife, Dorothy. Sitting next to Morgan in *Dauntless Dotty* and leading the mission was General O'Donnell, who was beginning a new chapter in his long fight against the Japanese. General Hansell had planned to lead the mission himself, but he was forbidden due to his knowledge of Ultra and Magic, the secret decryption of German and Japanese codes, which barred him from missions over enemy territory and the possibility of capture. He reluctantly watched as Morgan and O'Donnell prepared for takeoff.[40]

Weighing in at almost 140,000 pounds fully loaded, Morgan advanced the throttles, and everyone held their breath as *Dauntless Dotty* roared down the runway and slowly picked up speed. Losing an engine now would be disastrous. After using practically every inch of the mile-and-a-half-long runway, Morgan lifted her off. *Dotty* was airborne, and another 110 B-29s would follow behind her. Carrying a combined total of over 277 tons of bombs, the B-29s were on their way.

* * *

Like the Yawata raid five months earlier, a number of reporters would also accompany the more than 1,200 men of the 20th Air Force on their way to Tokyo that morning. Corporal Knox

Burger, a correspondent for *Yank* magazine, joined the mission in the lead formation with a crew from the 497th Bomb Group. His account was published a month later:

It was early morning and getting light fast. The crew made conversation as we stood around the *Lucky Lynn*, the B-29 that was to take us to Tokyo. Our pilot, Captain Leonard Cox of Tulsa, Oklahoma, recalled that the Japs had executed airmen for "bombing civilians" after the Doolittle raid on Tokyo in 1942.

"Can't we tell them we're sorry?" asked Staff Sergeant Frank Crane, a little plaintively. Crane, a gunner, is from Oshkosh, Wisconsin. He's the one Catholic on the crew and he carries a rosary.

"Better check us out on those beads, Frank," someone said as we climbed into the plane. We had heard so many conflicting reports about Tokyo's strength that no one knew what to expect.

Shortly afterward, we started to taxi out to the runway. Ours was the first squadron to take off. The *Lynn* was carrying a lot of weight and for 10 seconds or so it was hard to tell whether we were off the ground or not.

A gang of engineers just beyond the end of the runway looked up as we went over. I don't know just how far above them we were, but I noticed their knees were bent a little as they waved and they looked ready to dive into a nearby ditch.

Then the land dropped away and we were over coral shoals, flying 50 feet above the water. Captain Cox, who holds the Distinguished Service Cross and the Distinguished Flying Cross [medals] for services rendered with the Eighth Air Force in 1942 and 1943, expressed relief at getting airborne.

"Habba habba habba," he said happily to no one in particular. "Chop chop chop chop chop." It was the only nonsense he permitted himself; for the rest of the flight he was all business.

I crawled back to where the three waist gunners were sitting. Crane was watching the other ships in the formation. Staff Sergeant George Wright of Tyler, Texas, held up *Crime and Punishment*.

"This is a hell of a thing to be reading on the way to Tokyo," he said. Wright is part Indian and used to be a tankman.

Sergeant Larry Beecroft, who is 28 and looks like an *Esquire* undergraduate, was reading Steinbeck's *Pastures of Heaven*.

Someone brought a box of food back to the waist. Crane and Beecroft bitched because all the turkey sandwiches had been eaten.

Back in the tail, Sergeant Bill Stovall, a Regular Army GI from San Francisco, California, test-fired his guns. His 20mm jammed, and when he came forward to get a screwdriver I went back to his position. The tail gunner on a B-29 has to be able to keep himself happy or else he'll go nuts. It's like being alone in a small box for maybe 15 hours at a clip. There was a harmonica back there, a girl's picture and a pair of panties.

Time passed. By 1030 hours we had started chain smoking back in the waist. An hour later the captain told us to put on our flak suits.

In a few minutes the interphone crackled again. "Navigator to all gunners. We've sighted Japan."

Far ahead, jutting out of the clouds, was a beautiful snow-covered mountain. We recognized it from the pictures on captured postage stamps and currency – Fujiyama.

There was an excited interphone exchange as we approached the IP [initial point for the bomb run].

"If this stuff gets thicker, we may have to drop the bombs blind."

"Open the cowl flaps." The ship shuddered and slowed down a little.

"Hansen, keep your eyes straight ahead." Lieutenant Al Hansen of Missouri Valley, Iowa, is the *Lynn's* bombardier.

"Better not point the guns that way. They'll ice up." We were more than five miles high.

"Boy, that's rugged country down there." And it was. We were passing over a mass of steep, coppery mountains. Rivers and roads wound through the ravines.

"You should be able to see a town underneath us now, Hansen," said the navigator, Lieutenant Jack Ehrenberg of Passaic, New Jersey, who had been in England with Captain Cox.

"Flak at 8 o'clock, low." A cindery, innocent looking puff, thousands of feet below us.

"Fighter, at 3, low." The Zero looked small.

The target was hazy, but free of clouds as we went in for the run. There were a few flak bursts, level, but far away at 3 o'clock.

Then, up ahead, we saw two sticks of bombs fall ladder-like from the lead plane, *Dauntless Dotty*, piloted by Major Robert K. Morgan, who flew the famous *Memphis Belle* over Europe. Almost simultaneously, Lieutenant Hansen's casual Mid-Western voice said: "Bombs away."

The *Lynn* had delivered her child. Lifting a little, she seemed to gain speed. The first planes to bomb Tokyo since Doolittle were on their way home.

Our wing ship, the *Little Gem*, began to edge over closer to us. A line of flak bursts, which had been walking up on her from behind, passed harmlessly to one side. The almost nude woman painted on her fuselage blushed in the noon sun.

Far below us, two fighters circled for altitude. At that distance the fighters and flak looked as though they were fighting somebody else's war. A few minutes later the Zeros were sitting up there, waiting for the next squadron. As we pulled away, we passed over fighter fields from which tiny planes were taking off.

Then came the well-ordered, drab-looking Tokyo business district. The tail gunner described the columns of smoke rising from the target area.

There was a leak on the interphone, and we could hear, very faintly, one voice after another saying, "Bombs away," as the ships behind us went over the target.

The radio operator, Sergeant Mel Griffith of St. Louis, Missouri, picked up a message from another ship whose crew could see a B-29 going down. Stovall stopped talking. Interphones were silent.

Then, unaccountably we heard swing music. It sounded very far away and after a while an American announcer's practiced voice came in. It was Thanksgiving back home and the announcer was saying something about giving thanks.[41]

* * *

By the time the bomb bay doors of the last B-29 groaned closed, 860 high-explosive and incendiary bombs, each weighing 500 pounds apiece, had fallen on Tokyo. But much like the Yawata raid five months earlier, in which only a single bomb had landed in the target area, the results of the first Tokyo raid were also disappointing. Only 24 B-29s were able to bomb the primary target, with poor results, before the weather closed in and totally obscured the target area. The remaining B-29s attacked secondary targets along the docks and urban area of Tokyo.[42]

While the physical damage to the Nakajima Musashino plant was only minor, the psychological impact of the raid was huge. The front page of the *Honolulu Star-Bulletin* said it all: "VITAL TOKYO TARGETS HIT – Tokyo Gets Taste Of Things To Come In Blistering Raid."[43]

Almost three years after Pearl Harbor, the B-29s had struck the heart of the Japanese Empire, in plain view of the Emperor's Palace and millions of his subjects, and there was nothing they could do to stop them. The beginning of the end had begun.

9

Miracle Over Nagoya

1945

On January 3, 1945, a photograph was taken that would have a profound effect on my life. Soaring almost six miles high that day over Nagoya, Japan, a formation of 10 B-29s from the 497th Bomb Group were in a running gun battle with upwards of 100 Japanese fighters as they fought their way to the target area.[1] On board the B-29 *American Maid*, Sergeant Jim Krantz, the 22-year-old left gunner, was on his seventh combat mission and had battled with fighters before, but usually the Japanese broke off their attacks when the gunners opened fire. Today was different. Despite the gunners firing almost 40,000 rounds of ammunition during the battle, the fighters continued to aggressively press their attacks on the formation as the bombers closed in on Nagoya. Only three of the B-29s would escape the attacks undamaged.[2]

Just after "bombs away," a Ki-61 fighter dove out of the sun and peppered the tail of *American Maid* with machine-gun and cannon fire. Without warning, Krantz's sighting blister suddenly blew out, and the explosive decompression sucked him out with it. Krantz wasn't wearing a parachute, but he was wearing something else that no other B-29 gunner had.

During his last mission a week earlier, Krantz was helping the CFC gunner, Staff Sergeant Alvin Hart, get into his flak suit when the top blister suddenly blew out. The force of the decompression lifted Krantz off his feet and left Hart with a cut over his eye, but otherwise both men were okay. However, Krantz realized that if the top blister was bigger, Hart would have popped right out of the fuselage "like a champagne cork out of a bottle." Krantz then looked at his own sighting blister and realized that it was more than large enough for a man to easily pass through.[3] After they returned to Saipan, Krantz scrounged up an old parachute harness and a heavy-duty web strap and began making a special harness that would be strong enough to hold him just in case his blister ever did blow out. What Krantz didn't know was how soon he'd have to use it.

On his very next mission, Krantz was left hanging outside of his B-29 almost six miles above Nagoya. A flight surgeon on a B-29 next to *American Maid* was manning a camera at the time and captured an incredible photograph of Krantz as he dangled helplessly outside the bomber.

I can still remember the first time I saw that photo when I was a little boy in the book my father had about B-29s, and my amazement when he pointed to it and said: "Look, that's a man hanging out there!" I instantly became obsessed with that photo and showed it to my friend

111

Andrew the next time he came over to play. We weren't quite old enough to read yet, but he shared my excitement as I pointed to it and exclaimed: "Look at his leg – there's his boot!"

There were lots of other great pictures in my father's book, but I always seemed to gravitate towards that single black and white photo of the man hanging outside of his B-29. That book is what started by fascination with the B-29, but I think it was really that one photo that did it. Even today when I look at that book (it's sitting next to me now), I still find myself drawn to that photograph. It wasn't until many years later that I finally discovered the whole story about what happened that day. I was thumbing through an issue of *Brief* magazine from 1945 when I suddenly saw that very same photograph from my childhood. The caption said: "This startling photo shows Sgt. Krantz hanging from his blister, thousands of feet above Japan."[4] I immediately read the article, and then I read it again. After all those years, I finally knew the story behind that remarkable photograph. But it turns out there was a lot more to that story than I realized at the time.

I later found another article about Krantz that was written by none other than Corporal Knox Burger, the *Yank* correspondent who flew with Captain Leonard Cox's crew on *Lucky Lynn* during the first Tokyo raid, whose story you just read in the previous chapter. Written on Saipan only days after his brush with death, below is Burger's story about what happened to Sergeant Jim Krantz over Nagoya that day. I think you'll find his story and photo just as compelling as I did:

In a war in which close shaves are practically SOP [Standard Operating Procedure], the story of Sergeant Jim Krantz, a B-29 gunner from Hickory Point, Tennessee, will go down as one of the narrowest escapes in the book. Krantz's gun blister blew out just after his ship, *American Maid*, had dropped bombs on Nagoya. Krantz went out with the blister – all the way out. He was saved by a harness he had devised himself in anticipation of just such an emergency. He was outside the ship for more than 10 minutes, almost six miles over Japan, and the temperature was 40 degrees below zero. After the first minute or so, he lost consciousness, his body, whipped by a 200-mile-per-hour wind, flogging the side of the fuselage. His oxygen mask was torn from his face as he passed out. He didn't have on winter flying clothes or a parachute.

It happened on the *Maid's* third trip to Nagoya. On the first trip over the city, the No. 3 fan [propeller] was torn from the engine and went spinning off into thin air, narrowly missing the fuselage. On the second, the top blister blew out. The top gunner, Staff Sergeant Alvin R. Hart of Glendale, California, fell to the floor unconscious from lack of oxygen.

Krantz hadn't liked the idea of a blister blowing, particularly since the side blisters are bigger than the top blister – plenty big enough for a man to go through. He didn't have too much faith in the regular safety belt, so he set to work making one of his own. It consisted of a broad waistband with a double-thickness extension to the floor and two straps over the shoulders. On the morning of this mission, he had told the other crewmen that he hadn't had time to stitch the floor attachment the way he wanted to. They kidded him.

There were lots of fighters, and the *Maid* was "flying the diamond" – she was the tail ship in the formation. A few minutes before Krantz's blister blew, every gunner on the plane called fighters coming in from six directions practically simultaneously. Back in the tail, Sergeant Donald Wilson of Bringhurst, Indiana, had credit for one enemy plane destroyed – an Irving [Nakajima J1N fighter]. About two minutes after Wilson had seen the Irving go down, a Tony [Kawasaki Ki-61 fighter] dove through the formation and got off a burst at the tail of the *Maid*. Wilson saw the glass in his window shatter, and felt a slight pain in his left hand. He was firing at two fighters hanging out at 6 o'clock, and didn't bother to look at the hand.

Just about this time – none of the crew members are positive of the chronology from here on in – Sergeant Dick Cook, 19-year-old right gunner from Erlanger, Kentucky, felt a whoosh of air behind him. He turned around. The left blister was gone; so was the gunsight and so was Krantz. He did a double take. This time he saw a foot hugged tight against the inside of the ship. He spoke into the interphone. It was out. Indicating the empty seat to the top gunner, he yanked off his oxygen mask and crawled over to the foot.

Hart, up in the top blister, looked down at the empty seat. "The first thing I thought of," he said later, "was the picture by Krantz's bed – the picture of his wife and kids." Already a white mist was filling the interior of the airplane. The people up front had felt the blister go, too. The sudden depressurization practically doubled them up in their seats.

Just then Wilson, back in the tail, glanced down at his hand. He had received a ring from his sister only the day before and he was very proud of it. The ring and the finger were gone. He pressed his interphone pedal. "Hey," he said, "my finger's shot off." There was a note of mild incredulity in his voice. "It's not bleeding." Then he turned his attention back to the Jap fighters.

In the waist, Cook leaned out of the open blister and was almost pulled through it by the tremendous slipstream. The buckle on Krantz's home-made floor harness had slipped, doubling the length of the extension. Cook managed to get his hand on Krantz's shoulder and pull. Then he ducked back into the waist to get oxygen.

"One of the last things I remember before I blacked out," says Krantz, "was feeling a hand on my shoulder. It felt good. I was glad someone was trying to help me get back in. When I first got out there, I looked down at Japan, and was glad I didn't have a chute. This way I'd never know when I hit. I don't think I was conscious for over two minutes. I tried to adjust my mask. Then I lost it. I tried to keep my leg in that hole. I knew I had to, so the guys could grab me. The gunsight was swinging on a cable just below the hole. I tried to get it between my legs and walk it backward – work back to where I could get my shoulder in the hole. The next thing I remember, I was fighting the guys off. They were trying to give me oxygen, and I was fighting as hard as when I was going out. They say you do the same thing coming to that you did going out."

In the ship flying alongside and a little ahead of *American Maid* was Captain Guy T. Denton Jr. of Dallas, Texas, a flight surgeon. Before the flight he had been hastily checked out on the camera. "I was working it because I didn't have anything else to do. When I first saw Krantz, he was three-quarters of the way out of the blister. His ship had dropped down and swung up beneath us. As they pulled away, half a minute later, I saw Krantz. He was still conscious, trying to adjust his mask. I took three quick pictures."

The airplane commander, Lieutenant John D. Bartlett of Bozeman, Montana, had just sent the radio operator, Staff Sergeant Robert Angell of East Dubuque, Illinois, back to administer first aid to the tail gunner when Hart spoke over the interphone: "Somebody better get back here quick if you're going to save Krantz." Bartlett motioned to his co-pilot, Second Lieutenant Frank Crowe of Baltimore, Maryland. The radio operator arrived back in the waist just ahead of Crowe. Angell's small-size walkaround [oxygen] bottle was used up, and he almost collapsed on the floor. He was handed another bottle. Then he reached out between Hart, who had climbed down from his blister, and the radar specialist, Staff Sergeant Russell Strong of East Hampton, Connecticut, and gave a haul. He saw that there wasn't room for him to do any good, so he continued on back to the tail to see about Wilson.

Just as Crowe arrived in the waist, he saw Krantz's left foot go out of the plane. The single strap holding the gunner to the airplane was rubbing hard against a jagged edge of the plastic blister. Strong had to duck back into the plane for oxygen, so Crowe took his place. He reached out. The wind tore at his hand, whipping it against Krantz's back. He grabbed Krantz's shoulder holster strap and pulled; it broke. The holster and its contents flew back past the tail. Crowe then managed to get hold of a strap of the safety harness. He and Hart could see Krantz's face, covered with frozen blood from minor cuts he'd received as he went through the blister.

They finally got his head and shoulders inside. His eyes were half-open, showing only the whites of his eyeballs, and his eyebrows were thick with frost. Except for the blood, his face was oyster white. They thought he was dead. Crowe slapped his mask on Krantz's face and turned the oxygen flow indicator to "Emergency." Hart shared his own mask with Crowe as they worked to get the rest of Krantz's body into the ship. At first Crowe would wave the oxygen away. "You get the feeling you can take care of yourself," he says. Both of them passed out several times.

Krantz regained partial consciousness and tried to fight off the oxygen mask. Crowe thinks he heard him say, "My feet are cold."

When the blister blew out, a lot of oxygen had been lost. The ship was over water by this time, and there were no more fighters. Crowe called Lieutenant Bartlett and asked him to drop down to where they could breathe without oxygen, but the interphone he used was out. Up front they were worried about gasoline, and losing that much altitude would have been dangerous.

Krantz was still halfway out of the airplane, and the others were just about at the end of their rope when a large hand reached between Crowe and Hart and pulled Krantz the rest of the way in. The hand belonged to the bombardier, Lieutenant Harrison K. Wittee of Minonk, Illinois.

Back in the tail, Angell had tapped Wilson on the foot. The tail gunner came out of his little chamber and held up his left hand. "Look," he said. "No finger." Together they went up to the compartment behind the waist guns. It was pretty warm in there, and Wilson's hand began to hurt. Angell bandaged it and gave him morphine. "Go back and get my finger, will you?" asked Wilson. "I want to wave it at the crew chief when we get back."

Carrying Krantz into the compartment, they gave him morphine and plasma to relieve shock. The floor was ankle deep in paper and bandages. When he came to he turned to Hart. "Al, do you ever pray?" he asked. "I prayed that if that blister broke, my belt would hold."

At this writing Krantz is in a hospital in Hawaii. His shoulder is bandaged up where he hit it as he knocked over the gunsight on the way out. Several fingers on his left hand are in bad shape from frostbite and other parts of his body are less seriously frostbitten.

They never found the ring, but they buried Wilson's finger up near *American Maid's* hardstand, and the crew is hoping he can rejoin them. Krantz probably will never fly again. At that, to call him lucky is the height of understatement.

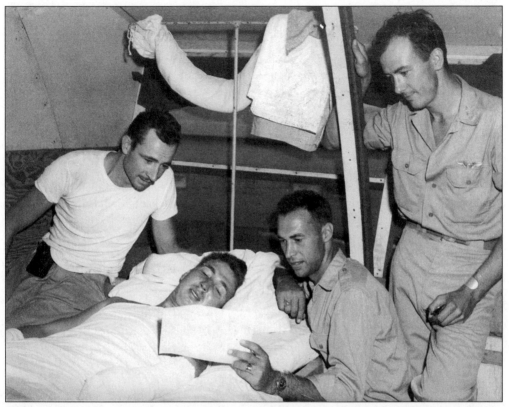

From a warm hospital bed on Saipan, Sergeant Jim Krantz looks at the photo of himself hanging outside of his B-29 almost six miles high over Nagoya along with his crewmates who saved his life. Left to right: Alvin Hart, Jim Krantz, Harrison Wittee and Frank Crowe. (National Archives 204973710)

A few minutes ago Sergeant Cook walked through the Quonset [hut] where I'm typing this. He looked at me and held up half a dozen thick straps. "Yeah," he grinned. "Think I'll build me a harness."[5]

* * *

After learning what happened over Nagoya that day, I just had to talk to Jim Krantz. I knew he would get a kick out of hearing from someone like me who fondly remembered that picture of him from my childhood, and I wanted to interview him for this book. I was also dying to know if he still had his harness after all these years.

I did some research and soon discovered that Krantz had sadly passed away about eight months before I found that article. It was heartbreaking to know that I'd come so close to being able to talk to him, but I was too late. After thinking it over for a few days, I decided to write a letter to his wife, Mildred, in hopes of learning more about Jim's recovery from the frostbite he suffered and his life after the war. Jim and Mildred had just celebrated their 70th wedding anniversary a month before he died. I never received a reply, but I later found out that Mildred passed away 11 days after I mailed her that letter back in 2012.

I almost gave up on this story after that, but it just seemed like there was more to it, like there was something that I was missing. So I began looking for other members of the *American Maid* crew who could tell me more about what happened that day over Nagoya. I soon discovered that Krantz, who said "I guess I'm a pretty lucky guy" as he lay recovering in a hospital bed after the incident, was much luckier than he realized.[6]

Four months after that day over Nagoya, the pilot of *American Maid*, Captain John Bartlett, returned home to help train new B-29 crews. His co-pilot, Lieutenant Frank Crowe, took over as aircraft commander and continued flying missions with most of the original crew. On June 1, while flying a different B-29, Lieutenant Crowe and the remaining members of the *American Maid* crew were shot down during a mission to Osaka, Japan. Seven men died in the crash. You'll recognize some of their names from the story above. Lieutenant Frank Crowe, pilot, and Staff Sergeant Robert Angell, radio operator, were both killed, along with two other original crew members.[7]

Three of the four men who bailed out and were captured by the Japanese were also original members of the *American Maid* crew: Lieutenant Harrison Wittee, bombardier; Tech Sergeant Alvin Hart, CFC gunner; and Staff Sergeant Russell Strong, radar observer. It was Wittee, Hart and Crowe who pulled Krantz back inside the B-29 that day.

There was also something else that I discovered. The name of the fourth man who bailed out sounded very familiar to me. Then I realized why. It was Sergeant Larry Beecroft. In the previous chapter, you read Corporal Burger's story about the crew of *Lucky Lynn* and the first mission to Tokyo. Beecroft was the gunner who was reading *Pastures of Heaven* on the way to Japan and looked like an *Esquire* undergraduate, according to Burger.

How Sergeant Beecroft ended up flying with the *American Maid* crew was another harrowing story. Less than two months after the first Tokyo raid, Beecroft and the crew of *Lucky Lynn*, while flying a B-29 named *Pacific Union*, were forced to ditch 430 miles out from Saipan when their No. 3 engine caught on fire and the flames rapidly enveloped the bomber. Just before touching down on the sea, an explosion rocked the center section of their B-29, and it broke in two as it hit the water. The impact and subsequent explosions released thousands of gallons of fuel that spread like a fiery blanket over the surface of the ocean. The few men who got out all suffered burns as they frantically swam through the fire surrounding the wreckage before it sank.

Beecroft was one of only four men to survive. Most of the men you read about on the first Tokyo mission were killed, including the pilot of *Lucky Lynn*, Captain Leonard Cox, and the CFC gunner, Staff Sergeant Frank Crane, who carried the rosary with him.[8]

Beecroft later joined up with the remaining crew of *American Maid* and continued flying missions until they were shot down on June 1, 1945.

As I continued my research into the fate of these men, I was hopeful that some of them might still be alive and could tell me more about Jim Krantz and what happened over Nagoya that day. It was too late to talk to Krantz or his wife, but maybe one of his crewmates could help me discover something new about his story that I didn't know before.

What I discovered instead was a nightmare.

This is what happened to the four survivors after they were shot down on June 1:

Lieutenant Wittee and Sergeant Beecroft were captured on June 2. Seven weeks later, on July 20, Wittee and Beecroft, along with 13 other American prisoners – all B-29ers – were loaded into a truck by the Kempeitai and taken to the Shinodayama military training grounds in Osaka. Bound and blindfolded, the Kempeitai walked the Americans over and sat them down in front of graves that had been dug the day before. A firing squad was assembled and armed with captured American .45 caliber pistols. The Kempeitai commander instructed them to aim at the prisoners' foreheads. Then the death sentence for the crime of "indiscriminate bombing" was read aloud. Then the order was given to fire.

The 15 Americans were immediately buried and the graves carefully hidden. The Kempeitai commander reminded his men to "keep it a top secret" after they buried the bodies.[9]

Sergeant Hart was captured on June 3 and was suffering from burns to his face. It was believed that he later died of "disease" while imprisoned by the Kempeitai, but I haven't been able to find much information about his death. When Hart's body was exhumed by American forces in 1946, both of his hands and all of his toes were missing.[10]

Sergeant Strong evaded capture until June 6. Eight weeks later, on July 31, Strong and another American prisoner held by the Kempeitai, Lieutenant James Price, a B-29 co-pilot who was shot down a week earlier and was the only survivor of his crew, were both suffering from diarrhea. Upon orders from the Kempeitai commander, the men were given stomach medicine to drink that was mixed with poison. Strong and Price died a few minutes after drinking the deadly concoction.[11]

The Kempeitai commander who ordered the executions of all these men, Lieutenant Colonel Hideo Fujioka, would also order the execution of 14 other B-29ers on August 5. One of those prisoners was Mr. Trabold's best friend, David McNeley.[12]

I was shocked when I discovered this. I had no idea who the man responsible for McNeley's death was until I began researching the fate of the *American Maid* crew. Now I knew his name: Hideo Fujioka. But that wasn't all I learned. Fujioka was ultimately responsible for the execution of 45 American prisoners of war. He killed some of the Americans himself. Fujioka was one of the shooters when Beecroft and McNeley were executed.

The last group of Americans Fujioka ordered to be killed were so close to making it home. On the very day that Japan surrendered, fearing that American forces could land at any time, Fujioka ordered the execution of the five remaining Americans in his custody, as well as the destruction of all records and evidence relating to the prisoners they had held. Even though the war was over, Fujioka told a subordinate earlier that morning that it would be "necessary to get rid of the remaining fliers held by the Kempeitai." The execution of these five Americans was later described as "neither formal nor orderly."[13]

At the Sanadayama Military Cemetery in Osaka, a freshly dug pit was waiting as a truck pulled to a stop carrying the five American prisoners. The back of the truck was covered so no one would see the eight Kempeitai or their prisoners, who were sitting blindfolded with their hands tied behind their backs, as the truck drove through the city.

The Americans were still wearing the same filthy clothing they were captured in as the Kempeitai unloaded them at the cemetery. The truck was also carrying a large assortment of survival gear and other equipment that had been captured with the Americans held by the Osaka Kempeitai, including parts salvaged from the wreckage of their B-29s. This was the evidence that Fujioka ordered to be destroyed, and his men began burning it.

While the evidence was being destroyed, the first American was led over to the pit. The other four remained under guard at the truck. In that moment, they may not have known what was coming, but they probably suspected it.

Picking through the evidence and burning what he could, one of the Kempeitai suddenly heard a "funny splashing noise" behind him next to the pit. When he turned around, he saw that the first American had just been beheaded with a sword. The noise he heard was blood spouting from the American's headless neck.[14]

As the Kempeitai executioner stood there with his bloody sword in hand, the other Kempeitai complimented him for his "extraordinary skill" in beheading the American. "It was a splendid work," the executioner later said. "Everyone … admired me."[15]

Then the next American was led over to the pit. He was made to kneel along the edge of it. And then the same Kempeitai raised his sword again. And then he swung his sword and sliced the American's head off.

Before the next American could be brought over to the pit, the executioner felt "slightly dizzy" and had to sit down. The other Kempeitai were impatient; the executions could not be delayed. The last three Americans were walked over to the pit. An interpreter told them to kneel. Then they were all shot with pistols, and their bodies dumped into the pit with the others. The rest of the captured equipment that couldn't be burned was dumped on top of the bodies, including the pistols that had just been used to kill the three Americans, and then it was all buried.[16] To cover up the murders, Fujioka's men were ordered to "maintain strict secrecy about the executions."[17]

Hideo Fujioka was later convicted of the 45 killings in 1949. He was also found guilty of withholding medical attention and medicine from the prisoners, and for allowing his subordinates to mistreat, beat and torture them. Fujioka was sentenced to life in prison for his war crimes.[18]

During the course of the war, 19 B-29s with 207 airmen on board were lost over the Chubu Army District that included Osaka (Japan was divided into eight Army Districts). From those B-29s, 57 Americans bailed out and were captured by the Japanese. None of them would return home alive. Some of the 57 Americans died from "disease" while imprisoned, but most would be executed by their captors.[19]

Back in January of 1945, as he lay recovering in a hospital bed in Hawaii, Jim Krantz said:

> Getting shoved out of a bomber by a blast of pressurized air when you're flying over Japan is something new in the way of an experience. But it's one that I would just as soon have missed. In a way it's a pretty unlucky thing to happen to anybody, but I'm certainly glad that it happened when it did and not on one of my earlier missions. If it had happened before, I wouldn't be around to tell the story.[20]

The irony was that getting sucked out of that blister was the luckiest thing that could have happened to Jim Krantz. Otherwise, he would have been shot down with his crew on June 1, 1945. And be it from the crash, or later at the hands of the Japanese, he would have died in Japan. I'm sure a day didn't go by when he didn't think about the friends he lost. Or why he survived, and they did not. I just wish that I could have talked to him about it.

10

The Price of Freedom

In the autumn of 2010, I discovered something extraordinary on eBay. I was on a real hot streak at the time. For the past few weeks, I'd been finding all of these amazing B-29 relics that were suddenly coming out of the woodwork, and I actually had money to spend, too. Life was good.

While searching for more lost history on eBay that night, I found another B-29 data plate. It's always exciting when you find a data plate, because you never know what kind of history you're going to discover when you look up its serial number. To my astonishment, this B-29 turned out to be a combat veteran with an incredible story. The funny thing was that I actually recognized it from some of my books. This B-29 was named *The Dragon Lady* after a character from the *Terry and the Pirates* comic strip. I remembered it because its nose art featured a giant portrait of the Dragon Lady fully in the nude, which made it very popular on Saipan. I even had an original photo of *The Dragon Lady* in my nose art collection.

The Dragon Lady touched down on Saipan less than a month after General Hansell arrived, and also flew on the first mission to Tokyo, which made it a very rare B-29. But what was really so incredible about this B-29 was that it was rammed head-on by a Japanese fighter – *and it survived*.

For the Japanese fighter pilots who were now facing the largest and most advanced bombers in the world, the ramming attacks were born out of desperation. Like its predecessor, the B-17, the B-29 could absorb a staggering amount of battle damage and still continue flying. Because the B-29 was so difficult to shoot down, the Japanese would resort to some drastic measures to combat the new bombers. After their first encounters with the B-29, the Japanese Army Air Force published instructions for its pilots on how to attack the bombers. A copy was later captured by American forces in the Philippines, and it contained chilling advice for downing a B-29:

> It is difficult to shoot down or set fire to an airplane such as a B-29 by gunfire. Warrant Officer Kimura of [4th Sentai] Flying Regiment on the B-29 raid of 15 June 1944 observed hits on one airplane, but, as the airplane did not burst into flames, he determined to ram it. Both airplanes went into a steep climb and finally into a spin. By such tactics an enemy B-29 was brought down. Once an attack is directed against an enemy airplane, it must be pressed to the limit with the intention of ramming. Do not allow a single airplane to escape.[1]

When the first B-29s appeared over Tokyo, the Japanese were so alarmed that they began forming special ramming units whose sole purpose was to literally crash their fighters into oncoming B-29s to destroy them. To prepare for their mission, the pilots received special training that included detailed briefings about the B-29 and culminated with actual flight training to perfect their attacks. The instructors also found it equally important to constantly "instill [the] trainees with patriotism" throughout their training.[2]

The ramming technique preferred by the Japanese was a direct frontal attack where the fighter impacted the B-29 head-on. With blistering closing speeds that left the bomber crews with only seconds to react, coupled with the element of surprise, frontal attacks were extremely difficult to defend against and were found to be the most effective tactic for inflicting damage on the B-29s, be it by ramming, or with cannon and machine-gun fire.[3] The Japanese conducted a thorough study of the ramming attacks, and they concluded in April that they were indeed a viable tactic for destroying B-29s. The 497th Bomb Group's intelligence officer on Saipan had already come to that sobering conclusion months earlier, when he lamented in his diary that most of their losses from Japanese fighter attacks were due to the fighters ramming their B-29s.[4]

In the heat of battle, many Japanese pilots outside of the special attack units would also launch ramming attacks on their own initiative. This was the case on August 20, 1944, when Sergeant Shigeo Nobe approached a formation of B-29s head-on over Yawata. Nobe radioed his flight leader that he was going to ram, and then he took aim at the lead B-29. What would become the first ramming attack proved to be devastating. As Nobe closed in on the lead B-29, flown by Lieutenant Colonel Robert Clinkscales, he banked his fighter and held his wings vertical like a knife, slicing into the bomber's left wing just outboard of the No. 1 engine. The wing exploded in a fireball as Nobe's fighter cartwheeled back through the formation. As the other crews watched in horror, the wreckage from the explosion sailed over the B-29 flying behind Clinkscales and collided with another B-29 in the formation. In just a matter of seconds, two B-29s were destroyed and 18 Americans were killed. Among the dead was Clinkscales' beloved cocker spaniel, Sally, the squadron mascot, who was riding in the cockpit with him and died with the crew.[5]

Nobe and his rear gunner were also killed in the attack, but as unbelievable as it seems, unlike a Kamikaze suicide attack, ramming a B-29 did not mean certain death. In fact, there were Japanese pilots who survived multiple rammings. One of the best known was Sergeant Kenji Fujimoto, who in the span of three days destroyed two B-29s by ramming and lived to tell about it.[6]

Four months after the first ramming attack by Sergeant Nobe, an extraordinary story was about to unfold in the skies above Japan. And were it not for a chain of events that culminated with the words before you on this page, what happened to *The Dragon Lady* on that winter day would have been largely forgotten. It all started on December 22, 1944, when *The Dragon Lady* was closing in on the Mitsubishi aircraft engine factory in Nagoya. The Japanese put up a vigorous defense of the city that day, and the B-29s encountered an estimated 175 fighters that made 508 passes at the bombers. The troubles for *The Dragon Lady* began when a 20mm shell from an attacking fighter pierced an oil line on the No. 2 engine and caused a severe oil leak. While the flight engineer was dealing with the crippled engine, more fighters began attacking B-29's formation over the target area, and that's when it happened.[7]

To this day, it is not known who the Japanese pilot was, but what is known is that he aimed his fighter directly at the cockpit of *The Dragon Lady* as he closed in to ram the bomber. What happened next was truly remarkable. Be it a miscalculation by the pilot, a last-second change of heart, or perhaps divine intervention, the fighter crashed into *The Dragon Lady* head-on, but the two airplanes did not explode when they collided. Maybe it was just plain old luck, but no matter how you try to explain it, what happened at the moment of impact was extraordinary.

Rocketing in at hundreds of miles per hour, the fighter slammed into the cockpit of *The Dragon Lady* at just the right angle to shatter the glass above the pilot's head, and then it simply bounced off the fuselage, like a stone skipping across a pond. The impact sent the fighter careening out of control over top of the bomber until it crashed into the tail, where it chopped off the top of its vertical stabilizer, before finally disappearing out of sight.

If that fighter had only been a hair lower, *The Dragon Lady* would have been destroyed, the crew would likely have all been killed, and you would not be reading these words right now. Incredible.[8]

Despite being heavily damaged, *The Dragon Lady* continued flying after the ramming, but it was now in serious trouble. The flak and fighter attacks had riddled the bomber with holes, and unbeknownst to the crew, four 500-pound bombs had failed to drop over the target and were now hung up inside the bomb bay. The bombardier was so busy shooting back at all the fighters that he didn't realize some of his bombs did not drop. The fighter attacks finally ended when *The Dragon Lady* crossed back over the coast and headed out to sea, but with oil streaming from the No. 2 engine, the entire 85-gallon oil tank was soon bled dry. With no oil pressure to control the pitch of its blades, the No. 2 propeller quickly ran away and began windmilling out of control. The pilot, Captain Howard Clifford, reduced airspeed to try to slow down the runaway propeller, but it was no use. The propeller shaft soon snapped under the strain, and the entire four-blade assembly violently separated from the engine. As the propeller flew off, it surged forward in front of the wing, and then drifted up and back before colliding with the No. 1 engine's propeller. The terrifying collision all but destroyed the blades and the entire airframe began shuddering from the damage.

After miraculously surviving a head-on ramming, the crew now found themselves seven hours away from Saipan in a severely damaged B-29 with only three functioning engines. To make matters worse, nightfall was approaching, and *The Dragon Lady* was shuddering so badly from the damaged propeller blades that it was impossible for the navigator to take a celestial fix of their position, but the crew would not give up. With the help of another B-29 that dropped back to guide them, they made it all the way back to Saipan and safely landed after nearly 15 hours in the air. For his skill in bringing his crew home in a severely damaged B-29, Captain Howard Clifford was awarded the Distinguished Flying Cross.[9] *The Dragon Lady* eventually returned to the air again after extensive repairs that included changing all four engines, but it had been so badly damaged that it never flew another bombing mission.

There weren't many B-29s that survived after being rammed head-on like *The Dragon Lady*. In all my years of collecting, this was the only piece I'd ever seen from a B-29 that did survive a ramming. What an incredible piece of history – I had to save it!

After watching the auction for a week, my chance to own this phenomenal artifact was finally here. It was around 10:30 p.m. on a Wednesday night, and as I clicked the button to bid with only seconds left, I was confident that no one could possibly want this data plate more than me. I knew that I would never find another B-29 data plate with a story behind it like this, and I was prepared to spend an awful lot of money to save it. But then the unthinkable happened. Someone outbid me. My bid of $617.99 somehow wasn't enough, and the auction was over. I remember just sitting at my desk for a few minutes, completely stunned, wondering who else besides me was crazy enough to spend that kind of money on a B-29 data plate?

For eBay's part, they did send me a nice message afterwards: "We're sorry you didn't win this time around. While this one got away, there's other stuff to find. Don't give up." That last sentence got me thinking. What if there was still a way? What if I contacted the buyer and tried to work out some kind of a deal? I wasn't going to give up yet; I would find a way![10]

Although eBay may have inspired me not to give up, they also made it hard to follow through as they were now hiding the identity of their bidders, and I had no way to know who bought the data plate. But I soon discovered there was a flaw to eBay's privacy policy. When a buyer left a seller feedback to rate their purchase, it listed the auction *and* the buyer's username. So all I had to do was wait for the feedback to appear, and then I'd know who the buyer was and I could contact them. Easy enough, I thought. (This has since changed and feedback is now totally anonymous.)

While I waited for the buyer to leave feedback, I took some time to learn more about where *The Dragon Lady's* data plate came from. The seller was an eBay dealer in southern California, and just as I suspected, the data plate came from a World War II Veteran's estate. And there were a lot more where it came from. The veteran who collected all of these data plates had served 30 years in the Air Force between World War II and the 1970s and had amassed quite a collection of souvenirs. Based on some of the other data plates that were being listed, he must have spent part of his career at Davis-Monthan Air Force Base in Arizona, home of the famous "boneyard" where military aircraft are stored. *The Dragon Lady* was also put into storage at Davis-Monthan after the war and was eventually scrapped in 1948, which is probably when he removed its data plate.

I wish I could have seen his collection when it was all together in one place. What a sight that must have been. But he had passed away, and it was all being sold on eBay now. The seller told me that the family went up to their late father's home about once a month to gather up "another load of his belongings" for him to sell, and he never knew what they were going to bring in next.[11] I bet his family had no idea what kind of history was passing through their hands, but at least they weren't just throwing everything away in the garbage, which happens a lot. In fact, I had just bought another B-29 data plate from them a week earlier. It was the data plate from *Tokyo Rose*, the first B-29 over Tokyo. That cost me $312.77, and I couldn't understand how the data plate from *The Dragon Lady* sold for double that a week later. I guess that's eBay for you.

After two anxious weeks, the feedback I was looking for finally appeared. I quickly typed up a message to introduce myself to the buyer, and I asked if he might be willing to work something out for the data plate. This was my last chance to save it, and it was all that I could think about when I went to bed that night. I didn't get much sleep.

The next morning, I got my answer. Much to my surprise, the buyer was not only a fellow collector, but he was also a Japanese citizen who was working here in America for a major university, and he was willing to trade *The Dragon Lady's* data plate for other World War II aviation relics. And if that wasn't great enough, he also mentioned that he had some other "historic B-29-related items" that I might be interested in as well.[12]

Was this really happening? It all seemed too good to be true, but the next day he sent me a list of all the B-29 relics in his collection. My jaw dropped when I saw what he had.

In a strange way, it was starting to make sense now why I had not won that auction. Otherwise, the opportunity to acquire these other relics never would have presented itself. It's funny how things work out like that. After a few weeks of negotiating, we came to an agreement where I would get all of the B-29 relics in his collection, including *The Dragon Lady's* data plate. The trade we agreed upon wasn't exactly even, because what I traded him was worth more than what I received in return, but that didn't matter to me. Some things are worth much more than money. Everything I got from him told a story, and they were stories that I wanted to explore and share with the world. I just didn't know at the time how big one of those stories would be, or the journey it would lead me on.

Even now, as I sit here typing these words, it's still hard to believe how this all came about. If the Japanese pilot who rammed *The Dragon Lady* had only been a few inches lower, this chapter would not be in this book. I cannot emphasize this enough: if that pilot had successfully rammed *The Dragon Lady* that day, you would not be reading this right now.

After the war, if that veteran had not removed *The Dragon Lady's* data plate and kept it as a souvenir for all those years, only for it to appear on eBay after his death, I never would have written about its story. And if I had won the auction for the data plate, I never would have met the Japanese collector and traded for his relics, and then the second part of this chapter would not have existed, either. Was it all by chance?

*   *   *

"They were waiting for us over Tokyo. It looked like the whole damn Jap air force."

January 27, 1945, is a date that probably doesn't mean anything to most people, but if you were on one of the B-29s that took off from Saipan that morning, you would never forget that day when you came back – *if you came back*. And even though I was born decades later, January 27, 1945, would become a day that I would never forget, either.

I first became interested in this mission after I bought a "WWII Navigator's Case" on eBay back in 2010, almost 10 months before I found *The Dragon Lady's* data plate. The old leather briefcase had literally been through the war and was really showing its age, but it was the contents of the case that caught my attention. From the auction pictures, it looked like it could be a treasure trove stuffed full of B-29 history, but I didn't have much else to go on. The seller didn't really know what he had either, so without knowing exactly what I was buying, I decided to gamble, and I won the auction for $297.18. I was in for quite a surprise.

The case had belonged to a B-29 radar observer with the 499th Bomb Group on Saipan, and it was literally bursting at the seams with his things from the war. Inside the case, I discovered his old mission reports, target profiles, aeronautical charts, target maps, radar scope images, photographs; the treasures went on and on. I even found propaganda leaflets that were to be dropped from his B-29 over Japan that he kept as a souvenir.

I was so happy I gambled on it, because that old leather case turned out to be a treasure trove of history that was beyond my wildest dreams. What was so fascinating to me was that most of these things had actually been used during his missions. I could look at the maps and other documents and see the notations he made while in the air. These things were actually there, in combat, over Japan.

One of the more interesting things I discovered in the case was a radar operator's report from January 27, 1945, that was filled out in pencil. Under the "remarks" column, the sergeant had jotted down a running commentary of the mission as it unfolded:

> Jap freighter fired on us – knocked out our No. 3 turbo
> Bombed small Jap town on mainland
> Could not get altitude – bad turbo
> Going out fast – too many fighters

After they landed back on Saipan, the sergeant added the following to his report:

> Jap freighter sitting out about 300 miles from coast of Japan fired on our formation and .50 caliber bullets knocked out one turbo. Boat radioed in our position and at least 175 fighters met our formation at coast. We could not reach altitude – went into coast alone – dropped bombs fast and got out fast. We had 27 fighter attacks.[13]

My first instinct with something like this is to try to find out more about the case and where it came from. The seller wasn't much help, though. He ran a consignment shop, and someone had brought the case in one day for him to sell. I couldn't get much more out of him than that, but for some reason, I always suspected that the case was found in the trash. It wouldn't be the first time something like that was thrown out with the garbage, and sadly, I know it won't be the last.

In all the years I've been collecting, one of the saddest things I ever saw was an old briefcase that had belonged to Staff Sergeant Russell Pollock, a B-29 radio operator, that was found in the garbage and then sold on eBay. The briefcase was filled with all of Pollock's service records and other effects from the war, including his Distinguished Flying Cross and other medals. Thankfully, it was saved and would now be cared for by collectors, but I couldn't believe that someone had thrown it all away as worthless trash.[14]

The radar operator's report had piqued my interest in the January 27 mission, but after the collector who had *The Dragon Lady's* data plate sent me the list of all the B-29 relics in his collection, my curiosity would grow into something much deeper. It was the last item on his list that did it. There was just something about it that intrigued me, and I had this feeling about it, like there was a lot more to the story. I can't really explain it any better than that.

This was the last relic on his list:

> A large piece of skin from Ki-45 Nick fighter that rammed B-29 *Haley's Comet* on January 27, 1945. It was recovered from the crash site in 1996. Has its original camouflage paint and readable stencil number.[15]

If reading his description had given me a "feeling," just imagine what it was like holding the wreckage in my hands for the first time. I've handled crash debris before, but there was something different about this. The first thing that struck me, as I opened the box and pulled away the bubble wrap, was how mangled it was. Every square inch of the aluminum was deformed and damaged in some way. I remember thinking to myself that it was hard to imagine the kind of force that would cause such destruction, even though I have witnessed those forces with my own eyes. (I've had the misfortune of witnessing a fatal plane crash.)

After I carefully removed the wreckage from the box, I paused for a moment before I went any further. The gravity of what I was looking at sunk in. People died here. This was as real as it gets.

As I began to examine the wreckage, I could see bits of clay and other debris that were still embedded between the crumpled aluminum from when it crashed. The serial number of the

Ki-45, stenciled in black, was still clearly readable. The clay had done such a remarkable job of preserving the wreckage that the original olive green paint was still almost perfectly intact, and there was practically no corrosion anywhere on the aluminum.

The collector didn't know what part of the airframe the wreckage came from, but based on how it was constructed, and comparing it to wartime photos, I surmised that it came from the rear cockpit where the radio operator sat. On the back side of the wreckage, I discovered some unusual red and black marks, and I couldn't figure out how they got there, or what made them. Then it hit me: they were from grease pencils bumping into the side of the cockpit, perhaps while studying a map or making notes. I thought about those forces again, and how a person had been sitting next to this piece when the fighter slammed into the ground. *Cold chills.*

I tried not to think about it, so I turned my attention back to the wreckage. How it all survived so perfectly preserved after being in the ground for over 50 years was truly astonishing.

By the time I finished examining the wreckage that evening, I felt a growing urge to learn all that I could about its final mission. I had to know more about this fighter and what happened to *Haley's Comet* on January 27, 1945. I began my research with the Ki-45 itself.

The Kawasaki Ki-45 was a twin-engine, two-seat fighter originally designed as a long-range bomber escort, but the fighter came into its own as an interceptor battling the B-29s. The Ki-45 that this wreckage came from, serial number 4065, was the most heavily armed variant and featured a 37mm cannon in the nose, a pair of 20mm cannons mounted obliquely between the cockpits, and a 7.7mm machine gun on a flexible mount for the radio operator. The upward-firing 20mm cannons were based on a tactic that was used by German night fighters over Europe with devastating effect. On the Ki-45, the cannons were mounted behind the cockpit and inclined upwards at a 30-degree angle to allow the pilot to approach a B-29 from below at night, unseen by the gunners, and rake its belly with cannon fire.[16]

The Allies had given the Ki-45 the code name "Nick," but its Japanese name, *Toryu*, was much more reflective of its new role: Dragon Slayer.

On the afternoon of January 27, 1945, the first of over 60 B-29s were closing in on Tokyo. At Mito airfield, home of the Hitachi Training Air Division, the alarm sounded and the airfield came alive as the crews scrambled to their fighters. Climbing into the cockpit of his olive green Ki-45, 20-year-old Sergeant Yuichi Kobayashi quickly started the engines. He was joined by 19-year-old Lance Corporal Natsuo Koibuchi, who would be riding in the rear cockpit as an observer. Having faced the Americans before without success, Kobayashi was determined to bring down a B-29. While chatting with the ground crew the previous day, Kobayashi turned to his crewmate and said: "Koibuchi, I will make a ramming next time!" Koibuchi's face turned pale and stiff at the thought.[17] Now, as the first formation of B-29s rumbled over the coast of Japan, today would be the day that Kobayashi would get his chance. With a final salute, the pair took off to meet the invading bombers. What happened next may never be known with absolute certainty.

A great air battle had erupted in the skies over Japan as Kobayashi flew into the fray. Hundreds of Japanese fighters rose to meet the B-29s, and they were putting up a ferocious defense of their homeland. The 73rd Bomb Wing had never encountered so many fighters before.

Leading the way to Tokyo that day were the 16 B-29s of the 497th Bomb Group, who would encounter a staggering 267 fighters that made 544 attacks on just their formation alone.[18] As Lieutenant Colonel Robert Morgan in *Dauntless Dotty* led the 497th into battle, his formation came under fighter attack 10 miles before they had even reached the coast of Japan. Up ahead, along the route to the target, swarms of fighters were climbing up to the formation's altitude and waiting for the Americans. Flying a full five minutes ahead of the next bomb group, Morgan's formation was about to face more Japanese fighters than anyone had ever seen before.

Fighting their way to Tokyo, Morgan later recalled how hundreds of fighters "hit us like a rain of meteors" as wave after wave swooped in for "close-encounter attacks" on his formation. So many fighters were attacking that some of the gunners ran out of ammo shooting back at them all. By the time the last B-29 had dropped its bombs and crossed back over the coast, the 73rd Bomb Wing had fired nearly 200,000 rounds of ammo during the battle.[19]

The B-29s also encountered intense flak beginning at landfall and continuing well past the target area, and there were at least two instances of the Japanese dropping air-to-air bombs on the formations as well. But it was the fighters – who were described as "hopped up" and "more aggressive and effective than ever before," with many pressing their attacks to within 100 feet of the bombers – that would inflict the greatest damage of all.[20]

One of the B-29s that came under heavy attack in the lead formation was *Thumper*, named after the rabbit in Walt Disney's *Bambi*. Piloted by Lieutenant Colonel Robert "Pappy" Haynes, *Thumper* was leading a four-plane element in the 497th's formation and was nearly rammed three times by Japanese fighters, some missing by only inches. After "bombs away," Haynes broke out of the melee and headed for the coast, but a lone fighter pursued *Thumper* out to sea. The fighter and *Thumper's* aft gun turrets were all out of ammo, but the fighter made pass after pass at the bomber's tail, attempting to ram it. Each time the fighter closed in, Haynes maneuvered *Thumper* away at the last second. This duel went on for 100 miles before the fighter gave up and turned back.[21]

Haynes was a veteran of 86 missions over Europe and North Africa, including the first raid on Berlin, but the January 27 raid on Tokyo was the roughest mission he ever encountered, he later said.[22] Only days after the battle, *Thumper's* bombardier, Lieutenant Raleigh Phelps, recalled:

> They were waiting for us over Tokyo. It looked like the whole damn Jap air force. In the scramble that followed, more than 500 separate attacks were made on members of our group.
>
> We figured afterward that more than 100 passes were made at *Thumper* – I counted 57 from the nose quarter alone. They barreled in without letup, usually alone, but sometimes in bunches. Some bored in to within 400 yards and then turned off. But others really pressed the attack, clearing us by inches.
>
> They went down in droves, but the rest kept coming. We downed six and damaged at least a dozen … But we lost planes, too, and our four-plane element happened to be the hardest hit of all. *Thumper* was the only one of the four that got back.[23]

After "bombs away," the air battle raged on as Morgan and his shot-up formation fought their way to the coast. Of his bombers that were still flying, only five remained undamaged.

Over the city of Funabashi, about 15 miles east of Tokyo, a Dragon Slayer found its prey. Sergeant Kobayashi spotted a lone B-29 from the 497th Bomb Group that had fallen out of formation and was badly damaged. This was the moment he'd been waiting for.

The B-29 that Kobayashi spotted had been under relentless fighter attack since it made landfall, and most of its crew were gravely wounded. Inside the shattered cockpit, the injured pilot was bleeding from his wounds, but he was still flying and fighting with everything he had. His co-pilot next to him had been hit in the head and through the chest and couldn't see due to all the blood in his eyes. Up in the nose in front of them, the bombardier was dead. Two of the gunners were also hit and one was unconscious, but the others were still fighting it out as the pilots desperately tried to reach the coast.[24] They would never make it.

Closing in to attack from behind, witnesses on the ground looked up in awe as Kobayashi dove and rammed his fighter into the B-29's left wing. The impact jolted the fighter, but it continued flying, leaving a trail of smoke and debris behind it. Kobayashi struggled to maintain control, but the damage was too severe. They were going down. After dropping some 20,000 feet, at the last moment, Kobayashi banked his fighter to avoid crashing into some homes and slammed into the ground. Yuichi Kobayashi and Natsuo Koibuchi were killed instantly.[25]

The B-29 that Kobayashi rammed continued flying east, but it too was mortally wounded.

In the peaceful countryside surrounding the small town of Shisui, far removed from the bombs falling on Tokyo, the residents were stunned when a B-29 appeared over the town. No one had ever seen a B-29 flying so low before, and to their horror, it was on fire and rapidly losing altitude. Streaming a thick trail of flames, the Japanese watched as the B-29 slowly circled their town. Then, in a flash, it suddenly exploded. With over 3,000 gallons of high-octane fuel on board, the bomber disintegrated in a massive fireball that left pieces of wreckage and body parts strewn across the countryside. A severed arm fell near one man who was working in his shed. In a rice paddy by the river, the upper half of a torso was found embedded in the mud. The wreckage continued to burn for almost two days before the flames finally died out.[26]

The 73rd Bomb Wing paid a heavy price that day. When it was all over, eight B-29s had been lost on the mission, and another 32 were damaged. One of the B-29s was rammed twice by Japanese fighters. The second ramming sheared off its left horizontal stabilizer and trapped the gunner in his mangled tail compartment, but the severely damaged bomber made it all the way back to Saipan with most of its controls knocked out and made a crash landing.[27]

The human toll of the mission was the heaviest of all: 77 men were missing. When the war ended, only seven of those missing men were found alive in Japanese prison camps.[28]

After the war, a U.S. Army investigation determined that the B-29 that exploded over Shisui was *Haley's Comet* from the 497th Bomb Group. *Haley's Comet* was one of the B-29s in the four-plane element led by *Thumper*. The other two bombers, *Werewolf* and *Shady Lady*, were also lost.[29]

In 1949, after multiple excavations of the crash site, the crew of *Haley's Comet* were buried with full military honors at the Zachary Taylor National Cemetery in Louisville, Kentucky. Due to the nature of their death, the crew was laid to rest together in a group burial because none of their remains could be identified.[30]

But that's not the whole story. Before *Haley's Comet* exploded, two of the 11-man crew managed to escape and parachute to safety. Both men were immediately captured and imprisoned at the Omori Prisoner of War Camp in Tokyo, where they would remain until the end of the war. And after an amazing discovery almost 66 years later to the day that *Haley's Comet* was lost, I would begin a solemn quest to find the family of one of those men.

*   *   *

In January of 2012, a little over a year after I acquired the Ki-45 wreckage from the Japanese collector, I found an old World War II scrapbook on eBay that came from an estate sale in

Upstate New York. I'd seen scrapbooks like it before, especially with so many of the Greatest Generation passing away now, but this one stood out from the rest.

What I couldn't believe about this scrapbook was that it belonged to the wife of Sergeant Albert Preisser. On that awful January day back in 1945, Albert Preisser was one of the nine men who died when *Haley's Comet* exploded. And now, 66 years later, his wife's scrapbook was for sale on eBay. I couldn't believe my eyes.

I was determined to be the new caretaker of the scrapbook, but the seller listed it with a really high starting bid and it didn't sell. A few days after the auction ended, I contacted the seller and asked if he was open to offers. Much to my dismay, the seller said that he'd listed it for a friend, and he no longer had the scrapbook. To make matters worse, his friend had just left town for a month. However, he'd be happy to pass along my offer when he returned.

While I was waiting to hear back about the scrapbook, I happened upon something else on eBay that captured my attention. It was the auction title that first caught my eye: "WW2 Love Letters (139) Serviceman Killed In Action Over Japan." The picture showed 139 letters stacked together that a B-29er had written home to his girl before he was killed, but the seller didn't have much more information than that. So I took a closer look at the letters to try to learn more about them, and that's when I noticed the name on the return address. It was Sergeant Al Preisser.

I couldn't believe it. These were all of the letters that Albert wrote home to his wife Shirley during the war, up until he was killed. Just like her scrapbook, they were now all for sale on eBay almost 66 years to the day since he died.

After contacting the seller, I learned that the letters came from the same estate sale as the scrapbook, and there were many people there buying things to resell on eBay. The seller said that he'd read most of the letters, which spanned from 1942–44, and that they gave a "history" of Sergeant Preisser, beginning with his training, marrying Shirley, then getting divorced, and finally going overseas. It came as a shock to me that Albert and Shirley were divorced. From what I had seen of her scrapbook, I never would have guessed it.

The last letter in the bundle was written on December 27, 1944, exactly one month before Albert was killed. The seller was kind enough to send me a partial copy of Albert's last letter. Knowing what would happen a month later, it was heartbreaking to read:

> When I hit the states again Shirl you can count on one thing – if I find the right person – I'm going to be married and have the life I've often read about, but the future will tell all – I guess. Yes Shirl I've seen plenty of this old world. More than I ever thought possible. To date I've got in eight missions. Six of these were over Japan proper and each one makes a guy think – and he thinks plenty, believe me – especially when the enemy fighters are coming in and the old ack-ack comes up at you. Thinking of home, what your folks are doing, if you'll ever see them again.[31]

I had to save these letters. Over the years, I've watched similar groups of letters sold on eBay that were also written by men like Albert who were later Killed in Action. Sometimes those same letters would appear on eBay again a short time later, only this time the person who bought the letters was now reselling them one letter at a time, so they'd make a lot of money. It sickened me to see these people profiting from the sacrifices of men who bravely fought and died for our freedom. I wasn't going to let that happen to Albert's letters.

My alarm went off a little after 9:00 a.m. on the day the auction was set to end. After a restless night thinking about the letters, I blindly felt for the iPhone sitting on my nightstand as I tried to wake up. I already had the eBay app loaded up from the night before, and when my eyes finally adjusted to the bright screen, I checked on the auction. Everything was looking good. My heart was beginning to race as the minutes ticked away. I kept thinking about what was in those letters, and what an incredible glimpse they would provide me into Albert's life. I couldn't wait to read them.

With only a few seconds left, my heart was about to beat out of my chest as I tapped the button to bid. The screen flashed. Then in bold, bright red letters, it said: "You have been outbid." And just like that, the auction was over.

I didn't want to get out of bed that day. After being cherished by Shirley for 70 years, going all the way back to 1942, the realization that Albert's letters would never again be together with her scrapbook was very hard to stomach. And it was all because I couldn't afford to bid more than $247.00 on the auction. I should have done more. I should have found a way.

I sulked for a while before it occurred to me that I might still be able to bring the letters and the scrapbook back together again. Even though I had not heard back from the guy yet about the scrapbook, and there was a real possibility that I might not be able to save it, I was trying to stay positive. In the meantime, just like I did with *The Dragon Lady's* data plate, I'd wait for the buyer to leave feedback, and then I would contact him about the letters.

When the feedback finally appeared, I wrote a short message explaining my interest in the letters, and then I anxiously waited to hear back from the buyer. I was hopeful that he might be willing to scan me a copy of Albert's last letter, and maybe he'd even consider selling me the letters once I saved up some more money. Hopefully I'd have the scrapbook by then, and I could reunite them. All I could do now was wait to hear from him.

But then the days turned into weeks. The weeks turned into months. And the months turned into years. Despite sending the buyer multiple messages, I never heard a word from him.

I was heartbroken, but I found solace in the fact that the buyer didn't start reselling the letters. At least they were all still together, as far as I knew. Only time will tell what will become of Albert's letters now. I still blame myself for losing them. (If the person who has Albert's letters is reading this, please get in touch with me at TrevorBMcIntyre@outlook.com.)

Two weeks later, I was still down on myself about losing the letters when I finally heard back about the scrapbook. The owner had accepted my offer! For $95.00, with shipping, I was now the new caretaker of Shirley's scrapbook. I took comfort in knowing that at least her scrapbook would be safe now. When the scrapbook arrived a few days later, I remember just staring at it for a while on my kitchen counter before I opened it. You can probably imagine what was going through my mind. Then I carefully lifted open the cover.

I didn't notice it at first, but the pages inside were made of a heavy construction-type paper that was dark black. The paper was so old that all of the pages were crumbling along the edges, leaving jagged confetti-like fragments all over my kitchen counter. In fact, the entire scrapbook was falling apart, but I didn't notice that either. No, it was what was on that first page that captured all of my attention when I opened it. Knowing what I knew, it was hard to look at. But I had to look.

In the center of the page, there was a large black and white portrait photo of Albert. He was wearing his dress uniform and had this playful smile on his face. With his hat slightly cocked over to one side, there was an air of confidence about him, like everything was going to be okay, even though the world was engulfed in war. He looked so happy and full of life. On the bottom left-hand corner, in red ink, he wrote a message to Shirley: "To Shirl, Loads of Love, Al."

Next to the portrait, Shirley pasted a small newspaper clipping announcing that Albert was overseas. It read in part:

> Sergeant Albert W. Preisser ... enlisted in the service October 27, 1941, and received his gunner's wings March 20, 1943 at Kingman Field, Arizona. Now a gunner on a B-29, Sgt. Preisser embarked in October, 1944 for overseas and is now based on Saipan. He has one enemy aircraft to his credit and his crew has destroyed three others. They have been on bombing missions over Tokyo and other Japanese cities and bases.

On each side of his portrait, there were two more clippings about Albert. The first said:

> B-29 Gunner Is Lost Over Japan ... Missing in action over Japan since January 27 is Sergeant Albert W. Preisser, waist gunner aboard a B-29 Superfortress.

The other clipping confirmed everyone's worst fears:

> Albert Preisser Listed As Dead ... A crew member of a bomber lost on a combat mission to Tokyo, Sergeant Albert W. Preisser has been listed by the War Department as officially dead.[32]

At the top of the page, directly above Albert's portrait, there was a photo of a Catholic priest. He looked young, maybe in his 30s, and wore glasses. He was dressed in a long black robe and seated in a chair reading a bible. Over his right shoulder, in the background, there was a statue of the Virgin Mary. I don't know who the priest was, but he must have comforted Shirley after her loss.

When I turned the page over, that's when I discovered it. It was a copy of a letter that was sent to Albert's mother just after the war ended. Shirley had hand-typed it herself from the original and pasted it in the scrapbook. The letter was written by Staff Sergeant Vere Carpenter, a B-29 radar observer, shortly after he was liberated from a Japanese Prisoner of War camp. Vere was one of the two men who miraculously escaped from *Haley's Comet* on that January day.

Vere had no memory of how he got out, but somehow he was blown clear when the B-29 exploded, and then he regained consciousness in time to pull the ripcord of his parachute as he was falling. (The wounded tail gunner, Sergeant Olinto Lodovici, bailed out before the explosion.)

What Vere did remember about that day was recounted in this letter to Albert's mother. He said that Al would have wanted her to know what happened on their last mission. "It's beyond us to understand the tragedies of war," Vere wrote.[33]

After having gone for so long without knowing what happened to her son, I tried to imagine what Albert's mother must have thought as she read this letter. But I could never imagine that.

When I reached the last paragraph of Vere's letter, it brought a tear to my eye the first time I read it. Even now, after having read it so many times, it still brings me to tears.

As I looked at the page opposite Vere's letter, I thought about what that one seller had told me about Albert and Shirley getting divorced before he went overseas. I don't know why they separated, but I do know they stayed friends and were prolific in the letters they wrote to each

One of the letters Shirley wrote to Albert after he went missing over Japan. It remains unopened to this day.

other. I was staring at three of those letters now. They were letters that Shirley had written to Albert, which she later pasted in the scrapbook, but there was something different about them. All of them had "Return To Sender" and "Verified" stamped on the envelopes, and someone had scribbled "Missing" on them. Then I noticed the postmarks. The letters were mailed 5, 10 and 12 days after Albert was killed. These letters were written knowing that Albert's B-29 was missing, long before anyone knew that he was dead. Shirley must have wanted these letters to be there, on Saipan, waiting for Albert when he came back.

The Army waited for two months, and then they sent the letters back to Shirley. The letters have remained sealed ever since she wrote them. They have never been opened or read.

I've always wondered what was in those letters, but it's not for me to know. They are Albert's letters, not mine. And they will remain unopened for as long as I'm on this earth.

As I slowly looked through the rest of the scrapbook, I found wedding photos, telegrams and other mementos, but my thoughts kept drifting back to that letter Vere wrote to Albert's mother. I don't know why, but I kept getting this feeling about it, like I should try to find Vere's family and give them a copy of his letter. Looking back on it now, I'm still at a loss for words to explain it. It just felt like something that I needed to do.

I decided then that no matter how long it may take me, I was going to find Vere's family.

* * *

I honestly didn't know what to expect as I began my quest to find Vere's family. Would they be excited to hear from me? Or would they even care? I've experienced both reactions before, and it's very disheartening when a family could care less about their own relative. But if nothing else, I at least had to try. For what Vere and his crew sacrificed for us, I owed him that much.

With the power of the internet at my fingertips, I began my search for Vere's family. I didn't have much luck at first. Carpenter is a very common name, and I wasn't even sure where to start looking. The only information I had was that Vere was from Utah, and as I soon learned, there's an awful lot of Carpenters in Utah. But after spending countless nights staring at my computer screen and connecting the genealogical dots, I finally tracked down a man named Larry who I thought was Vere's son. I felt nervous about calling him out of the blue, so I decided to send an e-mail instead. I wouldn't know how to explain all of this over the phone, anyway.

I lost track of how many times I wrote and rewrote that e-mail, but it was nearly 4:30 a.m. when I finally pressed "send." I had already decided by then that I wanted to write about *Haley's Comet* in this book, so I explained my long interest in his father's B-29 and that I was writing about his crew. Then I mentioned the scrapbook and his father's letter to Albert's mother that I wanted to share with his family. I thought it would be easier to understand why I was so interested in his father if I explained it from the point of view of a writer doing research, rather than coming across as just some guy on the internet. I've been ignored by other families I've contacted in the past, and I was really afraid that might happen here too. But less than five hours later, I received a reply. I remember feeling nervous as I clicked to open the e-mail, but then those nerves quickly gave way to a surge of excitement. I had found Vere's son!

In the days that followed, I was elated to share my research with him into *Haley's Comet* and what happened on that January day. It felt amazing to finally share all of this information with Vere's family, and they were so appreciative of my efforts. The most rewarding moment of all was when I sent Vere's son a copy of his father's letter. No one in his family had ever seen this letter before or knew that it even existed. You can imagine his feelings the first time he read it.

Of all the work I've done on behalf of veterans, sharing Vere's letter with his family was one of the proudest moments of my life. I only wish that I could have met Vere and thanked him for everything he did for our country. Vere passed away in 1995. He never talked much about the war, or his time as a prisoner. His son thought it was because he was such a humble man.[34]

Vere was imprisoned by the Japanese for seven months at the brutal Omori Prisoner of War Camp in Tokyo. For his first three months at the camp, Vere was kept isolated in solitary confinement. He rarely spoke about those three months.[35]

The Japanese considered Vere and his fellow B-29ers to be "special prisoners" who deserved special treatment. At Omori, the B-29ers were housed in a filthy, vermin-infested barrack that was fenced off from the rest of the camp. As "special prisoners," the B-29ers were not permitted to interact with the other prisoners, and they did not receive any medical attention for their wounds or ailments. But the cruelest treatment of all was that despite being subjected to the same forced labor, the B-29ers were only given half the food rations of the other prisoners.[36]

"They were forbidden to have medical treatment from us and their diet was considered worse than the rest of the camp, in spite of the fact that they were doing work carrying salvage material from the city," recalled Dr. Lloyd Goad, an Army doctor who spent over two years imprisoned at Omori, "and as a result of those conditions, many of the men were chronically ill for a long time and one man died, reported as a fact of starvation."[37]

One of the stories that Vere did share with his family happened after he was released from solitary confinement and joined the other "special prisoners." One day, at great risk to himself, Vere's cellmate managed to smuggle three large squash into their cell. After starving for so long on meager rations, the squash were like a feast. But they couldn't leave any traces behind for the guards to discover, so Vere and his cellmate had to eat the entire squash, including the seeds and the rind. That was one of the few days when Vere didn't go hungry.[38]

Another time, while working in the camp garden, Vere was starving and stole a turnip when he thought no one was looking. He quickly tried to eat it, but a guard caught him and drew his pistol. Under gunpoint, the guard made Vere walk out into the frigid waters of Tokyo Bay until the water was up to his nose. Then he was made to stand there, on the verge of drowning, until the guard was satisfied with the punishment.[39]

By the time the camp was liberated, Vere weighed less than 90 pounds.[40]

Decades after the war ended, Vere found himself back in Tokyo again during a layover at the airport. Looking out over Tokyo Bay, when his brother asked if he could see the area where he was held prisoner, Vere said that he could – but he had no desire to go there.[41]

Despite all of the hell he had suffered through at the hands of his captors, Vere never showed any hatred or animosity towards the Japanese people. In the 1980s, Vere and his wife even hosted an exchange student from Japan for a year. Vere treated her with the same love and kindness as though she were one of his own children.[42] What a remarkable and inspirational man Vere Carpenter was. I just wish that I could go back in time and meet him.

I've stayed in touch with Vere's son over the years, and I always send him any new information I find about *Haley's Comet* to share with his family. Thanks to a fellow researcher in Japan, Mr. Toru Fukubayashi, I was able to send him pictures of the crash site that were taken only hours after *Haley's Comet* was lost, including a photo showing a section of the fuselage where Vere's station was located, plus another of the crash site as it appears today. I was even able to give him the name of the Japanese soldier who captured his father after he landed.

When *Haley's Comet* exploded that day, the next thing Vere remembered was the wind blowing in his face as he was falling through the air. Vere's last memory was being inside *Haley's Comet* and preparing to bail out. The next thing he knew, he was falling, and the B-29 was gone. Dazed from the explosion, Vere's first thought was to try to fly like a bird, so he began flapping his arms up and down like wings. When he finally came to, he pulled the ripcord of his parachute and slowly descended to the ground. As Vere got closer to the ground, he could see villagers down below running towards him. Many were armed with farming tools and clubs. Vere tried to maneuver his parachute to get away from them, but it was no use.

When Vere hit the ground, he was swarmed by a mob of furious villagers who began beating him to death. They were getting some good licks in, Vere later recalled to his family, but then a huge Japanese man grabbed his arm and raised a club in the air over his head. Just before he swung, the man looked down at Vere's face. He paused, then threw his club to the ground. That Japanese man then saved Vere's life by keeping the other villagers at bay until some soldiers arrived.[43]

It's chilling to think what would have happened to Vere if that man had not been there. Vere's son told me that his father always said that he could still recognize that man if he ever saw him again. I wish we knew his name.[44]

I didn't think anything could ever compare to the feelings I had when I first shared Vere's letter with his family, but something came close a year later. It was when I discovered a very special picture of *Haley's Comet* for sale on a militaria website that I had never seen before. Vere's family had never seen the picture before, either. What was special about this picture was when it was taken. From the various clues I found in the photograph, I was able to determine that it was taken just before the January 27 mission. This was quite possibly the last photograph ever taken of *Haley's Comet* before she was lost.

When I bought the photo and had it enlarged, I also discovered that the B-29 parked in the background was none other than *Shady Lady*, the B-29 that was flying next to *Haley's Comet* on January 27 and was also lost during the mission. To this day, no one knows what happened to *Shady Lady*. No trace of the B-29 or its 11-man crew has ever been found.

In January of 2014, on the 69th anniversary of *Haley's Comet's* final mission, I surprised Vere's family with posters I had made from the photo. I think Vere would have liked that.

Throughout my journey researching *Haley's Comet* and discovering the forgotten stories of that January day in 1945, my thoughts have always returned to Vere's letter, and that last paragraph he wrote to Albert's mother. His family said it would be okay if I shared it with you. This is what Vere wrote:

> Al told me once he had a feeling he wouldn't be coming back. I tried to joke him out of thinking such things, but when I realized he really meant what he said, I asked him why he didn't stop flying if he felt that way. He just looked at me and said, "What if everyone quit just because they felt that way." I knew there was more to be said about it. He was willing to do his job even though he had to give his life. Thank God, we have men like Al. They are a symbol of true Americanship. I'm sure you are proud of the tribute he has given and even in your sorrow, it will be a consolation to know your son had such high ideals and was willing to fight and die for them.[45]

Albert Preisser was 25 years old when he died for his country. Thank God we have men like him.

*   *   *

Earlier in this chapter I wrote that after Sergeant Kobayashi took off in his Ki-45, we may never know what happened next with absolute certainty. I would be lying to you if I wrote otherwise. Throughout my research into what happened to *Haley's Comet* on January 27, 1945, I've found certain inconsistencies in some of the witness reports that I haven't been able to fully explain yet. This could just simply be the fog of war and the resulting confusion surrounding the events of that day, but I must remain diligent in trying to explain them.

We may never know with absolute certainty what happened that day, but my research into the loss of *Haley's Comet* and her crew will continue. I think what's most important, though, is not the minute details of how these men died, but to remember what they died for. These are their names. They paid the ultimate price for your freedom:

Joseph Bena Jr.
James F. Campbell
John J. Connell
Graydon V. Hardy
Cecil V. Hassell
Walter S. McDonell
William Pleus
Albert W. Preisser
David C. Williams Jr.

11

Thank God for the Marines

A month before his 53rd birthday in the summer of 1944, after his wife prepared one of his favorite meals of herring with rice and red beans, the distinguished general bid his family goodbye and set off for his new command. The night before he left, like all soldiers about to leave for war, he busied himself completing last-minute projects around the house for his family. The general focused on making some new shelves for the kitchen and other parts of his home, but he didn't have time to fix that stubborn draft in the kitchen. A crack in the floor was allowing cold air to blow up into the house, and it continued to worry him for months after he left. He later sent his wife detailed instructions on how to patch the crack until it could be properly fixed. He never stopped worrying about that draft in the kitchen.

The general's two oldest kids, 19 and 15, were at school when he left that afternoon, but his youngest daughter, just 9, had finished school early and was back home in time to see him off. She burst into tears as her father left. His daughter didn't know where he was going or when he would return, but as he stepped into his staff car and looked back for a final goodbye, the general already knew the fate that awaited him. Where he was going, the general would never see his family again.[1]

*   *   *

Lying halfway between the Marianas and Japan was a tiny godforsaken island named Iwo Jima. From the air, it looked like a burnt pork chop. It smelled even worse. The 8-square-mile island was formed by a volcano in ancient times that left its beaches covered in black volcanic ash, but unlike the Marianas, there were no lush tropical jungles to be found anywhere on the island. There wasn't even fresh water. In Japanese, its name meant "sulfur island," so named for the awful stench that hung over its barren landscape. The battle that began on its black shores was like nothing the United States had experienced before in its history. And God willing, nothing like it will ever be experienced again. For those who lived and fought and died there, Iwo Jima was Hell on earth.

After the capture of the Marianas, the strategic importance of Iwo Jima for both the Japanese and the Americans quickly became apparent. What made Iwo Jima so valuable was its topography. While there were other Japanese-held islands in the region, their mountainous terrain made them unsuitable for building large airfields that could support major air operations. Iwo

Jima, however, was flat and featured a broad plateau upon which the Japanese had already built two airfields, and a third airfield was under construction. In the hands of the Americans, those airfields would finally bring Japan within range of land-based fighters and provide a refuge for crippled B-29s.

As Japan's closest major outpost north of the Marianas, the radar station on Iwo Jima provided advance warning of B-29 raids, and the fighters based on the island could attack the bombers on the way to and from their targets, which forced them to fly longer routes to avoid the island. The proximity of Iwo Jima to the Marianas also meant that the B-29's airfields were now well within range of Japanese fighters and bombers. After the first B-29 appeared over Tokyo, the Japanese wasted no time in striking back. At 1:30 a.m. on November 3, 1944, nine Mitsubishi G4M Betty bombers appeared over Saipan and attacked Isley Field, but the bombers only inflicted minor damage and seven were shot out of the sky. A map was later discovered in the wreckage that showed the bombers had taken off from Iwo Jima.[2]

The Japanese launched two more small raids in the days that followed, but on November 27 they returned in force. Just after midnight, the air raid sirens wailed across Saipan as a pair of Betty bombers swept out of the night sky and attacked the airfield. General Hansell was standing on the edge of the runway watching the anti-aircraft fire with his deputy commander when one of the bombers suddenly appeared over the runway. Hansell later recalled:

> A couple of B-29s had been hit and were burning brightly. They lit up the sky, and the oncoming Japanese aircraft was clearly visible … It was making a low-level strafing attack down the runway we were standing on. There was no place to go. We hit the pavement with great force at just the same time. Tracers from the ground defenses were pouring into the Japanese bomber but it continued on course. Then, as it approached the end of the runway, it swerved slightly and plowed into the ground. The pilot evidently had been killed. The bomber hit with a roar about a hundred yards from us and was engulfed in flames. Just as we were rising to our feet, there was a violent explosion. Evidently it still had bombs aboard.[3]

The Japanese returned 12 hours later with 17 fighters and attacked Isley Field again in broad daylight. While speeding to the airfield in his jeep during the attack, General Hansell suddenly found himself face-to-face with a Japanese fighter on a strafing run as he came over a rise in the road. Hansell slammed on the brakes and dove under his jeep just as the fighter passed overhead. Hansell had luckily survived both attacks unscathed, but seven of his B-29s were destroyed and many more were damaged.[4] The Japanese launched another large raid on December 7, undoubtedly to celebrate Pearl Harbor Day, that lasted for 90 minutes and left two more B-29s destroyed and 23 damaged. On Christmas night, the Japanese returned with another large force of 25 aircraft that destroyed two B-29s and damaged many others.

By February, the Japanese had launched 22 raids against the Marianas with more than 80 aircraft. While 37 of the attackers were ultimately shot down, the raids were effective: 11 B-29s were completely destroyed, a further 49 were damaged, and 45 men were killed and over 200 were injured.[5] Iwo Jima had to be neutralized.

* * *

When General Tadamichi Kuribayashi left for his new command on Iwo Jima in the summer of 1944, he already knew that he would never see his family again. "This time maybe even my dead bones won't be sent back home," Kuribayashi said to his wife before he left, but he said it so casually that she didn't think he was serious.[6] The last time he saw his wife and their 9-year-old daughter, Takako, they were standing by the gate of their house as he drove away. Takako was inconsolable. After her father left, she sat down in the hall where she used to dance for him before school and wept for hours.

In the letters he wrote home from Iwo Jima in the months that followed, Kuribayashi often talked about seeing Takako in his dreams. After arriving on the island, he had a recurring dream of going home and taking walks with her and her mother around the neighborhood again. But sadly, he wrote, that wasn't something he could do now. Instead, he wanted her to study hard and do exactly as her mother told her, as that would put his mind at ease. In another dream, he wrote of seeing Takako all grown up and marveled at how tall she was.[7] Beyond his dreams, however, he would never get to see his daughter grow up.

When he arrived on Iwo Jima in June of 1944, General Kuribayashi had a unique insight about the men he would be fighting. Over the course of his military career, he came to know the Americans very well. Kuribayashi was a 30-year veteran of the Japanese Army and a direct descendant of samurai. After graduating from the Imperial Japanese Army Academy in 1914, Kuribayashi went on to study at the elite Army War College and upon graduation was honored with a saber personally presented to him by Emperor Taisho. In 1928, Kuribayashi sailed for America and would spend the next two years studying in the United States and traveling across the country in a Chevrolet he purchased himself. In between his travels, he studied English and American history at Harvard University. Kuribayashi was well liked and made many friends in the American military while he was attached to the U.S. Army's 1st Cavalry Division as an exchange officer. Kuribayashi then spent three years in Canada, where he served as a military attaché before returning to Japan in 1933.[8]

Kuribayashi spoke excellent English and admired the American people. He once wrote to his wife:

> The United States is the last country in the world Japan should fight. Its industrial potential is huge and fabulous, and the people are energetic and versatile. One must never underestimate the Americans' fighting ability.[9]

The energy and versatility of the American people, along with the country's industrial potential, became especially clear to Kuribayashi during a road trip from Kansas to Washington, D.C., in the winter of 1929. During his adventure across the country, Kuribayashi became stranded on the side of the road when his car broke down. When a passing car stopped to help him, Kuribayashi was shocked when a young girl, only 17 or 18 years old, got out and fixed his car for him. He later wrote to his brother how impressed he was that anyone in America over 16 years old with the right paperwork could drive, and that everyone knew how to perform routine maintenance on their cars. He was equally impressed that the housekeeper who looked over his residence could also own her own car. It was nothing like back home in Japan.[10]

In September of 1941, Kuribayashi was appointed Chief of Staff of the 23rd Army in China and took part in the Battle of Hong Kong that December. By 1943, he was promoted to commander of the 2nd Imperial Guards Division in Tokyo. A year later, Kuribayashi was personally selected by Prime Minister Hideki Tojo, one of Japan's biggest proponents for war against the United States, to defend Iwo Jima. Forming part of Japan's inner defensive ring, Iwo Jima was part of the Tokyo prefecture and was considered Japanese soil. An invasion of Iwo Jima was an invasion of the Japanese homeland. The gravity of what was at stake was made clear when Kuribayashi was given a personal audience with Emperor Hirohito before taking his new command. Iwo Jima would be defended at all costs.

During a meeting with the Prime Minister before he set off for Iwo Jima, Tojo reportedly instructed Kuribayashi to "do something similar to what was done on Attu" in his defense of the island. Attu was an island the Japanese had seized in Alaska's Aleutian Islands in 1942. When American forces landed to retake the island in May of 1943, the Japanese fought to the death, with practically the entire garrison being wiped out.[11]

Tojo expected Kuribayashi to also fight to the last man, but he may have had an ulterior motive in sending Kuribayashi to die on Iwo Jima. "It was because His Lordship the General was opposed to starting a war against the United States that Prime Minister Tojo disliked him and ordered him off to Iwo Jima," recalled Sadaoka Nobuyoshi, a civilian employee who worked for Kuribayashi.[12]

The loyal samurai he was, even though it meant certain death, Kuribayashi devoted himself to defending Iwo Jima wholeheartedly. In a letter to his brother before he left, Kuribayashi wrote:

> I may not return alive from this assignment but let me assure you that I shall fight to the best of my ability, so that no disgrace will be brought upon our family. I will fight as a son of Kuribayashi, the samurai, and will behave in such a manner as to deserve the name of Kuribayashi. May my ancestors guide me.[13]

Having lived in the United States and seeing its military and industrial might first-hand, Kuribayashi knew that he could not win the Battle of Iwo Jima. But he was also keenly aware of the American public's disdain for high casualties. To fight the Americans, Kuribayashi devised a brilliant plan. Taking full advantage of the island's terrain and the lessons learned from previous invasions, Kuribayashi's strategy was not to fight the Marines on the beaches as they came ashore, but to allow them to land and then wage a long battle of attrition that would keep the Marines pinned down and maximize casualties. Under Kuribayashi's defense-in-depth plan, the island's main defenses were moved inland away from the landing beaches to allow his men to fight the Marines from the protection of bunkers, caves and spider holes that were interconnected by miles of tunnels crisscrossing the island.[14]

The ultimate goal of Kuribayashi's strategy was to continue fighting as long as possible to deny the use of Iwo Jima for B-29 operations, and most importantly, to inflict the greatest number of casualties in the hope that the American public would falter in their support for an invasion of Japan, leading to a negotiated peace. (Kuribayashi's views about a negotiated peace to end the war were not shared by his superiors in Tokyo.)[15] To carry out his plan, Banzai charges were now strictly forbidden. No Japanese lives would be wasted in senseless attacks like those carried out in previous battles. Every man was expected to hold out as long as possible and inflict the most casualties. Each shot had to count.[16]

To inspire his forces, Kuribayashi wrote his "Courageous Battle Vows" and distributed them to his men. Copies were later found all over the island:

1. We shall defend this place with all our strength to the end.
2. We shall fling ourselves against the enemy tanks clutching explosives to destroy them.
3. We shall slaughter the enemy, dashing in among them to kill them.
4. Every one of our shots shall be on target and kill the enemy.
5. We shall not die until we have killed ten of the enemy.
6. We shall continue to harass the enemy with guerrilla tactics even if one of us remains alive.[17]

The terrain of Iwo Jima complimented Kuribayashi's strategy perfectly. The most prominent feature of the island was Mount Suribachi, a dormant volcano rising some 550 feet at the southern tip of the island. From the narrow neck at Suribachi, the center of Iwo Jima spread out 2½ miles wide and rose in terraces to a plateau that contained the island's valuable airfields. To the north, the terrain turned into a rocky nightmare of hills, ravines and caves that would conceal machine guns, mortars, artillery pieces, and Kuribayashi's command bunker 75 feet below ground.

Looking down from Mount Suribachi during his first inspection tour of the island, Kuribayashi realized that there were only two beaches on the entire island that could support a landing. He knew exactly where the Marines would come ashore. Kuribayashi would now transform Iwo Jima into the most heavily fortified island in the world, and he would make the Marines pay dearly for every inch of it.

With sulfur fumes filling the air, the living conditions on Iwo Jima were hellish as Kuribayashi's men began to build up the island's defenses. Since there was no source of fresh water on the island, an intricate system of cisterns and piping was built to collect rainwater for drinking. Each soldier was limited to one canteen of water per day. Fresh food was scarce. Flies and roaches were rampant. Due to the constant air raids, the garrison lived underground in caves that were unbearably hot.[18] On some parts of the island, the geothermal heat was so high that the soldiers could only dig in five or ten-minute shifts. As they tunneled deeper into the island, the heat became so extreme that the rubber soles of their shoes began to melt, but they pressed on to prepare for the coming invasion.[19]

While most Japanese officers were brutal to the men under their command, Kuribayashi was a commander who "overflowed with warmth" and made daily walks around the island to personally inspect the progress of the fortifications and talk to his men. During his time in China, Kuribayashi would often visit his wounded soldiers in the hospital, an unheard-of practice for such a high-ranking officer, and give them gifts of fruit.[20] Major Komoto Kumeji, who was called back to Tokyo before the invasion, recalled how Kuribayashi was a constant fixture in the lives of his men:

> He was always making inspection tours of the island and had a perfect memory for topography and natural objects. He personally directed the organization and construction of the defenses, and while so doing he would slip the cigarettes that were a gracious gift from the Emperor into the pockets of the hardworking troops, sharing them out.[21]

Under Kuribayashi's guidance, the island was honeycombed with 16 miles of tunnels connecting some 1,500 rooms carved out of the rock. Mortars and artillery pieces were preregistered on the landing beaches and could fire blind from protected positions without seeing their targets.

Blockhouses and pillboxes, made from reinforced concrete with walls several feet thick, were positioned to unleash a deadly crossfire as the Marines advanced inland.[22]

While Iwo Jima was being transformed into a fortress, Kuribayashi insisted on sharing the hardships of his men. He ate the same poor food his soldiers ate, refusing all the comforts afforded to officers of his stature. Kuribayashi was a soldier's soldier. He would soon be facing the largest force of U.S. Marines ever assembled for a single battle.[23]

*   *   *

After a 40-year career in the Marine Corps that stretched all the way back to 1905, 62-year-old Lieutenant General Holland M. "Howlin' Mad" Smith, the top Marine commander in the Pacific, was worried about Iwo Jima.

"This will be the bloodiest fight in Marine Corps history," Smith said to Fleet Admiral Chester Nimitz during a conference before the invasion. "We'll catch seven kinds of hell on the beaches, and that will be just the beginning." The old warrior paused, then added: "The fighting will be fierce, and the casualties will be awful, but my Marines will take the dammed island."[24]

Tension filled the room as Smith glared at Nimitz. "How much bombardment will we get before H-Hour?" Smith asked. Nimitz turned to Admiral Raymond Spruance, the commander of the Fifth Fleet, for the answer.

"Three days," Spruance replied.

Smith bristled, but controlled his rage: "Damn it, Ray, three days won't do the job. I need at least ten days of battleship and cruiser and carrier plastering. Otherwise the carnage will be unbelievable. God knows our losses will be horrible regardless of what we do."[25]

The best anyone could do was delay the invasion for 30 days to allow the Army Air Forces to continue bombing the island, but with General MacArthur's operations to retake the Philippines and the coming invasion of Okinawa in April, there was no more naval firepower to be had.

Three days of shelling was all the Marines would get.[26]

*   *   *

On February 18, 1945, a colossal invasion force of 495 ships and more than 100,000 men were bearing down on Iwo Jima. To supply the Marines for the coming battle, each transport ship carried 6,000 five-gallon cans of fresh water, medical supplies for a month, rations to feed the Marines for two months, gasoline for 25 days, spare parts for weapons, vehicles and communication equipment, and 30 days of general supplies. The Marines also had 100 million cigarettes on hand. It all added up to 1,322 pounds of supplies for each Marine.[27]

It was estimated that only 13,000 Japanese troops were on Iwo Jima, and after three days of Navy shelling, preceded by 72 straight days of bombing by the Army Air Forces, some were optimistic that the island would be captured in a matter of days.[28] In reality, the defenses on Iwo Jima had actually grown stronger during the bombardment. Despite a reconnaissance photo showing 5,000 bomb craters within one square mile alone on the island, some 22,000 Japanese soldiers were alive and waiting in their heavily fortified positions for the Marines to land.[29]

Iwo Jima was about to become the bloodiest battle in Marine Corps history.

As the sun began to rise over Iwo Jima on February 19, after a final meal of steak and eggs, followed by religious services, the Marines began boarding their amtracs (tracked landing vehicles) and landing craft. For the assault on Iwo Jima, the 5th Amphibious Corps under Major General Harry Schmidt had swelled to more than 70,000 men from three Marine divisions. Over half of the Marines were veterans of earlier fighting in the Pacific, and Schmidt had led the 4th Marine Division during the battles for Kwajalein and Saipan. But nothing the veteran Marines had experienced before could prepare them for Iwo Jima.

At 6:40 a.m., eight battleships, 19 cruisers and 44 destroyers opened fire on Iwo Jima. Thousands of tons of high-explosive shells rained down on the island. Gunboats swept in close to shore and unleashed thousands of rockets. Then the carrier planes took over at 8:05 a.m., dropping bombs, firing rockets and strafing the island. With H-Hour 35 minutes away, the Navy resumed its bombardment at 8:25 a.m. and blasted the landing beaches with another 8,000 high-explosive shells. Watching offshore, many wondered how any Japanese could survive the pounding.[30]

As the naval barrage lifted from the beaches and shifted inland, the first wave of amtracs came ashore at 9:00 a.m. Armed with 75mm cannons and machine guns to clear any beach defenses, the amtracs quickly became bogged down in the loose black sand as they struggled to climb up the steep terraces leading off the beach. Sporadic small-arms fire pinged off their armored hulls, but it was eerily quiet.[31]

The strange black sand that mired the amtracs on the beaches was an ancient volcanic ash that consisted of tiny, jagged particles of rock and volcanic glass. As the Marines following behind them would soon discover, trying to dig a foxhole in the sand was like "trying to dig a hole in a barrel of wheat" and was next to impossible.[32]

Three minutes later, the next wave of amtracs packed with Marines landed. Carrying anywhere between 70 and 120 pounds of gear, the Marines sank up to their calves in the black sand as they poured onto the beaches and charged up to the first terrace. The first reports from the beachhead came in a few minutes later. The terrain was awful, but casualties were light and resistance moderate. Optimism surged.[33]

Looking directly down on the landing beaches from their concealed fortifications within Mount Suribachi, the Japanese defenders watched and waited as the beaches became clogged with Marines and equipment. It was all part of Kuribayashi's plan to lure the Americans into a trap.

Within an hour of the first amtracs landing, there were now more than 6,000 Marines crowded on the beach. This was the moment Kuribayashi was waiting for. With his trap set, Kuribayashi gave the order to open fire. From mortars and machine guns to heavy artillery, the island fortress suddenly came alive, and hell was unleashed upon the Marines stuck on the beach. There was no place to hide.

Two miles out at sea, aboard the command ship *Eldorado*, General Smith and Admiral Turner were monitoring the radio traffic when the frantic reports began streaming in:

> 25th Regiment: Catching all hell from the quarry. Heavy mortar and machine gun fire. Troops inland two hundred yards but pinned down.
>
> 23rd Regiment: Taking heavy casualties and can't move for the moment. Mortars killing us.
>
> 27th Regiment: All units pinned down by artillery and mortars. Casualties heavy. Need tank support fast to move anywhere.
>
> 28th Regiment: Nearly across the neck but taking heavy fire and forward movement stopped. Machine gun and artillery fire heaviest ever seen.[34]

Many Marines would never make it off the beach alive. Others died in their landing craft, wiped out by artillery and mortar fire before they even reached the shore. They fell in increasing numbers, but slowly the Marines pushed forward through the hell-storm as more waves landed behind them.

Late in the afternoon of the first day, Robert Sherrod landed on Iwo Jima with the 24th Marine Regiment. Sherrod was continuing his coverage of the war for *Life* magazine and had previously landed with the Marines on Attu, Tarawa and Saipan, but what he saw on Iwo Jima was beyond anything he had experienced before. The Marines on Iwo Jima, Sherrod later wrote, died with the greatest possible violence. Nowhere in the Pacific War had he seen such mangled bodies. Many were cut squarely in half. Moving across the beach, he saw severed arms and legs blown 50 feet away from shattered bodies. In one spot, far away from a group of dead Marines, he saw a string of guts 15 feet long strewn across the sand.[35]

On Iwo Jima, the Marines could only advance and die, Sherrod said, paving with their bodies a way for the men who came behind them.[36] One veteran Marine later recalled:

> At Tarawa, Saipan, and Tinian, I saw Marines killed and wounded in a shocking manner, but not like the ghastliness that hung over the Iwo beachhead. Nothing any of us had ever known could compare with the utter anguish, frustration, and constant inner battle to maintain some semblance of sanity, clarity of mind, and power of speech. Everybody tells me they felt as I did. As long as you could speak, you believed you had a slim chance to live.[37]

Also going in with the Marines were the men of the Naval Construction Battalions, the Seabees, who would immediately begin work to expedite the flow of men and materiel off the beaches. During the first hours of the invasion, one landing ship hit the beach with a load of bulldozers and tanks. When the ramp dropped, the Seabee operating the first bulldozer was horrified by what he saw in front of him. There were so many dead Marines sprawled across the beach that there was no way to drive his bulldozer off without crushing their bodies. The Seabee didn't know what to do, but the ship had already been hit by artillery fire and the captain wanted to get off the beach as soon as he could. The Seabee had no choice but to drive his bulldozer over the dead Marines.[38]

Despite the murderous fire, 30,000 Marines were ashore by the end of the first day, and the 28th Regiment had pushed across the neck of the island and cut off Mount Suribachi from the rest of Iwo Jima. But the price was horrific: 2,321 Americans lay dead or wounded. All in just the first day.[39] At the White House, President Roosevelt was visibly shaken when he was informed of the casualties. It was the first time during the war that anyone had seen the President gasp in horror.[40]

Out on the command ship the next morning, General Smith reviewed the battle reports and openly wondered why the expected Banzai charges against the beachhead never materialized. Something was different about the commander of Iwo Jima. "I don't know who he is," Smith said, "but the Jap general running the show is one smart bastard."[41]

Kuribayashi's plan to make the Americans pay dearly for every inch of the island was working.

On the fifth day of the battle, after four days of ferocious fighting, a 40-man patrol from the 2nd Battalion, 28th Marines, scaled Mount Suribachi and raised the first American flag on Japanese soil. Down below, thousands of Marines and sailors were watching the patrol as they cautiously climbed up to the rim of the volcano. Using a section of pipe they found nearby for a flagpole, which was part of the rainwater catch system built by the Japanese, the Marines attached the flag to the pipe with a rope threaded through a bullet hole and raised it above the battle-scarred island.[42]

The sight of Old Glory flying high over Iwo Jima caused a sensation. The patrol's radioman, Raymond Jacobs, later recalled:

> Just moments after the flag was raised we heard a roar from down below. Marines on the ground, still engaged in combat, raised a spontaneous yell when they saw the flag. Screaming and cheering was so loud and prolonged that we could hear it quite clearly on top of Suribachi. The boats on the beach and the ships at sea joined in blowing horns and whistles. The celebration went on for many minutes. It was a highly emotional, strongly patriotic moment for us all.[43]

Down on the beach, General Smith and Secretary of the Navy James Forrestal were coming ashore just as the flag was raised. Looking up at the flag over Mount Suribachi, Forrestal turned to Smith and said: "Holland, this means a Marine Corps for another 500 years." His eyes filling with tears, Smith nodded in agreement.[44] "The raising of the flag high atop Suribachi was one of the proud moments of my life," Smith recalled after the war. "No American could view this symbol of heroism and suffering without a lump in his throat."[45]

When a larger replacement flag was brought up to Suribachi about two hours later, the image that Associated Press photographer Joe Rosenthal captured of the six Marines raising the flag would become the most recognized and reproduced photograph in history. Back home, where many thought the flag raising marked the end of the battle, the iconic photo lifted morale and would become the symbol of the 7th War Bond Drive that raised more than $26 billion for the war effort, but weeks of brutal fighting still lay ahead on Iwo Jima.[46]

Of the original 40-man patrol that scaled Mount Suribachi, only four would survive Iwo Jima unscathed. The rest were either killed or wounded in later fighting on the island.[47]

With Suribachi secured, the Marines continued pushing north across the island as the Seabees and Army Air Forces set to work behind them repairing Iwo Jima's airfields. Moving in with bulldozers behind the tanks, they began clearing Motoyama Airfield No. 1 of wrecked Japanese planes and shattered equipment in preparation for the first American planes to land on the island.

William Bradford Huie, a war correspondent and former Seabee, arrived on Iwo Jima to cover the battle with the Seabees. Huie later recounted the difficulties the Seabees faced on the island:

> Iwo Jima probably is the ugliest, filthiest island on earth. Everything about our operation there was difficult, dirty, and horrifying. That coarse, volcanic grit filled your shoes, cascaded down your neck, cut your face and eyes. The all-pervading odor was a mixture of incinerated or decaying flesh, sulfur fumes, sweat, excrement, and that sickening, pink "whorehouse powder" which the Japs smear on their stinking bodies. Sleep was impossible, and men deteriorated into incredibly filthy moles with split fingernails, swollen lips, begrimed faces, and comatose eyes.[48]

Working so close behind the front lines, the men frequently came under fire from the Japanese, but they carried on around the clock to rebuild and expand the chewed-up airfield. Their work would pay off much sooner than anyone expected.

* * *

In the spring of 2012, a dream of mine came true. During the overnight hours, while searching for something else, I discovered an amazing piece of Iwo Jima history on YouTube, of all places. It was color footage taken on the 13th day of the battle by a Marine cameraman, and the moment he captured was one that I had dreamed about seeing ever since I first read about it. I had always felt that footage of this historic event had to exist, and now, by sheer accident, I finally found it.

On March 4, 1945, 24-year-old Lieutenant Raymond Malo and his crew from the 9th Bomb Group were returning from their first mission to Japan when they discovered that they didn't have enough fuel to make it back to Tinian. The rookie crew had just arrived in the Marianas two weeks earlier, and before their first mission was even completed, they were now faced with one of the B-29er's biggest fears: ditching in the ocean.

"The first we knew that we couldn't make our base was about 360 miles out of Tokyo on the home run," recalled Staff Sergeant James Cox, the radio operator. "The bomb bay doors wouldn't shut after we made the [bomb] run and dragged so much that we were using gasoline too fast."

"I passed the word to throw out the loose equipment in case we had to make a water landing so no one would get hurt," Malo said.

"We tossed overboard all flak suits, the camera and expended all our ammunition," Cox added, "to lighten the ship."[49]

The crew was eventually able to get the bomb bay doors closed, but when they discovered that a fuel transfer pump had also failed, there simply wasn't enough usable fuel remaining to make it back to Tinian. The rough airfield on Iwo Jima was still under Japanese fire and no one had attempted to land such a large airplane there yet, but Malo only had two options.

"It was a case of trying the strip or ditching," Malo said. "We couldn't transfer fuel."[50]

Iwo Jima would be their only hope.

"They asked what the trouble was," Cox said, when he radioed Iwo Jima. "When I told them we were low on fuel and had jammed the bomb bay doors, they asked us whether we want to chance it, to land on the strip. Lieutenant Malo told me to say to try the strip."[51]

Coming in low over Suribachi, Malo circled the embattled island three times to size up the landing strip. On Tinian, the runways were 8,500 feet long and paved, but on Iwo Jima, Malo had barely 4,000 feet of dirt to land on. The crew didn't know it at the time, but the Japanese had just fired a volley of mortars at the airfield on which they were about to touch down. This would be the toughest landing Malo had ever attempted:

> We had to make three passes to feel for and see the ground to even get an idea what it would be like. It didn't look good. In the first place, it wasn't easy to make out the strip. That volcanic ash doesn't show much detail. Of course it isn't very long, just about the right size for fighter planes ... Everybody held on tight and I came in alongside Mount Suribachi. After using up about 600 feet of runway we touched down. Right away I put on the hydraulic brakes and co-pilot Lieutenant Ed Mockler of Park Falls, Wisconsin, pulled on the emergency brake.[52]

The B-29 bounced hard and skidded when Malo planted it down on the strip, kicking up plumes of dirt and sending scores of onlookers running, before finally screeching to a stop next to a Marine cameraman. Aside from knocking down the runway's windsock, the bomber was undamaged.

After taxiing back down the strip towards Suribachi and parking next to a Stinson OY-1, a light aircraft the Marines were using for artillery spotting within eyesight of the airfield, the B-29 was rushed by crowds of Marines and construction men as the engines were shut down and the relieved crew emerged. "One hatch opened and four or five men jumped and fell to their hands and knees," recounted Frank Crowe, one of the Marines who swarmed around the bomber. "What a contrast! Here were men so glad to be on the island that they were kissing it. A mile or two to the north were three Marine divisions who thought the place was hell on earth, its ground not even good enough to spit on."[53]

After emerging from the B-29, one of the crew shouted to the crowd surrounding his bomber: "Thank God for you Marines!"[54]

Iwo Jima had just saved its first B-29, but it came at a heavy price. After just 13 days of fighting, 2,419 Americans were dead, 504 were missing, and 11,429 were wounded, for a total of 14,352 casualties. And there were still thousands of Japanese troops left on the island who were determined to fight to the bitter end.[55]

About four hours after they landed, Malo had another big decision to make: stay on Iwo Jima until the strip could be lengthened, or try to take off now. If they stayed overnight, the construction men would have an additional 1,000 feet of runway completed for them by the morning, but being the biggest target on the island, the crew all agreed to leave as soon as possible. Malo later recalled:

We got off there as soon as we could … Course we were a good target for Jap fire, just about the biggest thing on the island, so after we borrowed some gas we decided to try a takeoff … So I gunned the motors, there's a lot of horsepower in four B-29 engines and held the brakes. Then just when they were turning at full power, I let go of the brakes and we started out like a shot. It was like a catapult. We got up all right and flew on down to our base without any trouble.[56]

In August of 2011, I was attending the 9th Bomb Group Association's reunion in Dayton, Ohio, when I met Don Mockler, the nephew of Lieutenant Edwin Mockler, Malo's co-pilot. I always had a big interest in Malo's historic landing, so it was a real treat to actually talk to someone with such a close connection to the crew. Out of curiosity, I remember asking Don if there was any footage of his uncle's crew landing on Iwo Jima. Being the first B-29 to land on the island, there must be something out there somewhere, I said, but we had never heard of any such footage existing.

Seven months later, my dream came true when I discovered color footage of their landing had just been uploaded on YouTube. The person who posted the video didn't know this was the first B-29 to land on Iwo Jima, but I recognized it from the photos that were taken that day and quickly confirmed it by the serial number on the B-29's tail. After getting over the shock, and watching the video about 20 times, I e-mailed Don to tell him about my discovery. I also told him that I was going to send the video to the 9th Bomb Group Association so it could be shared with the membership, but I wanted him to be the first to see it. I knew this video would be very meaningful to the Mockler family.

Six weeks after they landed on Iwo Jima, during a nighttime incendiary raid on the Kawasaki Urban Area, Lieutenant Malo's B-29 was shot down and crashed in Tokyo Bay. The entire crew was killed that night, except for Staff Sergeant Allan K. Hill, the CFC gunner, who was taken prisoner by the Kempeitai. What exactly happened to Malo's crew that night will never be known.

A month after he survived the downing that took the lives of his crewmates, Sergeant Hill was one of the 62 American prisoners of war held at the Tokyo Military Prison. They were all B-29ers who survived being shot down over Japan. The Tokyo Military Prison complex was surrounded by a 12-foot brick wall and contained five cell blocks and other wooden buildings with tile roofs. In addition to the Americans, some 500 Japanese prisoners were also held at the prison.

The American prisoners were confined in their own cell block building, which was walled off from the rest of the prison. Running down the center of the building was a row of 17 wooden cells, with a corridor along the front and back for the guards. The 62 Americans were divided up and locked inside the cells that were about 6 feet wide and 12 feet long. Vertical wooden timbers about 4 inches wide and spaced 3 inches apart like bars formed the front and back of each cell. The walls and floors were lined with thick wooden planks. The wooden door to each cell was secured with an iron lock. On each side of the lock, iron bars were mounted between the timbers to prevent the prisoners from reaching it. A crude faucet and a chamber pot for a toilet completed the cells. Since their arrival from the Tokyo Kempeitai headquarters 16 days earlier, none of the Americans had been allowed out of their tiny cells. They were blindfolded when they arrived and never saw what was around them.

On the night of May 25, 1945, the Tokyo Military Prison erupted in flames during a massive B-29 incendiary raid on Tokyo. The guards quickly evacuated all of the Japanese prisoners to safety as the fire spread through the complex, but upon orders from the warden, Toshio Tashiro, the American prisoners were all left in their cells to die.

Some of the Americans managed to break out as the fire enveloped the prison, but the guards cut them down with swords as they fled for their lives. The guards later bragged about the Americans they killed that night. The other helpless Americans banged and yelled and pleaded for their lives as the flames closed in, but the guards would not save them. They all burned to death in their cells as the fire swept through the wooden building.

All 62 Americans held at the prison, including Staff Sergeant Allan Hill, died that night.[57]

When American forces exhumed their charred remains after the war, a large number of the prisoners were found with fractured leg bones. It was never determined if their legs were broken before or after they died in the fire.[58] Allan Hill's remains were never identified.

In the video I discovered of their landing on Iwo Jima, you could clearly see Lieutenant Edwin Mockler hanging out of his cockpit window as they taxied past the Marine cameraman. You can imagine what it must have been like for the Mockler family to finally see that video of him 67 years after he died. The wreckage of their B-29 and the remains of Raymond Malo, Edwin Mockler and six others from their crew have never been found. They remain lost, but not forgotten, somewhere in the southern waters of Tokyo Bay to this day.

* * *

After 25 brutal days of combat, Admiral Nimitz declared Iwo Jima secured on March 16 and announced that organized Japanese resistance had ended. To the Marines still fighting against the fierce but shrinking pockets of Japanese on the northern part of the island, the declaration was met with disbelief. "If this dammed place has been secured," one Marine said upon hearing the news, "I wonder where in the hell all the Nip fire is coming from?"[59]

Later that evening, with thousands of his men dead and practically all of their supplies gone, an exhausted but still defiant General Kuribayashi sent his farewell message to the Imperial General Headquarters in Tokyo:

> The battle is entering its final chapter. Since the enemy's landing, the gallant fighting of the men under my command has been such that even the gods would weep. In particular, I humbly rejoice in the fact that they have continued to fight bravely though utterly empty-handed and ill-equipped against a land, sea, and air attack of a material superiority such as surpasses the imagination.
>
> One after another they are falling in the ceaseless and ferocious attacks of the enemy. For this reason, the situation has arisen whereby I must disappoint your expectations and yield this important place to the hands of the enemy. With humility and sincerity, I offer my repeated apologies.
>
> Our ammunition is gone and our water dried up. Now is the time for us all to make the final counterattack and fight gallantly, conscious of the Emperor's favor, not begrudging our efforts though they turn our bones to powder and pulverize our bodies.
>
> I believe that until this island is recaptured, the Emperor's domain will be eternally insecure. I therefore swear that even when I have become a ghost I shall look forward to turning the defeat of the Imperial Army into victory.
>
> I stand now at the beginning of the end. At the same time as revealing my inmost feelings, I pray earnestly for the unfailing victory and security of the Empire. Farewell for all eternity.[60]

As important as Iwo Jima was to Japan, the only support Kuribayashi received after the invasion came on the evening of the third day, when a Kamikaze strike launched from the mainland sank the aircraft carrier *Bismarck Sea* and damaged four other American ships in the waters off the island. The Japanese Navy also sent submarines to attack the Americans but were unsuccessful. For the remainder of the battle, the defenders of Iwo Jima were on their own. In the face of such overwhelming firepower, it was a testament to Kuribayashi's strategy and leadership that his men were able to hold out as long as they did. And they were not done fighting yet.

Ten days after Nimitz declared Iwo Jima secured, after waiting for the right moment, Kuribayashi gathered all the men he could muster for one final attack against the Americans. The 4th Marine Division had already left Iwo Jima by then, and the last elements of the 5th Division were due out the next day. The 3rd Marine Division and an Army infantry regiment were still mopping up, but Kuribayashi carefully planned his attack where it would cause the most damage. Under the cover of darkness, they would slip through the lines and strike the American encampments near the airfields that were packed with Army Air Force men who were not trained or equipped for ground fighting. (Ironically, the encampments were also home to the P-51 fighter pilots of the VII Fighter Command, who were only 12 days away from launching their first mission escorting the B-29s over Japan.)

Even though the battle was lost and any attack would be futile, for a Japanese soldier to surrender now would bring great shame upon himself and his family. To die in the final attack would be an "honorable death."

Just before dawn on March 26, Kuribayashi personally led some 400 of his men into battle. He wore no insignia on his uniform, and he carried nothing that could identify him. He would die as a common soldier. Kuribayashi's attack took the Americans completely by surprise. Without warning, the sleeping fighter pilots, mechanics and ground personnel were awakened by the crash of grenades and suddenly found themselves facing hordes of Japanese soldiers who had silently appeared out of the darkness. This was no insane Banzai charge, the American survivors later said, but a carefully planned and timed attack. Many men were caught asleep in their tents and never knew what hit them.[61]

As the Japanese swept through the encampments, they slashed open tents, tossed in grenades, and then charged in after the blast to finish off the occupants before moving on. The Americans fought back with any weapon they could find. One group of cooks only had kitchen utensils to defend themselves with. Others could only hide or play dead until the Japanese had passed. By the time it was over later that morning, Kuribayashi's attack had left a trail of death and destruction a mile long through the encampments before his men were finally wiped out. Lying inside and around the blood-splattered tents, 53 Americans were dead. Another 112 were wounded.[62]

What became of General Kuribayashi remains a mystery to this day. It was said that he was seriously wounded in his right thigh during the attack, but he pressed on with one of his men carrying him on their back. No one who saw his final moments lived to tell about it. On Iwo Jima, Kuribayashi had lived like his soldiers, and he died like his soldiers. His body was never found.[63]

The battle for Iwo Jima was officially over on March 26. In just 35 days, the vicious fighting had resulted in nearly 26,000 American casualties, including 6,821 dead. All in just 35 days.[64]

More Marines earned the Medal of Honor for actions on Iwo Jima than any other battle in American history. In all, 27 Medals of Honor were awarded for actions on Iwo Jima, 13 of them posthumously, and 22 were awarded to Marines. Seven of the Marines who received the Medal of Honor had dove on top of hand grenades to protect their buddies. Private First Class Jacklyn Lucas, who lied about his age and enlisted when he was only 14, miraculously survived after diving on two grenades and would become the youngest American to receive the Medal of Honor since the Civil War. Lucas was 17 years old.[65]

Of the approximately 22,000 Japanese soldiers entrenched on Iwo Jima when the invasion began, only 216 would be captured alive during the battle, and many of those were noncombatants from a Korean labor battalion. In the months that followed, the U.S. Army garrison that took over Iwo Jima captured 867 Japanese soldiers and killed another 1,602 during the final mopping up, but an untold number were still alive on the island and continued to be killed or captured over the next year.[66] The last two remaining Japanese soldiers finally surrendered in 1949, almost four years after the battle ended.

*   *   *

On March 14, 1945, Major General Graves B. Erskine said the following during the dedication of the 3rd Marine Division cemetery on Iwo Jima:

> There is nothing I can say which is wholly adequate to this occasion. Only the accumulated praise of time will pay proper tribute to our valiant dead. Long after those who lament

their immediate loss are themselves dead, these men will be mourned by the nation. They are the nation's loss.

There is talk of great history, of the greatest fight in our history, of unheard of sacrifice and unheard of courage. These phrases are correct, but they are prematurely employed. The evidence has not sufficiently been examined. Even the words and phrases used by historians to describe the fight for Iwo Jima, when the piecemeal story of our dead comes to light, will still be inadequate.

Victory was never in doubt. Its cost was … What was in doubt, in all our minds, was whether there would be any of us left to dedicate our cemetery at the end, or whether the last Marine would die knocking out the last Japanese gun and gunner.

Let the world count our crosses. Let them count them over and over … Let us do away with names, with ranks and rates and unit designations, here. Do away with the terms regular, reserve, veteran, boot, old timer, replacement. They are empty, categorizing words which belong only in the adjutant's dull vocabulary.

Here lie only Marines.[67]

The Fourth Marine Division cemetery on Iwo Jima, March 1945. The Marine laid to rest in the bottom left of the photo, Robert Steinhardt, was only 18 years old when he died on Iwo Jima. Four months later, Robert's older brother, Herbert Steinhardt, a 22-year-old fighter pilot, was Killed in Action in China. (80-G-412517 courtesy of the Naval History & Heritage Command)

Letters from Iwo Jima

While making my nightly search through eBay in the summer of 2011, I discovered one of the most incredible pieces of military history that I've ever seen. The auction I found that night was for a handwritten letter from the "Iwo Jima battlefield," but it turned out to be so much more.

I've always been interested in Iwo Jima and the battle that took place there, but I didn't really collect things from Iwo Jima. The focus of my collection had always been about the B-29ers and saving their history. I had a few things from Iwo Jima that I picked up over the years, mainly some souvenir paperweights that the Seabees had made by melting down the prop blades from the destroyed Japanese aircraft they found on the island, but that was about it.

Looking back on it now, I don't remember how I stumbled across that letter from Iwo Jima that night, but I knew right away that it was something special. And even though it wasn't something that I collected, I also knew that I had to save it. When the auction ended a few days later, I thought I had lost the letter for good when I was outbid at the last second. But then a funny thing happened. For some reason, the high bidder wasn't able to complete the purchase, so the seller, whose father wrote the letter, offered it to me for my original bid. I don't know if it was fate or fortune, but the letter was available again, and I was not going to lose it a second time.

A week later, a plain white envelope arrived in my mailbox. After carefully opening it, I was soon holding in my hands an extraordinary piece of history that was like nothing I had ever seen before – or since. And it only cost me $342.50.

The two-page letter I discovered on eBay was written on Iwo Jima five days after the invasion began by Lieutenant George W. "Bill" Haynes, a Marine who served in the same battalion that raised the first American flag on Mount Suribachi. Back home in Mississippi, his wife Dorothy knew that her husband was on Iwo Jima from the news reports about his division, and she also knew about the horrific casualties that the Marines were suffering as the battle unfolded. What she didn't know was whether her husband was alive. That's what this letter was for. This was the first letter that Lieutenant Haynes wrote home after he landed on Iwo Jima to let his wife and young son know that he was still alive.

As I held the letter in my hands for the first time, I tried to imagine what it must have been like when Haynes sat down to write it. What do you tell your wife after storming the beaches of Iwo Jima? What do you say after thousands of Marines have fallen around you? I tried to imagine what his wife must have thought when she read this letter, and the relief she must have felt in knowing that her husband was still alive when so many others were not. Try as I might, I couldn't imagine what any of this must have been like. Unless you were there, no one could ever imagine it.

After five days of brutal fighting and unspeakable horrors, this is what Lieutenant Haynes wrote home to his wife from Iwo Jima:

Iwo Jima
24 Feb., '45

Sweetheart –
I'm still alive by the Grace of God. I've had plenty of close ones as has everyone else who is still living. A sniper shot my binoculars off me, I got a little sliver of mortar shrapnel in my "seat," and have some grenade flash burns and fragments in my left hand. These are superficial, however, and I didn't have to go to the aid station with them, so don't worry. I'm okay except that I'm worn out – five days and nights under constant mortar, artillery and machine gun fire. I can't tell you in this letter how many men I've lost – but this thing has been pretty terrible. I guess you've heard the news broadcasts, tho.

We (2nd Bn, 28th) raised the first American flag over Japan. Iwo Jima is part of the Jap islands. It was all open beach where we landed, and you can't imagine what we went thru to get to the top of Suribachi Yama. We fought for 3 days, gaining in mere yards. The Nips had a system of caves, trenches, sniper pits etc. up on the mountainside that were really ingenious. Most of them are dead now. We've had one counter attack, but I believe they are under control. (One of them is lying about 20 feet from me, now, and things are beginning to stink.)

Naval gunfire and artillery helped a lot, but the only way to get the little bastards was to come up here with grenades, flamethrowers, etc. and burn 'em out. My machine gun platoon had an 8-hr. battle day before yesterday with a Japanese Nambu machine gun outfit. They knocked one of my guns out, but we finally annihilated them – I'm enclosing the insignia from the Lt. who was in charge of them. Give it to Bill. They held up our advance a long time.

Incidentally, Honey, I had a very happy 28th Birthday – we hit the beach under a hail of mortars and machine gun fire on Feb. 19th!

I have no paper – this is the back of a letter some Nip had on him. Hope you don't mind.

I can write only one letter – phone Mama. The battle isn't over, but I believe I'll make it okay, now. God has been good to us, Dot – Thank him for us.

I love you and Bill –
Bill[1]

Incredible. Just imagine what must have been going through his mind as he searched for the words to explain what he had just been through. I don't think any words could ever fully explain Iwo Jima. I don't think our language even has words for something so terrible. But for having been written right there on the battlefield during a break in the fighting, his short letter was the best account I'd ever seen of the first days of the battle.

I was also struck by the way Haynes described his wounds so dismissively and assured his wife that he was okay and not to worry. I think that's normal for all service members who find themselves in harm's way, but there was a lot more to the story behind those wounds than he let on. For his actions during which he was hit by those grenade fragments, Lieutenant Haynes would be awarded the Silver Star for valor. I later found a copy of his Silver Star Citation:

> When one of his men fell seriously wounded by a volley of fire from hostile snipers, First Lieutenant Haynes braved an enemy hand grenade barrage to move forward and evacuate the wounded man. Picking the casualty up bodily, he carried him to a safe position thirty yards to the rear and administered medical aid until a corpsman arrived. By his courage, initiative and inspiring action under hostile fire, First Lieutenant Haynes upheld the highest traditions of the United States Naval Service.[2]

When Admiral Nimitz declared Iwo Jima secured, he famously said of the men who fought and paid such a heavy price for the island: "Among the Americans who served on Iwo island, uncommon valor was a common virtue." Lieutenant Haynes exemplified the Americans who served on Iwo Jima.[3]

I was deeply honored to be the new caretaker of Haynes' first letter home from Iwo Jima, but that was only part of the story. There was another letter written on the back of his letter, but I couldn't decipher what it said. The letter was written in Japanese.

At some point during the battle, Haynes discovered a two-page letter while searching the body of a dead Japanese soldier, and he kept it as a souvenir. By the fifth day of the battle, with no other paper to be had, Haynes took that Japanese letter and wrote home to his wife on the back of it. I'd never seen anything like this before: letters from opposing soldiers written on the same pieces of paper, and from one of the greatest battles of all time. What an extraordinary piece of history.

As I looked over the Japanese letter and studied all of its intricately written characters, I was shocked to find "B-29" clearly written in the letter. I couldn't believe it at first, but there it was: B-29. I had to find out what this letter said.

Back when I began researching the loss of *Haley's Comet*, one of the first people I contacted was a researcher in Japan named Toru Fukubayashi. Mr. Fukubayashi had extensively researched all the B-29s that were lost over Japan during the war, and he was kind enough to send me a large file of documents from the U.S. Army's post-war investigation into the loss of *Haley's Comet*. It occurred to me one night that he might be just the right person to help me with the Iwo Jima letter, and it turned out I was right. He was very interested in the letter and offered to translate it for me. With the help of Mr. Fukubayashi and his friend, Ms. Yukako Ibuki, the contents of the Japanese letter from Iwo Jima was finally revealed after 70 years.

I'd read about Japanese soldiers on Iwo Jima who wrote final messages home to their families before the battle, but their letters could not be mailed once the island was cut off before the invasion. I wondered if that's what this letter could be? I even told Mr. Fukubayashi that I was hoping he would find a name in the letter that could help us get a copy of it to the soldier's family.[4]

But instead of a final goodbye, I was surprised to learn that the letter had actually been written to a soldier on Iwo Jima from an old army buddy in Japan. Based on the information in the letter, it was written about two weeks after *Tokyo Rose* appeared over Tokyo, before the first raid.

When I received the translation from Mr. Fukubayashi, I felt honored to be the first American to ever read this letter. But to be honest, I couldn't stop thinking about where it came from. I thought about that dead Japanese soldier Haynes mentioned in his letter, who was lying just 20 feet away as he wrote, and I wondered if there was a connection. I wondered about the smudges on the paper that looked like blood stains. Did this letter come from him?

This is what the Japanese letter from Iwo Jima said:

In reply to your letter:

We are in the middle of autumn, and it's getting a little cold in Japan. But I'm working in good health as usual, so please make your mind easy about that.

On hearing you are very well and are doing your best in your service, I'm glad and feel relieved. As you know, the enemy B-29s have made scouting flights three times over the Imperial Capital and once over the Kure area. We've certainly made up our minds to receive enemy attacks on Japan proper, and I want to say we have made impregnable preparations in case of emergency. So I'd like to cry out, "Those of you who are on the front line, rest your minds please!"

According to your previous letter, Kawachi, Irie and Hiroyasu are also there. I feel a bit nostalgic hearing their names, but they are not such intimate friends of mine. But when enlisted, we might feel better if there are such acquaintances in the unit.

Lt. Azuma is also there, you say, it might be the "Maboroshi Unit" again? In our days of the Independent Infantry in guard of northern Manchuria, we had some difficulties regarding the "illusion," but on the front line, I think it won't be of so much bother.

Although I can approximately imagine what you want to write, let's leave it here about me and I will do as I will.

I will let you know some recent news from Japan.

The other day, I made a business trip to Ishiyama in Ohmi. Fortunately, as the business finished unexpectedly early, I visited Ishiyama Temple and then Mii Temple. The weather was perfect, so everything was so good. (I'm afraid it sounds like poison for you who are on the front line, but please be patient.) Of course, I was alone.

I looked out over Lake Biwa from the garden of Mii Temple, thinking it was here that Lady Murasaki wrote the "Tale of Genji" in the ancient time. Then I suddenly remembered a scene of the [romance] movie "Aizen-Katsura." Ms. Sanae Takasugi and Mr. Saburi were looking at a motor boat on Lake Biwa from Mii Temple. It was just the same situation. But, I was alone.

Perhaps next Sunday, I hope to come back there with my future wife.

Well, this is just a joke. When I think of you or Keisuke, some changes have been born in my mind. I'd like you to think that I'm a little different man from what I used to be.[5]

I remember taking out the letters and just staring at them after I read the translation. My eyes slowly shifted back and forth between the two sides – American and Japanese. *American and Japanese.* I still couldn't get over the fact that something like this even exists: two letters from opposing soldiers written on the same pieces of paper. Think about what that means.

A small part of me wanted to celebrate for having found such a unique piece of history, but this wasn't something that I could celebrate. No, the humanity in me would not allow it. These two pieces of paper actually came from a Japanese soldier on Iwo Jima. He was carrying them when he died. His hands had once held what was now in my hands. It didn't seem real – but it was.

My thoughts drifted, and I wondered about that Japanese soldier and who he was. I wondered how important this letter must have been for him to carry it to his death. I wondered what he would think of me, an American, holding his letter 70 years later. I wondered how he died.

But none of my questions will ever be answered. The identity of the soldier will never be known because his name was not in the letter. While there were some clues about his unit, the letter could have been written to any of the 22,000 Japanese soldiers on the island. Maybe they would have wanted it that way.

As I continued looking back and forth at the letters, a great sorrow came over me. I just kept thinking how sad it was that this Japanese soldier would never know how our two countries, once bitter enemies, have since grown to become such strong and peaceful friends. I think that is what I was trying to understand as I stared at the letters from Iwo Jima. I wonder what they would think of us now.

* * *

The story of the letters from Iwo Jima did not end with the translation. There was another letter from Lieutenant Haynes that his son later sent me a copy of. The letter was to his sister back home and was written seven weeks after the letter you just read. The letter wasn't from Hawaii, though, where the 5th Marine Division returned after leaving Iwo Jima, but from Oakland, California.

Just six days after he wrote that first letter home to his wife, Haynes' life would be changed forever. This is what he wrote to his sister:

Ward 40-A
U.S. Naval Hospital
Oakland, California
April 18, 1945

Dear Mary Etta,
Guess by this time I've successfully come thru the "Valley of the Shadow." I absorbed two pieces of shrapnel and four bullets – still paralyzed, of course, but maybe the operation I'm going to have will help me! I'm suffering from severe pains in my legs and back which the Dr's say is caused by pinched nerves. The bullet that finally "downed" me went thru my liver, broke my back (3rd lumbar), fractured my pelvis, and came out the left side of the small of my back. But, I'm still here!

Arrived here in the states by plane from Pearl Harbor 4 days ago. Don't know how long I'll be here in Oakland. Write me when you can – give my regards to Bunk and my love to Mary Faith and Johnnie.
Love –
Bill[6]

Bill Haynes would spend the rest of his life confined to a wheelchair due to the wounds he suffered on Iwo Jima. That letter from the hospital, his son told me, was actually written for him by a nurse as he lay paralyzed from the waist down in excruciating pain. Despite everything he had been through, and the uncertainty of the future, it was clear in the letter that his spirit remained unbroken. He never gave up or stopped fighting.

What made his story even more remarkable is when I later learned that Haynes could have easily avoided fighting in the war altogether. Haynes had already served four years in the Marine Corps before the war and was discharged in 1939. When the war broke out, he was a captain in the Mississippi Highway Patrol, which was an essential job that exempted him from military service. If he wanted to, Haynes could have sat out the war and stayed home in Mississippi. But the United States was attacked, and Haynes saw it as his duty to fight for his country. He re-enlisted in the Marines as a private and was sent to Officer Candidate School, where he earned his commission.[7]

Haynes would never walk again after the horrific wounds he suffered, but he didn't let that stop him from achieving his dreams. After spending three-and-a-half years recovering in Navy hospitals, Haynes enrolled in law school. He went on to practice law in his hometown of Utica, and in 1966 he was appointed as a judge by the Governor of Mississippi.[8]

Haynes passed away in 1984 at the age of 67.

When I think about the sacrifices of men like Bill Haynes, and all of America's veterans from all the wars throughout our nation's history, I'm saddened that the sacrifices of so many are remembered by so few. Being remembered is exactly what led Haynes' son to put his Iwo Jima letter on eBay. He later told me that his children weren't interested in his father's things from the war, and he was trying to get them into the hands of people who would appreciate the history behind them. What a heartbreaking decision that must have been.[9]

Not long after I bought Haynes' letter, his son told me that he had also made the decision to sell his father's uniform and a few other small things, including that letter from the hospital. From the pictures he sent me, the uniform looked like it hadn't been touched since the end of the war. But there was something else in the pictures that deeply moved me the moment I saw it. Included with the uniform was the small bible that Lieutenant Haynes carried with him on Iwo Jima. It reminded me of the bible my uncle carried with him when he stormed Omaha Beach on D-Day.

I was struck by how the two bibles, carried by different men fighting different enemies thousands of miles apart, were so similar. You could tell from their appearance that both bibles had clearly been through a hell that none of us will ever understand, but they held together and survived, just like the men who carried them.

It was important that all of these things stayed together, so I tried to buy Haynes' uniform and bible, but someone else offered more money for them than I could. Iwo Jima militaria is highly sought after, and there was only so much that I could afford to spend. I offered his son $450.00. It was a fair offer, I thought. But it just wasn't enough. I wanted to offer more to ensure that I'd save everything, but I had just quit my job a month earlier and money was tight. The glory days of spending whatever it took to save these pieces of history were gone.

I don't know where his uniform and bible are today, but they're out there somewhere with another collector. Maybe one day I can reunite Haynes' uniform and bible with his letter and display them in his honor, but that's another dream.

In the decades after the war, I don't know if Haynes ever talked to a B-29er about Iwo Jima, but I did. I remember one B-29er in particular, a tail gunner, who I asked one day what Iwo Jima was like when he had to make an emergency landing there. I'll never forget his answer. Iwo Jima was not a pleasant place, he said, but he was sure glad it was there. Every B-29er who landed on Iwo Jima felt the same way.

In the weeks after Iwo Jima was captured, the XXI Bomber Command saw an immediate decrease in the number of B-29s that were being lost. In February, 3.2 percent of all the B-29s that took off on missions during the month were lost. The following month, when Iwo Jima became available for emergency landings, the loss rate plummeted to just 1.2 percent. This dramatic decrease in losses was attributed in part to the fact that 82 B-29s had made emergency landings on Iwo Jima in March alone.[10]

By the end of the war, 2,251 B-29s would make emergency landings on Iwo Jima. We'll never know how many of those B-29s could have made it back to the Marianas without landing, but when you do the math, Iwo Jima potentially saved the lives of *thousands* of B-29ers. They were all sure glad that island was there, and they never forgot what the Marines sacrificed for them.[11]

For some B-29ers, like Raymond Malo, Iwo Jima only prolonged the inevitable. But for many other B-29ers, like the one I talked to, Iwo Jima saved their lives. We can't ask him about it now, but to have helped save the lives of so many others, even though it came at such a great cost to himself, I think Bill Haynes was the type of man who would've deemed his sacrifice worth it.

I think they all would have been proud of the lives they saved.

After heavy flak knocked out two of their engines over Tokyo, severely damaging their bomber and wounding the right gunner, a thankful B-29 crew are all smiles after crash landing on Iwo Jima. (National Archives 204982049)

13

Japan's Invisible Ally

By January of 1945, it became painfully clear that the war was not going well for the XXI Bomber Command. As combat operations steadily increased, the B-29s continued to suffer unacceptable losses that were not due to the Japanese, and General Hansell had very little to show for it.

With the mechanical problems that had long plagued the bombers still persistent, it was not uncommon for 20 or more B-29s to abort during a single mission because of engine failures and other problems. Then, after fighting through the weather and mechanical problems to reach Japan, the crews were failing to hit their targets. The strike photos revealed a number of missions where only 7 percent or less of all the bombs dropped had fallen within 1,000 feet of the aiming point. For one mission in December, out of the 566 bombs that were dropped, only six actually hit the target. On other missions, the weather was so bad that no one knew where the bombs had fallen.[1]

In the two months since the first mission to Tokyo, 70 B-29s had been lost, and 419 men were dead or missing. The flak and fighter attacks left another 87 men wounded. The loss of so many lives for so little in return was made even harder to stomach by the fact that more B-29s had been lost due to mechanical failures, weather, human error and unknown causes, than by enemy action.[2]

Demoralized by the mounting losses and the poor bombing results, an alarming increase of "very subtle but significant psychological problems" began to develop among the combat crews. There were very few cases of individual breakdowns or hysteria, but what the flight surgeons did discover, and how quickly it was spreading among the men, was just as concerning. "A more mature but nonetheless ominous phenomena developed," stated one report. "A dull, dutiful 'flying of missions' set in with the quietness of an incipient epidemic. Most crews discerned their duty and set about performing it, technically, to the best of their ability, but with an emotional tone so hopeless and devoid of lustre that our operational efficiency could not but suffer."[3]

To add to the growing despair, before the capture of Iwo Jima, there was little hope of rescue for the crews that had to ditch in the 1,500 miles of ocean between the Marianas and Japan. Of all the B-29s that ditched in January, only 9 percent of the crew members were rescued. The cumulative effect of all these problems caused the crews to lose confidence in the B-29. With so many B-29s being lost due to mechanical failures, the crews were now beginning to fear their own airplanes and mission orders more than the Japanese.[4]

Back in Washington, General Arnold was growing more impatient by the day with the slow progress and demanded better results. After investing an unprecedented amount of money and resources into the B-29 program, the bombers were now in the best position to destroy Japan's war industries, but to Arnold's dismay, that wasn't happening. A big shakeup was coming for the 20th Air Force. With better bases now available in the Marianas, the 58th Bomb Wing would be leaving the China-Burma-India Theater in the coming months and moving to Tinian. The XX Bomber Command would then be absorbed into the XXI Bomber Command, and all five B-29 bomb wings would now be based in the Marianas on Saipan, Tinian and Guam.

General Arnold had also made another big decision that would have far-reaching consequences. On January 7, Brigadier General Lauris Norstad, the Chief of Staff of the 20th Air Force, traveled to Saipan and informed General Hansell that he was being relieved of his command. Hansell was blindsided by the news. As part of Arnold's reorganization, Hansell was offered the XX Bomber Command until it moved to the Marianas, where he would then become the Vice Commander of the XXI Bomber Command, but Hansell knew it wasn't a good idea to "replace a commander and leave him in a subordinate position in his own outfit," so he declined the job. Hansell later recalled:

> The XXIst had enormous potential. Given time to perfect its tactical performance and the growing might of the mounting accretions of new [bomb] wings, it held tremendous portent for the future ... Time, however, was not available to the XXIst Bomber Command. General Arnold was demanding measurable results – *now* ... In all fairness to General Arnold, he can not be blamed for his impatience ... He was under constant pressure and criticism from his associates on the Joint Chiefs of Staff and from higher authority to explain what his Twentieth Air Force was accomplishing.[5]

Arnold's demand for results had also cost General Wolfe his job at the XX Bomber Command three weeks after the first Yawata raid. The consummate gentleman that he was, Hansell felt that he should have been given more time to improve his operations, which amounted to only six weeks of combat missions to Japan, but he never showed any bitterness over Arnold's decision. Hansell returned home and was given command of a training wing, an assignment he requested and Arnold personally approved.[6]

Meanwhile, the pressure on Arnold from the President and the Joint Chiefs for the B-29s to get results was taking a toll. Ten days after Hansell was informed that he was being relieved, Arnold suffered his fourth serious heart attack in less than two years.[7] The man that Arnold selected to replace Hansell had also replaced Wolfe five months earlier, and had a reputation as a no-nonsense, tough-as-nails commander who solved problems and got results. If the B-29 was to live up to its potential, this was the commander who could do it. His name was Curtis E. LeMay.

LeMay also had another reputation, as one B-29er wrote upon hearing the news: "General LeMay has taken over the Bomber Command and he is going to get us all killed."[8]

With an ever-present cigar or pipe clenched in the right side of his mouth to conceal his facial paralysis caused by Bell's palsy, which left him with a scowling expression and fueled the rumors that he never smiled, LeMay was a formidable figure. After earning his pilot wings in 1929, LeMay began his long flying career in fighters before later moving on to bombers. In 1938, he was regarded as the best navigator in the Air Corps after two highly publicized flights that demonstrated the potential of land-based heavy bombers. LeMay was the lead navigator of six B-17s that flew 15 hours non-stop from Miami to Peru, a feat the Air Corps had never attempted before, and he also navigated a flight of three B-17s that successfully intercepted an Italian ocean liner 600 miles off the Atlantic coast that was broadcast live to millions of listeners by NBC radio.[9]

LeMay's reputation as a problem solver began in the early days of the war. Six months after Pearl Harbor was attacked, 35-year-old LeMay was given command of the new 305th Bomb Group and tasked with training the group for combat against the Germans. However, the bomb group had just been activated three months earlier and was desperately lacking in men, equipment and airplanes. LeMay would have to build an entire bomb group from scratch, and he only had a few short months to do it. Five months later, LeMay led his men on their first bombing mission to German-occupied France.

Prior to their first mission, LeMay was examining strike photos from earlier missions when he made a shocking discovery: most of the bombs being dropped were not hitting their targets. Even more disturbing was that no one knew where half of the bombs had fallen.[10]

The problem, LeMay discovered, was that no one believed they could fly a straight and level bomb run for more than 10 seconds without being shot down by German anti-aircraft fire. As a result, the bombers were taking evasive actions during the bomb runs and scattering their bombs all over the place. The German anti-aircraft gun that everyone dreaded was a fearsome 88mm cannon that could lob a 20-pound high-explosive shell well beyond 30,000 feet. The shells were fused to explode at predetermined altitudes and unleashed a deadly burst of shrapnel that appeared as thick black puffs of smoke when they exploded. LeMay studied the problem by working out a firing procedure for the German flak batteries and calculated how many rounds it would take to hit a target the size of a B-17 at 25,000 feet. Using an old artillery manual left over from his days in college, which he just happened to pack in his footlocker before he left for England, LeMay calculated that it would take 372 rounds to hit a B-17 flying straight and level at that altitude.[11]

LeMay was now confident that they could fly a straight bomb run for much longer than 10 seconds and survive, but that only solved half of the problem. The bombs also had to be dropped in a concentrated pattern that would saturate the target area, and the only way to do that was by flying the bombers together in a tight formation. LeMay's solution was to develop a new combat formation that not only provided a concentration of defensive fire against attacking fighters, but also the tightest concentration of bombs on the target.

When the 305th Bomb Group flew its first bombing mission, LeMay personally flew the lead B-17 at the head of the formation and led his group on a seven-minute bomb run straight in to the target. The results were spectacular. The 305th put more than twice the number of bombs on the target that day than any other bomb group, and none of his bombers were lost to flak. It was a revolution. The combat formation and other bombing procedures LeMay pioneered would go on to be adopted by the entire 8th Air Force.[12]

By the spring of 1944, at 37 years old, LeMay was the youngest two-star general in the entire U.S. Army, a rank he attained from a captain in just four years. LeMay's rapid promotions did not come from political connections or associations. He rose through the ranks by leading from the front and solving difficult problems. LeMay was a commander who got things done.

When LeMay arrived to take over the XX Bomber Command in India, and five months later the XXI Bomber Command in the Marianas, he found many of the same problems he had faced with the 305th Bomb Group. LeMay immediately began implementing new operating procedures that included a new combat box formation and other techniques to increase bombing accuracy, a new maintenance system, and more training for the crews. (Hansell had already begun implementing many of these changes when he was relieved.) But over a month after LeMay took over the XXI Bomber Command, not much had seemingly changed. Like Hansell before him, LeMay continued to wage a strategic bombing campaign against Japan with high-altitude daylight precision raids, exactly what the B-29 was designed to do, but the bombing campaign was failing.

The XXI Bomber Command had been assigned 11 high-priority targets to attack, but after three months of operations and over 2,000 sorties, not one of those targets had been destroyed. The B-29s were still not hitting their targets, losses in men and aircraft continued to rise, and crew morale was plummeting. The same pressure that had cost both Wolfe and Hansell their jobs was now building upon LeMay. Something had to change.[13]

Ironically, the best mission to date came on January 19, Hansell's last day of command. Bombing in clear weather, the B-29s heavily damaged the Kawasaki Aircraft factory at Akashi. All of the main buildings of both the engine and the aircraft plant were either damaged or destroyed, and 40 percent of the bombs fell within 1,000 feet of the aiming point.[14] The mission proved that high-altitude precision bombing could work, but the clear weather over the target was an anomaly. The most important target of all, the infamous Nakajima Musashino aircraft plant in Tokyo, better known to the B-29ers as Target 357, had remained virtually untouched after seven missions had been launched against the factory since November. The results were appalling: only 4 percent of the factory was damaged for the loss of 32 B-29s and 279 men.[15]

The major cause for the poor bombing was due to what some were calling Japan's invisible ally: the weather. A review of the weather over Japan since December revealed that there were only 15 days in the past three months that would have permitted visual bombing over Tokyo and Nagoya. In February alone, only 19 percent of all the B-29s over Japan had been able to actually see the targets they were bombing. Even during the best weather months over Japan, there might be seven clear days a month that would permit visual bombing, but based on the records LeMay reviewed, the average was more like just three or four days a month.[16]

The weather conditions were so bad that even Lieutenant General Millard Harmon, the overall commander of the Army Air Forces in the Pacific, publicly stated that the weather over Japan was the worst in the world, and that Tokyo was proving to be the most difficult precision bombing target of the war. (Harmon was later killed when his aircraft disappeared without a trace while en route to Hawaii from Kwajalein.)[17]

The B-29 was capable of bombing through the clouds using radar alone, but the capabilities of its radar were greatly diminished at high altitude, and together with the poor training that the radar observers received, the accuracy was abysmal. Lieutenant Raleigh Phelps, the bombardier of the B-29 *Thumper* piloted by Colonel "Pappy" Haynes, explained the difficulties of bombing Japan during an interview with *Brief* magazine in February of 1945:

> Weather over Japan isn't the kind of trouble for a B-29 that it would be for medium bombers. At our operating altitudes of 30,000 plus feet, we are above ordinary turbulence, in the clear air of the sub-stratosphere. But the extremely variable weather underneath us can play hell with visibility. Half a dozen different decks of clouds, at varying altitudes and

maybe moving in opposite directions, sweep across each other like camera shutters, and the target is alternately clear and obscured so that we may have to bomb by [radar] instrument.

It can change in a flash too. The lead plane may find the target wide open. The trailing planes may find it completely socked in by clouds. In addition, as you approach Japan at B-29 altitude, you encounter great westerly gales that whip with unbelievable force across the big islands from the mainland of Asia. They hit velocities of as much as 250 miles an hour, sometimes even higher. Bucking head winds in the approach, we have had ground speed as low as 60 miles an hour, even with the terrific power of our engines. One B-29 actually found itself flying backwards on one occasion.

It's a kind of Buck Rogers war at those altitudes and under those conditions. A temperature may be down to 60 below zero, and those terrific winds and heights, a bad weather condition underneath, a complicated plane to handle – and then flak all around and sometimes hordes of Jap fighters to make things really difficult. The speeds are amazing too, with those winds. If we fly downwind, we sometimes hit better than 500 miles an hour in level flight and you can see how much time a bombardier has for his computations. Why, we're 10 miles past our target before the bombs even hit it.[18]

(On April 1, 1945, Lieutenant Raleigh Phelps was flying with another crew as an observer when their B-29 crashed into the waters off Saipan and exploded just after takeoff, killing all on board. The B-29 they were flying was *Joltin' Josie, The Pacific Pioneer*, the first B-29 to arrive in the Marianas.)

The ferocious winds that Lieutenant Phelps described was a phenomenon that no one had encountered before during bombing operations over Europe. The B-29ers had unknowingly discovered the jet stream, a fast-flowing air current that can exceed 200 miles per hour, and no one knew how to deal with it. Trying to accurately bomb under these conditions proved to be next to impossible because the bombardiers and their revolutionary Norden bombsights simply could not compensate for such powerful and unpredictable winds. From the B-29's high operating altitude, the bombs were falling nearly six miles through multiple layers of weather that widely scattered them. "I can't think of a better way to describe the problem than to say it is like running full speed toward the eighteenth hole on a golf course and trying to drop a little white ball into the hole," recalled one B-29 pilot. "If you want to simulate battle conditions a little more realistically, let someone stand off with a shotgun and pelt you as you race by!"[19]

The severe winds encountered over Japan caused some peculiar incidents. Incredibly, some crews reported that their B-29s seemed to hover motionless in the air against the headwinds, while others said they began flying backwards. The weather had become such a problem that weathermen began flying missions to personally observe and report on the conditions over Japan. They also experienced the fierce winds firsthand, as reported by *Brief* magazine in the early months of 1945:

During three months of flying over the Empire, the weathermen encountered conditions they couldn't believe themselves. Most amazing phenomenon was the velocity of the westerly gales from Asia. With four great engines going full blast, turning out 8,800 horsepower, the big planes sailed steadily backwards on several occasions, like an 80-mile-an-hour plane in a 90-mile wind tunnel. Weathermen described that sensation as the eeriest they had ever experienced. Sometimes the Superforts would hang motionless for half an hour, like a seagull soaring into the wind.[20]

With the weather and other factors preventing the B-29s from hitting their targets, LeMay now found himself in the most difficult position of his career. When General Norstad informed him that he would be taking over the XXI Bomber Command, he warned LeMay that if he didn't get results with the B-29, he would be fired. Norstad added that if the B-29 didn't get results, it would eventually lead to a massive amphibious invasion of Japan that would probably cost half a million or more American lives.[21] The solution to getting around the weather and actually putting the bombs on the target, if there was a solution to be found, could dramatically affect the outcome of the war. The pressure on LeMay had never been greater.

(The same winds that were preventing the B-29s from hitting their targets would ironically be used by the Japanese to carry high-altitude balloon bombs thousands of miles across the Pacific to attack the American homeland. Loaded with incendiary and high-explosive bombs, the Japanese would launch over 9,000 of these balloon bombs that were intended to start massive forest fires and terrorize the Western United States. The balloon bombs were found as far inland as Michigan and failed to produce any sizeable fires, but five children and an expecting mother were killed when a bomb they discovered in the Oregon forest exploded as they examined it. As recently as 2019, these balloon bombs were still being found in the forests of North America.)

* * *

On February 16, the U.S. Navy launched its first carrier-based aircraft strikes against Japan. The raiders left a path of destruction across the Tokyo area and even damaged the Nakajima Musashino aircraft plant, the stubborn target that the B-29ers had been trying to knock out since November. After reading about the success of the raids, General Arnold vented his frustration in a private letter to his deputy, Lieutenant General Barney Giles, about the B-29's poor results and the ramifications. Arnold fumed: "I would not be surprised any day to see the control of the 20th Air Force pass either to Nimitz or MacArthur."[22]

By the end of February, after losing 33 B-29s and almost 300 men over the past five weeks, with little to show for it, it was clear to LeMay that he could not destroy his targets by using the same strategy based on his experience in Europe. That was a different war with different weather, and high-altitude precision bombing had proven to be nearly impossible over Japan. Over 200 of his B-29s had also been damaged by flak and fighter attacks during those five weeks alone, some so severely that they had to be scrapped.[23]

If the B-29 was to succeed in its mission, LeMay would have to make some drastic changes in the way he was using the bombers. Back in 1942, before the 305th Bomb Group's first mission, LeMay had studied the earlier strike photos to get a clear understanding of how well the American bombing campaign was working. Two years later, LeMay once again found himself staying up late at night and studying all the photos they had of every target in Japan. He also poured over the intelligence reports on Japanese anti-aircraft defenses around the targets.

LeMay soon realized that something was missing in all the photos and reports he was looking at. In Europe, the Germans defended their war industries with a combination of anti-aircraft guns that included smaller guns for low-level attacks and larger cannons for high-altitude bombers. But in Japan, LeMay did not see any of the low-level guns around the targets.[24]

LeMay knew that if you went over a German target in a bomber at low altitude, you'd be cut to pieces. But over Japan, with no significant low-level defenses, their large anti-aircraft guns that were lobbing shells up past 30,000 feet would be rendered impotent. The bombers would be moving too fast for the flak gunners to coordinate their fire.[25]

A radical idea was beginning to form. If he sent the B-29s in low at night, well below the ferocious winds and clouds that blanketed the targets, the bombing accuracy would dramatically improve, and he wouldn't have to wait for favorable weather before launching a mission. A low-level attack would also eliminate the long climb to high altitude, which was putting a tremendous strain on the B-29's engines and causing failures, and the fuel that would be saved meant the B-29s could carry more bombs. There would also be no need to assemble the bombers in formations, which consumed extra fuel. Instead, the B-29s could attack their targets individually in a long bomber stream under the cover of darkness.

It was a radical departure from the bombing techniques that LeMay himself had pioneered over Europe, but this was the answer he was looking for. The Japanese would never expect the B-29s to come in low at night. All LeMay needed now was a target to test his idea. That choice was easy, as one report stated:

> Tokyo, one of the world's three largest cities with a population of 7,000,000 (1940 population figure), is the hub of Japanese industry and commerce. With the exception of heavy industry, the city has substantial portions of almost every Japanese business enterprise. Concentrations of such key war industries as machines and machine tools, electronics, precision instruments, petroleum, and aircraft and aircraft parts are within the city limits. Tokyo is also a vital transportation and communications center and the terminus of a majority of the main railroads on the island of Honshu. In addition, it is the administrative seat of government and of the great industrial concerns which comprise Japan's war machine.[26]

With hundreds of identified targets within the city limits, ranging from aircraft and engine factories to the Nippon Typewriter Company, which was now making gun parts, Tokyo was overflowing with war production. In addition to large industries, there were also more than 15,000 small factories with five or more employees in Tokyo alone. But what couldn't be identified from the reconnaissance photos were the thousands of tiny "household industries" spread throughout the city that supplied the larger factories with parts. An intelligence report described these household industries as "thousands of little shops often located in a front or back room of individual residences, or small 'factories' consisting of hardly more than a couple of lathes operated by a few people." Japan's war industry was heavily dependent upon these small subcontractors and their supply of parts, which were used in the assembly of everything from rifles to airplanes. In effect, Tokyo had been transformed into one giant war factory.[27]

How to destroy thousands of factories that were spread out over such a wide area was the next problem LeMay had to solve. Sending the B-29s in low below the weather would ensure they hit their targets, but the key to LeMay's plan would be the type of bomb they would be dropping.

From the outside, the M-69 was an innocent-looking sheet metal pipe that was only 19 inches long and weighed 6½ pounds. The bomb was so simple to manufacture that it was now being made in factories that used to make bed springs and wallpaper before the war. It looked more like a rainspout from someone's house than one of the most destructive bombs in history. Packed inside the hexagon-shaped pipe was a sticky substance that looked like raspberry jelly, but it smelled unmistakably like gasoline. Created by mixing a thickening agent with ordinary gasoline, the deadly concoction was called "gel gas," but it was better known as napalm.

The way the bomb worked was ingenious. When an M-69 hit the ground, a three to five second delay fuse was activated, and then an explosive charge blasted fiery globs of napalm up to 100 feet away. What made the bomb so effective was that it was designed to penetrate factory roofs, fall on its side, and then eject the napalm horizontally. The napalm splattered on everything in its path and instantly produced a searing mass of flames six to eight feet high. If you poured it on the ground, each M-69 contained enough napalm to form a flaming puddle three feet across.[28]

The target area LeMay selected was 11 square miles in size and was the most heavily built-up section of Tokyo's sprawling urban-industrial area. With an average population of 103,000 people per square mile, it was one of the most densely populated areas in the world. An estimated 1.1 million people lived in the target area, and most of them worked in the household industries or the surrounding factories. After the 1923 earthquake and fires that devastated Tokyo, many temporary wooden barracks were built to house the homeless. By 1945, in what was now the target area, a large number of these temporary structures had "degenerated into highly congested slum areas" and were never rebuilt as the city had planned.[29] Sergeant Knox Burger later described the target area for *Yank* magazine:

> The slum was a mass firetrap of flimsy frame houses and shops which housed a big percentage of the population in Tokyo. The streets through the area ranged from broad avenues to shoulder-width lanes winding between jam-packed houses. Several large factories turned out parachutes and airplane parts, but the real economic strength of the area lay in the thousands of domestic industries that had sprung up with war. Not many of the householders had refrigerators or electric stoves – drill presses were installed instead. And a lathe had come to be a common back-room fixture.[30]

It was no secret that Japan's cities were highly susceptible to fire. The U.S. Army had previously conducted tests in which four Japanese-style dwellings were constructed: two in the typical fashion found in the target area, and two that complied with the latest Tokyo fire regulations. When the test buildings were set on fire, the typical dwellings that made up about 95 percent of all the structures in the target area burned to the ground in only 12 minutes.[31]

At the behest of Arnold and Norstad, the XXI Bomber Command had already launched several incendiary raids, beginning under Hansell, to further test the vulnerability of Japan's cities to fire. All of these missions were flown at high altitude and had disappointing results. Hansell launched the first night incendiary raid against Tokyo's industrial area back in November, dropping nearly 65 tons of incendiaries, but the results were unobserved due to the weather. Hansell had also been dropping a combination of high-explosive and incendiary bombs on the majority of the missions he launched before he was relieved, including the first raid on Tokyo.[32]

As disappointing as the previous incendiary raids were, the February 25 mission did show promise. Bombing from as high as 31,000 feet through a solid overcast, the M-69s were widely scattered by the winds over Tokyo and failed to saturate the target area, but when added all together, the numerous fires that burned across Tokyo destroyed a combined one square mile of the city. The results of the mission reaffirmed LeMay's conclusion that sending the B-29s in low at night would not only guarantee a tight concentration of M-69s to saturate the target area, but the resulting fires would merge into a massive conflagration that would quickly overwhelm Tokyo's firefighting capabilities.[33] Under the right conditions, driven by high winds and low humidity, the fires would be unstoppable.

LeMay realized that this attack could devastate Tokyo's war industries and maybe even shorten the war, but he also knew that the fires would undoubtedly kill a lot of Japanese civilians, and that raised a moral question about the type of bombing he was planning. When he first unveiled his plans to a small group of his officers, LeMay made it clear that his change in tactics was not intended to be terror bombing, and he did not look upon Japanese civilians as targets. However, since the Japanese had dispersed their war industries throughout the urban areas of their cities, there was simply no other way to knock out those industries.

"The President and General Arnold want results now," LeMay said during the meeting, alluding to the pressure he was under. "I was sent here to win the war in the air without an invasion."[34]

LeMay went on to explain that he wasn't giving up on high-altitude precision bombing, but since the weather conditions were predicted to remain unfavorable for the foreseeable future, he concluded that they had no choice but to change tactics. If the weather was clear, they would still fly daylight precision missions, but until then, they had to try something new.

"Aren't firebomb attacks on cities the type of terror bombing used by the RAF that our air force has been trying to avoid?" an intelligence officer asked.[35]

The officer was referring to the Royal Air Force's recent incendiary attack on Dresden, Germany, that devastated the city and killed some 25,000 people (German propaganda initially claimed 200,000 were killed in the attack). The high number of civilian casualties led many, including Winston Churchill himself, to question the "area bombing" of German cities at that stage in the war, which some in the press were decrying as terror bombing.[36]

"I know there may be some who will call it uncivilized warfare, but you simply can't fight a war without some civilian casualties," LeMay responded. "We didn't start this war, but the quicker we finish it, the more lives we will save – and not just American. We want to avoid killing civilians if possible, but keep in mind that the Japanese workers who manufacture weapons are part and parcel of their military machine. My first duty is to protect and save as many of our crews as possible."[37] Looking around the room, LeMay added: "I'm sure General Arnold will permit us to burn all of Tokyo if that's what it takes to win the war. The reality is that the only way we can destroy Japan's military targets is to burn down every city that has military targets."[38]

By the end of the meeting, LeMay's staff officers were still divided over his plans for a low-level attack. Some thought it was suicide. Others believed they could pull it off, especially with the element of surprise, but almost everyone felt some level of uncertainty. LeMay had studied the problem from every angle and weighed the risks, including the fact that his own flak experts warned that he would lose 70 percent of his B-29s by going in so low over Tokyo, and then he made the decision that only he could make.[39] The mission would proceed.

As the planning for the raid continued, to ensure his bombardiers hit their targets, LeMay would direct each Bomb Wing to send a squadron of Pathfinder B-29s ahead of the main force to mark the target area with 100-pound napalm bombs. The Pathfinders would drop their bombs to form a giant flaming "X" on the target area, with each corner marking one of the four aiming points.[40] The number of B-29s assigned to each of the aiming points ensured that no less than 60 tons of incendiaries would rain down upon each square mile of the target area.

Following behind the Pathfinders, the bombardiers were simply instructed to drop their bombs on the "dark spots" where no fires were burning yet. They couldn't miss.[41]

*   *   *

LeMay's plan was such a radical departure from American bombing doctrine that he decided not to seek General Arnold's approval beforehand. The field order for the mission, code-named *Meetinghouse 2*, was sent to Washington only a day before the B-29s would begin taking off, which effectively precluded a response or intervention from Arnold, who was still recovering from his fourth heart attack.[42] LeMay's reasoning for this reflected his character as a commander. If the mission was a disaster, and Arnold had approved it, Arnold would share in the blame for its failure, and the entire B-29 program and the 20th Air Force would be in jeopardy. But by not informing his boss, Arnold would be insulated from any accountability, LeMay could be fired, and Arnold would "still have a chance to make something" out of the B-29s.[43]

The responsibility for the mission, and the accountability, would rest solely on LeMay.

On the morning of March 9, General Norstad arrived on Guam to assess how operations were progressing under LeMay. Like Arnold, he also didn't know what LeMay was planning until he arrived on the day of the mission. Norstad was enthusiastic when he was briefed about the mission and alerted the 20th Air Force's public relations staff to be prepared for "what may be an outstanding strike," but as LeMay recalled after the war, it was his neck on the line if the mission was a disaster, not Norstad's.[44]

Later that morning, after a week of practice missions with an emphasis on radar bombing and another mission to the Nakajima Musashino aircraft plant (which couldn't be bombed because the weather was so bad), the combat crews all gathered in the briefing rooms at their bases. Rumors had been circulating for days that something big was in the works. On Guam, Brigadier General Thomas Power, the 314th Bomb Wing commander who would be leading the mission, began the briefing. A sea of young and anxious faces clung to his every word.

"We're making some tactical changes on this mission, gentlemen," the general announced. "Our three wings from Saipan, Tinian, and Guam are going to put 300 planes over Tokyo at night. This will be the largest B-29 mission of the war."[45]

Then General Power dropped a bombshell: the bombing altitudes would range from 5,000 to 8,000 feet. No one could believe what they were hearing.

"5,000 feet, you have to be kidding!" a voice in the back called out. Thoughts of the disastrous 1943 low-level attack on the Ploesti oil refineries in Romania, in which 54 B-24 bombers were lost, filled everyone's minds. "It's suicide," said another.

LeMay sat quietly puffing on his pipe, showing no emotion.

"I would not lead this mission and we would not be sending you if we thought it was an unreasonable risk," Power said. "General LeMay has had more combat experience in heavy bombers against both the Germans and the Japanese than anyone in the air force. His losses on missions are the lowest of any combat commander. We've lost more crews from engine and mechanical failure than from Japanese opposition."[46]

Power went on to explain the reasoning behind the dramatic change in tactics, and then he informed his men what was at stake: "This is the most important mission of the war. Success will mean that our troops may not have to invade Japan. I know you all have the guts to make this mission a success."[47] Power then turned to LeMay, who was still sitting quietly with his pipe, and asked if he wanted to add any comments.

"No," LeMay said, shaking his head, "you have said it all much better than I could."[48]

While the combat crews were in their briefings, out on the hardstands, the ground crews were busy bombing up the B-29s with incendiaries and making their final preparations. The M-69 incendiary bombs came preloaded in large 500-pound clusters that contained 38 individual bombs that were fused to separate in the air and shower the target with bombs. With all the weight saved by not needing the extra fuel to climb to high altitude, the B-29s could be loaded with up to 40 clusters apiece, for a total of 1,520 M-69 bombs. By dropping a cluster every 50 feet, a single B-29 could sow thousands of fires over a path 300 feet wide and up to 2,000 feet long, nearly 14 acres in size. For the coming raid, LeMay would be sending 325 B-29s over Tokyo.[49]

Later that evening, in Japan, Major General Shutsu Matsumura delivered a radio address to the nation in celebration of Army Day. Matsumura's assessment of the war was unusually candid:

> Since late last year the enemy air raids have become severe. I expect that the raids will be intensified more than ever as the war situation progresses. I cannot but be indignant over the enemy's blind bombings of harmless Japanese people ... Should the brutal Americans think that severe air raids would break the fighting spirit of the Japanese people, then this would be a fool's dream.
>
> The war situation has developed so much that we may anticipate a decisive battle to be waged upon the mainland of Japan. Should, however, the enemy invade the Japanese mainland, all the officers and men of the fighting forces will turn into a mass of bullets against the enemy attack and into a massive citadel of defense. The true value of the Imperial forces under the command of the great sovereign will then be displayed. The indignation of the 100 million people who firmly maintain the prestige of the fundamental character of the people of Japan is so great that we Japanese fully believe in victory.
>
> We must make America realize that Japan cannot be invaded under any circumstances. However frequently the enemy may come to Japan, this country will smash the invader each time. We are determined to fight longer than the enemy. We fight on to the last. I believe the highest peak of war morale is to fight the enemy with the conviction of sure victory.[50]

A great armada was nearing Tokyo as its residents listened to General Matsumura. Bloated with tons of incendiaries, it had taken almost three hours for all of the B-29s to take off from their bases in the Marianas. As the bombers closed in on Japan, the crews picked up a Japanese radio station playing American songs like "Smoke Gets in your Eyes," "My Old Flame" and "When Strangers Meet." An English-speaking announcer was also heard to say: "When you play with fire you are liable to get burned." The crews nervously chuckled.[51]

During his radio address, General Matsumura told the Japanese people that the "darkest hour came just before the dawn." As the first Pathfinders crossed over the coast of Japan, the darkest hour was now upon them.[52]

14

The Night Tokyo Died

A strong wind had been blowing all day across Tokyo as Funato Kazuyo, a 6th grade student, slept peacefully in her bed. Funato was from a large family, with three older brothers, two younger sisters and a baby brother. The war had scattered her family, but by chance, they were all together in Tokyo that night when the B-29s came.

"When mother woke me, all was in a terrible uproar," Funato recalled, as the first B-29s roared over the city, "great loud noises everywhere." As Funato's father, a medical volunteer, rushed to his post at a nearby school when the bombs started falling, Funato's mother quickly moved her and her younger sister and baby brother into the shelter dug beneath her father's shop. Meanwhile, her three older brothers ran to help fight the fires that were flaring up nearby. Funato's youngest sister, Teruko, was staying at her grandmother's house that night, but no one knew if they were safe. All Funato's mother could do now was comfort her children and wait for the raid to pass.[1]

Locked in a small cage inside a filthy old horse stable at the Kempeitai prison in downtown Tokyo, just a stone's throw away from the Emperor's Palace, 23-year-old Lieutenant Raymond "Hap" Halloran was suddenly awakened by people screaming. Hap was a B-29 navigator and had spent the last six weeks subjected to brutal beatings and interrogations after he was shot down on January 27. As he woke, Hap heard the unmistakable roar of airplanes flying overhead. "I couldn't imagine what the hell was happening," Hap recalled. "At first I thought the planes were Japanese, but soon I realized it was our B-29s, because I could see the orange glow of a fire in the distance."[2]

Following the 100-pound napalm bombs dropped by the Pathfinders to mark the target area, thousands of smaller M-69 bombs were now beginning to rain down on Tokyo as the main force moved in. As the clusters separated between 2,000 and 2,500 feet above the ground, scattering their deadly payload of M-69s across the sky, a three-foot-long cloth streamer unfurled from the tail of the bombs to slow and stabilize their descent. Watching from the ground, you could clearly see the bombs descending to earth as the fires lit up the sky. "They did not fall; they descended rather slowly, like a cascade of silvery water," recalled Lars Tillitse, a Danish diplomat living in Tokyo. "One single bomb covered quite a big area, and what they covered they devoured."[3]

One of the first B-29s over the target area was flown by Colonel "Pappy" Haynes. Major Manila Shaver, an intelligence officer flying on board as an observer, later recounted:

We arrived over the target a little ahead of schedule, but already some planes had set their fires and I could see whole blocks aflame. I saw the Jap searchlights ahead dip low at first, as if they were looking for low-flying Navy fighters. Then they swung up and caught us squarely. Colonel Haynes flew our plane into a 10,000-foot column of smoke, which screened us from the lights and any flak.

Coming out on the windward side, we went into our bomb run at more than 250 miles per hour. The glare from the searchlights was blinding and made it almost impossible to see flak bursts. We were bounced around crazily in updrafts from the flames below. I can remember saying the little prayer I always repeat over a target: "Please, let us get these bombs out before we're hit, if we're going to be hit." The instant we dropped our load, we were hit in the belly by flak and I added a little postscript: "Please, God, did you have to make it that close?" I found out later that we had been hit in the wing and tail, too.

Tokyo below now looked like all the open hearths in Pittsburgh. The searchlights were still tracking us. As we passed out of range, the light on us would blink once, and then a new battery would pick us up. We saw one fighter that fired some tracers under us, and as we passed over Chiba peninsula, we drew some automatic fire. Then we headed out to sea and home.[4]

From his rooftop lookout post at the Sophia Catholic University in Tokyo, Father Gustav Bitter was taken by the sight of the M-69s as they fell to earth. "It was like a silver curtain falling, like the *lametta*, the silver tinsel that we hung from Christmas trees in Germany so long ago," Father Bitter recalled. "And where these silver streamers would touch the earth, red fires would spring up."[5]

Father Bitter was a former German soldier who fought in the First World War and had entered the priesthood after spending two years in a Prisoner of War camp in England. As head of the school's civil defenses, Father Bitter was at his rooftop post during all of the previous B-29 raids, which most Japanese considered to be more of a "nuisance" than anything else, and he had also witnessed the Doolittle raid back in 1942. What was unfolding before him now was like nothing he had ever seen before. As the sky filled with B-29s, Father Bitter watched as the red and yellow flames reflected on the "silvery undersides" of the bombers, making them appear like "giant dragonflies with jeweled wings against the upper darkness" as they swept low over Tokyo and unleashed a rain of fire upon the city. Father Bitter later remembered:

In about 40 minutes the city is an ocean of flames. We are also hit by about 90 bombs. Several buildings are on fire. Quick action extinguishes most fires, only one school building is hopelessly ablaze, cannot be saved. Our whole neighborhood is on fire. B-29s swoop down and on the wings of these silvery ghosts we see ghastly reflections of the fire. The air is unbearably hot, a gale of firesparks sweeps over the city. The skin burns and the eyes get sore. It is an "*infernum*" (hell) like that which Dante so masterly describes in his *Divina Commedia*.[6]

Standing in the garden behind his house on the south side of Tokyo, miles away from the target area, French journalist Robert Guillain watched as the B-29s set to work "sowing the sky with fire," and a "huge borealis" grew over the target area as the fire began to "scythe its way through" the wooden city. Guillain wrote after the war:

The bright light dispelled the night and B-29s were visible here and there in the sky ...
Their long, glinting wings, sharp as blades, could be seen through the oblique columns
of smoke rising from the city, suddenly reflecting the fire from the furnace below, black
silhouettes gliding through the fiery sky to reappear farther on, shining golden against the
dark roof of heaven or glittering blue, like meteors, in the searchlight beams spraying the
vault from horizon to horizon ... All of the Japanese in the gardens near mine were out of
doors or peering up out of their [shelter] holes, uttering cries of admiration – this was typically Japanese – at this grandiose, almost theatrical spectacle.[7]

Back on Guam, the XXI Bomber Command's Public Information Officer, St. Clair McKelway,
walked into the operations center around 2:00 a.m. to await the first strike reports. Aside from
a small number of men on duty, the principal staff officers were all asleep in their quarters, but
there was LeMay, sitting by himself on a wooden bench, smoking a cigar. (LeMay wanted to
lead the mission himself, but he was forbidden from flying over enemy territory because he had
been briefed about the atomic bomb project.)[8]

LeMay cracked a smile when he saw McKelway and admitted that he was sweating out the
raid. "A lot could go wrong," LeMay said. "I can't sleep. I usually can, but not tonight."

McKelway sat down next to LeMay, and the two began chatting. LeMay had a reputation for
being a stern man of few words, but tonight he was unusually talkative. "I never think anything
is going to work until I've seen the pictures after the raid," LeMay said, "but if this one works
we will shorten this damned war out here."

Glancing down at his watch, LeMay concluded that they wouldn't get the first strike reports
for another half hour, and he asked McKelway if he'd like to have a Coca-Cola. "I can sneak in
my quarters without waking up the other guys and get two Coca-Colas and we can drink them
in my car," LeMay said. "That'll kill most of the half hour."[9]

After driving the short distance to his quarters, LeMay returned to his car with the cokes.
Handing one to McKelway, they sipped their drinks in the dark, overlooking the jungle, and
then for some reason LeMay started talking about India, where McKelway had also been
stationed. "The way all those people are in India gets you down," LeMay said, recalling the
extreme poverty he saw there. "It makes you feel rotten."

Unlike other generals, McKelway later recalled that he didn't feel the "presence of rank"
with LeMay as they talked. What he felt instead was the presence of a "good young guy doing
a stupendous job, feeling the right things, keeping his head, and wanting to get the war over
with."[10]

When they drove back to the operations center a half hour later, the first strike report was
just coming in: "Bombing the primary target visually. Large fires observed. Flak moderate.
Fighter opposition nil."[11] Then more messages began streaming in. They all reported a massive
conflagration. Tokyo was burning.

Hunkered together in the bomb shelter under her father's shop with her mother and two
siblings, the fires were now completely out of control when Funato Kazuyo's oldest brother
rushed into the shelter and told them to run to a nearby school before the flames cut off their
escape route. "The drone of the planes was an overwhelming roar, shaking earth and sky," Funato
recalled, when she emerged from the shelter. "Everywhere, incendiary bombs were falling."[12]

The sky was glowing bright red as Funato ran with her mother, little sister and baby brother.
When they finally reached the shelters behind the school, they realized they were nothing

more than open trenches dug in the ground. With nowhere else to go, Funato's mother led her children into a trench and waited for the rest of her family. As more B-29s thundered overhead, suddenly bombs began crashing down near the school, blasting flaming globs of napalm in all directions.

"We're all going to die!" someone screamed in terror, as a wall of flames bore down on the school. "If we stay here we'll die!" someone else yelled. "Let's run!"

With her baby son slung on her back, Funato's mother gathered her children and followed the others as they ran away from the school. "The sound of incendiary bombs falling, '*Whizzz*,' the deafening reverberations of the planes, and the great roar of fire and wind overwhelmed us," Funato recalled.[13] Outside the school, they found her father and three brothers, who were coming back to get them. Holding hands, the family rushed to a nearby park, where they thought they'd be safe, but the park was already jammed full of people and they couldn't get in. Their only hope now was to backtrack through the fire and try to make it to nearby Sunamachi, which had been bombed a few weeks earlier and had many vacant lots that wouldn't burn.

Funato's family made it as far as the Shinkai Bridge.

"The wind and flames became terrific," Funato said. "We were in Hell. All the houses were burning, debris raining down on us." As they fought their way through the fire, a sudden gust of wind swept Funato's mother off her feet. She rolled away and disappeared into the flames and black smoke with her baby still on her back. Funato's father and brother jumped after her. They also disappeared.[14]

With the fire closing in around them, Funato and her siblings all crouched together at the foot of the bridge. Her two brothers looked around for an escape, but they were completely surrounded by flames. Then off to the side of the road, just barely visible through the fire, they spotted a ditch that had been dug for shelter. As the four of them dashed through the flames to reach the ditch, the cotton hood that Funato's little sister was wearing caught on fire.

Tumbling into the ditch, they frantically tried to remove Hiroko's hood, but it was tied tightly over her head. Hiroko tried to pull it off herself, burning her hands. Finally, they tore it off and beat out the flames. Outside the ditch, everything was burning around them as the four lay together on their stomachs. Suddenly, Funato's oldest brother screamed and leapt out of the ditch with his back on fire. Her other brother jumped up and yelled for him, only to be swept away by the wind.

Funato and her little sister were all alone now. Hiroko's hands were badly burned, and she was screaming in agony. As firebrands rained down upon them, and the air became hotter and hotter, Funato was overcome with fear and thought about making a run for it with her sister, which would have been certain death. But then another young girl crawled up to them. She was also separated from her family, she said, as she slid her body over Hiroko to help protect her.

Surrounded by fire with no way to escape, the three little girls huddled together in the bottom of the ditch. Hiroko cried for water for her hands, but there was no water to give her. In desperation, Funato dug a small hole in the bottom of the ditch and placed her sister's hands in it. The dirt was cool and made her hands feel better.[15]

While the three girls clung to each other in the ditch, the streets of Tokyo had become "rivers of fire," as Ishikawa Koyo, a police cameraman, recalled: "Everywhere one could see flaming pieces of furniture exploding in the heat, while the people themselves blazed like matchsticks … Under the wind and the gigantic breath of the fire, immense incandescent vortices rose in a number of places, swirling, flattening, sucking whole blocks of houses into their maelstrom of fire."[16]

At 7,500 feet over Tokyo, Lieutenant Colonel Robert Morgan was trying to keep *Dauntless Dotty* straight and level in the turbulent air as he began his bomb run, but it was hard to stay focused. The images he saw, Morgan later said, were things that "few human beings who ever lived would witness." As hundreds of searchlights swept madly across the smoke-filled skies, appearing like some sort of a "hellish Hollywood premiere night," and anti-aircraft shells burst like fireworks above them, Morgan could clearly see other B-29s around him silhouetted against the fires raging below. Flying through the smoke, large pieces of flaming debris, lifted skyward by the powerful heat thermals from the fires, floated past the bomber as Morgan closed in on the target.[17]

Inside *Dauntless Dotty*, those same updrafts that were buffeting the bomber also brought with them a smell that no one would forget that night. It was the smell of burning flesh. The horrific stench caused some crews to gag and vomit, and a few men even passed out.[18]

Looking out from the cockpit, Morgan could see the Emperor's Palace illuminated by the nearby flames, but otherwise untouched. The crews had been instructed not to bomb it. *Dauntless Dotty* continued on the bomb run, shuddering through the violent turbulence and engulfed in smoke, as Morgan fought to hold her on course. Finally, the bombardier shouted "bombs away!" as seven tons of incendiaries dropped from the cavernous bomb bay. Having delivered his bombs on his 45th combat mission of the war, Morgan turned *Dauntless Dotty* around, passing the snow-capped Mount Fuji glowing in the night, and headed for Saipan.[19]

Down below, 27-year-old Hisashi Tsukakoshi was desperately trying to reach the safety of a firebreak a few blocks away from his home. "The whole city seemed to be on fire," Tsukakoshi recalled. "I was nearly overwhelmed with the heat, the screaming noise, the burning, shocking flames."[20] As he fought his way through the blazing streets, Tsukakoshi was hit by ferocious blasts of heat and wind that knocked him from his feet. Again and again, Tsukakoshi pulled himself up and staggered forward until another blast knocked him back down. Bodies were strewn all around him. Some were still alive, but unable to move against the winds. Others were already dead, burning in the street. Tsukakoshi pushed forward through the firestorm. "Burning debris showered all over me, the embers and sparks sticking mercilessly to my clothing," he said. "Several times my clothes flared up in a blaze, and I had to stop to beat out the fires."[21]

By the time Tsukakoshi made it to within a block of the firebreak, he nearly collapsed and didn't think he could go on. Clinging to a telephone pole to hold himself up, he desperately gasped for breath, but was left choking by the scorching air that painfully stung his throat and lungs. Everywhere he looked, furious cyclones of fire whirled about, consuming everything they touched. The houses all around him were ablaze. With the "roar of an avalanche," one after another, the houses came crashing down as the fire devoured them.

Tsukakoshi thought he was about to die. He could see his skin start to blister, but strangely, he felt no pain. At least he would die quietly without any thrashing about, he thought to himself.

Suddenly, an elderly man dashed out of a nearby house that had erupted in flames. He ran towards Tsukakoshi for help, but then he stumbled and collapsed a few feet away. The old man tried to pick himself up, but he didn't have the strength and fell back on the ground. With his arms wrapped around the telephone pole, Tsukakoshi watched helplessly as the old man struggled. Then from out of the sky, a flaming piece of debris landed on the old man's hood, setting it on fire.

Tsukakoshi told himself that he could not let the old man burn alive in front of him. Summoning all of his strength, he staggered over to his side and tried to beat out the flames, but the fire continued to spread. As the old man's hair began to burn, Tsukakoshi tried in desperation to tear the hood off, but it was firmly tied down with a string below his neck. Tsukakoshi pulled and clawed with all his might, but he couldn't break the string or undo the knot.

Then, to his horror, Tsukakoshi suddenly realized that his own clothes were on fire again. After beating out the flames, he staggered back to the telephone pole and fell against it. When he turned to look back, the old man was dead.

With his last ounce of strength, Tsukakoshi stumbled forward again, beating out the flames on his clothing as he went, until he finally reached the firebreak. Tsukakoshi would now be safe for the rest of the night, but most were not so sure of their survival.[22]

Locked in his cage at the Kempeitai prison, Hap Halloran was in fear for his life as the fires raged out of control. "I was frightened out of my mind, 'cause fire really scares me," recalled Hap, who listened to the wind howling like a tornado outside. "I was convinced I was going to burn to death."[23] From his cage, Hap could hear women and children screaming as they ran to escape the inferno. People were jumping into the moat that surrounded the Emperor's Palace to get away from the flames, but Hap didn't know that at the time. The howling winds and their screams of terror were all that he could hear. There was a small window at the back of the horse stall where Hap's cage was located, but it was always covered with a black cloth. But on that night, with the firestorm winds reaching upwards of what Hap estimated to be 100 miles an hour, the cloth was blown open. For the first time, Hap could see outside. It looked as if the whole universe was on fire.[24] Then the smoke began filling his cage, and he could feel the heat as the end of the stable went up in flames, which spread to the roof. Finally, the guards came into the stall where Hap was caged, but they weren't there to take him to safety. After shackling his hands and feet, ensuring that he couldn't possibly escape, the guards left Hap to die in his cage.[25]

Looking out from the cockpit of his B-29, 26-year-old Captain Charles Phillips saw what appeared to be a giant thunderstorm up ahead as he crossed over the coast of Japan. With three combat missions already under his belt, flying through the cloud on his approach to the target appealed to Phillips, since it would conceal his bomber from the flak gunners below. But the moment Phillips entered the cloud, he suddenly realized it was not a thunderstorm at all. Towering miles into the sky, Phillips had just flown into a roiling cloud of smoke that was so turbulent that it took all of his skills as a pilot to keep his B-29 under control.

Flying over the firestorm at 7,800 feet, Phillips could actually see burning pieces of window and door frames sailing past his airplane. They later found pieces of charred bamboo stuck in the air intakes of the engines. "The odor was overpowering," Phillips recalled after the war. "It was the smell of a great fire, but it was also the smell of death."[26]

As Phillips flew deeper into the smoke, the tremendous heat thermals rising from the fires were so powerful that his B-29 began to climb uncontrollably like a rocket. With all 57 tons of his bomber bouncing around "like a leaf in a windstorm," Phillips throttled his engines back to idle, but his B-29 continued to climb at an incredible 2,000 feet per minute, and his airspeed surpassed 350 miles per hour. If Phillips tried to force the B-29 back down to his assigned altitude, the enormous stress on the wings would cause a structural failure and rip the airplane apart. There was nothing Phillips could do but hold on and let the bomber climb. When they finally topped out, the B-29 had soared to almost 14,000 feet.

With help from his navigator and radar observer, Phillips got back on course and finally dropped his bombs on the target. But before his crew could catch their breath, they broke out of the smoke into clean air and were suddenly caught in a violent downdraft that sent them plunging out of control. Phillips and his co-pilot were not wearing their seat belts, and the sudden plunge lifted them out of their seats and pinned their shoulders against the roof of the cockpit. They both held on to their control yokes for dear life before slowly sinking back down into their seats and regaining control of the bomber. When the crew checked the airframe for damage, they discovered that the actuators on the forward bomb bay doors had been ripped off, leaving the doors swinging freely in the wind, but otherwise their B-29 was undamaged.

"It seemed certain the wings would be torn off our B-29," Phillips said, recalling the most severe turbulence he had ever experienced in his life. "The fact that my crew and I survived at all in such terrifying turbulence is a tremendous tribute to the strength and stoutness of the old Superfort."[27]

When the first bombs began falling on Tokyo, factory worker Hidezo Tsuchikura collected his young daughter and son and ran to the nearby Futaba School for shelter. The school was a large three-story building made of concrete, and its basement had been expanded into a large air-raid shelter that could hold over 500 people. Tsuchikura and his children were among the first to arrive in the basement, but it soon filled with a steady stream of people. If there was a panic, or the building collapsed, there would be no hope for his children, Tsuchikura concluded, so he led them out of the basement to find better shelter. With its wide doors, Tsuchikura decided that the gym would be the safest place to wait out the raid, and it was near the school's large swimming pool.

For those living in the surrounding wooden homes, they looked to the concrete building as a beacon of safety and rushed to the school. Within 10 minutes, over 1,000 people had crowded into the gym alone. Tsuchikura became uneasy as he looked around at all of the people. He pushed his way out of the gym and took his children up to the second floor, but it too quickly filled with people. Looking out of the windows, Tsuchikura could see the fires were rapidly advancing toward the school. Not feeling safe in a place that was so crowded, he led his children up to the third floor. "The fires were incredible by now, with flames leaping hundreds of feet into the air," Tsuchikura recalled. "There seemed to be a solid wall of fire rolling toward the building."[28]

All of the school's rooms and hallways were now jammed as more people flooded into the school to escape the flames. With so many people crowded into the building, the air became stifling and hard to breathe. Many were already gasping for breath. For the sake of his children, who were visibly growing weaker by the minute and begging to go home, Tsuchikura decided to move again to the only place left that could offer them safety: the roof.

Stepping over and around the people lying on the stairs, Tsuchikura and his children slowly climbed up the staircase until they finally reached the roof. Opening the door, they walked into a nightmare. "On the roof it was like stepping into hell," he said. "Pieces of flaming wood and sparks rained down from the sky or shot horizontally through the air."[29]

With smoke and firebrands filling the sky, the night air was still incredibly hot three stories above the ground, but it was much easier to breathe now out in the open. Tsuchikura and his children sat down near a large water tank, and for the first time in many minutes, he watched them smile. He had made the right decision to climb up to the roof. He told his children to stay down, and then he slowly stood up to see what was happening around them. In the sky above, B-29s were still coming over Tokyo in an endless stream as the flames leapt high over the city. The noise, Tsuchikura said, was a "continuing, crashing roar."

As he peered over the edge of the roof, he was horrified to see "fire-winds filled with burning particles" rushing up and down the streets in waves as adults and children ran for their lives. Everywhere he looked, hordes of people were desperately running away from the school, only to be enveloped in a "devil's cauldron of twisting, seething fire."

"The flames raced after them like living things, striking them down," Tsuchikura recalled. "They died by the hundreds right in front of me."[30]

The nightmare unfolding before him, "a real inferno straight out of the depths of hell itself," reminded Tsuchikura of the paintings he'd seen of Purgatory. It was all too much for him to take in. He felt dizzy and closed his eyes as he started to faint, but then just as suddenly, the screams from his 5-year-old daughter brought him out of his stupor. When he opened his eyes, he saw his daughter standing there on fire. Sparks had fallen from the sky and landed on her back, setting her clothes ablaze. Tsuchikura frantically scooped water out of the nearby tank with his hands and beat out the flames, but then his son screamed that he too was on fire. Leaping to his son, Tsuchikura picked him up and plunged him into the water tank. As he pulled him out of the water, his son pointed and screamed again: this time it was Tsuchikura who was on fire.

For the next 90 minutes, surrounded by raging fires, Tsuchikura had to keep dunking himself and his children in the water tank to keep from burning alive. The air was so hot that the water on their clothes turned to steam each time they emerged from the tank. With his children wrapped in his arms, there was nothing more he could do now but wait for the fires to burn out.[31]

Three hours after the raid began, the last B-29s dropped their bombs and turned home for the Marianas. The glow from the fires behind them could still be seen 150 miles away.

15

It's All Ashes

"Let's go back where it's already burned," the girl said to Funato Kazuyo at the first sign of dawn, as they peered out of the ditch where they had been sheltering near the Shinkai Bridge. "Everyone will probably be safe and will return there. You'll be able to go home then." Funato felt safe with the girl and didn't want to leave her, but their homes were in opposite directions. Reluctantly, Funato and the girl parted ways, never to see each other again.[1]

As Funato and her little sister, Hiroko, slowly walked up to the Shinkai Bridge, where her family became separated only hours earlier, they saw dead bodies everywhere. When the fires swept over the area, countless people had jumped into the river to escape the flames, but there was no escape. Some rivers and canals had actually boiled during the firestorm.[2] "Dead bodies covered the water," Funato recalled of the river. "Some people had tried to escape by running under the bridge but they, too, had been roasted."[3]

Crossing over the bridge, Funato saw "charcoal-black people" who were burned beyond recognition and still smoldering as she led her sister to a police station at the foot of the bridge for help. All that remained of the station were the concrete walls. No policemen were there. Funato leaned Hiroko up against the concrete wall and waited. It occurred to her that her father and brothers might come back this way, and then they could all go home together.

Funato and her sister waited, but their family never came.

Hiroko, in terrible pain from her burns, was asking for water, so Funato decided they would try to walk home themselves. When they arrived home later that morning, they found nothing but a burnt-out pile of rubble where their house had been. The fire was so intense that it melted the glass bottles in her father's store. The only thing left standing was a concrete water cistern they had in front of their house. A dead man was in the cistern now, his body hanging halfway out.

With nowhere else to go, Funato and her sister sat down on the concrete steps that once led to her father's store and waited. Soon a young woman came over and said their oldest brother, Koichi, was nearby. Funato found him sitting on a burnt-out truck. He was trembling and couldn't see when she walked up to him. Tears streamed down his face when he realized his sisters were alive. He thought they were all dead.

A short time later, Funato's father appeared with her other brother, Yoshiaki, as more survivors slowly returned to the neighborhood. "The people who came back were like ghosts, uttering no words," Funato remembered. "They simply staggered back, thinking somebody might be where their houses had been."[4] Funato's father had a first aid kit and began treating Hiroko's burns. She had been terribly burned, he said to her, but told her not to worry because daddy was here.

As the morning went on, the family waited for Funato's mother to return. What they didn't know was that her mother was already there, but no one recognized her. "Her clothes were all charcoal," Funato recounted. "Her hair, too. She was covered from head to toe by a military blanket and she was barefoot." By some miracle, she was still alive. But her baby was missing.

Funato's father asked his wife what happened, but she didn't answer. There were severe burns on her back and elbows where she had been carrying the baby. Looking at her mother's injuries, Funato realized that her baby brother had burned to death on her mother's back as she desperately tried to escape the firestorm. "Where Takahisa's legs had touched her body there were horrible burns," Funato said. "Her elbows, where she was probably holding him to keep him from falling off, were burned so that you could see the raw flesh."[5]

At the Sophia Catholic University, the campus quickly became a refuge for hundreds of survivors. Father Bitter recalled:

> When all the small wooden houses round us were burnt down to the ground, it became evident that the campus of the university was a place of safety. Refugees began to pour in by the hundreds. All were silent and calm, but the horror they went through reflected in their faces. There was no disorder. Every available room was used for shelter. That night we took in 876 victims of the air raid. When I went through all the buildings I saw unbelievable misery. I heard of many tragedies which made my heart bleed; they all realized the hopelessness of the situation, but there was no sign of unrest or revolutionary tendencies. They took all that very stoically with the remark "*shikata ga nai*" (it cannot be helped). When the first food was given out, it was done most orderly, just as if nothing had happened. When early in the morning I took my bicycle and went through the city, I saw long processions of bombed out people carrying the few things they had saved and were heading for the country to find shelter. All the caravans I met had an atmosphere of deep silence about them – they were exhausted, depressed, unhappy, but in no case in a radical mood.[6]

After spending the night on the roof at the Futaba School with his two children, Hidezo Tsuchikura decided to leave the building at the first sign of dawn. Walking over to the doorway leading down from the roof, only 10 yards away from where they had spent the night, Tsuchikura was sickened by what he saw. Just inside the smoke-filled doorway, piled atop the smoldering staircase, more than a dozen bodies were "sprawled about in grotesque positions." The stench of burning flesh nearly made him vomit.[7] He told his children to stay back as he looked down the hallway for a way out. Hundreds of "smoking and steaming" bodies blocked the way, making it impossible to go on. There were two other stairways leading down from the roof, but they were also choked with bodies.

Tsuchikura had by now discovered that 12 other people had also survived on the roof. Everyone was in shock and barely spoke, but all agreed that they should wait until everything inside the school burned out before they tried to get off the roof. About an hour later, one of the men found an emergency fire escape and led the group down from the roof. When Tsuchikura finally reached the ground and looked to see what happened inside the school, his worst fears were realized. "The entire building had become a huge oven three stories high," he recalled.

"Every human being inside the school was literally baked or boiled alive in heat. Dead bodies were everywhere in grisly heaps."[8]

But the swimming pool behind the school was the most horrible sight of all. The pool had been filled with water when Tsuchikura arrived, but now there wasn't a drop of water in it. It was full of dead bodies. Over a thousand people – men, women and children – were jammed into the pool.

Tsuchikura gave thanks for his safety, and hurried away with his children. Of the some 3,000 people who sought shelter in the school that night, only 15 would walk out alive the next morning.[9]

Before dawn that morning, Captain Shigenori Kubota, a doctor at the Imperial Japanese Army Medical School, was leading his rescue unit through the city to reach the Honjo ward of Tokyo. As his convoy of six vehicles slowly made their way deeper into the fire zone, the roads became "thoroughfares of rubble and destruction" clogged with wreckage and the twisted bodies of the dead. Kubota's men had to keep stopping to clear a path for their vehicles. The burnt flesh of the bodies crumbled like charcoal in their hands as they moved the dead out of the way.[10]

Leading his convoy onward, Kubota and his men finally reached the Sumida River, which they would have to cross to reach Honjo. Kubota was horrified by what he saw:

> The entire river surface was black as far as the eye could see, black with burned corpses, logs, and who knew what else, but uniformly black from the immense heat that had seared its way through the area as the fire dragon passed. It was impossible to tell the bodies from the logs at a distance. The bodies were all nude, the clothes had been burned away, and there was a dreadful sameness about them, no telling men from women or even children. All that remained were pieces of charred meat. Bodies and parts of bodies were carbonized and absolutely black. The whole area was still covered with smoke, the smoke that had asphyxiated these people even as they leaped into the water to save themselves from the fire storm.[11]

Along the banks of the river, Kubota saw rows upon rows of dead bodies stacked like cordwood by the tides. Standing next to the bridge they had to cross was the concrete skeleton of a huge building wrapped in smoke. Inside, his men discovered mountains of roasted bodies. There was no one left alive to rescue.

Kubota and his men pushed on, and later that morning they set up an aid station inside a school building that was already overflowing with survivors when they arrived. As his medical team set to work, victims streamed in with every kind of injury imaginable, but the ones that worried him the most were those suffering from smoke inhalation. Many of them would die in the days that followed from the damage to their lungs. There was nothing Kubota could do for them.[12]

Miles away from the target area at the Omori Prisoner of War Camp in Tokyo Bay, Ernest Norquist, a U.S. Army medic who was captured during the fall of the Philippines and survived the Bataan Death March in 1942, had watched with the other prisoners as the fires blazed in the distance that night. The next morning, Norquist departed the camp with a work detail and traveled into the city. He was shocked by what he found:

> Even we prisoners, who had suffered so much, did not glory in what we saw – miles of desolation – block after block of charred ruins, as far as the eye could see, where yesterday

had stood the flimsy dwellings and shops. Twisted tin, smoldering wood, miscellaneous household goods, and what not lay in blacken heaps. There was the stench of burnt flesh and the suffocating smell of smoke in the air. Women stood weeping, with children on their backs. Ragged, tired looking men pushed carts or carried bundles that held all their rescued earthly possessions. Some didn't even have the bundle. The homeless must number thousands.[13]

At the Kempeitai prison, Hap Halloran thought he was going to burn to death when the horse stable he was caged in caught on fire during the raid. As he lay shackled in his cage, unable to escape, the fire consumed one end of the wooden stable and quickly spread to the roof. Hap could feel the heat as the flames closed in, but then a miracle happened. Someone climbed onto the roof and put out the fire, saving the lives of Hap and the other B-29ers caged in the stable.

The next morning, an interpreter came into Hap's stall and told him what had happened during the night. He was very polite as he explained the situation to Hap, like he was trying to be informative. The interpreter described the devastation and how bodies were stacked many feet high in the streets and thousands more were floating in the river. Then the interpreter looked at Hap and said: "I regret to advise you that at our meeting this morning the decision was made to execute you B-29ers."[14]

A few days later, Hap was pulled out of his cage and told to take off his shoes. This was his death sentence, Hap thought, as he was blindfolded, bound, and loaded into a truck. A short drive later, the truck stopped and Hap was tossed off the back. When the guards stood him up and removed his blindfold, he was surprised to see that he was at the Ueno Zoo. The guards marched Hap through the zoo until they came to a tiger cage. After six weeks in captivity with very little food, Hap now weighed only 125 pounds, down from 212 pounds when he was captured. He hadn't showered or shaved since he left Saipan on his final mission, and his body was covered in open, running sores from the lice and fleas that infested the stable he was held in.

The guards took Hap into the tiger cage, stripped him naked, and tied his hands to the bars above his head. Hap didn't know what was going to happen next, but he soon figured it out when a long procession of Japanese civilians began to file by and glare at him. The purpose of it all, he later said, was to show the people of Tokyo that the B-29ers were not "super beings" and not to fear them. "I was a pathetic sight, standing there, skinny as a rail, with a long, filthy beard, shivering from the cold, with my body covered with running sores from lice and fleas," Hap recalled.

Hap was left tied up in the cage overnight. The next morning, he was moved to the Omori Prisoner of War Camp, where he would remain until the end of the war.[15]

The evening after the raid, some of Funato's relatives arrived with a pull cart and helped her family evacuate to an unburnt part of the city. Her father would later go back in search of her sister, Teruko, her grandmother and her oldest brother, Minoru, who leapt out of the ditch with his back on fire, but no trace of them was ever found. Suffering from severe burns, her sister Hiroko's condition worsened in the days that followed. Most of the hospitals had burned down, but her father found a small one that could take her. Hiroko's face was badly burned, and her bandages quickly became soaked with blood and pus. There were so few bandages available that the family had to take them home and wash them for reuse.

On the ninth day, it was Funato's turn to bring the clean bandages back to the hospital for her sister. Walking into the small concrete room with only one bed, she saw Hiroko asleep with her eyes open. Funato was confused and asked her why she was sleeping with her eyes open. She didn't answer. Funato reached over and tried to close her sister's eyes, but they wouldn't close. She called her sister's name again. Hiroko didn't answer.

Then her father walked in. He told her that Hiroko had just died.

It wasn't the burns or the smoke that caused Hiroko's death. It was tetanus, a serious infection caused by bacteria that live in the soil. As they huddled together in the ditch during the fire, not knowing what else to do to ease her pain, it was Funato who covered Hiroko's burnt hands with the cool dirt. Her father assured her that it wasn't her fault, but she was inconsolable. Funato blamed herself for her sister's death.[16]

*   *   *

"All this is out," General LeMay said with a cigar clenched in his teeth, sweeping his hand over a table full of reconnaissance photos, as he stood in his pajamas. "This is out – this – this – this." It was around midnight on Guam, and LeMay had just been woken up by telephone a few minutes earlier after the first post-strike photos of Tokyo were rushed through the photo lab.[17]

With his bedroom full of staff officers, LeMay was trying to light a stubborn cigar when the photo interpretation officer walked in with the photos and spread them on the table. Everyone stood back so LeMay could look at the photos first, but his cigar still refused to light. As his officers anxiously waited, the general's dogged persistence in lighting his cigar made it clear that anyone who dared to interrupt him would be obliterated.[18] Finally, the cigar gave in, and LeMay leaned over the table for a closer look at the photos. Some of the fires were still burning, and a smoky haze obscured part of the city, but the destruction was undeniable. Against the darker surrounding sections of the city that were untouched by the flames, the vast burned-out swathes of Tokyo appeared white in the photos, like the ground was covered in snow.

LeMay studied the photos for about a minute before making his pronouncement. Then he stood up and looked at the officers surrounding the table. As his cigar slowly swept from side to side in his mouth, like the barrel of a gun turret, LeMay didn't say a word. His face was expressionless as he looked at his men.

"It's all ashes," General Norstad said, breaking the silence as he bent over the photos, "all that and that and that." The devastation revealed in the photos was staggering. Nearly 16 square miles of Tokyo had been destroyed in just a matter of hours.[19]

"The heart of this city is completely gutted by fire," LeMay's aide wrote in his diary. "It is the most devastating raid in the history of aerial warfare."[20]

After struggling for months to put bombs on their targets, the reconnaissance photos showed that 22 industrial targets and "many other unidentified industries" had been completely destroyed or damaged. The Japanese later calculated that over 267,000 buildings and houses were lost in the fires, and over a million people were left homeless. Nearly a quarter of all the buildings in Tokyo were destroyed or damaged.[21]

The human toll of the raid will never be known with any certainty. The estimates range broadly from 83,000 to over 100,000 killed that night. Some put the number of dead as high as 130,000. Many thousands, perhaps tens of thousands, were cremated by the fires or washed out to sea in the rivers. Their bodies would never be found or counted. Of all the deaths caused by air attacks on Tokyo over the course of the entire war, 90 percent occurred during this single night. It took almost a month to remove all of the bodies.[22]

For LeMay, his losses for the mission were surprisingly light. Of the 325 bombers taking off that night with over 3,300 men, 14 B-29s were lost, 42 were damaged by flak, and 96 men were dead or missing. Only two of the B-29s lost were known to have been downed by flak, and the 74 Japanese fighters that were spotted during the raid did not inflict any damage on the bombers.[23]

The lack of fighter opposition reaffirmed another controversial decision LeMay had made. To save additional weight, LeMay ordered the B-29s to fly without any ammunition loaded in their gun turrets. After studying Japan's night-fighter capabilities, coupled with the raid's element of surprise, LeMay concluded that there would not be any effective fighter opposition, and the ammo – and some of the gunners themselves – would not be needed. However, three of his bomb groups still flew the mission fully armed, and other crews ignored the order and loaded their guns anyway. Several gunners from the 314th Bomb Wing were flying low enough to actually shoot back at some of the searchlights that were tracking their B-29s, knocking out two of them.[24]

The success of the raid proved that the Japanese were totally unprepared for a low-level attack, just as LeMay had predicted. In what General Thomas Power called the "greatest single disaster incurred by any enemy in military history," LeMay had destroyed 15.8 square miles of the Japanese capital with 1,665 tons of incendiaries.[25]

For the first time, after nine frustrating months of operations from the CBI to the Marianas, the B-29s had finally dealt a decisive blow to Japan. Morale soared and cases of psychological disorders plummeted. The new maintenance system LeMay put into action had also dramatically improved the reliability of the B-29, and the men regained confidence in their airplanes. As one report after the raid put it, the B-29 was finally "established as an efficient and reliable combat aircraft."[26]

The B-29 had come into its own, but there was no time to celebrate. "Finally Curtis LeMay had hit upon a strategy that worked, and, gladiator that he was, he bore in now for the kill," Colonel Robert Morgan recalled. "Rest and airplane endurance be damned – he'd found a way into the enemy's center, and now he was going to pour fire through it."[27]

In the days that followed, LeMay would launch four more incendiary raids in rapid succession to keep the pressure on the Japanese and deny them time to counter his new tactics. LeMay would push his men and the B-29s harder than they had ever been pushed before.

When the blitz ended 10 days later, four of Japan's largest cities – Tokyo, Nagoya, Osaka and Kobe – lay in ruin. For the loss of 21 B-29s and 145 men, LeMay's B-29s had dropped 9,917 tons of incendiaries and destroyed over 32 square miles of urban-industrial area.[28]

It would take over a month waiting on the resupply ships before the next incendiary raid could be launched. General LeMay had literally run out of firebombs.

16

Voices from the Past

When I was growing up in Orlando in the 1980s and early 1990s, like a lot of American boys who came before me, my friends and I were obsessed with war. For a big part of my childhood, "playing war" was my favorite thing to do. I loved watching the old war movies on TV and then re-fighting those battles amongst the houses of my neighborhood with my friends, but some of our neighbors didn't exactly like us using their shrubbery as bunkers. Our fathers didn't seem to mind what we were doing, probably because they had grown up doing the same thing, but they did have to draw a line when we started digging a foxhole in my friend's front yard.

Some of my fondest memories growing up were the airshows of that era, where the warbirds I saw in the movies and built models of came alive in the skies above me. One time at the airshow in Kissimmee, Florida, my best friend Graham and I each manned a waist gun in a B-24 bomber that was parked on display. As the other warbirds flew overhead during the show, we called out approaching fighters to each other just like we'd seen in the movies, and then we wildly swung those replica machine guns back and forth across the sky and pretended to shoot down hundreds of German Messerschmitt fighters.

While we were busy playing, I noticed there was an older man standing over by the ball turret a few feet away from us. I'm not sure why I noticed him, but I remember thinking that it was weird how he was just standing there looking down at that gun turret all by himself. After what seemed like an eternity, he slowly walked over and asked us how many fighters did we shoot down. We talked for a few minutes, in the way that a curious grandson would talk to his grandfather, and it turned out that he was a B-24 ball turret gunner and had flown missions over Germany during the war. We both thought that was pretty cool.

There were more World War II Veterans like him who walked through the B-24 after he left, but most of them were lost in their thoughts and barely said a word to anyone. Then there were the others, who just stood outside the bomber and wouldn't come any closer.

I remember another World War II Veteran I saw that day who I've never been able to forget. He was standing just outside the rope line and was facing the waist gunner window where I was playing, maybe 30 feet or so away. He was wearing dark sunglasses and a blue hat that had his bomb group on it. I couldn't see his eyes, but it was like he was looking *through me* as I swung that gun back and forth across the sky. The airshow was in full swing by then and there were airplanes flying overhead and dazzling the crowd with their routines, but he just stood there the whole time and stared at that B-24 in silence. I've always wondered what he was thinking about that day, and why he would not – or could not – come any closer. Some 30 years later, I've seen Vietnam Veterans react the same way when they see the UH-1 Huey helicopter at our local veterans park.

Back then, as I gleefully played inside that B-24, the horrors of war were something that I couldn't understand at that age. And how could I, only knowing "war" from the old movies I watched on TV and the pictures I saw in books. For me, freedom had always been free. I didn't know anything about the price of freedom, or what war does to a person.

The irony, as I look back on it now, is that I was actually witnessing the traumatic effects that the war had on my uncle, but I didn't understand what I was seeing. My Uncle Mac was a D-Day veteran who survived the war, but he never *overcame* the war. This was long before the days when there were people who our veterans could talk to for help, so my uncle turned to alcohol instead.

I was too young back then to understand why my uncle was always drunk. He wasn't a mean or abusive drunk; he only drank to forget. But there wasn't enough alcohol in the world to make him forget the horrors he saw on Omaha Beach, or the victims of the Malmedy massacre, or the starved and tortured human beings inside those concentration camps.

As I grew older and learned more about the war, I slowly began to understand what my uncle went through, and why he tried to find peace in the bottom of a bottle. The movie *Saving Private Ryan* really opened my eyes. My uncle was an Army combat engineer who landed on Omaha Beach with the 2nd Ranger Battalion on D-Day. The horrific opening battle sequence of *Saving Private Ryan* followed the 2nd Rangers on Omaha Beach. That's what my uncle went through when he was 20 years old.

As the years went by and my interest in the B-29 turned into an obsession, I also wanted to better understand what the B-29ers went through during the war. I read lots of books, but none of them really captured what it was like for these young men. And there are no movies like *Saving Private Ryan* to help us better understand a B-29er's war. My search for understanding continued for years, and even after talking to some B-29ers who were actually there, I still didn't really know what it was like for them.

Then late one night in 2011, everything changed. While doing some research on something else, I came across a fascinating website called Japan Air Raids.org, a bilingual digital archive about the air raids conducted against Japan during the war. As I browsed through the website, I found a grainy old recording of the Army Air Forces' official radio program, *The Fighting AAF*, that featured a recording made on March 31, 1945, in the cockpit of a B-29 during an actual bombing mission over Japan. I'd never heard of *The Fighting AAF* radio show before, but I soon learned that it was a weekly radio program that featured reports from the Army Air Forces around the world.

When I clicked "play," the broadcast began with an announcer explaining that I was going to fly a B-29 mission over the mainland of Japan. There was no script or prearranged dialog or sound effects, he said. This was the real thing, a true report of what took place during the mission. "When the combat reporter speaks of flak, you'll know that at that very moment it was cutting the sky around him, real and hard and deadly," the announcer said. "When he speaks of enemy fighters closing in, you'll know that he could look over his shoulder and see them circling for the kill." The B-29 was named *The City of Muncie*, he added, and its pilot was Lieutenant Frank Crowcroft.[1]

The combat reporter who made the recording I was about to hear, Staff Sergeant Harold Brown of the AAF 1st Combat Radio Team, captured the action that day as he sat between the pilots with a Boosey & Hawkes wire recorder, which magnetically records sounds on a thin steel wire fed between two spools. For security reasons, Brown couldn't say what they were bombing, but I looked it up, and their target was the Omura Naval Air Station on Kyushu, Japan's southern home island. The invasion of Okinawa was set to begin the next day, and the raids on Kyushu's airfields were intended to draw Japan's fighters away from Okinawa and destroy their airfields to prevent them from attacking the invasion force.[2]

As Brown began his commentary from the flight deck, I started hearing sounds that I never thought I'd ever hear: the drone of the engines, the nervous whistling and chatter of the crew as they approached the target, and then – most incredibly of all – the sound of the machine guns firing back as the crew fought a running gun battle with swarms of Japanese fighters. For as long as I can remember, I had always wanted to know what a B-29 mission over Japan was like. On the night I found this recording, I came the closest that I will ever be to knowing.

This is a transcript of the recording Harold Brown made on March 31, 1945:

> While we're moving in on the target of Japan, I should like to say this is a daylight mission, and the weather is crystal clear. Our bombardier, Lieutenant Charlie Henderson, is all smiles with expectations.
>
> We are now two minutes to the bomb run. No fighters, no flak, as yet. Weather remains crystal clear, a beautiful sunny day.
>
> We have observed some surface craft in some inland waterways here. Through the right window I can observe a portion of the Japanese coastline. It's a peaceful, pastoral scene.
>
> One minute to our bomb run. No flak, no fighters, as yet. Things are too peaceful and we are uneasy. Tension among the crew is high, but everyone is calm.
>
> We're moving closer to our bomb run now. One unidentified plane at 2 o'clock low has just been reported by our tail gunner, Staff Sergeant Wolf.
>
> Our bombardier is getting ready now, everything has been cleared. Moving on the bomb run, he's huddling over that intricate instrument in front of him.
>
> Now I can look out my compartment window here and see that unidentified plane. We are by the way, on the bomb run at the present time. The unidentified plane is some distance off, lower than our line of flight, however, keeping up on a parallel speed with us. Probably using his plane as radio to radio our position, altitude and speed.
>
> We are now on the bomb run. As yet, our bomb bay doors have not opened.
>
> Our giant bomb bay doors have just yawned open. This is it, we're starting in.
>
> Our aircraft commander, Lieutenant Frank Crowcroft, is holding her on course while our bombardier gets ready. Everyone is tense. Straight course into target.
>
> An unidentified plane, a fighter, is still tagging along parallel with us.
>
> Up ahead, I can see puffs of ack-ack coming up, black puffs of smoke, straight ahead. We're moving into it.
>
> A fighter has been reported at 1 o'clock. We're holding our course on our bomb run.
>
> Another fighter has been reported at 2 o'clock high, now he's at 3, 5.
>
> Our bombardier is crouching over his delicate instrument now. Everyone is holding course.
>
> To my right, I can see puffs of ack-ack still coming up, also straight ahead. We are running into a curtain of anti-aircraft fire at the present time. And I should – We're jockeying now, as we move into it. Getting a little rough. A fighter is coming in at 4 – Bombs away!
>
> The bomb bay doors are closing.

General Henry H. "Hap" Arnold, Commanding General of the U.S. Army Air Forces. (U.S. Air Force Museum)

The first XB-29 prototype under construction at Boeing's Plant 1 in Seattle. (USAAF)

A Japanese torpedo bomber takes off to attack Pearl Harbor.
(NH 50603 courtesy of the Naval History & Heritage Command)

This remarkable photo of Pearl Harbor was taken from a Japanese aircraft just as the
attack began and captured the moment a torpedo struck the battleship *West Virginia*.
(NH 50930 courtesy of the Naval History & Heritage Command)

Japanese soldiers triumphantly take down the American Flag after the fall of Corregidor. (NH 73223 courtesy of the Naval History & Heritage Command)

Three American prisoners are questioned by the Japanese during the Bataan Death March. None of them would survive the war. Captain James Gallagher, right, died shortly after this photo was taken. His remains have never been found. (National Archives 74252422)

The first XB-29 prototype gleams in the Seattle night. (USAAF)

A- THROTTLE CONTROLS	F- EMERGENCY HAND BRAKES	K- AILERON TAB CONTROL
B- SUPERCHARGER CONTROLS	G- AISLE STAND	L- RUDDER
C- PILOT'S CONTROL STAND	H- SEAT POSITION CONTROL	M- AUXILLIARY BOARDS
D- TEST EQUIPMENT	I- ELEVATOR TAB CONTROL	N- RADIO COMPASS CONTROL
E- PROPELLER FEATHERING CONTROLS	J- CO-PILOT'S CONTROL STAND	O- COMMAND RADIO CONTROLS

The cockpit of the first XB-29 prototype. A large panel with test instruments (D) is installed where the bombardier would normally sit. Nearly 4,000 B-29s would be built during the war. (USAAF)

The third XB-29 prototype passes by Mount Rainier during a test flight high over Washington State.
(U.S. Air Force Museum)

As America's armed forces swelled with manpower after Pearl Harbor, the factories of America
surged with *womanpower*. Mrs. Virginia Young, right, whose husband was killed at Pearl Harbor,
was among the millions of women who joined the war effort. (National Archives 196352)

The B-29's fuselage was built in five sections that were then bolted together along with the wings during final assembly to form a complete airplane. The forward cabins seen here were attached to the bomb bay assemblies with 165 bolts. (U.S. Air Force Museum)

The B-29 production line at Boeing-Wichita in December 1943. The B-29 at the far right was lost six months after this photo was taken when it ditched in the Bay of Bengal after bombing Bangkok, Thailand, on June 5, 1944, killing four of its crew. (U.S. Air Force Museum)

A gleaming, factory-fresh B-29 in flight over the United States. (U.S. Air Force Museum)

The B-29's unique cockpit later inspired George Lucas when creating the *Millennium Falcon* for *Star Wars*. (U.S. Air Force Museum)

Final preparations underway at the 40th Bomb Group's forward base in China for the first mission to Japan. The B-29 in the foreground was destroyed in a fire three weeks later. (National Archives 204832029)

As smoke rises from the target area below, a B-29 comes under attack by a Japanese fighter over Manchuria on July 29, 1944. Three B-29s were lost that day. (National Archives 204840129)

The *Eddie Allen* was named in honor of aviation pioneer Edmund T. Allen. During a later mission over Tokyo, the *Eddie Allen* was so badly damaged that it never flew again. (U.S. Air Force Museum)

Only 15 days after it rolled out of the Bell Bomber Plant in Georgia, the aptly named *Rush Order* was dropping bombs on Japan from its forward base in China. (National Archives 204829815)

This photo appeared on the cover of *Newsweek* in 1944 with the ominous headline: *B-29 Superfortress: Black Shadow Over Japan*. Two months later, this B-29 and four of its crew were lost while attempting an emergency landing in China due to an engine failure and a runaway prop. (U.S. Air Force Museum)

Ding How was the 21st B-29 to roll off the production lines and flew on the first mission to Japan. Most of its crew were killed two months after this photo was taken when their new B-29 crashed on takeoff. The author later discovered the data plate from *Ding How* for sale on eBay. (National Archives 204830819)

Bombs away over Rangoon. The B-29 on the left was later one of the 26 B-29s that were lost during the costly May 25, 1945, mission to Tokyo. (U.S. Air Force Museum)

The crew of the *Gen. H.H. Arnold Special* before a mission to Japan. The *Gen. H.H. Arnold Special* was later interned by the Soviets and reverse engineered to produce their own copy of the B-29, the Tupolev Tu-4, after the crew made an emergency landing in Russia. (National Archives 204960950)

General Haywood Hansell Jr. arrives on Saipan in *Joltin' Josie, The Pacific Pioneer*, the first B-29 to land in the Marianas. This photo was autographed by Hansell on Saipan and was later found for sale on eBay by the author and purchased for $7.90. (USAAF/Trevor McIntyre)

Generals O'Donnell, Harmon and Hansell discuss the upcoming bombing operations against Japan. The B-29 behind them, *Pacific Union,* was lost two months after this photo was taken (chapter 9), and General Millard Harmon's plane disappeared without a trace a month later. (National Archives 193867554)

Captain Ralph Steakley (far right) and the crew of *Tokyo Rose*, the first B-29 to fly over Tokyo, after their daring photo-reconnaissance mission over the heart of the Japanese Empire. (National Archives 204972152)

Major Robert Morgan, the pilot of the famed B-17 *Memphis Belle*, and his crew prepare to board *Dauntless Dotty* for the first mission to Tokyo. Parked next to *Dauntless Dotty* in the background is *The Dragon Lady*, a month before it was rammed by a Japanese fighter. (National Archives 204972610)

A formation of B-29s pass by Mount Fuji on their way to Tokyo. (National Archives 204834836)

A Japanese Ki-45 "Dragon Slayer" fighter attacks a formation of B-29s over Japan.
(National Archives 204835769)

Flak bursts over Nagoya on June 26, 1945. Two B-29s were lost to flak over Nagoya that day, and one bomb group alone suffered flak damage to 21 of the 33 B-29s it sent on the mission.
(National Archives 204835908)

With its wing blown off by a direct flak hit, a B-29 goes down in flames over Japan.
(National Archives 204835919)

After being hit by cannon fire from a Japanese fighter, this B-29 was so severely damaged when its No. 3 propeller spun off and sliced through the fuselage that it broke in half when it crashed on Saipan, but the crew survived their harrowing 17-hour mission to fight another day. (National Archives 204972415)

The crew of *Special Delivery* clean their B-29. *Special Delivery* was lost a month later when the crew were forced to ditch 100 miles off Saipan, killing two of the crew. (National Archives 204974318)

Haley's Comet shortly before it was lost on the bloody January 27, 1945, mission to Tokyo that cost the lives of 70 men and eight B-29s (chapter 10). (USAAF/Trevor McIntyre)

After flying 3,100 miles nonstop from China, General Curtis LeMay, left, is greeted on Guam by Generals Haywood Hansell and Roger Ramey, where LeMay would soon assume command of the XXI Bomber Command from Hansell. (National Archives 193867572)

These six photographs were published in Japan during the war:

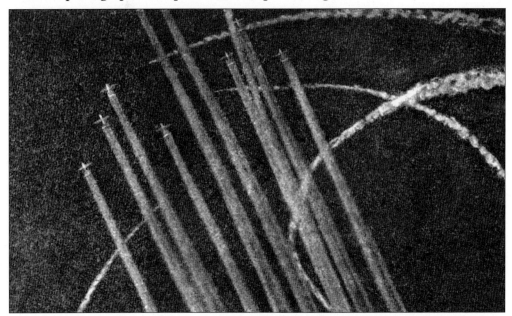

A formation of B-29s under heavy attack by Japanese fighters. The white streaks are contrails (condensation trails) produced by the engine exhaust at high altitude. (Asahigraph)

· Gathered in front of a Ki-45 "Dragon Slayer" fighter, Japanese fighter pilots are instructed how to attack a B-29. The preferred method was a direct frontal attack. Right: The moment a B-29 was rammed near Tokyo, which sheared off one of its engines. The crippled bomber flew on before it was brought down by more fighter attacks and crashed off the coast of Choshi Point. There were no survivors. (Asahigraph)

The crew of *Uncle Tom's Cabin No. 2* put up a valiant fight over Tokyo, but their B-29 plunged into Tokyo Bay after being overwhelmed by Japanese fighters and rammed twice. Some of the wreckage was recovered from the waters of the bay and placed on public display in a Tokyo park. (Weekly Report; Asahigraph)

A captured B-29er, Lieutenant Ernest Pickett, is shown off by members of the Kempeitai, the brutal Japanese military police. Pickett survived his torture and imprisonment and returned home after the war, weighing only 97 pounds when he was liberated. (Unknown/Trevor McIntyre)

Smoke rises from Iwo Jima after B-24s pound the island. The Army Air Forces bombed Iwo Jima for 72 straight days leading up to the invasion. Mount Suribachi can be seen at the bottom right of the island, and the long beach above it where the Marines would come ashore. (National Archives 204983412)

The Fifth Marine Division cemetery on Iwo Jima with Mount Suribachi in the distance. This was just one of the three Marine cemeteries on the island. (80-G-412518 courtesy of the Naval History & Heritage Command)

The first B-29 saved by Iwo Jima. Running low on fuel, Lieutenant Raymond Malo's crew landed the first B-29 on the embattled island and were welcomed by a swarm of curious Marines (chapter 11). (U.S. Air Force Museum)

Lieutenant Raymond Malo and crew after their emergency landing on Iwo Jima. (National Archives 204982046)

The *Enola Gay* crew that bombed Hiroshima. Back row, left to right: John Porter (maintenance officer, not on flight crew), Theodore "Dutch" Van Kirk, Thomas Ferebee, Paul Tibbets, Robert Lewis, Jacob Beser. Front row, left to right: Joseph Stiborik, George Caron, Richard Nelson, Robert Shumard, Wyatt Duzenbury. William "Deak" Parsons and Morris Jeppson not pictured. (National Archives 204972604)

Hiroshima after the atomic bomb was dropped. The aiming point for the bomb, the unique T-shaped Aioi Bridge, is seen in the center of the photo. (National Archives 204836316)

The *Bockscar* crew that bombed Nagasaki. Back row, left to right: Charles Sweeney, Charles Albury, Fred Olivi, Kermit Beahan, James Van Pelt, Jacob Beser. Front row, left to right: John Kuharek, Abe Spitzer, Raymond Gallagher, Ed Buckley, Albert Dehart. (National Archives 204972616)

This patient was standing about 1.2 miles away from ground zero when the atomic bomb detonated and suffered flash burns to the side of his exposed face and neck, but his hat and clothing protected him from additional burns. This and other examples led Japanese officials to conclude that "defenses were possible against the bomb," and instructions were issued to wear white clothing because "white reflects radiation." (National Archives 204836172)

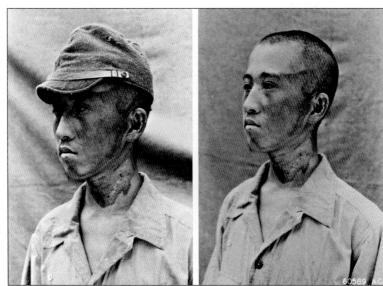

American and Allied Prisoners of War at the Omori prison camp in Tokyo Bay welcome their liberators from the U.S. Navy. The flags were made by the prisoners from the parachutes that were used to drop supplies to the camp by B-29s after Japan surrendered. During the "mercy missions," the B-29s airdropped 4,470 tons of food, medicine, and supplies to an estimated 69,000 Allied prisoners held at 158 camps across Japan, China, Manchuria, and Korea. (National Archives 520992)

The Japanese sign the Instrument of Surrender aboard the USS *Missouri* in Tokyo Bay on September 2, 1945, officially ending World War II, as General Douglas MacArthur and Allied representatives look on. (National Archives 23658002)

"It is my earnest hope and indeed the hope of all mankind that from this solemn occasion a better world shall emerge out of the blood and carnage of the past—a world founded upon faith and understanding—a world dedicated to the dignity of man and the fulfillment of his most cherished wish—for freedom, tolerance and justice." —*General Douglas MacArthur, September 2, 1945.*

[Gunfire]

That burst you're hearing – [gunfire] – That's answering the fighters. There's a fighter at 11 o'clock.

As you hear this plane jar in our microphone, it's our gunners going after the fighters coming in.

We are trying now to dodge the anti-aircraft fire – [gunfire] – Another burst from our guns.

Another fighter at 4 o'clock high. Our tail gunner is after him. I can feel the jar in this plane.

Anti-aircraft fire is all around us now. A fighter is high at 3. Our bombardier has put his instrument away and is now manning guns in front.

A fighter is coming in at 4 o'clock high. I am reporting this as I hear it on the intercom – [gunfire] – There's another burst from our guns.

Fighter – A fighter coming in at 7 o'clock, a fighter, and at 7 o'clock, 11. Our bombardier is getting a sight on him.

We're still riding it out. We're over our target, we've dropped our bombs, and we're moving.

Anti-aircraft fire is still around us – [gunfire] – there's – there's another burst. A fighter at 11 o'clock high – at 11 o'clock high and our – [gunfire] – bombardier moves around now.

[Gunfire]

You got 'em!

[Gunfire]

We got 'em! There goes one, we got 'em! On that last burst we got a fighter!

There's a fighter at 9 –

Here comes a fighter at 1 o'clock.

A fighter coming in at 4 o'clock low.

We expected it on this one, we're getting it! One at 4, one at 3, those are fighters reporting in.

They're holding off now, they're not coming in.

There's one at 6 o'clock right below us. Went right in front of us down here but he was out of range.

Now that – [gunfire] – There's another burst, that one that cut across in front of us, a fighter at 3 o'clock level.

There's a fighter smoking off to our right. We don't know whether we got him or not, or who got him, but he's smoking.

That – [gunfire] – I spoke about a little while ago – [gunfire] – is still hanging along – [gunfire] – parallel with us – [gunfire] – That was our bombardier. That was our bombardier in front on a burst. A fighter just made a pass at us directly ahead, but turned away before he got in range.

There's some up here at 9 o'clock reported by our gunners. A squadron of fighters.

Here comes one turning in – No he decided to turn away. We're still over Japanese territory.

There goes a fighter to our right spiraling down smoking.

About 28 fighters have been reported by our waist gunner at 9 o'clock. They haven't as yet come in.

Our left waist gunner, Sergeant Siegel, says that flight – those three flights of fighters are still hanging on.

Three flights of fighters are still hanging on our wingtip to the left. They're still waiting, they haven't as yet come in, although they look like they're coming.

That flight of about 30 Jap bombers are – Jap fighters rather, are still hanging on. About 30.

We're just passing over the Japanese coastline again and out to the open sea, and that water looks awfully good. We want to put miles and miles between us and the Japanese islands right now.

Those fighters over to our left that I talked to you about a moment ago are not coming in.

We're passing away. We can see the waves lapping up on the shores down below us, and we're heading out to the open sea.

Those planes we saw a moment ago that we thought was a fighter element turned out to be some of our own '29s and how welcome, and how welcome they look.

We're now putting miles between us and the Japanese coastline. Our '29 is functioning beautifully, smoothly, as we streak away toward the Marianas.

And that's our mission completed.

This is your AAF combat reporter returning you now to the United States.[3]

I couldn't believe what I just heard. The sound of those machine guns and Lieutenant Charlie Henderson shooting down that fighter, it was all just so incredible. I could even hear the clanking of the shell casings as they tumbled down inside the gun turret after he fired his guns. It gave me cold chills when I heard those machine guns firing, and then Brown exclaiming: "We got 'em! There goes one, we got 'em! On that last burst we got a fighter!"[4]

I never thought that I'd ever hear a B-29 gun turret in action, let alone shooting down a fighter. What made the recording even more special for me is that I actually have a B-29 gun turret in my collection that's just like the one Henderson used to shoot down that fighter. And now I had just heard one in action over Japan.

What an extraordinary piece of history Brown recorded that day. But before I could fully absorb what I just heard, the second half of the broadcast began with the announcer boasting that the gunners on *The City of Muncie* had shot down three Japanese fighters that day, and their mission covered a distance of 3,400 miles and took 17 hours to fly. The announcer then said that we were going to hear from some of the wives and mothers of *The City of Muncie's* crew, who'd also been listening to the broadcast. In the Los Angeles studio was Mrs. Frances Devesci, the mother of Lieutenant Robert Smith, the navigator, who was the youngest member of the crew. Next was Mrs. Sarah Siegel in the New York studio, the wife of Sergeant Leroy Siegel, the left gunner. And from San Francisco was Mrs. Viva Crowcroft, the wife of Lieutenant Frank Crowcroft, the pilot.

Listening to these women talk about their men was something I never expected to hear, either. They were all so proud. Congratulations were in order all around for the crew, but not just for the success of the mission. Mrs. Siegel explained that Mrs. Crowcroft had just given birth to a baby girl, Susan, only a month before, and the wife of the flight engineer, Lieutenant Melvin Greene, was expecting a baby any day. Lieutenant Charlie Henderson's wife, Betty, was also expecting a baby in May. Mrs. Crowcroft came on last and joked that Frank had done such a good job handling *The City of Muncie* that she might even trust him to take Susan out in her carriage.

The broadcast ended with the AAF orchestra playing "The Bombardier Song," written by Bing Crosby. The song's final verse looked to the future, when the war was finally over, and the men would see a world that's free when they flew home again. Hearing those words about flying home again brought tears to my eyes, because I already knew then what those millions of listeners that evening in 1945 didn't know.

Exactly seven days after that recording was made, *The City of Muncie* was rammed by a Japanese Ki-45 fighter over Nagoya. The impact was devastating. Bursting into flames after its left wing was sheared off, *The City of Muncie* rolled over on her back and spun to earth from 20,000 feet.

Back in the gunners' compartment, the centrifugal force from the spin was so great that Sergeant William Price couldn't move. The last thing he remembered thinking was: "Mom is going to give me hell for this."[5] When he woke up, Price was floating through the air and thought he was in heaven. Then he looked up and saw his parachute and realized where he was. Price had no memory of how he got out, or of pulling the ripcord of his parachute. Sergeant Leroy Siegel later said that Price had dove head-first through his sighting blister. Siegel followed him out. They were the only ones to escape from the back of the B-29.[6]

In the forward cabin, the collision ripped a hole in the fuselage large enough for Lieutenant Melvin Greene and Lieutenant Robert Smith to jump through. No one else from *The City of Muncie* got out alive. As he fell through the air, Smith pulled the ripcord of his parachute, but something went wrong. His parachute did not fully open. Smith was last seen by Sergeant Siegel on the ground near the wreckage, unconscious but still alive. He died a short time later.[7]

Hearing those words at the end of the broadcast about seeing a world that's free when they flew home brought me to tears, because eight of those men from *The City of Muncie* would never see a world that's free or fly home again. It was just 17 days after Robert Smith's 20th birthday.

*   *   *

The recording that Harold Brown made that day was such an incredible piece of history that I had to share it with as many people as possible. With permission from Japan Air Raids.org, I put a copy of the recording and a brief story about the mission on my website. I was also able to obtain a great photo of the crew from the 29th Bomb Group Association to go with the recording. It was really something to see the smiling faces of all these young men from the recording. Crowcroft, Henderson, Smith – they were all there, standing tall and proud next to their B-29. These men gave their lives for our freedom, and I couldn't think of a better way to honor their sacrifice than by making this recording available for everyone to hear. I shared it with everyone I knew, including a friend who flew B-29s during the Korean War. The recording left him limp, he said.

A few years went by, and then one night I received an e-mail from someone I didn't know. Her name was Ann, but everyone called her Andy, she said, after her father, Charles Andrew Henderson, *The City of Muncie's* bombardier. She was born six weeks after her father died that day over Nagoya.[8]

Andy went on to explain that she had just found my website and listened to the recording of her father's mission. She had an old copy of the recording that was given to her years ago by Bill Price, the right gunner, but the audio on my recording was so much clearer. She was stunned, she said, as she listened to the crew talking in the background. One of those voices was her father.

This recording is the only time that she has ever heard her father's voice.

When I first posted the recording on my website, I was hoping that some of the family members of the crew would find it, as I knew what it would mean for them to hear it. I never dreamed that Charlie Henderson's daughter would find it, or that this recording would be the only time that she would ever hear her father's voice. I don't have the words to express how all of this made me feel. I was just so proud that my work had reached Charlie's daughter, and that it had such an impact on her. But there was something that I didn't tell her.

Back in 2010, when I traded with the Japanese collector for the data plate of *The Dragon Lady* and the wreckage from the Ki-45 that rammed *Haley's Comet*, I also got something else from him. Included in the trade were two pieces of wreckage from a B-29 that was shot down over Japan. The first piece was a section of aluminum skin that had part of the United States "star and bar" national insignia painted on it. The piece was big enough that I could tell it came from the top left point of the star. The second piece was a section of control surface fabric that still had almost all of its original silver paint intact. Even though the B-29 was the most advanced bomber in the world, its control surfaces (the rudder, elevators and ailerons) were all covered in fabric. Both of these pieces had the date of the crash stamped on the back of them in Japanese. That date was April 7, 1945, the day that *The City of Muncie* was rammed.

There was a possibility that this wreckage came from her father's B-29.

I did some research after I acquired the wreckage and discovered that five B-29s were lost over Japan that day, one of which was *The City of Muncie*. I was hoping to identify which B-29 the wreckage came from, but the collector couldn't tell me much about it, or who the previous owners were when I tried to trace its history back to 1945.

I had always intended to send Andy pictures of the wreckage after she got in touch with me, but since my research had failed to identify which B-29 it came from, it fell by the wayside. A few years later, while I was working on this chapter, it occurred to me that I still needed to send her pictures of the wreckage. Even though there was only a 20 percent chance it was from her father's B-29, I knew she would still like to see it. I had not e-mailed Andy in a few years, so I got back in touch to see if the e-mail address I had for her was still current. I mentioned that I wanted to send her pictures of something that might be connected to her father's B-29, but I didn't say what it was.

A few hours later, I heard back from Andy. She was touched that I remembered her, and then she said something that left me speechless: did I know that today was her father's birthday? Of all the days that I could have e-mailed her, it just happened to be Charlie Henderson's birthday![9]

I had no idea that it was her father's birthday when I sent that e-mail. It made me think of what Mr. Trabold and I had talked about, and how I thought that some things happen for a reason.

After talking to Andy, I was inspired to take another look at the wreckage and my research into its identity. Just like before, my research was inconclusive, but there was one clue left that I had not fully explored yet. There was a name written on the old envelope that the wreckage came in. It could be the person who took the wreckage from the crash site in 1945, or maybe it's the name of a Japanese collector who owned it at some point over the years. I reached out to a fellow researcher in Japan for help with the name, but so far we haven't had any luck in identifying this person. The name on the envelope is C.S. Okumura. If you have any information about that name, please get in touch with me at TrevorBMcIntyre@outlook.com.

We'll probably never know for sure which B-29 this wreckage came from, so I plan to display the pieces in honor of all 51 men who died on the five B-29s that were lost on that April day. I think they would like that, all of them being remembered together. As the first American to hold this wreckage since 1945, I am honored to be the caretaker of these artifacts, and I humbly accept the responsibility that comes with them. I see it as my duty now to ensure the sacrifices of those 51 young men who gave their lives that day are not forgotten. I won't let them down.

*   *   *

To listen to the actual recording of *The City of Muncie's* mission on March 31, 1945, visit my website at TrevorMcIntyre.com. Thanks to the work of Harold Brown and the crew of *The City of Muncie*, now we can all know what a B-29 mission over Japan was like. It still gives me cold chills.

17

Flying for Uncle Sam

This chapter was supposed to be an intimate profile of Ben Kuroki, a humble farmer from Hershey, Nebraska, who served his country with honor and distinction during World War II. But I failed you, the reader. Ben Kuroki passed away before I could interview him for this chapter.

For someone who I had never met, Ben's death really affected me. I admired him so much for what he stood for and fought against, and now the world was suddenly a lesser place without him. It's hard to admit this, but I never felt an urgency to get in touch with Ben as I was working on this book. I know it sounds naive, but I always thought that he would be just a short phone call away when I was ready to write this chapter. Then my world came crashing down in September of 2015, when I saw on the news that Ben Kuroki had died.

I had a grand vision for this chapter, but that has all changed now. I struggled for weeks to figure out how to write this story without Ben's help. It hurt to think about all of those questions that I wanted to ask him, and the opportunity I let slip away. I'll never forgive myself for not reaching out to Ben when I had the chance.

Maybe I was too hard on myself, but my failure left me in a deep depression, and part of me wanted to forget all about this chapter and what could have been. But then I became determined to fight my way through it for Ben. His story is too important to be left untold in this book. I could not fail Ben, and I could not fail you, the reader, for a second time. The best I can do now is to simply tell you about Ben's life, and how he inspired me.

Ben, I hope I can do your story justice.

*   *   *

The day after Pearl Harbor was attacked, Ben Kuroki and his younger brother Fred left their family's small farm to join the U.S. Army. Ben was 24 years old, slight in stature, and the epitome of small-town Nebraska: soft-spoken, hardworking and honest. Ben came from a poor, hardworking family who, like so many other Americans, struggled through the Great Depression and the Dust Bowl. With nine brothers and sisters, the food wasn't always plentiful when he was growing up, but life was getting better on his family's farm as 1941 drew to an end.

Then everything changed after Pearl Harbor. Everything changed because Ben was the son of Japanese immigrants. For the next four years, Ben Kuroki had to fight two wars: one against the Axis powers, and the other against racial prejudice. The latter, he said, was the toughest at times. "I had to fight like hell for the right to fight for my own country," Ben often said.[1]

Growing up in Nebraska as a Nisei, a person born in the United States to Japanese immigrants, Ben had never experienced any racial prejudice before, but that all changed when he tried to join the Army. After passing a physical and signing the enlistment forms, Ben was told to go home and wait. Two weeks passed and Ben still had not heard from the Army, so he called the recruiting station. Some of his friends had already left for basic training, but for some reason Ben had not been called up yet. He soon learned why. The Army didn't know what to do with Americans of Japanese ancestry.[2]

Ben was angry that the Army didn't want him, but he was determined to fight for his country. A few days later, Ben heard on the radio that the Air Corps was signing up men at Grand Island, Nebraska. Ben called first and asked if they cared about a man's last name, what he looked like or where his family came from. The sergeant replied that he got $2.00 for every man he signed up, and he didn't care who he was. Ben and his brother drove 150 miles to Grand Island and enlisted in the Army Air Forces.[3]

During the train ride to basic training, Ben and his brother were talking when another recruit suddenly yelled: "What are those two lousy Japs doing in this Army? I thought this was the American Army." Ben Kuroki's second war against racism had begun.[4]

His first months in the Army would be the toughest period of Ben Kuroki's life. Ben had never even visited Japan, but many viewed him as Japanese instead of American, which led to endless harassment and verbal abuse. Even in uniform, he was still looked upon with anger and suspicion. Because of his appearance, Ben was subjected to weeks of KP (kitchen patrol) duty, washing pots and pans and peeling potatoes in the kitchen. Ben felt like he was being punished for the way he looked, but he didn't dare complain to his superiors. When he was off duty, Ben stayed alone in his barracks while the others went into town. He quietly kept to himself for fear of being kicked out of the Air Corps for the slightest infraction. Without any explanation, his brother Fred was kicked out after two weeks and sent to the Army to dig ditches. Ben didn't even get to say goodbye before his brother left. He was lonelier now than ever before.[5]

Most people wouldn't even speak to Ben, but behind his back they would stare and point while whispering to one another. Then there were the others who yelled racial insults at him. The drunks he feared the most – they always wanted to fight.

Despite all the harassment and abuse, Ben Kuroki's spirit could not be broken. He was determined to prove his loyalty and fight for his country. With the encouragement of a handful of friends he made who saw past his race, he was going to do just that. After graduating from clerical school, Ben was sent to Barksdale Field in Louisiana to await his next assignment. Ben had long dreamed of flying and was fascinated by the B-24 bombers he saw at Barksdale, but he was afraid to go near one out of fear someone would think he was a Japanese spy. Ben was finally assigned to a B-24 bomb group as a clerk typist, but twice his name was left off the roster when the group moved to a new base. Both times he had to beg – with tears in his eyes – to stay with his group.[6]

In the fall of 1942, Ben's bomb group moved overseas to England and was the first B-24 outfit to face the Germans. Ben still dreamed of joining a crew, but he was not allowed to fly. Ben was persistent and didn't give up. During his free time, Ben helped out on the flight line and studied the .50 caliber machine guns to the point where he could assemble one blindfolded.

Ben's persistence finally paid off when Jake Epting, one of the pilots he'd been begging to get into combat with, came to see Ben after he returned from a five-day gunnery school near London. A gunner on Epting's crew had lost some fingers due to frostbite, and he needed a new gunner if Ben wanted the job. Before Epting approached Ben, he asked his crew if they would fly with a man who looked Japanese. Everyone agreed that Ben's looks did not matter. If he could do the job, he was more than welcome. On December 7, 1942, one year after Pearl Harbor was attacked, Ben Kuroki's dream came true: he was now a full-fledged gunner on a B-24 combat crew.[7]

On his first bombing mission, Ben saved the life of his crew's tail gunner, who was severely wounded when a piece of flak struck him in the head. Ben later described that first encounter with flak as terrifying, but strangely, he experienced peace. For the first time, Ben felt like he belonged. No one in the bomb group questioned his nationality or his loyalty after that first mission.[8]

Ben's tenacity quickly earned him the nickname "Most Honorable Son" because, in the words of Epting, Ben was "a most honorable son of America." The nickname was soon painted on their B-24's fuselage next to Ben's gun turret.[9]

After spending 11 weeks bombing Axis targets in North Africa and Italy, Ben's outfit was ordered back to England. While en route, Ben's B-24 became hopelessly lost and the pilots had to make a forced landing in rugged terrain when they ran out of fuel. The crew didn't realize it at the time, but they had just landed in Spanish Morocco, a neutral territory, and were immediately captured. Later that day, the crew was taken to a nearby town, where a Spanish officer informed them that they would be spending the rest of the war in prison. That did not appeal to Ben, and he soon hatched a plan to escape to freedom in French Morocco, some 20 miles away.

Under the cover of darkness, Ben made his escape. For the better part of two days, he was constantly on the run. To blend in with the locals, he fashioned a turban out of his shirt and turned his raincoat inside out, but people still stared at him. Ben was shot at twice before his luck ran out on the second day when Arab sentries captured him near the border. Ben was returned to prison and reunited with his crew, who told him the Spanish soldiers admired his guts for escaping.[10]

Ben and his crew were soon flown to Spain, where they were interned in a hotel, and within three months they were back in England. It was rumored that the American Government secured their release in trade for a new Buick.[11]

Before Ben returned to combat, he was interviewed on BBC Radio by Ben Lyon, who starred in Howard Hughes' epic film *Hell's Angels*. The Hollywood star introduced Ben Kuroki to millions of listeners and highlighted his stoic determination to fight for his country.[12]

Ben Kuroki had flown his fair share of tough missions, but nothing could have prepared him for what was coming. On August 1, 1943, Ben fought in one of the bloodiest air battles in history. Targeting "Hitler's Gas Station" with nearly 200 B-24 bombers, Operation *Tidal Wave* was a massive low-level bombing raid that was launched to destroy Germany's vital oil refineries in Ploesti, Romania. The plan was for the bombers to come in low and fast and overwhelm Ploesti's defenses, but what the planners didn't know was that the Germans had turned Ploesti into one of the most heavily fortified targets in all of Europe. And with a sophisticated early warning system in place, the Germans would know exactly when the Americans were coming.[13]

What was supposed to be a surprise attack turned into a deadly ambush. The carnage that ensued in the skies over Ploesti would become known as Black Sunday.

Ben was manning his B-24's top turret when his formation dropped down to tree-top level and began their bomb run into Ploesti. As they neared the target, the air around Ben's bomber suddenly filled with explosions and murderous anti-aircraft fire. The German trap had been sprung. The bombers were flying so low that the gunners began exchanging point-blank fire with the German flak batteries. For the first time, the crews could actually see the soldiers shooting at them. The German guns were everywhere, even appearing out of haystacks and church steeples to rake the low-flying bombers.[14]

Ben could do nothing but watch as the bombers around him were hit one after another. "We went in at 50 feet into terrible anti-aircraft fire," Ben later said. "Our planes would crash and we could see our buddies burning in their planes."[15]

As they approached the target area, the B-24 flying next to Ben was hit and burst into flames. Ben watched helplessly as the bomber sank to the ground and exploded in a fireball. Ben was friends with every man on that bomber. In the blink of an eye, they were all gone.[16]

Then Ben's bomb group commander, Lieutenant Colonel Addison Baker, was hit. Baker's B-24 was on fire and he could have made a belly landing, but he stayed in formation and led his bombers another three miles to their target and dropped his bombs. Before the mission, Baker told his men that he would get his B-24 over the target even if it fell apart. "He got his ship over the target all right – we were close behind him," Ben recalled. "And we saw it when it fell apart, flaming to the earth."[17] Baker and his co-pilot, Major John Jerstad, were both posthumously awarded the Medal of Honor for their actions over Ploesti that day.

The losses suffered during the Ploesti raid were horrifying. Of the 178 B-24s dispatched on the mission, 54 bombers were lost, and 310 men were killed. Hundreds more were wounded or captured. Only 33 of the bombers that returned were fit to fly the next day. Ben's squadron alone had launched nine bombers on the mission, but only two returned home.[18]

Back at base later that night, there was no line at the mess hall for dinner. Ben was hungry, but he couldn't eat when he thought about all the men who should have been standing in line and weren't there. Ben was exhausted from the 13-hour mission and tried to sleep, but the sight of all the empty bunks haunted him. Ben didn't sleep for three nights.

The morning after the raid wasn't any easier. The men always got up at 6:00 a.m. and there was usually a lot of playful yelling between the tents, but the only shouting Ben heard that morning was from his co-pilot; he was yelling hysterically for his best friend, who he watched die in the B-24 next to him.[19] The survivors of Ploesti would carry the horrors of the battle with them for the rest of their lives.

Ben had one mission left after Ploesti before he completed his tour of 25 combat missions and could go home, but he still had something to prove. He and his crewmates had a saying about their missions: "On the way to the bombing target, we were flying for Uncle Sam. The minute we dropped the bombs and we turned around, we were flying for ourselves. All we wanted to do is get back to base and live another day."[20]

Ben could have gone home after his 25th mission and spent the rest of the war far away from the fighting, but against the advice of his buddies, who all said that he'd done enough for one man, he volunteered to fly five more missions. Ben later said those extra missions were for America and all Americans of different races, religions and skin colors.[21]

On his 30th and final mission, Ben's luck almost ran out over Munster in north-west Germany. Ben was manning his top turret when he felt the radio operator tug on his leg. As Ben looked down, a flak burst suddenly hit his turret and shattered its plexiglass dome. The force of the explosion was so violent that it knocked Ben out. The radio operator pulled him out of the turret and revived him with oxygen, but incredibly he didn't have a scratch on him. The dome of his turret, however, had a hole in it big enough for Ben to fit his entire head through. If he hadn't been looking down when the flak exploded, he would have been killed.[22]

After serving 15 months overseas, Ben Kuroki returned home to a hero's welcome. His story appeared in *Time* magazine, the *New York Times*, and other newspapers all across the country, who heralded the return of a hero fighting a dual war.[23] Ben's first train ride in uniform had been a dreadful experience, but now complete strangers bought him drinks and congratulated him. Back home in Nebraska, the biggest department store in Omaha included Ben's picture in their window display of "Nebraska's Heroes," and his local drugstore wanted to display his medals. The top radio station in Omaha even visited Ben on his parents' farm for an interview.

Following a well-deserved visit home, the Army sent Ben to Santa Monica for more rest and recuperation at the Edgewater Beach Hotel. California had changed a lot while Ben was overseas. To provide "every possible protection against espionage and against sabotage," President Roosevelt signed an executive order on February 19, 1942, that granted the Secretary of War and military commanders the power to designate military areas across the United States from which any or all persons could be excluded. With this unprecedented power, during the spring of 1942, some 120,000 people of Japanese ancestry were forced from their homes on the West Coast and relocated to internment camps, where they were placed under armed guard. Some were foreign nationals, but the majority were American-born citizens who looked just like Ben.[24]

According to a *Time* magazine reporter, Ben was probably the first Nisei to walk the Santa Monica beaches since the "great evacuation of Japanese from California after Pearl Harbor."[25]

The time that Ben spent in California was a period of great highs and lows. The roller-coaster began when Ben was invited to tell his story on a nationwide radio show hosted by Ginny Simms, a famous singer and actress. Before the broadcast, Ginny took Ben and two other servicemen to dinner at the world-famous Brown Derby restaurant, a Hollywood landmark. For a humble farmer from Nebraska, dining with movie stars felt like a dream. Back at the radio station, the producer had some bad news. An NBC executive had decided that the "Japanese American question" was too controversial to air, and Ben was not allowed to go on the show. After all he had been through, there were still many who couldn't see past his race. Ben was devastated. "They wouldn't let me on the air because I'm a Jap," he later said. Ben cried himself to sleep that night.[26]

A few days after the radio show fiasco, Ben was scheduled to give a speech at the prestigious Commonwealth Club in San Francisco, which had hosted speeches from every President since Abraham Lincoln. A newspaper announced his appearance with the headline "JAP TO ADDRESS S.F. CLUB."[27] Ben was still shaken and wanted to cancel the speech, but it was too late to back out now. On the day of his speech, the newspapers were filled with the first accounts of the Bataan Death March. As news spread about the atrocities Japan committed after the fall of Bataan in April of 1942, the American public became enraged when they learned about the thousands of American and Filipino prisoners of war who died during the 60-mile forced march to Japanese prison camps. When Ben arrived at the club, he saw angry people carrying signs in front of the building. He was afraid to be seen on the street, even in uniform, and quickly rushed inside.[28]

When it was time to give his speech, Ben was shaking in fear as he took to the stage before a crowd of 600 people. Looking into the audience, Ben kept thinking that he could see the fury over Bataan in their eyes. He'd rather be on a bombing mission than standing at that podium. He nervously began his speech by thanking everyone for the invitation to speak, and then explained that a soldier's job was to fight, not talk, but he was going to do the best he could. Ben then said:

> I've spent most of my life in Hershey, Nebraska, which isn't where they make Hershey candy bars. Hershey is so small that probably none of you has ever heard of it. Before the war the population was about 500; now I guess it's about 300.
>
> I didn't even live in Hershey; my father had a farm a mile north of town. I remember the farmers used to go to town every Saturday night and stand in groups on the street corners talking about their cows and horses. We've lived on that farm since 1928, and after I finished high school I helped my father work it until the war came along.
>
> The last two years are what really matter, though, and maybe I can tell you something about them, even if I don't know much about making speeches. That's one thing the Army didn't teach me, though it taught me a lot of other things, and the experience I went through as a result of being in the Army taught me even more.
>
> I learned more about democracy, for one thing, than you'll find in all the books, because I saw it in action. When you live with men under combat conditions for 15 months, you begin to understand what brotherhood, equality, tolerance and unselfishness really mean. They're no longer just words.
>
> Under fire, a man's ancestry, what he did before the war, or even his present rank, don't matter at all. You're fighting as a team – that's the only way a bomber crew can fight – you're fighting for each other's life and for your country, and whether you realize it at the time or not, you're living and proving democracy.[29]

Ben had taken the stage fearful that he would be booed, or worse, but then something incredible happened: the audience became enthralled with his story. With his nerves calmed by bursts of applause, Ben poured his heart out for the next 40 minutes. When he was finished, the audience erupted and gave Ben a 10-minute standing ovation. Looking into the cheering crowd, he now saw people crying in admiration. Ben had trouble holding back his own tears. The audience was so captivated by Ben's story that he returned to the stage two more times to say a few more words.

Ben's speech was so compelling that magazines and newspapers across the country reprinted it, and it was even translated into Japanese and broadcast on short-wave radio to Japan. Looking back today, scholars say that Ben Kuroki's speech at the Commonwealth Club was a major turning point in the mistrust and bitterness against Japanese Americans. Ben later said that giving that speech was one of the most important things he ever did during the war.[30]

With his wealth of combat experience, Ben could have taken an easy assignment as a gunnery instructor for the rest of the war, but he wanted to keep fighting for those who couldn't. He turned his attention to the Pacific next, and to the one bomber that could strike Japan: the B-29.

A week after his Commonwealth Club speech, Ben reported to an Army replacement center in Salt Lake City for his next assignment. Ben told the interviewing officer that he wanted to fight in the Pacific, but the officer was very curt: "You'll go where we send you." Later that night, Ben wrote a long letter to Colonel Warren Williams of the 2nd Air Force, the training command for new B-29 bomb groups. Colonel Williams' brother had introduced himself to Ben after his Commonwealth Club speech and told him to write to the colonel if he ever needed help. Ben pleaded his case to fight in the Pacific:

> I don't want a nice, soft setup as a gunnery instructor. There's a war in the Pacific that I should be part of, not only because I'm an American citizen but I have a personal score to settle. Because it's the Japanese Fascists who are responsible for stirring up so much hatred in this country against the Nisei. Am I asking too much? All I want is to fight in the Pacific.[31]

Four days later, Ben received orders transferring him to the B-29 field at Salina, Kansas. Ben's plea had worked, but when he arrived at Salina, the runaround started again. He waited for weeks to get assigned to B-29 training, but nothing was happening. When his orders finally did come through, there was no mention of a B-29 assignment. Instead, he was ordered to report to several relocation camps for public relations work. This was not the way Ben wanted to spend the rest of the war. Ben's new assignment was to give speeches and urge the young Nisei in the camps to join the U.S. Army's 442nd Infantry Regiment, which was composed almost entirely of Japanese Americans. (The 442nd would go on to fight with distinction in Europe and became the most decorated combat unit in American history.)

Ben didn't know what to expect as he was driven to the first camp, but what slowly came into view appalled him. Ringed with high barbed wire fences and guard towers was the massive Heart Mountain War Relocation Center in Wyoming, which held almost 11,000 internees at its peak. At the gate, Ben felt uneasy as the guards looked him over and checked his identification. Would they try to shoot him if he ran, he wondered? The guards were armed with rifles and wore the same uniform as Ben, but inside the camp, the people looked just like him. Ben had heard stories about the camps, but he couldn't believe what he was seeing. Was this really America? [32]

Inside the camp, Ben was treated like a movie star. Everyone had read about him in the newspapers and wanted to meet him. No one had ever seen a Nisei war hero before. The camp newspaper later said that to the Nisei, Ben Kuroki was their first national hero.[33]

But not everyone in the camps welcomed him. Some of the older Japanese Americans, many of whom had lost everything they owned when they were evicted from their homes, along with a small faction of dissidents who vehemently opposed military service until their rights were restored, despised Ben for fighting for the same government that had forced them into the camps. All of this weighed heavily on Ben, and he kept thinking about his own family and how lucky they were to be safe back in Nebraska. But what if they had also been forced into one of these camps, he thought to himself. Would he still want to fight for America? Ben didn't have an answer.[34]

Later that day, the whole camp gathered to sing "Auld Lang Syne" as the camp director drove Ben back to the train station. Ben watched them singing through the barbed wire as the car pulled away. The director told him how important his visit had been for morale inside the camp, and then he mentioned how the Nisei had volunteered to save the local bean crop the previous fall. The Nisei had saved the crop, but the locals still put up signs in their town like the one Ben saw hanging in a barbershop window: "No Japs Wanted Here."[35]

The visits to the camps took a toll on Ben – the armed guards and the barbed wire; the young Nisei asking how things were in the outside world. None of it made any sense. Ben needed some time to collect himself. With a 15-day furlough coming up, he decided to spend part of his time in Colorado with his younger sister and her husband. Outside the train station in Denver, Ben was about to get into a cab when another man suddenly jumped in and slammed the door in his face. Then the man looked up at Ben and shouted: "I don't want to ride with no lousy Jap!"[36]

Ben was speechless and just stood there, in full uniform with silver wings and combat ribbons on his chest, as the cab sped away. After 30 bombing missions, Ben Kuroki still could not get a cab in his own country.

A few days later, Ben received a letter from his sister back home. She wrote that she didn't know how to tell him about the news she just heard. By the second sentence, the letter had fallen out of his hands. Ben's best friend, Gordy Jorgenson, had been killed by the Japanese while fighting in the Solomon Islands.[37]

Ben staggered out of his barracks in disbelief and wandered aimlessly for hours in the cold while thinking about Gordy. When they were kids, Gordy had saved Ben's life when he fell through the ice into a frozen river. He thought about all of their adventures and hunting trips while growing up. He thought about Gordy's wife and baby back home. The Japanese had just killed his best friend – Ben was now more determined than ever to go back to war again.

After a phone call to Colonel Williams, in which he explained what happened to Gordy, Ben soon had orders to report to an airfield in Nebraska where the 505th Bomb Group was being formed. When Ben checked in with the operations officer, he was told to come back the next morning. The runaround was starting all over again, he thought. But the next day, he finally got the news he was waiting for: he was assigned to a new B-29 crew as the tail gunner.[38]

For the next three months, as his crew trained for combat, everything was going well until Ben's pilot, James Jenkins, was called in to see the intelligence officer one day. A new War Department regulation had just come down from Washington, and it stated that no person of Japanese ancestry could fly combat in the Pacific.[39] Ben was shocked by the news, but he'd come too far to give up now. Ben reached out to his friends for help, and soon there were letters and telegrams pouring into the War Department on his behalf. His most powerful advocate was Congressman Carl Curtis of Nebraska, who asked General George C. Marshall – the U.S. Army Chief of Staff – to personally review Ben's case. After a tense period of waiting, a letter arrived from Secretary of War Henry Stimson himself: Ben was exempt from the regulation and could remain with his crew.

Ben Kuroki would now be the first Japanese American to fly combat missions in the Pacific.

While the Secretary of War had personally granted an exemption for Ben, there were still some people who didn't want him to fly in the Pacific. At Mather Field in California, Ben's crew were making the final preparations to their B-29 before leaving for the Pacific when Jenkins suddenly ran up looking for Ben. He had a mad look on his face and asked him for the letter from Secretary Stimson. "Haven't got time to explain now," Jenkins said. "Just get it."[40]

Ben dug the letter out of his bag and handed it to Jenkins, who rushed away with it. Ben was confused and wondered what was happening now. With their engines already started and warming up, Jenkins finally came running back with a big smile on his face. The last of the crew jumped aboard and Jenkins quickly taxied the B-29 out to the runway for takeoff.

Ben got the rest of the story after they took off. At the last minute, an intelligence officer and some FBI agents had been trying to remove Ben from the crew and demanded that Jenkins delay taking off. The FBI had also tried to pull Ben off his B-29 before they left Nebraska, but this time the agents were armed. Jenkins showed the Stimson letter to the men and tried arguing with them, but it was no use. The agents refused to budge, so Jenkins ignored them and quickly took off before anyone could stop them.[41]

Ben's new home in the Pacific was Tinian Island, and it was a very dangerous place for a Nisei to be. As soon as they landed, an officer warned the crew that there were still a lot of Japanese soldiers on the island, and at night they snuck into the camps in search of food and water. They were also stealing American uniforms. "So anything that even looks like a Jap," the officer explained, "the guards shoot first and ask questions afterwards." Everyone immediately turned to look at Ben.[42] From that moment on, Ben didn't go anywhere without his crewmates with him.

The first time Ben walked into the mess hall, everyone stopped eating and glared at him. One soldier even began reaching for his pistol. Luckily, Ben was with his crew, but it would take time for the others to get to know him. The most perilous time for him was when darkness fell. That's when the shooting started. It always began with a single shot, then several more. Soon everyone was nervously shooting at shadows and noises beyond the perimeter of the camp. Bullets whizzed by so close that Ben and his crewmates had to lay on the floor of their tent until things calmed down. Ben would often wake up in the middle of the night and need to go to the latrine, but the risk of being mistaken for a Japanese soldier made it suicidal to leave his tent at night. His buddies joked that he deserved a Purple Heart for "bladder damage." During his first month on Tinian, Ben felt safer flying missions than he did on the island.[43]

All of the dangers Ben faced on the ground and in the air took a toll on him. One night, Ben was walking back to camp alone when a group of American soldiers confronted him.

"Look, there's a Jap," one of the soldiers said.

"Don't shoot, I'm an American," Ben pleaded, but the soldiers didn't believe him.

"C'mon, let's shoot the bastard."[44]

Ben then woke up screaming from the nightmare.

Ben started having terrible nightmares soon after arriving on Tinian. He never slept well and often needed a shot of whiskey just to fall asleep, but the alcohol didn't stop the dreams. As Ben flew more missions, the nightmares became so bad that he was constantly waking up in terror throughout the night. There was one dream that kept occurring over and over again, and it terrified Ben. In the nightmare, Japanese soldiers came into his tent with knives to kill him. After his 10th mission, Ben had the nightmare again. This time he tried to wake up, but couldn't. Maybe it wasn't a dream after all, Ben thought, and they really *were* stabbing him. Ben struggled and screamed until he finally woke up covered in sweat. He couldn't take it anymore, so he went to see the flight surgeon and told him everything. The next day, Ben was told that he was being sent home. "You've done more than your share in this war," the flight surgeon said.[45]

By now, Ben had flown 40 missions: 30 in Europe and North Africa, and 10 against Japan. If anyone deserved to go home, it was Ben Kuroki. But he kept thinking about all those people in the relocation camps, and his best friend, Gordy. He couldn't stop fighting now.

"I know what my body can take and all I need is a rest, sir," Ben said to the flight surgeon. "I don't want to go back now." The flight surgeon stared at Ben, then shrugged his shoulders. Instead of going home, Ben was sent to Hawaii for a rest. After he returned, Ben was ready to fight again.[46]

Months later, when the news broke that Japan had finally surrendered and World War II was over, Ben Kuroki was lying in a hospital bed on Tinian. He had survived 58 bombing missions without a scratch, but ironically, it would be a fellow American who nearly killed him.

It all began after he returned from his 28th mission to Japan. Ben and his crew were relaxing and having a few drinks when a very drunk and angry soldier started a fight with Ben over who was more patriotic. Before he knew what was happening, the soldier stabbed him in the head with a knife. As Ben collapsed to the ground, one of his crewmates, Master Sergeant Russell Olsen, jumped in to protect him from the attacker. Olsen probably saved Ben's life. When Ben woke up, he was in the hospital with 24 stitches in his head. If the knife had cut a little deeper, the doctors said he would have died.[47]

In the Kuroki family, there was a legend about lucky ears. It was said that any boy born into the family with a tiny hole near the top of each ear was special and would live a very long and lucky life. Ben was the only one in his family with ears like that, and he had miraculously survived 58 combat missions and a near-fatal stabbing. The legend was true.[48]

* * *

Three days after he arrived home from the Pacific, Ben gave a speech at the New York Herald Tribune Forum at the Waldorf-Astoria Hotel in New York City. The panel of speakers joining Ben on stage included General George C. Marshall, who was seated next to Ben, and the President of the Philippines.[49] I can still remember the first time I read the speech Ben gave that night, and how his words moved me. This is part of what Ben said:

> Not only did I go to war to fight the Fascist ideas of Germany and Japan, but also to fight against a very few Americans who fail to understand the principles of freedom and equality upon which this country was founded ... I fought with a lot of men in this war, all kinds, a Polish gunner, a Jewish engineer, a German bombardier and even a full-blooded Dakota Indian. I saw men wounded, and whatever land their grandfathers came from, their blood was always the same color. And whatever church they went to, the screams of pain sounded just about the same.
>
> I've had 58 bombing missions now, and I'm still tired enough so my hands shake, and plenty of nights I don't sleep so good. I'd like to go home to Nebraska and forget the war, and just lie under a tree somewhere and take it easy. It's hard to realize that the war is not over for me. Not for a lot of us, Jewish-Americans, Italian-Americans, Negro-Americans, Japanese-Americans. While there is still hatred and prejudice, our fight goes on. Back in Nebraska on our farm, when I planted a seed, I knew that after a while I'd get a crop. That's the way it was with a lot of us in this war: we went to plant the seeds to bring in a crop of decency and peace for our families and our children.
>
> Back in high school in Nebraska, one of the things they taught me was that America is a land where it isn't race or religion that makes free men. That's why I went to Tokyo. I went to fight for my country, where freedom isn't color, but a way of life, and all men are created equal until they prove otherwise.[50]

After he returned home from the war, Ben embarked on his 59th and most difficult mission: his fight against racial intolerance. Using his own money and small donations, Ben went on speaking tours across the country and told his story to schools and civic clubs. His story would touch many lives. Six decades after Ben spoke to her 8th grade class in 1946, one student recalled how Ben's story had "opened our eyes to the reality and cruelty of racial prejudice," and that her entire class benefited from that awakening.[51]

Ben Kuroki was a true American. And his story made me want to be a *better* American. I'm sorry that I never got to meet you, Ben. I hope we can all live up to the legacy you left behind.

Harold Brown interviews Ben Kuroki for *The Fighting AAF* radio show after his 27th mission to Japan. (National Archives 204972348)

18

The Red, White and Blue

If you've ever watched an honor guard perform the military funeral honors for a veteran, it's something you'll never forget. After the rifle squad fires a three-volley salute, followed by the playing of Taps, the American flag is gently lifted and displayed to the family. Before the flag is folded and presented to the family on behalf of a grateful nation, you will hear these words explaining what the colors of the flag represent:

> The blue field represents the sky that overlooks our land and denotes the watchfulness of God the Eternal.
> The red stripes tell us of the blood, sweat and tears that have been offered and conquered by our comrades' devotion to the responsible freedom of his country.
> The white stripes boldly proclaim the peace that he helped to bring to our future generations.[1]

At our local veterans park, I've attended a number of these memorial services for veterans who've passed away. I'm not a good enough writer to express how moving the ceremonies are, so I won't even try to put those feelings down on paper. Instead, I'll just say that it's something that every American needs to see, especially those who didn't serve in the military.

When I discovered the magnitude of the story you're about to read, and then considered how to go about telling it, I found myself thinking back to all those memorial services I've attended at our veterans park over the years, and to those words about the American flag. As you begin to read this story and take it all in, I think you'll understand why.

It all began on the evening of July 27, 1945, when 30 B-29s from the 504th Bomb Group lifted off from Tinian and headed for Japan. Their objective that night was the continuation of Operation *Starvation*, the aerial mining campaign to choke off Japan's seaways and paralyze its merchant fleet. Japan relied heavily on the import of raw materials from its conquered territories in Asia to feed both its war machine and its people, and to cut off this vital flow of supplies, the XXI Bomber Command began Operation *Starvation* in late March of 1945 when it sent over 100 B-29s to mine the Shimonoseki Strait. In the months that followed, the B-29s would sow minefields in every major seaway and harbor, ranging from the Sea of Japan to the Inland Sea, and even Tokyo Bay itself. The mines would have a devastating effect on Japan's merchant fleet.[2]

At the controls of one of the bombers that took off that July night was 25-year-old First Lieutenant Raymond Shumway, the aircraft commander. The last few missions had not gone well for Shumway and his crew. Mechanical problems had plagued their B-29, and they were only able to complete one mission out of their last three. On what would now be their seventh combat mission, the crew were hopeful that their streak of bad luck was over as they settled in for the long 15-hour flight ahead.

The target that night for their load of 1,000-pound mines was the Shimonoseki Strait, a narrow channel between Honshu and Kyushu islands. The strait was the only passage that connected the Sea of Japan to the Inland Sea and was a natural bottleneck, vulnerable to mining. (The Inland Sea is a major body of water that separates three of Japan's four home islands.) Since American submarines had practically shut down the two southern entrances to the Inland Sea, the majority of all shipping en route to the Japanese homeland was now passing through the Shimonoseki Strait. Shutting down the channel would dramatically impact Japan's economy and war effort.[3]

Seven hours after they took off, Shumway's B-29 was flying smoothly as the coast of Japan slowly appeared on their radar scope. The bomber was on course and proceeding to the target area, but then something went terribly wrong. After crossing over the coast, without warning, the oil pressure on the No. 1 engine suddenly dropped to zero, and the propeller began to run away and overspeed the engine. Shumway leaned forward and pressed down on the red switch to feather the blades, which would stop the propeller from turning, but there was no oil left in the system for the feathering pump to work. Whatever had failed on the engine, it caused a total loss of the engine's 85-gallon oil supply.

Shumway could only watch helplessly as the propeller began windmilling dangerously out of control. By now they were over the Japanese mainland and in serious trouble. Glancing down at his instrument panel, Shumway realized the No. 1 engine tachometer was reading almost 4,000 RPM, far exceeding the safe limit. He had to act fast. Shumway immediately turned the bomber around, reduced airspeed, and headed back to the open sea as the flight engineer shut down the engine. To lighten their load, the bombardier planted his mines in a small bay along the Inland Sea on the way out. With the propeller still windmilling out of control, the crippled bomber slowly headed back out to sea and took up a course for Iwo Jima.

Looking out of his window, Shumway watched as the propeller shaft began to glow red hot from the propeller turning the engine over without any oil. As they continued to put miles between themselves and Japan, the propeller shaft turned white hot, and then it began shedding pieces of molten metal like shooting stars. There was nothing the crew could do but ride it out as long as they could. The farther away they could get from Japan, the safer they'd be if they had to bail out.

Sometime after 1:00 a.m., at the very moment the co-pilot was ribbing the flight engineer about having to jump, the propeller shaft on the No. 1 engine disintegrated under the strain. What happened next was the stuff of nightmares. Stretching more than 16 feet in diameter and weighing 865 pounds, the massive propeller assembly broke free and slammed into the No. 2 engine. The terrifying impact rocked the B-29 down to its rivets and peppered the airframe with shrapnel. To the crew, it almost felt like they had stopped for a moment in mid-air.

Within seconds, flames began streaming from the No. 2 engine. Shumway tried to feather the No. 2 propeller while the flight engineer discharged the fire extinguisher, but nothing was happening. When he turned and looked out over the left wing, he couldn't believe what he saw. The whole propeller assembly on the No. 2 engine had been ripped away in the collision and was gone. In the blink of an eye, the entire left wing went up in flames. At that point in the mission, their B-29 still had nearly 4,000 gallons of high-octane fuel on board. With ruptured fuel cells feeding the inferno, there was nothing more the crew could do. Their only chance now was to get out before the bomber exploded. Shumway gave the order to bail out.

Following the emergency procedures ingrained during training, the co-pilot lowered the landing gear and opened the hatch in the cockpit floor to bail out (the nose gear had to be lowered to exit through the hatch), and the bombardier flipped the switch to open the bomb bay doors for the gunners in the aft compartment. The crew scrambled to escape as fast as they could. Into the dark night below, the co-pilot jumped first, dislocating his shoulder on the way out, and was followed by the bombardier, flight engineer and navigator. The radio operator was still sending out a distress call, but he would jump as soon as he could.

Back in the aft compartment, the gunners rushed forward to jump from the rear bomb bay. Pulling the bulkhead hatch open, they discovered the bomb bay doors had only opened a few inches and stopped. They were trapped. The gunners frantically tried to beat the doors open, but they were running out of time. Shumway was starting to lose control of the bomber and every second counted. In desperation, two of the gunners tried jumping on the doors. With all their weight, the doors suddenly broke open and the two men tumbled out of the bomb bay. The third gunner was right behind them and about to jump. The radar observer was last seen going back to his station to put on his survival gear, but no one had seen or heard from the tail gunner after the order was given to bail out.

Up in the cockpit, as the fire raged out of control, Shumway held on as long as he could for the others to get out. When he finally jumped, the B-29 was in a flat spin and completely engulfed in flames. After escaping from the death spiral, Shumway realized as he was falling that the bomber, being in a flat spin, was coming down almost on top of him. If he pulled the ripcord now, he would surely be killed when his parachute opened. With no other choice, Shumway had to continue freefalling until he was clear of the B-29.

When he finally pulled the ripcord, a few seconds passed before he felt the jolt of his parachute opening. The next thing Shumway knew, he plunged into the churning seas of the Pacific Ocean. Shumway had jumped so low that if he'd waited any longer, he would not have survived the impact.

Parachuting into water was extremely dangerous, even in calm seas, because you could easily become tangled in your parachute and drown. Ray Shumway had just landed under some of the worst conditions imaginable, and he now had to get out of his parachute as fast as possible. Feeling his way down the straps in the dark water, Ray quickly unfastened his parachute harness and kicked away from the shroud lines. When he was free, he pulled the cords to inflate his yellow Mae West life vest. Before letting his parachute harness go, he reached for the one-man life raft attached to the bottom of the harness. The raft came packed with a small cylinder of carbon dioxide gas, and after yanking out the safety pin, it swiftly inflated when Ray turned the valve on. Only a month earlier, before their first mission, Ray and his crew were trained how to use the life rafts in Tinian harbor. That training would now save his life.

As Ray climbed into the tiny raft and tried to get settled, he suddenly heard someone yelling for help off in the distance. The seas were so rough that Ray couldn't see very far around him, but by following the sound, he frantically made his way towards the cries for help. After paddling for 15 minutes, Ray came upon his radio operator, 32-year-old Sergeant Sam Kidd, from Texas. Sam didn't have a life raft and was drowning. Ray got to Sam just in time and pulled the six-foot tall Texan into his small raft as best he could. After nearly drowning, Sam was not doing well and began vomiting from all the salt water he ingested, and then he passed out. To keep him breathing, Ray had to hold Sam's head above the water after he lost consciousness. The raft just wasn't big enough for the two of them. Sam was safe for now, but in the Pacific, danger was never far away.

To help him swim, Sam had taken his shoes and socks off after he hit the water. When Ray finally pulled him into the raft, there wasn't enough room for Sam to fit, so his legs and bare feet were left dangling over the side. All of this thrashing about had not gone unnoticed. Suddenly, three sharks appeared and began circling the raft. Sensing an easy prey, the sharks edged closer and closer to Sam's feet with each pass. With blood in the water from the cuts on Sam's legs, it was only a matter of time now before they attacked.

Sam was still unconscious and couldn't be moved, so Ray did the only thing he could: he pulled out his .45 automatic and started shooting at the sharks.

The first shots scared the sharks away, but then five more appeared and began circling. One of the sharks came so close that Ray could have reached out and touched it. With its dorsal fin protruding above the surface, Ray followed the shark as it sliced through the water next to the raft. Then, to his horror, the shark suddenly turned and lunged for Sam's feet. By the time he could fire, the shark's jaws were less than two feet away from Sam. Ray carefully took aim and placed his bullet six inches in front of the shark's nose. The water erupted like a geyser as the slug hit next to Sam's foot. Frightened by the impact, the shark recoiled and splashed Ray with its tail as it darted away. His quick shot had scared the predator off before it was too late, but more kept coming.

Ray would fire 16 shots at the sharks that first night.

When the new dawn broke, Sam regained his senses and was able to turn over in the raft. It was very uncomfortable, but they discovered that they could both squeeze into the small raft if Sam sat between Ray's legs and leaned back against his chest. They crammed themselves in so tight that they couldn't move their legs, but at least Sam was safe from the sharks now.

As they bobbed in the stormy seas, Ray and Sam talked about what they had just been through. Did the rest of the crew make it? They saw everyone from the cockpit get out before it was too late, but they didn't know about the gunners or their new radar observer, who was on his first mission with the crew. Ray and Sam were all alone now and didn't see any other survivors. Searching the storm-filled skies, they didn't see any airplanes looking for them, either.

Before they bailed out, the navigator had given Sam their position to radio in, but something went wrong. As they scanned the horizon for search planes, Sam explained that their radio frequency was jammed, and he was unable to send out a distress call before he jumped. That meant that no one knew what happened to them, or where to start looking for survivors.

With that sobering revelation, Ray was afraid the search might take longer than they could survive. The Pacific was a big ocean, and there were almost 1,600 miles between their base on Tinian and the target area. That was greater than the distance between New York City and Dallas. For all anyone knew, they could be anywhere along those 1,600 miles. Ray's life raft carried a small amount of drinking water and rations, but not knowing how long they would be adrift, they decided not to touch any of it for 48 hours.

Later that day, their hopes of being rescued soared when they spotted some Navy fighters approaching overhead. They were the first friendly aircraft they had seen since hitting the water. Ray quickly fired a red signal flare to get their attention. During daylight hours, the flare was supposed to be visible for up to three miles, but the pilots didn't see it. The fighters flew right over them and disappeared out of sight. They were all alone again.

As the day went on, the storms continued and the waves grew higher and higher. The tiny raft wasn't made to support two large men and it was now partially under water. From the raft sitting so low, Ray and Sam seemed to go through as many waves as they rode over. The storms were getting worse as evening approached, and by the time night fell, the waves had become mountains 30 feet high. Ray and Sam held on as tight as they could as they were cast about by the raging seas.

Later that night, when the savage waves reached a crescendo, their worst fears were realized. As they rode the next wave higher and higher, the crest began to curl, and then the wave broke with them on top of it. The violent crash flipped the raft over like a toy and hurled Ray and Sam headfirst into the water. Gasping for air as they surfaced, they found themselves separated and without a life raft in 30-foot seas at night. That tiny raft was now the difference between life and death. Ray and Sam fought with everything they had to get back to it. Thrashing against the fierce waves in a fight for their lives, they were finally able to recapture the raft and climb back in. Luckily, the sharks did not return while they were struggling in the water. The storm must have kept them down in deeper waters, Ray thought.

By morning, the giant waves had dissipated and the sun slowly rose over choppy seas. Ray and Sam had survived another night lost in the Pacific, but Sam was now facing a life-threatening situation. During his scramble to escape from the B-29, he had gashed open his legs as he forced his way through the cramped compartment and jumped from the nose hatch. All of those open wounds, having been submerged in seawater since he landed, were now badly infected. Without a first aid kit and antibiotics, and a way to keep the wounds dry, there was nothing Sam or Ray could do to stop the infection from spreading.

The blazing sun and no water to drink were also taking a heavy toll on both men. With no protection from the sun, all of their exposed skin was now covered in painful burns and blisters that only accelerated the effects of dehydration. Coupled with his leg infections, Sam was in bad shape and getting worse with each passing hour. If they were going to be rescued, it had to happen soon, before it was too late. As they drifted in the growing swells, Ray and Sam kept searching the skies for help, but no one was coming.

Back home in the United States, Ray and Sam's wives had no idea that their husbands were in a struggle for their lives. The Army had not even notified them yet that their husbands had disappeared on their last mission and were now Missing in Action. News traveled slowly in those days, but they would undoubtedly know soon that something had happened when the daily letters from their husbands suddenly stopped arriving. Ray and Sam each had a small child waiting for them back home. Surrounded by an unforgiving ocean, all they could think about now was their families and how desperately they wanted to see them again. They weren't giving up, but in the open waters of the Pacific, time was not on their side.

Sometime before noon on the second day, Ray and Sam's battered spirits were suddenly lifted when they heard the faint but familiar groan of airplane engines. Off in the distance, hazy at first, but becoming clearer, they spotted a pair of B-29s several miles away. With renewed hope, Ray set off a smoke signal to get their attention. If they weren't rescued today, they might not survive another stormy night. As the bright orange smoke billowed into the sky, the B-29s continued flying on a steady course. Then the lead B-29 began to peel off, its wings glinting in the sun as it banked, and it slowly turned in their direction. They saw the smoke!

Ray fired off two more red flares as the B-29 approached, and then he released a packet of fluorescent green sea marker dye in the water around their raft. Ray and Sam were doing everything they possibly could so the crew would see them. The B-29 swept down low and took aim directly at the raft. With tears in their eyes, Ray and Sam rejoiced as the gleaming Super Dumbo, a B-29 equipped for air-sea rescue, roared right over top of them. Finally, someone knew they were alive.

The B-29 swung around and made a couple more passes to look them over, and then the crew dropped a large life raft with extra supplies. With all the energy they had left, Ray and Sam paddled feverishly through the waves to reach the raft, but they could only get within 10 feet of it before the winds swept it away. Even though they lost everything, at least their position was now known.

After a final pass, the B-29 flew away and they were all alone again. All Ray and Sam could do now was pray that someone was coming for them.[4]

* * *

More than 80 miles away from Ray and Sam's small life raft, an American submarine was patrolling Japan's home waters for downed American flyers when a call for help crackled over its radio. The radioman aboard the USS *Whale*, a Gato-class submarine with a 60-man crew, immediately responded and learned that a Super Dumbo had spotted survivors in the water from an unknown crash. But before they would transmit their location, the Super Dumbo insisted on authentication to confirm they were really talking to an American submarine and not the Japanese.[5]

For their part, the *Whale* was also suspicious of the report. Not only was the Super Dumbo using an outdated reference point, but their authentication was not according to procedure. It could be the Japanese setting a trap for them.[6]

The *Whale* had good reason to be cautious. A few days earlier, while searching for another downed flyer, the *Whale* picked up a transmission about an airplane coming in to ditch near them. The *Whale* radioed the distressed aircraft and gave their position, but no one replied. There were no aircraft within sight or on radar. Nothing more was ever heard from these voices on the radio. Five hours later, the *Whale* had to crash dive when an unidentified aircraft began closing on its position. It was later believed that the voices they heard may have been the Japanese.[7]

After some back and forth between the radio operators, the authentication problems were finally worked out, and the survivors' position was transmitted to the *Whale*. When the location was plotted on a chart, it was discovered that the downed flyers were 80 miles away and well inside a restricted area that was too dangerous for submarines to enter.[8]

The fate of the survivors was now in the hands of the *Whale's* captain, 30-year-old Lieutenant Commander Freeland Carde, Jr., and the decision he had to make that morning could easily result in the loss of his submarine. If Carde attempted a rescue, not only was there the danger of being attacked by the Japanese in broad daylight, but there were also mines in the area that were difficult to spot. The *Whale* had recently experienced a heart-stopping encounter with a mine that came within five feet of striking its hull. If that mine had exploded, it would have destroyed the submarine and killed most of his crew. On the other hand, if Carde stayed out of the restricted area and did nothing, it would probably cost the survivors their lives.[9]

Carde was now faced with one of the most difficult decisions he would have to make as a submarine commander. As he considered his options, a recent incident would weigh heavily on his decision that morning, and it had been haunting him for days.

Five days earlier, the U.S. Navy's Third Fleet had launched hundreds of carrier-based aircraft in a massive strike against the remnants of the Imperial Japanese Navy anchored at Kure in the Inland Sea. For its part of the operation, the *Whale* was assigned to a lifeguard station off the Bungo Channel, the southern entrance to the Inland Sea, to rescue any flyers who went down returning from the strike. The *Whale* was in for a busy day.

Just before noon, a TBM torpedo bomber that was badly damaged during a glide-bombing attack on a Japanese heavy cruiser radioed the *Whale* that it was coming in to ditch alongside the sub. A few moments later, a fighter radioed that he was also coming in to ditch. At that time there were about 300 aircraft passing overhead from the strike, and the *Whale's* crew had difficulty spotting which of the planes were going to ditch. The TBM finally appeared and ditched about 300 yards off the *Whale's* starboard bow. As the sub moved in and began picking up the three crewmen, the fighter came into view and ditched nearby.

With the TBM crew safely aboard, the *Whale* headed for the fighter pilot, but he was now in serious trouble. The pilot had ditched his plane perfectly and was then seen climbing out onto the wing, where he appeared to slip and fall into the water. As the *Whale* approached, the crew could see the pilot's one-man life raft had been opened, but it wasn't inflated. The crew could also see flak damage on the fighter's belly tank, which may have continued up into the cockpit.

To rescue the pilot, Carde had ordered the dive planes on the submarine rigged out so a man could stand on one and simply pull the pilot out of the water, but he soon realized this was a mistake. The seas were too rough for that type of rescue, and with the dive planes out, it made it impossible for the *Whale* to come up close alongside the pilot. The sub would now have to carefully maneuver a short distance away to avoid hitting the pilot with the dive plane.

As the submarine cautiously neared, a crewman heaved a life ring to the pilot, but he didn't reach for it. The men on deck could see his yellow Mae West life vest flapping in the waves. Like his life raft, for some reason his Mae West wasn't inflated either. Had flak peppered the cockpit?

The *Whale* inched closer, but the pilot was barely floating now and couldn't keep his head above the water. The crew watched helplessly as he slowly stopped moving. They were running out of time. Just before a swimmer could dive for him, when the submarine was only 25 feet away, the pilot slipped beneath the waves and disappeared.

Despite all efforts to find him, the pilot was never seen again.[10]

The heart-wrenching experience of watching a man die just beyond their reach had a profound effect on the *Whale's* crew. As Carde later wrote in his patrol report, it was an incident that few of his men would ever forget, and it undoubtedly weighed heavily on his mind as he contemplated what to do about the survivors in the restricted area.[11]

After considering all the risks, Carde made his decision. They were going in for the rescue.

The following was reconstructed from the *Whale's* War Patrol Report that day:

> 10:12 a.m.: Report of survivors 80 miles away in a restricted area received from a Super Dumbo. The *Whale* is proceeding to the area. Informed COMSUBPAC [Commander, Submarine Force, U.S. Pacific Fleet] of intentions. Requested air cover and authorization to enter the restricted area.
>
> 11:36: An unidentified aircraft is picked up on radar six miles away and closing with no IFF [Identification, Friend or Foe]. The *Whale* crash dives for safety.
>
> 12:00 p.m.: Surfaced in five-foot seas. A rush of water flooded into the conning tower when the hatch was opened, soaking the crew in the conning tower and control room.

12:02: A U.S. Navy PBM patrol bomber is spotted overhead and contacted by radio. The PBM had no IFF and was believed to have been the aircraft that forced the *Whale* to crash dive, which only angered the soaked crew. The PBM had no information about the survivors the *Whale* was searching for.

2:13: Five miles away from the restricted area. The *Whale* slowed and began circling while trying to contact the Super Dumbo that was supposed to be covering the survivors. No contact was made. Still awaiting authorization from COMSUBPAC to enter the restricted area.

3:15: Received instructions from COMSUBPAC to leave restricted area immediately after picking up survivors and not to enter a restricted area again without authorization. COMSUBPAC mistakenly believed the *Whale* had already entered the restricted area, when in fact the submarine was still circling on the outskirts.

3:35: All attempts to contact the Super Dumbo that was supposed to be covering the survivors have gone unanswered. A relief Super Dumbo was due on station at 3 o'clock, but it could not be raised, either. The *Whale's* captain makes the risky decision to enter the restricted area without air cover and proceeds at flank speed to the last known location of the survivors.

4:00: A life raft is spotted in the distance. The *Whale* changes course to intercept.

4:02: A second life raft is spotted.

4:15: Second Lieutenant James Brechtbill, navigator, is rescued.

4:17: The second life raft was found to be empty. It was determined that the raft had been dropped to the survivors from a B-29.

4:37: A lookout spots a red flag being waved from another life raft. The *Whale* changes course to intercept.

4:40: A lookout spots what appears to be a man in the water wearing a Mae West life vest. A thorough search reveals nothing.

4:55: Another life raft is spotted.

4:57: A Super Dumbo finally appears overhead and is contacted by radio to join the search.

5:15: With help from the Super Dumbo dropping smoke bombs and zoom climbing to guide the submarine in, Second Lieutenant George Lomas, co-pilot, is rescued. Lomas had a dislocated shoulder and was in bad shape. The Super Dumbo continues searching for more survivors.

5:19: Another life raft is spotted. The man in the raft jumped up and down to attract the crew's attention.

5:25: Staff Sergeant Kirk Icenhower, flight engineer, is rescued.

5:27: The Super Dumbo spots another life raft. The *Whale* changes course to intercept while the Super Dumbo orbits the raft and drops flares to guide the submarine in.

5:51: Corporal Warren Bartlett, right gunner, and Sergeant Harold Windberg, CFC gunner, are rescued. The Super Dumbo continues to search for more survivors.

5:59: A floating Japanese mine is spotted, reaffirming the dangers of the restricted area.

6:00: By plotting where the rescued flyers were picked up, and after determining the order in which they bailed out, the *Whale's* crew was able to estimate the B-29's course and the probable location of any remaining survivors. This information was relayed to the Super Dumbo, and it began searching the suggested sectors.

6:24: The Super Dumbo spots another life raft and drops smoke bombs to mark its location. The *Whale* changes course to intercept.

6:47: First Lieutenant Raymond Shumway, aircraft commander, and Sergeant Sam Kidd, radio operator, are rescued. Kidd was in very bad condition and suffering from shock, sunburn and water immersion.

6:50: The *Whale* and Super Dumbo continue searching for more survivors.

8:35: No more survivors have been spotted, so signal rockets are fired from the *Whale* in hopes of receiving a response. No answer is received.

11:00: The search ends for the night. With seven survivors from Lieutenant Shumway's 11-man crew safely aboard, the *Whale* departs the restricted area at flank speed under escort by the Super Dumbo.[12]

Still missing that night were Flight Officer Henry Goldstein, bombardier; Staff Sergeant Frank Blackett, left gunner; Sergeant Yearby Ashby, tail gunner; and Corporal Jack Atanis, radar observer. They remain Missing in Action to this day.

A week after he was rescued, while still aboard the *Whale*, Ray wrote a letter home to his family. It must have been hard for him to put into words, but he explained everything he had just been through, including those terrible days and nights in the raft. When he finally spotted the submarine coming for them, Ray wrote that he cried when he realized they would not have to spend another night at sea.[13]

Lieutenant Raymond Shumway's crew. Back row, left to right: Kirk Icenhower, Henry Goldstein, Mickey Merrian, James Brechtbill, George Lomas, Raymond Shumway. Front row, left to right: Yearby Ashby, Warren Bartlett, Frank Blackett, Harold Winberg, Sam Kidd. (USAAF/Bruce Cairns)

As Ray and Sam were pulled aboard the *Whale*, Lieutenant Knute Lee, a Navy fighter pilot who was rescued by the *Whale* four days earlier, noticed that they were both badly sunburned and covered in blisters. When they finally got them on deck, the crew realized that Ray and Sam, after all they had been through, were more dead than alive.[14]

After being crammed in the tiny raft for so long without any water or food, Ray and Sam were so weak that they couldn't walk when they were rescued, but they had miraculously survived. The two men had been in the water for 42 hours.[15]

* * *

The story you just read took a tremendous amount of time to research and write. Going into it, I didn't know where that research was going to take me, but it soon became an obsession.

My interest in Ray and Sam's incredible story of survival began in September of 2017, when I discovered Ray's uniform for sale on eBay. When I clicked on the auction that September night, I had no idea what kind of a story I was about to discover. The ribbons I saw on Ray's uniform, which signify the medals he was awarded, was the first clue that I was looking at something very special. I'd been collecting long enough to know that this was not your typical B-29 pilot's uniform.

As I looked over the auction, I noticed the seller had done a little research before he listed the uniform, and he included a very condensed version of Ray's story in the listing. I took that information and quickly confirmed some of the facts. Everything seemed to check out, but there was still a lot of research left to do.

Within minutes of clicking on the auction, I made up my mind that I was going to bid on Ray's uniform – and I was going to win it. It was such an incredible story – and I didn't even know the half of it yet – that I just felt like I had to save his uniform at any cost. I still had a lot of questions about what happened to Ray and his crew, but on that night, there was really only one big question on my mind: how was I going to pay for it all?

To be perfectly honest with you, at that moment in time, I was broke.

Six years earlier, I decided that it was time to make a drastic change in my life. I was almost 31 years old then, and I was working harder than ever before at my job at the restaurant, but I was going nowhere in life. It felt like I was running in place, and no matter how hard I tried, I never moved an inch. You could say that I made a living, but I wasn't living. *I was dying.*

Without knowing what the future had in store for me, only that it had to be better than what I was doing now, I decided to quit my job and chase my dreams of becoming a writer.

Dreams are never easy, though. I had not drawn a paycheck since I left the restaurant, and what little money I had saved ran out years ago. To keep myself going, I'd been selling off some warbird parts from my collection as I needed money. It helped a lot that I lived with my parents, but I was at the point now where I had to start selling some things that I never planned to sell. My B-29 parts were safe, as I'd never sell any of those, but I'd collected a lot of other World War II aircraft parts over the years, and one by one, I was having to sell them. After so much time and effort, it was hard to watch my collection dwindle, but it was either that or give up my dreams and go back to a dead-end job with no future. And I was *never* going back.

The night I discovered Ray's uniform, I started looking for something that I could sell to help pay for it. I had some B-24 parts listed on an aviation marketplace, but I needed something else just in case they didn't sell in time. That's when I remembered something unique that I had.

Many years ago, I was a big collector of World War II Japanese bayonets. I began collecting in my early teens after my parents gave me a Japanese rifle for Christmas. I was fascinated by this piece of history, which had been brought back from the war, and I soon found a bayonet to complete my new rifle at a gun show. That's when I discovered how many different bayonet variations there were, and I was hooked after that.

By the time my interests shifted to the B-29 in my early 20s, I had amassed a sizeable collection of bayonets. I'd sold most of them after I left my job six years ago, but I still had some special ones left. One of them was the earliest bayonet I'd ever seen from the Nagoya Arsenal. It had a three-digit serial number and was in great condition for having survived a world war. I really didn't want to sell it, but when I asked myself if I had to choose between this bayonet and saving Ray's uniform, which would I choose? I didn't give it a second thought after that. The bayonet was going up for auction.

There were five days and 17 hours left on the auction for Ray's uniform when I put the bayonet on eBay. I set the starting bid at $200, which was a fair price considering its rarity, and I listed it as a five-day auction so I'd know exactly how much money I could spend on Ray's uniform. The irony that the sale of a Japanese bayonet would help me save the uniform of a B-29 pilot who bombed Japan during the war was not lost on me. Or the irony that Nagoya, the city where the bayonet was made, also happened to be the target on Ray's first combat mission.

While I counted down the days, I continued researching Ray's final mission, and I soon made a huge discovery. Navy history is far from my normal studies, but with luck on my side, I unearthed a copy of the USS *Whale's* War Patrol Report from 1945. Searching through the pages, I had to wipe my eyes when I found it, but there on page 31, at 1847 hours (6:47 p.m.) on July 29, 1945, was the log entry for when Ray and Sam were rescued. Reading those words that were written so long ago, it almost felt like I was there that day. I was supposed to be working on another chapter in this book at the time, but after I discovered that report, I became so engrossed in Ray's story that it was all I could think about. Nothing else mattered now. All I wanted to do was learn more about those harrowing days and nights in the summer of 1945.

After four more days consumed by research, Sunday evening finally came. My bayonet auction was about to end, and I had a lot riding on it. Depending on what it sold for, it could be the difference between saving Ray's uniform or losing it forever. With such a unique story behind it, that uniform was something a collector would really treasure and hold on to. This would probably be my only chance to save it. Hurricane Irma was pounding Florida that evening as I counted down the final minutes of the bayonet auction. My heart sank a little more as each second passed, and then it was all over. There were no bids.

I checked on Ray's uniform again. There were 17 hours and 34 minutes left. The bidding was holding steady at $256.00. Now what? There was nothing else that I could sell in less than 17 hours. For a few minutes, I just sat there and stared at the pictures of Ray's uniform. I felt helpless. But feeling helpless and *being* helpless are two very different things. This wasn't over for me yet!

I snapped out of it and quickly took stock of what I had to work with. I had a little over $200 in my PayPal account from some P-40 parts I sold the previous week, and together with the little money I had saved, plus whatever else I could find around the house, I scraped together just over $400. That was a lot of money for someone like me, but I didn't think it would be enough to save Ray's uniform. The seller had first listed it with a $450 Buy It Now price, but he quickly removed that option once the bidding skyrocketed. That meant the seller thought he could get a lot more money for it now. All I could do was hope for the best.

The next day, I woke up to the sound of rain from Hurricane Irma. I didn't get much sleep. Thinking about Ray's story and worrying about money had kept me tossing all night. You'd think that I'd be used to all of this by now, since I've been here so many times before with Sally's grouping and other auctions, but it hasn't gotten any easier. I know I'm just one man and I can't save everything, but Ray's story had really taken hold of me. I tried not to think about what would happen if I couldn't save his uniform.

Later that evening, as I sat at my computer and nervously counted down the final minutes of the auction, I listened to a 1942 recording of the Army Air Corps song to lift my spirits. One of the verses talked about living in fame or going down in flames. I sure felt like that right now.

With 10 minutes to go, the bidding was up to $266. My hands were getting sweaty.

Under four minutes now. The bidding climbed to $298. The other collectors had already placed 17 bids, and I knew more were coming. It wasn't looking good for me.

I typed in $431.99 and waited for the clock to wind down. It was everything I had.

With around 30 seconds left, the high bid shot up to $340 – not good.

With four seconds left, my heart was pounding out of my chest as I clicked on the button to bid. The screen flashed, and it said in green that I was the high bidder. Then just as quickly, the screen flashed again, and the page began to reload as the auction ended. Someone could have outbid me there at the end, but I wouldn't know until the page loaded. Come on internet, work faster! Then I saw it: "You won this auction."

How I reacted was a funny thing. I was instantly relieved, but I wasn't happy. No, that's not true. I *was* happy, but I wasn't filled with joy. After saving something as important as this, normally I'd be euphoric, but this was different. Instead of celebrating, I started crying.

This has never happened to me before. Even with Jerry's scrapbook, when there were times that I wanted to, I never broke down. Something was different about this. I can't really explain what it was, but maybe it just hit me how sad it was to see Ray's uniform on eBay in the first place. Or maybe it was because today was September 11. Maybe it was both.

Two days later, after putting almost all the money I had into my PayPal account, I sent my payment to the seller. The final price for Ray's uniform, with shipping, was $396.95. Talk about cutting it close. All I had to do now was wait for the post office to deliver it.

*   *   *

While I waited for Ray's uniform to arrive, I turned my attention to another World War II uniform I found on eBay a few days earlier. I didn't know the story behind it yet, but I had a feeling there was something special about it too.

I could tell from the 20th Air Force patch on the left shoulder, the engineering specialist patch on the right sleeve and the silver wings on the left breast, that this uniform belonged to a B-29 flight engineer. The technical sergeant who wore this uniform had earned an assortment of ribbons you typically find on a B-29er's uniform, but one of them alluded to a story that I had to know more about. Below his silver wings, there was an Asiatic-Pacific Campaign ribbon with two service stars (also known as battle stars), an Air Medal ribbon for meritorious achievement in aerial flight, and most significant of all, a Purple Heart ribbon for wounds received in combat.

Who was this B-29er? I searched the auction pictures for clues, but there was no name written in the uniform. The seller didn't know who it belonged to, either.

The only clue I could find was a handwritten number inside the uniform at the back of the neck. To the untrained eye, it looked meaningless, but that number was actually a special code known as a laundry number that was used to identify a soldier's clothing and equipment. The number contained the first initial of the soldier's last name, followed by the last four digits of his serial number. For example, A-1234. With millions of men in the Army, the laundry numbers were not unique to each soldier, but they were specific enough for use within the soldier's unit.

A few years ago, a British historian created a website where you can search U.S. Army enlistment records from the war. As I'm typing this now, the database contains almost 9 million records. What makes the website such a phenomenal research tool is that you can search the database by laundry number. To my surprise, the website revealed that there were 80 men with that same laundry number during the war. It was going to take some time to go through them all, but at least I had somewhere to start now.[16]

I could feel the adrenaline surging as I began my quest to learn who this B-29er was and how he earned his Purple Heart. Once I discovered his story, I'd do everything I could to save his uniform. I was flat broke, but I'd figure the money part out later, just like I always do.

My focus now was to learn as much as I could about this veteran. Was he wounded by flak, or by a fighter attack? Could he have been injured bailing out, or while ditching? With some luck, I'd know soon enough. My spirits were high as I began researching each name online for information. From enlistment records to obituaries, there's an incredible amount of information available on the internet, and I was going to search through all of it.

As I pored over the records, I kept thinking about the patch that was sewn over the right breast of the uniform. It was called the Honorable Discharge Emblem, but to the soldiers, it was better known as the Ruptured Duck. The emblem featured a golden eagle with spread wings perched within a ring, but the eagle looked more like a duck; hence the nickname. The emblem was issued in the form of a lapel pin and a patch to signify that the wearer had been honorably discharged from the service. Due to a shortage of civilian clothing, the patches allowed returning veterans to continue wearing their uniforms for up to 30 days after they were discharged.

I couldn't help but to wonder about all the people and places this veteran had visited in his uniform after he got home from the war. Back in those days, magazines like *National Geographic* published guides for civilians that showed all the various ribbons that could be found on a veteran's uniform and what they meant. I wondered how many people had noticed his Purple Heart ribbon and asked where he was wounded? I wish he was here right now to tell that story one more time.

In the past, I've sometimes been lucky and discovered stories written by the veteran himself or members of his crew. In a few cases, I even found video interviews. It's always a long shot, but maybe I would find something from this veteran. The thrill of the hunt kept me going. It was only a matter of time before I found him and could piece together his story.

A few hours later, I completed my search of all 80 names on the list – I found nothing.

I wish there was a happy ending that I could share with you, but there's not. With no way of knowing who the uniform belonged to, and with no money to spend, I had to let it go. The auction ended a few days later. It sold for $87.00.

Outside of the veteran's family – and who knows how many of them are still alive, or even care to remember – this B-29er's story, a Purple Heart recipient who shed blood for his country, will be lost forever. What a price to pay.

*   *   *

On a Thursday afternoon in mid-September, Ray Shumway's uniform began its journey to North Georgia at the Trabuco Canyon Post Office in the foothills of California's Santa Ana Mountains. Thanks to the tracking updates from the post office, I was thrilled to see Ray's uniform was soon on an airplane headed east across the country to Atlanta. Less than 48 hours later, the package had moved through my local post office and was now out for delivery. A short time later, the tracking information was updated again. All it said was "No Access." The package was not delivered, but sometimes my neighborhood's parcel lockers are already full, so maybe the mail carrier just didn't have anywhere to put it. That was on a Saturday.

By Monday it was hard to contain my excitement. I couldn't wait to see Ray's uniform. But when the mail came that afternoon, there was still no package, and the tracking had not been updated since Saturday. I was starting to get that sinking feeling in my stomach. After all this, I didn't want to think about his uniform getting lost in the mail. The next day, I woke up feeling more tired than when I went to bed. Surely it would be here today. After a quick check of the mail that afternoon, my worst fears were realized: Ray's uniform was nowhere to be found.

Not knowing what else to do, I got in my truck and sped over to the post office as fast as I could. Living in a small town, we have an equally small post office, with only one lady behind the counter. It looked like she was having a bad day when I walked in. I explained the situation and handed her a printout of the tracking information. With a nod, she disappeared into the back. She couldn't hear me, but I was whispering "please, please, please" to myself as she searched.

"Here it is," she said at last. After churning inside me for days, the sight of that box coming around the corner in her hands melted all my fears and anxieties away. Ray's uniform was finally here. I thanked her and sped home as fast as I could.

I wasn't sure how I was going to react when I saw Ray's uniform. Maybe I shouldn't admit this, but when I started opening the box, I told myself to keep it together and don't cry. Ever since I discovered it on eBay that night, this story has moved me in ways that I cannot explain. Now that I was just seconds away from holding a piece of that story in my hands, I wasn't sure what was going to happen. With a deep breath, I carefully pulled the uniform out of the box. I gently unfolded it on my kitchen counter, mindful of its nearly 75-year age, and then I took a step back to take it all in. It was overwhelming – but I was too excited to cry.

I wish you could feel what I felt in that moment, because there are no words to describe it. Looking at Ray's uniform with his silver pilot wings and those special ribbons, above all else, it really brought home to me that Ray's story wasn't just some words on paper. These were *real people*. These were *real lives* that were lost and saved on that July night in 1945. And with this uniform, I now had something tangible to help tell their story and ensure they are never forgotten. It was worth every penny it cost to save it.

*   *   *

With Ray's uniform safely in my possession, this is usually where my journey would come to an end, but not this time. Something kept pushing me to continue chasing this story. I can't explain what it was, but I learned a long time ago to always listen to my intuition, so that's just what I did.

In the weeks that followed, I continued to uncover new information about Ray and Sam's story that I had somehow missed before. The eyewitness account I found from Lieutenant

Knute Lee proved to be an eye-opening discovery. Standing on the *Whale's* deck that day, Lee described Ray and Sam as being "more dead than alive" when they were rescued, and that Sam "seemed to hover between life and death for days" as the *Whale's* pharmacist's mate slowly nursed him back to health on the submarine.[17]

What happened to the rest of Ray's crew after the war also captured my interest. From my earlier research, I already knew that Ray had passed away in 1981, before I was even a year old. As I dug deeper into the crew, I learned that the other survivors were all gone now as well – except for one. As hard as I searched, I could not find anything about this man passing away.

Could there really be a crew member still alive from that night, 72 years later? It didn't seem possible, but the more that I searched and found nothing, the more convinced I became.

I focused all my efforts, and I soon found a man who appeared to be his son. After some more searching, I found an e-mail address for him too. By now it was just before Thanksgiving, so I waited a few days before I contacted him. In the meantime, I spent hours trying to write the perfect e-mail to introduce myself. Even though I've sent out countless e-mails and letters like this over the years, it's always awkward when you contact someone out of the blue. I try to show that I'm sincere and not some weirdo on the internet, but you never know how someone is going to react. Sometimes I'll get a response right away, but other times I've been completely ignored.

I wasn't sure what to expect in this case, but after crafting the best e-mail that I could, I pressed "send" and hoped for the best. The next evening, I found a reply in my inbox. After a deep breath, I learned that he was indeed the man I thought he was. Unfortunately, his father had passed away back in 1988, and that meant there were no living survivors from Ray's crew.

But I couldn't feel sad because there was a lot to be happy for now. The man I was talking to was none other than the son of Sergeant Sam Kidd! I couldn't believe how lucky I was.

With all that I had discovered, I felt a responsibility now, not only as a man trying to save the history of the B-29ers, but as an American, to share a story with Sam's son, Sam Jr. A few hours later, I sent him some photos of Ray's uniform. I wanted to draw his attention to the ribbons below Ray's silver pilot wings; specifically, to the striped ribbon on the end. That was the ribbon for the Soldier's Medal, I said, the U.S. Army's highest award for non-combat valor. And then I explained what it was for. Ray was awarded the Soldier's Medal for saving his father's life.[18]

As I soon learned from his son, Sam Kidd was a very modest man. Like so many of his generation, Sam did not talk about the war. His son had never heard the story about Ray saving his father's life until I shared it with him.[19]

You can probably imagine what it must have been like for Sam Jr. to hear that story for the first time. It was an honor to share it with his family.

Shortly after Ray's uniform arrived here, I was looking at a copy of his Soldier's Medal Citation, which summarized his actions in saving Sam's life, when I noticed that it was dated September 11, 1945. That was exactly 72 years *to the day* that I won his uniform on eBay. Was it all a coincidence?

In the days that followed, Sam Jr. dug out an old box filled with his father's papers from the war. He'd never looked through any of it before, but he thought he should check and see if there was anything inside the box that might help with my research into Ray's crew and their final mission. We were in for a big surprise. Inside the box, perfectly preserved among the other wartime documents, he discovered all the letters his father wrote home to his mother during the war.

When Sam Jr. began reading what was in his father's letters, from the daily life on Tinian to combat and everything in between, it quickly became clear that they were a treasure trove of history. Knowing what they would mean to someone like me, he graciously sent me copies to help with my research. It was amazing to read in Sam's own words what happened on that July night and in the days that followed.

In the same box with the letters, his son also found some old photographs of Ray's crew. It was so moving to see all of their young faces, some of whom would never come home again. But for me, the photo from August 14, 1945, was the most compelling of them all. Taken just minutes after the survivors stepped off the submarine at Guam, the photo showed Sam, the flight engineer and the two surviving gunners all dressed in Navy dungarees and standing in front of a Quonset hut. Sam had a slight grin on his face, no doubt happy to be back on dry land again. To be standing there after all these men had been through made for quite a photograph.

I noticed that Ray, his co-pilot and navigator were not in the photo with the rest of their crew, and there's a funny story behind that. To get back to the Marianas, Ray's crew and the other men the *Whale* had rescued were all transferred under the cover of darkness to another submarine, the USS *Blackfish*, in the waters off Japan. The survivors boarded the *Blackfish* just in time to learn that its seawater distillers were broken. With a limited supply of fresh water on board, that meant that no showers would be allowed during the voyage back to Guam. No one had showered during their time on the *Whale*, either. After spending over two weeks crammed inside the submarines without a shower, Ray and the other two officers were so anxious to get cleaned up when they reached Guam that they didn't wait around to have their picture taken first.[20]

With the discovery of the photos and letters spurring him on, Sam Jr. continued searching for more of his father's things from the war. He soon found something he had not seen in many years: a carousel tray of 35mm slides his father had taken during the war. Beginning when Sam arrived on Tinian in June of 1945, the 50 delicate slides captured moments in history all the way through to the end of the war when he came home. To go with his photos, Sam had also written a short description for each slide, which proved to be invaluable all these years later. But the biggest surprise of all was that the 50 slides were all in color.

It would still be a few weeks before I saw the photos with my own eyes, but I already knew that they would be a remarkable glimpse into a B-29er's life on Tinian, and being in full Kodachrome color, they were extremely rare. I've been collecting for a long time now, and even I don't have any original color slides from Tinian in my collection.

To ensure his father's photos last forever, Sam Jr. had all 50 slides scanned and put on a disc. I was honored to receive a copy a short time later. The first time I looked at the photos, I began scanning through them for a quick overview before going back to look at each one in detail, but I was stopped in my tracks when I came upon the photo of Ray, Goldy and Mickey squeezed together in a one-man life raft. Sam's letter home on July 20, 1945, told the rest of the story.

Six days before their first combat mission, Ray's crew drove down to Tinian harbor for a demonstration on how to use the one-man life raft. Sam just happened to bring his camera along and captured four amazing photos that morning. The first two photos were all business as the instructor jumped into the water and demonstrated how to inflate and climb into the raft. After the demonstration was over, with some time to spare before a training flight later that afternoon, the next photos showed the crew swimming and playing around on the rafts.

If I'm honest, it was hard to look at that photo of Ray, Goldy and Mickey all together on that raft. A month later, Ray and Sam would be fighting for their lives in just such a raft. They were the lucky ones, though. After he bailed out, Henry "Goldy" Goldstein, the bombardier, was never seen again. The third man in the photo, Mickey Merrian, was the crew's original radar observer – his replacement on that July night, Jack Atanis, was never seen again either.

The last photo Sam took that day included Yearby Ashby, the tail gunner. When their B-29 went out of control and fell into a flat spin, the survivors believed that the centrifugal force must have pinned down Yearby, Frank and Jack inside the bomber and prevented them from escaping. It was tough to see these young men so happy and full of life in Sam's photos, knowing they would be dead a month later.[21]

After the war ended, with 17 exposures left in his Eastman camera, Sam also documented his long voyage home aboard the troopship USS *Winged Arrow*. The series of photos he took on November 10, 1945, passing under the Golden Gate Bridge into San Francisco Bay and docking after 16 days at sea, were breathtaking. Sam had captured a moment in history as thousands of veterans returned home from a very long and brutal war in the Pacific. To see all of their smiling faces, in color, as they stepped onto American soil again, some for the first time in years, while a band played and bold signs overhead proclaimed, "Welcome Home" and "Thru These Portals Return The Best Damn Soldiers In The World," it just blew me away.

As I told Sam Jr., those color photos are a real historical treasure. Kodachrome film was very sensitive to heat, which is why you don't find many wartime color photos from the Pacific. We are so lucky this film survived its time on Tinian.

If all these photos and letters weren't incredible enough, the biggest surprise of all came when Sam Jr. discovered a letter written by Ray himself on the submarine 10 days after they were rescued. In the two-page letter, typed on green USS *Whale* stationary, Ray described everything he and Sam had just been through. I couldn't believe my eyes the first time I saw it.

A copy of Ray's letter is sitting next to me now as I'm typing this. Looking over at it, I think back to when I first saw his uniform on eBay, and how there was so much waiting to be discovered about his story. To now have a copy of that letter, plus all of Sam's photographs and everything else, to display with Ray's uniform is nothing short of miraculous. It's funny how things work out.

*   *   *

This would normally be a great place to end this story, but as anyone who does historical research will tell you, when you open one door, it often leads to many other doors. And that's exactly what happened with this story.

While looking through all the material Sam Jr. sent me, I found something in one of his father's letters that I just had to follow up on. Ever since I learned how bad a shape Sam was in when he was rescued, I've wanted to know more about the man who slowly nursed him back to health on the submarine. In one of his letters, Sam simply referred to him as "Doc" and praised him for the job he did. Doc was a Navy pharmacist's mate, also known as a corpsman, and was responsible for all the medical care aboard the USS *Whale*. (On smaller vessels and submarines, a pharmacist's mate acted as the ship's doctor because there were not enough doctors to go around.)

Based on everything I've learned about Sam's leg infections, and his severe dehydration after being exposed to the harsh elements for 42 hours without a drink of water, it's safe to say that Doc saved Sam's life. I had to find out who Doc was.

For the next few hours, I scoured the internet for even the slightest clue to Doc's identity, but there was nothing to be found. I even looked for a roster of the *Whale's* crew, but I came up empty-handed. I wasn't off to a good start. My big break finally came a few days later when I read the letter Sam wrote home to his wife on August 18, 1945, four days after he returned to Tinian. Halfway down the second page, to my surprise, I found a name and address for a B.F. Olsen. Sam wrote that Olsen was the pharmacist's mate on the USS *Whale* who took such good care of him, and he wanted his wife to keep his address for him. Now I had something to start with!

I went to work and quickly discovered that Doc was Mr. Blaine F. Olsen from Brigham, Utah. In that moment, I had dreams of talking to Doc and asking him all about his time aboard the USS *Whale*, much like I had dreams of talking to Sam. But those dreams were not meant to be. I was too late – Doc passed away in 2010.

Sometimes I think that I was born too late in life. If I had just 10 extra years, there would have been so many more World War II Veterans who I could have talked to. It hurts to think about what could have been if only I'd known about Doc and this story a few years earlier.

After staring at Doc's obituary on my screen for a few minutes, and wondering about all of the questions that I'd never know the answers to, I felt like I had to open another door in this story. So that's just what I did. By the end of the night, after a lot of research, I found Doc's son.

When I later heard back from him, and he confirmed that Doc Olsen was indeed his father, I had to stop for a moment to let it all sink in. It almost didn't seem real, but I was now in touch with the families of both Sam Kidd and Doc Olsen.

I soon learned that Doc Olsen, just like Sam, was also very modest about his time in the service. In all the decades after the war, until the day he died, Doc never said a word to anyone about the life he saved on his submarine in the summer of 1945.[22]

It was really something to think that if I had not made the effort to find his son, Doc's family never would have known about him saving Sam's life all those years ago. What happened a few weeks later, though, was the most remarkable of all. Almost 73 years after their fathers last saw each other, it was my distinct honor to introduce by e-mail the son of Sam Kidd to the son of Blaine "Doc" Olsen. They spoke on the phone a short time later. As you can imagine, they had a lot to talk about.

* * *

My spirits soared after reuniting the Kidd and Olsen families, but that euphoria didn't last for long. After everything I had discovered about this story, there was still something missing. And to be frank, it was really starting to bother me.

I don't know why, but I kept thinking about that fighter pilot the *Whale* couldn't reach in time to save. I firmly believe that the sight of him slipping beneath the waves just beyond their reach was the decisive factor in Commander Carde's decision five days later to go after those survivors 80 miles away in the restricted area, which turned out to be Ray and Sam. But who was that fighter pilot? There was nothing in the *Whale's* War Patrol Report that could help me identify him. The report didn't even mention the type of fighter he was flying, let alone which aircraft carrier he was from. That fighter pilot was the missing piece of this story, and not knowing his name had been eating away at me for months.

Then late one night, for reasons that I can't explain, I pulled up that grainy copy of page 17 in the *Whale's* War Patrol Report. I soon found myself staring again at those chilling words that described the pilot's death. That awful vision of him slipping away unfolded over and over again in my mind. I couldn't get it out of my head.

I've lost track of how many times I've studied the words on that page. But no matter how many times I tried, there was nothing there that could identify him. I don't know why I keep doing this. I don't know why I keep torturing myself.

As his death replayed in my mind, my eyes drifted up the page and settled on the report about the TBM torpedo bomber that ditched moments before him. The names of its three-man crew from Torpedo Squadron 34 were right there in front of me. I had looked them all up before, though, and found nothing. I sank further into my chair and just stared at that page.

And then for more reasons that I can't explain, I decided to look up that TBM crew one more time. That's when a funny thing happened.

I don't know how I missed it before, but I found a newspaper article from 2010 about a Torpedo Squadron 34 reunion in California. Reading through it, I discovered that the name of the reunion organizer was the same name that appeared in the *Whale's* report about the TBM. How did I miss this? The article mentioned this man's hometown in California, and when I did some more searching, I could only find one man in that area with the same name. This had to be the guy I was looking for. Could he *really* still be alive, though? It had been almost 73 years since that day in 1945, and he would have to be well into his 90s by now. As hard as I tried, I couldn't find an obituary for him, but I couldn't find an obituary for Sam either, so that really didn't mean anything.

My hopes weren't very high, but I did find an address and phone number for him. I had no way to know if they were current, though. What should I do? Thinking back on past experiences with cold calls that didn't go so well, I decided to write a letter instead of calling. Part of my reasoning was that if he had passed away, I wanted to be respectful, and I figured it would be easier on the family if I sent a letter instead of calling. These letters are never easy to write, even for a writer, so to prove that my interest was sincere, I printed out the pages from the *Whale's* report that had his name on them and included them with my letter.

I sent everything out by Priority Mail that Monday, and I followed the tracking updates as the letter made its way out to California. It was delivered in two days, just like the post office said it would be. Then I anxiously waited to hear something. And waited. And waited.

By the third day, I was coming to terms with reality: I was too late – *again*.

That night, feeling utterly depressed and defeated, I found myself staring at page 17 again. Still the same words. Still the same awful vision of that pilot slipping away, over and over again. There was nothing new in those words, but I couldn't stop staring at them. If only I had known sooner.

Three days turned into a week. All hope was lost.

On the eighth day, a Tuesday, I woke to find a voicemail on my phone from a number that I didn't recognize. It was probably another telemarketer, I thought, as I pressed play. Still half asleep, my head collapsed back on my pillow as I waited for the message to begin. Then an unfamiliar voice came through the speaker. What was he selling? My eyes shot open – I couldn't believe what I was hearing. Unlike the past week, I jumped out of bed with a purpose that day.

A few hours later, I was seated at my desk and feeling more excited than nervous. Arranged in front of me was my phone, a tall cup of water, a blank piece of paper and a marker pen. As I prepared myself for what was about to happen, I fiddled with the marker's cap and kept telling myself how important this was. The paper started to move as I scribbled on it, so I weighed the top corner down with a bottle of water so I could take notes with one hand. With everything positioned in front of me, it was now or never. I pressed "call," put the phone to my ear, closed my eyes, and took a deep breath.

From the moment he said "hello," I felt this burst of warmth envelop me. There was an undeniable spirit in his voice, an exuberance for life, and it was infectious. *My God, I felt alive again*! After so many dark days of depression, the sun was shining again, and I couldn't contain the giddy smile on my face.

You see, I was talking to Mr. Bill Steenberg, the TBM pilot who was rescued by the USS *Whale* on July 24, 1945. My dream had finally come true!

I was amazed to learn that Bill was 94 years young and still going just as strong as ever. He moved a little slower now, he admitted, but I could tell that he had not lost his zeal for life. As we talked about the war, cherry-picking the good memories from the bad, he became so animated as he recalled those defining years of his life. If I didn't know any better, from just the energy in his voice alone, I'd swear that he was in his 30s, tops.

For someone like me, a relatively young guy almost 60 years his junior, who battles with the highs and lows of life every day, just listening to him speak was so uplifting. Even as I sit here now reminiscing about that day, his words still fill me with inspiration. I could learn a lot from this man.

I had a million questions that I wanted to ask Bill that day, but there were two that stood out from the rest. First, did he remember Ray and Sam?

It had been almost 73 years since those weeks they spent together aboard the *Whale*, and sadly, any memories Bill had of Ray and Sam had since faded. But I couldn't feel disappointed, because just being able to talk to someone who was actually on the submarine with them was a huge thrill.

The second big question I had was about that fighter pilot who I kept seeing slip away. Did he know anything about him?

Bill's voice suddenly turned somber. I struck something that had been bothering him, too, for a very long time. Bill said that everyone on the submarine was heartbroken over his loss, but he didn't know anything else about the pilot or who he was.

I felt myself slouching in my chair. If anyone knew something about that pilot, it would be Bill. He's probably the last person alive who was there that day, but he didn't know anything that could help me. As amazing as this phone call was, I was starting to feel defeated again.

But then Bill surprised me. Even though more than seven decades had passed, Bill still vividly remembered that the pilot was flying an F6F Hellcat that day, and it wasn't a Hellcat from his aircraft carrier, the USS *Monterey*. This revelation gave me a renewed hope. With enough work, maybe I could figure out who that pilot was after all.

Bill and I talked for over half an hour that day. We could have talked a lot longer, but I didn't want to keep him. When it came time to say goodbye, I had something special that I wanted to say to Bill. I had dreamed about a phone call like this, I explained, but I never thought that dream would ever come true. For as much as I hoped and prayed, I honestly never expected to find someone who was actually on the USS *Whale* that day, let alone talk to them. "Thank you for making my dream come true," I said. "I'll never forget this phone call for as long as I live."

Many years from now, I will one day tell my grandkids about that phone call. That's how much it meant to me.

Later that night, while still on a high from talking to Bill, I began my new mission to identify the pilot of that Hellcat. My plan was to assemble a list of all the U.S. Navy personnel who died that day, and then eliminate all the names except for Hellcat pilots. Then I would research each name for more information and clues. This was going to be a big job.

By the end of that night, I was shocked to discover that on July 24, 1945, the Navy had lost 165 men in combat. And that was *just* the Navy, not including Army or Marine combat losses, on just one day of a 1,365-day war. When I dug deeper, I found that 112 of the 165 men who died that day were from one ship, the destroyer escort USS *Underhill*, when it was sunk by a Japanese Kaiten manned suicide torpedo.[23]

I then discovered that the Third Fleet lost 52 pilots and crewmen during the air strikes against Kure that day. One of those men was the fighter pilot I was looking for. As I went through the names on the list, I tried to stay focused on the mission at hand, but in all honesty, it was hard not to think about all of these brave young men who sacrificed their lives and would never see the world at peace. I tried not to let it get to me, but it did. I pushed through it, and I discovered that five Hellcat pilots were lost that day.

Now that I knew my pilot was one of those five men, I began researching each name. There's an old saying that you should remember someone for how they lived, not for how they died. As I studied their bright but short lives, it seemed like all I could find about these men were stories of how they died. But in their deaths, I saw the selflessness that defined their young lives.

Ensign William Hall, 23, from Pennsylvania, had just attacked the seaplane base at Otsu when he was seen to do a wingover and immediately dove to attack the base again. No one knows for sure, but it was believed that Hall was peppered by 20mm anti-aircraft shells as he dove on the target. Hall never pulled out of the dive. His Hellcat exploded when it crashed in a nearby inlet. No trace of Ensign Hall was ever found.[24]

Commander Porter Maxwell, 31, from West Virginia, was leading his squadron of Hellcats near Kure when his fighter was struck by anti-aircraft fire. Porter's wingman said the tail of his Hellcat seemed to fall apart under the withering fire. His wingman watched as Porter bailed out, but his parachute did not fully open. With his parachute streaming behind him, Porter continued to free-fall until he impacted the water. He was killed instantly. After the war, his remains were recovered and laid to rest in West Virginia. Porter was on his second combat tour in the Pacific.[25]

Lieutenant Kenneth Neyer, 22, from Kansas, was shot down by a Japanese fighter while coming to the aid of a lone American pilot locked in a vicious dogfight with four Japanese fighters over the Bungo Channel. No trace of Lieutenant Neyer was ever found.[26]

Lieutenant Commander Charles Sawers, 28, from Tennessee, was shot down by anti-aircraft fire while attacking Kure harbor and crashed in the Inland Sea. No trace of Lieutenant Commander Sawers was ever found.[27]

Hall, Neyer and Sawers remain Missing in Action to this day.

Six days after my research began, after hours upon hours of work, when I came to the very last name on the list, I finally found my fighter pilot. His name was Lieutenant Robert Zimmerman.[28]

It felt like a great weight was suddenly lifted off me. After all those sleepless nights, and all those awful visions and nightmares of him slipping away, I finally knew his name.

In the days that followed, I was able to reconstruct the events of his final mission. On the morning of July 24, 1945, Zimmerman was flying alone over Kure Harbor on a photo-reconnaissance mission. Inside the fuselage of his specially modified Hellcat, a large camera was mounted to photograph the Japanese fleet anchored at Kure. During a photo pass over the harbor, Zimmerman's Hellcat was hit by anti-aircraft fire. It will never be known for sure, but I believe Zimmerman was severely wounded at that time as well.

All of the pilots attacking Kure that day had been briefed on the location of the lifeguard submarines that were stationed in the waters off Japan in case they were hit, and Zimmerman immediately headed for the closest one, the USS *Whale*. Based on what Bill told me about his own experiences that day, it was about a 20-minute flight from Kure to reach the *Whale*. Zimmerman was only a few minutes behind Bill, and it's possible that he was photographing the same Japanese heavy cruiser, the *Tone*, that Bill had just bombed when he was hit.

We'll never know for sure what was going on in the cockpit as he struggled to reach the *Whale*, but we do know that Zimmerman, a tough Chicagoan, was a highly experienced pilot on his second combat tour, and as I soon discovered, he had been in this exact situation once before.

Less than a year earlier, during his first combat tour, Zimmerman was shot down by anti-aircraft fire while attacking a Japanese airfield in the Philippines. The damage to his fighter was so severe that he could only stay airborne for a few minutes before he was forced to ditch. After more than eight hours in the ocean, Zimmerman was found floating 10 miles offshore and rescued by an American destroyer. During that same tour, Zimmerman had also made a barrier crash landing on his aircraft carrier, presumably due to battle damage, and he also shot down two Japanese aircraft and destroyed a third on the ground.[29]

If anyone could be prepared for the struggle he was facing that day over Kure, it was Lieutenant Robert Zimmerman. But his wounds from the anti-aircraft fire were too severe. He must have passed out from all the blood loss after he climbed out of the cockpit and fell into the water. He was so close to making it home.

While I was unearthing all of this information, I found something that I honestly never thought I'd see. On the website dedicated to the squadron he served his first combat tour with, Fighting Squadron 31, I found a photograph of Lieutenant Zimmerman. The photo was taken at the end of his first combat tour in 1944. Dressed in all of his flight gear, Zimmerman was sitting in the cockpit of his Hellcat and smiling for the camera. He looked so young and happy. Less than 10 months after that photo was taken, Zimmerman was gone. He was only 24 years old.[30]

I couldn't wait to share all of this with Bill, as I knew it would mean so much to him, but I decided to wait a few weeks before I called him. After all it took to discover who that Hellcat pilot was, it was hard to just sit on all of this information now, but I think I made the right decision. You'll soon understand why.

*   *   *

While I counted down the days before I could call Bill, I received a surprising e-mail from Sam Jr. He and his wife, Sherry, would be driving through North Georgia soon and he wanted to know if we could meet somewhere and talk. We quickly made plans to meet at our local veterans center, where I served as curator. With the small military museum we had inside the veterans center as a backdrop, it was the perfect place for us to meet.

It soon occurred to me that Sam Jr. had never talked to anyone before who could explain what happened to his father's B-29 that night, so I decided to surprise him with a special presentation at the veterans center. Searching through my collection, I found a number of things that would give him a better understanding of what his father went through, and I prepared an informal presentation centered around those items.

Ten days later, on a beautiful Sunday afternoon in July, another dream of mine came true: I met the son of Sergeant Sam Kidd. It was such a privilege to give Sam Jr. a full briefing about his father's last mission. I began by showing him some original target maps that were actually used on a B-29 in combat, and I pointed out their target area that night and where they bailed out. The maps also illustrated the vast distances that the B-29ers had to fly between their bases and Japan, and just how lucky Ray and Sam were to be rescued. A lot of crews were not so fortunate.

I knew Sam Jr. had never heard of a "runaway prop" before, so I explained what that was and how it led to the crew having to bail out that night. We know from Sam's letters that he struggled to get out, so using a large-scale model of a B-29 and a cutaway poster of the bomber's interior, I showed him where his father and the others jumped from, and I talked about the men who didn't survive and what probably happened to them. I also brought Baldwin's parachute to show him, and I talked about Mr. Trabold and some of his experiences during the war.

One of my favorite things I brought to show Sam Jr. was an original, unrestored, World War II B-29 radio operator's chair. The chair was little more than a stool with a simple backrest, complete with its horsehair cushion, but it was the exact type of chair that his father used during the war. The chair may have looked old and ratty, but they built things to last back then, so I didn't hesitate to invite Sam Jr. to sit down on it. Like his father, Sam Jr. is also a tall man, and the chair was not a comfortable fit for either of them. "Just imagine sitting there for a 14-hour mission, or longer," I said, adding that Mr. Trabold's longest mission was 19 hours. I truly don't know how they did it.

As much as I enjoyed sharing all of these things with Sam Jr., nothing could compare to the moment I showed him Ray's uniform. As I carefully removed the uniform from its protective cover and placed it on the table in front of him, it struck me how far I'd come with this story. After almost a year of research, to now be standing there next to Sam Jr. with Ray's uniform, as I pointed to the Soldier's Medal ribbon that Ray was awarded for saving his father's life, it was such a beautiful and moving experience. I never could have dreamed of a moment like this.

We spent about two-and-a-half hours together before Sam Jr. and his wife had to leave. I wish they could have stayed longer, but they still had a couple of hours of driving ahead of them. With hearty hugs and handshakes, we bid our goodbyes and left that day filled with happy memories that will last a lifetime. I wish all of my stories ended like that.

A few days later, Sam Jr. e-mailed me to let me know that he'd safely arrived back home in Texas, and to express his appreciation for everything I did at the veterans center. Then he said something that left me totally speechless. After talking it over with his family, Sam Jr. said he wanted to give me the coveralls that his father was given to wear aboard the USS *Whale* after he was rescued. I was so touched that the Kidd family would want to entrust something so important to me. I even asked Sam Jr. if he was sure he wanted to do it. He was.

Sam's coveralls are here with me now. We don't know when Ray and Sam last saw each other, but it was probably when they left Tinian to come home. With Sam's coveralls and Ray's uniform here, it feels like they have been reunited again. What an incredible journey it was to get here.

*   *   *

Nine days later, it was time to call Bill and tell him about Lieutenant Zimmerman. I waited for this exact day because it had a lot of significance in Bill's life. The date was July 24, 2018 – exactly 73 years to the day since Bill was shot down and rescued by the USS *Whale*. In modern times, it's what veterans now call their "Alive Day," the day they came close to death. What better day to call Bill and tell him all about that Hellcat pilot who he'd spent the last 73 years wondering about?

Despite my best-laid plans, it didn't quite work out that way; we kept missing each other's calls and were never able to connect. But the next day, we finally caught each other at home at the same time. I guess 73 years and one day isn't too bad, either.

Bill is always sunny and upbeat when we talk, but he really came alive when I explained why I had wanted to talk to him so badly the day before. He was so touched that I remembered, and he thanked me for thinking about him on that day. I jokingly asked Bill if it felt like it had been 73 years since he was shot down. He laughed and said that it didn't feel like it had been that long ago.

I didn't tell Bill this, but in that moment, in 2018, I thought to myself how incredible it was to actually be talking to a pilot who was shot down during World War II. I guess it just hit me, again, how truly lucky I was to find Bill.

We shared a few more laughs about getting old, and then I told Bill that there was another reason why I had wanted to talk to him yesterday. "I have some very good news to tell you," I began. I explained that after our last conversation about the Hellcat pilot, he had inspired me to take another look at the events of that day. As I continued, I could hear the anticipation in Bill's voice. He knew that I was building towards something big.

Then I broke the news: "I figured out who the Hellcat pilot was!"

I wish you could have heard Bill's reaction when I told him Zimmerman's name. It was like an explosion of joy and relief and happiness. It was such a beautiful moment that it makes me teary-eyed now just thinking about it.

The first question Bill asked me was what aircraft carrier Zimmerman was from. I could tell it was one of those questions that he'd wondered about since 1945.

"Zimmerman was with Fighting Squadron 27 on the USS *Independence*," I said.

"Oh, I'll be darned!" Bill said, surprised.

We talked a little while about Zimmerman and the events of that day, and then I told Bill that I had another surprise for him. It was the photo I found of Zimmerman in the cockpit of his Hellcat after his first combat tour. Seeing that photo for the first time meant an awful lot to me, but just imagine what it would mean to Bill. I told him that I'd send him a copy of it.

If all this news wasn't great enough, I still had one more surprise left. During my research, I found a map that showed the exact location where Zimmerman had ditched that day, which was also the same location where Bill ditched. I knew right away that this map was something that Bill would love to show to his family, so I told him that I'd send a copy of it with Zimmerman's photo.

It was such a thrill to hear the excitement in Bill's voice as I shared all of this with him. Over seven decades after that life-changing day, I was finally able to give him the answers to those questions that had haunted him for so long. I think it brought him some peace, and more importantly, it gave him closure. And for that I am most proud.

We talked for almost 20 minutes that day before Bill had to leave for a doctor's appointment. I told him to tell his doctor for me that he'd better take good care of him, because he was a national treasure. Bill laughed and said that he would.

After we said our goodbyes, I sat at my desk for a few minutes and reflected on the past few weeks. So many dreams of mine had come true that it almost didn't seem real. I never expected to find someone like Bill, let alone anyone who was on the USS *Whale* during that summer in 1945. But most of all, I never expected to make a new friend.

Bill has lived a long and full life, and I don't know how many more years he will be with us, but I'm going to make the most of our new friendship.

You really never know where those doors are going to take you.

*   *   *

As I look back on this journey, I always find myself returning to that night in September of 2017, when I first discovered Ray's uniform on eBay, and the moment I realized that I was looking at something very special. Knowing everything I know now, it makes me emotional just thinking about it all, but I'm going to push through it and write the end of this story.

What first caught my eye when I saw Ray's uniform that night, as I looked past his silver pilot wings, were the colors of his Soldier's Medal ribbon. They are the colors of the American flag.

The Red, White and Blue, and all that they represent, are personified by men like Ray and Sam. But if they were here today, and you asked them about it, they would say they were just doing their job, and the real heroes are the ones who never came home. They would tell you the real heroes that July night were Henry Goldstein, Frank Blackett, Yearby Ashby and Jack Atanis.

They are the heroes who died for the Red, White and Blue.

19

Downfall

The Trinity explosion. (National Archives 558571)

"Now we are all sons of bitches," test director Kenneth Bainbridge said to Robert Oppenheimer, as they stood 5.7 miles away from ground zero and watched a boiling mushroom cloud rising above the Trinity test site.[1] The date was July 16, 1945. In a barren stretch of New Mexico desert that Spanish Conquistadors had named *Jornada del Muerto*, "Route of the Dead Man," at 5:29 a.m., the world's first atomic bomb exploded in a blinding flash that was seen 250 miles away. The monstrous explosion unleashed from the bomb's 13-pound plutonium core was equivalent to some 20,000 tons of TNT. The resulting fireball was hotter than the surface of the sun and melted the desert sand, turning it to glass.

After almost three years of work and $2 billion, the 20 or so scientists and military men at the control bunker were at first jubilant and congratulated each other on their success, but then the mood turned somber. "We knew the world would not be the same," recalled Oppenheimer, the 41-year-old theoretical physicist and director of the Manhattan Project's secret Los Alamos weapons laboratory that developed the bomb. "A few people laughed, a few people cried. Most people were silent."[2] Soon to be known to the world as the father of the atomic bomb, Oppenheimer would later recall being reminded of a verse from the *Bhagavad Gita*, an ancient Hindu scripture, as he took in the awesome forces they had just unleashed: "Now I am become Death, the destroyer of worlds."[3] The atomic bomb was born.

Half a world away in Germany, the leaders of the "Big Three" Allied powers – Harry Truman, Winston Churchill and Joseph Stalin – were gathering for the Potsdam Conference on the outskirts of Berlin to discuss the future of Germany and post-war Europe. After the start of the conference was postponed because Stalin was late in arriving from Moscow, Truman took advantage of the delay and embarked on a driving tour of the war-ravaged capital. As recorded in the President's travel log that day, the destruction of Berlin was total and complete:

> Every building we saw was either badly damaged or completely destroyed. This once beautiful city, capital of a proud nation, that housed four and one-quarter million inhabitants, now wrecked beyond repair, is a distressing example of the results that follow the loss of moral appreciation of others and attachment to false prophets. But much more distressing than the ruined buildings was the long, never-ending procession of old men, women and children along the autobahn and the country roads. Wandering aimlessly and probably without hope, they clutter the roads carrying their small children and pushing or pulling their slender belongings. In this two hour drive we saw evidence of a great world tragedy – the beginning of the disintegration of a highly cultured and proud people.[4]

A veteran himself of the First World War, the "absolute ruin" of Berlin would leave a lasting impression on Truman, who wrote in his diary: "Never did I see a more sorrowful sight, nor witness retribution to the nth degree."[5]

Truman would spend part of the afternoon reviewing the famed "Hell on Wheels" 2nd Armored Division outside Berlin. Stretching as far as the eye could see, over 1,000 tanks and vehicles from the division, along with their crews, were parked along the autobahn to welcome the President. Riding in one of the division's reconnaissance vehicles, it took 22 minutes for the President to reach the end of the line. This stunning display of military might represented just one of the 16 armored divisions operating in Europe when Germany surrendered on May 7.[6]

Later that evening, Secretary of War Henry Stimson, who was also at Potsdam with the President, received an urgent message from Washington:

> Operated on this morning. Diagnosis not yet complete but results seem satisfactory and already exceed expectations. Local press release necessary, as interest extends great distance. Dr. Groves pleased. He returns tomorrow. I will keep you posted.[7]

The coded message was from George Harrison, Stimson's special consultant on the Manhattan Project, and confirmed the successful test of the world's first atomic bomb. "Well, I have been responsible for spending two billions of dollars on this atomic venture," Stimson said to his assistant. "Now that it is successful I shall not be sent to prison in Fort Leavenworth."[8]

Stimson immediately took the message to Truman, who was "greatly interested" in the results, as Stimson noted in his diary. Churchill was also "greatly cheered up" when he heard the news the next day, but it was decided not to inform Stalin about the test, or even divulge the existence of the Manhattan Project to the Soviets. (Stalin was already aware of the Manhattan Project through the network of Soviet spies operating in the United States.)[9]

A second message about the test arrived the next day that "highly delighted" Truman, but it was also in code and gave few details. The awesome power that the United States now possessed was arguably not fully appreciated by Truman until five days after the test, when a full report prepared by Major General Leslie Groves, the director of the Manhattan Project, arrived by special courier from Washington. Before he presented it to the President, Stimson read the report, marveling at how the test "revealed far greater destructive power than we expected."[10] Later that afternoon, Truman was captivated as Stimson read the report aloud for the President, who was "immensely pleased" and "tremendously pepped up" by its contents. Stimson then went to see Winston Churchill, but the Prime Minister had to leave for a meeting before he could finish the report.[11]

The next day, after reading the full report, Churchill told Stimson that he'd noticed that something had changed with Truman the previous day during their meeting with Stalin. Churchill had no idea what it was, but Truman was clearly "fortified by something that had happened" because he "stood up to the Russians in a most emphatic and decisive manner" against "certain demands that they absolutely could not have." After reading the report, it all made sense now. "Now I know what happened to Truman yesterday," Churchill said. "I couldn't understand it. When he got to the meeting after having read this report he was a changed man. He told the Russians just where they got on and off and generally bossed the whole meeting."[12]

In his initial dealings with Stalin, Truman was negotiating under the belief that the United States needed Stalin's help to defeat Japan by entering the war and tying up its massive army in Manchuria. The Soviets and Japanese had signed a neutrality pact in 1941 and were not engaged in hostilities, but with the plans for an invasion of Japan already underway, a Soviet attack on Manchuria would prevent Japan from moving those troops back to the home islands to fight the Americans during the coming invasion. At the Yalta Conference in February of 1944, Stalin had already secretly agreed to enter the war with Japan within three months of Germany being defeated, but only after certain conditions were met, including the restoration of rights and territory that Russia had lost during the Russo-Japanese War in 1904.[13]

Truman later recalled that there were many reasons for him to travel to Potsdam, but the most urgent reason, in his mind, was to "get from Stalin a personal reaffirmation of Russia's entry into the war against Japan." The consensus among the Joint Chiefs of Staff was that the Soviets' entry into the war would hasten the defeat of Japan, and thereby save American lives.[14] What was most important to Truman in the coming campaign to defeat Japan, as he outlined to the Joint Chiefs, was to reduce the loss of American lives to the maximum extent possible. Truman recalled:

> The Chiefs of Staff were grim in their estimates of the cost in casualties we would have to pay to invade the Japanese mainland. As our forces in the Pacific were pushing ahead, paying a heavy toll in lives, the urgency of getting Russia into the war became more compelling. Russia's entry into the war would mean the saving of hundreds of thousands of American casualties.[15]

On July 18, before he received the Trinity report from Groves, Truman wrote in a letter to his wife that he had obtained from Stalin what he came to the conference for: the Soviet Union would enter the war with Japan on August 15. "I'll say that we'll end the war a year sooner now and think of the kids who won't be killed!" Truman wrote. "That is the important thing."[16]

But after Groves' report about the Trinity test was fully digested by Truman and others, there was now a growing question about whether the Soviets would truly be needed in the war against Japan. Stimson felt that with the new weapon, the United States "would not need the assistance of the Russians to conquer Japan" and end the war.[17]

The question of Soviet intervention in Manchuria took on a new meaning after Truman began meeting with Stalin and saw firsthand "what we and the West had to face in the future" with the Soviets. Stalin fully expected to share in the occupation of Japan after the war, but after his experience at Potsdam, where he saw the beginning of the Sovietization of Eastern Europe that would eventually lead to the Cold War, Truman was so alarmed that he became determined not to allow the Soviets any part in the control of Japan.[18] "The Russians were planning world conquest," Truman recalled after the war.[19]

With the atomic bomb, could the war now be won much sooner, without the help of the Soviets?

*   *   *

Back at the Trinity test site, in the minutes after the first atomic detonation, thoughts had also turned towards swiftly ending the war with Japan. Shortly after the explosion, Brigadier General Thomas Farrell, the Deputy Commander of the Manhattan Project, and Robert Oppenheimer left the command bunker and drove back to base camp 10 miles away from ground zero.

"The war is over," Farrell said, as he walked up to his boss, General Leslie Groves.

"Yes, after we drop two bombs on Japan," Groves replied. He then turned to Oppenheimer and quietly congratulated him: "I'm proud of all of you."[20]

Years later, Groves recalled: "We were both, I am sure, already thinking of the future and whether we could repeat our success soon and bring the war to an end."[21]

Following the test, Farrell summed up his thoughts in the report for the Secretary of War that would have such a profound effect on Truman:

> As to the present war, there was a feeling that no matter what else might happen, we now had the means to insure its speedy conclusion and save thousands of American lives. As to the future, there had been brought into being something big and something new that would prove to be immeasurably more important than the discovery of electricity or any of the other great discoveries which have so affected our existence.[22]

While the mushroom cloud still loomed over the Trinity test site that Monday morning, 1,000 miles away, the preparations for the first atomic strike against Japan were already well underway.

The morning before the test, the commanding officer of the heavy cruiser USS *Indianapolis*, Captain Charles McVay, received orders for a secret mission. The *Indianapolis* had just undergone major repairs after being damaged by a Japanese Kamikaze during the Battle of Okinawa, and it would now be returning to duty the next morning on one of the most important missions of the war. When McVay was briefed that Sunday morning by Rear Admiral William Purnell and

Captain William "Deak" Parsons, he was told that the *Indianapolis* was to deliver a "small but vital top-secret cargo" at high speed to Tinian after a brief stopover at Pearl Harbor. McVay was not told what the cargo was, but it was stressed to him that the cargo was so important that it was to be guarded even after the life of his vessel. If the *Indianapolis* was in danger of sinking during the voyage, the cargo would be saved at all costs, going so far as to secure it in a lifeboat, if necessary.[23]

Two Army officers would accompany the cargo and it would be guarded around the clock by Marines, but no one else was to go near it. McVay was mystified, but he knew not to ask questions. With his orders in hand, McVay returned to his ship and later that afternoon the *Indianapolis* steamed down to San Francisco and docked at the Hunters Point Navy Yard. Only three of his officers knew they would sail the next day.

At 3:00 a.m. that morning, the loudspeakers on the *Indianapolis* came alive with an announcement to prepare to get under way. No one knew what was going on or why they were suddenly going to sea. "I cannot tell you the mission," McVay said to his small group of senior officers gathered on the bridge, "but every hour we save will shorten the war by that much." McVay went on to explain that within an hour, a top-secret cargo would be brought aboard. A large wooden crate would be stowed on the hangar deck and placed under armed guard. The flag lieutenant's cabin would be occupied by two Army officers who were escorting the cargo. They were not to be disturbed.[24]

An hour later, two Army trucks pulled to a stop next to the *Indianapolis*. One of the trucks was carrying a massive wooden crate, but the other appeared to be empty except for a small metal cylinder that stood about 2 feet tall. As a gantry crane picked up the crate and deposited it on the hangar deck, two sailors slid a crowbar through a ring on top of the cylinder and picked it up on their shoulders, dangling the cylinder between them. While the crate was being secured on the hangar deck, the two sailors carried the cylinder to the flag lieutenant's cabin, where a series of pad eyes were welded to the floor and fitted with steel straps on hinges. The cylinder was placed in the middle and the straps were closed over it, forming a cage to contain what was essentially a sealed, lead-lined bucket. One of the Army officers escorting the cargo, who was actually the Manhattan Project's Chief of Foreign Intelligence posing as an artillery officer, secured the straps with a lock.[25]

At 8:36 a.m., only four hours after the first atomic bomb was detonated, the USS *Indianapolis* and its precious cargo passed beneath the Golden Gate Bridge and headed out to sea. There was no turning back now.

*   *   *

"Right now, gentlemen, approximately 520 B-29s are dumping 3,000 tons of bombs on Osaka," General Arnold announced on June 15, 1945, to the nearly 100 reporters crowded into the XXI Bomber Command's War Room on Guam. "Just a year ago today, in the first B-29 raid against the Japanese homeland, 68 Superforts hit Yawata with 215 tons. And just about two years before that, Jimmy Doolittle's raiders hit Tokyo with 12 tons of bombs."

For the staff officers looking on, it was hard to tell which figure shocked the reporters the most: the incredible amount of bombs that were raining down on Osaka at that very moment, or the revelation that the Doolittle Raiders had carried so few bombs in their daring attack.

"That will give you some indication of the growth of the Air Forces during three years of war against the Jap mainland," Arnold continued. "As for the future – well, in the year beginning

July first, we will dump more than 2,000,000 tons of bombs on the Empire." Arnold grinned when he saw the look of disbelief on everyone's face. "That means the strategic Air Forces out here will drop 1,300,000 tons, and the tactical bombers will handle more than 700,000 tons. All of this on an area less than a third the size of Germany."

"But General," one reporter spoke up, "does that mean you don't expect the war to be over by next July?" Ever since Germany surrendered, the reporters had been hounding Arnold and many others with the same question: when will the war be over? Arnold was blunt with the reporter:

> Look, maybe you know when the war will be over. Frankly, I don't, and neither does anyone else in the Air Forces. We can only operate on the basis of long-range planning. That is our schedule for the next year. If the Japs quit before then, fine and good. If they don't, we will have a larger dose to hand out during the next year. If necessary, we will keep going until we have accomplished the utter destruction of all of Japan's cities, down to the last household still turning out war goods for the Empire. We have worked out our strategic bombing plan – which will be very similar to the one we used in Europe ... Right now we have our schedule for a year. When that year is over – and if the Jap still hasn't given up – we will proceed to continue the program and step it up.[26]

As candid as Arnold was, he couldn't divulge that there actually was one man in the Army Air Forces who felt that he knew when the war would be over. That man was General Curtis LeMay.

The morning after he arrived on Guam, LeMay gave Arnold a briefing on his plan to destroy Japan's remaining industrial facilities. When LeMay began his firebombing campaign back in March, he ran out of incendiary bombs after five missions and had to wait over a month before launching the next fire raid. Three months later, his supply of bombs had steadily improved, but now LeMay had another problem: he was running out of targets.

LeMay began his firebombing campaign by going after Japan's five most important industrial cities: Tokyo, Osaka, Nagoya, Yokohama and Kobe. By June 15, the same day that Arnold watched over 500 B-29s depart for Osaka, LeMay had burned out over 103 square miles of Japan's "big five" industrial cities alone. These five cities were so "thoroughly gutted" that they were "no longer considered essential targets except for occasional pinpoint 'policing' attacks."[27]

With the "big five" cities in ruins, LeMay turned his attention to the industrial centers located in more than 60 other cities across Japan. These smaller cities could be successfully attacked with fewer B-29s, which allowed LeMay to divide his forces and attack multiple cities simultaneously. "With the destruction of these cities, Japan would have few of the things needed to supply her Army, Navy, and Air Force, and couldn't continue fighting," Arnold later said. "We had done the same thing in Germany with much more difficult targets and much more intense antiaircraft fire, not to mention the Luftwaffe's tough opposition."[28]

Arnold was so impressed with the plan that he asked LeMay the same question the reporters had been dogging him with: when was the war going to end? "I didn't have an answer," LeMay recalled. "I told him I was too busy fighting it to figure that out."[29] Since he was now on the spot, LeMay told Arnold to give him 30 minutes and he'd have an answer for him. "My staff and I were convinced, when we came up with this plan ... that we had a good chance of defeating Japan before the invasion," LeMay recalled, but he'd never given the question much thought before.[30]

Gathering his staff, LeMay looked at the targets they had left and calculated how long it would take to destroy them. "We looked at ... what we had left to do and we couldn't find any targets that were going to be in existence after about the first of September ... we couldn't see much of a war going on after that time," LeMay recounted.[31]

Satisfied that he had an answer, LeMay returned and gave Arnold his assessment. "I told General Arnold that with those targets gone, there wouldn't be any targets left," LeMay said. "I could then start to work over the Japanese rail network, but that wouldn't take long." Based on his best estimate, LeMay concluded that the war would be over by the first of October.[32]

"October 1, we will see," Arnold cautiously wrote in his diary after LeMay's briefing.[33]

Later that night, after eating dinner with Admiral Nimitz, Arnold returned to his quarters to find a preliminary report had just arrived about the strategic bombing campaign against Germany and its effect on the war. The report concluded that the bombing campaign had not only hastened the end of the war, but it had a disastrous effect on Germany's war production. The report emphasized that the strategic air offensive had "effectively paralyzed the German war economy" and contributed in a decisive manner to the "early and complete victory which followed." The report also noted that Japan's war industries were more vulnerable to air attack than Germany's, and that unlike Germany, Japan was powerless to stop American air attacks.[34]

With LeMay's briefing still fresh in his mind, the revelations in the report led Arnold to consider the implications regarding Japan. "I didn't see the whole report then, naturally, but reading that much of it caused me to do some serious thinking about Japan," Arnold recalled. "If our bombing did have that effect upon the national and industrial collapse of Germany, certainly the same amount of bombing, or perhaps less, would have a worse effect upon Japan."[35]

Two days later, Arnold received a cable from General Marshall in Washington. President Truman had called a meeting in the coming days with the Joint Chiefs of Staff to discuss the strategy to defeat Japan and force its unconditional surrender. Marshall wanted Arnold's opinion on a controversial question: "Can we win the war by bombing?"[36]

"If we could win the war by bombing, it would be unnecessary for the ground troops to make a landing on the shores of Japan," Arnold recalled. "Personally, I was convinced it could be done. I did not believe Japan could stand the punishment from the air that Germany had taken."[37]

Later that afternoon, Arnold decided that LeMay should immediately fly back to Washington and brief the President and the Joint Chiefs at the upcoming meeting. "After thinking and talking it over, I was convinced LeMay probably had more information on the subject of 'bombing Japan' than anyone else, so I proposed that he go to the meeting of the Joint Chiefs of Staff and make the presentation to the President," Arnold remembered.[38]

After scrambling the rest of the afternoon to pack for the sudden trip, LeMay and 15 men from his staff took off from Guam that night in a B-29 and headed for the United States. With LeMay at the controls, they flew directly to Hawaii, stopping only to refuel, before continuing non-stop to Washington. When they landed, they had flown 4,650 miles in 38½ hours – a new record.[39]

For the next six days, LeMay and his staff would be in constant meetings at the Pentagon with everyone from General Marshall to members of the press. On the afternoon of June 18, while the Joint Chiefs were preparing to brief President Truman at the White House, LeMay held a conference in General Norstad's office at the Pentagon. One of the officers in attendance was Major James Cozzens, a famous novelist in civilian life, who was now working for General Arnold at the Office of Information Services at the Pentagon. General LeMay made quite an impression that day on Cozzens, who observed in his diary:

LeMay is stocky, full-faced and dark. He had a dead cigar in his mouth when he came in and he never moved it for three quarters of an hour, though talking around it well enough when occasion arose. The superficial first impression was that he was dumb or gross; but he has one of those faces that grows on you – a real intelligence and even a kind of sweetness – as though he would not do anything mean, or even think anything mean, though he is well known to be a hard man, and you can see that, too – becoming more apparent the longer you look at him. Around the motionless cigar he spoke sensibly.[40]

After the war, Cozzens confided to a friend: "I have seldom been more impressed by anyone than by LeMay who once put his chest against mine, my back being against the wall of General Fred Smith's office [Smith was the Deputy Chief of the Air Staff] and said … that whoever fixed up this idea ought to be socked." Cozzens didn't elaborate on what LeMay was referring to.[41]

* * *

Later that afternoon at the White house, the Joint Chiefs and the Secretaries of War and the Navy began their meeting with President Truman to discuss the details of the campaign against Japan and their strategy moving forward. The decision Truman was facing that afternoon would be the hardest he would have to make since assuming the Presidency after Franklin Roosevelt died from a stroke two months earlier, and potentially hundreds of thousands of American lives were at stake.

In the memo that Fleet Admiral William Leahy, the President's Chief of Staff, sent out to the Joint Chiefs alerting them of the meeting, Leahy said that Truman specifically wanted "an estimate of the losses in killed and wounded that will result from an invasion of Japan proper," as well as estimates to defeat Japan by blockade and bombardment. Leahy added that Truman intended to make his decisions on the campaign "with the purposes of economizing to the maximum extent possible in the loss of American lives."[42]

In the discussions between the Joint Chiefs and field commanders in the months leading up to the meeting, two distinct strategies emerged for defeating Japan. The Army favored an invasion of the Japanese home islands to defeat its forces on the battlefield, while the Navy and Army Air Forces preferred a strategy of blockade and bombardment to force Japan to surrender.

The night before the meeting, Truman wrote in his diary: "I have to decide Japanese strategy – shall we invade Japan proper or shall we bomb and blockade? That is my hardest decision to date. But I'll make it when I have all the facts."[43]

The plan that was recommended to Truman that June afternoon was a combination of the two.

"The Kyushu operation is essential to a strategy of strangulation and appears to be the least costly worthwhile operation following Okinawa," General Marshall said, as he outlined the strategy for Truman. The plan to defeat Japan was broken down into two phases and would begin with an invasion of Kyushu, Japan's southern island, followed by a massive invasion of the Tokyo (Kanto) Plain on Japan's main island, Honshu, four months later. To weaken Japan as much as possible before the invasion, the naval blockade and air bombardment would continue unabated.[44]

"The basic point is that a lodgement in Kyushu is essential, both to tightening our strangle hold of blockade and bombardment on Japan, and to forcing capitulation by invasion of the

Tokyo Plain," Marshall continued. "We are bringing to bear against the Japanese every weapon and all the force we can employ and there is no reduction in our maximum possible application of bombardment and blockade, while at the same time we are pressing invasion preparations."[45]

While General Arnold felt that air power alone could win the war, in a cable to Marshall before the meeting, he expressed his support for the plan to invade Kyushu, which would gain new air bases for 40 groups of heavy bombers to further bombard Japan. But Arnold was emphatic that priority should be given to B-29 attacks, and that all restrictions hindering such operations should be removed so that the bombers could "drop the greatest number of bombs in the shortest possible time," a reference to the administrative delays LeMay had been experiencing with the Navy in getting enough bombs and supplies.[46] Arnold was calling for the "complete destruction of Japan proper" through air power, and he recommended that the plans for an invasion of Honshu be kept on a "live but postponed basis."[47]

The possibility of defeating Japan through air power without an invasion was brought up at the meeting, but no one in the room thought it was a practical strategy. General Marshall felt that "air power alone was not sufficient to put the Japanese out of the war" because "it was unable alone to put the Germans out." Major General Ira Eaker, who was representing Arnold at the meeting, also agreed with Marshall, as did Generals MacArthur and Eisenhower, who cabled their opinions to the Joint Chiefs.[48]

In the hours before the meeting at the White House, Arnold had a "long, spirited talk" with MacArthur at his headquarters in the Philippines about a number of issues, including how to end the war. "He gets excited and walks the floor, raises his voice," Arnold wrote in his diary after the meeting with MacArthur. "I thought I was one of the few who did it." When Arnold brought up the idea that air power alone could defeat Japan, MacArthur said that he believed that bombing could do a lot to end the war, but in his final analysis, "doughboys will have to march into Tokyo."[49]

The Joint Chiefs also agreed with MacArthur's analysis that an invasion of the home islands was the only way to force the unconditional surrender of Japan, but Truman was concerned about the casualties from such a massive and prolonged operation. The issue of the casualties that American forces might suffer during an invasion of Japan was first raised in a report to the Joint Chiefs on August 30, 1944. Based on the ratio of American to Japanese casualties during the Battle of Saipan, the report reached a chilling conclusion:

> In our Saipan operation it cost approximately one American killed and several wounded to exterminate seven Japanese soldiers. On this basis it might cost us half a million American lives and many times that number in wounded to exterminate the Japanese ground forces that conceivably could be employed against us in the [Japanese] home islands.[50]

This shocking estimate is probably what led General Norstad to warn LeMay when he took over the XXI Bomber Command that if he didn't get results with the B-29s, "it will mean eventually a mass amphibious invasion of Japan, to cost probably half a million more American lives."[51]

The "Saipan Ratio" was also an important factor for the dramatic increase in men drafted for U.S. military service, which rose from 60,000 to 80,000 men per month in January of 1945, and then to 100,000 a month in March. Another report was also released in March which concluded that between mid-1945 and the end of 1946, the U.S. Army alone – not including Navy and Marine losses – would need 720,000 replacement troops for "dead and evacuated wounded" in fighting against Japanese forces.[52]

In the weeks before the June 18 meeting, Truman had also met with former President Herbert Hoover to discuss various issues, including his thoughts on ending the war. Hoover submitted to Truman his "Memorandum on Ending the Japanese War" outlining his ideas, which included his assertion that defeating Japan could cost between 500,000 and 1,000,000 American lives.[53]

Truman was so alarmed by Hoover's casualty estimates, and the responses from those he shared the memo with – none of whom questioned Hoover's numbers – that it led him to call the June 18 meeting with the Joint Chiefs.[54]

A copy of Hoover's memo, as well as an earlier memo Hoover sent to Stimson with the same casualty estimates, were also given to Marshall's deputy, General Thomas Handy, for analysis by the Operations Division Staff. Handy's staff concluded that Hoover's "estimated loss of 500,000 lives due to carrying the war to conclusion under our present plan of campaign is considered to be entirely too high" and his estimates deserved "little consideration."[55]

The "present plan of campaign" Handy referred to was underlined for emphasis in the memo, and it did not entail defeating every last bastion of resistance throughout the Japanese Empire. Instead, it was believed that if the Japanese were "ever willing to capitulate short of complete military defeat in the field," its leaders would do so when faced with an invasion of the home islands, coupled with the Soviet Union entering the war, which would "convince them of the hopelessness of their position" and force their surrender to avoid further destruction.[56]

In his two memos, Hoover envisioned the frightening scenario of having to destroy all of Japan's forces spread out across the home islands and Asia in costly last-ditch battles. "If we fight out the war with Japan to the bitter end, we will need to put 1,000,000 men to attack the Japanese home islands and possibly 2,000,000 on the Asiatic mainland, as Japan has armies of 3,500,000 men left," Hoover warned.[57]

Hoover's casualty estimates for a long drawn-out campaign to defeat Japan gave Truman pause, but during the meeting at the White House, Marshall was vague on the subject of casualties. "Our experience in the Pacific War is so diverse as to casualties that it is considered wrong to give any estimate in numbers," Marshall said. He then presented the casualty figures for the last four major campaigns in the Pacific, and the Normandy campaign in Europe, as a reference point for the President. Marshall added that General MacArthur's operations from March 1944 until May 1945 had resulted in 13,742 Americans killed, compared to 310,165 Japanese killed, a ratio of 22 to 1.

"There is reason to believe that the first 30 days in Kyushu should not exceed the price we have paid for Luzon," Marshall continued. "It is a grim fact that there is not an easy, bloodless way to victory in war and it is the thankless task of the leaders to maintain their firm outward front which holds the resolution of their subordinates." The figures that Marshall provided showed 31,000 American casualties (dead, wounded and missing) for Luzon, which was the most favorable American-to-Japanese casualty ratio of the battles shown on the chart.[58]

Marshall then read aloud a telegram from General MacArthur, who believed the proposed operation to invade Japan was "the most economical one in effort and lives that is possible," and that "sooner or later a decisive ground attack must be made." MacArthur was fully behind the plan, which he believed presented "less hazards of excessive loss than any other that has been suggested," and recommended no changes.[59]

What Marshall didn't mention was that only days earlier, MacArthur's staff had estimated 105,050 casualties for the first 90 days on Kyushu, plus 12,600 non-battle casualties. When Marshall asked for clarification and advised that the President was "very much concerned as to the number of casualties we will receive," MacArthur replied that the estimate was "purely academic" for planning purposes, and that he "did not anticipate such a high rate of loss."[60]

Marshall had also received four other casualty estimates that ranged from 49,000 in the first 30 days to 220,000 total battle casualties, but none of these estimates were shared with Truman.[61]

As the discussions continued and drifted away from casualty projections, Truman turned to Admiral Leahy and asked for his views of the situation. Leahy reminded everyone in the room that the President "had been interested in knowing what the price in casualties for Kyushu would be and whether or not that price could be paid." Leahy pointed out that the troops on Okinawa had suffered 35 percent casualties, and if this percentage was applied to those to be employed on Kyushu, the similarity of the expected fighting would give a good estimate of the casualties to be expected.[62] The brutal fighting on Okinawa had cost the lives of 12,520 Americans and left more than 36,000 wounded. Over 92,000 Japanese soldiers, plus a horrifying number of Okinawan civilians that some estimates put as high as 150,000, were also killed.[63]

Admiral Ernest King, the Chief of Naval Operations, spoke up and said that on Okinawa "there had been only one way to go," and that meant "a straight frontal attack against a highly fortified position," whereas on Kyushu, the "landings would be made on three fronts simultaneously and there would be much more room for maneuver." In King's opinion, a realistic casualty figure for Kyushu would lie somewhere between the Luzon and Okinawa operations, which in the data provided to the President were 17,000 and 41,700 casualties, respectively.[64]

There is no record in the official minutes of the meeting to indicate that anyone did the actual math and applied the 35 percent casualty figure to the Kyushu operation as Leahy had suggested, but the figure would have shocked the President. If 35 percent of the troops participating in the invasion of Kyushu became casualties, that would equate to over 268,000 Americans dead, wounded and missing.

When the meeting turned to Japanese troop strength on Kyushu, it was estimated that there were about 350,000 troops on the island. In reality, Japan's military planners had accurately predicted that Kyushu would be the site of the coming invasion, and they began a massive buildup to reinforce its defenses. In less than two months, about 900,000 Japanese troops would be on the island, which was larger than the American invasion force.[65]

The subject of casualties fell by the wayside as the meeting moved on, but two days later, King protested that the casualty information provided to the President was "not satisfactory," and he pointed out that Admiral Nimitz had estimated 49,000 casualties for just the first 30 days. King went on to say that he believed a fair estimate of Navy casualties alone would be at the same rate as Okinawa, but Marshall felt it was "unnecessary and undesirable for the Joint Chiefs of Staff to make estimates, which at best can be only speculative."[66] What is evident from the minutes of the meeting is that Truman never received a clear answer to his question about casualties.

By the end of the meeting, after considering every possible strategy to defeat Japan, the Joint Chiefs of Staff were unanimous on the course moving forward. Truman was also in agreement, but he expressed his hope that there was "a possibility of preventing an Okinawa from one end of Japan to the other."[67]

Operation *Downfall*, the invasion of Japan, was approved by President Truman.[68]

Downfall was broken down into two phases. Phase one, Operation *Olympic*, was set for November 1, 1945, and would see southern Kyushu invaded with a projected force of 766,700 men. Phase two, Operation *Coronet*, was tentatively set for March 1, 1946, pending a review of the tactical situation following Kyushu, and would be a massive invasion of the Tokyo Plain on Honshu to seize the Tokyo-Yokohama area with over one million men.[69]

In support of Operation *Coronet*, the U.S. Navy would assemble a massive fleet that included 33 aircraft carriers, 74 smaller escort carriers, 23 battleships, 364 destroyers, 326 destroyer escorts and 189 submarines. The Navy's carrier-based airplanes alone would number 3,600 for the invasion.[70]

For planning purposes, the date for the end of organized resistance by Japan was estimated to be November 15, 1946.[71] In the period prior to Operation *Coronet*, the Army Air Forces were planning to drop more bombs on Japan than were dropped on Germany during the entire war.[72]

*   *   *

The day after Truman approved *Downfall*, General LeMay finally met with the Joint Chiefs of Staff to present his plans for ending the war. Despite Arnold's wishes, Truman did not attend the briefing. LeMay began the briefing with some general remarks about the XXI Bomber Command's operations and why he thought the war would be over by October 1, and then his staff gave detailed presentations about their operations and plans. It wasn't a polished briefing like the Joint Chiefs were used to, however. Instead of fancy charts and graphs, LeMay's staff had to use the only thing they had available on Guam – a two-foot-wide roll of brown butcher paper – to hand-make all of their charts and drawings for the presentation.[73]

As LeMay and his staff laid out their plans, he noticed that the Joint Chiefs were disinterested and had a completely blank expression on their faces. "They paid absolutely no attention to us," LeMay recalled. "Marshall was sleeping or dozing through most of it. Admiral Ernest King, the chief of Naval Operations, reacted with disbelief and a complete lack of interest, just as the Navy brass always had."[74]

The decision to invade Japan had already been made, and the Joint Chiefs didn't seem to care what a 38-year-old two-star general from Ohio State who was making $798.91 a month had to say about ending the war. "Here were these dumb kids coming in, saying they were going to end the war for him," LeMay recalled of Marshall, who he didn't blame for dozing off during the briefing, as he looked like he needed the sleep.[75]

By the time he left Washington, LeMay had come to realize that the entire U.S. Army General Staff believed that to end the war, they had to invade Japan just as they had invaded Europe. "The conventional wisdom was still that you can't do anything with strategic air power and that was that" LeMay recalled.[76]

When LeMay landed back on Guam on July 4, his deputy operations officer, Colonel David Burchinal, recalled how the XXI Bomber Command accelerated their operations:

> After that trip we made a change: from there on, we were going to fly max effort ... We were going to burn the crews out. To hell with crew rotation, we were going to burn them out because we thought we could end the war ... It was just max effort from there on out to knock the Japanese out of the war. Night and day.[77]

LeMay now had four months to prove that his B-29s could end the war without a costly invasion.

Little Boy and Fat Man

"Heed this warning and evacuate these cities immediately." (USAAF)

Read this carefully as it may save your life or the life of a relative or friend. In the next few days, four (or more) of the cities named on the reverse side will be destroyed by American bombs. These cities contain military installations and workshops or factories which produce military goods. We are determined to destroy all of the tools of the military clique which they are using to prolong this useless war. But, unfortunately, bombs have no eyes. So, in accordance with America's well-known humanitarian policies, the American Air Force which does not wish to injure innocent people now gives you warning to evacuate the cities named and save your lives.

America is not fighting the Japanese people but is fighting the military clique which has enslaved the Japanese people. The peace which America will bring will free the people from the oppression of the military clique and mean the emergence of a new and better Japan.

You can restore peace by demanding new and good leaders who will end the war.

We cannot promise that only these cities will be among those attacked but at least four will be, so heed this warning and evacuate these cities immediately.[1]

The B-29s had dropped propaganda leaflets over Japanese cities before, but there was something ominous about these new leaflets that began fluttering to the ground in July of 1945. Across the bottom of the leaflet, below an actual photo of B-29s unleashing thousands of firebombs over Japan, were the names of 12 Japanese cities. At least four of the cities, the leaflet warned, would be bombed in the coming days. The *Daily Target* newspaper on Saipan ran the startling headline "B-29 Command Now Calling Its Shots" as front-page news after the leaflets were dropped and added: "The 20th Air Force is now calling its shots, telling the Japs in advance just which of their cities are going to be bombed next by Superforts."[2]

As LeMay's B-29s reigned over Japan with virtual impunity in the summer of 1945, LeMay and his staff created the leaflets to further demonstrate to the Japanese people that their leaders were powerless to protect them. Masuo Kato, a reporter with the Domei News Agency, recalled what happened after the leaflets were dropped:

> Before the bombs fell, the bombers roared overhead, dropping leaflets that told where and when the next strike would be made. Flee for your lives, the leaflets said, the B-29s are coming. At first the people believed their leaders, who told them these leaflets meant nothing. "The Allies," they said, "only wish to frighten you. Remain calm and stay at your posts." The B-29s came with the airy nonchalance of Babe Ruth pointing to the exact spot in right field where his game-winning home run was to be delivered, and those who had believed their leaders died by the thousands.[3]

Within 48 hours of the leaflets being dropped, five cities on the list were bombed. LeMay was now telling the Japanese exactly where he was going to bomb, and they were helpless to stop him.

The ability of LeMay to "call his shots" reflected just how powerful the Army Air Forces had become since the war began. When Pearl Harbor was attacked, the Army Air Forces had 152,000 men and 12,297 aircraft of all types in service, over half of which were training aircraft. Three–and-a-half years later, the Army Air Forces now had nearly 12,000 aircraft operating against Japanese forces alone. Overall, the Army Air Forces had swelled to almost 65,800 aircraft and more than 2.2 million men, over a million of whom were serving overseas.[4]

From its rocky beginnings, the XXI Bomber Command was a well-oiled machine by July of 1945. When LeMay took over in January, the B-29s of the 73rd Bomb Wing were flying an average of 61.9 hours a month. Six months later, the B-29s were now flying over 120 hours a month. The 20th Air Force had grown to more than 94,000 men, and with five Bomb Wings operating from the Marianas, LeMay had almost 1,000 B-29s flying against Japan. And more were on the way.[5]

With the capture of Okinawa after a brutal 82-day battle, the Japanese homeland was now just a 90-minute flight away for American fighters and bombers. In July, Lieutenant General

Jimmy Doolittle arrived on Okinawa to begin setting up the 8th Air Force for operations against Japan. After Germany surrendered, the 8th Air Force returned home from Europe and began training with B-29s for the Pacific. Doolittle's first two bomb groups were set to arrive on Okinawa during the first week of August.

The arrival of Jimmy Doolittle and the 8th Air Force was part of a larger reorganization of the air war in the Pacific. With the war over in Europe, General Arnold turned to his commanders who had been so successful in the air war against Germany to prepare for the final offensive against Japan. General Carl Spaatz was given command of the new United States Strategic Air Forces in the Pacific, which would direct the strategic air assault against Japan with the 20th and 8th Air Forces and was modeled after the command Spaatz led in Europe. The headquarters of the 20th Air Force was also moved from Washington to Guam, where it absorbed the XXI Bomber Command, and was placed under the command of Major General Nathan Twining.[6]

As for General LeMay, after briefly assuming command of the 20th Air Force until Twining arrived, he then became Spaatz's Chief of Staff. LeMay did not have the rank to command the new Strategic Air Forces (Spaatz was a four-star general), but in reality, LeMay continued his work as if nothing had changed. "I was kind of pleased that Spaatz would pick me for his chief of staff," LeMay recalled. "Knowing Spaatz, I knew I would be running the whole damned thing anyway."[7]

By November of 1945, with the combined strength of both the 20th and 8th Air Forces, Spaatz and LeMay would have 1,600 B-29s operating against Japan.[8] Back home in the United States, B-29 production was surging, with a record-breaking 375 built in July alone, a rate of 12 new bombers a day. A staggering 3,441 B-29s had been built to date, and hundreds more would roll out of the factories in August.[9]

To help pay for the coming Battle of Japan, the 7th War Loan Drive was launched on May 14, only a week after Germany surrendered, with the goal of raising $14 billion for the war effort. At a time when the average pay for a factory worker was $44.39 a week, the Treasury Department was seeking to raise $7 billion from individual Americans alone, the most ever sought from the American public. A pamphlet about the 7th War Loan laid out what was at stake:

> The Battle of Japan has just begun. It must be backed up, paid for, fought for by a free people, intent on sweeping the Pacific clear of fascist hate – forever.
>
> With the war in the West our first and major concern, we have not yet been able to go all-out in the East. But neither has the Jap.
>
> The war to crush Japan will be bigger, tougher, and longer than most Americans expect. The Allied Military Command has estimated that it will take years, not months.
>
> The destruction of Japan's armies has not yet reached the annual rate of normal replacements – between 200,000 and 250,000 men a year. And the Jap, as our men in the Pacific know, fights to the death.
>
> As far as Japan is concerned, the outer Empire – and the men who defend it – are expendables. The Jap will fight the Battle of Japan from inside the inner Empire, of which Iwo Jima was an outpost. And Iwo Jima, according to Admiral Nimitz, was a pattern of the resistance our forces may expect to meet in future offensives.

The single greatest obstacle to our crushing of Japan is distance. While in the Battle of Europe supply ships from our bases in England had only an overnight run to make, ships in the Pacific have long-reach round trips taking up to 5 months to make.

To crush Japan will take time, heroic and backbreaking effort, overpowering equipment.

Millions of fighting men – freshly outfitted and equipped – will have to be moved from Europe halfway around the globe; and supplied day-in, day-out by hundreds of new ships now building.

More of everything will be needed. More B-29s. More tanks, half-tracks, jeeps and trucks. More rockets, mortars, airborne radar.

These are just some of the 101 ways in which your dollars are needed more than ever to bring America's might to its full strength – so that we may crush our foe the faster, make an end of killing, and bring our men back home.[10]

When the "Mighty 7th" War Loan Drive concluded after six weeks, over $26 billion had been raised, the most of any war loan drive during the war.[11]

*   *   *

While LeMay's leaflets were warning the Japanese which of their cities were doomed, on the other side of the world in Germany, President Truman released the Potsdam Declaration from Berlin that called for the immediate and unconditional surrender of Japan – or it would face prompt and utter destruction:

1. We – the President of the United States, the President of the National Government of the Republic of China, and the Prime Minister of Great Britain, representing the hundreds of millions of our countrymen, have conferred and agree that Japan shall be given an opportunity to end this war.
2. The prodigious land, sea and air forces of the United States, the British Empire and of China, many times reinforced by their armies and air fleets from the west, are poised to strike the final blows upon Japan. This military power is sustained and inspired by the determination of all the Allied Nations to prosecute the war against Japan until she ceases to resist.
3. The result of the futile and senseless German resistance to the might of the aroused free peoples of the world stands forth in awful clarity as an example to the people of Japan. The might that now converges on Japan is immeasurably greater than that which, when applied to the resisting Nazis, necessarily laid waste to the lands, the industry and the method of life of the whole German people. The full application of our military power, backed by our resolve, will mean the inevitable and complete destruction of the Japanese armed forces and just as inevitably the utter devastation of the Japanese homeland.
4. The time has come for Japan to decide whether she will continue to be controlled by those self-willed militaristic advisers whose unintelligent calculations have brought the Empire of Japan to the threshold of annihilation, or whether she will follow the path of reason.

5. Following are our terms. We will not deviate from them. There are no alternatives. We shall brook no delay.
6. There must be eliminated for all time the authority and influence of those who have deceived and misled the people of Japan into embarking on world conquest, for we insist that a new order of peace, security and justice will be impossible until irresponsible militarism is driven from the world.
7. Until such a new order is established and until there is convincing proof that Japan's warmaking power is destroyed, points in Japanese territory to be designated by the Allies shall be occupied to secure the achievement of the basic objectives we are here setting forth.
8. The terms of the Cairo Declaration shall be carried out and Japanese sovereignty shall be limited to the islands of Honshu, Hokkaido, Kyushu, Shikoku and such minor islands as we determine.
9. The Japanese military forces, after being completely disarmed, shall be permitted to return to their homes with the opportunity to lead peaceful and productive lives.
10. We do not intend that the Japanese shall be enslaved as a race or destroyed as a nation, but stern justice shall be meted out to all war criminals, including those who have visited cruelties upon our prisoners. The Japanese Government shall remove all obstacles to the revival and strengthening of democratic tendencies among the Japanese people. Freedom of speech, of religion, and of thought, as well as respect for the fundamental human rights shall be established.
11. Japan shall be permitted to maintain such industries as will sustain her economy and permit the exaction of just reparations in kind, but not those which would enable her to re-arm for war. To this end, access to, as distinguished from control of, raw materials shall be permitted. Eventual Japanese participation in world trade relations shall be permitted.
12. The occupying forces of the Allies shall be withdrawn from Japan as soon as these objectives have been accomplished and there has been established in accordance with the freely expressed will of the Japanese people a peacefully inclined and responsible government.
13. We call upon the government of Japan to proclaim now the unconditional surrender of all Japanese armed forces, and to provide proper and adequate assurances of their good faith in such action. The alternative for Japan is prompt and utter destruction.[12]

The instrument for the "prompt and utter destruction" of Japan had already arrived in the Marianas. In the hours before the Potsdam Declaration was released, the USS *Indianapolis* dropped anchor at Tinian with its secret cargo. As a flotilla of small craft swarmed around the ship, the *Indy's* crew crowded the decks to get a look at the mysterious cargo, but just like before, watching the wooden crate and small cylinder being offloaded was anticlimactic. Still, everyone could sense that this was something important. The high-ranking officers who came aboard to watch the unloading and knew what was in the crate didn't say a word to anyone, but their broad smiles told the two Army officers who'd escorted the cargo that the Trinity test had been a success. As the cargo was brought ashore and driven away under heavy security, only a handful of men knew that the first atomic bomb had arrived.

The use of the new bomb against Japan had already been approved by the President, but Truman had made his decision with a heavy heart. The day before the Potsdam Declaration was released, Truman wrote in his diary:

> We have discovered the most terrible bomb in the history of the world. It may be the fire destruction prophesied in the Euphrates Valley Era, after Noah and his fabulous Ark.
>
> Anyway we "think" we have found the way to cause a disintegration of the atom. An experiment in the New Mexican desert was startling – to put it mildly. Thirteen pounds of the explosive caused the complete disintegration of a steel tower 60 feet high, created a crater 6 feet deep and 1,200 feet in diameter, knocked over a steel tower ½ mile away and knocked men down 10,000 yards away. The explosion was visible for more than 200 miles and audible for 40 miles and more.
>
> This weapon is to be used against Japan between now and August 10th. I have told the Sec. of War, Mr. Stimson, to use it so that military objectives and soldiers and sailors are the target and not women and children. Even if the Japs are savages, ruthless, merciless and fanatic, we as the leader of the world for the common welfare cannot drop this terrible bomb on the old Capital [Kyoto] or the new [Tokyo].
>
> He & I are in accord. The target will be a purely military one and we will issue a warning statement asking the Japs to surrender and save lives. I'm sure they will not do that, but we will have given them the chance. It is certainly a good thing for the world that Hitler's crowd or Stalin's did not discover this atomic bomb. It seems to be the most terrible thing ever discovered, but it can be made the most useful.[13]

As Truman was writing those words in his diary, a new report on the estimated casualties from an invasion of Japan had arrived at the War Department, and its conclusion was shocking. In an effort to gain a new perspective on the issue of casualties independent from the Army, Dr. William Shockley, who would later go on to win the Nobel Prize in physics, was commissioned to write a report on the casualties that could be expected from an invasion of Japan. In his initial report on July 21, Shockley proposed that a study be initiated to "determine to what extent the behavior of a nation in war can be predicted from the behavior of her troops in individual battles." Shockley concluded in his report:

> If the study shows that the behavior of nations in all historical cases comparable to Japan's has in fact been invariably consistent with the behavior of the troops in battle, then it means that the Japanese dead and ineffectives at the time of the defeat will exceed the corresponding number for the Germans. In other words, we shall probably have to kill at least 5 to 10 million Japanese. This might cost us between 1.7 and 4 million [American] casualties including 400,000 and 800,000 killed.[14]

Stimson had also reached a similar conclusion a few weeks earlier in a memo to the President:

> There is reason to believe that the operation for the occupation of Japan following the landing may be a very long, costly and arduous struggle on our part. The terrain, much of which I have visited several times [before the war], has left the impression on my memory of being one which would be susceptible to a last ditch defense such as had been made on

244 The Heroes We Needed

Iwo Jima and Okinawa and which of course is very much larger than either of those two areas ... The Japanese are highly patriotic and certainly susceptible to calls for fanatical resistance to repel an invasion. Once started in actual invasion, we shall in my opinion have to go through with an even more bitter finish fight than in Germany. We shall incur the losses incident to such a war and we shall have to leave the Japanese islands even more thoroughly destroyed than was the case with Germany.[15]

A fanatical, last-ditch battle is exactly what Japan was preparing for. On April 8, the Imperial General Headquarters in Tokyo unveiled its strategy to win a "decisive battle" against the United States that would save Japan. The *Ketsu-Go* Operation was a comprehensive plan to defend the Japanese home islands against the coming invasion and relied heavily upon "Special Attack Units," or suicide attacks, to defeat the Americans.

Under the provisions of *Ketsu-Go*, by the end of June, the Japanese had stockpiled thousands of aircraft for the coming invasion, most of which were to be used for Kamikaze attacks, and thousands more were due to be completed by September. The Japanese were also rushing to complete hundreds of new airfields to disperse these aircraft throughout the home islands. Many of these airfields were simple strips that used caves as hangars to conceal their location.[16]

By the middle of August, the Japanese would have 18,000 pilots and 10,700 operational aircraft available, plus another 7,200 aircraft that were awaiting repairs or modifications, and over 100 million barrels of aviation fuel. During the invasion, the Japanese envisioned sending waves of 300–400 Kamikaze aircraft against the American invasion force every hour.[17]

While the production of naval special attack boats was falling behind schedule, by the end of June, the Japanese had more than 2,800 suicide motorboats ready for use, which would be laden with explosives and rammed into ships and landing craft. Almost 450 underwater special attack crafts, ranging from midget submarines to manned torpedoes, were also ready by June.[18]

The *Ketsu-Go* planners had also anticipated that southern Kyushu, as well as the Tokyo Plain, would be targeted for invasion, and emergency preparations to build up the defenses on Kyushu began immediately in April. These preparations were accelerated the following month when it was concluded that the Americans could invade as early as late June, and additional Army divisions were moved to reinforce the island's defenses.[19]

As Kyushu was being reinforced, the Japanese also undertook a massive mobilization of new troops to strengthen its homeland armies, which amounted to some 1.5 million additional soldiers. This would give Japan over 3.5 million troops to defend the home islands alone. In addition, *Ketsu-Go* would also draw upon the entire Japanese citizenry in what it called "every citizen a soldier" to form guerrilla units and internal security forces to fight the Americans.[20]

On June 23, to further bolster its civilian forces and enlist the "full participation of the entire nation in prosecuting the war to the end," a new law expanded the People's Volunteer Corps into a paramilitary fighting force. The corps was not volunteer, however, and mandated service for all Japanese men aged 15–60, and all Japanese women aged 17–40, who were not already serving in the military. This equated to tens of millions of Japanese civilians who were formed into militia units led by military personnel.[21]

Only three days after the People's Volunteer Corps was expanded, Prime Minister Kantaro Suzuki took to the airwaves and told the Japanese people that the losses they exacted upon the enemy during the Battle of Okinawa were so severe that the Americans were getting tired of the war. The strategic situation for the coming "final decisive battle on the homeland" would favor the Japanese, Suzuki said, but he also warned that victory hinged upon the "determination and effort of Japanese people." Individual life or death was unimportant, he added. The Japanese people must all do their part and "fulfill obligations to win sacred war."[22]

The determination that was expected of the Japanese people was made clear in the People's Handbook of Resistance Combat, which said: "Should the enemy invade our mainland, 100 million of us, as the Special Attacking Forces, must exterminate them to protect our native soil and maintain our everlasting empire."[23]

To fight the invading Americans, the Japanese began a research program in 1944 to develop simple weapons to arm its military and civilian forces. For the Volunteer Corps, a crude black powder rifle was developed that used steel pipe for the barrel and projectiles formed from sections of bar stock. The rifle was so simple that any small factory or smith shop could manufacture it in quantity. Crossbows, spears, short bows and even ceramic hand grenades were also put into production and issued.[24] Based on the lessons learned during the Battle of Okinawa, in which suicide attacks had knocked out 221 American tanks in two months, the Japanese continued producing a variety of explosive devices that were designed to be carried by a soldier or a civilian, who would then lunge at a tank and blow themselves up. Similar devices would also be used by the Japanese Navy's suicide divers, who would wait in the waters off the landing beaches and then blow themselves up along with passing landing craft during the invasion.[25]

The preparations for the "final decisive battle" even reached as far as Japan's schoolchildren. One Japanese schoolgirl, who was mobilized to fight under the People's Volunteer Corps, was issued a simple stitching awl (a small-pointed tool) and told:

> Even killing just one American soldier will do. You must prepare to use the awls for self-defense. You must aim at the enemy's abdomen.[26]

*   *   *

While the Japanese were producing a variety of crude, last-ditch weapons to arm its people, inside a secluded and heavily guarded compound on the northwest coast of Tinian, a small group of Americans were hard at work on the most advanced weapons in the world. Inside one of the three specially built and air-conditioned buildings that were far removed from the other facilities in case of an accident, Project Alberta personnel from the Manhattan Project's Los Alamos laboratory, along with technicians from the Army Air Forces' elite 1st Ordnance Squadron, began assembling the first atomic bomb for use against Japan. After more than two years of work, the Manhattan Project had developed two different types of atomic bombs that would be known as Little Boy and Fat Man, nicknames that reflected their size and shape.

Little Boy was a gun-type weapon and was incredibly simple. Measuring 10 feet long with a diameter of only 28 inches, one crewman recalled that the 9,700-pound bomb looked like "an elongated trash can with fins." The heart of the Little Boy bomb was a 6-foot-long cannon barrel contained within the bomb casing. At the breach of the barrel, a "bullet" of uranium-235 was inserted along with a powder charge. When the charge was ignited, the bullet was shot down the barrel into the "target" fixed at the muzzle, which was another mass of uranium-235. The impact of these two subcritical masses formed a supercritical mass and initiated a chain reaction that resulted in a colossal explosion.[27]

The gun-type mechanism of Little Boy was so simple that General Groves decided that a test of the bomb was not needed before it was used in combat. The production of uranium-235 was also so time-consuming that there simply wasn't enough stockpiled to use for a test.[28]

In contrast to the simplicity of Little Boy, Fat Man was an implosion-type weapon and incredibly complex. Stretching over 10 feet long and ballooning in the center to 5 feet in diameter, Fat Man was a massive 10,300-pound bomb based on the design tested at Trinity. At the heart of the bomb was a spherical core of plutonium-239 that was surrounded by an enormous 5,300-pound sphere of high explosives. What made the Fat Man design so complicated is that the explosives surrounding the core were made from almost 100 separate castings that were machine finished and assembled into hexagonal and pentagonal pyramid-shaped blocks, which the scientists called lenses, that fitted together like the pattern of a soccer ball to form a sphere around the core. The blocks then had to be precisely detonated within a microsecond of each other to form a symmetrical explosive wave that would compress the core into a supercritical mass. This was a difficult challenge to overcome, and some initially thought it would be impossible to do before the war ended, but the Trinity test proved that the implosion design worked.[29]

Two days after the USS *Indianapolis* delivered the uranium bullet and the crate containing the Little Boy bomb to Tinian, the Japanese finally responded to the Potsdam Declaration. In an afternoon press conference, Prime Minister Kantaro Suzuki told the world that the Japanese Government did not "find any important value" in the Potsdam terms, and there was "no other recourse but to ignore it entirely and resolutely fight for the successful conclusion of the war."[30]

Suzuki believed that Japan could fight on for another two or three years, but there were some inside the Japanese Government who were already seeking a peaceful end to the war.[31]

With so much destruction being wrought upon Japan, Foreign Minister Shigenori Togo felt that it was not feasible to continue fighting and the war should be ended immediately. Togo hoped to bring the war to a negotiated end with the help of the Soviet Union. Working through Japan's ambassador in Moscow, Naotake Sato, Togo's foremost objective was to keep the Soviets out of the war and induce a friendly policy towards Japan, which he considered to be of "utmost urgency," and then to seek their mediation with the United States. However, there was no agreement on the peace terms that Japan was prepared to offer.[32]

On July 12, Togo sent a "very urgent" cable instructing Sato to inform the Soviets that Emperor Hirohito desired the war to be "quickly terminated." But so long as the United States insisted upon unconditional surrender, Togo warned that the "Japanese Empire has no alternative but to fight on with all its strength for the honor and existence of the Motherland."[33]

The Japanese proposed to send a Special Envoy to Moscow to discuss the matter, which Togo made clear would not be for "mediation in anything like unconditional surrender," but this was ultimately rejected by the Soviets because Japan was not offering a "concrete plan" to end the war. Truman was informed about these overtures by Stalin during the Potsdam Conference, but the Soviet leader said there was "nothing new" in Japan's proposal for talks.[34]

From his post in Moscow, Sato advised Togo that Japan had no choice "but to accept unconditional surrender or terms closely equivalent" to end the war, but Togo was firm that an unconditional surrender was not acceptable. If the United States insisted "unrelentingly upon unconditional surrender," Togo said in a cable to Sato, then the "Japanese are unanimous in their resolve to wage a thoroughgoing war."[35]

What Togo didn't know was that all of his cables were being intercepted and read by the Americans. The United States had cracked the Japanese diplomatic code before the war began, and the White House was receiving daily summaries of all diplomatic communications to and from Tokyo. While the revelations in the cables did provoke discussions at the highest levels of the American Government about modifying the long-held policy of unconditional surrender, which stemmed from the belief that the present war resulted from the failure to secure the unconditional surrender of Imperial Germany during the First World War, what was clear from the cables was that Japan had no intention of accepting the Potsdam terms.[36]

"In the face of this rejection," Secretary Stimson recalled, "we could only proceed to demonstrate that the ultimatum had meant exactly what it said when it stated that if the Japanese continued the war, 'the full application of our military power, backed by our resolve, will mean the inevitable and complete destruction of the Japanese armed forces and just as inevitably the utter devastation of the Japanese homeland.' For such a purpose the atomic bomb was an eminently suitable weapon."[37]

President Truman was much blunter in his reaction to Japan's rejection to the Potsdam terms, as he recalled after the war: "They told me to go to hell, words to that effect."[38]

On the same day that Japan rejected the Potsdam terms, five C-54 transports landed on Tinian carrying the last components needed to complete the Little Boy bomb, the uranium target assembly segments, and the plutonium core and initiator for the first Fat Man bomb (the Fat Man bomb case would arrive five days later). Under the supervision of Captain William "Deak" Parsons, the director of the Manhattan Project's Ordnance Division at Los Alamos and commander of Project Alberta on Tinian, Little Boy was fully assembled and completed on July 31.[39]

The first atomic bomb was now ready to drop on Japan. After spending $2 billion on its development, all that was needed now was favorable weather.

Armorers prepare to load the Little Boy atomic bomb into the *Enola Gay*. (National Archives 76048710)

21

The Victory Boys

"All right, you Victory Boys," a corporal from headquarters shouted through the doorway of the Quonset hut. "Off and on. Let's get on the beam. You've got to be at the combat room at 1500." The corporal paused, then smirked: "Extra special briefing for you Victory Boys."[1]

Sitting on his bunk and trying to put his shirt on, Sergeant Abe Spitzer from New York was in no mood for the ribbing. The corporal was joking, but the way Abe felt in that moment, he could have jumped up and smashed his face in. "Ever since we'd arrived on the island, they'd called us that, the men in all the other squadrons," Abe recalled. "We were the 'Victory Boys' or 'Glory Boys' or the 'Errol Flynns' or the 'Guys Who're Going to Win the War for Us.'"[2]

In the two months since the combat crews of the 509th Composite Group arrived on Tinian, the other B-29ers on the island had first looked upon this secretive group with curiosity, and then with growing contempt. The 509th never flew missions with the other bomb groups, and the men had their own separate compound and seemed to be living the high life while focusing on training instead of combat. Even their B-29s were unusual and had their own parking area away from the other bomb groups. Code-named Silverplate for the project that produced them, the 509th's single squadron of B-29s were specially built by Martin-Omaha with all of the latest improvements and other special modifications not found on other B-29s. Stripped of all unnecessary weight and armament except for the tail turret, and boasting the latest fuel-injected engines with Curtis Electric propellers that were fully reversible to provide extra braking (reverse thrust) upon landing – something that no other B-29s in the Marianas had – the Silverplate B-29s had superior high-altitude performance and could easily out-turn smaller fighters at 30,000 feet.[3]

The 509th had the hottest bombers in the world, but no one knew what they were doing on Tinian, or why the crews never flew regular missions. Walking past the 509th's compound, the combat crews from the other bomb groups would often pelt the roofs of their Quonset huts with rocks and taunt the men inside. "Hey, Glory Boys," they'd jeer. "When're you guys ever gonna fly a mission?" It didn't help that when the 509th's ground crews first arrived on Tinian, they told everyone that the 509th was "going to end the war in a hurry" when their combat crews got there.[4]

An anonymous clerk from one of the other bomb groups wrote a poem mocking the 509th and circulated it around the island. Entitled "Nobody Knows," it began:

Into the air the secret rose,
Where they're going, nobody knows.
Tomorrow they'll return again,
But we'll never know where they've been.
Don't ask us about results or such,
Unless you want to get in Dutch.
But take it from one who is sure of the score,
The 509th is winning the war.[5]

Whatever it was that the 509th was doing, everyone sarcastically agreed that they were "winning the war." All of this was wearing men like Abe Spitzer thin, and the last thing he wanted to hear was more mocking. "All right, off your butts," the corporal shouted again into the hut. "You guys do more sack time than all the rest of the squadrons put together."[6]

Moving slow in the oppressive heat, Abe and his four crewmates gathered themselves and began making their way over to the briefing hut, where the rest of their crew was already waiting for them. Abe had not slept well that night. He kept thinking about the Golden Gate Bridge in San Francisco, and how he told himself to take a good look as they overflew it on their way out to the Marianas, because he'd probably never see it again.

At 33 years old, Abe was an old man by combat crew standards. He wasn't even supposed to be on flying status because of his "weak" eyes, but he pestered the higher-ups and got a waiver. With the briefing coming up and the mission that would follow, he was now wondering if he should have just kept his mouth shut and stayed on the ground. Abe was proud to be a B-29 radio operator and would never complain, but with the dangers he was about to face, he kept thinking about the saying: "It's better to be a live coward than a dead hero."[7]

All of these thoughts had left Abe tossing and sweating all night as he reflected on the past 11 months he'd spent in the 509th, and how different it was from every other bomb group in the Army Air Forces. That past September, his squadron mates first realized they were "in on something new and big" when they met their new commanding officer, Lieutenant Colonel Paul Tibbets, shortly after arriving at Wendover Field in the bleak Utah desert near the Bonneville Salt Flats. Standing before his men assembled at the base theater, Tibbets introduced himself and told the men that they had been selected to form a new type of combat group that would be self-sufficient and could operate anywhere in the world. They would be asked to carry out a mission that, if successful, would bring the war to a rapid conclusion. But they had to trust him, Tibbets said, because they would not be told what their mission was until they were ready to perform it.

Security was of the utmost importance. Over the coming months, as the crews underwent intensive training to hone their skills, Tibbets warned that there would be no second chances when it came to security breaches. The men were to keep their mouths shut. Any speculation about the nature of their mission, even among themselves, would not be tolerated. "Gentlemen, much is going to be expected of you," Tibbets said. "If it all works out, it will have been worth it."[8]

As time went on, the crews understood that they were training to drop something everyone called the "gimmick." It would shorten the war by six months, maybe more, they were told, but no one knew what exactly the "gimmick" was. It was obviously a new type of bomb, Abe concluded, and it was obviously going to be very powerful, but that was all anyone knew.[9]

As Abe and his crewmates walked up to the briefing hut that afternoon, they were about to get their first sense of just how powerful the "gimmick" really was.

"We aren't Japs," one of Abe's crewmates joked to the MP (military police) standing guard at the door. "Can't you tell? We're on your side. Remember?" Most MPs would have grinned and joked back, but this one must be under strict orders, Abe thought, because he didn't smile or say a word. There were other MPs standing around the Quonset hut, whose windows were all covered to keep prying eyes away, and they were all armed. One by one, the MP at the door checked their names off a list and motioned them inside.[10]

"The long low room was already filled with cigarette smoke, and it was hot, the kind of enervating, tropical heat that's unknown back in the States," Abe recalled. Taking their seats on the hard wooden benches, Abe winked at the officers of his crew who were seated towards the front of the hut. Captain Beahan, the bombardier, winked back and grinned. The day before, the crew had voted to name their B-29 *The Great Artiste* in honor of Beahan, who was "popular with the girls wherever he went."[11]

At exactly 3:00 p.m., Colonel Tibbets, who Abe described as a "short, rather muscular, easygoing man with a boyish smile," walked in to begin the briefing. Tibbets was a highly experienced bomber pilot and was no stranger to smoky briefing rooms. In 1942, Tibbets led the first American bombing mission against German-occupied Europe. After completing 43 missions in Europe and North Africa, Tibbets then spent over a year flight-testing the B-29 and training new crews.[12]

By the spring of 1944, the development of the atomic bomb had reached the point where the problem of delivering it to a target now needed urgent attention, even though it would still be more than a year before the first bomb was even built. Since the Army Air Forces would be responsible for dropping the bomb in combat, a specialized tactical unit would have to be formed solely for this purpose.[13] With his proven leadership as a combat commander and a wealth of experience with the B-29, Tibbets was chosen in September of 1944 to organize, train and lead the world's first atomic strike force, the 509th Composite Group. The 509th was given high priority and Tibbets had the authority to requisition anything he needed to carry out his mission by using the code word "Silverplate" to break any impasse. In the months that followed, the 509th would grow into a fully independent, self-contained organization of 1,800 men with a squadron of B-29s and a squadron of C-54 transports.[14]

One of the early challenges Tibbets faced was how to drop such a powerful bomb – and there was still no consensus among the scientists on exactly how powerful it would be – without destroying the B-29 that dropped it. It was immediately clear to Tibbets that conventional bombing methods would not work, so Tibbets would also have to develop the tactics for safely dropping the bomb.[15] As Tibbets recounted after the war, his job was to organize and train a bombing force for the purpose of dropping a bomb that hadn't been built yet on a target that hadn't been chosen.

When all of this responsibility was thrust upon him in 1944, Tibbets was only 29 years old.[16]

Less than a year later, Tibbets now stood at the front of the briefing hut and prepared to address his men. After 11 months of intensive training, this was the moment they had all been waiting for. All eyes were on Tibbets as he began to speak:

> The moment has arrived. This is what we have all been working towards. Very recently the weapon we are about to deliver was successfully tested in the States. We have received orders to drop it on the enemy.[17]

Even though these men would be dropping the first atomic bomb in history, they were still not told what kind of bomb it was. The word "atomic" was not said at any time during the briefing.

Tibbets nodded to the two intelligence officers, and as they removed the cloth from the blackboards to reveal the reconnaissance photos, he announced that Hiroshima would be the primary target, followed by Kokura and Nagasaki. As Tibbets laid out the details of the mission, he assigned three B-29s to scout the weather over the three cities ahead of the main strike force. Tibbets had strict orders to only drop the bomb visually, so the weather over the target had to be perfect. Tibbets would fly the B-29 carrying the bomb, and he would be accompanied to the target by two additional B-29s, one that was equipped with special instruments to measure the blast, and the other with cameras to document the strike. A seventh B-29 would be staged on Iwo Jima as a backup in case a mechanical problem developed with the strike aircraft.

Satisfied with the operational details of the mission, Tibbets called upon Captain "Deak" Parsons to brief the men about the bomb they were going to drop. Parsons wasted no time and got right to the point:

> The bomb you are going to drop is something new in the history of warfare. It is the most destructive weapon ever produced. We think it will knock out almost everything within a three-mile area.[18]

Parsons' revelation was met with a stunned gasp. No one could believe what they were hearing. "It couldn't be possible," Abe later wrote in his diary. "Why, this wasn't real, it couldn't be – this was some weird dream conceived by one with a too vivid an imagination."[19]

As the crews sat in shocked silence and tried to digest what they had just heard, Parsons told the men that scientists and tens of thousands of workers all across the United States had been working for years on this "instrument of destruction," and the experiments they conducted had cost hundreds of millions of dollars. To prepare the crews for what was to come, Parsons walked over to a film projector and signaled its operator. Loaded into the machine was footage of the Trinity test, but nothing happened when the operator flipped the switch. As they fiddled with the machine, it suddenly started and ripped up the top-secret film.[20]

Parsons told the operator to turn the projector off, and then he walked back to the front of the hut. "The film you are not about to see," Parsons said, as a roar of laughter broke the tension, "was made of the only test we have performed." Parsons then went on to describe the Trinity test:

> This is what happened. The flash of the explosion was seen for more than ten miles. A soldier 10,000 feet away was knocked off his feet. Another soldier more than five miles away was temporarily blinded. A girl in a town many miles away who had been blind all her life saw a flash of light. The explosion was heard fifty miles away. For those of us who were there, it was the beginning of a new age.[21]

Abe felt a cold chill go through him as he listened to Parsons describing the test. Back in the States, he remembered how they had snickered when they were told that the "gimmick" could shorten the war by six months. No one was snickering now. Abe's crew would be flying next to Tibbets with the instruments to record the effects of the blast.[22]

Tension filled the room again as Parsons turned to a blackboard and began drawing the shape of a mushroom:

No one knows exactly what will happen when the bomb is dropped from the air. That has never been done before. But we do expect a cloud this shape will rise to at least 30,000 feet and maybe 60,000 feet, preceded by a flash of light much brighter than the sun's.[23]

Parsons paused to let his words sink in, and then he turned to one of the intelligence officers, who brought forward a box full of tinted goggles similar to those worn by welders. Holding up a pair for all to see, Parsons explained that the goggles would be worn by every man over the target area. Then he slipped the goggles over his eyes and showed the men how to adjust the knob to change the amount of light admitted by the glass. Over the target area, the knob must be turned to its lowest setting, he said.[24]

After Parsons was finished, Tibbets spoke to the crews again. He began with a warning:

You're now the hottest crews in the Air Force. No talking – to anyone. No talking even among yourselves. No letters. No writing home. No mentioning of the slightest possibility of a mission.[25]

After going over some more operational details of the mission, followed by a briefing from the Air-Sea Rescue officer, Tibbets concluded the briefing by telling his men how proud he was of them, as Abe recalled:

The Colonel began by saying that whatever any of us, including himself, had done before was small potatoes compared to what we were going to do now. Then he said the usual things, but he said them well, as if he meant them, about how proud he was to have been associated with us, about how high our morale had been and how difficult it was not knowing what we were doing, thinking maybe we were wasting our time and that the "gimmick" was just somebody's wild dream. He was personally honored, and he was sure all of us were, to have been chosen to take part in this raid which, he said – and all the other big-wigs nodded when he said it – would shorten the war by six months. "At least six months," he added emphatically. And you got the feeling that he really thought this bomb would end the war, period.[26]

They would all know soon enough.

*   *   *

"I hope you don't have to use these," Captain Donald Young said, as he slipped a small pillbox to Tibbets in the mess hall. Tibbets had just finished a helping of pineapple fritters and was about to leave for the final midnight briefing when Young, the 509th's flight surgeon, quietly walked over to his table. Young was trying to be cheerful, but there was nothing cheerful about what he had just handed to his friend.

"Don't worry," Tibbets said, stashing the pillbox in his pocket. "The odds are in our favor."[27]

A few days earlier, during a private conversation with Parsons about the upcoming mission, Parsons had asked Tibbets a question that he hadn't given much thought to: what do we do if we're shot down?[28] Parsons would be flying with Tibbets as the "weaponeer," the bomb commander, and would have final authority on all matters concerning the bomb during the mission. With his intimate knowledge of the bombs and all of their secrets, the thought of being captured gave him reason for concern. "I'll be goddamned if I want to fall in their hands," Parsons said, thinking about what the Japanese did to Americans who were captured.[29]

Tibbets was confident they'd return from the mission, but now he had to be realistic. There was a chance they could be shot down, and if they were captured alive, Tibbets had no doubt that they would be subjected to intensive questioning and torture to extract the secrets of the atomic bomb.

"I've got a .45 and I might be inclined to use it if I was about to be captured," Tibbets said, after considering the alternatives. As Tibbets and Parsons talked it over, Young walked by and joined the conversation. In the days that followed, Young mulled over the question before finally telling Tibbets that it would be easier to take a pill than shoot himself.[30]

Now only hours before takeoff, Young quietly handed Tibbets a pillbox with 12 cyanide capsules inside, one for each member of the crew. No one else knew about the cyanide except for Parsons, who slipped his pill in a matchbox. The other pills would only be passed out during an emergency, and their use would be left up to each man. No one would be ordered or urged to commit suicide to avoid capture.[31]

With the capsules stashed in a pocket on his flight suit, Tibbets walked into the crew lounge at midnight on August 6, 1945, to begin the final briefing before takeoff. Abe noticed that the colonel looked a little tired and tense, but he still smiled as he greeted his men.

Tibbets had tried to get a few hours of sleep before the briefing, but his nerves were wound too tight. Instead, he passed the hours by playing poker with his old friends, Major Thomas Ferebee, a bombardier, and Captain Theodore "Dutch" Van Kirk, a navigator. Both men had served on his B-17 crew in Europe and North Africa, and with their proven skills, they were among the first men Tibbets recruited for the 509th. In a few short hours, they would all be embarking on a mission that could end the war. None of them could sleep.

With takeoff now less than three hours away, as Tibbets took his place at the front of the lounge to address his men, he quickly got to the point:

> I'm going to keep this short because there is not much left to say. I want you to remember this bomb we are going to drop is different from any you have ever seen or heard about. Secondly, I want you to remember that it contains a destructive power equal to about 20,000 tons of TNT.[32]

The briefing only lasted 15 minutes. Everyone knew their jobs and what was expected of them. Just before the crews were dismissed, Tibbets called upon the 509th's chaplain, 27-year-old Captain William Downey, to say a prayer. Downey asked for everyone to bow their heads, and then he began reading the special prayer he composed for this mission on the back of an envelope:

> Almighty Father, Who wilt hear the prayer of them that love Thee, we pray Thee to be with those who brave the heights of Thy heaven and who carry the battle to our enemies. Guard and protect them, we pray Thee, as they fly their appointed rounds. May they, as well as we, know Thy strength and power, and armed with Thy might may they bring this war to a rapid end. We pray Thee that the end of the war may come soon, and that once more we may know peace on earth. May the men who fly this night be kept safe in Thy care, and may

they be returned safely to us. We shall go forward trusting in Thee, knowing that we are in Thy care now and forever. In the Name of Jesus Christ. Amen.[33]

After the briefing, Tibbets returned to his hut to gather his flight gear and "smoking equipment" for the long flight ahead, which consisted of cigars, cigarettes and pipe tobacco. With everything in hand, a truck pulled up at 1:15 a.m. to take Tibbets and his crew to their B-29.[34]

When they arrived a few minutes later at the *Enola Gay*, the name Tibbets had given his B-29 in honor of his mother, they couldn't believe what they saw. Ringed with bright floodlights, photographers and film crews, the *Enola Gay* looked like the star of a Hollywood premiere. In all, almost 100 people – ranging from generals and scientists to MPs – were standing around the aircraft when the crew arrived.[35] The sendoff had been ordered by General Groves back in Washington, who wanted a pictorial record made of the mission. Tibbets knew beforehand that there would be some "routine picture-taking" before takeoff, but this was like a "full-scale Hollywood premiere treatment." For the next hour, the crew were treated like movie stars as the photographers bayed for their attention in between the handshakes of well-wishers.[36]

Finally, at 2:20 a.m., after the last group photo was taken, Tibbets told the crew that it was time to go to work. Settling into their seats in the cockpit, Tibbets and his co-pilot, Captain Robert Lewis, started going through their pre-flight checklist.

"All set, Dooz?" Tibbets said to his flight engineer, Staff Sergeant Wyatt Duzenbury, after completing the 27 checks on the list.

"All set, Colonel."[37]

With everyone at their stations, Tibbets looked out from his cockpit window and waved for the cameras, and then Duzenbury started the engines.

"This is Dimples Eight-Two to North Tinian Tower," Lewis called over the radio, after the engines were warmed up. "Ready for taxi out and takeoff instructions."

"Tower to Dimples Eight-Two," the tower replied. "Clear to taxi. Takeoff on runway A for Able."[38]

Following a jeep out to the runway, Tibbets slowly taxied the *Enola Gay* into position and rolled to a stop at the west end of Runway Able. As the crew completed their final checks, the jeep raced ahead down the mile-and-a-half-long runway to look for any obstructions. When it reached the far end, the jeep flashed its lights and then sped off to join the fire trucks and ambulances that were waiting along the runway in case they crashed.

"Dimples Eight-Two to North Tinian Tower," the radio crackled from the *Enola Gay*. "Ready for takeoff on Runway Able."

"Dimples Eight-Two, Dimples Eight-Two, cleared for takeoff," the tower replied.[39]

And with those words, 30-year-old Colonel Paul Tibbets advanced the throttles, and the overloaded *Enola Gay* slowly began lumbering down the runway, using nearly every inch of the strip before Tibbets finally lifted her off the ground.[40]

The time was 2:45 a.m. Special Bombing Mission Number 13 was underway.

22

A New Type of Bomb

"We're starting," Parsons said, tapping Tibbets on the shoulder. Tibbets nodded as Parsons and Lieutenant Morris Jeppson, the assistant weaponeer, made their way into the bomb bay of the *Enola Gay*. "Judge going to work," Tibbets radioed back to Tinian, where General Farrell and a handful of scientists were monitoring the radio.[1]

Inside the cramped bomb bay, Parsons and Jeppson carefully worked their way around the bomb to a removable catwalk that was installed behind the tail of Little Boy. From their perch, Parsons would begin a procedure that less than 24 hours ago had not been planned: arming the bomb in flight. Little Boy was originally designed to be loaded into the B-29 fully armed except for three green safety plugs that prevented the activation of its electrical firing circuits, but after Parsons watched four B-29s crash in flames attempting to take off the day before, he realized that a disaster could occur if the *Enola Gay* crashed with an armed bomb. The resulting fire could ignite the powder charge inside the breach and detonate the weapon, destroying all of North Field.[2]

A few hours after he watched the B-29s crash, Parsons brought up his concerns at the meeting that morning. "If we crack up and the plane catches fire, there is a danger of an atomic explosion that could wipe out half of this island," Parsons said to his startled colleagues. Farrell winced and suggested they'd all have to pray that such a disaster would not happen. Parsons had a better idea, proposing that he arm the bomb after takeoff.

"Are you sure you can do that?" Farrell asked.

"No, but I've got all day to learn," Parsons said.[3]

Parsons had spent hours rehearsing the procedure after the meeting, but as he squeezed in behind the tail of Little Boy, now was the moment of truth. As Parsons went to work opening up the rear of the bomb and removed an armor plate to reach the breach plug, Jeppson read off each step from a checklist that had been typed up only hours earlier. When each step was completed, Jeppson reported it over the interphone to Tibbets, who then radioed a prearranged code for each step of the process back to Farrell and the scientists on Tinian. By the time Parsons completed the most important steps – the insertion of the powder charges and tightening the breach plug – Tinian was fading out of radio range, but Farrell had no doubt of Parsons' success.[4]

With the bomb now fully armed, the crew relaxed and settled in for the long mission ahead. Having gone with little sleep over the past 48 hours, Tibbets knew that he needed to get some rest so he'd be "reasonably sharp for the work ahead." But first, he decided to check on his men back in the aft compartment. Crawling on his hands and knees through the bomb bay tunnel, Tibbets slid over a raised section of the tunnel floor that had been cut out and rebuilt to make room for the massive H-frame and shackle assembly needed to carry the atomic bombs, which was just one of the many special modifications found only on the Silverplate B-29s. Glancing down through the plexiglass viewing port, Tibbets could see the top of the 9,700-pound bomb directly below him and the single-point shackle it was hanging from as he continued back through the tunnel.[5]

When the bomb was being loaded that afternoon, Tibbets noticed that it had the usual messages scribbled on it that you'd typically find on bombs about to be dropped on the enemy, but one had more significance than the others. It was addressed to Emperor Hirohito and signed "From the boys of the *Indianapolis*." The message was written after news of the ship's fate reached Tinian.[6]

Just after midnight on July 30, only four days after delivering its secret cargo to Tinian, the USS *Indianapolis* was sailing alone without escort to Leyte when an explosion suddenly rocked its starboard bow. Another explosion followed seconds later near midship, knocking out two engines and most electrical power. Unbeknownst to the crew, lying some 1,500 yards away, a Japanese submarine had fired a spread of six torpedoes at the *Indianapolis*. Two of the torpedoes found their mark. The explosions blew off the ship's bow and split the *Indianapolis* down to its keel.

The *Indianapolis* rolled over and sank in 12 minutes, taking some 300 men down with her. About 100 men died from their wounds within the first hours. The rest faced slow, horrific deaths from dehydration, exposure and shark attacks as they floated together in groups, most with nothing but life vests. No one knew the *Indianapolis* was lost until three days later when a Navy patrol bomber just happened to spot a group of survivors, and only then did rescue operations begin.

When the last survivor was pulled from the water almost five days later, of the 1,195 sailors and marines on board the *Indianapolis* when the torpedoes struck, only 316 men were rescued alive.[7]

"Have you figured out what we're doing?" Tibbets asked his tail gunner, Tech Sergeant George Caron, after he swung down into the aft compartment.

"Hell, Colonel, I'd probably get in trouble with the security around here," Caron jokingly replied. "I don't want to think."

Caron was a B-29 armament specialist and instructor whose expertise with the bomber's gunnery system stretched back to 1943, when he was assigned to the Boeing-Wichita factory to test and troubleshoot the complicated system. He later worked with Tibbets testing the B-29 before the colonel asked him to join the 509th. With the two machine guns in his tail turret, Caron was the *Enola Gay's* only defense against fighters.

"We're on our way now," Tibbets said to his trusted gunner. "You can guess anything you want."

"Is it a chemist's nightmare?" Caron asked, recalling an article he'd read years ago about British experiments with some type of superweapon.

"Not exactly, but you're warm," Tibbets said.

The two chatted a little while longer before Tibbets crawled back into the tunnel, only to feel a sudden tug on his foot. Thinking something was wrong, he popped back into the compartment and saw Caron standing there.

"Are we splitting atoms today, Colonel?"

"That's about it," Tibbets said, impressed that Caron had figured out the secret, before disappearing back into the tunnel.[8]

Up in the forward cabin, Parsons and Jeppson were keeping a watchful eye on their special instrument panel that was connected by cables to Little Boy and monitored the bomb's electrical system. With its assortment of volt meters, circuit breakers and switches, the two men could test the bomb's various circuits from this panel to ensure all of its systems were functioning properly. The soft glow of the green indicator lights told them everything was normal as Tibbets emerged from the tunnel and made his way back up to his seat.

By now, other members of the crew were taking naps, and with nothing important to do for the time being, Tibbets reclined his seat back and made himself comfortable using his life vest and a parachute pack. Against the rhythmic drone of the engines, he quickly dozed off, while Lewis had a bite to eat and watched the autopilot.[9]

Flying a few miles behind the *Enola Gay*, Sergeant Abe Spitzer was staring blankly at his radios on board *The Great Artiste* when he started to doze off, but then quickly jerked himself awake. Looking around the cabin, three of his crewmates were sound asleep, including the pilot, Major Charles Sweeney. "I didn't see how it was possible [to sleep]," Abe recalled. "There was too much to think about, too many other star-filled nights to remember and too much hoping that there'd be another such night. And not being sure that there would be."[10]

A few minutes after 6:00 a.m., the *Enola Gay* rendezvoused at 9,300 feet over Iwo Jima with *The Great Artiste* and *Necessary Evil*. After a final circle around the island, with the *Enola Gay* in the lead, the three B-29s proceeded towards Japan in a loose formation. Tibbets had only managed to get about an hour of "fitful but useful" sleep, but he felt relaxed as he puffed on his pipe and filled the cockpit with its sweet aromatic smoke.[11]

Just under two hours away from the target, Jeppson climbed into the bomb bay and removed the three green safety plugs from the upper left side of the bomb. After inserting three red arming plugs in their place, Little Boy's firing circuits were now complete. "The bomb is now alive," Lewis wrote in his mission log. "It is a funny feeling knowing it is right in back of you."[12]

Another hour passed before the weather report came in from the B-29 flying high over Hiroshima. Monitoring the radio on *The Great Artiste*, Abe wrote down the message, decoded it, and then passed it to Sweeney. Returning to his seat, Abe put on his heavy flak vest and then keyed the interphone. "It's okay, boys, clear sailing," Abe announced to his crew. "Hiroshima it is."

"How much longer?" Pappy Dehart, the tail gunner, asked. "I've aged at least another thirty years already."

"It won't be long now," Abe said. "I can almost taste that whiskey we'll be getting back at the base."[13]

Abe sounded confident as he announced the target, even a little cocky, he later admitted, but he didn't really feel that way. In that moment, as he looked up ahead at the *Enola Gay* and its "silver fuselage sparkling in the bright morning sunlight," and thinking what a perfect target it was for enemy gunners, Abe felt that the "end of the world" was approaching. "I began getting that familiar feeling," he recalled, "the one you almost always have on a mission, just before you reach the target, the feeling that your stomach has fallen out of the plane some place, and then a chill begins down in your feet and travels right up to your shoulder blades, and you shiver, and the chill goes back down to your feet. Back and forth. Several times. After that, you begin sweating, and at the same time your teeth chatter a little."[14]

That chilling feeling as they neared the target was still new to Abe. Only two weeks earlier, his crew had completed their first combat mission to Japan. And just like everything else with the 509th Composite Group, their combat missions were like no other in the 20th Air Force.

When the Fat Man bomb was under development, Parsons and Tibbets realized that a high explosive version of the bomb would be highly beneficial to the 509th for training purposes. The Pumpkin bombs, as they would be called, were practically identical to the Fat Man atomic bomb on the outside and had the same ballistic characteristics but were filled with 6,300 pounds of high explosives. In late July, the 509th began dropping these massive "blockbuster" bombs on targets across Japan, which provided a perfect cover story to further conceal the group's real purpose. The tactics that Tibbets developed for dropping the atomic bomb in combat would also be used during the Pumpkin missions, including the sudden 155-degree diving turn after bomb release to put as much distance as possible between the target and the B-29. This allowed the crews, who still didn't know what their true mission was, to unknowingly rehearse the upcoming atomic strike in a real combat environment.[15]

Now, as the *Enola Gay* made a gentle left-hand turn onto the IP, the Initial Point of the bomb run to the target, followed by *The Great Artiste* and *Necessary Evil*, Abe was nervously sweating as he waited for the flak bursts and fighters to appear as they closed in on Hiroshima.

"Okay, I've got the bridge," Ferebee said, pointing from the nose of the *Enola Gay*.

"No question about it," Van Kirk agreed, as he looked over Ferebee's shoulder and compared it to a reconnaissance photo. The aiming point Ferebee selected for the mission was the unique T-shaped Aioi Bridge in the center of Hiroshima, about 2,000 feet away from the headquarters of the Japanese Second Army. Located just above a fork in the Ota River, there was no other bridge like it in the entire city, and even from their altitude at over 30,000 feet, it clearly stood out.

"It's all yours," Tibbets said, as he switched on the autopilot and handed control over to Ferebee for the bomb run. Ferebee was now flying the *Enola Gay* through his bombsight, which was connected to the autopilot and allowed him to make course corrections as they approached the target.[16] As Ferebee concentrated on the bomb run, Tibbets slid back in his seat and looked out over the center of Hiroshima as it "shimmered in the early morning sunlight." Then by habit, he scanned the skies for the first signs of flak or fighters, but the skies were empty.[17]

"We're on target," Ferebee announced. With one minute to go before bomb release, Ferebee flipped a switch that activated a high-pitch radio tone that sounded in the crew's headsets. The tone would cease the instant the bomb was released.[18]

Watching from the nose of *The Great Artiste* about a mile behind the *Enola Gay*, Captain Beahan, the bombardier, readied himself to drop the three blast instruments to measure the shock wave, which would descend by parachute and transmit the data back to the three Project Alberta scientists flying on board. Sitting about 15 feet behind Beahan at the rear of the compartment, Abe was bracing himself as the final seconds ticked away before the bomb's release. Abe recalled what happened in the minutes that followed:

> Fifteen seconds … The tone signal continues; I hadn't even noticed its beginning although, right then, it seemed to be the loudest tone signal in the world; I thought it would deafen me. When it broke, when the signal faltered, that was the second for "bombs away."
>
> When the signal broke, our job was simple; we were to make a 60-degree bank and get the hell away, quick, far away and fast … I was set; everybody was set, everybody except

the Japs down there. I had my arc-welder's glasses pulled far down over my eyes, for the maximum protection ... My head was against the hatch; my legs were braced; my eyes were closed tight.

I drew in a breath, and held it ... And considered the possibility that I might never breathe again ... Then the tone signal broke.

What happened after that takes time to tell, much more time than it took to happen; after all, I found out later that exactly one-tenth of one-millionth of a second was required for the bomb to explode and only an unmeasured infinitesimal instant of time for it to drop, less than a minute.

It was precisely 8:15 a.m. [Hiroshima time] when the "bombs away" signal was given, and not even a complete minute of time had elapsed before the flash came.

The events I'm describing now were not all seen by me; they couldn't have been. I have only one set of not-very-good eyes. I've pieced the story together from what I've been told by the rest of our crew aboard – Major Sweeney, Captain Beahan, Van Pelt, Kuharek, Pappy Dehart, Ed Buckley, and Ray Gallagher – as well as the scientists and the men on the other two ships.

When the tone signal broke, I continued to hold my breath or thought I did; I believe all of us thought we did. My fists were clenched together, and my head was still resting against the hatch.

Almost immediately I could feel the plane go into a steep bank, and we were going faster – or so it seemed – than I ever remember, so fast it felt as if the plane might fall apart in midair, might shatter into a thousand pieces. The speedometer, Van Pelt, our navigator, told me later, registered 280 miles per hour.

Then, even though my eyes were shut, I could see – through the lids, as I remember it, although that may be physically impossible (I don't know) I only know that's the way it seemed – a strange purple light. I opened my eyes. The purple light, now half-blue, completely illuminated the inside of the plane, so brightly that my eyes blinked involuntarily, and I closed them again, then opened them, quickly.

Not more than 50 seconds had elapsed since the tone signal broke.

After that, there was a sharp slap against the plane, and we dropped; how far I don't know; it wasn't far, a few hundred feet, perhaps, but at the same time the plane vibrated violently and I thought – all of us thought – we'd been hit by flak. What seemed like a second hit followed almost immediately, then a third. All this in about ninety seconds.

I threw off my goggles and ran to the navigator's window. It was at that second, when I first looked out the window, my eyes blinking from the brightness of the blinding purple light, enveloping the earth below and the sky above, that I felt, fearfully felt, that I was having an hallucination, that I had bumped my head against the side of the plane and was, perhaps temporarily, seeing something that didn't exist, that couldn't possibly exist. Below us, spread out almost as far as I could see, was a great fire, but it was like no ordinary fire. It contained a dozen colors, all of them blindingly bright, more colors than I imagined existed, and in the center and brightest of all, a gigantic red ball of flame that seemed larger than the sun. Indeed, it seemed that, somehow, the sun had been knocked out of the sky and was on the ground below us and beginning to rise again, only coming straight up toward us – and fast. At the same time, the ball itself spread outward, too, until it seemed to cover the entire city, and on every side the flame was shrouded, half-hidden by a thick, impenetrable column of grey-white smoke, extending into the foothills beyond the city and bursting outward and rising toward us with unbelievable speed.

Then the ship rocked again, and it sounded as if a giant gun – some large artillery or cannons – were firing at us and hitting us from every direction. The purple light was changing to a green-blue now, with just a tinge of yellow at the edges, and from below the ball of fire, the upside down sun, seemed to be following the smoke upward, racing to us with immeasurably fast speed – although, we at the same time, though not so quickly – were speeding away from what was left of the city.

Suddenly, we were to the left of the pillar of smoke, and it continued rising, to an estimated height, I later learned, of 50,000 feet. It looked like a kind of massive pole that narrowed toward the top and reached for the stratosphere. The scientists later told us they believed the pole was as much as four or five miles wide at its base and a mile and a half or more wide at the top.

As I watched, hypnotized by what I saw, the column of smoke changed in color, from a grey-white to brown, then amber, then all three colors at once, mingled into a bright, boiling rainbow. For a second it looked as though its fury might be ending, but almost immediately a kind of mushroom spurted out of the top and travelled up, up to what some say was a distance of 60,000 to 70,000 feet. I've never been in Yellowstone Park, but from the movies I've seen I'd say it was something like a tremendous Old Faithful, or rather, a thousand or a million Old Faithful's boiling over at the same time; the whole column seethed and spurted, but the mushroom top shot out in every direction, like giant waves during an ocean storm.

Then, quite suddenly, the top broke off the column, as if it had been cut away with a sharp blade, and it shot still further up; how far I don't know; nobody did or does; not even the pictures show that, and none of our apparatus could measure it exactly. Some said it was 80,000 feet, some 85,000, some even more. When you start talking about distances like that, it doesn't matter much. To me, it seemed as if it reached the top of the sky, like Jack's Beanstalk. Jack could climb up now; there was nothing between the top of the pillar and the roof of the world.

After that, another mushroom, somewhat smaller, boiled up out of the pillar, and the first cloud, the one that had broken away, spread into a kind of horizontal petal, still boiling and again changing color, to a pure clean white on the outside and a delicate pink toward the center.

Major Sweeney had turned the ship, and once or twice – I was too nervous and excited to notice exactly how many times, and afterward no one else could remember either – we circled the remains of the city below. Not that we could see much; everything was still covered with the thick, dirty smoke, at first a light grey, then, while we watched – changing to a darker grey, turning finally to a black around the edges. All of Hiroshima was hidden by the smoke, and interspersed everywhere were huge, boiling fires. Pappy Dehart in the tail, who had the best place for observation, said a few buildings in what might have been the suburbs, or at least the edges of town, were visible, as we broke away to start back.

When we wheeled around, someone spoke, for the first time since the signal for "bombs away." I don't know who it was, but someone who was standing close enough for me to hear said, "I wonder if maybe we're not monkeying around with things that are none of our business."

I didn't answer. I couldn't have said a word without my voice breaking. My hands were clammy and, yes, shaking, too. I merely nodded my head. It was not an answer to the observation; yet I'm not sure my nodding wasn't answer enough.

I sat down at the radio. I didn't look any more; I couldn't have. I'd seen so much in the last few minutes – it was less than five, probably, since the bomb had dropped – that I couldn't have absorbed anything else, and later, when I thought it over, it seemed to me as if the entire, unforgettable, unbelievable event might have been just a short, very brief, bad dream. Not real, not anything that actually happened to anybody. It was too much like a Buck Rogers cartoon. Or the H.G. Wells stories I used to read in school. Such things simply don't happen in real life; at least they never had before, and what had happened now had taken place so quickly it was easy to think it was just something you'd imagined.[19]

The moment the bomb was released, the *Enola Gay* was instantly five tons lighter and leapt upwards as Little Boy fell away. Just like he'd practiced so many times before, Tibbets immediately pushed the bomber into a 155-degree diving turn to the right, with a steep 60-degree bank, to put as much distance as possible between himself and the target. Months earlier, the scientists had told Tibbets that the minimum distance a B-29 could be expected to survive the shock wave from the explosion was eight miles away from the point of detonation. Tibbets did the calculations and concluded that this unorthodox maneuver was their "best bet for survival," even though it put considerable strain on the airframe.[20]

As he pulled the goggles down over his eyes in the middle of the turn, Tibbets quickly discovered that he couldn't see the instrument panel in front of him through the dark glass. He ripped the goggles off and threw them to the floor. Ferebee was so fixated watching the bomb fall that he forgot all about his goggles. When the bomb exploded 43 seconds later, a brilliant flash lit up the cockpit as the *Enola Gay* roared away from Hiroshima. Ferebee later said that it felt as if a giant flashbulb had gone off a few feet from his face. More so than the flash, Tibbets was startled by a tingling sensation in his mouth and the taste of lead. He was later told by the scientists that it was the "radioactive forces" unleashed by the bomb interacting with the fillings in his teeth.[21]

Strapped into his wooden seat in the tail gunner compartment, Caron was directly facing the city when the bomb exploded. Even with his goggles on, which made the sun appear as only a faint glimmer, the flash was so intense that it caused him to forcibly blink his eyes. When he regained his vision and took the goggles off, the first thing Caron saw was a strange shimmering in the air radiating up towards them. Before he could warn the crew, the shock wave from the explosion, traveling at the speed of sound, rocked the *Enola Gay*.

"Flak!" Tibbets yelled, thinking they were under fire.

"No, no," Parsons said. "That's not flak. That's it – the shock wave. We're in the clear now.[22]

A few seconds later, Caron yelled that another one was coming. The bomber was rocked again when the second shock wave hit. Then just as suddenly, the *Enola Gay* was back in calm air.

After the shock waves passed, Tibbets called back to Caron and asked if he could see anything yet. With the gun turret protruding from the back of his compartment blocking his view below, Caron said he couldn't see anything because the turret was in the way. Then all of a sudden, a giant mushroom cloud appeared over the turret as it shot up into the sky. "Holy Moses, here it comes!" Caron said over the interphone.[23]

As Tibbets banked the *Enola Gay* around and Hiroshima came into view, a feeling of "shock and horror" swept over the crew. No one could believe what they saw. "The city we had seen so clearly in the sunlight a few minutes before was now an ugly smudge," Tibbets recalled. "It had completely disappeared under this awful blanket of smoke and fire."[24]

Back in the tail, Caron was busy snapping pictures of the mushroom cloud as it rose high over the city. Before they took off, a photographer handed Caron a large camera and told him to "shoot anything you see" after the strike. Even though he knew nothing about photography, one of the pictures Caron took that day would soon be seen all across Japan, where it appeared on leaflets urging the Japanese to surrender.[25]

"Fellows, you have just dropped the first atomic bomb in history," Tibbets finally announced over the interphone to his stunned crew.[26]

Once everyone was over the initial shock, Tibbets had each man report his observations over the interphone, which were recorded on a wire recorder set up in the aft compartment. A recording was also made of everything said during the bomb run. (After landing, the recording was handed to an "information officer" and was never seen again. If you have any information about the lost recording or its whereabouts, please contact me at TrevorBMcIntyre@outlook.com.)[27]

By 8:31 a.m. Hiroshima time, 16 minutes after the bomb was dropped, the *Enola Gay* was on its way back to the Marianas. As they turned for home, Tibbets was inundated with questions about the atomic bomb and the project that produced it. For over an hour, the crew had a "lively conversation" about the bomb and the end of the war. Tibbets tried to answer all of their questions, but Parsons had to chime in when Ferebee wondered if the bomb had rendered them all sterile. Parsons assured him that such a danger was remote.[28]

Aboard *The Great Artiste*, the mood was much more subdued on the flight back, as Abe recalled:

> On our way back we each had a dry C-ration sandwich and more black coffee, Army style. Usually, on the return from a mission there's a lot of talking. Everyone relaxes a little. The danger is passed, and you're glad, damn glad, to be still alive.
>
> But this time hardly any of us had anything to say. A couple of times over the interphones I spoke to Ray and Pappy.
>
> "You fellows still around?" I'd ask.
>
> "Don't know," Ray said, "the angels are still waving and winking."
>
> "I think I'd just as soon have missed it," Pappy answered. "Come to think of it, I won't be mentioning it to my grandchildren. Not ever. I don't think it's the kind of thing to be telling kids. Not what we saw."
>
> I knew what he meant. Or thought I did. It might have been that what we witnessed was too fantastic. Or simply that what we'd gone through was too different from anything any of us had ever experienced before … and too horrible to describe adequately. Or perhaps the rest were, as I was, frightened by the very idea that in less time than it takes to draw a single breath a whole city can be (and was) largely demolished by one medium-sized bomb dropped from one not-very-large plane. Not thousands of both. One of each.
>
> About all I could think of on that flight back was that maybe we really were playing around with something that wasn't any of our business; maybe we had gone too far. We might have made winning a war too easy. Or too difficult. Or too awful. I couldn't be sure which.

And then, too, I kept thinking that the war was surely all over now, that certainly the Japs would surrender immediately and that I was safe and might be going home soon.

It never occurred to me that there'd ever be another mission or that any nation, any people could possibly ask for more of it.

And, finally, I'll admit that, because I'm human, I was a little glad and somewhat smug. For months we'd been taking a ribbing from all the other bomber groups. They'd made fun of us and called us the "Victory Boys." Well, we'd proved our point; it hadn't been just talk. We'd done it, and I was glad. We could dish out our own Bronx cheers from here on in.

When we circled over Tinian for the landing, we'd been gone exactly thirteen hours, and we were exhausted. I had even slept for a few minutes on the way back.

But as we stepped off the ship, all the brass in the world was around, especially the kind with stars, and the movie cameras and spotlights and microphones were there again. General Carl A. Spaatz greeted Colonel Tibbets and presented him with the Distinguished Service Cross. It wasn't much of a ceremony, and the Colonel was too fatigued to do more than smile wanly and shake the General's hand.

The rest of us were hurried into the interrogation room and each given an extra large shot of whiskey before the questioning began.

I didn't say much, personally. I told them what I had seen and, as best I could, what I had felt when the bomb exploded. The latter was a foolish question, unanswerable and completely meaningless. What had I felt? Frightened, of course. But more than that, much more; you're always frightened on a mission. Everyone is, afraid and uncertain, not sure you'll ever return and wanting terribly to return – to go back, to the base, home, to be at that moment anywhere except the place you are. And what else? Well, I didn't say it then, but I'll say it now, and I'll repeat it again and again if anyone asks me. I felt that we were seeing a thing that man should never see, that was too big for the human mind really to understand and, moreover and more important, that even in a war, even in a war in which the enemy in the Pacific had been the most sadistic, most inhuman, most cruel, most hateful enemy in history, we had unleashed a force too great to be understood and properly feared. That we had, in short, learned how to kill too many thousands too quickly.

I thought all that, but, when they asked me the simple question, "What was it like?" I replied in a simple sentence. "It was hell," I said, "absolute hell." I think everyone understood, and I am sure that was about all it was necessary to say.[29]

Half a world away in the North Atlantic, on the fourth day of his voyage home from Potsdam aboard the USS *Augusta*, President Truman was handed a message from Washington while he was eating lunch with some of the ship's crew:

Big bomb dropped on Hiroshima August 5 at 7:15 p.m. Washington time. First reports indicate complete success which was even more conspicuous than earlier test.[30]

"This is the greatest thing in history," Truman said to the sailors around him, after reading the message. "It's time for us to get home."[31]

A few minutes later, Truman was handed a second message:

Following info regarding Manhattan received. "Hiroshima bombed visually with only one tenth cover at 052315A. There was no fighter opposition and no flak. Parsons reports 15 minutes after drop as follows: 'Results clear cut successful in all respects. Visible effects greater than in any test. Conditions normal in airplane following delivery.'"[32]

Truman was "greatly moved" by the messages and what it could mean for the end of the war. Overcome with joy, he leapt to his feet and drew the room's attention by loudly tapping the side of his glass. With all eyes on the President, Truman announced to the stunned sailors that a new bomb had just been dropped on Japan that had more power than 20,000 tons of TNT. The mess hall erupted in cheers and applause. "I could not keep back my expectation that the Pacific war might now be brought to a speedy end," Truman recalled.[33]

In the hours that followed, radio bulletins from Washington broke the news of the atomic bomb to the world, along with a warning to Japan: "If they do not now accept our terms," the President said in a prepared statement, "they may expect a rain of ruin from the air, the like of which has never been seen on this earth."[34] The fate of Japan was now in the hands of its leaders.

The Fat Man atomic bomb. The atomic bombs were so large that special loading pits had to be constructed for the B-29s to back over top of in order to load the bombs. (National Archives 519397)

23

Evacuate Your Cities

In the hours following the first atomic strike, the Japanese 12th Air Division began to investigate the attack on Hiroshima. The report they later transmitted to Tokyo was intercepted and decoded by the Americans:

1. Report on the bomb used (and estimates) and resulting conditions: A violent, large, special-type bomb, giving the appearance of magnesium, was dropped over the center of the city of Hiroshima this morning by a formation of three or four planes (it is also said that there was only one plane; some say that the bomb was attached to a parachute). It is estimated that, after being dropped from a plane, the bomb exploded at a certain altitude above the ground (500 to 1,000 meters). There was a blinding flash and a violent blast. (Over the center of the city the flash and the blast were almost simultaneous, but in the vicinity of the airfield [south of the city] the blast came two or three seconds later.) Then a mass of white smoke billowed up into the air.
2. The flash was instantaneous, burning objects in the immediate vicinity, burning the exposed parts of people's bodies as far as three kilometers away, and setting fire to their thin clothing.
3. The blast leveled completely or partially as many as 60,000 houses within a radius of three kilometers, and smashed glass blocks, etc.
4. Losses: The majority of the houses within the city were completely or partially leveled. The conflagration spread all over, and many important areas were destroyed by fire. The majority of government buildings were either leveled or destroyed by fire. Many people were injured by burns from the flash and by objects shattered by the blast, particularly by glass fragments, and, as far as was observed, [word missing] one-third of the residents were either seriously or slightly injured.[1]

A second report from the 12th Air Division continued:

1. Because conflagration broke out suddenly and the spread of the fire was rapid, we think that 70 or 80 percent of the people in the city were casualties.
2. As a result of the horrible catastrophes brought about by the recent air raid, there appears to be a gradual increase in the circulation of wild and fantastic rumors.

Moreover, there have been an increasing number of cases in which the fighting spirit of victims and eyewitnesses has been broken. However, in this prefecture [west of Hiroshima] the mobile police officials are doing everything in their power to [words missing] the spread of such frenzied rumors, and are using every means at their disposal to provide against this in advance. In order to calm the people's fears, they are particularly stressing the fact that, even in the recent air raid, those who took refuge immediately in the safe underground shelters escaped injury completely.[2]

A Japanese Navy report from nearby Kure added the following:

1.   The concussion was beyond imagination, demolishing practically every house in the city.
2.   Present estimate of damage: About 80 percent of the city was wiped out (destroyed or burned). Only a portion of the western section escaped the disaster. Casualties have been estimated at 100,000 persons.
3.   Relief squads have been dispatched to the area to assist the Army in rescue operations. About 1,000 Army troops and 10,000 [words missing] medical supplies were moved in by dawn on the 7th.[3]

While the ruins of Hiroshima were still smoldering, the B-29s began dropping new leaflets over Japan's cities with a dire warning:

To the Japanese people:
America asks that you take immediate heed of what we say on this leaflet.
   We are in possession of the most destructive explosive ever devised by man. A single one of our newly developed atomic bombs is actually the equivalent in explosive power to what two thousand of our giant B-29's can carry on a single mission. This awful fact is one for you to ponder and we solemnly assure you it is grimly accurate.
   We have just begun to use this weapon against your homeland. If you still have any doubt, make inquiry as to what happened to Hiroshima when just one atomic bomb fell on that city.
   Before using this bomb to destroy every resource of the military by which they are prolonging this useless war, we ask that you now petition the emperor to end the war. Our president has outlined for you the thirteen consequences of an honorable surrender. We urge that you accept these consequences and begin the work of building a new, better, and peace-loving Japan.
   You should take steps now to cease military resistance. Otherwise, we shall resolutely employ this bomb and all our other superior weapons to promptly and forcefully end the war.
   EVACUATE YOUR CITIES.[4]

On the evening of August 9, President Truman addressed the nation by radio from the White House. Most of his speech dealt with news from the Potsdam Conference and the future of post-war Germany, but then Truman turned to the war with Japan and the atomic bomb:

Our meeting at Berlin was the first meeting of the great Allies since victory was won in Europe. Naturally our thoughts now turn to the day of victory in Japan.

The British, Chinese, and United States Governments have given the Japanese people adequate warning of what is in store for them. We have laid down the general terms on which they can surrender. Our warning went unheeded; our terms were rejected. Since then the Japanese have seen what our atomic bomb can do. They can foresee what it will do in the future.

The world will note that the first atomic bomb was dropped on Hiroshima, a military base. That was because we wished in this first attack to avoid, insofar as possible, the killing of civilians. But that attack is only a warning of things to come. If Japan does not surrender, bombs will have to be dropped on her war industries and, unfortunately, thousands of civilian lives will be lost. I urge Japanese civilians to leave industrial cities immediately and save themselves from destruction.

I realize the tragic significance of the atomic bomb.

Its production and its use were not lightly undertaken by this Government. But we knew that our enemies were on the search for it. We know now how close they were to finding it.

And we knew the disaster which would come to this Nation, and to all peace-loving nations, to all civilization, if they had found it first.

That is why we felt compelled to undertake the long and uncertain and costly labor of discovery and production.

We won the race of discovery against the Germans.

Having found the bomb we have used it. We have used it against those who attacked us without warning at Pearl Harbor, against those who have starved and beaten and executed American prisoners of war, against those who have abandoned all pretense of obeying international laws of warfare. We have used it in order to shorten the agony of war, in order to save the lives of thousands and thousands of young Americans.

We shall continue to use it until we completely destroy Japan's power to make war. Only a Japanese surrender will stop us.[5]

The President's warnings were not empty threats. As Truman was addressing the nation, a second atomic bomb had already been dropped on Japan.

24

A New Gimmick

"We're going to have another test hop in the morning," whispered Master Sergeant John Kuharek, *The Great Artiste's* flight engineer, to his crewmates as they huddled in the corner of their Quonset hut. "There's a new kind of 'gimmick' and we're going to test it." It was 9:30 p.m. on August 7, 1945, one day after Hiroshima was bombed, and Kuharek had just walked in with the news that no one wanted to believe.

"For God's sake, why?" Staff Sergeant Edward Buckley, the radar observer, said. "They're bound to surrender tomorrow. No doubt about it."

"I'm just telling you what they told me," Kuharek shrugged, "and there may be another mission, too. If there is, our crew will probably drop the new one."

"You're kidding," Abe said in disbelief. But Kuharek wasn't kidding. He'd just been talking to Major Sweeney and Captain Beahan when they told him the news about the test hop the next day.

"There couldn't be another mission," Buckley said.

"The war's over," Pappy Dehart spoke up. "It's just a matter of waiting until the little bastards admit it."

"Right," Kuharek sarcastically said, as he unlaced his shoes and got ready for bed. "You're exactly right. You guys know all the answers. I made the whole thing up."[1]

The crew joked around some more as they got ready for bed, but no one mentioned what Kuharek had said. Deep down, they knew he wasn't joking. They had all just spent the last 12 hours listening to the radio and expected to hear any minute that Japan had surrendered, but the news they were waiting for never came. Even after Hiroshima, the Japanese were still fighting.

Abe tried to sleep that night, but he kept thinking about the new bomb Kuharek had mentioned, something bigger and more effective than the first, and why the Japanese had not surrendered yet. None of it made sense. "I smoked almost a full pack of cigarettes before morning," Abe recalled.[2]

While Abe was tossing in his bunk that night, the people of Japan were also uneasy after learning about Hiroshima. Over the airwaves that day, after the American broadcasts had blanketed Japan with President Truman's statement about the atomic bomb, the Imperial Headquarters were forced to announce that a "new type" of bomb that caused "considerable damage" had been used against Hiroshima and was under investigation. The development and use of the new bomb was attributed to America's "beastly nature and impatience to end the war," and "disappointment over slow progress of invasion plans." Listeners were warned to "strengthen air defense precautions" and "guard against enemy propaganda." Another broadcaster said that the use of the new bomb was a manifestation of the enemy's "beastly nature in [a] desperate attempt to shorten [the] war," and that the authorities will "indicate measures to combat it."[3] A domestic broadcast reported:

> The enemy has exposed his cold bloodedness and atrocious nature more and more in killing people by use of this new type bomb. It is believed that the enemy, being faced with difficult conditions, is feeling impatient to turn the war into one of short duration. Hence he has begun to use this type of bomb.[4]

A Domei News Agency broadcast about the bomb concluded:

> It is the accepted rule that a new weapon will show considerable results when it makes its debut, but usually loses its effectiveness with the passing of time and the appearance of countermeasures. It is important that we have firm faith and trust in the leadership of our authorities and show strong resistance against the psychological offensive of the enemy, which is backed by a brutal, murderous war.[5]

Tokyo promised the listeners that "adequate countermeasures would be found to combat the new weapon," but the true scale of the devastation in Hiroshima was kept from the Japanese people. Japan's military leaders, however, were fully aware of the troubling reports that were coming in from Hiroshima. Some of them recorded their thoughts in their diaries that day.[6]

Lieutenant General Torashiro Kawabe, Vice Chief of the Imperial Army General Staff, wrote:

> As soon as I arrived at the office I looked through the reports on the air attack by new bomb on Hiroshima performed on the morning of the 6th. I was shocked tremendously. I once saw the studies made by B Ken [Japanese research institute]. The study made by [unclear words] was regarded by us as hopeless. However, the enemy has turned it into reality and it seems that they have used this against us with great success … It is too late to have regrets or to cry over this. If we expended time crying, the war situation will deteriorate further and become more difficult. We must be tenacious and active.[7]

Vice Admiral Matome Ugaki, Commander of the 5th Air Fleet, wrote:

> At about 0825 yesterday two or three B-29s came over Hiroshima and dropped two or three large-type bombs with parachutes attached. They exploded about fifty meters above ground with a terrific flash and explosion, with a result that about 80 percent of the houses in the city were leveled and burnt out. Casualties suffered reached over 100,000.
>
> A radio broadcast from San Francisco this afternoon said that seventeen hours before an atomic bomb had been dropped for the first time in history, on Hiroshima, an army base … it is clear that this was a uranium atom bomb, and it deserves to be regarded as a real wonder, making the outcome of the war more gloomy.

We must think of some countermeasures against it immediately, and at the same time I wish we could create the same bomb.[8]

* * *

After another restless night, Abe woke up on August 8 with a roaring headache and no energy. Having missed breakfast, he lay back in his bunk and listened to the radio. The Japanese still had not surrendered. "All the news still concerned the Hiroshima raid, and there wasn't a word about a possible surrender, not even a surrender offer," Abe recalled. "About the only new development was that President Truman had warned the Japs again that unless they gave up, the bombs would keep on coming, and coming, and coming."[9]

The radio announcer then explained that the first bomb had destroyed most of the city, and that the heat from the explosion reached "approximately 150 million degrees Fahrenheit," followed by a wind "traveling as much as 500 to 1,000 miles an hour." It was all a charming thought the morning before a raid, Abe thought to himself. "Oh, what a beautiful morning," Gallagher hummed as he moved about the hut, "oh, what a beautiful day." Buckley threw a shoe at him, and Abe heaved a book. They both missed.[10]

Over 1,500 miles away from Tinian, a team of investigators dispatched from Tokyo looked down upon Hiroshima in disbelief as they circled above the city. Surveying the destruction from the air, Dr. Yoshio Nishina, the physicist leading Japan's efforts to develop its own atomic bomb, quickly concluded that "nothing but an atomic bomb could have inflicted such damages."[11] However, the team leader, Lieutenant General Seizo Arisue, remained unconvinced. Looking out over the city, Arisue would only concede that the Americans had used an "unconventional" type of bomb.

After landing at an airfield just south of the city, the officer in charge of the field rushed up to greet the team as they stepped off the plane. The whole side of his face had been badly burned by the flash. "Everything which is exposed gets burned, but anything which is covered even only slightly can escape burns," the officer exclaimed. "Therefore it cannot be said that there are no countermeasures."[12]

The following report from Hiroshima was later intercepted and decoded by the Americans:

1. The substance of this bomb is not an ordinary explosive charge or incendiary material. We conclude that it is an atomic bomb. It is dropped from a single plane or several planes, not necessarily with a parachute.
2. The explosion occurred about 300 meters south of the Gokoku Shrine in the center of Hiroshima, at a height of approximately 350 meters.
3. The force of the blast, at a point on the ground at the center of the explosion, is estimated at 6 kilograms per square centimeter (enough to knock a man down). However, more accurate and careful examination will be necessary.
4. We are quite sure that the burns were caused by the flash, which includes infra-red to gamma rays. Moreover, we suspect that beta rays may also be involved. Apparently the duration of the flash is more than momentary.
5. Some of the fires were caused by highly inflammable materials (such as straw, thin boards, paper, black cloth, etc.) which caught fire from the flash.

6.   People were killed principally by being crushed or burned to death in collapsing houses. Eighty percent of the wounded were burned and the outlook for their recovery is not favorable.
7.   This type of bomb explodes [word missing] an ordinary bomb and produces an intense blue-white flash. The flash usually burns exposed skin. Since the emission of light lasts for some time, the immediate loss of [words missing] is low. If the exposed parts are covered, one can avoid burns.

Note: At this point there is a fragmentary sentence which appears to state that, since the blast travels at a speed much slower than that of the flash, it is possible for persons at a distance from the center of the explosion to avoid injury, "if steps are taken immediately upon perceiving the flash."

The report concluded with a list of "countermeasures" for the atomic bomb, which included removing all glass windows at once to avoid injuries, and rebuilding houses as half-underground shelters. Japanese people were also to dress in heavy clothing that would leave as little of their bodies exposed as possible and wear white underwear. "Other points are as in ordinary air raid precautions," the report concluded.[13]

* * *

"It sure looks like a storm is brewing up," Buckley said, looking up at the dark clouds. "It looks like all hell might break loose in a minute."

Abe and his crewmates had just landed after testing the new bomb Kuharek mentioned the night before. The new "gimmick" was a Fat Man bomb, minus the plutonium core, that they dropped in the waters near Tinian to test the bomb's complex firing system. The final test before a Fat Man bomb would be used in combat had now been completed.

"Yeah," Pappy Dehart agreed, looking up at the sky. "May storm for days, too. This is the rainy season."

"Couldn't possibly take off in weather like this," Gallagher said. "It'll probably ground every ship on the base."

"Maybe for days," added Buckley. "Maybe for weeks."

By the time they finished lunch, the weather was looking better. "There's a pre-flight briefing at 1600," Kuharek announced to his crewmates, confirming that the mission would proceed.

"Wonderful!" Abe sarcastically thought to himself. "Great!"[14]

In the few hours they had to themselves before the briefing, the crew split up and wandered off to be alone. "It was a time when you wanted to be alone," Abe recalled. "I stayed in the hut, nursing my headache and trying to keep my mind occupied with something. Anything except what was coming up."[15]

While Abe kept himself busy writing letters home, under heavy security, a mustard yellow Fat Man bomb was being loaded into the forward bomb bay of *Bockscar*, the Silverplate B-29 his crew had just conducted the test drop from. The bomb's unusual color was a heavy coat of zinc chromate primer to keep it from rusting.

The first Fat Man bomb was originally scheduled to be dropped on August 11, but Tibbets had asked Parsons if the bomb assembly team could advance their schedule two full days to

August 9, because bad weather was forecast for the next five days. As Tibbets recalled after the war, the decision to drop two atomic bombs within days of each other was to demonstrate to Japan that the United States had an "endless supply of this superweapon for use against one Japanese city after another," and it would mark the beginning of the "rain of ruin" that President Truman promised if the Japanese did not surrender. With bad weather in the forecast, it was imperative to drop the second bomb without delay.[16]

For the upcoming strike, since *The Great Artiste* was already outfitted with the special equipment to record the effects of the blast and reinstalling everything in another B-29 would be too time consuming, Abe's crew would fly *Bockscar* on the mission instead, while Captain Frederick Bock's crew would fly *The Great Artiste*. Just like the Hiroshima mission, *The Great Artiste* would again drop three blast instruments to measure the shock wave of the explosion. The sight of these instruments descending by parachute led many Japanese to mistake them as bombs. It was known that these instruments had survived the Hiroshima blast and landed on the ground intact, and this gave Project Alberta physicist Luis Alvarez an idea.

Before the war, Alvarez had known a Japanese physicist at Berkley, Ryokichi Sagane, who was now at the University of Tokyo. With the help of two other Project Alberta physicists who also knew Sagane from Berkley, Alvarez wrote a letter to their former colleague urging him to convince Japan's leaders to surrender. A copy of the letter was then secured inside each of the three instrument canisters:

Headquarters
Atomic Bomb Command
August 9, 1945
To: Prof. R. Sagane

From: Three of your former scientific colleagues during your stay in the United States

We are sending this as a personal message to urge that you use your influence as a reputable nuclear physicist, to convince the Japanese General Staff of the terrible consequences which will be suffered by your people if you continue in this war.

You have known for several years that an atomic bomb could be built if a nation were willing to pay the enormous cost of preparing the necessary material. Now that you have seen that we have constructed the production plants, there can be no doubt in your mind that all the output of these factories, working 24 hours a day, will be exploded in your homeland.

Within the space of three weeks, we have proof-fired one bomb in the American desert, exploded one in Hiroshima and delivered the third this morning.

We implore you to confirm these facts to your leaders, and to do your utmost to stop the destruction and waste of life which can only result in the total immolation of all your cities if continued. As scientists, we deplore the use to which a beautiful discovery has been put, but we can assure you that unless Japan surrenders at once, this rain of atomic bombs will increase manyfold in fury.[17]

*   *   *

By 1:00 a.m. on August 9, after their third and final briefing in the past nine hours, Abe and his crew had gathered all of their flight gear back at their hut and were waiting for a truck to pick them up. Sitting "long-faced and solemn" on the edges of their bunks, barely a word was spoken as they waited. "I think everybody on our crew was more frightened, really downright terrified, than we had been the first time," Abe recalled, "but, after all, we were, in a sense, veterans now, and even though the bomb we were to carry was 'slightly larger and much more efficient, much more,' we didn't feel we had to be Superman this time."[18]

Abe had noticed during the briefings that the same people had said practically the same things in practically the same way as the Hiroshima briefings, only the details were different. With storms along their route to Japan, the rendezvous with the two escort B-29s, *The Great Artiste* and *Big Stink*, was moved from Iwo Jima to a small island off the southern coast of Kyushu. The three B-29s would then proceed to the primary target, Kokura, or the secondary target, Nagasaki. Flying ahead of the strike aircraft, the *Enola Gay* (flown by a different crew) would scout the weather over Kokura, and *Laggin' Dragon* would scout the weather over Nagasaki.

After loading all their gear in the truck, Abe and his crewmates took a long, and some thought maybe their last, look at their hut as they drove away.

"Isn't a bad place to live, compared to some," Gallagher said, looking back.

"Depends on what you're comparing it with," Buckley spoke up. "Compared to a farmhouse in Ohio, now, it isn't much."

"Shut up," Gallagher said.[19]

A handful of men from the other crews were waiting to wish Abe and his crew good luck when they pulled up to *Bockscar*, along with some photographers, scientists and the brass, but it wasn't a big production like the Hiroshima mission. There had been rumors of a Japanese attack against Tinian since the first bomb was dropped, and Abe noticed that only a few lights were on around the field. It was nothing like the "Hollywood premiere" that awaited the crew of the *Enola Gay*.

"It wasn't raining yet, but every few minutes there'd be a flash of lightning or a bolt of thunder," Abe recalled when they arrived at *Bockscar*. "We'd been expecting a suicide raid ever since Hiroshima ... there'd been two alerts, but still no sign of a raid. Not even an observation plane."[20]

As an extra precaution, *Bockscar* would not break radio silence even while on the ground, which could alert the Japanese of the mission. Instead, the crew would use signal lights to communicate with the control tower before takeoff. After the last pictures were taken, and the final handshakes and well wishes were given, the crew climbed aboard to begin their pre-flight checks.

"Give the little bastards our regards," someone said to Abe.

"Don't worry," Abe said. "See you soon."

"I'll save a drink for you, Abe," another man said. "I'll save a lot of drinks."

"Thanks," Abe grinned. "I'll be needing them."

"Take care of yourself, old man, and good luck."[21]

By 3:35 a.m., all four of *Bockscar's* engines were running smoothly, but then Kuharek discovered that he couldn't transfer fuel from the bomb bay tanks. This meant that the fuel in the tanks was not usable. Kuharek informed Major Sweeney of the problem, who climbed out of the cockpit and conferred with Tibbets. He quickly returned and told the crew that the mission would proceed.

At 3:45 a.m., as Sweeney advanced the throttles and began the long takeoff roll, Abe nervously looked back at the bomb. Unlike Little Boy, there was no way to arm a Fat Man bomb in flight. Except for the green safety plugs, the bomb was fully armed when it was loaded into the bomb bay. Abe recalled that frightening takeoff:

> I took a last fleeting look at the bomb nestling cozily behind me, turned to look at my wife's picture and with a wave of my hand and a "We're on our way again, Hon," strained forward to watch the needle on the speedometer – 100 – 110 – 120. Normally, at 120 mph, we're supposed to leave the ground, but we didn't. The wheels hadn't lifted an inch. I could hear the Major swearing, and again I glanced back at the bomb, looking harmless and peaceful, and I thought, Oh, God, if we crash with that thing, there won't be any pieces to worry about. Plane or people. Nothing. Not even an island, probably. Just a bubble in the sea where Tinian had been.[22]

Just like the *Enola Gay* three nights earlier, *Bockscar* finally took to the air after using practically every inch of the runway. Wiping the nervous sweat off his face, Abe tried to settle down for the long flight ahead. Ever since the first briefing that afternoon, he'd been thinking about the way the intelligence officer had described the new bomb they would be dropping. "Bigger and better," the officer kept repeating. Bigger perhaps, Abe thought, but better was a poor choice of words. "I doubted if that were the way to describe a bomb that would kill more people," Abe recalled.[23]

The "bigger and better" bomb they were carrying had just arrived on Tinian a week ago, but it almost didn't make it past California. On August 2, three Silverplate B-29s arrived on Tinian after a 6,500-mile journey from the United States. The bomber piloted by Captain Edward Costello, call sign Victor 95, would soon have the name *Laggin' Dragon* painted on its nose next to a weary-looking green dragon, a parody of the squadron's insignia of a ferocious, fire-breathing dragon. The name and artwork was created by the bombardier, Lieutenant John Downey, because his crew was lagging so far behind the rest of the 509th Composite Group when they finally received the last of the 15 Silverplate B-29s assigned to the group.

Crammed inside Costello's brand-new B-29 as it rolled to a stop that day were 19 men and their baggage, a statue of the Virgin Mary, miscellaneous cargo and parts, and two slot machines salvaged from the Wendover officers' club after it burned down. But the most important cargo of all was the Fat Man bomb assembly F31, minus the plutonium core, hanging in the forward bomb bay.[24] The second atomic bomb had arrived.

The three Silverplate B-29s that landed on Tinian that day each carried a Fat Man bomb assembly with them (minus the cores), but the bomb carried by *Laggin' Dragon*, and its crew, were nearly lost in a freak accident. On July 24, *Laggin' Dragon* lifted off from Wendover under sealed Top Secret orders. Expecting to proceed to Tinian to join the rest of the 509th, the crew was surprised when they opened their orders after takeoff and discovered they were to proceed to Kirkland Field in New Mexico instead, where a Fat Man bomb assembly would be loaded into their forward bomb bay.

The next day, with the bomb and two security agents on board, the crew flew on to Mather Field in California. Before departing for Hawaii the following day, the personnel at Mather were required to inspect the emergency equipment on every aircraft going overseas. This created a problem for the security agents guarding *Laggin' Dragon*, because only the crew were permitted inside the bomber. A compromise was reached, and the ground personnel were allowed to inspect the life rafts and survival gear stowed in the B-29's two life raft compartments, which were accessible from the outside of the aircraft through doors on the upper fuselage above the wings.

When *Laggin' Dragon* departed for Hawaii the next day, disaster nearly struck. Only seconds after takeoff, a loud "whap" was heard and the bomber began to violently shake and sink toward the ground. Costello tried to pull the nose up, but the controls were jammed. Yelling to his co-pilot for help, both men pulled back on their control yokes as hard as they could until the aircraft slowly responded. Fearing they were about to crash, Costello turned to line up with a clearing ahead when the controls suddenly freed up and the shaking subsided. Once they reached a safe altitude, the pilots brought *Laggin' Dragon* back around for an emergency landing.

Back on the ground, it was discovered that the door latch on one of the life raft compartments wasn't secured after the inspection. When *Laggin' Dragon* lifted off, the life raft was ejected when the door blew open and became wrapped around the horizontal stabilizer, jamming the elevator. After repairs, the crew took off about 12 hours later and proceeded to Tinian without incident.[25]

*   *   *

"For God's sake, what is it?" Abe asked over the interphone. Back in the tail gunner compartment, as *Bockscar* approached the rendezvous point off the coast of Japan, Pappy Dehart had just reported an unidentified airplane off in the distance behind them.

"Hold it," Dehart finally said after a long pause. "Hold it. Okay. Relax. It's a '29."

"Jesus God!" Barnes said. "I don't mind telling you –"

"Shut up," Abe shouted, as something crackled over the radio. "Keep quiet." It was the weather report from the *Enola Gay* over Kokura. The primary target was clear. A few moments later, *Laggin' Dragon* reported in from Nagasaki. It was also clear.[26]

Sweeney announced to the crew that Kokura would be the target just as they arrived at the rendezvous point. The B-29 that Dehart spotted behind them was *The Great Artiste*, and the two bombers quickly joined up and waited for *Big Stink* to arrive. Sweeney had orders to remain at the rendezvous point for no more than 15 minutes before proceeding to the target.

After circling for 45 minutes, with *Big Stink* still nowhere to be found, the two B-29s finally proceeded to the target area, but the mission was now hopelessly behind schedule. (*Big Stink* was circling at the wrong altitude and never saw the other B-29s.)

By the time *Bockscar* began its bomb run on Kokura, the weather had closed in.

"No drop!" Beahan yelled, huddled over his bombsight. "No drop!" The target was completely obscured by smoke and clouds. With orders to only drop the bomb visually, Beahan, who was celebrating his 27th birthday that day, had to abort the bomb run.

Sweeney swung *Bockscar* around and made a second bomb run, but the target was still obscured.

"No drop," Beahan called again.

"A few bursts of flak, Major," Dehart reported from the tail.

A third bomb run was attempted, but it was hopeless. The conditions over the target were only getting worse. As Sweeney conferred with Beahan and Commander Frederick Ashworth, the bomb commander, about what to do next, Dehart suddenly spotted some fighters climbing to intercept them. "Fighters below and climbing rapidly," Dehart reported. "Four of them. Climbing rapidly."

After spending almost an hour over Kokura, Sweeney finally turned for their secondary target. "We got the hell out, and we turned as quickly as any plane ever turned, and we headed straight for Nagasaki," Abe recalled. "The fighters followed us a little way, and when I looked back I could still see the flak bursts; in fact, the whole sky seemed to be black with flak bursts, but they were in the distance now, and we didn't have to worry about them."[27]

Bockscar was now running dangerously low on fuel as they headed for Nagasaki. After spending so much time over the rendezvous point and Kokura, Kuharek reported to Sweeney that they only had 1,500 gallons of fuel left. They would never make it to Iwo Jima, let alone Tinian. Their only hope was to try for Okinawa. Calling Ashworth up to the cockpit, Sweeney explained that they only had enough fuel left to make one pass over the target. If Nagasaki was also obscured, what would they do with the bomb? If they didn't drop it on the target, they may have to let it go in the ocean, Sweeney said, or there was a slim chance they might be able to make it to Okinawa with the bomb still aboard, but with all the extra weight, the odds were very slim. Ashworth struggled with the decision. Even though it was against orders, when faced with the alternatives, he decided they would drop the bomb by radar if they had to.[28]

When *Bockscar* began its bomb run on Nagasaki a few minutes before 11:00 a.m., just as the crew feared, the city was obscured by clouds. Glued to their radar scopes, Buckley and the navigator worked out minor course corrections while Beahan searched in vain for the target below. Two minutes out, Beahan shouted that he still couldn't see the target.

Bockscar droned on with less than a minute to go before they dropped by radar.

"I've got it!" Beahan suddenly yelled. With just 30 seconds left on the bomb run, Beahan found a hole in the clouds and took over with his bombsight.[29] Abe recalled what happened next:

> We let go with the bomb at 11:01 [Nagasaki time], August 9, 1945, an hour, a moment and a day to be remembered … As soon as the bomb was off the ship went into a sharp turn, then a dive to pick up speed. Immediately a flash of light, more intense by far than the one at Hiroshima, filled the plane, crept into every corner, stole up under my goggles and forced my eyes open with its intensity. And again, the sky was filled with it, and all around there was nothing but the light, the light of a color I am unable to describe, partly purple, partly blue, with a touch of red and yellow. A combination of blended, bright colors no artist could paint – or ever has, at least – and no novelist could put it in words – or, again, has yet done.
>
> The ship shuddered, once … twice … three times. Then a brief pause, then a fourth and a fifth blast rocked the ship, knocking some papers from my desk to the floor, nearly pushing me off my seat.
>
> Sweeney leveled out the ship, and I was at the window again, my goggles in my hand, staring out, my eyes still blinking with the intensity of the light. How I got there I don't know. There I was, and I was looking out at a technicolor world and a technicolor sky.
>
> The ball of fire was greater this time, wider and reaching higher into the sky, and the smoke was thicker and blacker and seemed to rise even more rapidly than it had at Hiroshima, and the colors, the browns, the purples, the greens, the yellows, the reds, were brighter. Huge rings of smoke, the circumference of which reached around most of the city, reached hungrily upward. There was another blast, a sixth, and this time the plane seemed to drop several hundred feet and rocked nervously from side to side.

"Hey, Abe," said Barnes, the [bomb] commander's assistant, who was at my side, "we'd better get the hell out of here. That stuff is dangerous."

"Tell it to Sweeney," I answered, and I wasn't gagging. The Major may have heard me, or, more probably it was coincidence, but he kicked the plane over into another dive, and we pulled away. Just in time, not a second too soon to avoid colliding with the great column of smoke which now continued upward, on and on until we couldn't see the top of it any longer; then, as before, the top of the mushroom broke off, sharp and clean, and rushed up and away, and another, smaller mushroom was formed, and below, as we rushed away from the maelstrom, the fires reached toward us, hungrily, and the city was now completely obscured by the smoke, multi-colored, white and grey and black and brown, all at the same time, and the smoke extended far beyond the limits of the city itself, hiding everything from our view, even the port which had been filled with ships, many of them probably already loaded with troops.

"Olivi," I shouted, "Lieutenant, get out the camera. Let's get some pictures of this." Olivi's hands fumbled with the camera, and what we got weren't very clear pictures; the negatives were foggy, like double-exposures, the kind you make for a gag at a party. Only this was no gag and no party. This was a double-exposure of death and destruction. And, looking at the picture, no one would ever laugh. No one would ever even smile.

Another blast, and the ship shuddered again.

"What's that, flak?" Olivi wanted to know.

"Heh," I said. "Heh, heh! Who's able to man a gun down there? Dead Japs, maybe? Japs with wings?"

"Oh, yeah," Olivi answered. "I can see what you mean."

We circled the area, just once, and fast; our speedometer showed 200, but it seemed to me we weren't moving at all; we appeared to be caught in a huge magnet, drawing us closer and closer to that still-rising column of smoke. The Major pushed out the throttles; we were at top speed now, but still going slow. Crawling.

"I've never seen anything like it," said the [bomb] commander. He paused, shuddered as if he'd had a sudden chill, then added, speaking with a strange, hesitant emphasis, "and I hope I never do again."

"I guess it's something we'll never forget," said Barnes who was just behind us. "I know I never will."

"Don't worry," I replied. "It'll stay with us, what we've just seen. I mean we don't have to worry about forgetting a single detail."

"No, I guess not," Barnes added, a peculiar, faraway look in his eyes. "I guess we won't have to worry about that."

We were speeding away now, but the smoke was still rising, and a second mushroom had broken off the column, and a third was rapidly forming again.

"Better get your report out, Abe," said Sweeney.

"Yeah, guess you're right. Better get my report out." I was a little dazed, from shock and fright and surprise. It was the greatest moment of my Army career, the first time – and the only one, I'm sure – when the whole world, hundreds, thousands, millions of people – were waiting for my report. Back at Tinian they had no idea what had happened to us; they may have thought – we found out later they had – that we'd never reached our destination. After all, we were two and a half hours overdue; we had spent close to two hours over the Empire dropping one bomb. No American plane had been over enemy territory for so long a period during the entire war. That we survived was, again, the luck of the gods. Or, more likely, the stupidity of the Japs. In any case, we'd set a second record that day, not only in dropping a bomb, but in sweating out the possibility of enemy action for a longer time than any crew in any theater of war – ever. We had, therefore, gained a double victory.

It was 12:15 [Tinian time] when I sent my long-to-be-remembered message. The mission was a success; the new, improved atomic bomb – "Fat Boy," it was called by the brass, to distinguish it from "Little Boy," which was the unofficial name of the first bomb – had succeeded. Nagasaki was obliterated. Thousands had died an instant death, and more thousands would die later, much later and much more painfully.[30]

* * *

Two hours after they dropped their bomb on Nagasaki, *Bockscar* was flying on fumes as it circled over a busy airfield on Okinawa, but no one was answering Sweeney's urgent radio calls for landing instructions. Abe tried on his radio set, but he couldn't raise anyone, either. In desperation, Sweeney finally decided that they were coming in to land with or without clearance. He yelled back to Olivi to get ready to start shooting off the signal flares to alert the control tower.

As Sweeney brought *Bockscar* around and lined up for landing, Olivi began shooting off the flares as fast as he could. The color of each flare signified a certain type of emergency, such as wounded on board, and Olivi was shooting off every flare they had in an attempt to clear the runway. Back in the aft compartment, the crew smelled the smoke and thought they were on fire.

The fireworks display worked, and the runway cleared as Sweeney brought *Bockscar* in for a "hot" landing. Throwing the props into reverse, *Bockscar* roared to a stop just before it reached the end of the runway. "Bless those reversible props," Abe said to himself. When Kuharek later measured the remaining fuel, he discovered that they only had five minutes of fuel left when they landed.[31]

"You all right?" an out-of-breath captain shouted up into the cockpit, expecting the worst. "Anybody hurt? Anything wrong?"

"We're fine," Sweeney answered. "Nobody's hurt. Nothing's wrong. We're just fine."

"You heard the news?" the captain asked.

"I think so," Sweeney said. "I think we know all about the news."

"Russia's declared war on Japan," the captain said. "And, oh yeah, a couple of hours ago they dropped another atomic bomb. On Nagasaki."

"No kidding," Sweeney said. "On Nagasaki. Well, I'll be a son of a bitch."

"We'll all be sons of bitches," said Buckley. "Won't we, fellows?"

"Yeah," Abe and his crewmates agreed. "We'll all be sons of bitches."[32]

25

The Sacred Decision

Between August 9 and 10, Lieutenant General Torashiro Kawabe, the Vice Chief of the Imperial Japanese Army General Staff, wrote the following entries in his diary as the Supreme Council for the Direction of the War met in Tokyo:

1. Soviets finally started this morning [declared war against Japan]. My estimate was wrong. However, now that things have come to this end, we can give no thought to peace. We should have expected at least partly such an event during the war. There is nothing to reflect on now. We simply have to rely on the honor of the Japanese people and continue fighting. I was very cautious and almost cowardly in approaching [war with the Soviets], once however this has come to pass, I can never think of peace or surrender. Whatever the end, we have no choice but to try. I confirmed my decision and came to the office.
2. The Vice Minister of the Army Matsumoto also visited me and he did not oppose my decision.
3. After I came to the office, I prepared a memo as follows about what came to my mind: Decision: No change with regard to continuing the war (with the United States as the main enemy).

Actions to take:
1. Within the whole nation we should declare martial law. I will push for this and if necessary we will change the government and the Army and Navy will take control.
2. As for operations, all the overseas armies and air general army understand their missions and will conduct strong resistance along the Manchurian border line. When the time comes to abandon Manchuria, the main formations will withdraw to southern Korea. China will be left generally in the present status. Those in Mongolia should gradually retreat to North China.
3. About the Manchurian Emperor, he should be moved to Japan.
4. Measures to stop unrest among the military units. One means is a statement from the Minister of the Army.

    I waited for the Chief of the Army General Staff to come to the office and explained my proposals to him. As usual he did not show a clear indication of his views. However, he did not express any disagreement. I do not wish to "make waves" at this time and decided to wait and see as the situation develops and also to await further information.

5.   I heard that there would be a meeting of the Supreme War Direction Council at 1030 and visited General Anami at the office of the Army Minister. He was cheerful as usual, he told me: "Good, I'll take your opinion as representative of the entire Army General Staff." I said, "I hope you do well in today's conference, the meeting should be very stormy." Then the minister answered: "It will be rough, but I will risk my life," and after saying this he stood up. He said to himself, "If what I insist can not be accepted I will resign and have myself conscripted into a unit in China so I can fight there." And then he laughed and showed his high spirit. Some people might say that he lacks ability and he is too optimistic or he is possessed by something, but I thought that he was really dependable in such a difficult situation, keeping up his spirit and charging ahead.[1]

On the morning of August 9, Japan's six-member Supreme Council for the Direction of the War held its first meeting following the attack on Hiroshima. With the creation of such a devastating weapon, Foreign Minister Shigenori Togo believed that the atomic bomb now offered a reason for the military to terminate the war, and he proposed to accept the Potsdam Declaration with the condition that the Emperor would remain in power.

General Korechika Anami, the Army Minister, rejected Togo's proposal and insisted upon the continuation of the war. If there was "room for negotiations," however, Anami argued that to maintain the national polity, Japan should insist upon four demands to end the war: the Emperor's position would be guaranteed, there would be no Allied occupation of Japan, Japan's armed forces would disarm themselves, and the Japanese Government would prosecute the country's alleged war criminals.[2] Both the Army and the Navy General Staff Chiefs concurred with Anami's position, splitting the council into two opposing groups.

After several hours of debate, the council received word that afternoon that a second atomic bomb had just been dropped on Nagasaki. The debate continued, but the council was hopelessly deadlocked. Even after two atomic bombs had been dropped on their country, plus the Soviet Union's declaration of war, the council still could not reach a consensus to end the war.

After the meeting concluded, the council members reconvened at 2:30 p.m. for a cabinet meeting at Prime Minister Kantaro Suzuki's residence. This "endless, inconsequential meeting," in the words of one Army officer, stretched on for nine hours, but an agreement on the path forward could not be reached.[3]

General Kawabe wrote in his diary:

The cabinet meeting lasted from 1430 to 2030, with about a one hour recess. The results of this are not known to me at this time as I write this diary, but there were forceful arguments like the big waves smashing into a massive rock which was the insistence made by the Army Minister. This is the atmosphere I can surmise.[4]

With the members of both the cabinet and the Supreme Council still deadlocked after a day of meetings, Prime Minister Suzuki and Foreign Minister Togo rushed to the Imperial Palace and were immediately granted an audience with the Emperor. After informing Emperor Hirohito that a decision to end the war was not forthcoming from either the Supreme Council or the cabinet, Suzuki proposed convening an Imperial Conference that night to break the impasse. This was an unprecedented move because the council and the cabinet were supposed to achieve unanimity before presenting a matter and their decision to the Emperor for his sanction. To bring a matter before the Emperor, who the Japanese regarded as a living God, that was still open to debate was unheard of, but there were no other options. The Emperor nodded in approval of Suzuki's plan.[5]

Just before midnight, the council members assembled in the Emperor's air raid shelter buried beneath a hill next to the Imperial Palace. Protected by thick concrete walls and massive steel doors, the musty air inside the wood-paneled conference room was sweltering as the council members took their seats behind two parallel tables and prepared to present their cases to the Emperor. The arguments had not changed since the first meeting 14 hours earlier: to accept the Potsdam terms with one or four conditions attached, or to continue the war.

At the head of the room, behind a small table draped with an elegant golden brocade and a large gold screen for a backdrop, a simple wooden chair awaited the arrival of the Emperor. In all, 11 men sat rigidly in silence until rising to bow as the Emperor, impeccably dressed in his Army uniform, entered the room and took his seat.

General Kawabe wrote in his diary:

> Late in the evening there was an Imperial Conference. The Chief of the General Staff attended. The Army Minister after the Diet meeting joined the Imperial Conference and did not return to the office. At 2000, the Vice Chief of the Navy General Staff Onishi came to visit me. He said that morale of the Navy General Staff remained still high and expressed the hope that the ministry department on the Army side would strongly support pushing forward [continuing the war]. After Onishi departed I laid myself on the sofa in my room and awaited the return of the Chief of the Army General Staff … I started thinking of the fortunes of this Imperial nation which could be determined within these few hours. Even if we continue the war, I will die and even if we reach peace, we will perish. I thought that it is better to continue the war so that the whole nation will perish in this land and maintain the everlasting greatness of the Japanese race. Without this determination how could we find the way out in this state of death.[6]

After the full text of the Potsdam Declaration was read aloud for the Emperor, followed by Prime Minister Suzuki summarizing the day's meetings and the impasse over the conditions Japan should seek to end the war, Foreign Minister Togo stated his case for accepting the Potsdam terms.

"The military situation is now more favorable to the United States and Britain given the current state of the enemy forces and because of Soviet participation in the war, so it is difficult for us to demand that they change the terms of the [Potsdam] ultimatum any further," Togo said. "From their standpoint, it seems there is no room for compromise through negotiations."

Togo went on to say that it would not be reasonable to add too many conditions to their acceptance of the Potsdam terms, and then he explained why three of the four suggested demands should be abandoned or negotiated at a later date. "However, our position about the Imperial House is non-negotiable, because it will be the fundamental basis for the future development of our nation," Togo said, seeking to ensure the future of the Emperor. "Therefore, it is essential that our demands focus upon this [one] issue."

"I totally agree," Navy Minister Yonai said.

"I totally disagree," retorted Army Minister Anami.

While Anami agreed that the Emperor must be preserved, he again rejected Togo's proposal because Japan would "lose its life as a moral nation" if they accepted the Potsdam Declaration. Even if they had to accept the declaration, Anami argued that their four conditions must be accepted by the Allies, and he could not agree with the idea of making a proposition to "an immoral nation like the Soviet Union" to end the war.

"We should live up to our cause even if our hundred million people have to die side by side in battle," Anami added. "We have no choice other than to continue the war by all means. I am confident that we are ready for the battles. I am sure we are well prepared for a decisive battle on our mainland even against the United States."

Anami then warned that Japan's armed forces, which were spread out across Asia and the Pacific, "might not be willing to retreat unconditionally," and that they "may well face a civil war at home" with those determined to fight the war to the end.

The Chief of the Army General Staff agreed with Anami. "We are prepared for a decisive battle on our mainland," General Yoshijiro Umezu said. "Although the Soviet entry into the war is disadvantageous to us, we are still not in a situation where we should be forced to agree to an unconditional surrender. If we surrender unconditionally now, we have no excuse to make to those who have sacrificed their lives during the war." At the minimum, Umezu added, the four conditions should be included before any concessions were made.

The President of the Privy Council, Kiichiro Hiranuma, then spoke up and said that he wanted to pose some questions before expressing his own views on the situation. After questioning Togo about the past attempts to seek the Soviet Union's mediation with the Allies for peace terms and the matter of war criminals, Hiranuma turned to the Army Minister and the Chief of the Army General Staff. "You claim that we can still pursue the war but I have doubts because air raids will go on every day and every night," Hiranuma said. "And are you confident in our defense against atomic bombs?"

"Though we haven't made sufficient progress so far in dealing with air raids, we should expect better results soon since we have revised our tactics," Umezu said. "But there is no reason we should surrender to our enemies as a result of air raids."

Hiranuma went on to question the Navy Minister and Prime Minister Suzuki before expressing his own opinion. What mattered most, Hiranuma said, was the preservation of the *kokutai*, the "body of the nation," Japan's national polity. The four conditions that General Anami argued for sounded reasonable to Hiranuma, but if there was "no hope for negotiations," or if they were confident in their battle plans, then he felt that Japan "must continue the war."

"In summary, I argue that we must push forward if we are confident; if not, we will not be able to continue the war however strong our Army and Navy are," Hiranuma said. "And we have to preserve the *kokutai* and maintain the Imperial House at any rate, even if the whole nation must die in the war."

After hours of debate, the council members were still hopelessly deadlocked. That left the matter up to the only person in the room who could break the impasse. "I deeply regret that we could not reach a consensus despite the deliberations for many hours," Prime Minister Suzuki said. "This matter is extremely important and it is indeed a critical question as the President of the Privy Council described. Since opinions are still divided, we have no choice but to ask for the *seidan* [the Emperor's sacred decision]."

Rising from his seat, Suzuki presented himself before the Emperor and declared: "We would ask for *go-seidan* and accept His Majesty's opinion as the final decision of the council."

As the Emperor stood to render his sacred decision, the council members leapt to their feet and bowed as the Emperor began to speak. "I have given serious thought to the situation prevailing at home and abroad and have concluded that continuing the war can only mean destruction for the nation and a prolongation of bloodshed and cruelty in the world," the Emperor said. "I cannot bear to see my innocent people suffer any longer. Ending the war is the only way to restore world peace and to relieve the nation from the terrible distress which it is burdened."

Citing the Army's failure to complete the promised fortifications along Kujukuri Beach to defend Tokyo against the coming invasion, the Emperor had harsh words for those asserting that the "key to national survival lies in a decisive battle in the homeland." The experiences of the past, the Emperor pointed out, showed that "there had always been a discrepancy between plans and performance." With the beach fortifications months behind schedule, and the equipment for the troops who would be fighting there insufficient, how could Japan "repel the invaders" when the enemy landed?

"I cannot help feeling sad when I think of the people who have served me so faithfully, the soldiers and sailors who have been killed or wounded in far-off battles, the families who have lost all of their worldly goods – and often their lives as well – in the air raids at home," the Emperor continued. "It goes without saying that it is unbearable for me to see the brave and loyal fighting men of Japan disarmed. It is equally unbearable that others who have rendered me devoted service should now be punished as instigators of the war."

"Nevertheless," the Emperor concluded, "the time has come when we must bear the unbearable." The Emperor then rendered his sacred decision to accept the Potsdam terms with the one condition outlined by Foreign Minister Togo.[7] As the Emperor wiped the tears away from his face with a white glove, the council members, overcome with emotion, burst into wails. It was exactly 2:30 in the morning.[8]

* * *

To carry out the Emperor's will, the cabinet quickly reconvened and voted to accept the Potsdam terms with the condition that the Emperor would remain in power. General Anami had doubts that the Americans could be trusted, and he stated to the other cabinet members that unless there was "positive evidence that the royal family can be preserved," the Army would continue the war.[9]

Anami then asked Prime Minister Suzuki a pointed question: if Japan could not confirm that the "sovereign power of the Emperor will be recognized," would he accept the policy of continuing the war? In a low voice, Suzuki answered yes. If the future of the Emperor could not be assured, Japan would continue fighting.[10]

Later that morning, General Kawabe wrote in his diary:

> If I am allowed to make presumptuous remarks, the Emperor's decision was not the result of the arguments in the Imperial Conference (again this is only my presumption). In essence, His Majesty has no expectation of favorable results in future operations. In short, His Majesty has lost completely his trust in the armed forces. And this opinion is probably not just limited to His Majesty. It may be that the mistrust of the armed forces that has

accumulated in both His Majesty and among the civilians has only been finally articulated in an absolute and clear manner in His Majesty's words.

What acute pain is in my heart as a member of the armed forces. What a pity that none of the leaders of the Army and Navy could say that they could guarantee certain victory in the future. Both Army and Navy General Staff Chiefs who are supposed to assist His Majesty were not able to promise certain victory in the future. I heard that they said: "Although we can not promise a certain victory we can not say that there will be certain defeat." What indecisive words! Note I am not criticizing that statement. I am shocked that their statement is a picture of reality. I myself insisted that we continue fighting and kept encouraging myself. However, if I had been asked whether I could assure certain victory, what answer could I have given that would have differed much from those words issued by the two chiefs of the general staffs? I was bound by the feeling "I do not want to surrender. I do not want to admit I am defeated, even in the face of death."[11]

While the cables announcing Japan's conditional acceptance of the Potsdam terms were slowly making their way through diplomatic channels to the Allies, General Anami returned to the Army Ministry to brief his senior staff officers. "I do not know what excuse I can offer but since it is the decision of His Majesty that we accept the Potsdam proclamation there is nothing that can be done," Anami said to his men, who were shocked not only by the Emperor's decision, but by his loss of faith in the Army. "The really important consideration is that the Army act in an organized manner. Your individual feelings and those of the men under you must be disregarded."

Anami then warned his officers that the war was not over yet: "Since the Imperial decision is predicated upon the assumption that the Allies will guarantee the preservation of our national polity, it is too soon to say that the war has already ended. The Army must therefore be prepared either for war or for peace."[12]

Later that day, the Domei News Agency announced in a radio broadcast to the world that in accordance with the Emperor's wishes to "restore the general peace" and "put an end to the untold sufferings engendered by the war," the Japanese Government was ready to accept the Potsdam terms, but with "the understanding that the said declaration does not comprise any demand which prejudices the prerogatives of His Majesty as a Sovereign Ruler."[13]

The decision to openly broadcast the announcement was a shrewd calculation by Japan's Foreign Office. Since the official cables would be slow in reaching the Allies through diplomatic channels, it was reasoned that broadcasting the announcement would not only prevent a third atomic bomb from being dropped on Japan, but the news would be cause for celebration as it quickly spread among the Allied peoples, and it could compel their governments to accept Japan's conditional offer. To get the announcement past the Army censors, who would never allow the broadcast to go through, the Foreign Office secretly directed Domei to translate the message into English and transmit it in Morse code. By the time the Army learned about the broadcast the next morning, the announcement had spread across the world.[14]

When news of the broadcast reached the White House, hours before the official cable arrived through the Swiss Government, President Truman summoned Admiral Leahy and Secretaries Byrnes, Stimson and Forrestal to discuss Japan's offer. Huddled in the Oval Office later that morning, as a cheering crowd grew outside the White House, Truman turned to each man for their opinion on two fundamental questions: could they allow the Emperor to continue and still expect to eliminate the warlike spirit in Japan, and could they even consider a message with so large a "but" as the kind of unconditional surrender they had fought for?[15]

Secretary of War Stimson had always felt that it would be advantageous to retain the Emperor because he was the "only symbol of authority which all Japanese acknowledged," which would be critical for the capitulation of Japan's armed forces. Admiral Leahy concurred and said Japan's proposal should be accepted, because they would be able to "use the Emperor in effecting the surrender."[16] With Soviet forces driving through Manchuria, Stimson also believed that it was important to accept the surrender as quickly as possible before the Soviets could get near the Japanese homeland and lay claims to occupy it.[17]

Secretary of State Byrnes was much less certain that anything less than unconditional surrender should be accepted. It should be the United States, Byrnes argued, not Japan that should state the conditions of the surrender. Secretary of the Navy Forrestal then suggested that in their formal reply, the United States could indicate its willingness to accept, but could "define the terms of surrender in such a manner that the intents and purposes of the Potsdam Declaration would be clearly accomplished."[18]

The President agreed, and Byrnes drafted a reply which stated that from the moment of surrender, the authority of the Emperor and the Japanese Government "shall be subject to the Supreme Commander of the Allied powers." The Emperor would remain on the throne for the time being, but the ultimate form of Japan's new post-war government, and what role the Emperor would have – if any – as part of that new government, would be "established by the freely expressed will of the Japanese people."[19]

On August 11, with the concurrence of Britain, China and the Soviet Union, the official reply was handed to the *Chargé d'Affaires* of the Swiss Legation in Washington for transmission to Tokyo. The future of the Emperor would be left for the Japanese people to decide.

*   *   *

"For God's sake, let's get some sleep," Abe said, as someone shook his shoulder. It was still dark outside, but for some reason all of the lights inside the hut were on as Abe glanced at his watch.

It was 5:30 a.m. "Wake up, Abe," Gallagher said. "There's a strike going out; briefing at 0600." As Abe slowly pulled himself out of his bunk and reached for his shoes and socks, he joined the chorus of his crewmates in cursing the Japanese, the U.S. Army, the Air Corps, the officers responsible for the mission, and anyone who would wake someone up at 5:30 in the morning. Abe was on his third cup of coffee that morning before he said a pleasant word to anyone.[20]

The date was August 14, 1945. It had been three days since the Allies replied to Japan's surrender offer, and with no response yet from Tokyo, the 20th Air Force was about to resume its bombing operations in a very big way. After news first broke of Japan's surrender offer on August 10, General Spaatz contacted General Norstad in Washington by teletype for guidance on the mission scheduled for that night. Since there was no official confirmation that Japan had surrendered, Norstad said the mission should proceed as planned. When Spaatz later decided to cancel the mission due to bad weather, it was misinterpreted by the press as a cease-fire order. This created a "very delicate and critical problem" for the President, General Marshall advised Spaatz by teletype the next day, because a resumption of the bombing would then give the appearance that the negotiations had failed and would lead to "a storm of publicity and

confusing views." To avoid any more confusion, Spaatz was ordered to cease all bombing operations at once and recall any B-29s that were already on the way to their targets.[21]

For the B-29ers, the Domei news flash had taken everyone by surprise and led to a "delir-
ious celebration" throughout the Marianas. But then, as the hopeful hours turned into nerve-
wracking days and no official surrender announcement came, the celebration quickly gave way
to anger. Everyone knew the war was over, but the war didn't seem to be ending.[22]

By August 13, with only silence from the Japanese, Marshall dispatched an urgent message to
MacArthur and Spaatz: "The President directs that we go ahead with everything we've got."[23]

The B-29s were back in the war again. Following up by teletype, General Arnold directed
Spaatz to resume his operations against Japan "at once" and wanted to know the maximum
number of B-29s he could send out. "1,000 looks like a very good minimum to me," Arnold
said. "Can you reach it? What can you do about this at once?" In his typical fashion, Arnold
was wasting no time and demanded immediate action. "The maximum number possible must
be sent over Tokyo so as to impress the Japanese officials that we mean business and are serious
in getting them to accept our peace proposals without delay," Arnold continued. "What number
can be used effectively over Tokyo?" Spaatz replied that Tokyo was "not a good target except
for the atomic bomb," and then he listed the targets they had selected. Over the next 24 hours,
Spaatz would be sending "at least 900 airplanes" to attack targets across Japan.[24]

As Abe and his crewmates walked into the briefing room on the morning of August 14, they
quickly realized the enormity of the strikes that were set to begin that afternoon and would
carry on late into the night. "The briefing room was crowded this time; this was to be no three-
plane mission," Abe recalled. "It was to be the greatest air-sea blast in history, with hundreds of
planes ... no one knew how many; planes were to take off not only from Tinian but from bomber
bases all over the Pacific, and to be supplemented by a surface fleet that would strike along the
entire coast of Japan."[25]

While Abe was taking his seat in the briefing room that morning, back in Tokyo, General
Anami was just finishing breakfast with Field Marshal Shunroku Hata, the commander of
the Second Army that was headquartered at Hiroshima. At Anami's request, Hata had flown
in from Hiroshima to personally report on the effects of the atomic bomb, and to urge the
Emperor to reject the Allied reply and continue the war.

During their investigation, Hata's team discovered that survivors whose skin was covered
in dark clothing had suffered flash burns through the fabric, but curiously, the "blast had been
reflected by white clothing." This was observed on survivors who were wearing both black and
white clothing at the time of the blast and suffered burns beneath the black clothing but not the
white. Hata's investigation also found that the bomb had not affected the roots of sweet potato
plants "just an inch or so below the surface." This indicated that "defenses were possible against
the bomb," Hata said. Anami was delighted by the revelation and insisted that Hata inform the
Emperor and urge His Majesty to resist the calls to surrender.[26]

Elsewhere in Tokyo that morning, and in other major cities across Japan, B-29s were dropping millions of leaflets that contained a copy of Japan's surrender offer and the reply from the
Allies, all of which had been kept secret from the Japanese people:

> These American planes are not dropping bombs on you today. American planes are drop-
> ping these leaflets instead because the Japanese Government has offered to surrender and
> every Japanese has a right to know the terms of that offer and the reply made to it by the

United States Government on behalf of itself, the British, the Chinese, and the Russians. Your government now has a chance to end the war immediately. You will see how the war can be ended by reading the two following official statements.[27]

At the Imperial Palace, a chamberlain rushed down the halls to the room of Koichi Kido, the Lord Keeper of the Privy Seal and Emperor Hirohito's closest adviser. Rousing him from bed, the chamberlain handed Kido one of the leaflets that had just fallen on Tokyo. As he examined the leaflet and its verbatim copy of Japan's offer to surrender, Kido was immediately "stricken with consternation" when he realized what would happen if the leaflets fell into the hands of the troops, who knew nothing about the surrender negotiations with the Allies.[28] The leaflet Kido held in his hands that morning could now destroy any hope of peacefully ending the war.

*   *   *

When the Allied reply was received on August 12, the same arguments that had so divided the Supreme Council and the cabinet before the Emperor rendered his sacred decision had once again hopelessly deadlocked the members as they deliberated how to respond to the Allies.

Within hours of receiving the reply, the Army and Navy Chiefs of Staff met with the Emperor and advised His Majesty that the terms were "absolutely unacceptable." Japan, they said, had only one alternative: reject the terms and "fight to the very last." With great pleasure, Umezu said, the armed forces would die for the Emperor and their country. Even though "millions of soldiers and sailors would be lost in the last-ditch defense," Umezu saw no other way. The Allied terms were "impossible" and would lead to the "internal destruction" of the country and must be rejected.[29]

When the cabinet ministers met later that day to discuss the Allied reply, Togo opened the meeting with a cogent argument for why the terms should be accepted. While Togo admitted that the Allied reply was not "entirely reassuring" as to the future of the Emperor, he found it inconceivable that the "overwhelming loyal majority" of the Japanese people would not wish to preserve the Imperial system. Since this question would be left for the Japanese people to decide, Togo believed that the Emperor's position, subject to some modification, "would for all practical purposes remain secure."[30] To demand any changes in the wording of the reply with regards to the Emperor would probably fail, Togo warned, and to continue debating the point with the Allies would give rise to those calling for the abolition of the Imperial system altogether, in which case Japan would have no choice but to break off the negotiations and continue the war. For this reason, Togo concluded that Japan should accept the Allied reply as it stood.[31]

As reasonable as Togo's argument was, General Anami quickly rose to counter. For the Army Minister, and others at the meeting, the Allied reply was totally unacceptable because it stated that the authority of the Emperor would be "subject to" the Supreme Commander of the Allied powers, and that Japan's new form of government would be decided by the Japanese people. Since Japan's national polity had been handed down by the Gods, Anami and others argued, it could not be put to the people to decide.[32]

As Anami continued his assault against the reply and launched into his old arguments against disarmament and occupation, Togo became heated and declared that adding further stipulations would be "highly improper" and would only lead the Allies to conclude that Japan intended to break off the negotiations. To revive old questions that had already been resolved by the Emperor's sacred decision was to show disrespect for that decision, Togo added, and to advocate a continuation of the war by raising these issues again, which would likely produce a break-down in the negotiations, was acting "in a manner contrary to reason."[33]

Despite Togo's impassioned arguments, he was failing to sway the other cabinet members to his side. "The situation looks extremely bad," Togo confided to his Vice Minister over a phone call during a break from the meeting. "It's a difficult problem. The atmosphere at the meeting is definitely against acceptance of the Allied note."[34]

As the cabinet meeting continued, Togo was shocked when Prime Minister Suzuki suddenly began spouting the same hardline views as General Anami. Not only was the Allied reply unsatisfactory because it did not guarantee the preservation of Japan's polity, Suzuki said, but there was also the issue of disarmament. "If disarmament is to be forced on Japan, there is no alternative to continuing the war!" Suzuki said. "To be disarmed by the enemy would be unbearable for a Japanese soldier and under such circumstances the Allied reply is unacceptable."[35]

If the Allies refused to concede to their demands, then Suzuki declared that there would be "no other way than to fight it out."[36]

Togo was livid over Suzuki's wavering opinions, but he respectfully countered that while the Prime Minister's views were "worthy of consideration," unless there was some prospect for victory, Japan should negotiate for peace. By now Togo recognized that his position was untenable, so to stall for more time before a formal vote on the matter could be taken, he proposed that the meeting be adjourned until the official communication was received from the Allies. The ministers agreed and the meeting was quickly adjourned.[37]

As the ministers were leaving, Togo took Suzuki aside into another room and unloaded on the Prime Minister. "What are you thinking of?" Togo fumed. "I completely disagree with you. This is no time to bring up the question of disarmament. Incessant bandying of words over the ultimatum from the enemy is profitless. Unless we are prepared for a breakdown of negotiations, there is no alternative but to accept their reply as it stands. As the premier is well aware, the Emperor wants to end the war. It goes without saying that his opinion, as Commander-in-Chief, should prevail."[38]

Only hours before the cabinet meeting, Togo had met with the Emperor to discuss the reply from the Allies. After the two analyzed each point of the message, the Emperor said that he considered the reply to be "satisfactory" and that it "should be accepted as it stood." The Emperor then instructed Togo to inform Suzuki of his wishes, which he did as soon as he left the Imperial Palace. But now Suzuki was openly going against the desire of the Emperor.[39]

"I warn you," Togo said, emphasizing each word to Suzuki, "if you and the cabinet insist on continuing the war I will be forced to report my opposing view directly to the Emperor!"[40]

Later that evening, Suzuki privately met with Koichi Kido, the Emperor's adviser, at the Imperial Palace to discuss the impasse over the reply. Kido understood the argument of those who were "anxious to guard the national polity," but he explained to Suzuki that based upon the careful study by the foreign ministry, there was "nothing objectionable" in the message. There was no alternative but to accept the reply. "If the Potsdam Declaration is rejected at this stage and if the war continues, Japan will have to sacrifice additional millions of innocents, due to bombings and starvation," Kido said. "Even if a serious disturbance occurs on the home front because of accepting the Potsdam terms, we shall have only to sacrifice our lives. Without wavering or hesitation, let us carry out the policy to accept the Potsdam Declaration!"

Kido's willingness to sacrifice his life to carry out the Emperor's desire for peace had stirred something inside Suzuki, who was captivated by his call to action. "Let us do!" Suzuki said, deeply moved by his words.[41] Kido's frankness had brought Suzuki back in line with the Emperor's wishes to end the war, but while the Prime Minister was now fully behind accepting the Allied reply, General Anami and the others still refused to budge.

The next morning, Kido heard those arguments firsthand when General Anami arrived at his office. Anami was "full of bounce" and "smiling brightly" as the two men, who'd known each other for years, exchanged pleasantries, but then Anami turned grave as he began to speak. "Japan will be destroyed if the Allies' demands are accepted," Anami said. "We must by all means have the Emperor reconsider and conduct a final decisive battle in the homeland." If Japan made one last effort, Anami believed it would be possible to end the war more to their advantage.

"That will not do," Kido said, as he repeated the same argument he used to convince Suzuki that the Allied reply was acceptable. Anami, however, could not be swayed. Kido then pointed out, hypothetically, what would happen if the Emperor rescinded Japan's peace offer and issued a proclamation for a final decisive battle. "Remember, Japan has already notified the Allies that we are willing to accept the Potsdam terms," Kido said. "If the Emperor should now turn his back on this official note, the Allies and the rest of the world would then regard him as a fool or a lunatic. It is unbearable to have His Majesty insulted that way. You may have your own ideas, but I have no alternative but to follow my own policy."

As he exhaled a long drag from his cigarette, Anami's demeanor suddenly changed. "I understand your position quite well, *Kido-san*," Anami said, laughing. "I knew you would say something like that." Anami then paused, his face turning grim, and said: "But the atmosphere in the Army is indeed tense."

As Anami stubbed out his cigarette and left, Kido pictured the Army Minister "forcibly holding the lid on a furiously boiling cauldron." The young officers under Anami were rumored to be so incensed by the surrender offer that a coup was imminent, and Kido himself was said to be targeted for assassination for being a "false counselor" to the Emperor and advocating peace. How long could Anami control his men before they boiled over?[42]

A few minutes later that morning, the commander of the Kempeitai, Lieutenant General Sanji Okido, suddenly appeared in the Prime Minister's office. Suzuki had not arrived yet, so Okido warned his chief cabinet secretary that if Japan surrendered, the Army would rise in revolt against the government. "We cannot take the responsibility for what happens," Okido snapped. "The Kempeitai urges that the war be continued. Tens of millions of lives may be sacrificed, but we must not surrender!"[43]

In the hours that followed, both the Supreme Council and the cabinet met to further discuss the Allied reply, but just as before, they were still deadlocked. After some nine hours of debate, a discouraged Suzuki addressed his cabinet: "I admit that when I first read the Allied reply I did not see how it could be accepted. I was resolved to fight to the last, scorching the earth behind our heroic defenders." But then Suzuki explained that after he reread the note again and again, he decided that the "Allies had no sinister purpose in mind." Since "His Majesty's heart cried out for one thing only – the end of the war and restoration of peace," Suzuki said it was his desire and duty to follow the Imperial will. He would therefore report to the Emperor and again ask for his sacred decision.[44]

After the meeting was adjourned, General Anami went to Suzuki's office where he found the Prime Minister talking with a visitor, a Navy doctor. "Mr. Prime Minister, would you please wait another two days before calling an Imperial Conference?" Anami asked.

"Now is the time Anami; we must not miss the opportunity," Suzuki said. "I am sorry." Realizing that further discussion was useless, Anami silently bowed and left the Prime Minister's office.

"Why not wait for a while?" the doctor asked after Anami left. "Would it matter so much?"

"Any delay would be dangerous," Suzuki sighed. "If we miss this chance for ending the war, the Russians may come not only into Korea, Manchuria, and Sakhalin Island, but into Hokkaido [Japan's northern home island]. This would be a fatal blow to the very foundation of our country. No, we must settle this business while the negotiations are confined to one primary party, the United States."

"But Mr. Prime Minister, General Anami may kill himself," the doctor said.

"Yes," Suzuki said, pausing at his office door before leaving. "That is possible. I am sorry."[45]

Later that evening, Togo privately met with fellow Supreme Council members Umezu and Toyoda. After two hours of talks, during which the two chiefs of staff continued their arguments from earlier in the day, Vice Admiral Takijiro Onishi suddenly burst into the room. Onishi was the Vice Chief of the Navy General Staff and the father of the Kamikaze. "Let us formulate a plan for certain victory, obtain the Emperor's sanction, and throw ourselves into bringing the plan to realization," Onishi said, with tears in his eyes, after learning that the Emperor had lost faith in the armed forces. "If we are prepared to sacrifice 20,000,000 Japanese lives in a special attack [Kamikaze] effort, victory shall be ours!"[46]

Onishi's plea only elicited silence from the chiefs, so he turned to Togo and demanded his opinion. "If only we had any real hope of victory," Togo said quietly, "no one would for a moment think of accepting the Potsdam Declaration; but winning one battle will not win the war for us."[47]

Leaving Onishi behind to sulk, Togo stopped by the Foreign Ministry on his way home to look through the latest news and telegrams from Japan's overseas offices. After days of silence from his government, the vitriol Togo saw in the foreign news against Japan for stalling the negotiations impressed upon him the "growing gravity of our peril." Japan was running out of time.[48]

During the ride home that night, Togo thought more about Onishi's plan. "Even if we offered the sacrifice of twenty million Japanese lives, they would but fall easy prey to machines and gunfire," Togo concluded. "We could bear anything, if it promised a return; the arrows and bamboo spears of which the military men were prating promised none. The soldiers' ignorance of the nature of modern warfare was beyond my understanding."[49]

By the time he arrived home, Togo was determined that no further delay could be tolerated. A final decision on their reply to the Allies must be reached the next day.

Now, as the leaflets rained down across Tokyo and other cities with the details of Japan's offer to surrender on the morning of August 14, Koichi Kido was "stricken with consternation" because his government's secret surrender negotiations with the Allies had just been exposed to the Japanese people, who had been indoctrinated to believe that sacrificing one's life for the Emperor was the "highest possible calling," and surrender was the ultimate dishonor.[50]

While many Japanese would probably dismiss the leaflets as more American propaganda, Kido knew that a significant number would believe the leaflets because earlier ones that listed the next cities to be bombed were always accurate. Kido recalled after the war:

> In the past two or three days the military services had gradually stiffened their attitude [against peace negotiations] ... Now, here, such leaflets were being distributed at this

juncture! If they should fall into the hands of the troops and enrage them, a military coup would become inevitable and make extremely difficult the execution of the planned policy [to surrender]. It would bring about the worst possible situation for our country.[51]

The only way to avert a disaster now would be to immediately convene another Imperial Conference before the fanatics in the armed forces could act. As Kido rushed to arrange an audience with the Emperor to inform him of the new developments, just as he feared, a military plot to overthrow Japan's Government and continue the war was already in motion. Kido would have to act fast.

*   *   *

Later that morning, Abe and his crew took off from Tinian on what everyone hoped would be their last combat mission of the war. Since *The Great Artiste* was still outfitted with its special instrumentation in anticipation of a third atomic strike, the crew was flying another Silverplate B-29 that morning, *Straight Flush*.

"This is going to be like playing soldier," Gallagher said, as the crew winged their way towards Japan with a massive 10,000-pound Pumpkin bomb.

"I know, I know," Captain Albury, the pilot, agreed. "This is boy's stuff; this is for the Scouts. I thought they were saving us for the men's work."

"I hear they've got some more of the atomic babies ready in case this doesn't do the trick," Buckley added.

"Yeah, just in case it's needed," Gallagher said, before pausing. "But if there's any more of that hot stuff to be dropped, I think they ought to let someone else have the experience. I don't think it'd be fair for us to hog all the glory, do you, fellows?"

"No," answered Abe, sarcastically. "We'd be glad to do it, but it just wouldn't be fair for us to have all the breaks. I'll willingly let somebody else do it; I'm no pig; I'll not mind letting someone else get famous, a little famous, anyway."[52]

The rumor Buckley heard about more atomic bombs wasn't that far from the truth. Most of the components for the third atomic bomb were already in place on Tinian, and General Spaatz had already voiced his opinion on what the next target should be. During his teletype conference with Arnold and Norstad earlier that morning, while the Allies were still waiting for Japan's reply, Spaatz made it clear that he wanted to drop the next atomic bomb on Tokyo. "Recommend utmost urgency be given to placing 3rd atomic bomb here to be dropped on Tokyo," Spaatz advised.

"On future Centerboard [atomic bombings], we will keep you advised on time and target," Norstad replied. "We have nothing new in that subject at this time. Your target recommendation is being considered."[53]

After the strike on Nagasaki, General Groves met with General Marshall to discuss their future operations with the atomic bomb. Since Groves was convinced that Japan would surrender soon, they decided to hold all shipments of fissionable material to Tinian until August 13. If the Japanese still had not surrendered by then, the shipments would resume and the third atomic bomb, subject to approval by the President, would be ready to drop in less than a week.

By August 13, the plutonium core for the third bomb was ready and awaiting orders at Los Alamos, but Groves decided to hold the shipment in light of Japan's surrender offer. In the meantime, the Project Alberta personnel on Tinian continued assembling three additional Fat Man units for drop testing and stood ready to prepare the third atomic bomb if the surrender negotiations broke down.[54] In less than three weeks, Los Alamos was also on schedule to produce a new Fat Man bomb approximately every 10 days, and discussions on the most effective use of these bombs, either by dropping them in rapid succession on cities or employing them in a tactical role in support of the invasion forces, were already underway.[55]

Three hours after takeoff, Abe was closely monitoring his radio for a special code word that all the crews had been briefed about. When the code word was transmitted, the crews were to immediately abort their missions, drop their bombs in the ocean and return to base, for it meant that the Japanese had surrendered. The code word for the end of the war was "Utah."[56]

While Abe remained glued to his radio as they closed in on Japan, at the Army Ministry in Tokyo, a steady rush of junior officers flocked to General Anami's office when word spread through the building that he had just returned from a second Imperial Conference with the Emperor. Standing among the officers waiting for the general were some of the very men who were planning a coup to continue the war. The plotters had already approached Anami with their plans for him to assume power by declaring martial law and overthrowing the Suzuki cabinet, but Anami was noncommittal at first. After discussing the matter with General Umezu, he was now firmly against a coup.[57]

As Anami walked into his crowded office that afternoon, having come directly from the Imperial Palace, the general was "noticeably pale" and "choked with emotion" as he prepared to address his officers.[58] During the conference, only three men had spoken against accepting the Allied reply as it stood. Their arguments before the Emperor were brief.

General Umezu:

> I apologize for the unfavorable turn of events which must be a disappointment to Your Majesty. If Japan is to accept the terms of the Potsdam Declaration at this time, the preservation of our national structure becomes a grave issue. Under existing conditions, the national polity would be destroyed. Therefore we would like to determine once more the real intentions of the United States. We have lost the war anyway, so if we can be sure of maintaining our national structure we are ready to resign ourselves. However, if our national polity cannot be preserved, we must be ready to sacrifice the entire nation in a final battle.[59]

Admiral Toyoda:

> There is no certain assurance that we can win victory by continuing the war, but in view of the fact that we have once resolved to fight a decisive battle on the homeland with the entire nation prepared for suicidal warfare, I cannot see why we cannot resolve to negotiate on such a matter as the national polity.[60]

General Anami:

> If it is impossible to question the Allies again about the safety of the Emperor system, it would be better to fight on, for there are still chances to win. And if not win, at least to end the war on better terms than these.[61]

After Anami sat down, the Emperor rose and began speaking:

> I have listened carefully to each of the arguments presented in opposition to the view that Japan should accept the Allied reply as it stands without further clarification or modification, but my own thoughts have not undergone any change. I have surveyed the conditions prevailing in Japan and in the world at large, and it is my belief that a continuation of the war promises nothing but additional destruction. I have studied the terms of the Allied reply and have concluded that they constitute a virtually complete acknowledgment of the position we maintained in the note dispatched several days ago. In short, I consider the reply to be acceptable.
>
> I realize that there are those of you who distrust the intentions of the Allies. That is, of course, quite natural, but to my mind the Allied reply is evidence of the peaceful and friendly intentions of the enemy. The faith and resolution of this nation as a whole, therefore, are factors of paramount importance.
>
> I appreciate how difficult it will be for the officers and men of the Army and Navy to surrender their arms to the enemy and to see their homeland occupied. Indeed, it is difficult for me to issue the order making this necessary and to deliver so many of my trusted servants into the hands of the Allied authorities by whom they will be accused of being war criminals. In spite of these feelings, so difficult to bear, I cannot endure the thought of letting my people suffer any longer. A continuation of the war would bring death to tens, perhaps even hundreds, of thousands of persons. The whole nation would be reduced to ashes. How then could I carry on the wishes of my Imperial ancestors?
>
> The decision I have reached is akin to the one forced upon my Grandfather, the Emperor Meiji, at the time of the Triple Intervention. As he endured the unendurable, so shall I, and so must you.
>
> It is my desire that you, my Ministers of State, accede to my wishes and forthwith accept the Allied reply. In order that the people may know of my decision, I request you to prepare at once an Imperial Rescript so that I may broadcast to the nation. Finally, I call upon each and every one of you to exert himself to the utmost so that we may meet the trying days which lie ahead.[62]

Now Anami had to break the news to his officers that there was no hope of continuing the war. "It was decided at the Imperial Conference this morning to terminate the war," Anami announced to his stunned officers. "I must apologize for not meeting your expectations."

"For what reason did you change your resolve, Minister?" asked one of the men, as the room broke down in tears.

"I could not resist the Emperor's own desires any longer," Anami said after a long pause. "Especially when he asked me in tears to forbear the pain, however severe it might be, I could not but forget everything and accept it. Moreover, His Majesty said he was confident that the national polity would be guaranteed." For those who'd been plotting a coup, Anami had a warning: "Now, if you try to rise in revolt, kill Anami first!"[63]

With those words, the officers fell silent and shuffled out of the Army Minister's office. Anami's pronouncement had convinced many of the plotters to abandon their plans, but a number of the rebel officers were still determined to save Japan from the shame of surrender.[64]

*   *   *

"Son of a bitch," Beahan said, observing the poor results after dropping his Pumpkin bomb on the Toyota Auto Works factory in Koromo. "I guess I've forgotten how to handle this kid stuff."[65]

A few bursts of flak followed Abe and his crew as they departed the target area, but it was all out of range. Down below, after the devastation they witnessed at Hiroshima and Nagasaki, it looked as though their Pumpkin bomb had virtually no effect on the target. "From where we were, it looked as if we'd pelted the city below with bean shooters," Abe recalled. "It seemed as if we'd done nothing at all; we'd flown all this way and risked our necks for no visible result. No columns of smoke, no blazing balls of fire, no instant impact of giant explosion."[66]

While the Koromo strike was "simple and easy" for Abe's crew, it was also their most frightening mission of the war. No one talked about their fears out loud, but Abe could feel the trepidation "in the atmosphere" during the mission. "It's difficult to explain the reason, except that we, all of us, knew that the war was so nearly ended, that we'd had our two tough missions – there couldn't be any tougher than those to Hiroshima and Nagasaki – that we'd really succeeded in knocking them out, that now it was merely a matter of doing a little more waiting," Abe recalled. "Nobody wants to die, ever, of course, but especially nobody wants to die during the last hours of a war."[67]

At the exact moment their Pumpkin bomb was falling on Koromo, 150 miles away in Tokyo, officials from Japan's Home Ministry, who had no idea that their country was about to surrender, were meeting to discuss ways to cope with America's newest weapon. To counter the effects of the atomic bomb, the Home Ministry would instruct the Japanese people to wear white clothes, because "white reflects radiation" from the bomb. "A man clad in white will not sustain burns at a distance, but will be burned if his flesh is exposed," they concluded. "Since white material is unavailable, people are to be instructed to use bedsheets to make clothing. The war will continue."[68]

After nearly 12 hours in the air, Abe and his crew returned to Tinian to find that the war still had not ended. For the entire flight, Abe had been monitoring the radio for the code word "Utah," but the broadcast never came. As they filed into the 509th's briefing hut after the mission, the only "news of any importance" that awaited Abe and his crew were the two Red Cross girls serving coffee and donuts. The sight of real American women lifted everyone's spirits, but it was only a temporary distraction from the pall that hung over the crews. Abe recalled:

> That night everybody on the island who could find a bottle got as drunk as the liquor available would allow. And, in our case, that was quite drunk, really very intoxicated. We kept the radio on, and we listened, between drinks, not very hopefully. There were rumors from Washington and more rumors from Tokyo, and word, unofficially, from Switzerland of an unofficial surrender offer, and more talk about more atomic bombs being dropped ... I went right on drinking. And, I thought, I'll keep drinking, every night, every goddamned day until the goddamned war ends. I'd never understood before why people wanted to drink, but I did then. There are certain things you want to forget and to ignore and not to think about, for a few hours, for a few glorious, forgetful hours, and even the next morning, that's fine, too. So you have a hangover; so your head aches; that's fine; that's dandy. You can concentrate on that instead of what you want to forget.[69]

While Abe and his crewmates were drowning their sorrows that night, back in Tokyo, a small group of rebel officers had launched a coup to overthrow the government and continue the war. Using forged orders to deceive the Imperial Guards into aiding their plot, the rebels succeeded in taking over the grounds of the Imperial Palace for a few hours while the Emperor remained safe in his quarters. Only hours earlier, a phonograph recording had been made of the Emperor reading the Imperial Rescript that terminated the war, which would be broadcast to the Japanese people the next day. The rebel officers knew the odds were against them, but if they could isolate the Emperor from all outside contact and prevent the recording from being broadcast, they believed their actions would inspire the Army to rise up and continue fighting. The rebels would spend hours searching through a maze of darkened rooms in the Household Ministry Building for the recordings, but they were secured in a hidden safe that the troops stood no hope of finding. Ironically, their search efforts were hampered by a city-wide blackout due to an incoming B-29 raid.[70]

By 8:00 a.m. on August 15, the rebellion was over, and order was restored at the Imperial Palace without a shot being fired. The only casualties were two Army officers who were murdered earlier in the night after refusing to cooperate with the plot.[71]

Later that day, at noon, the Emperor's words would be broadcast to the nation and the Japanese people would finally learn that the war had been lost. When it was announced that the Emperor would be addressing the nation, a teacher at the Sophia Catholic University in Tokyo asked his students what they thought the Emperor was going to say. Most of the students thought the Emperor was going to announce that Japan had dropped an atomic bomb on Washington. No one expected to hear that Japan had surrendered.[72]

At the Army Minister's residence, General Anami took his last breath at 8:00 a.m. Unable to bear the shame of defeat, General Anami committed *seppuku*, ritual suicide, to atone for losing the war. Many others would kill themselves in the hours and days following the Emperor's broadcast. (Most Japanese would come to accept defeat and move on with their lives, but the last soldier did not surrender until 1974.)[73]

Back at his hut on Tinian that morning, Abe was outside doing his laundry while a steady stream of B-29s were landing from the previous night's mission. A lot of the crews had rigged up homemade washing machines using whatever parts they could find to do their laundry, but Abe had nothing more than a bar of soap and washbowl. As the radio played inside his hut, Abe halfheartedly scrubbed the grime from his clothes, but nothing really came clean. It was just going through the motions that mattered to Abe and nothing else.

A few minutes after 9:00 a.m., as Abe was hanging his half-clean laundry out to dry on the clothesline, an announcement suddenly came over the radio. It was official: Japan had surrendered. The war was finally over.

After three years in the Army, Abe had thought a lot about what he'd do when he heard that news. But instead of cheering and jumping for joy, Abe calmly finished hanging up his laundry. A few shouts could be heard echoing across the camp as the news broke, but in that moment, the mood was more subdued than celebratory.

"Except for the radio, the hut was almost quiet when I went inside," Abe recalled. "Men seemed to be standing or sitting or lying where they had been when they had first heard the news."

As the news slowly sunk in, Gallagher reached over and shook Abe's hand.

"You happy, Abe?" Gallagher asked, his voice breaking.

"Yeah," Abe said. "I'm happy."

"So am I," Gallagher said. "Only I'm not happy like I thought I'd be. It's not like I thought it'd be at all. You know what I mean?"

"Yeah," Abe said. "I know what you mean."[74]

*   *   *

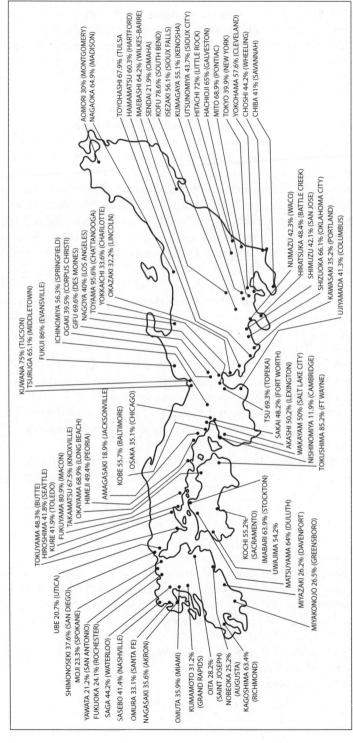

The results of General LeMay's bombing campaign. This map shows the destruction of Japanese cities compared to American cities of a similar size. The destruction of Nagoya alone was equal to 40 percent of Los Angeles being destroyed.

After the war ended, the U.S. Army Air Forces interrogated hundreds of Japanese military, civilian and industrial leaders to gain an insight into the war from the enemy's perspective. Their statements about the B-29 and its devastating effect on Japan's war effort were eye-opening:

"The war was lost when the Marianas were taken away from Japan and when we heard the B-29s were coming out … We had nothing in Japan that we could use against such a weapon … If the B-29s could come over Japan, there was nothing that could be done." Prince Naruhiko Higashi-Kuni

"Without B-29s the defeat of Japan could not have been effected." Rear Admiral Iwao Kawai

"Fundamentally, the thing that brought about the determination to make peace was the prolonged bombing by the B-29s." Prince Fumimaro Konoye

"Superfortresses were the greatest single factor in forcing Japan's surrender. These planes burned out Japan's principal cities, reduced military production by fully 50 percent and affected the general livelihood of the Japanese people." Rear Admiral Toshitano Takata

"It can be said that Japan lost the war only because of the superiority of the Allied air force, without which the Allies would never have won." Rear Admiral Tadao Kato

"The B-29 was the main force that brought about Japan's defeat … During the last stages of the war you started broadcasting the names of the cities to be bombed and it was very effective." Sukehide Kabayama, Publicity Bureau of the Foreign Office

"One of the biggest things leading to the surrender was the bombing of industrial cities of Japan. Your bombing of small industrial cities and the use of fire bombs was very effective." Lieutenant General Masakazu Kawabe

"The result of the mining [of Japan's seaways and harbors] by B-29s was so effective against shipping that it eventually starved the country. I think you probably could have shortened the war by beginning earlier." Captain Kyuzo Tamura

"The people in general began to abandon the effort to continue [the] war as incendiary attacks by B-29s became more frequent and severe. Therefore the final decision [to surrender] may be attributed totally to the Allied air power." Shigeru Yoshitomi, Ministry of Interior

"The destructive power of incendiary attacks against wood-constructed Japanese homes was terrific … An incendiary raid will practically burn out a city … owing to the destruction of large factories and the loss of small factories scattered throughout a city in the way of home industries, the production of parts decreased rapidly and thus hindered the entire war program." Vice Admiral Rokuzo Sugiyama

"I myself recognized the B-29 as a very superior weapon … It seemed to me unavoidable that in the long run Japan would be almost destroyed by air attack so that merely on the basis of the B-29s alone I was convinced that Japan should sue for peace. On top of the B-29 raids came the atomic bomb, immediately after the Potsdam Declaration, which was just one additional reason for giving in and was a very good one and gave us the opportune moment to make open negotiations for peace. I myself, on the basis of the B-29 raids, felt that the cause was hopeless." Prime Minister Kantaro Suzuki[75]

26

The End

On August 24, 2011, I had one of the most unforgettable days of my life: I got to stand in the forward bomb bay of *Bockscar* at the National Museum of the United States Air Force in Dayton, Ohio. I was in Dayton that week to complete a very special mission during the 9th Bomb Group Association's annual reunion, which I was honored to attend as a guest. Since 1987, the veterans who served together in the 9th Bomb Group had been meeting every year to renew old friendships and remember their fallen brothers from the war. The time that I spent with those B-29ers would have a profound and lasting impact on my life.

The events that led me to Dayton that summer, as improbable as they were, all started a year-and-a-half earlier, when I found a large collection of old letters for sale on eBay. The letters had been written during the war by a B-29 tail gunner who served with the 9th Bomb Group on Tinian. They looked like a pretty interesting collection, but with only so much money to spend, they just didn't strike me as something that I needed to save, so I didn't plan to bid on them.

A week later, when the auction was in its final hours, and I was half asleep after a long day at work, for reasons that I still cannot explain, I placed a bid on the letters without thinking about it, and then I went to bed. The next morning, I was surprised to learn that for $57.53, I was now the new owner of all these letters. I had no idea what I was going to do with them, and I kept asking myself why I even bid on them in the first place.

When the package arrived a few days later, I discovered that these were all of the letters that the tail gunner had written home to his mother during the war. There were 150 letters in all, ranging from his first day in the Army to his voyage home after the war, and his mom had hand-numbered each one of them on the envelope in the order they arrived. As I slowly read through the letters, I decided to do some more research on the man who wrote them. Aside from some limited information on the 9th Bomb Group Association's website, there wasn't much to be found about him on the internet. I naturally assumed that the letters came from his estate sale after he passed away, but I couldn't find his obituary anywhere.

Then one night, I read in one of the letters where he asked his parents to send him an ID bracelet. He was very specific about what he wanted engraved on the bracelet, including his hometown. That's when it dawned on me that I should try searching his name and hometown together, which I had not done before. When I clicked "search," I still couldn't find his obituary, but I did find something else: a phone book listing with his address. The address looked very familiar, so I pulled out one of the old envelopes, and I noticed that it was the same exact address that he mailed all of these letters to during the war. Could he really still be alive and living in the same house after all these years?

I wasn't sure what to do next, and I was afraid to just call the phone number out of the blue. If he had passed away, or was in bad health, I didn't want to cause his family any more pain by asking about the letters. I decided that the best thing to do was contact the 9th Bomb Group Association and see if they knew anything about him. I was in for a big surprise: the man who wrote the letters was still very much alive!

When I first read through the letters, I kept thinking to myself how I wish I could have talked to this man, because there were so many questions that I wanted to ask him about his experiences. A couple of days after I contacted his bomb group association, that wish came true when I talked to him on the phone. To actually hear his voice, the man behind the letters, who I thought was dead, was an experience that is simply beyond words. It was like I was reaching back in time.

There were so many questions that I wanted to ask him, but first I had to know one thing: how in the world did his letters end up on eBay?

As incredible as it seems, it turned out that he had no idea that his mother had kept all of his letters after the war, or that they had been hidden away in the attic of his childhood home for the last 65 years. The letters were only found after he hired an auction company to clean out some things in his attic, but no one told him about the old box of letters they discovered as they were going through everything. He never knew that the workers found the letters, or that they took them to be auctioned off with the other things. The person who later bought the letters kept them for a year or so before putting them on eBay, and that's when I found them.

The last time he saw any of these letters was when he mailed them home during the war. Almost 70 years later, you can imagine his surprise when his bomb group association called one day and told him that some guy in Georgia had all of his letters from the war and wanted to talk to him!

As we continued talking on that Sunday afternoon, I knew there was one question that he wanted to ask me. I could tell that he was a humble man and was too polite to ask, so I quickly put his mind at ease. "These are your letters," I said. "They do not belong to me. I'm going to get them back to you." He was thrilled to hear this and even offered to repay me for them, but that was out of the question. His service to our country was more than enough payment, I said.

For some reason these letters had come into my possession, and I considered it an honor to be able to return them to their rightful owner. Little did I know, those letters would change my life.

I always had big dreams, but I never really did anything about them. There was always an excuse, some stupid reason not to act, and I would tell myself that now was not the right time to go chasing after my dreams. Then the months turned into years; then the years turned into a decade.

I was working harder than ever before at my job, but I was going nowhere. Every night after work, when I should have been sleeping, but couldn't, I would lay awake in bed and listen to the song "Down in a Hole" by Alice in Chains, because that's exactly where I was. I was stuck in life. It felt like I was on an endless grind straight to the grave, a one-way path to oblivion, and for what. What was the point? Was this all there was?

I kept thinking to myself that there had to be more to life than this. *There had to be*. A lot of you reading this right now know exactly what I mean.

But then I found these letters. Or maybe the letters *found me*. And the story surrounding them inspired me to finally go after my dreams of becoming a writer.

Those letters are the reason why I'm sitting here right now typing these words. They were also the reason why I had to quit my job at the restaurant after working there for 12 years. There was no other way that I could get the time off from work so I could travel up to Dayton and return the letters. After all the letters had been through, I wasn't going to risk sending them in the mail. I had to return the letters in person, and if that meant that I had to quit my job, then I was going to do it. And that's exactly what I did.

To finally meet this man at the reunion with his fellow B-29ers, and then give him a hug and return his long-lost letters, it was one of the proudest moments of my life. It was worth losing my job over. (Never give up on your dreams. Be bold and dare greatly!)

The day after I returned the letters, the Air Force Museum opened its doors an hour early to give the 9th Bomb Group Association a private viewing of their B-29. As we all gathered next to *Bockscar* that morning, around 50 of us in all, I was shocked when a museum official took down the barrier strap and invited us all to take an up-close look at the bomber. We couldn't get inside the cockpit, of course, but we had free rein to look over and actually touch the airframe. This was a once-in-a-lifetime opportunity to get up close with a Silverplate B-29, and I was going to relish every second of it.

With my camera in hand, I could hardly contain myself as we filed through the open barrier and walked up to the nose of the second-most famous B-29 in history. I stopped for a moment to take a picture of the nose art, but there was really only one place that I wanted to see above all else. Leaving the others behind, I ducked under the fuselage and was soon standing in the open bomb bay where the Fat Man atomic bomb that was dropped on Nagasaki had once hung. For someone like me, I thought this was about as good as it gets, but then it got even better. I think the veterans must have had the same idea as me, because soon there was a steady stream of B-29ers ducking in and out of the bomb bay. I couldn't believe I was actually standing there inside the bomb bay with all of these B-29ers, or how lucky I was to just listen as they reminisced about the war. I was too lost in the moment to realize it at the time, but I would never have another experience like that again for the rest of my life.

It was very dark in the bomb bay and I couldn't see much above me, but the flash from my camera provided some fascinating glimpses. I really wanted to get a good look at the bomb bay tunnel cut-out that was made for the special H-frame and shackle that was needed to carry an atomic bomb, a modification found only on the Silverplate B-29s, but I didn't have a flashlight. Using my camera's flash, I could see that the H-frame and most of the specialized equipment for the bombs were long gone, but some of the electrical junction boxes were still there, and the tunnel cut-out was right above me. After studying these things in old pictures from the war, it was really something to see it all in person.

As I continued snapping pictures, one of the B-29ers pulled out a small flashlight and began inspecting the bomb bay. We both had a good laugh when I complimented him for doing such a thorough pre-flight inspection, and I jokingly asked what else he had hidden away in his pack. His name was Charles Chauncey, and he had this big, fun-loving grin that I'll never forget. Chauncey was the co-pilot of *Goin' Jessie*, a B-29 famous for being the top performing B-29 against Japan after completing 50 straight combat missions without an abort. Chauncey flew 35 missions himself, and on July 9, 1945, his crew had the honor of dropping the 2,000,000th ton of bombs dropped by the Army Air Forces during World War II. Thanks to Chauncey, I was able to see everything in the bomb bay while we chatted about all things B-29. I'll always be grateful to him for sharing some of his stories with me – and his flashlight.[1]

Of all the pictures I took in the bomb bay that morning, my favorite one shows the forward bulkhead hatch and the tunnel cut-out while a B-29er stands below looking up. The window in that hatch is the same one that Abe kept looking back through during their long takeoff roll with the bomb. I just wish that I had known about Abe's story back then. It wasn't until years later that I discovered the little book he wrote in 1946 about his experiences. I'd have given anything to talk to him about the history he witnessed, but that wasn't meant to be.

After all he lived through during the war, Abe was killed in a car accident on his way home from work in 1984. He was only two minutes away from his home when he died.[2]

I wrote Abe's story based on his book and the diary he kept during the war. I hope I did you proud, Abe! Looking back on the time I spent with *Bockscar*, that whole experience is all the more special to me now knowing that Abe flew on this B-29, and our hands had touched the same places on the airframe. The next time I visit *Bockscar*, Abe and his crew will all be in my thoughts.

But as I stood in the bomb bay that morning, my thoughts drifted to another Silverplate B-29, *Laggin' Dragon*, and its crew. I was standing in the very spot where the Fat Man bomb they delivered to Tinian was dropped on Nagasaki. Less than a year earlier, I found four B-29 data plates on eBay that came from the estate of an Air Force veteran. The airman had removed the data plates after the four B-29s in his squadron were retired and stripped of any usable parts before being scrapped. After talking to the seller and researching the serial numbers, I discovered that these data plates came from the last four B-29s in the entire United States Air Force, which were operated by a radar evaluation squadron at Naha Air Base on Okinawa.

I didn't have much money at the time, so I decided not to bid on the first data plate, which didn't have any combat history. But the next data plate the seller listed I had to save at all costs. It came from the last operational B-29 in the U.S. Air Force. After 17 years of service, through World War II, Korea and the Cold War, the Boeing B-29 Superfortress was officially retired by the United States when this B-29, serial number 42-65234, made its final flight on June 21, 1960.[3]

A few years earlier, I found a piece of a cabin insulation blanket that also came from this same B-29, and I always wondered what other pieces might be out there. I never dreamed of finding its actual data plate for sale on eBay, of all places.

The biggest shock of all came a few days later, when the seller listed his two remaining data plates. They were the data plates from two of the Silverplate B-29s assigned to the 509th Composite Group for combat operations during the war, *Luke the Spook* and *Laggin' Dragon*.[4]

In all my years of collecting, I'd never seen anything from a Silverplate B-29 before. I now had the opportunity to actually own a piece of two of them. But to buy these data plates was going to take all the money I could find, just like when I found Sally's things on eBay.

I managed to win the auctions for all three data plates, but after scraping together every last penny I had, I still didn't have enough money to pay for them. To make up for the shortfall, I had to pawn this massive gold bracelet I bought years earlier after watching a few too many episodes of *The Sopranos*. It turned out to be the best dumb purchase I ever made, because gold prices had since skyrocketed, and I could not have bought the data plates without it.

When I held the data plates in my hands for the first time, I wondered if that airman realized the history he saved when he removed them back in 1960. *Laggin' Dragon* had such a unique story and place in history. It was the last of the 15 Silverplate B-29s assigned to the 509th for combat operations, and it was lagging so far behind the rest of the group that its bombardier gave it the name *Laggin' Dragon* out of frustration. Then the crew almost crashed in a freak accident as they left California, but *Laggin' Dragon* survived to deliver the Fat Man bomb to Tinian and went on to fly the weather recon mission over Nagasaki on that fateful day.[5]

Laggin' Dragon was a B-29 that helped make history, and I was so fortunate to have a piece of it to help keep its story alive. My only regret, as I stood there thinking to myself in the bomb bay, was that I didn't bring the data plate with me to Dayton. What a reunion that would have been.

*   *   *

When I ducked out of the bomb bay and walked around *Bockscar* that morning, there were small groups of B-29ers and their families surrounding the bomber. The veterans were all talking about the war. Being so close to a B-29 again had awakened something inside them.

I watched as the memories came over them like waves. Their eyes would light up and this energy would return, like they were young again, as the stories poured out of them. They were suddenly back in that time and place that forever changed their lives. If I looked hard enough, I swear I could see them all as kids again.

But then those waves of nostalgia would crest, and they would fall silent when the bad memories came. You could see it; the pain, the haunting. Old wounds that never fully healed. That youthful spark would fade from their faces, and they'd look like old men again.

Then it would repeat, the highs and the lows, as it all came rushing back.

Something changed inside me that morning in Dayton. I remember one of the veterans was showing me where his own B-29 was shot-up by flak one night. He pointed up to the fuselage and explained how he "almost got it" that time, a softer way of saying he was almost killed. Then that awkward silence followed, as it always does. I knew what he was thinking: why did I live, when so many others did not?

I didn't know what to say. There was nothing that I *could* say. Finally, one of us spoke – I don't remember who – and then I turned around and walked over beneath the wing by myself. That's when it happened. For some reason, I just stopped and looked around at all of these veterans, and then I suddenly felt this profound sense of responsibility. How will the B-29ers be remembered when they're gone?

Listening to their stories that morning, I thought about the heavy price they paid for victory. When Japan surrendered, the 20th Air Force had lost 502 B-29s to all causes and suffered 3,415 battle casualties. Including training losses, 772 B-29s were lost during the war.[6]

But their sacrifices prevented an even greater tragedy had the war continued. For the coming invasion of Japan, almost half a million Purple Hearts were stockpiled for the anticipated casualties. My uncle might have been one of those casualties when he landed with the First Army on Kujukuri Beach during Operation *Coronet*, if the invasion had taken place.

The B-29ers were the heroes we needed, but they would never call themselves heroes. They were just doing their job, like the one who "almost got it" that time, and their stories needed to be told and remembered. I realized that morning what I had to do now.

As I slowly continued walking around *Bockscar* and watched all of these veterans with their families, I thought to myself how lucky I was. In a few more years, they would all be gone. We had all heard that shocking figure back then that around 1,000 World War II Veterans were dying each day in this country, but it's hard to wrap your head around something like that. It just didn't seem real. But what happened next left no doubt in any of our minds that we had reached the final page in the final chapter of the Greatest Generation.

Just before the museum opened its doors to the public, a photographer asked all of us to form a long sweeping line in front of the B-29 for a group photo. After he took our picture, the photographer wanted to get one of just the veterans standing with the B-29. As we walked over and gathered behind the photographer – the wives, the children, the grandchildren and friends – when we turned around, we were greeted with a sight that I will never forget. All of a sudden, the group became hushed. You could feel it, like the mood had changed, but I didn't understand what was happening until I turned around and looked back to where we had all just been standing.

When the war ended in 1945, the 9th Bomb Group had over 2,200 men in its ranks. Standing before us now were just 16 veterans.

I remember fighting back the tears as I stood witness to this extraordinary group of men. They were all in their late 80s and 90s now. Some were frail and had to use a wheelchair to get around the museum; another leaned against a cane to steady himself. But they all stood together. They were a cross-section of America. They came from all parts of the country, from all backgrounds and walks of life, and when our nation needed them the most, they bravely answered the call and fought for our freedom. You could still see it, that sense of duty running through their veins.

The look in their eyes belied their age as they proudly stood, and their spirit inspired us all as we looked upon those 16 out of 2,200 men.

This was the Greatest Generation. This was *the end*. And I was a witness.

Epilogue

On the 75th anniversary of the bombing of Hiroshima, I posted a picture on Facebook of Colonel Paul Tibbets waving from the cockpit of the *Enola Gay* just before takeoff on August 6, 1945, with the caption "75 years ago today." A few hours after I posted the photo, a gentleman from Australia posted the following comment: "Not something to celebrate." This was my reply:

> For the people of the United States, after three years and eight months of war, when news first broke about the atomic strike on Hiroshima, it was cause for celebration. When you consider what our young men would be facing three months later [during the invasion of Japan], had the war continued, I do not fault any of them for celebrating the strike.
>
> What we celebrate today is the fact that in the 75 years since two atomic bombs were dropped on Japan, no one else on this earth has been in the terrible position of having to make the decision President Truman had to make in the summer of 1945. And for that we should all celebrate and thank God.

The controversy over the use of the atomic bomb began before the first bomb was even dropped, and it still continues to this day. Did the atomic bomb have to be used? Would Japan have surrendered by October, without the need for an invasion, as General LeMay believed? Based on all of the research I did for this book, I'm going to give you my honest answer: I don't know. And neither does anyone else.

No one knows what would have happened if the atomic bombs had not been dropped. Entire books have been written on the subject, both for and against the use of the bomb, and the proponents of both viewpoints do have evidence to support their arguments. Despite the best-laid plans, we have learned from the past that there will always be unforeseen events that can alter the course of history. Just ask the people of Kokura, who narrowly escaped the second atomic bomb.

We will never know how the war would have ended if the bombs had not been dropped, and it's just as simple as that. Instead of arguing over the "what ifs" of World War II, humanity would be better served if we all worked together to ensure that another war like it never happens again.

There is also the question of the morality of the atomic bomb and the killing of so many civilians. The death toll from the atomic bombs will never be known for certain. The best estimate is that both attacks combined killed between 100,000 and 200,000 Japanese men, women and children.[1] To put that horrifying number into perspective, it is estimated that between 200,000 and 300,000 Chinese men, women and children were killed by Japanese soldiers after the fall of Nanking alone. Following the Doolittle Raid in 1942, the Japanese also killed upwards of

250,000 Chinese civilians by every means imaginable, including biological warfare, in retaliation for helping the raiders.[2]

Even after the war ended, civilians continued to die in horrific numbers. Of the more than 2.7 million Japanese that were captured by the Soviets in Asia, two-thirds of whom were civilians, 347,000 would die in captivity after the fighting was over. An estimated 179,000 Japanese civilians died during the first winter of captivity in Manchuria alone. And I could go on.[3]

Some estimates put the total death toll from the war, including disease and famine, as high as 85 million people. The Soviet Union alone lost upwards of 27 million people by some estimates, and China lost 20 million. Japan's death toll was 3.1 million, while the United States lost over 405,000 people to all causes. During the Holocaust, approximately 6 million Jews were murdered across Europe. For us living in modern times, the human cost of World War II was so great that it is beyond comprehension.

But was the use of the atomic bomb, and more broadly, the firebombing of Japan's cities, all of which destroyed almost 180 square miles of urban-industrial area and killed some 330,000-plus people, morally justified to help bring the war to an end? I don't have an answer to that question, either. You'll have to decide all of this for yourself. I just hope that this book has provided you with enough information to draw your own conclusions.

The only thing I can offer you now are the words of Father John Siemes, a German-born Jesuit priest and professor at Tokyo's Sophia Catholic University, who was teaching in Hiroshima at the time of the attack and was wounded by the blast. His account of the attack and the days that followed was included in the Manhattan Project's report about the bombings. Father Siemes wrote:

> None of us in those days [after the bombing] heard a single outburst against the Americans on the part of the Japanese, nor was there any evidence of a vengeful spirit. The Japanese suffered this terrible blow as part of the fortunes of war … something to be borne without complaint. During this war, I have noted relatively little hatred toward the allies on the part of the [Japanese] people themselves, although the press has taken occasion to stir up such feelings. After the victories at the beginning of the war, the enemy was rather looked down upon, but when [the] allied offensive gathered momentum and especially after the advent of the majestic B-29s, the technical skill of America became an object of wonder and admiration.
>
>   The following anecdote indicates the spirit of the Japanese: A few days after the atomic bombing, the secretary of the University came to us asserting that the Japanese were ready to destroy San Francisco by means of an equally effective bomb. It is dubious that he himself believed what he told us. He merely wanted to impress upon us foreigners that the Japanese were capable of similar discoveries. In his nationalistic pride, he talked himself into believing this. The Japanese also intimated that the principle of the new bomb was a Japanese discovery. It was only lack of raw materials, they said, which prevented its construction. In the meantime, the Germans were said to have carried the discovery to a further stage and were about to initiate such bombing. The Americans were reputed to have learned the secret from the Germans, and they had then brought the bomb to a stage of industrial completion.
>
>   We have discussed among ourselves the ethics of the use of the bomb. Some consider it in the same category as poison gas and were against its use on a civil population. Others

were of the view that in total war, as carried on in Japan, there was no difference between civilians and soldiers, and that the bomb itself was an effective force tending to end the bloodshed, warning Japan to surrender and thus to avoid total destruction. It seems logical to me that he who supports total war in principle cannot complain of war against civilians. The crux of the matter is whether total war in its present form is justifiable, even when it serves a just purpose. Does it not have material and spiritual evil as its consequences which far exceed whatever good that might result? When will our moralists give us a clear answer to this question?[4]

The debate continues.

*   *   *

There's something that I need to tell you about this book, and I wasn't sure if I should share this or not. As deeply personal (and scary) as it is to talk about, I think it's something that you should know. What I'm about to tell you, as I'm typing these words now, no one else knows about. Maybe those around me have seen it or suspected it, but I've never talked about any of this before now.

Writing this book took a heavy toll on me.

When I started this project, as a new writer with no writing experience and only an 8th grade education, I had absolutely no idea what I was doing. I didn't know anything about writing or story telling (and maybe I still don't), but I did know something about hard work. I knew that if I worked hard enough, I could make my dreams come true. If I devoted myself and gave it my all, I knew that I could write this book. I never had any doubts about that. But I never could have imagined how long it would take me, or what some of these stories would do to me.

It took me a long time to write this book. All told, it consumed over 10 years of my life. There were some stretches during those 10 years, some for months at a time, when I did not want to work on this book or even think about it. And it wasn't because I was lazy or my heart wasn't in it, it was because some of these stories were just so difficult to write about that I had to walk away for a while.

I've never told anyone this before, but writing about these stories caused me pain, and nobody likes pain. Nobody *likes* to hurt. It's not something you do for fun.

I would find these great stories about these B-29ers, men like Sergeant Larry Beecroft and his crew during the first mission to Tokyo, only to discover that they later died in such horrific ways. "They're all dead," I'd softly say to myself, after learning about the horrible fate that so many of these young men suffered. And then I'd go to that dark place again – and again, and again.

It was easier to just walk away and stop working on this book when the pain became unbearable, but I always came back to it. As much as it hurt, I always reminded myself that these were real men with real lives and real families that I was writing about, and whatever I was feeling or going through, as real as it was, it was *nothing* compared to what they went through. I owed it to them to keep going. I had to push forward and finish this book for them.

I've learned that pain is something you never forget. And if some of these stories have pained you in the same way they've pained me, then everything I put myself through will be worth it, because it means that you will never forget these men who gave their lives for you.

We all know that freedom isn't free, but most people really don't know the *price* of freedom. Now you do.

*   *   *

One of the stories that took the biggest toll on me was Lieutenant Robert Zimmerman, the Navy fighter pilot that the USS *Whale* couldn't reach in time to save. I had nightmares about his death – *a lot of nightmares*. I kept seeing him slipping beneath the waves, over and over again. This was before I knew his name, when he was just an unknown pilot whose death was recounted in the *Whale's* War Patrol Report. Those nightmares were the reason why I worked so hard to figure out who he was. The nightmares finally ended after I discovered his name.

I never asked him, but I wonder if Bill Steenberg had those same nightmares.

Another story that really affected me was that of Captain James Shumate and his crew. He was the pilot of the last B-29 shot down over Japan on August 8, 1945. Shumate and most of his crew were killed when their B-29 was hit by flak and spun to earth in flames before exploding over the city of Tachikawa, a suburb of Tokyo. I wasn't able to tell you his story earlier in this book, but I want to share it with you now. This book would not be complete without it.

In the spring of 2019, I began researching Shumate's story when his effects from the war began appearing on eBay after his widow passed away. The seller had everything from the telegram informing his wife that he was missing, to his medals that were presented to her in a ceremony after the war. When I contacted the seller and realized what he had, I asked if I could make him an offer for everything. Being the pilot of the last B-29 shot down over Japan during World War II, I explained to him, made this a historically significant grouping, and it was important that everything remain together for posterity.

Maybe I shouldn't have been so honest, but I also explained to him that he'd make more money if he split everything up and sold it piece by piece. I told him that I was an honest person, and I wanted to be upfront and honest with him about that. I couldn't afford to pay him what he'd make by selling it all piece by piece, but I was hoping that we could work something out to keep everything together, I explained, because it would be a shame to split it all up after being together for 75 years. This was real history that needed to be saved and preserved for future generations.

The seller said that he would consider an offer for everything, so I offered him $800. I didn't even have that much money to my name, but I'd figure it out, like I always do.

With the first round of auctions for Shumate's effects already under way, the seller said that he wanted to see how things went first, and then he would consider my offer. He added that he wasn't in a hurry to sell everything, because he was retired and needed all the funds he could generate. In other words, he was going to try to make as much money from all this stuff as he could. And that's exactly what he did by splitting everything up and listing them in over 50 different auctions.

I wanted to tell the seller what I really thought about him, but I had to remain cordial. I still wanted to save some of these things, and that meant that I'd have to deal with him, so I had to keep my mouth shut and be polite. I'm very tempted to tell you now what I think about him, but I don't want to use that kind of language in this book. So I'll just say this: I hope he enjoyed all the money he made off the death of Captain James Shumate. I hope he sleeps well at night.

To maximize his profits, the seller made it a point to emphasize in the auctions that Shumate was killed flying the last B-29 shot down during the war. He even talked about his widow, calling her by her first name, like he knew her or something. In one of the listings, the seller wrote that he was "honored to have the opportunity" to share Shumate's history with the people who were "fortunate enough to obtain these historic pieces." It's easy to talk about honor, but this guy didn't know the first thing about it.

The bidding for Shumate's effects quickly got out of control. By flaunting the way he died, the seller hit on something, because the bidders went wild. I started off trying to keep everything together, but there was no way that I could compete. I couldn't believe what some of these things were selling for. I finally decided that I was going to stop bidding on the auctions altogether, because I was only helping the seller make more money. And I just couldn't live with that.

After thinking it over, I decided to sell some more things from my collection, and then I would try my hardest to save Shumate's Purple Heart, the medal he was posthumously awarded after he was killed. This Purple Heart was the symbol of James Shumate's ultimate sacrifice for our country, and it was presented to his grieving widow after the war. I had to do everything I could to save it.

In the weeks that followed, I sold some more warbird parts from my collection that I'd been keeping for just such an emergency. I actually had money to spend by the time the seller listed the Purple Heart, but then the auction suddenly disappeared. I already knew what happened: eBay had a rule against selling Purple Hearts. Someone had reported the auction, and eBay took it down.

I contacted the seller again, and he said that he was going to relist it in a week or so as a Buy It Now listing instead of an auction. He was hoping for a quick sale before eBay caught him again.

A week later, when it reappeared on eBay, I could only shake my head in disgust. The seller listed the Purple Heart for $1,000 or best offer.

I really don't want to use that kind of language in this book, but I think you can imagine what I said to myself when I saw his asking price. For a moment, though, I did think about buying it for $1,000. I had enough money by then to cover it, but I just could not stomach the thought of giving that sleazy seller $1,000 and further enriching him over the death of James Shumate. It just wasn't right. This whole thing wasn't right.

But what should I do? I still had a chance to save his Purple Heart, but I knew that I had to act fast before eBay pulled the listing down again. What should I offer? I don't collect Purple Hearts, so I wasn't very familiar with their prices, but I had started paying attention to what they were selling for on other websites. In all honesty, being the pilot of the last B-29 shot down over Japan, I concluded that James Shumate's Purple Heart was probably worth a lot more than $1,000.

Still, I couldn't live with the thought of giving him all that money. It was an agonizing decision, but I decided to offer him $650 for the Purple Heart. That was hard to stomach, but I knew from his messages that he was nervous about eBay penalizing him for relisting it, so I figured he might be inclined to quickly accept my offer before eBay or another buyer could act.

I submitted my offer, and then I nervously waited. I waited all night, and still nothing. When I finally went to bed, I kept thinking about that Purple Heart. I even dreamed about it when I drifted off, but I hardly slept at all. I checked my e-mail a couple times through the morning as I tossed and turned, but nothing. Finally, that afternoon, I saw the e-mail that I dreamed about. It was from eBay, and it said that my offer had been accepted.

I did it. I saved Captain James Shumate's Purple Heart.

In that moment, I remember feeling the same way I felt when I won Ray's uniform on eBay a few years earlier. I was relieved that I'd saved Shumate's Purple Heart, and I was thankful that I now had something tangible to help tell his story with, but I was also depressed. It was all just so sad. None of this ever should have happened.

*   *   *

The story of James Shumate took a toll on me. Not only because of what happened to him during the war, and what happened to his effects after his widow died, but because of what happened to his radio operator, Staff Sergeant Serafino Morone.

Of the 12 men who were on board *The City of Phoenix* that day, the name Shumate had given his B-29 in honor of his hometown, only his radio operator, Staff Sergeant Serafino Morone, and his flight engineer, Master Sergeant Lester Morris, were able to bail out and parachute to safety. Both men were immediately captured and turned over to the Kempeitai.

At the headquarters of the Tachikawa Kempeitai, Morone and Morris were beaten and interrogated for information. Morris later recalled how he passed out three times during the interrogation. The Kempeitai would ask him a question, but before he could answer, they would beat him over the head with clubs until he was unconscious. After they knocked him out, they would throw a bucket of cold water on him to bring him to, and then the beatings would start all over again.[5]

The day after they were captured, the Kempeitai pulled Morone out of his cell, tied his hands behind his back, and blindfolded him. Morris was left lying in his cell, still dazed from the beatings and not fully conscious.

To "lift up the morale of the people," who were "very low in their spirits" because of the continued bombing, the Kempeitai commander ordered Morone to be exhibited to the civilians and "handed over to the populace to be beaten." This would "bolster up their war spirit, the spirit to continue the war," the commander said to a subordinate.[6]

With his hands bound behind his back and his eyes blindfolded, Morone was barefoot and wearing only shorts as three of the Kempeitai walked him out through the front gate of their headquarters. On each side of him, a Kempeitai walked with an arm stiffly locked through Morone's arms to control his movements as they led him out to the street. A crowd of civilians were already there, waiting for the American to appear.

The civilians followed behind in a long procession as the Kempeitai paraded Morone down the street to a nearby school. The school had a playground with a basketball court where the children played. All of the arrangements had already been made.[7]

When Morone and his guards arrived at the school, a massive crowd of people were gathering in a circle surrounding the basketball court. The Kempeitai walked Morone through the crowd, past the children's playground, and over to a basketball post on the side of the court. The basketball post was a simple wooden post, square on all sides, and about four inches wide. At the top of the post there was a wooden backboard with a steel hoop attached to it. A net hung from the hoop.

Just before the prisoner arrived, another Kempeitai had walked up to the basketball post carrying a long wooden board. The board was about five feet long and four inches wide. The Kempeitai placed the long board across the post at shoulder-height. Then he hammered nails through the long board into the post, one by one, as the crowd watched and waited for the American to arrive.[8]

Morone was tied up to the basketball post, with his face against the post. His bare back was facing the crowd. The Kempeitai untied his hands from behind his back, and then, pulling his arms out wide, they tied his wrists to the long board that was nailed at shoulder-height across the post. It looked like he was being crucified, witnesses later said.[9]

The crowd surrounding the court continued to grow. Some said there were as many as 2,000 people there, maybe more. Some of them were carrying clubs.

After Morone was firmly tied up to the post and unable to escape, the Kempeitai began forming lines of people from the crowd. A poster was displayed next to Morone that said: "This Prisoner of War was one of the persons who bombed Tokyo." Children from the elementary school were also there. Some of them got in line with the adults.[10]

With the preparations completed, a man wearing a Civilian Defense Corps uniform announced to the crowd that "through the good will of the Kempeitai," the people were "being permitted to beat an American Prisoner of War."[11]

For the next two hours, under the supervision and instruction of the Kempeitai, hundreds of Japanese stepped forward from the lines and took turns beating Morone with bamboo sticks.

A witness later said: "As he was being struck you could see that it was painful. He would move his head, move his body or twitch his legs." It was a systematic, orderly and efficient beating. The Kempeitai made sure of that.[12]

After two hours, Morone was "mumbling in a delirium" when the Kempeitai finally halted the beatings. They only stopped because an air raid alarm sounded.[13]

The Kempeitai untied Morone and laid him face-up on a stretcher that belonged to the school. They carried him across the basketball court, past the children's playground, and into a hallway at the back entrance of the school. Morone was "partly unconscious," but somehow he was still alive and breathing.[14]

A doctor came and checked Morone's pulse. Then he examined his mouth and eyes, but he did nothing for him. The doctor walked away and left Morone lying on the stretcher in the hallway while the others stood around and waited. Morone tried to speak, but no one in the hallway spoke English or understood what he was trying to say.[15]

As the men waited in the hallway, a Kempeitai warrant officer arrived from headquarters. He was accompanied by an officer from the Japanese Army Air Forces. No one in the hallway had ever seen this officer before, but the Kempeitai commander had ordered the warrant officer to take him along. The officer was a lieutenant, and a long sword hung from his waist.[16]

The men waited in the hallway for another 10 or 15 minutes, until one of the Kempeitai shouted down the hall that everything was ready. Two of the Kempeitai picked up the stretcher holding Morone, and then the group left the school through the back entrance and made their way down the road. No civilians were following them as they had earlier in the day.

As the group passed by a hospital, a doctor came running up to them. He talked to the Kempeitai in charge of the detail, but the doctor wasn't there to help the American. He only wanted permission to watch the "ceremony." Permission was granted, and the doctor joined the group as they continued walking down the empty street.[17]

When the group arrived at the temple grounds, they carried Morone on the stretcher through the graveyard to a secluded corner of the cemetery. There, the Kempeitai sergeant major was waiting. Two men from the city council were also there, as were the two grave diggers and the pit they had just finished digging.[18]

Two more doctors from the hospital also arrived, but at no time did they render aid to Morone. They were only there to watch the "ceremony," like the other doctor.[19]

As one of the men called the temple priest over, the lieutenant and one of the Kempeitai picked Morone up from the stretcher and sat him on the edge of the pit. He was facing forward and looking down into his grave as the others gathered around for the "ceremony."

The lieutenant stepped back and drew his long sword from its sheath. From a pail of water, he reached in and took some of the water in his hand, and then he sprinkled the water over the long, shimmering blade of his sword. Then he walked up to Morone, who was still alive and sitting on the edge of the pit, and stood off to his side.

Morone just sat there, his bruised and battered body covered in blood from the beatings. He didn't say anything, or even try to speak.[20]

As the others watched in silence, the lieutenant raised his long sword high in the air above his head. Then, with all of his strength, he swung the blade down and through Morone's neck, slicing his head off in one swoop.[21]

The "ceremony" was completed.

Morone's decapitated head and body were put into the pit, and then the two grave diggers quickly covered him up with dirt as the rest of the group dispersed.[22]

Serafino Morone was murdered six days before the war ended. He was 24 years old.

To cover up the killing, the Kempeitai asked the doctor who joined them on the way to the cemetery to fill out Morone's death certificate for their report. Under cause of death, the doctor was told to write "burned completely." The Kempeitai also changed their report to show that only one American had been captured alive instead of two.[23]

The only remaining survivor from Shumate's crew, Master Sergeant Lester Morris, remained in the custody of the Kempeitai for a week after he was captured. On August 15, the day the Emperor announced that Japan had surrendered, Morris was transferred to the Omori Prisoner of War Camp and finally received medical attention for the wounds he suffered while bailing out.

Morris later recalled that it sounded like two flak bursts had hit their B-29 when they were shot down, and one must have hit the right wing, he thought, because they started to roll over immediately. He remembered Shumate yelling for "bombs away" and trying to right the ship, but his controls must have been severed. Morris turned around and saw that Shumate had his control yoke all the way over, but it was no use.

As their B-29 rolled over out of control, Morris hit his head on something and was knocked out. When he came to, they were upside down and on fire. He remembered looking at the altimeter on his instrument panel, and how it was spinning like a top as they fell to earth. Morris looked around the cabin, but he didn't see anyone. He only saw the flames coming towards him. Looking to his left, the No. 3 engine was just outside the escape hatch next to him, and its prop was still turning.

Morris figured it was all over for him, but he thought that it would be better to be chopped up by the prop blades than burned alive, so he pulled the escape hatch and jumped. He was surprised when he found himself floating through the air, and although still dazed, he had the presence of mind to pull the ripcord of his parachute. When he hit the ground, Morris realized that one of the prop blades had sliced through his right leg on the way out, severing his Achilles tendon at the heel, and it felt like his skull was fractured, but he was alive.

After he was captured, the Japanese refused to give Morris any medical treatment for his wounds. Morris thought he was going to lose his leg from the infection, but when he arrived at Omori, an American doctor who'd been captured at Bataan three years earlier saved his leg using medical supplies from the Red Cross that the Japanese had been withholding from the prisoners. It was also at Omori that Morris met up with the survivors from Lieutenant Frank Crowcroft's crew, Lieutenant Greene and Sergeants Siegel and Price. They were all in the same squadron together. Morris survived his imprisonment and returned home after the war.[24]

Six weeks after Serafino Morone was murdered, when the U.S. Army Graves Registration Teams began scouring Japan to locate and recover the remains of American servicemen, some of the same Kempeitai who took part in his torture and killing returned to the cemetery on orders from their commander. Under the cover of darkness, they dug up Morone's body and cremated his remains to conceal the true cause of his death. The Kempeitai commander told one of his men that it would be "best not to talk to other people about this."[25]

After the war, the Kempeitai commander was convicted for Morone's death and sentenced to life in prison. The identity of the lieutenant who beheaded Morone was never determined.[26]

(By 1958, all surviving Japanese war criminals, including those sentenced to life in prison for their crimes, were granted clemency and released from prison. They would live the rest of their natural lives as free men.)

* * *

I first became aware of what happened to Serafino Morone many years ago while researching another B-29 crew that was lost during the war, but I didn't look any further into it at the time. His torture and death were just too awful to put myself through to learn more about it. But after I became the caretaker of Shumate's Purple Heart, I forced myself to learn as much as I could about his murder.

One of the first places I looked for information about Morone was the website "Find a Grave," which is an online database of cemetery records. It was there that I learned that Morone was laid to rest after the war at the National Memorial Cemetery of the Pacific in Honolulu, Hawaii. When I clicked on the photos tab, my eyes were immediately drawn to a photograph that still gives me cold chills to this day. It was taken from another B-29 that was flying in formation next to *The City of Phoenix* on its final mission. The photo captured the moment just after their B-29 was hit and began to roll out of control.

I couldn't believe what I was looking at. There on my screen, with fire streaming from its No. 3 engine, was an actual photo of Shumate's B-29 as it rolled over and fell away from the formation. I'd seen photos of B-29s going down before, but nothing so close as this. You could clearly see the open bomb bays and everything.

I just sat there, numb, and stared at that photograph. I couldn't imagine the horror that was going through the minds of those young men when it was taken. They all knew what was happening. They all knew they had to get out or die.

Then I thought about the other men in the formation that day, like the person who took that photograph, and how they watched their buddies go down in flames. It was broad daylight, and the skies were clear. They could all see it happening. What does that do to a person? How do you deal with something like that?

When I looked at the "Find a Grave" pages for the rest of the crew, I found another photo of their B-29 that was taken a split second later. In this photo, their B-29 was entering a dive as it continued to fall away. Those are two of the most haunting photographs that I have ever seen of a B-29. I still get cold chills every time I see them.

A short time later, I also found the "Record of Trial" for the war crimes trial against the Kempeitai commander, which contained all of the graphic witness testimony about Morone's torture and murder. There were 296 pages in the report, and I read every single one of them. More than once. I spent a few weeks going through all the testimony in that report. That was not a happy time in my life.

*   *   *

My research into what happened to Serafino Morone, and forcing myself to write about it, took a toll on me. I didn't have a lot of nightmares about it, like I did with Zimmerman's death, but there are images in my mind of Morone being beaten and executed that I will never be able to forget.

The murder of Mr. Trabold's best friend, David McNeley, and those 13 other B-29ers also really got to me. As did what happened to the survivors from Jim Krantz's crew, and those five Americans the Osaka Kempeitai murdered the day the war ended. Sadly, they were not the only American prisoners to be "disposed of" as the war was ending, but those horrific stories could fill another book. They were all so close to making it home.

Of all the research I've done, even predating this book, I've spent the most time investigating the loss of *Haley's Comet*. It all began when I acquired that piece of wreckage from the Ki-45 fighter that rammed *Haley's Comet*, and then my research turned into an obsession a year later when I found that scrapbook Sergeant Albert Preisser's wife put together after he died. The story of *Haley's Comet* has always affected me for some reason, and my research into the loss of Albert and his crew continues to this day. I hope to go to Japan one day and visit the field where it all ended. Something is calling me there.

The story of Staff Sergeant Allan K. Hill, the CFC gunner from Lieutenant Raymond Malo's crew, the first to land a B-29 on Iwo Jima, also took a toll on me. You read about him earlier, and how his crew were shot down and crashed in Tokyo Bay six weeks after their emergency landing on Iwo Jima. Allan was the only one to survive that night, but he died a month later in the Tokyo Military Prison fire. The prison held 62 American Prisoners of War, all B-29ers, and they all died that night. Some were murdered by the guards as they tried to escape the flames, but most of them burned to death in their cells. Allan Hill's remains were never identified, and he's still listed as Missing in Action to this day. That was a tough one for me.

The Tokyo fire raid was also incredibly difficult to write about. No one wants to write about children dying. I dreaded it. There were nightmares. That's all I care to say about it.

There were some stories that were just too horrible to even try to write about. Like what happened to the crew of Lieutenant Marvin Watkins after their B-29 was shot up by Japanese fighters and rammed over central Kyushu on May 5, 1945. Watkins and his entire crew managed to safely bail out before their B-29 exploded that day, but Watkins would be the only survivor.

Two of Watkins' crewmates were shot by Japanese civilians and then stabbed to death after they landed. A third was machine-gunned by Japanese fighters as he descended helplessly in his parachute, but they all missed. Circling back around to attack again, one of the Japanese pilots used the wing of his fighter to slice through the shroud lines of the parachute, sending the American plunging to his death.

The left gunner, Corporal Robert Johnson, landed without injury, but he was soon surrounded by an angry mob of Japanese civilians. Johnson drew his pistol and began firing as the mob closed in, but there were too many of them. He was doomed. With the last bullet he had left, Johnson put the pistol to his head and killed himself.

If the others had known the fate that awaited them, they would have done the same thing.

Watkins was sent to Tokyo for further interrogation after he was captured, but the other six survivors from his crew were turned over to Japanese doctors at Kyushu University, who used them for horrific medical experiments and vivisections. That's a term you don't hear very often – vivisection. It means they were dissected while they were still alive. [27]

* * *

A lot of these stories put me in a very dark place when I was writing about them. It was really hard sometimes to keep pushing forward with this project. There's only so much death and destruction that a person can take. Even from the outside, decades after the war, as a human being, it does something to you. So many deaths; so many horrible deaths.

But in all of those dark places that I found myself, when I was at my lowest, there were always rays of light that penetrated the darkness and brought me back. Some of those stories you've already read about, like when I found Bill Steenberg, but I want to share a few more with you now.

A few weeks after I finished writing about Staff Sergeant Allan K. Hill in my chapter about Iwo Jima, a funny thing happened. When I do my nightly eBay search for all things B-29, I only look at the auction listings before moving on. But for some reason, on that night, I got this feeling that I should check out the "Buy It Now" listings too, which I rarely ever look at because it's usually just stuff that no one wants. As I scrolled through the listings, I came across an old B-29 gunner's manual that was published by General Electric during the war. I see these manuals all the time and this one didn't look like anything special, but when I looked closer at the listing title, my heart skipped a beat. The listing title had the name Allan K. Hill in it.

In disbelief, I clicked on the listing and looked over the pictures. The first page of the manual had a place for the owner to write their name in it, and there in blue cursive letters was the name Allan K. Hill. Could this really be Allan's manual?

I quickly checked the enlistment records, and there was only one Allan K. Hill who served in the U.S. Army during World War II. This had to be his manual, but it just seemed so improbable. What were the chances of it surviving for 75 years after his death, and then it suddenly shows up on eBay now, of all times, after I was just writing about him?

By now it was getting late, and I had to make a decision. I was still in disbelief, but I decided to make the seller an offer, and then I went to bed. The next day, the manual was mine for $100.

I did some more research that afternoon, and what was even more curious about this manual is that it came from the estate sale of a former Prisoner of War. He must have been a B-29er, I thought, but when the seller sent me his name, I discovered that he was actually a B-17 ball turret gunner who was shot down and captured by the Germans. How he ended up with this manual is still a mystery to me.

When the manual arrived a few days later, I was delighted to see that many of the pages were filled with hand-written notes. The listing had a couple of pictures that showed some of these pages, but there were too many to show all of them. As I carefully flipped through the pages, I still wasn't totally convinced that this manual had belonged to the same Allan K. Hill that I had just finished writing about. But then I came to a page in the back of the manual, a page that the seller had not taken a picture of. The page had a hand-written list of all the men in his B-29 crew. The first name at the top was Ray Malo. And Mockler was there too, along with the rest of them.

This really was Allan's manual. What were the chances?

It was only a month after I found Allan's manual that James Shumate's effects began appearing on eBay. As I was selling off some things from my collection so I could try to save his Purple Heart, I found something else on eBay that is still hard to believe. It was the Distinguished Flying Cross that was awarded to Lieutenant Walter S. McDonell, the pilot of *Haley's Comet*.

Nothing else mattered to me at that point. My only purpose in life now was to save that medal, whatever it took. I honestly didn't think I'd be able to save it, and a lot of sleepless nights followed. But I did – I won the auction for $347.00. I was prepared to spend a lot more, and I didn't care what it cost. To me, this was something that was worth much more than money.

I talked to the seller, but he couldn't tell me much about the medal or where it came from. He bought it at an auction about 10 years earlier in Minnesota, McDonell's home state. He did ask the auction people if they had anything else that belonged to McDonell, but this was all they had. They handled a lot of consignments and had no idea who McDonell was, he said.

The seller mentioned that he collected the medals of Killed in Action service members, and he must have had McDonell's medal on display somewhere in the past, because he included a placard with it that had some information about McDonell and the loss of *Haley's Comet*. I noticed it said at the bottom that no information was known regarding McDonell's award of the Distinguished Flying Cross. In other words, the seller didn't know what actions had earned him this medal.

I naturally assumed that McDonell was awarded the Distinguished Flying Cross for one of his missions over Japan, but I decided to do some more research into it. I was in for a surprise. I never knew this before, but McDonell had actually served a previous combat tour flying B-24 bombers with the 1st Anti-Submarine Squadron. I was shocked to discover that Lieutenant Walter S. McDonell was awarded the Distinguished Flying Cross for sinking a German U-boat off the coast of Portugal on July 7, 1943.

When McDonell and his crew spotted the surfaced U-boat in broad daylight that day, he immediately dove in to attack. Normally, the U-boats would crash dive for safety, but this U-boat's captain decided to fight it out with the Americans. This is the report I found that the Anti-Submarine Command released about the battle:

> Diving in to attack in a hail of shellfire that ripped through all sections of the plane, pilot McDonell dropped almost to water level before releasing depth charges on the U-boat. The attack was carried out despite injury to almost half of the plane crew and damaging of all instruments from an explosion of a U-boat shell in the nose of the aircraft. The wounded bombardier dropped his depth charges in a perfect straddle of the sub, which was seen by the waist gunners to break in two near the conning tower. The rear section of the boat rose 10 to 12 feet out of the water, turned over and then settled with no forward motion. With four of his crew in need of immediate medical attention, the pilot set his course for his base. Although the wounds were serious, all of the crew are out of danger and on the road to recovery.[28]

With this information, I was able to determine that the submarine McDonell and his crew sank was U-951, which was on its first war patrol. There were no survivors.

A short time after the attack, McDonell's incredible story about sinking the U-boat appeared in newspapers all across the country. His story was even featured in *Time* magazine. I had never seen any of these stories when I researched him before, the reason being that they all misspelled his last name with two n's instead of one, so they didn't show up during my searches.

Having spent years researching the loss of *Haley's Comet*, I feel so honored to be the caretaker of McDonell's Distinguished Flying Cross. This medal, along with his Purple Heart and other medals whose current whereabouts are unknown, was presented to McDonell's mother after his death. I hope that I can do her proud by keeping her son's memory alive.

With McDonell's medal safely in my possession, I turned my focus back to Shumate's Purple Heart, and I began selling off even more warbird parts so I'd be ready when the seller listed it. I saved his Purple Heart three weeks later, and that's when another funny thing happened.

While doing my nightly search through eBay, I came across a B-29er's officer uniform. It looked to be in pristine condition, but aside from the 20th Air Force patch on the left shoulder, everything else – from the rank to the ribbons – had been stripped off the uniform. I could see a name written inside it, but I couldn't make out what it said, so I asked the seller about it, out of curiosity. He told me the name was H.A. Salm and the uniform came from an estate sale, but he didn't know anything else about it.

When I looked up that name, I discovered that Henry Alexander Salm was not only a decorated B-29 pilot, but he actually served in the same bomb squadron with James Shumate! That was all I needed to hear, and I won the auction a few days later for $45. I was the only bidder.

While Salm's uniform was making its way to Georgia, the package containing Shumate's Purple Heart and a little black notebook arrived from Arizona. The notebook was something that I decided to bid on at the last minute. There wasn't anything special about it, and I guess that's why no one was really bidding on it. But it did belong to Shumate, so I thought I'd try for it. I won the auction for $26. To go with the Purple Heart and the notebook, the seller also sent me an old newspaper clipping about Shumate and his crew, as well as his Social Security card from 1936. He didn't charge me for those items.

After I opened the box, I spent a long time just staring at Shumate's Purple Heart. His name was engraved on the back of it, and as I looked at that name, James L. Shumate, I thought about how he died. I thought about his wife and the little girl he left behind, and about what happened to all of his effects 75 years later. It was all so sad. Then I picked up the little black notebook and slowly flipped through the pages. Shumate had actually used this on Guam, and it was sent home to his wife with the rest of his things after he died. Inside the front cover, he wrote "Shumate, J.L." and "Fightin' 6th," for the 6th Bomb Squadron.

The pages of the notebook were filled with his mission notes and the names of the pilots who flew each mission. I didn't really pay any attention to the names until I came to the last page he filled out. That's when I realized that I was looking at the last entry he made in this notebook before he was killed. They were the details of what would be his final mission. At the top half of the page, Shumate drew a diagram of the formation they were going to fly over the target that day, along with each pilot's name and their position in the formation. Below it, he made another list of all the pilots flying on the mission. That's when I discovered that Salm's name was on that page.

Not only did Henry Alexander Salm know James Shumate, but according to the diagram he drew in his notebook before he died, Salm was flying right behind Shumate when he was shot down. He would have clearly seen Shumate's B-29 going down in flames right in front of him. *And I had just bought his uniform on eBay.*

It still leaves me speechless to think how these items found themselves together again after 75 years. What were the chances?

Henry Salm passed away in 2016. He was 97 years old and lived quite a life, from what I've read about him. I just wish that I could have talked to him about his friend James Shumate.

I thought that was going to be the end of this story, but after a whole year went by, another door into Shumate's story was suddenly opened. I was browsing through a B-29 Facebook group one evening when I came across a post about bailing out of a B-29. Scrolling through the replies, I froze when I saw that haunting photo of Shumate's B-29 going down. I soon learned that the man who posted the photo, Mark Miller, was the nephew and namesake of Sergeant Mark Miller, Shumate's right gunner. If that wasn't incredible enough, another gentleman who posted in the thread, Anthony Ferraro, was the grandson of Staff Sergeant Harold Brennan, Shumate's CFC gunner. Both of their family members were killed that day. (I later learned that it was Brennan's grandson who posted those two photos on "Find a Grave.")

Once I realized who they were, I mentioned Shumate's effects being sold on eBay a year earlier and my interest in his story, and then we all got in touch by e-mail. They had also seen the auctions and tried to save his things but didn't have much luck. The seller was very rude and disrespectful when they contacted him. He even blocked Brennan's grandson from bidding on Shumate's effects. I guess he must have told the seller what he really thought about him, as I had wanted to.

Being in touch with the families was another dream come true for me. They answered all the questions I had about Shumate's crew, and they graciously shared two private letters with me. The first was written by Master Sergeant Lester Morris after he returned home, and it included his recollection of being shot down and captured. The second letter was from Shumate's brother, who traveled to Japan after the war ended to find out what happened to him. He eventually found the crash site, which he identified as Shumate's B-29 by the serial numbers on the engines and the machine guns, and he located the grave where the Japanese buried the crew. None of this was known by the Army until he went to Japan to find his brother.

I also learned more about Lester Morris, who everyone called Cliff. He and Miller were both from New Jersey, and after he came home from the war, Miller's widow, Betty, visited Cliff in the hospital as he recovered from his injuries. Betty was hoping that he could tell her something about the fate of her husband, who was still listed as missing at that time, but Cliff didn't know what happened to him. Miller and the rest of the crew were declared dead in early 1946, even though the crash site and their remains had not been found yet.

In 1949, Miller was laid to rest at Arlington National Cemetery in a common grave with four other members of his crew, including Brennan. Their remains could not be identified due to the nature of their death. Shumate was laid to rest in California that same year.

Cliff and Betty kept in touch with each other after the war. Betty lived alone with her young daughter, and Cliff would visit them and help with things around the house. They grew closer as time went on. In 1947, Cliff and Betty were married.

In the summer of 2020, some of Shumate's effects appeared on eBay again. This time they were being sold by a so-called "collector" who'd bought them from the original seller a year earlier. He had Shumate's Distinguished Flying Cross and Air Medal, among other things. I immediately alerted the families after I discovered the auctions, and since I didn't have any money to spend, I was hoping they'd be able to save some of these things, especially his medals. Brennan's grandson said he would do all that he could to save them.

Just like before, the seller made sure to flaunt the fact that everything belonged to the pilot who was killed in the last B-29 shot down over Japan. In the auction for Shumate's Distinguished Flying Cross, the seller actually bragged that he "had the good sense to pick up most of his [Shumate's] stuff right here on eBay." It was disgusting. The bidders went wild for Shumate's medals, but Brennan's grandson was determined not to lose them again. Thankfully, he saved everything.

A short time later, I was horrified to discover that this same "collector" was also trying to sell a fake Purple Heart that he had engraved with Shumate's name. He was trying to pass off this forgery as the original Purple Heart that was presented to Shumate's widow after his death. You could tell from the style of the engraving that it was clearly a forgery, but to make it more convincing to the untrained eye, he included with it a newspaper clipping about Shumate and some photos that came from the original seller. I couldn't understand how someone could do something so despicable. How could someone sell a fake Purple Heart? Who are these people? Who would try to profit from the death of an American hero? How can they sleep at night?

Someone paid $300 for that fake Purple Heart. I still get upset just thinking about it.

As sickening as it was to see this low-life profit from his death, I took comfort in knowing that a lot of James Shumate's effects were now being cared for by Brennan's grandson, with whom they would finally get the respect they deserve. I'm so happy that I was able to connect with the Miller and Brennan families, and I'm forever grateful for all of the information they shared with me as I was researching Shumate's crew. We've remained in touch ever since.

There's one more thing about this story that you should know. It's something that happened decades after the war ended, and I wasn't sure at first if I should mention it or not. I talked to the family about it, and they said it would be okay if I shared this with you. It's not something that's easy to talk about, but maybe it could help someone else.

Like many returning veterans, Cliff Morris would spend the rest of his life trying to deal with the trauma he suffered during the war. As the years went by, it appeared that Cliff had moved on from the war. He loved his family, and he worked hard for them. But then in 1977, Cliff was forced into early retirement from his job at Bell Labs. With Betty and their son working full-time, and his stepdaughter married and out of the house, Cliff found himself home alone with just his memories.

In 1979, on the 34th anniversary of his crew being shot down, Cliff took his own life.

If there is anyone reading this right now who is hurting like Cliff was hurting, who is struggling with something like my uncle and so many other veterans have struggled with, I want you to know that there are people who care for you and are here to help you. It's okay to ask for help. Please reach out to the Veterans Crisis Line by dialing 988 and then press 1, or visit veteranscrisisline.net. You are not alone in this.

*   *   *

I began this book by telling you about Sergeant Gerald Bonne, the 20-year-old tail gunner whose B-29 disappeared without a trace on July 13, 1945, and the scrapbook I found on eBay that his mother put together after he died. It only seems right that I should end the book now by telling you the rest of the story.

I wrote the opening about Jerry and his scrapbook over the Christmas holidays. My family celebrated Christmas in Florida that year at my brother's house, but I stayed home here in Georgia.

I stayed home because I wanted to be alone when I wrote about Jerry. *I had to be alone* when I wrote about him. That was the toughest Christmas I've ever had. But it wasn't because I was lonely, or that I was missing my family – it was tough because of what I was writing about. There's just something about Jerry's story that hits me so hard. Even now, I'm getting choked up about it. (I just had to stop typing this to wipe my eyes.) I don't know why his story affects me so much.

Writing the opening about Jerry and his scrapbook, from purely a technical standpoint – and by that I mean finding the right words and putting them on paper – was the hardest thing that I've ever written about. The words did not come easy. The words are not coming so easy now, either. But I have to push through it, because I have to tell you what happened after I wrote about Jerry.

When I finished writing about Jerry that night, before I organized all my papers and put my typewriter away, I just sat there for a few minutes and thought about his life. His scrapbook was sitting next to me, and I remember looking over at it and thinking about the rest of his crew who disappeared with him that night. I knew all of their faces well. Inside the scrapbook, there was a large photograph of Jerry's crew standing in front of their B-29. I spent a lot of time staring at that photo while I was trying to write about Jerry. From the uniforms they were wearing, I could tell the photo was taken here in the United States during their training before going overseas. Jerry still had corporal stripes on his uniform, so it was probably taken a few months after his 20th birthday, before he was promoted to sergeant. It was mind-boggling to think that he was still a teenager only a few months before that photo was taken. They all had to grow up so fast back then.

As I was sitting there looking over at the scrapbook and thinking about that crew photo, this feeling suddenly came over me that I should look up the other members of his crew, like there was something that I was missing or needed to see. And that's when another funny thing happened.

The first person I googled from Jerry's crew was his pilot, Lieutenant James Crim. Scrolling through the search results, I was maybe halfway down the page when I found a newspaper article that had been published just a month earlier. The article was about a gentleman named Silver Crim and his older brother, James Crim, who "flew B-29 bombers during World War II" and "died shortly before the end of the war."[29]

The first thing I noticed in the article was a picture of Silver sitting in his home office. He was holding the officer's cap that belonged to his brother. On the wall behind him, there was an old leather flight jacket displayed in a frame, and there were black and white photographs of his brother and family around the frame. I thought about that crew photo again, but I didn't see it anywhere on his wall. I knew then what I had to do. I was going to give Silver a copy of this photo.

Since it was the holidays, I told myself that I should wait a little while before I contacted the reporter, who would hopefully put me in touch with Silver. I also needed some time to recover after writing about Jerry, to be honest with you. I just needed to take a step back and not think about his story for a while. I needed to find some happiness again, for my own mental health.

Four months went by before I contacted the reporter.

When I finally felt up to it, I was happy to learn that the reporter, J.P. Lawrence, was a veteran himself, so he knew what all of this would mean to Silver. Barely an hour had passed before I heard back from him, and he was more than happy to put us in touch.

In my first e-mail to Silver, I told him that I had some things related to his brother and his B-29 crew that I wanted to send him, but I didn't tell him what those things were. I did explain that I found all of these things in Jerry's scrapbook, but I didn't tell him the whole story behind it. I was saving that for the letter I was going to include with the crew photo. I wanted it all to be a surprise.

As you can imagine, Silver was overcome with emotion when he learned all of this. He had so little of his brother's things, he said, mainly just a lot of wonderful memories of his big brother Jimmy, and he wanted to reimburse me for making copies of what I had. Then he apologized if he wasn't making sense "through the tears of joy."[30] Reimbursing me was out of the question, of course. His family had given enough, and I told him that this was the very least that I could do for him. It was an honor to do this for Lieutenant Crim's family.

It was so moving to see how excited Silver was about all of this. Jimmy had died three weeks before his 14th birthday, but no one knew that at the time. It wasn't until weeks later that the families finally learned that their loved ones were missing. I later noticed that the telegram that was sent to Jerry's mother to inform her that her son was Missing In Action was dated August 1, 1945; August 1 was also Silver's birthday. I never asked him about it, but Silver may have been celebrating his birthday when he learned that his big brother was missing.

Silver went on to join the Air Force because of his brother, and he retired as a lieutenant colonel. In one of the pictures I saw in the reporter's article, there was a photo of Jimmy standing beside the prop blade of his B-29. Standing next to Jimmy, someone had photoshopped an image of Silver in his Air Force uniform so they could be together, as adults, in the same photograph.

I couldn't wait for him to see the photo of his brother proudly standing there with his crew. I asked the reporter about it, and he didn't remember seeing the photo when he visited Silver at his home. This would be his first time seeing it, a new 72-year-old photo of his big brother, and it was all happening because I had found Jerry's scrapbook on eBay. What a moment this was going to be.

To go along with the photo, I put together a whole folder of information about his brother's crew and their final mission. From Jerry's scrapbook, I made copies of the letters that were sent to his mother by their squadron commander and chaplain after they disappeared. I knew these letters would mean a lot to Silver and his family. I also included a copy of the Missing Air Crew Report for his brother's crew, and the mission report with all the details about the mission they flew the night they disappeared. I didn't know if Silver had seen any of this information before, so I wanted to make sure his family had copies of everything.

What was interesting about the Missing Air Crew Report was how little information it contained. According to the report, the last time anyone saw Lieutenant Crim's B-29 was when they took off from Guam. But the letters I discovered in Jerry's scrapbook told a different story. Some of the crews saw an aircraft explode over the target area that night, but no one could definitively say that it was a B-29 they saw. There was even mention of a navigator who saw parachutes descending in the night sky. None of this appeared in the official report, however. It was all so intriguing.

After I assembled all of this information in the folder, I wrote a letter to Silver explaining what everything was, and the story of how I found Jerry's scrapbook. I closed the letter by telling him that I would be thinking of his brother and the rest of his crew during the upcoming Memorial Day Ceremony at our local veterans park. His brother and his crew were the epitome of the Greatest Generation, I wrote, and their sacrifice is not forgotten.

When Silver received the package a few days later, just as I suspected, he had never seen that photo of his brother and his crew before. You can imagine what that photo meant to him.

In the weeks that followed, I discovered that I had a target map in my collection that was actually used on that very mission when their B-29 disappeared. The map showed all of the targets in the Kawasaki area, including the petroleum center that the 315th Bomb Wing attacked on July 13, 1945. I also found some reconnaissance photos that were taken of the target area before and after it was bombed. The photos and the map were in a large binder that someone from the 315th Bomb Wing had put together on Guam just after the war ended. I found it on eBay years earlier. Using the target map, the reconnaissance photos and the information that was in the mission report, you could trace the exact route that the crew flew that night into the target area.

I also discovered something else. Two weeks after their B-29 disappeared, the 315th Bomb Wing returned to Kawasaki to attack three more oil refineries that were located next to the petroleum center they targeted on July 13. I discovered that none other than Tech Sergeant Harold Brown joined one of the crews that night and recorded the mission for *The Fighting AAF* radio show. I had actually listened to this recording countless times before, but for some reason I never realized that this was the same target area where Jerry and his crew were lost. Even though the recording was made almost two weeks after they disappeared, Brown's chilling description of hundreds of searchlights sweeping across the sky as bursts of flak went off all around them, some so close that the explosions lit up the flight deck, were important clues to the disappearance of their B-29. The squadron commander wrote to Jerry's mother that other crews had seen his B-29 get hit by anti-aircraft fire over the target area, but this wasn't mentioned in the official report, either. With Brown's recording, we now had a real understanding of just how intense that anti-aircraft fire was.

I sent all of this information to Silver and his son, and together with everything else I had sent them, it gave the family a whole new insight into what might have happened to Jimmy's crew on that July night in 1945. Jimmy's family is hopeful that this information can be used in the future to begin searching the waters around the target area in Tokyo Bay, where we believe the wreckage of his B-29 is located. Silver has also submitted DNA samples to the Defense POW/MIA Accounting Agency in the hopes that one day it can be used to identify his brother's remains.

Only time will tell if their B-29 is ever found, but if the information I discovered does one day lead to the recovery of the crew, I can't help but think how it all started because of an old scrapbook I found on eBay back in 2014. Was it all by chance?

Postscript

It's now the summer of 2021, and I'm writing these words as I'm finishing up the third draft of this book. I didn't plan on writing a postscript like this (or any postscript), but there's something that I need to tell you: Mr. Trabold passed away on November 12, 2020.

It had been a long time since I last heard from Mr. Trabold, and after the pandemic started, I sent him an e-mail to see how he was doing and if there was anything that I could send him. He never replied, and I later heard from someone else who knew him that he had been in bad health. I didn't know that Mr. Trabold had passed away until three months later.

After coming to terms with the death of my friend and favorite B-29er, I was now faced with a dilemma. How was I going to inform you, the reader, of his passing? After thinking it over, I decided not to make any changes to the chapter I wrote about him in this book, because to me, even though he's gone now, Mr. Trabold will always be here in spirit. I hope you'll forgive me for not telling you about his passing until now. It just seemed right for him to live on in that chapter, as he does in the hearts of all the people he touched during his 97 years on this earth.

Blue skies, Mr. Trabold. I'll never forget you, my friend!

There's also one more thing that I need to tell you. In December of 2020, while going back over the prologue of this book, I started thinking about Jerry again and how his scrapbook had led me to Silver Crim. I had not heard anything from Silver in a long time, so out of curiosity, I did a Google search to see if there was any news about the search for his brother's B-29. I didn't find any news about a search, but I did find an obituary. Silver Crim had passed away that April.

I was heartbroken that Silver never found out what happened to his big brother before he died. I contacted his son that night to express my condolences, and I also told him that Jerry's scrapbook and the disappearance of his crew would be in this book, which would hopefully bring some awareness to their story, and to please let me know if there was ever any news about the search for their B-29. I heard back from his son the next day. There wasn't any news about the search for Lieutenant Crim's B-29 since we last spoke, he said, but his family was still hopeful that one day the Defense POW/MIA Accounting Agency would conduct a search of the waters around the target area in Tokyo Bay.

I thought that was the end of the story for now, but just four days after I sent that e-mail to Silver's son, something incredible happened. While browsing through Facebook that evening, I just happened to see a news article from Japan about a fisherman who snagged an old landing gear leg from a large airplane in his net while fishing in Tokyo Bay. You can probably already guess where this is going.

I could tell right away from the pictures that this was a B-29 main landing gear leg, and when I looked more into the story, I discovered that it was pulled up in the vicinity of Kawasaki, the target area where Jerry and his crew disappeared that night. Could this landing gear be from their B-29?

I immediately alerted Silver's son, and I told him that he was not going to believe the article I just saw. I sent him the link and some pictures, and I confirmed that the landing gear definitely came from a B-29 (I had one just like it from a scrapped B-29). He in turn alerted the proper authorities here in the United States, who now have the coordinates where the landing gear was found and other pertinent information. Due to the pandemic, no further action could be taken at that time, but we are all hopeful that a search will be launched one day to recover more wreckage.

I've also been in touch with the Defense POW/MIA Accounting Agency and have offered to help them identify any wreckage that's recovered in the future, and I've shared my thoughts on how some of the wreckage, depending on what it is, could positively identify this as Lieutenant Crim's B-29. As I'm writing this now, there are currently more than 72,000 American service members still Missing in Action from World War II alone. With the discovery of this landing gear, it may lead to some of those men finally coming home again.

While there were other B-29s that crashed in Tokyo Bay during the war, and this landing gear could very well be from one of them, I'm more optimistic now than ever before that Jerry and his crew will be found. I can't wait to see how this story ends!

To my readers,

From the bottom of my heart, I'd like to thank you for reading this book. Writing is the loneliest art form, and every aspiring writer dreams that someone will read their work one day. Thank you for making my dreams come true! If you'd like to write to me, I'd love to hear from you so I can personally thank you for reading my book.

I hope the stories in this book have given you a better understanding of World War II, and that you will share these stories with others. As we enter a new age in America where our children will grow up never knowing a World War II Veteran, it is up to all of us now to ensure that the Greatest Generation is never forgotten. Without their sacrifices, there would be no America today. They gave their lives for our freedom, and we all have a duty now to ensure their sacrifices were not in vain. That's why I wrote this book. We can't let them down!

Sincerely,
Trevor B. McIntyre

Write to me!

TrevorBMcIntyre@outlook.com

Or visit TrevorMcIntyre.com for my current mailing address.

If you have or know of any B-29 parts or militaria in need of a new home, please contact me. My dream is to one day build a museum dedicated to the B-29ers, and I am always looking for artifacts to help tell their story!

Acknowledgments

"It's never too late to be what you might have been."

I can honestly say that this book would not exist without my publisher, Duncan Rogers. As a new and inexperienced writer, Duncan took a huge gamble when he signed me based on nothing more than a proposal and a rough sample chapter, and even though this project took much longer to complete than I ever could have imagined, he always stood by me. Thank you, Duncan, for taking a chance on me!

One of the biggest challenges in writing a book about events that happened so long ago is that practically all of the people involved have since passed away. Fortunately, many of them wrote about their experiences after the war. Thank you to Hap Arnold, Haywood Hansell Jr., Curtis LeMay, Abe Spitzer, and to the countless others, both American and Japanese, who took the time to record their experiences with the B-29. You have all given us a gift of immense historical value.

To the late Toru Fukubayashi of the POW Research Network Japan, thank you for all of the incredible work you did researching the B-29s that were lost over Japan during the war. The documents you mailed to me from Japan at your own expense were crucial to my research into the loss of *Haley's Comet*. Your work lives on and will be treasured by historians for decades to come.

Jim Bowman, thank you for everything you've done to ensure the B-29ers of the 73rd Bomb Wing are not forgotten. Among his many projects, Jim spent two months scanning all of the 73rd Bomb Wing mission reports at the National Archives, and then he made all of those files available to people like me. I salute you, Jim!

The team at JapanAirRaids.org have also done an incredible job of compiling information from the National Archives about the bombing operations against Japan and making it all available on their website. Cary Karacas and David Fedman, thank you for all the hard work you have done to share this information with the world.

To the 40th Bomb Group Association, who created an online archive featuring their wartime records and stories for the benefit of all, you have my eternal thanks.

Thank you to Sam and Sherry Kidd, Don Mockler, Larry Carpenter, Anthony Ferraro, Mark Miller, Bruce Cairns, Milt Martin, Joe Chovelak, Rollin Maycumber, Larry Miller and Kurt Stauffer for your help with my research on some of the stories in this book.

Chuck Giese and Brad Pilgrim, thanks for your help when I needed those measurements of the B-17 and B-29 engine cowlings!

To William Burr and the National Security Archive, thank you for creating a magnificent digital collection of primary source documents about the atomic bombs and the end of the war. During the pandemic, when travel to libraries and archives was not possible, your digital collection was invaluable to my research for this book.

To the late Paul Vasconi, Phil Avery, Melody Headrick, George Damato, Gary Austin and Mike Crowe, I wish you guys were here to see this!

And last but not least, thank you to my parents, Rod and Jill McIntyre, for always believing in me and supporting me as I worked to make my dreams come true. None of this would have been possible without you!

Notes

Chapter 1: The Greatest Gamble of All

1. Rhodes, Richard, *The Making of the Atomic Bomb* (New York: Touchstone, 1988), p. 314.
2. Einstein, Albert and Szilard, Leo, "Einstein-Szilard letter to President Franklin D. Roosevelt, 2 August 1939," *Franklin D. Roosevelt Presidential Library and Museum* <http://docs.fdrlibrary.marist.edu/psf/box5/a64a01.html> (accessed 19 January 2019).
3. Arnold, H.H., *Global Mission* (New York: Harper & Brothers, 1949), p. 15.
4. Arnold, *Global Mission*, p. 189.
5. Craven, W.F. and Cate, J.L., *The Army Air Forces in WWII: Volume VI, Men and Planes* (Illinois: University of Chicago Press, 1955), p. 176.
6. Arnold, *Global Mission*, pp. 163–164, 167–168, 182–183.
7. Arnold, *Global Mission*, pp. 102–105.
8. Craven and Cate, *AAF Vol. VI*, p. 173.
9. Craven and Cate, *AAF Vol. VI*, pp. 175, 173.
10. Craven and Cate, *AAF Vol. VI*, pp. 120, 175.
11. Craven and Cate, *AAF Vol. VI*, Cate, p. 174.
12. Craven and Cate, *AAF Vol. VI*, pp. 172–173.
13. Collison, Collison, *The Superfortress is Born: The Story of the Boeing B-29* (New York: Duell, Sloan & Pearce, 1945), p. 21.
14. Roosevelt, Franklin D., "Message to Congress on Appropriations for National Defense, 16 May 1940," *The American Presidency Project* <www.presidency.ucsb.edu/ws/index.php?pid=15954> (accessed 29 January 2019).
15. Churchill, Churchill, "We Shall Fight on the Beaches," *International Churchill Society* <www.winstonchurchill.org/resources/speeches/1940-the-finest-hour/we-shall-fight-on-thebeaches> (accessed 30 January 2019).
16. Craven and Cate, *AAF Vol. VI*, p. 13.
17. Craven and Cate, *AAF Vol. VI*, p. 13.
18. Churchill, Churchill, "Their Finest Hour," *International Churchill Society* <www.winston-churchill.org/resources/speeches/1940-the-finest-hour/their-finest-hour> (accessed 30 January 2019).
19. Collison, *Superfortress*, p. 42.
20. Office of the Historian, "Summary of the Three-Power Pact Between Japan, Germany, and Italy, Signed at Berlin, September 27, 1940," *Office of the Historian, US Department of State* <https://history.state.gov/historicaldocuments/frus1931-41v02/d100> (accessed 31 January 2019).
21. Hansell, Haywood S. Jr., *Strategic Air War Against Japan* (Alabama: Airpower Research Institute, Air War College, Maxwell Air Force Base, 1980), pp. 3–4.
22. Collison, *Superfortress*, pp. 109–110.

23. Collison, *Superfortress*, p. 110.
24. Collison, *Superfortress*, pp. 4, 110–111.
25. Call, Helen, "Get a load on that wing," *Boeing Magazine*, Vol. XIV, No. 9 (September 1944), pp. 8–9, 18.
26. Collison, *Superfortress*, p. 8.
27. Call, "Wing," p. 9.
28. Call, "Wing," p. 9.
29. Craven and Cate, *AAF Vol. VI*, pp. 21–27.
30. Hansell, Haywood S. Jr., *The Strategic Air War Against Germany and Japan: A Memoir* (Washington, D.C.: Office of Air Force History, United States Air Force, 1986), p. 30.
31. Hansell, *Air War Against Germany and Japan*, pp. 31–41. Craven and Cate, *AAF Vol. VI*, p. 276.
32. Hansell, *Air War Against Germany and Japan*, p. 36. Craven and Cate, *AAF Vol. VI*, pp. 243–246.
33. Hansell, *Air War Against Japan*, p. 6.
34. Naval History and Heritage Command, U.S. Navy, "Overview of The Pearl Harbor Attack, 7 December 1941," *Naval History and Heritage Command* <www.history.navy.mil/ research/library/online-reading-room/title-list-alphabetically/p/the-pearl-harbor-attack-7december-1941.html> (accessed 11 February 2019).
35. Roosevelt, Franklin D., "Fireside Chat, 9 December 1941," *The American Presidency Project* <www.presidency.ucsb.edu/documents/fireside-chat-12> (accessed 11 February 2019).
36. National Archives of Australia, "The bombing of Darwin – Fact sheet 195, Japanese air raids on Darwin and northern Australia, 1942–43," *National Archives of Australia* <www.naa.gov. au/collection/fact-sheets/fs195.aspx> (accessed 12 February 2019).
37. McWilliams, Bill, *Sunday in Hell: Pearl Harbor Minute By Minute* (New York: Open Road Media, 2014), p. 747.
38. McWilliams, *Sunday*, pp. 747–748.
39. McWilliams, *Sunday*, pp. 760–762.
40. McWilliams, *Sunday*, p. 763.
41. McWilliams, *Sunday*, pp. 780–781.
42. McWilliams, *Sunday*, p. 789.
43. Schoettler, Carl, "U-boat skipper recalls good hunting off East Coast," *The Baltimore Sun* <www.baltimoresun.com/news/bs-xpm-1992-11-02-1992307117-story.html> (accessed 17 February 2019).
44. Schoettler, "U-boat skipper."
45. Warnock, A. Timothy, "The U.S. Army Air Forces in World War II: Air Power Versus U-boats: Confronting Hitler's Submarine Menace in the European Theater," *Internet Archive* <https://archive.org/details/AirPowerVersusUboats> (accessed 17 February 2019).
46. Collison, *Superfortress*, pp. 116, 118.
47. Roosevelt, Franklin D., "Fireside Chat, 23 February 1942," *The American Presidency Project* <https://www.presidency.ucsb.edu/documents/fireside-chat-6> (accessed 18 February 2019).
48. Craven, W.F. and Cate, J.L., *The Army Air Forces in WWII, Volume I, Plans and Early Operations, January 1939 to August 1942* (Washington, D.C.: Office of Air Force History, 1983), p. 282.
49. Miller, Mark James, "When a submarine attacked Goleta," *Santa Maria Times* <https:// santamariatimes.com/news/opinion/editorial/commentary/guest_commentary/when-a-submarine-attacked-goleta/article_6d0e3a7b-3e62-56eb-8ff8-f1994932b86e.html> (accessed 18 February 2019).
50. 4th Anti-Aircraft Command, "History of the 4th Anti-Aircraft Command, Western Defense Command, January 1942 to July 1945," *CUFON* <www.cufon.org/pdf/BattleOfLosAngeles.pdf> (accessed 19 February 2019). Craven and Cate, *AAF Vol. I*, pp. 283–286.
51. Craven and Cate, *AAF Vol. I*, pp. 285–286.
52. Craven and Cate, *AAF Vol. I*, p. 280.

53. Craven and Cate, *AAF Vol. VI*, p. 91.
54. Craven and Cate, *AAF Vol. I*, pp. 527–528.
55. Craven and Cate, *AAF Vol. VI*, pp. 98–99.
56. Siegel, Adam B., "Wartime Diversion of U.S. Navy Forces in Response to Public Demands for Augmented Coastal Defense," *Naval History and Heritage Command* <www.history. navy.mil/ research/library/online-reading-room/title-list-alphabetically/w/wartime-diversionus-navy-forces-response-public-demands-augmented-coastal-defense-cna.html> (accessed 21 February 2019).

Chapter 2: The War of Production

1. Roosevelt, "Fireside Chat, 23 February 1942."
2. Roosevelt, "Fireside Chat, 23 February 1942."
3. United States War Production Board, Conservation Division, "Get In The Scrap: A Plan for the Organization of the School Children of America in the National Salvage Program," 1 September 1942, *Southern Methodist University Library* <http://digitalcollections.smu.edu/ cdm/ref/collection/hgp/id/524> (accessed 16 March 2019).
4. War Production Board, "Get In The Scrap."
5. Life Magazine, "U.S. Auto Plants Are Cleared For War," *Life Magazine*, Vol. 12, No. 7 (1942), pp. 19–21.
6. Roosevelt, Franklin D., "Fireside Chat, 28 April 1942," *The American Presidency Project* <www. presidency.ucsb.edu/documents/fireside-chat-5> (accessed 18 February 2019).
7. Roosevelt, "Fireside Chat, 28 April 1942."
8. U.S. Treasury Department, War Finance Division, "Handy Reference Guide to 4th War Loan," 15 January 1944, *U.S. National Archives and Records Administration* <www.archives.gov/education/lessons/war-bonds.html> (accessed 23 June 2019).
9. UNT Digital Library, "Back the Attack!" and "For Freedom's Sake" war bond posters, *University of North Texas Digital Library* <https://digital.library.unt.edu/ark:/67531/metadc196/> <https:// digital.library.unt.edu/ark:/67531/metadc600/> (accessed 20 June 2019).
10. Duke University Libraries, "Brief History of World War Two Advertising Campaigns, War Loans and Bonds," *Duke University Libraries* <https://library.duke.edu/specialcollections/ scriptorium/ adaccess/warbonds.html> (accessed 20 June 2019). UNT Digital Library, "I gave a man!" war bond poster, *University of North Texas Digital Library* <https://digital.library.unt.edu/ark:/67531/ metadc462/> (accessed 20 June 2019).
11. Collison, *Superfortress*, p. 115.
12. Collison, *Superfortress*, pp. 103–104.
13. Vander Meulen, Jacob, *Building the B-29* (Washington: Smithsonian Institution Press, 1995), pp. 26–31.
14. Roosevelt, Eleanor, "Women In Defense", Office For Emergency Management, 1941, *National Archives and Records Administration* <https://archive.org/details/gov.archives.arc.38686> (accessed 14 July 2019).
15. Colman, Penny, *Rosie the Riveter: Women Working on the Home Front in World War II* (New York: Crown Publishers, 1995) p. 46.
16. Colman, *Rosie*, p. 70.
17. Colman, *Rosie*, pp. 15–16.
18. Colman, *Rosie*, p. 71.
19. Colman, *Rosie*, pp. 57–58.
20. Colman, *Rosie*, p. 106.
21. Boeing Aircraft Company, *This is Boeing* (Washington: Boeing, date unknown), p. 10.

22. Vander Meulen, *Building the B-29*, p. 59.
23. Vander Meulen, *Building the B-29*, pp. 27–28. The 1,664 figure includes 14 pre-production YB-29s for service testing.
24. Vander Meulen, *Building the B-29*, p. 27.
25. Boeing Aircraft Company, "Jigsaw Picture in 40,000 Parts," *Boeing Magazine*, Vol. XIV, No. 10 (October 1944), p. 10. Craven and Cate, *AAF Vol. VI*, p. 209.
26. Vander Meulen, *Building the B-29*, pp. 47, 51.
27. Vander Meulen, *Building the B-29*, pp. 81, 65.
28. Vander Meulen, *Building the B-29*, pp. 26–29.
29. Collison, *Superfortress*, p. 140.
30. Collison, *Superfortress*, p. 141.
31. Robbins, Robert M., "Eddie Allen and the B-29," in Marshall (ed.), Chester, *The Global Twentieth Vol. III* (Tennessee: Global Press, 1988), pp. 19, 27. Putt, Donald L., "The B-29 Superfortress," *Air Force Magazine*, Vol. 27, No. 7 (July 1944), pp .6–7.
32. Putt, "B-29," p. 7.

Chapter 3: Tempting Fate

1. Robbins, "Eddie Allen," p. 25.
2. Robbins, "Eddie Allen," pp. 26, 14, 15.
3. Collison, *Superfortress*, p. 59.
4. Robbins, "Eddie Allen," pp. 14–16.
5. Robbins, "Eddie Allen," p. 16.
6. Robbins, "Eddie Allen," p. 16.
7. Boeing Aircraft Company, "World Wide Wings," *Boeing Magazine*, Vol. XIV, No. 7 (July 1944), p. 17.
8. Call, Helen, "Birth of the B-29," *Boeing Magazine*, Vol. XIV, No. 7 (July 1944), p. 18. Collison, *Superfortress*, pp. 136–137.
9. Cima, Anthony P., *The Thrilling Story of Boeing's B-29 Superfortress* (New York: Playmore, 1944), p. 30.
10. Stout, Wesley W., *Great Engines and Great Planes* (Michigan: Chrysler, 1947), p. 2.
11. Wright Aeronautical Division, Curtis-Wright Corporation, "Historical Engine Summary," *Aircraft Engine Historical Society* <www.enginehistory.org/Piston/Wright/C-WSpecsAfter1930.pdf> (accessed 3 January 2021). Vander Meulen, *Building the B-29*, pp. 86–88.
12. Collison, *Superfortress*, p. 141.
13. Collison, *Superfortress*, pp. 142–143.
14. Robbins, "Eddie Allen," p. 27.
15. Robbins, "Eddie Allen," p. 27.
16. Robbins, "Eddie Allen," p. 28.
17. Collison, *Superfortress*, p. 144.
18. Robbins, "Eddie Allen," p. 29.
19. Wright, Wiley R., *Aircraft Accident Classification Committee Report on Boeing Aircraft Company Model XB-29, Serial No. 41-003, February 18, 1943* (Washington: U.S. Army Air Forces, 1943), exhibit 8.
20. Robbins, "Eddie Allen," p. 29.
21. Wright, *XB-29*, exhibits 4, 5, 12.
22. Wright, *XB-29*, part III, summary and recommendations.

Chapter 4: We Are Going to Build It

1. Boeing Aircraft Company, "Boeing Statement On Bomber Crash," *Boeing News*, Vol. 2, No. 5 (24 February 1943), pp. 1, 3.
2. Collison, *Superfortress*, p. 149.
3. Robbins, "Eddie Allen," p. 33.
4. Collison, *Superfortress*, pp. 149–150.
5. Birdsall, Steve, *Saga of the Superfortress* (New York: Doubleday, 1980), p. 16.
6. Beasley, Norman, *Knudsen: A Biography* (New York: McGraw-Hill, 1947), p. 366.
7. Wolk, Herman S., *Cataclysm: General Hap Arnold and the Defeat of Japan* (Texas: University of North Texas Press, 2010), pp. 78–79.
8. Birdsall, *Saga*, p. 16.
9. Birdsall, *Saga*, p. 16.
10. Birdsall, *Saga*, p. 16.
11. Birdsall, *Saga*, p. 16.
12. Welty, G.D., "Magnesium Alloys in Aircraft-Engine Construction," *SAE Transactions*, Vol. 27 (1932), p. 112, *JSTOR* <www.jstor.org/stable/44436648> (accessed 10 January 2021).
13. Wright Aeronautical Corporation, *Wright Cyclone 18 Aircraft Engine, Series C18BA* (New Jersey: Wright, 1942), pp. XII, 51.
14. Stout, *Great Engines*, p. 18.
15. Headquarters, Eighth Air Force, *Engine Fires* (Texas: Eighth Air Force, date unknown), p. 4.
16. Wright, *XB-29*, exhibit 14.
17. Wright, *XB-29*, exhibit 14.
18. Wright, *XB-29*, exhibit 14.
19. Wright, *XB-29*, exhibit 11.
20. Robbins, "Eddie Allen," p. 27.
21. Wright, *XB-29*, part III, summary and recommendations.
22. Wright, *XB-29*, exhibit 9.
23. Wright, *XB-29*, exhibit 6, 7, 11.
24. Wright, *XB-29*, part III, summary and recommendations.
25. Wright, *XB-29*, part III, summary and recommendations.
26. Wright, *XB-29*, part III, summary and recommendations.
27. Wright, *XB-29*, exhibit 11, 14.
28. Wright, *XB-29*, exhibit 12.
29. Wright, *XB-29*, exhibit 15.
30. Wright, *XB-29*, part III, summary and recommendations.
31. Putt, "B-29," p. 7.
32. Wright, *XB-29*, part III, summary and recommendations. Robbins, "Eddie Allen," pp. 33–35.
33. Birdsall, *Saga*, p. 17.
34. Birdsall, *Saga*, p. 17.
35. Birdsall, *Saga*, p. 17.
36. Birdsall, *Saga*, p. 17.
37. Birdsall, *Saga*, p. 17.
38. Collison, *Superfortress*, p. 153.
39. Collison, *Superfortress*, p. 153.
40. Vander Meulen, *Building the B-29*, p. 90. Stout, *Great Engines*, p. 23.

Chapter 5: The Battle of Kansas

1. Gurney, Gene, *Journey of the Giants* (New York: Coward-McCann, 1961), p. 103.
2. Boeing Aircraft Company, "Trailblazer," *Boeing Magazine*, Vol. XIV, No. 7 (July 1944), p. 2.
3. Herman Arthur, *Freedom's Forge: How American Business Produced Victory in World War II* (New York: Random House, 2012), p. 309.
4. Collison, *Superfortress*, p. 151.
5. Wolfe, Kenneth B., "The Men of the B-29s," *Air Force Magazine*, Vol. 27, No. 9 (September 1944), p. 5.
6. Wolfe, *B-29s*, p. 5.
7. Mitchell, John H., "Service Testing of the Early B-29s," in Marshall (ed.), Chester, *The Global Twentieth Vol. II* (Tennessee: Marshall, 1987), p. 18.
8. 58th Bomb Wing, *B-29 Familiarization File* (Georgia: 58th Bomb Wing, 1943), p. 2.
9. U.S. Army Air Forces, *Erection and Maintenance Instructions for Army Model B-29 Airplane, T.O. 01-20EJ-2* (Illinois: U.S. Army Air Forces, 1944), p. 93.
10. U.S. Army Air Forces, Office of Statistical Control, *Army Air Forces Statistical Digest, World War II* (Washington, D.C.: Office of Statistical Control, 1945), Table 50.
11. Collison, *Superfortress*, pp. 162–163.
12. Vander Meulen, *Building the B-29*, p. 54.
13. Wolfe, "B-29s," p. 6.
14. Oliver, Philip G., *Hellbird War Book* (location unknown: A.F. Kalberer, undated), pp. 12–17.
15. Birdsall, *Saga*, p. 26.
16. Harvey, Alva, "Birth and Deployment of the B-29," in Marshall (ed.), Chester, *The Global Twentieth Vol. I* (Minnesota: Apollo, 1985), pp. 21–22.
17. Birdsall, *Saga*, p. 23.
18. Wolfe, "B-29s," p. 8; Army Air Forces, *Statistical Digest*, Table 214.
19. U.S. Army Air Forces, Office of Flying Safety, *How Not To Fly The B-29* (Illinois: U.S. Army Air Forces, 1945).
20. Army Air Forces, *Statistical Digest*, Table 46, 213.
21. Army Air Forces, *Statistical Digest*, Table 213.
22. Arnold, H.H., *Report of the Commanding General of the Army Air Forces to the Secretary of War, 4 January 1944* (location unknown: Arnold, 1944), p. 1.
23. Carter, Kit C. and Mueller, Robert, *The Army Air Forces in WWII: Combat Chronology, 1941–1945* (Alabama: Albert F. Simpson Historical Research Center, Air University, 1973), p. 245.
24. Carter, *Combat Chronology*, p. 245.
25. Army Air Forces, *Statistical Digest*, Table 4, 84.
26. Army Air Forces, *Statistical Digest*, Table 4.
27. Army Air Forces, *Statistical Digest*, Table 47, 50, 79, 81.
28. Birdsall, *Saga*, p. 36.
29. Wood, F.G. Jr., "40th Bomb Group History Report, January 1944," *40th Bomb Group* <www.40thbombgroup.org/Archives/40thBG_Files/40th_Jan44.pdf> (accessed 14 August 2014).
30. Tanner, Dean, Olson, Mrs. George, Cooney, Wilbur and Ponder, J.D., "George Olson and the Blown Blister Accident over Texas," *40th Bomb Group* <www.40thbombgroup.org/memories/Memories55.pdf> (accessed 14 August 2014).
31. Tanner, "George Olson."
32. Stoumen, Lou, "Superbases," *Yank*, Vol. 3, No. 5 (21 July 1944), p. 4.
33. Stoumen, "Superbases."
34. Mackey, Bill, "Lucas & Crew Show a B-29 to the President," *40th Bomb Group* <www.40thbombgroup.org/memories/Memories31.pdf> (accessed 14 August 2014).

35. Birdsall, *Saga*, p. 36.
36. Birdsall, *Saga*, p. 37.
37. Roth, Morton, "Going Overseas, Part 1," *40th Bomb Group* <www.40thbombgroup.org/ memories/Memories22.pdf> (accessed 14 August 2014).
38. Cate, James L., *History of the Twentieth Air Force: Genesis* (Washington, D.C.: AAF Historical Office, 1945), p. 198; Gurney, *Journey*, p. 52.
39. Werrell, Kenneth P., *Blankets of Fire: US Bombers over Japan during World War II* (Washington: Smithsonian Institution Press, 1996), p. 94.
40. Birdsall, *Saga*, p. 36.
41. Putt, "B-29," pp. 4–6.
42. Vander Meulen, *Building the B-29*, p. 34.
43. Agather, Victor, "The Battle of Kansas (Part 1)," *40th Bomb Group* <www.40thbombgroup.org/ memories/Memories11.pdf> (accessed 14 August 2014).
44. Gurney, *Journey*, p. 51.
45. Arnold, *Global Mission*, p. 479.
46. Arnold, *Global Mission*, p. 479.
47. Gurney, *Journey*, p. 53.
48. Collison, *Superfortress*, p. 175; Wood, F.G. Jr., "40th Bomb Group History Report, March 1944," *40th Bomb Group* <www.40thbombgroup.org/Archives/40thBG_Files/40thBG_ Mar44.pdf> (accessed 14 August 2014).
49. Wood, "40th Bomb Group, March 1944."
50. Wood, "40th Bomb Group, March 1944."
51. Mathers, Ira, "The Battle of Kansas, Part II," *40th Bomb Group* <www.40thbombgroup.org/ memories/Memories13.pdf> (accessed 14 August 2014).
52. General Electric, "The Battle of Kansas (Part 1)," *40th Bomb Group* <www.40thbombgroup. org/ memories/Memories11.pdf> (accessed 14 August 2014).
53. Call, Helen, "The Minute Men of Kansas," *Boeing Magazine*, Vol. XV, No. 6 (June 1945), p. 7.
54. Hall, Robert L., "The Battle of Kansas, Part II," *40th Bomb Group* <www.40thbombgroup.org/ memories/Memories13.pdf> (accessed 14 August 2014).

Chapter 6: The Global 20th

1. Wood, F.G. Jr., "40th Bomb Group History Report, April 1944," *40th Bomb Group* <www.40thbombgroup.org/Archives/40thBG_Files/40thBG_Apr44.pdf> (accessed 14 August 2014). Edmundson, James V., "Birth and Rise of the Twentieth Air Force," in Marshall (ed.), Chester, *The Global Twentieth Vol. IV* (Tennessee: Global, 1992), pp.60–61.
2. Oliver, *Hellbird*, p. 27. Wood, "40th Bomb Group, April 1944."
3. Smith, Hibbard A., "Going Overseas, Part II," *40th Bomb Group* <www.40thbombgroup.org/ memories/Memories24.pdf> (accessed 14 August 2014).
4. Mitchell, "Service Testing," p. 20. Arnold, *Global Mission*, pp. 479–480.
5. Cate, *Twentieth Air Force*, p. 199. Birdsall, *Saga*, p. 43.
6. Cate, *Twentieth Air Force*, p. 199.
7. O'Keefe, James, "Going Overseas, Part II," *40th Bomb Group* <www.40thbombgroup.org/ memories/Memories24.pdf> (accessed 14 August 2014).
8. Hilton, Robert, *B-29 Superfortress Combat Chronicles* (Texas: Squadron/Signal, 2012), p. 14. Sinclair, Boyd, "Running On Time In a Timeless Land," *CBI Order of Battle* <www.cbihistory. com/part_vi_ba_railway2.html> (accessed 19 August 2019).
9. Oliver, *Hellbird*, p. 33.

10. Oliver, *Hellbird*, p. 34.
11. Carmichael, M.E., "The Battle of Kansas (Part 1)," *40th Bomb Group* <www.40thbombgroup.org/memories/Memories11.pdf> (accessed 14 August 2014).
12. Vander Meulen, *Building the B-29*, p. 96.
13. Birdsall, *Saga*, p. 44.
14. Wright, *Wright Cyclone 18*, pp. 1–5.
15. XXI Bomber Command, *Flight Engineer's Information File* (location unknown: XXI Bomber Command, 1945), Regulation 55–108.
16. McNair, William N., "40th Bomb Group History Report, September 1944," *40th Bomb Group* <www.40thbombgroup.org/Archives/40thBG_Files/40thBG_Sep44_Main.pdf> (accessed 14 August 2014).
17. Brief, "Cover," *AAFPOA Brief*, Vol. 2 No. 14 (6 March 1945), p. 2.
18. XXI Bomber Command, *Combat Crew Manual* (location unknown: XXI Bomber Command, 1945), Section XII, p. 18.
19. Cima, *Thrilling Story*, p. 4.
20. Gurney, *Journey*, p. 71.
21. Craven, W.F. and Cate, J.L., *The Army Air Forces in WWII, Volume Five: The Pacific: Matterhorn to Nagasaki, June 1944 to August 1945* (Washington, D.C.: Office of Air Force History, 1983), p. 85.
22. Wood, F.G. Jr., "40th Bomb Group History Report, May 1944," *40th Bomb Group* <www.40thbombgroup.org/Archives/40thBG_Files/40th_May44.pdf> (accessed 14 August 2014).
23. Wood, "40th Bomb Group History, May 1944."
24. Lowman, Clarence P., "45th Bomb Squadron History Report, May 1944," *40th Bomb Group* <www.40thbombgroup.org/Archives/45thSQ_Files/45thSq_May44.pdf> (accessed 14 August 2014).
25. Wood, "40th Bomb Group History, May 1944."
26. Werrell, *Blankets of Fire*, p. 99.
27. Gottlieb, Irving L., "44th Bomb Squadron History, June 1944," *40th Bomb Group* <www.40thbombgroup.org/Archives/44thSQ_Files/44thSQ_Jun44.pdf> (accessed 14 August 2014).
28. Rooney, Bill, "Bill Rooney remembers: A Catholic chaplain named Adler," *40th Bomb Group* <www.40thbombgroup.org/memories/Memories38.pdf> (accessed 14 August 2014).
29. Adler, Bartholomew, "First B-29 Combat Mission – 5 June 1944," *40th Bomb Group* <www.40thbombgroup.org/memories/Memories9.pdf> (accessed 14 August 2014).
30. Gurney, *Journey*, p. 81.
31. Matthews, Ira V., "Setting the Record Straight, Story 80," *40th Bomb Group* <www.40thbombgroup.org/matthews/Ira80.htm> (accessed 14 August 2014).
32. Gottlieb, "44th Bomb Squadron History, June 1944."
33. Gottlieb, "44th Bomb Squadron History, June 1944."
34. Stoumen, Lou, "B-29 Raid on Japan," *Yank*, Vol. 3, No. 5 (21 July 1944), pp. 2–4.
35. The San Francisco News, "Japan Bombed," *The San Francisco News*, Vol. 42, No. 142 (15 June 1944).

Chapter 7: Friends Through History

1. Trabold, Charles, "S/Sgt Burton K. Baldwin's parachute" (2005).
2. R.S. (2005) "B-29 stuff." Email (19 January 2005).
3. Trabold, Charles (2005) "B-29s." Email (20 January 2005).
4. Trabold "B-29s." Email (20 January 2005).
5. Trabold "B-29s." Email (20 January 2005).
6. Trabold "B-29s." Email (20 January 2005).

7. Trabold, Charles (2010) "Air Medal Roster." Email (22 February 2010).
8. Trabold "Air Medal Roster." Email (16 February 2010).
9. Baldwin, Burton K., "Flight Log of Burton K. Baldwin" (1944–1945).
10. Birdsall, *Saga*, p. 53.
11. Trabold "B-29s." Email (21 January 2005).
12. Trabold "Air Medal Roster." Email (22 February 2010).
13. Trabold "Air Medal Roster." Email (22 February 2010).
14. Trabold, Charles (2011) "Nov 5th Mission to Singapore." Email (1 June 2011).
15. Trabold "B-29s." Email (20 January 2005).
16. Trabold, Charles (2014) "B-29 ammo can markings." Email (12 March 2014).
17. Trabold, Charles (2014) "B-29 APU walkaround video." Email (23 October 2014).
18. O'Keefe, James J., "The Day We Flew the Superstitious Aloysious," in Marshall (ed.), Chester, *The Global Twentieth Vol. II* (Tennessee: Marshall, 1987), pp. 80–83.
19. Veth, K.L., "Shootout at Palembang," *American Aviation Historical Society Journal*, Vol. 25 No. 1 (spring 1980), pp. 72–73.
20. Birdsall, *Saga*, p. 62.
21. Birdsall, *Saga*, pp. 62–63.
22. Trabold, Charles (2010) "B-29 Parachute." Email (9 February 2010).
23. Baldwin, "Flight Log."
24. Birdsall, *Saga*, p. 81.
25. Baldwin, "Flight Log."
26. Mann, Robert A., *The B-29 Superfortress Chronology, 1934–1960* (North Carolina: McFarland, 2009), p. 79.
27. Mann, Robert A., *The B-29 Superfortress: A Comprehensive Registry of the Planes and Their Missions* (North Carolina: McFarland, 2004), p. 12.
28. Trabold "B-29 Parachute." Email (10 February 2010).
29. Baldwin, "Flight Log."
30. Trabold "B-29 Parachute." Email (10 February 2010).
31. Trabold "B-29 Parachute." Email (10 February 2010).
32. Trabold, Charles (2010) "C-87s and the fwd bases." Email (12 December 2010).
33. Trabold, Charles (2011) "New Photo." Email (24 January 2011).
34. Trabold "New Photo." Email (24 January 2011).
35. Brief, "India Wing," *AAFPOA Brief*, Vol. 2, No. 33 (17 July 1945), p. 13.
36. Picklum, Neysa McNeley, "Personal Story of David Frederick McNeley," *North Des Moines High School Wall of Honor* <www.nhwallofhonor.com/pages/storyofahellbirdcrewmcneley1942+.html> (accessed 28 March 2017).
37. Trabold "Air Medal Roster." Email (24 February 2010). Trabold, Charles (2012) "B-29 book news." Email (3 May 2012). Picklum, "McNeley."
38. Picklum, "McNeley."
39. Office of the Staff Judge Advocate, Headquarters Eighth Army, U.S. Army, "United States of America vs. Hideo Fujioka," *Philipps-University Marburg* <www.online.uni-marburg.de/icwc/yokohama/Yokohama%20No.%20T328.pdf> (accessed 22 September 2019), pp. 63–64.
40. Trabold "B-29 book news." Email (3 May 2012). Picklum, "McNeley."
41. Trabold, Charles (2010) "Holy smokes!" Email (24 August 2010).
42. Trabold "Holy smokes!" Email (24 August 2010).
43. Trabold "Holy smokes!" Email (28 August 2010).
44. Trabold "Holy smokes!" Email (24 August 2010).
45. Trabold "Holy smokes!" Email (30 August 2010).
46. Trabold "Holy smokes!" Email (25 August 2010).

47. McIntyre, Trevor (2010) "Holy smokes!" Email (30 August 2010).
48. Trabold "Holy smokes!" Email (25 August 2010).
49. W.M. (2010) "eBay Item #180551889315." Email (6 September 2010).
50. McIntyre, Trevor (2010) "VICTORY!!" Email (7 September 2010).
51. 462nd Bomb Group, "Bombing Equipment in B-29 Airplane," *U.S. Army Air Forces* (11 February 1944).
52. Hoisington II, Perry M., "Thurman W. Sallade Commendation," *462nd Bomb Group* (4 March 1945).
53. 462nd Bomb Group, "Special Orders Number 89," *U.S. Army Air Forces* (2 April 1944).
54. Trabold, Charles (2010), "Today's findings!" Email (28 September 2010).
55. Trabold "Today's findings!" Email (21 September 2010).

Chapter 8: The Beginning of the End

1. Bowers, William T., "Ben Salomon and the Medal of Honor," *U.S. Army Medical Department, Office of Medical History* <https://history.amedd.army.mil/corps/dental/leaders/citation.html> (accessed 3 September 2019).
2. Bowers, "Ben Salomon."
3. Bowers, "Ben Salomon."
4. Bowers, "Ben Salomon."
5. Bowers, "Ben Salomon."
6. Frank, Richard B., *Downfall: The End of the Imperial Japanese Empire* (New York: Penguin, 1999), p. 29.
7. Frank, *Downfall*, p. 29.
8. Frank, *Downfall*, p. 29.
9. Sherrod, Robert, "Saipan: Eyewitness Tells of Island Fight," *Life Magazine*, Vol. 17, No. 9 (28 August 1944), p. 80. Sherrod, Robert, "Nature of the Enemy," *Time Magazine*, Vol. 44, No. 6 (7 August 1944), p. 27.
10. Sherrod, "Nature of the Enemy," p. 27.
11. Frank, *Downfall*, p. 29.
12. Sherrod, "Nature of the Enemy," p. 27.
13. Cook, Haruko Taya, "The myth of the Saipan Suicides," *MHQ: The Quarterly Journal of Military History*, Vol. 7, No. 3 (spring 1995), p. 17.
14. Cook, "Saipan Suicides," p. 17.
15. Sherrod, "Nature of the Enemy," p. 27.
16. Cook, "Saipan Suicides," p. 19.
17. U.S. Air Force, "The Air Force Story: Chapter 24: Air War Against Japan," *YouTube* <www.youtube.com/watch?v=m7JgXOxOAeQ> (accessed 5 September 2012).
18. Griffith, Charles, *The Quest: Haywood Hansell and American Strategic Bombing in World War II* (Alabama: Air University Press, 1999), p. 145.
19. U.S. Air Force, "General Emmett O'Donnell Jr.," *U.S. Air Force* <www.af.mil/About-Us/Biographies/Display/Article/106016/general-emmett-odonnell-Jr./> (accessed 6 September 2019).
20. Hansell, *Air War Against Japan*, p. 34.
21. Yank, "Building the Base," *Yank*, Vol. 3, No. 28 (29 December 1944), p. 5.
22. Prideaux, Tom, "The B-29ers," *Impact*, Vol. 3, No. 9 (Sept–Oct 1945), p. 60.
23. Speer, Bob, "Official Photographers of Japan," *USASTAF Brief*, Vol. 2, No. 36 (7 August 1945), p. 6.
24. Speer, "Official Photographers," p. 6.
25. Zamperini, Louis and Rensis, David, *Devil at my Heels: A Heroic Olympian's Astonishing Story of Survival as a Japanese POW in World War II* (New York: Harper, 2011), p. 161.

26. Martindale, Robert R., *The 13th Mission: The Saga of a POW at Camp Omori, Tokyo* (Texas: Eakin, 1998), p. 176.
27. Takai, Koji and Sakaida, Henry, *B-29 Hunters of the JAAF* (Oxford: Osprey, 2001), p. 26.
28. Speer, "Official Photographers," p. 6. Brief, "Recon and Raid," *AAFPOA Brief*, Vol. 2, No. 2 (12 December 1944), p. 5.
29. Speer, "Official Photographers," pp. 6–7.
30. Brief, "Recon and Raid," p. 5.
31. Mann, *Superfortress Registry*, p. 37.
32. Speer, "Official Photographers," p. 7.
33. Dixson, Walter Clay, *From Tyler, Texas to Tokyo: The Pacific War Letters and Photograph Collection of Captain Elmer R. Dixson* (Texas: Historic Aviation Memorial Museum, 2002), pp. 53, 51.
34. Dixson, *From Tyler*, p. 53.
35. Brief, "Recon and Raid," p. 14.
36. Brief, "Recon and Raid," p. 14.
37. Brief, "Recon and Raid," p. 14.
38. Unknown, "Death to fliers, Japanese warn," undated newspaper clipping, Thurman Sallade papers.
39. Brief, "Recon and Raid," p. 14.
40. Hansell, *Air War Against Japan*, p. 37.
41. Burger, Knox, "Lynn Delivers Her Child," *Yank*, Vol. 3, No. 28 (29 December 1944), pp. 2–3.
42. Headquarters, 73rd Bomb Wing, "Tactical Mission Report, Mission No. 7: Tactical Narrative, Bombing Data," *73rd Bomb Wing* (24 November 1944).
43. Honolulu Star-Bulletin, "VITAL TOKYO TARGETS HIT," *Honolulu Star-Bulletin*, Vol. 51, No. 16,285 (24 November 1944).

Chapter 9: Miracle Over Nagoya

1. Krantz, James R., "Head First Over Japan," *AAFPOA Brief*, Vol. 2, No. 9 (20 January 1945), pp. 3–4.
2. 73rd Bomb Wing, "Consolidated Statistical Summary, Mission No. 17: Ammunition Consumption Data; Aircraft Lost and Damaged," *73rd Bomb Wing* (3 January 1945).
3. Krantz, "Head First," p. 4.
4. Krantz, "Head First," p. 4.
5. Burger, Knox Burger, "Trapeze Act Over Japan," *Yank*, Vol. 3, No. 39 (16 March 1945), pp. 8–9.
6. Krantz, "Head First," p. 15.
7. U.S. Army Air Forces, "Missing Air Crew Report 14593," *National Archives Catalog* <https://catalog.archives.gov/id/91156180> (accessed 15 September 2019).
8. U.S. Army Air Forces, "Missing Air Crew Report 11221," *National Archives Catalog* <https://catalog.archives.gov/id/91106509> (accessed 15 September 2019).
9. Office of the Staff Judge Advocate, Headquarters Eighth Army, U.S. Army, "United States of America vs. Hideo Fujioka," *Philipps-University Marburg* <www.online.uni-marburg.de/icwc/yokohama/Yokohama%20No.%20T328.pdf> (accessed 22 September 2019), p. 62.
10. Fukubayashi, Toru, "Allied Aircraft and Airmen Lost Over the Japanese Mainland During WWII: Chubu Army District," *POW Research Network Japan* <www.powresearch.jp/en/ pdf_e/ pilot/chubu.pdf> (accessed 25 October 2016). Memorial Branch, QM, Headquarters Eighth Army, U.S. Army, "Report of Disinterment for Identification: Unknown X-51, 6 May 1946," *73rd Bomb Wing (VH) POW Honor Roll* <www.exciteableitalian.com/POW%20 Honor%20Roll/ The%2055/19%20HART/02%20identification/Identification1.htm> (accessed 1 February 2021).

11. Judge Advocate, "U.S. vs. Fujioka," pp. 62–63.
12. Judge Advocate, "U.S. vs. Fujioka," pp. 63–64.
13. Judge Advocate, "U.S. vs. Fujioka," pp. 64–65.
14. Office of the Staff Judge Advocate, Headquarters Eighth Army, U.S. Army, "United States of America vs. Jiro Hamamoto," *Philipps-University Marburg* <www.online.uni-marburg.de/ icwc/ yokohama/Yokohama%20No.%20T364.pdf> (accessed 22 September 2019), p. 6.
15. Judge Advocate, "U.S. vs. Hamamoto," p. 5.
16. Judge Advocate, "U.S. vs. Hamamoto," p. 5.
17. Judge Advocate, "U.S. vs. Fujioka," p. 65.
18. Judge Advocate, "U.S. vs. Fujioka," p. 1.
19. Fukubayashi, "Chubu Army District."
20. Krantz, "Head First," p. 3.

Chapter 10: The Price of Freedom

1. XXI Bomber Command, "Jap Instructions On Fighting B-29s," Air Intelligence Report Vol. 1 No. 3 (22 March 1945), p. 15.
2. Takaki, *B-29 Hunters*, p. 29. United States Strategic Bombing Survey, *Japanese Air Weapons and Tactics* (Washington, D.C.: Military Analysis Division, 1947), pp. 27–29.
3. Strategic Bombing Survey, *Japanese Air Weapons*, pp. 29–30. Takaki, *B-29 Hunters*, p. 45.
4. Strategic Bombing Survey, *Japanese Air Weapons*, p. 27. Dossett, Walter B. Sr, "The Diary of Major Walter B. Dossett, Sr.," *497th Bomb Group B-29 Memorial* <www.497thbombgroupb29. org/personal%20accounts/Dossett,%20Walter%20B.%20Personal%20Account%20497th.pdf> (accessed 1 October 2019).
5. Takaki, *B-29 Hunters*, pp. 14–16.
6. Takaki, *B-29 Hunters*, p. 93.
7. 73rd Bomb Wing, "Consolidated Statistical Summary, Mission No. 14: Analysis Of Attacks By Enemy Aircraft," *73rd Bomb Wing* (22 December 1944).
8. 73rd Bomb Wing, "Consolidated Statistical Summary, Mission No. 14: Narrative Flight Engineer's Report, 497th Bomb Group," *73rd Bomb Wing* (22 December 1944).
9. Headquarters Twentieth Air Force, "Distinguished Flying Cross Citation: Captain Howard M. Clifford," *497th Bomb Group B-29 Memorial* <www.497thbombgroupb29.org/records/ DFC%20 citations%20.pdf> (accessed 17 August 2016).
10. eBay (2010), "Sorry, you didn't win." Email (27 October 2010).
11. D.M. (2010), "eBay item #310258647546." Email (12 October 2010).
12. M.S. (2010), "Dragon Lady acceptance plate." Email (12 November 2010).
13. Brusgulis, Peter, "Radar Operators Report: 27 January 1945," (27 January 1945).
14. eBay, "eBay item #150768246531," *eBay* <http://cgi.ebay.com/ws/itm150768246531> (accessed 16 March 2012).
15. M.S. (2010), "Dragon Lady acceptance plate." Email (13 November 2010).
16. Strategic Bombing Survey, *Japanese Air Weapons*, p. 42.
17. Nakamura, Taizo, "A B-29 rammed by a Ki-45 Nick Over Funabashi," *Pacific Wrecks* <https:// pacificwrecks.com/aircraft/ki-45/4067/history.html> (accessed 14 November 2010).
18. 73rd Bomb Wing, "Consolidated Statistical Summary, Mission No. 22: Combat Data," *73rd Bomb Wing* (27 January 1945).
19. Morgan, Robert and Powers, Ron, *The Man Who Flew The Memphis Belle* (New York: New American Library, 2002), p. 298. 73rd Bomb Wing, "Consolidated Statistical Summary, Mission No. 22: Ammunition Consumption Data," *73rd Bomb Wing* (27 January 1945).

20. 73rd Bomb Wing, "Consolidated Mission Report, Mission No. 22: AA and Air-to-Air Bombing; Tactical Narrative; CFC Gunnery," *73rd Bomb Wing* (27 January 1945).
21. Speer, Bob, "Pappy's Boys Report: The Jap is Good," *AAFPOA Brief*, Vol. 2, No. 13 (27 February 1945).
22. Speer, "Pappy's Boys Report," p. 4.
23. Speer, "Pappy's Boys Report," pp. 5, 15.
24. Abeare-Welch, Angelique, "Memorial Day Memory – 1st Lt David C. Williams Jr. KIA, Japan, WWII & the Crew of B-29 Haley's Comet: Sgt Olinto F. Lodovici Statement to Casualty Branch, War Department, 10 November 1945," *Angelique's Rabbit Hole* <http://porphyrins.org/angeliques_rabbit_hole/?p=37> (accessed 2 December 2010).
25. Nakamura, "A B-29 rammed."
26. Sakurai, Tokuzo, "A B-29 Was Shot Down," *Shisui Hometown Research Society Newsletter No. 98* (1 October 2000).
27. 73rd Bomb Wing, "Consolidated Statistical Summary, Mission No. 22: Aircraft Lost and Damaged; Lost Aircraft," *73rd Bomb Wing* (27 January 1945).
28. 73rd Bomb Wing, "Consolidated Statistical Summary, Mission No. 22: Casualties," *73rd Bomb Wing* (27 January 1945). Fukubayashi, Toru, "Allied Aircraft and Airmen Lost Over the Japanese Mainland During WWII: Tobu Army District," *POW Research Network Japan* <www.powresearch.jp/en/pdf_e/pilot/tobu.pdf> (accessed 25 October 2016).
29. Headquarters, Eighth Army, "Resume of Official Records Pertaining to Crash of B-29 #42-24616, 27 January 1945," Headquarters, Eighth Army, U.S. Army (18 June 1948).
30. Eighth Army, "B-29 #42-24616."
31. Paul (2012) "eBay item #130631227141." Email (20 January 2012).
32. Albert Preisser newspaper clippings, author, date and publisher unknown.
33. Letter from Vere Carpenter to Mrs. Isabel Armstrong, 1945.
34. Carpenter, Larry (2012) "Vere D. Carpenter – book research." Email (23 October 2012).
35. Carpenter, Larry (2012) "Memories of Vere's War Experiences." Email (23 October 2012).
36. Martindale, *13th Mission*, pp. 204–206.
37. Martindale, *13th Mission*, pp. 206–207.
38. Carpenter, Larry, "Memories of Vere's War Experiences." Email (23 October 2012).
39. Carpenter, Larry (2016) "Haley's Comet news." Email (24 October 2016).
40. Carpenter, Larry, "Memories of Vere's War Experiences." Email (23 October 2012).
41. Carpenter, Larry, "Memories of Vere's War Experiences." Email (23 October 2012).
42. Carpenter, Larry, "Vere D. Carpenter – book research." Email (23 October 2012).
43. Carpenter, Larry, "Memories of Vere's War Experiences." Email (23 October 2012).
44. Carpenter, Larry, "Haley's Comet news." Email (24 October 2016).
45. Letter from Vere Carpenter to Mrs. Isabel Armstrong, 1945.

Chapter 11: Thank God for the Marines

1. Kakehashi, Kumiko, *So Sad to Fall in Battle: An Account of War Based on General Tadamichi Kuribayashi's Letters from Iwo Jima* (New York: Presidio Press, 2007), pp. 3–5.
2. Davis, Joseph T., *The Story of the 73rd: The Unofficial History of the 73rd Bomb Wing* (Texas: 73rd Bomb Wing, 1946), p. 48.
3. Hansell, *Air War Against Japan*, p. 41.
4. Hansell, *Air War Against Japan*, p. 40. Davis, *Story of the 73rd*, p. 49.
5. Werrell, *Blankets of Fire*, p. 128.
6. Kakehashi, *So Sad to Fall*, p. 3.

7.   Kakehashi, *So Sad to Fall*, pp. 5–7.
8.   Kakehashi, *So Sad to Fall*, pp. 110, 112–113, 37.
9.   Ross, Bill D., *Iwo Jima: Legacy of Valor* (New York: Vintage Books, 1986), p. 20.
10. Kakehashi, *So Sad to Fall*, p. 112.
11. Kakehashi, *So Sad to Fall*, p. 18.
12. Kakehashi, *So Sad to Fall*, p. 106.
13. Ross, *Iwo Jima*, p. 20.
14. Kakehashi, *So Sad to Fall*, pp. 51–54.
15. Kakehashi, *So Sad to Fall*, pp. 44–46.
16. Kakehashi, *So Sad to Fall*, p. 42.
17. Kakehashi, *So Sad to Fall*, p. 39.
18. Kakchashi, *So Sad to Fall*, p. 66.
19. Kakehashi, *So Sad to Fall*, p. 66.
20. Kakehashi, *So Sad to Fall*, pp. 31–32.
21. Kakehashi, *So Sad to Fall*, p. 31.
22. Bradley, James and Powers, Ron, *Flags of Our Fathers* (New York: Bantam, 2000), pp. 142–-143.
23. Kakehashi, *So Sad to Fall*, p. 76.
24. Ross, *Iwo Jima*, pp. 31–32.
25. Ross, *Iwo Jima*, p. 32.
26. Ross, *Iwo Jima*, p. 32.
27. Ross, *Iwo Jima*, p. 26.
28. Bradley, *Flags*, p. 135.
29. Bradley, *Flags*, p. 135.
30. Ross, *Iwo Jima*, pp. 60–61.
31. Ross, *Iwo Jima*, p. 65.
32. Sherrod, Robert, "The First Three Days," *Life Magazine*, Vol. 18, No. 10 (5 March 1945), p. 44.
33. Ross, *Iwo Jima*, p. 66.
34. Ross, *Iwo Jima*, p. 68.
35. Sherrod, "First Three Days," p. 44.
36. Sherrod, "First Three Days," p. 42.
37. Haynes, Fred and Warren, James A., *The Lions of Iwo Jima* (New York: Henry Holt, 2008), p. 96.
38. Huie, William Bradford, *From Omaha to Okinawa: The Story of the Seabees* (New York: E.P. Dutton, 1945), p. 46.
39. Ross, *Iwo Jima*, p. 81.
40. Ross, *Iwo Jima*, p. 81.
41. Ross, *Iwo Jima*, p. 80.
42. Bradley, *Flags*, pp. 204–205.
43. Haynes, *Lions of Iwo Jima*, p. 128.
44. Smith, Holland M. and Finch, Percy, *Coral and Brass* (Washington, D.C.: Zenger, 1979), p. 180.
45. Smith, *Coral and Brass*, p. 180.
46. Bradley, *Flags*, p. 3.
47. Ross, *Iwo Jima*, p. 103.
48. Huie, *Omaha to Okinawa*, p. 30.
49. Mockler, Don (2011) "First B29 Landing on Iwo Jima," transcript of Jack Hooley radio interview of Raymond Malo and James Cox, 5 March 1945. Email (2 September 2011).
50. Brief, "Iwo Echelon," *AAFPOA Brief*, Vol. 2, No. 17 (27 March 1945), p. 7.
51. Mockler, "First B29 Landing on Iwo Jima."
52. Mockler, "First B29 Landing on Iwo Jima."
53. Ross, *Iwo Jima*, pp. 276–277.

54. Bradley, *Flags*, p. 235.
55. Headquarters, Expeditionary Troops, Task Force 56, "Report of Planning, Operations, Iwo Jima Operation Enclosure B: Report No. 15, 5 March 1945," *HyperWar Pacific Theater of Operations* <www.ibiblio.org/hyperwar/PTO/Iwo/ComTaskForFiftySixIwoJima/ TaskFor FiftySix-EnclosureB.pdf> (accessed 27 November 2019).
56. Mockler, "First B29 Landing on Iwo Jima."
57. Office of the Staff Judge Advocate, Headquarters Eighth Army, U.S. Army, "United States of America vs. Toshio Tashiro," *Philipps-University Marburg* <www.online.uni-marburg.de/icwc/ yokohama/Yokohama%20No.%20T078.pdf> (accessed 14 November 2019), pp. 7–12.
58. Judge Advocate, "U.S. vs. Tashiro," p. 10.
59. Ross, *Iwo Jima*, p. 329.
60. Kakehashi, *So Sad to Fall*, p. 186.
61. Frederick, Robert O., "This is What Happened," *AAFPOA Brief*, Vol. 2, No. 21 (24 April 1945), pp. 6–7.
62. Frederick, "This is What Happened," p. 15. Ross, *Iwo Jima*, p. 336.
63. Kakehashi, *So Sad to Fall*, pp. 195–196.
64. Ross, *Iwo Jima*, p. XIII.
65. Ross, *Iwo Jima*, p. XIII. Bradley, *Flags*, pp. 174–175.
66. Ross, *Iwo Jima*, p. 341.
67. Ross, *Iwo Jima*, p. 324.

Chapter 12: Letters from Iwo Jima

1. Haynes, George W., letter from Iwo Jima to Dorothy Haynes, 24 February 1945.
2. 5th Marine Division, "Lieutenant George W. Haynes Silver Star Citation," *The Hall of Valor Project* <https://valor.militarytimes.com/hero/36739> (accessed 15 December 2019).
3. Ross, *Iwo Jima*, p. 329.
4. Kakehashi, *So Sad to Fall*, pp. 145–147.
5. Fukubayashi, Toru (2013) "The translation of the Iwo letter." Email (20 April 2013).
6. Haynes, Bill (2011) "Haynes hospital letter." Email (14 September 2011).
7. Culbertson, Jean, "Service Moves Haynes," *Clarion-Ledger* newspaper (14 June 1970).
8. Culbertson, *Haynes*.
9. Haynes, Bill (2011) "My father Iwo Jima." Email (14 August 2011).
10. 33rd Statistical Control Unit, "Monthly Activity Report: March," *XXI Bomber Command* (5 April 1945), p. 9.
11. Prideaux, "The B-29ers," p. 64.

Chapter 13: Japan's Invisible Ally

1. Sutherland, John H., *The Hundred Missions: The History of the 73rd Bomb Wing, Volume I* (Saipan: 73rd Bomb Wing, 1945), Mission No. 7, 8, 9, 10, 13, 14, 16. 73rd Bomb Wing, "Consolidated Mission Report, Mission No. 10: Bomb Impact Data," *73rd Bomb Wing* (3 December 1944).
2. Army Air Forces, *Statistical Digest*, Table 43. 33rd Statistical Control Unit, "Monthly Activity Report: February," *XXI Bomber Command* (1 March 1945), p. 9.
3. Burchinal, David A., "Analysis of Incendiary Phase of Operations Against Japanese Urban Areas, 9–19 March 1945," *XXI Bomber Command* (March 1945), pp. 39–40.

4. 33rd Statistical Control, "Monthly Activity: February," p. 10. Burchinal, "Incendiary Operations," p. 39.
5. Hansell, *Air War Against Japan*, pp. 48–49.
6. Hansell, *Air War Against Japan*, pp. 48–49, 139–143.
7. Werrell, *Blankets of Fire*, p. 139.
8. Werrell, *Blankets of Fire*, pp. 139–140.
9. LeMay, Curtis E. and Kantor, MacKinlay, *Mission with LeMay: My Story* (New York: Doubleday, 1965), pp. 154, 191.
10. LeMay, *Mission with LeMay*, p. 231.
11. LeMay, *Mission with LeMay*, p. 238.
12. LeMay, *Mission with LeMay*, pp. 234, 245.
13. Burchinal, "Incendiary Operations," p. 3.
14. 73rd Bomb Wing, "Consolidated Mission Report, Mission No. 20: Bomb Impact Data," *73rd Bomb Wing* (19 January 1945).
15. Burchinal, "Incendiary Operations," p. 3. Fukubayashi, "Aircraft Lost: Tobu Army District."
16. Burchinal, "Incendiary Operations," p. 4. LeMay, *Mission with LeMay*, pp. 343–344.
17. Speer, "Pappy's Boys Report," p. 5.
18. Speer, "Pappy's Boys Report," p. 5.
19. Lind, Wilfred N., "With a B-29 Over Japan – A Pilot's Story," *New York Times Magazine* (25 March 1945), p. 38.
20. Dugan, Richard L. and Speer, Bob, "Japan's Invisible Ally," *AAFPOA Brief*, Vol. 2, No. 19 (10 April 1945), pp. 3, 15.
21. LeMay, *Mission with LeMay*, p. 347.
22. Frank, *Downfall*, p. 60.
23. LeMay, Curtis E. and Yenne, Bill, *Superfortress: The B-29 and American Air Power* (New York: McGraw-Hill, 1988), p. 121. 73rd Bomb Wing, "Consolidated Statistical Summary, Mission No. 21" (23 January 1945); "Consolidated Statistical Summary, Mission No. 22" (27 January 1945), *73rd Bomb Wing* (1945). XXI Bomber Command, A-2 Section, "Tactical Mission Report: Mission No. 26" (4 February 1945); "Tactical Mission Report: Mission No. 29" (10 February 1945); "Tactical Mission Report: Mission No. 34" (15 February 1945); "Tactical Mission Report: Mission No. 37" (19 February 1945); "Tactical Mission Report: Mission No. 38" (25 February 1945), *XXI Bomber Command* (1945).
24. LeMay, *Mission with LeMay*, pp. 345–347.
25. LeMay, *Mission with LeMay*, p. 346.
26. XXI Bomber Command, A-2 Section, "Tactical Mission Report: Mission No. 40," *XXI Bomber Command* (10 March 1945), p. 1.
27. Office of the Assistant Chief of Staff, Intelligence, "Air Objective Folder Japan, No. 90.17, Tokyo Area," *U.S. Army Air Forces* (23 February 1944), p. T-8. XXI Bomber Command, "Effects of Incendiary Attacks," *Air Intelligence Report Vol. 1 No. 4* (29 March 1945), pp. 9–10.
28. Standard Oil Company, *M-69 … The Fire Bomb That Falls on Japan* (New York: Standard Oil Company, 1945), pp. 1–3.
29. United States Strategic Bombing Survey, *Effects of Incendiary Bomb Attacks on Japan: A Report on Eight Cities* (Washington, D.C.: United States Strategic Bombing Survey, 1947), pp. 67, 70.
30. Burger, Knox, "Fire Raid," *Yank*, Vol. 4, No. 23 (23 November 1945), p. 2.
31. Strategic Bombing Survey, *Effects of Incendiary Bomb Attacks*, p. 73.
32. Burchinal, "Incendiary Operations," p. 6. 73rd Bomb Wing, "Consolidated Mission Report, Mission No. 9: Tactical Narrative," *73rd Bomb Wing* (29 November 1944).
33. XXI Bomber Command, A-2 Section, "Tactical Mission Report: Mission No. 38," *XXI Bomber Command* (25 February 1945), p. 5.

34. Nutter, Ralph H., *With the Possum and the Eagle: The Memoir of a Navigator's War over Germany and Japan* (California: Presidio, 2002), p. 236.
35. Nutter, *Possum and the Eagle*, p. 237.
36. International Churchill Society, "Education – Bombing Germany: Again," *International Churchill Society* <https://winstonchurchill.org/publications/finest-hour/finest-hour-127/ education-bombing-germany-again/> (accessed 21 January 2020).
37. Nutter, *Possum and the Eagle*, p. 237.
38. Nutter, *Possum and the Eagle*, p. 237.
39. Werrell, *Blankets of Fire*, p. 152. McKelway, St. Clair, "A Reporter with the B-29s: III – The Cigar, the Three Wings, and the Low-Level Attacks," *The New Yorker Vol. XXI No. 19* (23 June 1945), p. 32.
40. XXI Bomber Command, "Mission No. 40," p. 2.
41. XXI Bomber Command, "Mission No. 40," p. 3. Hartman, Alan, "Hell for Honshu," *AAFPOA Brief,* Vol. 2, No. 21 (24 April 1945), p. 4.
42. 73rd Bomb Wing, "Consolidated Mission Report, Mission No. 29: Field Order No. 43, 8 March 1945," *73rd Bomb Wing* (10 March 1945).
43. LeMay, *Mission with LeMay*, p. 348.
44. Beckeméier, Theodore E., "Daily Diary: Major General Curtis E. LeMay: Resume of Events While Aide-De-Camp to Major General Curtis E. LeMay, June 25, 1943 to September 25, 1945: 9 March 1945," *Scribd* <www.scribd.com/doc/37161060/Curtis-E-LeMay-DailyDiary-1944-1945> (accessed 22 January 2020). Birdsall, *Saga*, pp. 179–180.
45. Nutter, *Possum and the Eagle*, p. 239.
46. Nutter, *Possum and the Eagle*, pp. 240–241.
47. Nutter, *Possum and the Eagle*, p. 241.
48. Nutter, *Possum and the Eagle*, p. 242.
49. XXI Bomber Command, "Mission No. 40," pp. 2–3.
50. Edoin, Hoito, *The Night Tokyo Burned* (New York: St. Martin's Press, 1987), pp. 56–57.
51. 497th Bomb Group, "Consolidated Mission Report, Mission No. 29: Radio Interceptions," *497th Bomb Group* (10 March 1945).
52. Edoin, *Tokyo Burned*, p. 56.

Chapter 14: The Night Tokyo Died

1. Cook, Haruko Taya and Cook, Theodore F., *Japan At War: An Oral History* (New York: The New Press, 1992), p. 345.
2. Marshall, Chester W. and Thompson, Warren, *Final Assault on the Rising Sun: Combat Diaries of B-29 Air Crews Over Japan* (Minnesota: Specialty Press, 1995), p. 132.
3. Tillitse, Lars, "When Bombs Rained on Us in Tokyo," *Saturday Evening Post*, Vol. 218, No. 28 (12 January 1946), p. 82.
4. Hartman, "Hell for Honshu," p. 4.
5. Martin, Harold H., "Black Snow and Leaping Tigers," *Harper's Magazine*, No. 1149 (February 1946), p. 153.
6. Assistant Chief of Air Staff – Intelligence, *Mission Accomplished: Interrogations of Japanese Industrial, Military, and Civil Leaders of World War II* (Washington, D.C.: U.S. Army Air Forces, 1946), p. 100. Martin, "Black Snow," p. 153.
7. Guillain, Robert, *I saw Tokyo Burning: An Eyewitness Narrative from Pearl Harbor to Hiroshima* (New York: Doubleday, 1981), pp. 181–182.
8. LeMay, *Mission with LeMay*, p. 10.

9.   McKelway, "A Reporter with the B-29s," p. 35.
10.   McKelway, "A Reporter with the B-29s," p. 36.
11.   McKelway, "A Reporter with the B-29s," p. 36.
12.   Cook, *Japan At War*, p. 345.
13.   Cook, *Japan At War*, p. 345.
14.   Cook, *Japan At War*, p. 346.
15.   Cook, *Japan At War*, pp. 346–347.
16.   Selden, Kyoko and Selden, Mark, *The Atomic Bomb: Voices from Hiroshima and Nagasaki* (New York: M.E. Sharpe, 1989), p. xiv.
17.   Morgan, *Memphis Belle*, p. 313.
18.   Morgan, *Memphis Belle*, p. 311.
19.   Morgan, *Memphis Belle*, p. 313.
20.   Caidin, Martin, *A Torch to the Enemy: The Fire Raid on Tokyo* (New York: Bantam, 1992), p. 176.
21.   Caidin, *Torch to the Enemy*, p. 177.
22.   Caidin, *Torch to the Enemy*, pp. 176–178.
23.   Miller, Donald L., *D-Days in the Pacific* (New York: Simon & Schuster, 2005), p. 327.
24.   Marshall, *Final Assault*, p. 132.
25.   Martin, Milt, "Hap Halloran Interview, Part 4 of 6," *YouTube* <www.youtube.com/watch?v=NNBtTCYML_4> (accessed 9 February 2020).
26.   Phillips, Charles L. Jr., *Rain of Fire: B-29s Over Japan, 1945* (California: B-Nijuku Publishing, 1995), p. 41.
27.   Phillips, *Rain of Fire*, p. 37.
28.   Caidin, *Torch to the Enemy*, p. 171.
29.   Caidin, *Torch to the Enemy*, p. 172.
30.   Caidin, *Torch to the Enemy*, p. 172.
31.   Caidin, *Torch to the Enemy*, p. 173.

Chapter 15: It's All Ashes

1.   Cook, *Japan At War*, p. 347.
2.   Strategic Bombing Survey, *Effects of Incendiary Bomb Attacks*, p. 102.
3.   Cook, *Japan At War*, p. 347.
4.   Cook, *Japan At War*, p. 348.
5.   Cook, *Japan At War*, p. 348.
6.   Assistant Chief of Air Staff, *Mission Accomplished*, pp. 100–101.
7.   Caidin, *Torch to the Enemy*, p. 173.
8.   Caidin, *Torch to the Enemy*, p. 174.
9.   Caidin, *Torch to the Enemy*, p. 170.
10.   Edoin, *Tokyo Burned*, p. 99.
11.   Edoin, *Tokyo Burned*, p. 100.
12.   Edoin, *Tokyo Burned*, p. 103.
13.   Martindale, *13th Mission*, p. 202.
14.   Miller, *D-Days in the Pacific*, p. 328.
15.   Miller, *D-Days in the Pacific*, p. 328.
16.   Cook, *Japan At War*, pp. 348–349.
17.   McKelway, "A Reporter with the B-29s," p. 37.
18.   McKelway, "A Reporter with the B-29s," p. 37.
19.   McKelway, "A Reporter with the B-29s," p. 37.

20. Beckemeier, "Daily Diary: Major General Curtis E. LeMay: 11 March 1945."
21. XXI Bomber Command, "Mission No. 40," p. 36. Strategic Bombing Survey, *Effects of Incendiary Bomb Attacks*, pp. 94, 102.
22. Strategic Bombing Survey, *Effects of Incendiary Bomb Attacks*, p. 102. Frank, *Downfall*, pp. 17–18.
23. XXI Bomber Command, "Mission No. 40," p. 47.
24. XXI Bomber Command, "Mission No. 40," pp. 4, 16.
25. LeMay, *Mission with LeMay*, p. 10. XXI Bomber Command, "Mission No. 40," pp. 6, 8.
26. Burchinal, "Incendiary Operations," p. 40.
27. Morgan, *Memphis Belle*, p. 315.
28. 33rd Statistical Control Unit, "Monthly Activity Report: March." XXI Bomber Command, A-2 Section, "Tactical Mission Report: Mission No. 40" (10 March 1945); "Tactical Mission Report: Mission No. 41" (12 March 1945); "Tactical Mission Report: Mission No. 42" (14 March 1945); "Tactical Mission Report: Mission No. 43" (16 March 1945); "Tactical Mission Report: Mission No. 44" (20 March 1945), *XXI Bomber Command* (March 1945).

Chapter 16: Voices from the Past

1. The Fighting AAF, "Fighting AAF Radio Shows: Fighting AAF, B-29 Mission Over Japan," *Japan Air Raids.org* <www.japanairraids.org/?page_id=20> (accessed 11 January 2011).
2. XXI Bomber Command, A-2 Section, "Tactical Mission Report: Mission No. 50," *XXI Bomber Command* (31 March 1945), p. 2.
3. Japan Air Raids.org, "Fighting AAF, B-29 Mission Over Japan."
4. Japan Air Raids.org, "Fighting AAF, B-29 Mission Over Japan."
5. Price, William E., "The Crew That Wasn't," in Marshall (ed.), Chester, *The Global Twentieth Vol. III* (Tennessee: Global Press, 1988), p. 340.
6. Price, "The Crew That Wasn't," pp. 340, 342.
7. Takaki, *B-29 Hunters*, p. 101. U.S. Army Air Forces, "Missing Air Crew Report 14232," *National Archives Catalog* <https://catalog.archives.gov/id/91151849> (accessed 18 March 2020).
8. Whitehouse, Andy (2014) "Charlie Henderson's daughter." Email (25 September 2014).
9. Whitehouse, Andy (2020) "Charlie Henderson's daughter." Email (23 March 2020).

Chapter 17: Flying for Uncle Sam

1. Stewart, Carroll, *The Most Honorable Son: Ben Kuroki* (Nebraska: Nebraska Printing Center, 2010), p. 30.
2. Lukesh, Jean A., *Lucky Ears: The True Story of Ben Kuroki* (Nebraska: Field Mouse Productions, 2010), p. 47.
3. Lukesh, *Lucky Ears*, p. 49.
4. Martin, Ralph G., *Boy from Nebraska: The story of Ben Kuroki* (New York: Harper & Brothers, 1946), p. 49.
5. Lukesh, *Lucky Ears*, p. 53.
6. Martin, *Boy from Nebraska*, p. 60.
7. Stewart, *Honorable Son*, p. 5.
8. Lukesh, *Lucky Ears*, p. 67. Stewart, *Honorable Son*, p. 8.
9. Lukesh, *Lucky Ears*, p. 68.
10. Martin, *Boy from Nebraska*, p. 126.
11. Lukesh, *Lucky Ears*, p. 72.

12. Stewart, *Honorable Son*, p. 10.
13. Miller, Donald L., *Masters of the Air: America's Bomber Boys Who Fought the Air War Against Nazi Germany* (New York: Simon & Schuster, 2006), p. 190.
14. Miller, *Masters of the Air*, p. 190.
15. United States Department of the Interior, War Relocation Authority, *Nisei in Uniform* (Washington, D.C.: U.S. Government Printing Office, 1944), p. 24.
16. Kuroki, Ben, *Ben Kuroki's Story* (Utah: Japanese American Citizens League, 1944), p. 14.
17. Kuroki, *Ben Kuroki's Story*, p. 12.
18. Miller, *Masters of the Air*, p. 192. Lukesh, *Lucky Ears*, p. 76.
19. Kuroki, *Ben Kuroki's Story*, p. 15.
20. Conscience and the Constitution, "In remembrance of Sgt. Ben Kuroki," *YouTube* <www.youtube.com/watch?v=DUqDZuSp2Io> (accessed 2 January 2016).
21. Lukesh, *Lucky Ears*, p. 77.
22. Lukesh, *Lucky Ears*, p. 78.
23. Stewart, *Honorable Son*, p. 16.
24. Martin, *Boy from Nebraska*, p. 126.
25. Department of the Interior, *Nisei in Uniform*, p. 23.
26. Roosevelt, Franklin D., "Document for February 19th: Executive Order 9066: Resulting in the Relocation of Japanese," *National Archives* <www.archives.gov/historical-docs/todaysdoc/?dod-date=219> (accessed 24 April 2020). Department of the Interior, *Nisei in Uniform*, p. 24.
27. Martin, *Boy from Nebraska*, p. 158.
28. Stewart, *Honorable Son*, p. 16.
29. Martin, *Boy from Nebraska*, p. 159. Kuroki, *Ben Kuroki's Story*, p. 3.
30. Stewart, *Honorable Son*, p. 17. Lukesh, *Lucky Ears*, p. 84.
31. Martin, *Boy from Nebraska*, pp. 161–162.
32. Martin, *Boy from Nebraska*, p. 164.
33. Martin, *Boy from Nebraska*, p. 166.
34. Lukesh, *Lucky Ears*, p. 88.
35. Martin, *Boy from Nebraska*, p. 167.
36. Stewart, *Honorable Son*, p. 18.
37. Martin, *Boy from Nebraska*, p. 170.
38. Martin, *Boy from Nebraska*, p. 171.
39. Martin, *Boy from Nebraska*, pp. 172–173.
40. Martin, *Boy from Nebraska*, p. 175.
41. Stewart, *Honorable Son*, p. 21.
42. Martin, *Boy from Nebraska*, p. 177.
43. Stewart, *Honorable Son*, p. 22.
44. Martin, *Boy from Nebraska*, pp. 182–183.
45. Martin, *Boy from Nebraska*, p. 186.
46. Martin, *Boy from Nebraska*, p. 186.
47. Lukesh, *Lucky Ears*, pp. 98–99.
48. Lukesh, *Lucky Ears*, pp. 1–2.
49. Stewart, *Honorable Son*, p. 26.
50. Baird, A. Craig, *Representative American Speeches: 1945–1946* (New York: H.W. Wilson Company, 1946), pp. 212–213.
51. Stewart, *Honorable Son*, p. 57.

Chapter 18: The Red, White and Blue

1. Sons of the American Legion, "Manual of Ceremony and Prayer," *The American Legion* <www.
    legion.org/sons/filelib/BroPrayerMn12.pdf> (accessed 26 September 2017).
2. Mann, *The B-29 Superfortress*, pp. 241–244.
3. XXI Bomber Command, A-2 Section, "Tactical Mission Report: Mission No. 47," *XXI Bomber
    Command* (27 March 1945), p. 2.
4. Shumway, Raymond E., letter to Lloyd Hale, 8 August 1945 (Sam Kidd, Jr., collection).
    Shumway, letter to his family, 8 August 1945, in Stroud (ed.), Martha Sue, *For Love of Country:
    The Price of Freedom* (Texas: Nortex Press, 2000), pp. 528–529. Kidd, Sam C., letters to LaNelle
    Kidd, 15 August, 17 August, 23 August, 24 August, 6 September, 26 September 1945 (Sam Kidd,
    Jr., collection).
5. U.S. Navy, "SS-239, USS WHALE Submarine War Patrol Report: 29 July 1945," *Issuu* <https://
    issuu.com/hnsa/docs/ss-239_whale> (accessed 10 October 2017).
6. U.S. Navy, "USS Whale: 29 July 1945."
7. U.S. Navy, "USS Whale: 24 July 1945."
8. U.S. Navy, "USS Whale: 29 July 1945."
9. U.S. Navy, "USS Whale: 24 July 1945."
10. U.S. Navy, "USS Whale: 24 July 1945."
11. U.S. Navy, "USS Whale: 24 July 1945."
12. U.S. Navy, "USS Whale: 29 July 1945."
13. Shumway, letter to his family, 8 August 1945, p. 529.
14. Lee, Knute, *Survivor: Knute's Wild Story* (Nebraska: Authors Choice Press, 2003), p. 169.
15. Shumway, Raymond E., letter to Lloyd Hale, 8 August 1945 (Sam Kidd, Jr., collection).
16. U.S. Army, "WWII U.S. Army Enlistment Records," *WWII U.S. Army Enlistment Records* <www.
    wwii-enlistment.com> (accessed 22 September 2017).
17. Lee, *Survivor*, p. 169.
18. Headquarters, 20th Air Force, "Raymond E. Shumway, Soldier's Medal Citation," *The Hall of
    Valor Project* <https://valor.militarytimes.com/hero/27689> (accessed 19 November 2017).
19. Kidd, Sam Jr. (2017) "Sgt Sam Kidd – WWII Veteran Research." Email (3 December 2017).
20. Kidd, Sam C., letter to LaNelle Kidd, 22 August 1945 (Sam Kidd, Jr., collection).
21. Kidd, letter to LaNelle Kidd, 24 August 1945 (Sam Kidd, Jr., collection).
22. J., Bruce. (2018) "WWII Veteran Blaine F. Olsen." Email (14 March 2018).
23. U.S. Navy, "U.S. Navy Casualties, Bureau of Personnel Entries by Date – 1945," *Naval-History.
    net* <www.naval-history.net/WW2UScasaaDB-USNBPbyDate1945.htm> (accessed 20 June
    2018).
24. U.S. Navy, VF-31, "Original U.S. WWII USN Pilot Distinguished Flying Cross KIA Named
    Grouping: Aircraft Action Report No. VF31-13, 24 July 1945," *International Military Antiques*
    <www.ima-usa.com/products/original-u-s-wwii-usn-pilot-distinguished-flying-cross-kianamed-
    grouping?variant=26171563205> (accessed 21 June 2018).
25. U.S. Naval Academy Virtual Memorial Hall, "PORTER W. MAXWELL, CDR, USN," *U.S.
    Naval Academy Virtual Memorial Hall* <https://usnamemorialhall.org/index.php/ PORTER_W._
    MAXWELL,_CDR,_USN> (accessed 21 June 2018).
26. Sakaida, Henry, *Imperial Japanese Navy Aces 1937–45* (London: Osprey Publishing, 1998), p. 95.
27. U.S. Naval Academy Virtual Memorial Hall, "CHARLES H. SAWERS, LCDR, USN,"
    U.S. Naval Academy Virtual Memorial Hall <https://usnamemorialhall.org/index.php/
    CHARLES_H._SAWERS,_LCDR,_USN> (accessed 21 June 2018).

28. U.S. Navy, "U.S. Navy Casualties, Bureau of Personnel Entries by Date – 1945: ZIMMERMAN, Robert O., LT., 121761," *Naval-History.net* <www.naval-history.net/WW2UScasaaDBUSNBPbyDate1945.htm> (accessed 20 June 2018).
29. Hudson, J. Ed, "A History of the USS CABOT (CVL-28): A Fast Carrier in World War II," *stexboat.com* <www.stexboat.com/books/cabot/cab03_05.htm> (accessed 27 June 2018).
30. Air Group 31, "Pilots of Fighter Squadron 31," *Air Group 31* <www.vf31.com/pilots/vf-31.html> (accessed 27 June 2018).

Chapter 19: Downfall

1. Bainbridge, Kenneth T., "A Foul and Awesome Display," *The Bulletin of Atomic Scientists*, Vol. XXXI, No. 5 (May 1975), p. 45.
2. Rhodes, *Atomic Bomb*, p. 676.
3. Rhodes, *Atomic Bomb*, p. 676.
4. Rigdon, William M., "Log of the President's Trip to the Berlin Conference: July 16, 1945," *StudyLib* <https://studylib.net/doc/8414894/log-of-the-president-s-trip-to-the-berlin-conference> (accessed 1 May 2020).
5. Ferrell, Robert H., *Off the Record: The Private Papers of Harry S. Truman* (New York: Harper & Row, 1980), p. 47.
6. Rigdon, "Berlin Conference: July 16, 1945."
7. Office of the Historian, United States Department of State, "Foreign Relations of the United States: Diplomatic Papers, The Conference of Berlin (The Potsdam Conference), 1945, Volume II: Document No. 1303," *Office of the Historian* <https://history.state.gov/historicaldocuments/frus1945Berlinv02/d1303> (accessed 13 May 2020).
8. Bundy, Harvey H., "Remembered Words," *The Atlantic*, Vol. 199, No. 3 (March 1957), p. 57.
9. Office of the Historian, "The Conference of Berlin: Vol. II: Document No. 1303."
10. Office of the Historian, United States Department of State, "Foreign Relations of the United States: Diplomatic Papers, The Conference of Berlin (The Potsdam Conference), 1945, Volume II: Document No. 1304, Document No. 1305," *Office of the Historian* <https://history.state.gov/historicaldocuments/frus1945Berlinv02/d1304>, <https://history.state.gov/historicaldocuments/frus1945Berlinv02/d1305> (accessed 13 May 2020).
11. Office of the Historian, "The Conference of Berlin: Vol. II: Document No. 1305."
12. Office of the Historian, United States Department of State, "Foreign Relations of the United States: Diplomatic Papers, The Conference of Berlin (The Potsdam Conference), 1945, Volume II: Henry Stimson diary, 22 July 1945," *Office of the Historian* <https://history.state. gov/historical-documents/frus1945Berlinv02/d710a-59> (accessed 13 May 2020).
13. Office of the Historian, United States Department of State, "Foreign Relations of the United States: Diplomatic Papers, The Conference of Berlin (The Potsdam Conference), 1945, Volume II: Henry Stimson diary, 23 July 1945," *Office of the Historian* <https://history.state.gov/historicaldocuments/frus1945Berlinv02/d1275> (accessed 13 May 2020). Office of the Historian, United States Department of State, "Foreign Relations of the United States: Diplomatic Papers, Conferences at Malta and Yalta, 1945: Agreement Regarding Entry of the Soviet Union Into the War Against Japan, February 11, 1945," *Office of the Historian* <https://history.state.gov/historicaldocuments/frus1945Malta/d503> (accessed 24 May 2020).
14. Truman, Harry S., *Memoirs by Harry S. Truman: Volume One: Year of Decisions* (New York: Doubleday, 1955), pp. 411, 387.

15. United States Department of Defense, *The Entry of the Soviet Union into the War Against Japan: Military Plans, 1941–1945* (Washington, D.C.: United States Department of Defense, 1955), p. 76. Truman, *Memoirs*, p. 314.
16. Truman, Harry S., "Letter from Harry S. Truman to Bess W. Truman, July 18, 1945," *Harry S. Truman Presidential Library and Museum* <www.trumanlibrary.gov/library/truman-papers/correspondence-harry-s-truman-bess-wallace-truman-1921-1959/july-18-1945> (accessed 13 May 2020).
17. Office of the Historian, "The Conference of Berlin: Vol. II: Henry Stimson diary, 23 July 1945."
18. Truman, *Memoirs*, pp. 411–412.
19. Truman, *Memoirs*, p. 412.
20. Groves, Leslie M., *Now It Can Be Told: The Story of the Manhattan Project* (New York: Da Capo Press, 1983), p. 298.
21. Groves, *Now It Can Be Told*, p. 298.
22. Office of the Historian, "The Conference of Berlin: Document No. 1305."
23. Newcomb, Richard F., *Abandon Ship! The Saga of the USS Indianapolis, the Navy's Greatest Sea Disaster* (New York: HarperCollins, 2001), pp. 18–19.
24. Newcomb, *Abandon Ship!*, p. 24.
25. Newcomb, *Abandon Ship!*, pp. 24–25.
26. Speer, Robert, "Five Star Report," *AAFPOA Brief*, Vol. 2, No. 32 (10 July 1945), pp. 3–4.
27. Prideaux, Tom, "B-29 Payoff," *Impact*, Vol. 3, No. 9 (Sept–Oct 1945), p. 90.
28. Arnold, *Global Mission*, p. 564.
29. LeMay, *Superfortress*, p. 143.
30. LeMay, *Superfortress*, p. 142.
31. Coffey, Thomas M., *Iron Eagle: The Turbulent Life of General Curtis LeMay* (New York: Crown Publishers, 1986), p. 174.
32. LeMay, *Superfortress*, pp. 143–144. Coffey, *Iron Eagle*, p. 174.
33. Huston, John W., *American Airpower Comes of Age: General Henry H. "Hap" Arnold's World War II Diaries: Volume 2* (Alabama: Air University Press, 2002), p. 326.
34. Wolk, *Cataclysm*, pp. 149–150.
35. Arnold, *Global Mission*, p. 566.
36. Arnold, *Global Mission*, p. 566.
37. Arnold, *Global Mission*, p. 566.
38. Arnold, *Global Mission*, p. 567.
39. Beckemeier, "Daily Diary: Major General Curtis E. LeMay: June 16, 1945."
40. Bruccoli, Matthew J., *James Gould Cozzens: A Time of War: Air Force Diaries and Pentagon Memos 1943–45* (South Carolina: Bruccoli Clark, 1984), p. 307.
41. Bruccoli, *Cozzens: A Time of War*, pp. viii–ix.
42. Kort, Michael, *The Columbia Guide To Hiroshima and The Bomb* (New York: Columbia University Press, 2007), pp. 201–202.
43. Ferrell, *Off the Record*, p. 47.
44. Kort, *Hiroshima*, p. 105.
45. Office of the Historian, United States Department of State, "Foreign Relations of the United States: Diplomatic Papers, The Conference of Berlin (The Potsdam Conference), 1945, Volume I: Document No. 598," *Office of the Historian* <https://history.state.gov/historicaldocuments/frus-1945Berlinv01/d598> (accessed 13 May 2020).
46. Arnold, *Global Mission*, pp. 567, 564–565.
47. Arnold, *Global Mission*, p. 567.
48. Office of the Historian, "The Conference of Berlin: Vol. I: Document No. 598."
49. Huston, *American Airpower*, p. 334.

50. Kort, *Hiroshima*, p. 241.
51. LeMay, *Mission with LeMay*, p. 347.
52. Kort, *Hiroshima*, p. 98.
53. Kort, *Hiroshima*, pp. 186–188.
54. Kort, *Hiroshima*, p. 99.
55. Kort, *Hiroshima*, pp. 195, 192.
56. Office of the Historian, "The Conference of Berlin: Vol. I: Document No. 598." Kort, *Hiroshima*, pp. 195–196.
57. Kort, *Hiroshima*, p. 193.
58. Office of the Historian, "The Conference of Berlin: Vol. I: Document No. 598."
59. Office of the Historian, "The Conference of Berlin: Vol. I: Document No. 598."
60. Kort, *Hiroshima*, pp. 250–251.
61. Kort, *Hiroshima*, p. 100.
62. Office of the Historian, "The Conference of Berlin: Vol. I: Document No. 598."
63. Frank, *Downfall*, pp. 71–72.
64. Office of the Historian, "The Conference of Berlin: Vol. I: Document No. 598."
65. Kort, *Hiroshima*, p. 87.
66. Kort, *Hiroshima*, p. 252.
67. Office of the Historian, "The Conference of Berlin: Vol. I: Document No. 598."
68. Office of the Historian, "The Conference of Berlin: Vol. I: Document No. 598."
69. Frank, *Downfall*, p. 118.
70. Hansell, *Air War Against Japan*, p. 121.
71. U.S. Department of Defense, *Entry of the Soviet Union into the War*, p. 76.
72. Hansell, *Air War Against Japan*, p. 119.
73. Coffey, *Iron Eagle*, p. 175.
74. LeMay, *Superfortress*, p. 143.
75. Coffey, *Iron Eagle*, p. 175.
76. LeMay, *Superfortress*, p. 143.
77. Kohn, Richard H. and Harahan, Joseph P., *Strategic Air Warfare: An Interview with Generals Curtis E. LeMay, Leon W. Johnson, David A. Burchinal, and Jack J. Catton* (Washington, D.C.: Office of Air Force History, 1988), p. 65.

Chapter 20: Little Boy and Fat Man

1. XXI Bomber Command, "Attention Japanese People," *Air Intelligence Report*, Vol. 1, No. 22 (4 August 1945), p. 21.
2. American News Service, "B-29 Command Now Calling Its Shots," *The Daily Target Saipan*, Vol. II, No.83 (29 July 1945).
3. Kato, Masuo, *The Lost War: A Japanese Reporter's Inside Story* (New York: Alfred A. Knopf, 1946), p. 8.
4. Army Air Forces, *Statistical Digest*, Tables 3, 83, 9.
5. Statistical Control, 73rd Bombardment Wing, *73rd Bombardment Wing Summary of Operations: Nov. 1943 Thru Aug. 1945* (Saipan: 73rd Bombardment Wing, 1945), p. 15. Army Air Forces, *Statistical Digest*, Tables 30, 91.
6. Hansell, *Air War Against Japan*, p. 69.
7. Coffey, *Iron Eagle*, p. 178.
8. Hansell, *Air War Against Japan*, p. 86.
9. Vander Meulen, *Building the B-29*, p. 54.

10. War Finance Division, U.S. Treasury Department, "Straight Talk about the 7th War Loan," U.S. Government Printing Office (1945).
11. Duke University Libraries, "Loans & Bonds."
12. Truman, *Memoirs*, pp. 390–392.
13. Ferrell, *Off the Record*, pp. 55–56.
14. Kort, *Hiroshima*, p. 223.
15. Kort, *Hiroshima*, p. 211.
16. MacArthur, Douglas, *Reports of General MacArthur: Japanese Operations In The Southwest Pacific Area: Volume II – Part II* (Washington, D.C.: Center of Military History, U.S. Army, 1994), p. 631.
17. United States Strategic Bombing Survey, *Japanese Air Power* (Washington, D.C.: Military Analysis Division, 1946), pp. 70–71, 42.
18. MacArthur, *Reports of General MacArthur, Vol. II*, p. 632.
19. MacArthur, *Reports of General MacArthur, Vol. II*, pp. 603, 622.
20. MacArthur, *Reports of General MacArthur, Vol. II*, pp. 591, 604. MacArthur, Douglas, *Reports of General MacArthur: MacArthur In Japan: The Occupation: Military Phase Volume I Supplement*, (Washington, D.C.: Center of Military History, U.S. Army, 1994), p. 117.
21. MacArthur, *Reports of General MacArthur, Vol. II*, pp. 627–629.
22. U.S. Office of War Information, *Japanese Propaganda: June 26, 1945* (California: U.S. Office of War Information, 1945).
23. Giangreco, D.M., *Hell To Pay: Operation Downfall and the Invasion of Japan, 1945–47* (Maryland: Naval Institute Press, 2009), p. 161.
24. Honeycutt, Fred L. Jr. and Anthony, F. Patt, *Military Rifles of Japan* (Florida: Julin Books, 1996), p. 150.
25. Frank, *Downfall*, pp. 172, 184.
26. Frank, *Downfall*, p. 189.
27. Rhodes, *Atomic Bomb*, p. 701.
28. Groves, *Now It Can Be Told*, p. 305.
29. Rhodes, *Atomic Bomb*, p. 577.
30. U.S. Office of War Information, *Japanese Propaganda: July 29 and 30, 1945* (California: U.S. Office of War Information, 1945).
31. Kort, *Hiroshima*, p. 388.
32. Kort, *Hiroshima*, pp. 277, 388.
33. Kort, *Hiroshima*, p. 279.
34. Kort, *Hiroshima*, pp. 283–284. Truman, *Memoirs*, p. 396.
35. Kort, *Hiroshima*, p. 283.
36. Kort, *Hiroshima*, pp. 55, 92.
37. Rhodes, *Atomic Bomb*, p. 693.
38. Kort, *Hiroshima*, p. 57.
39. Campbell, Richard H., *The Silverplate Bombers: A History and Registry of the Enola Gay and Other B-29s Configured to Carry Atomic Bombs* (North Carolina: McFarland, 2005), p. 40.

Chapter 21: The Victory Boys

1. Spitzer, Abe and Miller, Merle, *We Dropped the A-Bomb* (New York: Thomas Y. Crowell, 1946), p. 8.
2. Spitzer, *A-Bomb*, p. 8.
3. Campbell, *Silverplate Bombers*, p. 1. Tibbets, Paul W. Jr., Stebbins, Clair and Franken, Harry, *The Tibbets Story* (New York: Stein and Day, 1978), p. 169.

The Heroes We Needed

4.   Caron, George R. and Meares, Charlotte E., *Fire of a Thousand Suns: The George R. "Bob" Caron Story, Tail Gunner of the Enola Gay* (Colorado: Web Publishing, 1995), p. 189. Spitzer, *A-Bomb*, pp. 8–9.
5.   Tibbets, *Tibbets Story*, p. 191.
6.   Spitzer, *A-Bomb*, p. 9.
7.   Spitzer, *A-Bomb*, p. 6.
8.   Krauss, Robert and Krauss, Amelia, *The 509th Remembered: A History of the 509th Composite Group as told by the Veterans that Dropped the Atomic Bombs on Japan* (Michigan: Krauss, 2009), p. 34.
9.   Spitzer, *A-Bomb*, pp. vi, 6.
10.   Spitzer, *A-Bomb*, p. 10.
11.   Spitzer, *A-Bomb*, p. 5.
12.   Spitzer, *A-Bomb*, p. 14.
13.   Tibbets, *Tibbets Story*, p. 155. Groves, *Now It Can Be Told*, p. 254.
14.   Tibbets, *Tibbets Story*, p. 156.
15.   Tibbets, *Tibbets Story*, pp. 156–157.
16.   Tibbets, *Tibbets Story*, p. 160.
17.   Thomas, Gordon and Witts, Max Morgan, *Ruin from the Air: The Enola Gay's Atomic Mission to Hiroshima* (Michigan: Scarborough House, 1990), p. 281.
18.   Thomas, *Ruin from the Air*, p. 282.
19.   Spitzer, Abe, "Abe Spitzer's Diary: August 4, 1945," *Atomic Heritage Foundation* <www.atom-icheritage.org/sites/default/files/resources/Abe%20Spitzer%20Diary.pdf> (accessed 2 July 2020).
20.   Spitzer, *A-Bomb*, p. 12.
21.   Thomas, *Ruin from the Air*, p. 282.
22.   Spitzer, "Abe Spitzer's Diary: August 4, 1945."
23.   Thomas, *Ruin from the Air*, pp. 282–283.
24.   Thomas, *Ruin from the Air*, p. 283.
25.   Thomas, *Ruin from the Air*, p. 283.
26.   Spitzer, *A-Bomb*, p. 15.
27.   Tibbets, *Tibbets Story*, p. 204.
28.   Tibbets, *Tibbets Story*, p. 205.
29.   Christman, Al, *Target Hiroshima: Deak Parsons and the Creation of the Atomic Bomb* (Maryland: Naval Institute Press, 1998), p. 181.
30.   Tibbets, *Tibbets Story*, p. 205.
31.   Tibbets, *Tibbets Story*, pp. 204–205.
32.   Thomas, *Ruin from the Air*, p. 293.
33.   Thomas, *Ruin from the Air*, p. 294.
34.   Tibbets, *Tibbets Story*, p. 205.
35.   Thomas, *Ruin from the Air*, p. 297.
36.   Tibbets, *Tibbets Story*, p. 206. Thomas, *Ruin from the Air*, p. 297.
37.   Thomas, *Ruin from the Air*, p. 301.
38.   Thomas, *Ruin from the Air*, p. 301.
39.   Tibbets, *Tibbets Story*, p. 210.
40.   Tibbets, *Tibbets Story*, p. 211.

Chapter 22: A New Type of Bomb

1. Thomas, *Ruin from the Air*, p. 304.
2. Christman, *Target Hiroshima*, p. 183.
3. Tibbets, *Tibbets Story*, p. 199.
4. Tibbets, *Tibbets Story*, pp. 211–212.
5. Tibbets, *Tibbets Story*, pp. 213–214.
6. Tibbets, *Tibbets Story*, p. 201.
7. Hulver, Richard A. and Luebke, Peter C., *A Grave Misfortune: The USS Indianapolis Tragedy* (Washington, D.C.: Naval History and Heritage Command, 2018), pp. xxvii–xxx.
8. Tibbets, *Tibbets Story*, p. 213.
9. Tibbets, *Tibbets Story*, p. 214.
10. Spitzer, *A-Bomb*, p. 31.
11. Tibbets, *Tibbets Story*, pp. 215, 219.
12. Tibbets, *Tibbets Story*, p. 219.
13. Spitzer, *A-Bomb*, pp. 34–35.
14. Spitzer, *A-Bomb*, p. 35.
15. Campbell, *Silverplate Bombers*, pp. 72–74.
16. Tibbets, *Tibbets Story*, pp. 222–223.
17. Tibbets, *Tibbets Story*, p. 223.
18. Tibbets, *Tibbets Story*, p. 224.
19. Spitzer, *A-Bomb*, pp. 40–45.
20. Tibbets, *Tibbets Story*, p. 170.
21. Tibbets, *Tibbets Story*, p. 225.
22. Christman, *Target Hiroshima*, p. 192.
23. Caron, *"Bob" Caron Story*, p. 250.
24. Tibbets, *Tibbets Story*, p. 227.
25. Caron, *"Bob" Caron Story*, pp. 234, 258.
26. Tibbets, *Tibbets Story*, p. 227.
27. Tibbets, *Tibbets Story*, p. 228.
28. Tibbets, *Tibbets Story*, pp. 229–230.
29. Spitzer, *A-Bomb*, pp. 40–50.
30. Truman, *Memoirs*, p. 421.
31. Truman, *Memoirs*, p. 421.
32. Truman, *Memoirs*, p. 421.
33. Truman, *Memoirs*, p. 422.
34. Truman, *Memoirs*, p. 422.

Chapter 23: Evacuate Your Cities

1. War Department, Office of the Assistant Chief of Staff, G-2, "MAGIC – Far East Summary No. 507, 9 August 1945," *National Security Archive* <https://nsarchive.gwu.edu/documents/ atomic-bomb-end-world-war-ii/074.pdf> (accessed 4 August 2020).
2. War Department, "MAGIC" – No. 507."
3. War Department, "MAGIC" – No. 507."
4. Kort, *Hiroshima*, p. 233.
5. Truman, Harry S., "Radio Report to the American People on the Potsdam Conference," *Harry S. Truman Library and Museum* <www.trumanlibrary.gov/soundrecording-records/sr61-37radio-report-american-people-potsdam-conference> (accessed 26 July 2020).

Chapter 24: A New Gimmick

1. Spitzer, *A-Bomb*, p. 58.
2. Spitzer, *A-Bomb*, p. 59.
3. U.S. Office of War Information, *Japanese Propaganda: August 7, 1945*.
4. U.S. Office of War Information, *Japanese Propaganda: August 7, 1945*.
5. U.S. Office of War Information, *Japanese Propaganda: August 7, 1945*.
6. U.S. Office of War Information, *Japanese Propaganda: August 7, 1945*.
7. Kort, *Hiroshima*, pp. 310–311.
8. Kort, *Hiroshima*, pp. 318–319.
9. Spitzer, *A-Bomb*, p. 60.
10. Spitzer, *A-Bomb*, pp. 60–61.
11. Frank, *Downfall*, p. 270.
12. Frank, *Downfall*, p. 270.
13. War Department, Office of the Assistant Chief of Staff, G-2 "MAGIC – Far East Summary No. 515, 18 August 1945," *National Security Archive* <https://nsarchive.gwu.edu/documents/ atomic-bomb-end-world-war-ii/090.pdf> (accessed 4 August 2020).
14. Spitzer, *A-Bomb*, pp. 61–62.
15. Spitzer, *A-Bomb*, p. 62.
16. Tibbets, *Tibbets Story*, p. 236.
17. Krauss, *509th Remembered*, p. 114.
18. Spitzer, *A-Bomb*, p. 85.
19. Spitzer, *A-Bomb*, p. 89.
20. Spitzer, *A-Bomb*, p. 89.
21. Spitzer, *A-Bomb*, p. 90.
22. Spitzer, *A-Bomb*, p. 92.
23. Spitzer, *A-Bomb*, p. 81.
24. Krauss, *509th Remembered*, pp. 67, 161.
25. Krauss, *509th Remembered*, pp.67–68.
26. Spitzer, *A-Bomb*, p. 98.
27. Spitzer, *A-Bomb*, pp. 101–104.
28. Spitzer, *A-Bomb*, p. 109.
29. Spitzer, *A-Bomb*, p. 110.
30. Spitzer, *A-Bomb*, pp. 111–115.
31. Spitzer, *A-Bomb*, p. 120.
32. Spitzer, *A-Bomb*, pp. 119–120.

Chapter 25: The Sacred Decision

1. Kort, *Hiroshima*, pp. 311–312.
2. Kort, *Hiroshima*, pp. 69, 316.
3. Kort, *Hiroshima*, p. 316.
4. Kort, *Hiroshima*, p. 312.
5. Butow, Robert J.C., *Japan's Decision To Surrender* (California: Stanford University Press, 1974), pp. 165–167.
6. Kort, *Hiroshima*, pp. 312–313.
7. Hoshina, Zenshiro, *Secret History of the Greater East Asia War: Memoir of Zenshiro Hoshina* (Tokyo: Hara-Shobo, 1975), pp. 139–149. *National Security Archive* <https://nsarchive.gwu. edu/

documents/atomic-bomb-end-world-war-ii/075.pdf> (accessed 2 September 2020). Butow, *Japan's Decision*, pp. 175–176.

8. Hoshina, *Memoir of Zenshiro Hoshina*, pp. 139–149.
9. Kort, *Hiroshima*, p. 317.
10. Kort, *Hiroshima*, p. 317.
11. Kort, *Hiroshima*, p. 313.
12. Butow, *Japan's Decision*, p. 184.
13. War Department, Office of the Assistant Chief of Staff, G-2, "MAGIC – Diplomatic Summary No. 1233, 10 August 1945," *National Security Archive* <https://nsarchive.gwu.edu/documents/atomic-bomb-end-world-war-ii/077a.pdf> (accessed 1 September 2020). Truman, *Memoirs*, p. 427.
14. Butow, *Japan's Decision*, p. 186.
15. Truman, *Memoirs*, p. 428.
16. Truman, *Memoirs*, p. 428.
17. Kort, *Hiroshima*, p. 237.
18. Truman, *Memoirs*, p. 428.
19. Truman, *Memoirs*, p. 429.
20. Spitzer, *A-Bomb*, pp. 133–134.
21. Marshall, George C., "Carl Spaatz Papers Related To The Japan Air Raids: Eyes Only Message From General Marshall To General Spaatz, 11 August 1945," *Scribd* <www.scribd.com/document/37163410/Carl-Spaatz-papers-related-to-the-Japan-air-raids> (accessed 15 September 2020).
22. Speer, Bob, "The Last Mission," *USASTAF Brief*, Vol. 2, No. 40 (V-J Day Issue), p. 5.
23. Marshall, George C., "To General of the Army Douglas MacArthur and General Carl Spaatz, August 13, 1945," *The George C. Marshall Foundation* <www.marshallfoundation.org/library/digital-archive/to-general-of-the-army-douglas-macarthur-15/> (accessed 15 September 2020).
24. Arnold, H.H., "Carl Spaatz Papers Related To The Japan Air Raids: Special Radio Teletype Conference, 14 August 1945," *Scribd* <www.scribd.com/document/37163410/Carl-Spaatzpapers-related-to-the-Japan-air-raids> (accessed 15 September 2020).
25. Spitzer, *A-Bomb*, p. 134.
26. Brooks, Lester, *Behind Japan's Surrender: The Secret Struggle That Ended an Empire* (New York: McGraw-Hill, 1968), p. 256.
27. Brooks, *Japan's Surrender*, p. 256.
28. Brooks, *Japan's Surrender*, pp. 259–260.
29. Brooks, *Japan's Surrender*, p. 217.
30. Togo, Shigenori, *The Cause of Japan* (New York: Simon & Schuster, 1956), pp. 325–326. Butow, *Japan's Decision*, p. 194.
31. Togo, *Cause of Japan*, pp. 326–327.
32. Brooks, *Japan's Surrender*, p. 226.
33. Butow, *Japan's Decision*, p. 194.
34. Brooks, *Japan's Surrender*, p. 226.
35. Brooks, *Japan's Surrender*, p. 226.
36. Butow, *Japan's Decision*, p. 195.
37. Butow, *Japan's Decision*, pp. 195, 226.
38. Brooks, *Japan's Surrender*, p. 227.
39. Brooks, *Japan's Surrender*, p. 220.
40. Brooks, *Japan's Surrender*, p. 227.
41. Brooks, *Japan's Surrender*, pp. 230–231.
42. Brooks, *Japan's Surrender*, pp. 235–237.
43. Brooks, *Japan's Surrender*, p. 238.

44. Brooks, *Japan's Surrender*, p. 251.
45. Brooks, *Japan's Surrender*, pp. 251–252.
46. Butow, *Japan's Decision*, p. 205.
47. Brooks, *Japan's Surrender*, p. 253.
48. Togo, *Cause of Japan*, p. 332.
49. Togo, *Cause of Japan*, p. 332.
50. Brooks, *Japan's Surrender*, pp. 259, 270.
51. Brooks, *Japan's Surrender*, pp. 259–260.
52. Spitzer, *A-Bomb*, p. 135.
53. Norstad, Lauris, "Carl Spaatz Papers Related To The Japan Air Raids: Special Radio Teletype Conference, 14 August 1945," *Scribd* <www.scribd.com/document/37163410/Carl-Spaatzpapers-related-to-the-Japan-air-raids> (accessed 15 September 2020).
54. Groves, *Now It Can Be Told*, pp. 352–353.
55. Hull, John E. and Seeman, L.E., "Telephone Conversation Transcript, General Hull and Colonel Seeman – 1325 – 13 August 1945," *The National Security Archive* <https://nsarchive.gwu.edu/documents/atomic-bomb-end-world-war-ii/087.pdf> (accessed 2 September 2020).
56. Spitzer, *A-Bomb*, p. 134.
57. Brooks, *Japan's Surrender*, p. 256.
58. Brooks, *Japan's Surrender*, p. 276.
59. Brooks, *Japan's Surrender*, p. 264.
60. Brooks, *Japan's Surrender*, pp. 264–265.
61. Brooks, *Japan's Surrender*, p. 265.
62. Butow, *Japan's Decision*, pp. 207–208.
63. Brooks, *Japan's Surrender*, pp. 276–277.
64. Brooks, *Japan's Surrender*, pp. 279–280.
65. Spitzer, *A-Bomb*, p. 137.
66. Spitzer, *A-Bomb*, pp. 137–138.
67. Spitzer, *A-Bomb*, p. 136.
68. Brooks, *Japan's Surrender*, p. 290.
69. Spitzer, *A-Bomb*, pp. 138–139.
70. Brooks, *Japan's Surrender*, p. 304.
71. Brooks, *Japan's Surrender*, pp. 349, 311.
72. Brooks, *Japan's Surrender*, p. 353.
73. Brooks, *Japan's Surrender*, pp. 339, 380.
74. Spitzer, *A-Bomb*, p. 141.
75. Assistant Chief of Air Staff, *Mission Accomplished*, pp. 18, 92, 40, 23, 92, 25, 23, 31, 83, 76, 39.

Chapter 26: The End

1. Chauncey, Charles G., "We Named Our Plane 'Goin' Jessie' and She Became Top Performing B-29," in Marshall, Chester (ed.), *The Global Twentieth Vol. II* (Tennessee: Marshall Publishers, 1987), pp. 161–166.
2. Blum, Andrew, "I feel that the A-bomb has made another war impossible," *United Press International* <www.upi.com/Archives/1984/05/28/I-feel-that-the-A-bomb-has madeanother-war/1637454564800/> (accessed 12 November 2020).
3. Checkertale, "B-29's Complete Last Flight: Rarick Pilots Final Superfortress Flight," *Checkertale*, Vol. 1, No. 3 (July 21, 1960).
4. Campbell, *Silverplate Bombers*, pp. 194–198.

5. Krauss, *509th Remembered*, pp. 67–68.
6. Army Air Forces, *Statistical Digest*, Tables 43, 99, 101.

Epilogue

1. Frank, *Downfall*, p. 287.
2. Boister, Neil and Cryer, Robert, *Documents on the Tokyo International Military Tribunal: Charter, Indictment and Judgments* (New York: Oxford University Press, 2008), p. 537. Scott, James M., *Target Tokyo: Jimmy Doolittle and the Raid That Avenged Pearl Harbor* (New York: W.W. Norton & Company, 2015) p. xiv.
3. Frank, *Downfall*, pp. 325–326.
4. Manhattan Engineer District, *The Atomic Bombings of Hiroshima and Nagasaki* (New York: Manhattan Engineer District, 1946), p. 42.
5. Lester Morris letter to Jack Lamb, 20 November 1945. Mark Miller (2020) "Shumate Crew." Email (21 April 2020).
6. Office of the Staff Judge Advocate, Headquarters Eighth Army, U.S. Army, "United States of America vs. Shichisaburo Yajima," *Philipps-University Marburg* <www.online.uni-marburg.de/icwc/yokohama/Yokohama%20No.%20T066.pdf> (accessed 11 April 2019), pp. 186, 43, 27.
7. Judge Advocate, "U.S. vs. Yajima," p. 172.
8. Judge Advocate, "U.S. vs. Yajima," pp. 47, 84.
9. Judge Advocate, "U.S. vs. Yajima," p. 48.
10. Judge Advocate, "U.S. vs. Yajima," pp. 83, 173.
11. Judge Advocate, "U.S. vs. Yajima," pp. 172–173.
12. Judge Advocate, "U.S. vs. Yajima," p. 83.
13. Judge Advocate, "U.S. vs. Yajima," pp. 83, 174.
14. Judge Advocate, "U.S. vs. Yajima," p. 187.
15. Judge Advocate, "U.S. vs. Yajima," pp. 84–85.
16. Judge Advocate, "U.S. vs. Yajima," pp. 51–52.
17. Judge Advocate, "U.S. vs. Yajima," p. 53.
18. Judge Advocate, "U.S. vs. Yajima," p. 53.
19. Judge Advocate, "U.S. vs. Yajima," p. 142.
20. Judge Advocate, "U.S. vs. Yajima," p. 141.
21. Judge Advocate, "U.S. vs. Yajima," p. 53.
22. Judge Advocate, "U.S. vs. Yajima," p. 55.
23. Judge Advocate, "U.S. vs. Yajima," pp. 144, 56.
24. Lester Morris letter to Jack Lamb, 20 November 1945. Mark Miller (2020) "Shumate Crew." Email (21 April 2020).
25. Judge Advocate, "U.S. vs. Yajima," pp. 196–197.
26. Judge Advocate, "U.S. vs. Yajima," pp .262, 168–170.
27. Landas, Marc, *The Fallen: A True Story of American POWs and Japanese Wartime Atrocities* (New Jersey: John Wiley & Sons, 2004), pp. 192–194; 229–234.
28. Whitman, Howard, "U.S. Based Bombers Blast Ten Nazi Subs: Daily News, 28 August 1943," *Newspapers.com* <www.newspapers.com/newspage/435674188/> (accessed 12 March 2019).
29. Lawrence, J.P., "Korea: Silver Crim," *San Antonio Express News* <www.expressnews.com/military-city/article/Korea-Silver-Crim-10606717.php> (accessed 26 December 2016).
30. Crim, Silver (2017) "Message." Email (12 May 2017).

Bibliography

5th Marine Division, "Lieutenant George W. Haynes Silver Star Citation," *The Hall of Valor Project*
    <https://valor.militarytimes.com/hero/36739> (accessed 15 December 2019).
33rd Statistical Control Unit, *Monthly Activity Report: February*, XXI Bomber Command (1 March
    1945).
33rd Statistical Control Unit, *Monthly Activity Report: March*, XXI Bomber Command (5 April 1945).
58th Bomb Wing, *B-29 Familiarization File* (Georgia: 58th Bomb Wing, 1943).
73rd Bomb Wing, *Tactical Mission Report: Mission No. 7* (24 November 1944).
73rd Bomb Wing, *Consolidated Mission Report: Mission No. 9* (29 November 1944).
73rd Bomb Wing, *Consolidated Mission Report: Mission No. 10* (3 December 1944).
73rd Bomb Wing, *Consolidated Statistical Summary: Mission No. 14* (22 December 1944).
73rd Bomb Wing, *Consolidated Statistical Summary: Mission No. 17* (3 January 1945).
73rd Bomb Wing, *Consolidated Mission Report: Mission No. 20* (19 January 1945).
73rd Bomb Wing, *Consolidated Statistical Summary: Mission No. 21* (23 January 1945).
73rd Bomb Wing, *Consolidated Statistical Summary: Mission No. 22* (27 January 1945).
73rd Bomb Wing, *Consolidated Mission Report: Mission No. 22* (27 January 1945).
73rd Bomb Wing, *Consolidated Mission Report: Mission No. 29* (10 March 1945).
462nd Bomb Group, *Bombing Equipment in B-29 Airplane*, U.S. Army Air Forces (11 February
    1944).
462nd Bomb Group, *Special Orders Number 89*, U.S. Army Air Forces (2 April 1944).
497th Bomb Group, *Consolidated Mission Report: Mission No. 29* (10 March 1945).
Abeare-Welch, Angelique, "Memorial Day Memory – 1st Lt. David C. Williams Jr. KIA, Japan,
    WWII & the Crew of B-29 Haley's Comet," *Angelique's Rabbit Hole* <http://porphyrins.org/
    angeliques_rabbit_hole/?p=37> (accessed 2 December 2010).
Adler, Bartholomew, "First B-29 Combat Mission – 5 June 1944," *40th Bomb Group*
    <www.40thbombgroup.org/memories/Memories9.pdf> (accessed 14 August 2014).
Agather, Victor, "The Battle of Kansas (Part 1)," *40th Bomb Group* <www.40thbombgroup.org/
    memories/Memories11.pdf> (accessed 14 August 2014).
Air Group 31, "Pilots of Fighter Squadron 31," *Air Group 31* <www.vf31.com/pilots/vf-31.html>
    (accessed 27 June 2018).
American News Service, *B-29 Command Now Calling Its Shots*, The Daily Target Saipan, Vol. II,
    No.83 (29 July 1945).
Arnold, H.H., *Report of the Commanding General of the Army Air Forces to the Secretary of War, 4
    January 1944* (location unknown: U.S. Army Air Forces, 1944).
Arnold, H.H., *Global Mission* (New York: Harper & Brothers, 1949).

Arnold, H.H., "Carl Spaatz Papers Related To The Japan Air Raids: Special Radio Teletype Conference, 14 August 1945," *Scribd* <www.scribd.com/document/37163410/Carl-Spaatzpapers-related-to-the-Japan-air-raids> (accessed 15 September 2020).

Assistant Chief of Air Staff – Intelligence, *Mission Accomplished: Interrogations of Japanese Industrial, Military, and Civil Leaders of World War II* (Washington, D.C.: U.S. Army Air Forces, 1946).

Bainbridge, Kenneth T., "A Foul and Awesome Display," *The Bulletin of Atomic Scientists*, Vol. XXXI, No. 5 (May 1975).

Baird, A. Craig, *Representative American Speeches: 1945–1946* (New York: H.W. Wilson Company, 1946).

Baldwin, Burton K., *Flight Log of Burton K. Baldwin* (1944–1945).

Beasley, Norman, *Knudsen: A Biography* (New York: McGraw-Hill, 1947).

Beckemeier, Theodore E., "Daily Diary: Major General Curtis E. LeMay: Resume of Events While Aide-De-Camp to Major General Curtis E. LeMay, June 25, 1943 to September 25, 1945," *Scribd* <www.scribd.com/document/37161060/Curtis-E-LeMay-Daily-Diary-1944-1945> (accessed 22 January 2020).

Birdsall, Steve, *Saga of the Superfortress* (New York: Doubleday, 1980).

Blum, Andrew, "I feel that the A-bomb has made another war impossible," *United Press International* <www.upi.com/Archives/1984/05/28/I-feel-that-the-A-bomb-has-made-another-war/ 1637454564800/> (accessed 12 November 2020).

Boister, Neil and Cryer, Robert, *Documents on the Tokyo International Military Tribunal: Charter, Indictment and Judgments* (New York: Oxford University Press, 2008).

Bradley, James and Powers, Ron, *Flags of Our Fathers* (New York: Bantam, 2000).

Brief, "Recon and Raid," *AAFPOA Brief*, Vol. 2, No. 2 (12 December 1944).

Brief, "Cover," *AAFPOA Brief*, Vol. 2, No. 14 (6 March 1945).

Brief, "India Wing," *AAFPOA Brief*, Vol. 2, No. 33 (17 July 1945).

Brief, "Iwo Echelon," *AAFPOA Brief*, Vol. 2, No. 17 (27 March 1945).

Bruccoli, Matthew J., *James Gould Cozzens: A Time of War: Air Force Diaries and Pentagon Memos 1943–45* (South Carolina: Bruccoli Clark, 1984).

Bundy, Harvey H., "Remembered Words," *The Atlantic*, Vol. 199, No. 3 (March 1957).

Boeing Aircraft Company, "Boeing Statement On Bomber Crash," *Boeing News*, Vol. 2, No. 5 (24 February 1943).

Boeing Aircraft Company, "Jigsaw Picture in 40,000 Parts," *Boeing Magazine*, Vol. XIV, No. 10 (October 1944).

Boeing Aircraft Company, *This is Boeing* (Washington: Boeing, date unknown).

Boeing Aircraft Company, "Trailblazer," *Boeing Magazine*, Vol. XIV, No. 7 (July 1944).

Boeing Aircraft Company, "World Wide Wings," *Boeing Magazine*, Vol. XIV, No. 7 (July 1944).

Bowers, William T., "Ben Salomon and the Medal of Honor," *U.S. Army Medical Department, Office of Medical History* <https://history.amedd.army.mil/corps/dental/leaders/citation.html> (accessed 3 September 2019).

Brooks, Lester, *Behind Japan's Surrender: The Secret Struggle That Ended an Empire* (New York: McGraw-Hill, 1968).

Brusgulis, Peter, *Radar Operators Report: 27 January 1945* (27 January 1945).

Burchinal, David A., *Analysis of Incendiary Phase of Operations Against Japanese Urban Areas, 9–19 March 1945*, XXI Bomber Command (March 1945).

Burger, Knox, "Fire Raid," *Yank*, Vol. 4, No. 23 (23 November 1945).

Burger, Knox, "Lynn Delivers Her Child," *Yank*, Vol. 3, No. 28 (29 December 1944).

Burger, Knox, "Trapeze Act Over Japan," *Yank*, Vol. 3, No. 39 (16 March 1945).

Butow, Robert J.C., *Japan's Decision To Surrender* (California: Stanford University Press, 1974).

Caidin, Martin, *A Torch to the Enemy: The Fire Raid on Tokyo* (New York: Bantam, 1992).

Call, Helen, "Birth of the B-29," *Boeing Magazine*, Vol. XIV, No. 7 (July 1944).

Call, Helen, "Get a load on that wing," *Boeing Magazine*, Vol. XIV, No. 9 (September 1944).

Call, Helen, "The Minute Men of Kansas," *Boeing Magazine*, Vol. XV, No. 6 (June 1945).

Campbell, Richard H., *The Silverplate Bombers: A History and Registry of the Enola Gay and Other B-29s Configured to Carry Atomic Bombs* (North Carolina: McFarland, 2005).

Carmichael, M.E., "The Battle of Kansas (Part 1)," *40th Bomb Group* <www.40thbombgroup.org/memories/Memories11.pdf> (accessed 14 August 2014).

Caron, George R. and Meares, Charlotte E., *Fire of a Thousand Suns: The George R. "Bob" Caron Story, Tail Gunner of the Enola Gay* (Colorado: Web Publishing, 1995).

Cate, James L., *History of the Twentieth Air Force: Genesis* (Washington, D.C.: AAF Historical Office, 1945).

Carter, Kit C. and Mueller, Robert, *The Army Air Forces in WWII: Combat Chronology, 1941–1945* (Alabama: Albert F. Simpson Historical Research Center, Air University, 1973).

Chauncey, Charles G., "We Named Our Plane 'Goin' Jessie' and She Became Top Performing B-29," in Chester Marshall (ed.), *The Global Twentieth Vol. II* (Tennessee: Marshall Publishers, 1987).

Checkertale, "B-29's Complete Last Flight: Rarick Pilots Final Superfortress Flight," *Checkertale*, Vol. 1, No. 3 (July 21, 1960).

Christman, Al, *Target Hiroshima: Deak Parsons and the Creation of the Atomic Bomb* (Maryland: Naval Institute Press, 1998).

Churchill, Winston, "Their Finest Hour," *International Churchill Society* <www.winstonchurchill.org/resources/speeches/1940-the-finest-hour/their-finest-hour>(accessed 30 January 2019).

Churchill, Winston, "We Shall Fight on the Beaches," *International Churchill Society* <www.winstonchurchill.org/resources/speeches/1940-the-finest-hour/we-shall-fight-on-thebeaches> (accessed 30 January 2019).

Cima, Anthony P., *The Thrilling Story of Boeing's B-29 Superfortress* (New York: Playmore, 1944).

Coffey, Thomas M., *Iron Eagle: The Turbulent Life of General Curtis LeMay* (New York: Crown Publishers, 1986).

Collison, Thomas, *The Superfortress is Born: The Story of the Boeing B-29* (New York: Duell, Sloan & Pearce, 1945).

Colman, Penny, *Rosie the Riveter: Women Working on the Home Front in World War II* (New York: Crown Publishers, 1995).

Conscience and the Constitution, "In remembrance of Sgt. Ben Kuroki," *YouTube* <www.youtube.com/watch?v=DUqDZuSp2Io> (accessed 2 January 2016).

Cook, Haruko Taya, "The Myth of the Saipan Suicides," *MHQ: The Quarterly Journal of Military History*, Vol. 7, No. 3 (spring 1995).

Cook, Haruko Taya and Cook, Theodore F., *Japan At War: An Oral History* (New York: The New Press, 1992).

Craven, W.F. and Cate, J.L., *The Army Air Forces in WWII, Volume I: Plans and Early Operations, January 1939 to August 1942* (Washington, D.C.: Office of Air Force History, 1983).

Craven, W.F. and Cate, J.L, *The Army Air Forces in WWII, Volume V: The Pacific: Matterhorn to Nagasaki, June 1944 to August 1945* (Washington, D.C.: Office of Air Force History, 1983).

Craven, W.F. and Cate, J.L., *The Army Air Forces in WWII, Volume VI: Men and Planes* (Illinois: University of Chicago Press, 1955).

Culbertson, Jean, "Service Moves Haynes," *Clarion-Ledger Newspaper* (14 June 1970).

Davis, Joseph T., *The Story of the 73rd: The Unofficial History of the 73rd Bomb Wing* (Texas: 73rd Bomb Wing, 1946).

Dixson, Walter Clay, *From Tyler, Texas to Tokyo: The Pacific War Letters and Photograph Collection of Captain Elmer R. Dixson* (Texas: Historic Aviation Memorial Museum, 2002).

Dossett, Walter B. Sr., "The Diary of Major Walter B. Dossett, Sr," *497th Bomb Group B-29 Memorial* <http://www.497thbombgroupb29.org/personal%20accounts/Dossett,%20Walter%20B.%20Personal%20Account%20497th.pdf> (accessed 1 October 2019).

Dugan, Richard L. and Speer, Bob, "Japan's Invisible Ally," *AAFPOA Brief*, Vol. 2, No. 19 (10 April 1945).

Duke University Libraries, "Loans & Bonds: Brief History of World War Two Advertising Campaigns, War Loans and Bonds," *Duke University Libraries* <https://library.duke.edu/specialcollections/scriptorium/adaccess/warbonds.html> (accessed 20 June 2019).

Edmundson, James V., "Birth and Rise of the Twentieth Air Force," in Chester Marshall (ed.), *The Global Twentieth Vol. IV* (Tennessee: Global, 1992).

Edoin, Hoito, *The Night Tokyo Burned* (New York: St Martin's Press, 1987).

Einstein, Albert and Szilard, Leo, "Einstein-Szilard letter to President Franklin D. Roosevelt, 2 August 1939," *Franklin D. Roosevelt Presidential Library and Museum* <http://docs.fdrlibrary.marist.edu/psf/box5/a64a01.html> (accessed 19 January 2019).

Ferrell, Robert H., *Off the Record: The Private Papers of Harry S. Truman* (New York: Harper & Row, 1980).

Frank, Richard B., *Downfall: The End of the Imperial Japanese Empire* (New York: Penguin, 1999).

Frederick, Robert O., "This is What Happened," *AAFPOA Brief*, Vol. 2, No. 21 (24 April 1945).

Fukubayashi, Toru, "Allied Aircraft and Airmen Lost Over the Japanese Mainland During WWII: Chubu Army District," *POW Research Network Japan* <www.powresearch.jp/en/pdf_e/pilot/ chubu.pdf> (accessed 25 October 2016).

Fukubayashi, Toru, "Allied Aircraft and Airmen Lost Over the Japanese Mainland During WWII: Tobu Army District," *POW Research Network Japan* <www.powresearch.jp/en/pdf_e/pilot/ tobu.pdf> (accessed 25 October 2016).

General Electric, "The Battle of Kansas (Part 1)," *40th Bomb Group* <www.40thbombgroup.org/memories/Memories11.pdf> (accessed 14 August 2014).

Giangreco, D.M., *Hell To Pay: Operation Downfall and the Invasion of Japan, 1945–47* (Maryland: Naval Institute Press, 2009).

Gottleib, Irving L., "44th Bomb Squadron History, June 1944," *40th Bomb Group* <www.40thbomb group.org/Archives/44thSQ_Files/44thSQ_Jun44.pdf> (accessed 14 August 2014).

Griffith, Charles, *The Quest: Haywood Hansell and American Strategic Bombing in World War II* (Alabama: Air University Press, 1999).

Groves, Leslie M., *Now It Can Be Told: The Story of the Manhattan Project* (New York: Da Capo Press, 1983).

Gurney, Gene, *Journey of the Giants* (New York: Coward-McCann, 1961).

Hall, Robert L., "The Battle of Kansas, Part II," *40th Bomb Group* <www.40thbombgroup.org/
    memories/Memories13.pdf> (accessed 14 August 2014).

Hartman, Alan, "Hell for Honshu," *AAFPOA Brief*, Vol. 2, No. 21 (24 April 1945).

Harvey, Alva, "Birth and Deployment of the B-29," in Chester Marshall (ed.), *The Global Twentieth
    Vol. I* (Minnesota: Apollo, 1985).

Hansell, Haywood S. Jr., *Strategic Air War Against Japan* (Alabama: Airpower Research Institute,
    Air War College, Maxwell Air Force Base, 1980).

Hansell, Haywood S. Jr., *The Strategic Air War Against Germany and Japan: A Memoir* (Washington,
    D.C.: Office of Air Force History, United States Air Force, 1986).

Haynes, Fred and Warren, James A., *The Lions of Iwo Jima* (New York: Henry Holt, 2008).

Headquarters, Eighth Air Force, *Engine Fires* (Texas: Eighth Air Force, date unknown).

Headquarters, Eighth Army, *Resume of Official Records Pertaining to Crash of B-29 #42-24616, 27
    January 1945*, Headquarters, Eighth Army, U.S. Army (18 June 1948).

Headquarters, Expeditionary Troops, Task Force 56, "Report of Planning, Operations: Iwo Jima
    Operation, Enclosure B, 1 May 1945," *HyperWar Pacific Theater of Operations* <www.ibiblio.
    org/hyperwar/PTO/Iwo/ComTaskForFiftySixIwoJima/TaskForFiftySix-EnclosureB.pdf>
    (accessed 27 November 2019).

Headquarters, Twentieth Air Force, "Distinguished Flying Cross Citation: Captain Howard
    M. Clifford," *497th Bomb Group B-29 Memorial* <www.497thbombgroupb29.org/records/
    DFC%20citations%20.pdf> (accessed 17 August 2016).

Headquarters, Twentieth Air Force, "Raymond E. Shumway, Soldier's Medal Citation," *The Hall of
    Valor Project* <https://valor.militarytimes.com/hero/27689> (accessed 19 November 2017).

Herman, Arthur, *Freedom's Forge: How American Business Produced Victory in World War II* (New
    York: Random House, 2012).

Hilton, Robert, *B-29 Superfortress Combat Chronicles* (Texas: Squadron/Signal, 2012).

Hoisington, Perry M. II, *Thurman W. Sallade Commendation*, 462nd Bomb Group (4 March 1945).

Honeycutt, Fred L. Jr. and Anthony, F. Patt, *Military Rifles of Japan* (Florida: Julin Books, 1996).

Honolulu Star-Bulletin, "VITAL TOKYO TARGETS HIT," *Honolulu Star-Bulletin*, Vol. 51, No.
    16285 (24 November 1944).

Hoshina, Zenshiro, "Secret History of the Greater East Asia War: Memoir of Zenshiro Hoshina"
    (Tokyo: Hara-Shobo, 1975), pp. 139–149, *National Security Archive* <https://nsarchive.gwu.
    edu/documents/atomic-bomb-end-world-war-ii/075.pdf> (accessed 2 September 2020).

Hudson, J. Ed, "A History of the USS CABOT (CVL-28): A Fast Carrier in World War II," *stex-
    boat.com* <www.stexboat.com/books/cabot/cab03_05.htm> (accessed 27 June 2018).

Huie, William Bradford, *From Omaha to Okinawa: The Story of the Seabees* (New York: E.P. Dutton,
    1945).

Hull, John E. and Seeman, L.E., "Telephone Conversation Transcript, General Hull and Colonel
    Seeman – 1325 – 13 August 1945," *The National Security Archive* <https://nsarchive.gwu.edu/
    documents/atomic-bomb-end-world-war-ii/087.pdf> (accessed 2 September 2020).

Hulver, Richard A. and Luebke, Peter C., *A Grave Misfortune: The USS Indianapolis Tragedy*
    (Washington, D.C.: Naval History and Heritage Command, 2018).

Huston, John W., *American Airpower Comes of Age: General Henry H. "Hap" Arnold's World War II
    Diaries: Volume 2* (Alabama: Air University Press, 2002).

International Churchill Society, "Education – Bombing Germany: Again," *International Churchill
    Society* <https://winstonchurchill.org/publications/finest-hour/finest-hour 127/education-
    bombing-germany-again/> (accessed 21 January 2020).

Kakehashi, Kumiko, *So Sad to Fall in Battle: An Account of War Based on General Tadamichi Kuribayashi's Letters from Iwo Jima* (New York: Presidio Press, 2007).

Kato, Masuo, *The Lost War: A Japanese Reporter's Inside Story* (New York: Alfred A. Knopf, 1946).

Kidd, Sam C., letters to LaNelle Kidd, August–September 1945 (Sam Kidd, Jr., collection).

Kohn, Richard H. and Harahan, Joseph P., *Strategic Air Warfare: An Interview with Generals Curtis E. LeMay, Leon W. Johnson, David A. Burchinal, and Jack J. Catton* (Washington, D.C.: Office of Air Force History, 1988).

Kort, Michael, *The Columbia Guide To Hiroshima and The Bomb* (New York: Columbia University Press, 2007).

Krantz, James R., "Head First Over Japan," *AAFPOA Brief*, Vol. 2, No. 9 (20 January 1945).

Krauss, Robert and Krauss, Amelia, *The 509th Remembered: A History of the 509th Composite Group as told by the Veterans that Dropped the Atomic Bombs on Japan* (Michigan: Krauss, 2009).

Kuroki, Ben, *Ben Kuroki's Story* (Utah: Japanese American Citizens League, 1944).

Landas, Marc, *The Fallen: A True Story of American POWs and Japanese Wartime Atrocities* (New Jersey: John Wiley & Sons, 2004).

Lawrence, J.P., "Korea: Silver Crim," *San Antonio Express News* <www.expressnews.com/military-city/article/Korea-Silver-Crim-10606717.php> (accessed 26 December 2016).

Lee, Knute, *Survivor: Knute's Wild Story* (Nebraska: Authors Choice Press, 2003).

LeMay, Curtis E. and Kantor, MacKinlay, *Mission with LeMay: My Story* (New York: Doubleday, 1965).

LeMay, Curtis E. and Yenne, Bill, *Superfortress: The B-29 and American Air Power* (New York: McGraw-Hill, 1988).

Life Magazine, "U.S. Auto Plants Are Cleared For War," *Life Magazine*, Vol. 12, No. 7 (1942).

Lind, Wilfred N., "With a B-29 Over Japan – A Pilot's Story," *New York Times Magazine* (25 March 1945).

Lowman, Clarence P., "45th Bomb Squadron History Report, May 1944," *40th Bomb Group* <www.40thbombgroup.org/Archives/45thSQ_Files/45thSq_May44.pdf> (accessed 14 August 2014).

Lukesh, Jean A., *Lucky Ears: The True Story of Ben Kuroki* (Nebraska: Field Mouse Productions, 2010).

MacArthur, Douglas, *Reports of General MacArthur: MacArthur In Japan: The Occupation: Military Phase Volume I Supplement* (Washington, D.C.: Center of Military History, U.S. Army, 1994).

MacArthur, Douglas, *Reports of General MacArthur: Japanese Operations In The Southwest Pacific Area: Volume II – Part II* (Washington, D.C.: Center of Military History, U.S. Army, 1994).

Mackey, Bill, "Lucas & Crew Show a B-29 to the President," *40th Bomb Group* <www.40thbombgroup. org/memories/Memories31.pdf> (accessed 14 August 2014).

Manhattan Engineer District, *The Atomic Bombings of Hiroshima and Nagasaki* (New York: Manhattan Engineer District, 1946).

Mann, Robert A., *The B-29 Superfortress: A Comprehensive Registry of the Planes and Their Missions* (North Carolina: McFarland, 2004).

Mann, Robert A., *The B-29 Superfortress Chronology, 1934–1960* (North Carolina: McFarland, 2009).

Marshall, Chester W. and Thompson, Warren, *Final Assault on the Rising Sun: Combat Diaries of B-29 Air Crews Over Japan* (Minnesota: Specialty Press, 1995).

Marshall, George C., "Carl Spaatz Papers Related To The Japan Air Raids," *Scribd* <www.scribd.com/document/37163410/Carl-Spaatz-papers-related-to-the-Japan-air-raids> (accessed 15 September 2020).

Marshall, George C., "To General of the Army Douglas MacArthur and General Carl Spaatz, August 13, 1945," *The George C. Marshall Foundation* <www.marshallfoundation.org/library/digital-archive/to-general-of-the-army-douglas-macarthur-15/> (accessed 15 September 2020).

Martin, Harold H., "Black Snow and Leaping Tigers," *Harper's Magazine*, No. 1149 (February 1946).

Martin, Milt, "Hap Halloran Interview, Part 4 of 6," *YouTube* <www.youtube.com/watch?v=NNBfTCYML_4> (accessed 9 February 2020).

Martin, Ralph G., *Boy from Nebraska: The story of Ben Kuroki* (New York: Harper & Brothers, 1946).

Martindale, Robert R., *The 13th Mission: The Saga of a POW at Camp Omori, Tokyo* (Texas: Eakin, 1998).

Mathers, Ira V., "The Battle of Kansas, Part II," *40th Bomb Group* <www.40thbombgroup.org/memories/Memories13.pdf> (accessed 14 August 2014).

Matthews, Ira V., "Setting the Record Straight, Story 80," *40th Bomb Group* <www.40thbombgroup.org/matthews/Ira80.htm> (accessed 14 August 2014).

McKelway, St. Clair, "A Reporter with the B-29s: III – The Cigar, the Three Wings, and the Low-Level Attacks," *The New Yorker*, Vol. XXI, No. 19 (23 June 1945).

McNair, William N., "40th Bomb Group History Report, September 1944," *40th Bomb Group* <www.40thbombgroup.org/Archives/40thBG_Files/40thBG_Sep44_Main.pdf> (accessed 14 August 2014).

McWilliams, Bill, *Sunday in Hell: Pearl Harbor Minute By Minute* (New York: Open Road Media, 2014).

Memorial Branch, QM, Headquarters Eighth Army, U.S. Army, "Report of Disinterment for Identification: Unknown X-51, 6 May 1946," *73rd Bomb Wing (VH) POW Honor Roll* <www.exciteableitalian.com/POW%20Honor%20Roll/The%2055/19%20HART/02%20identification/Identification1.htm> (accessed 1 February 2021).

Miller, Donald L., *D-Days in the Pacific* (New York: Simon & Schuster, 2005).

Miller, Donald L., *Masters of the Air: America's Bomber Boys Who Fought the Air War Against Nazi Germany* (New York: Simon & Schuster, 2006).

Miller, Mark James, "When a submarine attacked Goleta," *Santa Maria Times* <https://santamariatimes.com/news/opinion/editorial/commentary/guest_commentary/when-a-submarine-attacked-goleta/article_6d0e3a7b-3e62-56eb-8ff8-f1994932b86e.html> (accessed 18 February 2019).

Mitchell, John H., "Service Testing of the Early B-29s," in Chester Marshall (ed.), *The Global Twentieth Vol. II* (Tennessee: Marshall, 1987).

Morgan, Robert and Powers, Ron, *The Man Who Flew The Memphis Belle* (New York : New American Library, 2002).

Nakamura, Taizo, "A B-29 rammed by a Ki-45 Nick Over Funabashi," *Pacific Wrecks* <https://pacificwrecks.com/aircraft/ki-45/4067/history.html> (accessed 14 November 2010).

National Archives of Australia, "The bombing of Darwin – Fact sheet 195, Japanese air raids on Darwin and northern Australia, 1942–43," *National Archives of Australia* <www.naa.gov.au/collection/fact-sheets/fs195.aspx> (accessed 12 February 2019).

Naval History and Heritage Command, "Overview of The Pearl Harbor Attack, 7 December 1941," *Naval History and Heritage Command, U.S. Navy* <www.history.navy.mil/research/

library/online-reading-room/title-list-alphabetically/p/the-pearl-harbor-attack-7-december-1941. html> (accessed 11 February 2019).

Newcomb, Richard F., *Abandon Ship! The Saga of the USS Indianapolis, the Navy's Greatest Sea Disaster* (New York: HarperCollins, 2001).

Norstad, Lauris, "Carl Spaatz Papers Related To The Japan Air Raids: Special Radio Teletype Conference, 14 August 1945," *Scribd* <www.scribd.com/document/37163410/Carl-Spaatzpapers-related-to-the-Japan-air-raids> (accessed 15 September 2020).

Nutter, Ralph H., *With the Possum and the Eagle: The Memoir of a Navigator's War over Germany and Japan* (California: Presidio, 2002).

Office of the Assistant Chief of Staff, Intelligence, *Air Objective Folder Japan, No. 90.17, Tokyo Area*, U.S. Army Air Forces (23 February 1944).

Office of the Historian, United States Department of State, "Foreign Relations of the United States: Diplomatic Papers, Conferences at Malta and Yalta, 1945: Agreement Regarding Entry of the Soviet Union Into the War Against Japan, February 11, 1945," *Office of the Historian* <https://history.state.gov/historicaldocuments/frus1945Malta/d503> (accessed 24 May 2020).

Office of the Historian, United States Department of State, "Foreign Relations of the United States: Diplomatic Papers, The Conference of Berlin (The Potsdam Conference), 1945, Volume I," *Office of the Historian* <https://history.state.gov/historicaldocuments/frus1945Berlinv01> (accessed 13 May 2020).

Office of the Historian, United States Department of State, "Foreign Relations of the United States: Diplomatic Papers, The Conference of Berlin (The Potsdam Conference), 1945, Volume II," *Office of the Historian* <https://history.state.gov/historicaldocuments/frus1945Berlinv02> (accessed 13 May 2020).

Office of the Historian, United States Department of State, "Summary of the Three-Power Pact Between Japan, Germany, and Italy, Signed at Berlin, September 27, 1940," *Office of the Historian* <https://history.state.gov/historicaldocuments/frus1931-41v02/d100> (accessed 31 January 2019).

Office of the Staff Judge Advocate, Headquarters Eighth Army, U.S. Army, "United States of America vs. Hideo Fujioka," *Philipps-University Marburg* <www.online.uni-marburg.de/icwc/yokohama/Yokohama%20No.%20T328.pdf> (accessed 22 September 2019).

Office of the Staff Judge Advocate, Headquarters Eighth Army, U.S. Army, "United States of America vs. Jiro Hamamoto," *Philipps-University Marburg* <www.online.uni-marburg.de/icwc/yokohama/Yokohama%20No.%20T364.pdf> (accessed 22 September 2019).

Office of the Staff Judge Advocate, Headquarters Eighth Army, U.S. Army, "United States of America vs. Shichisaburo Yajima," *Philipps-University Marburg* <www.online.uni-marburg.de/icwc/yokohama/Yokohama%20No.%20T066.pdf> (accessed 11 April 2019).

Office of the Staff Judge Advocate, Headquarters Eighth Army, U.S. Army, "United States of America vs. Toshio Tashiro," *Philipps-University Marburg* <www.online.uni-marburg.de/icwc/yokohama/Yokohama%20No.%20T078.pdf> (accessed 14 November 2019).

O'Keefe, James J., "Going Overseas, Part II," *40th Bomb Group* <www.40thbombgroup.org/memories/Memories24.pdf> (accessed 14 August 2014).

O'Keefe, James J., "The Day We Flew the Superstitious Aloysious," in Chester Marshall (ed.), *The Global Twentieth Vol. II* (Tennessee: Marshall, 1987).

Oliver, Philip G., *Hellbird War Book* (location unknown: A.F. Kalberer, undated).

Phillips, Charles L. Jr., *Rain of Fire: B-29s Over Japan, 1945* (California: B-Nijuku Publishing, 1995).

Picklum, Neysa McNeley, "Personal Story of David Frederick McNeley," *North Des Moines High School Wall of Honor* <www.nhwallofhonor.com/pages/storyofahellbirdcrewmcneley1942+.html> (accessed 28 March 2017).

Price, William E., "The Crew That Wasn't," in Chester Marshall (ed.), *The Global Twentieth Vol. III* (Tennessee: Global Press, 1988).

Prideaux, Tom, "B-29 Payoff," *Impact*, Vol. 3, No. 9 (Sept–Oct 1945).

Prideaux, Tom, "The B-29ers," *Impact*, Vol. 3, No. 9 (Sept–Oct 1945).

Putt, Donald L., "The B-29 Superfortress," *Air Force Magazine*, Vol. 27, No. 7 (July 1944).

Rhodes, Richard, *The Making of the Atomic Bomb* (New York: Touchstone, 1988).

Rigdon, William M., "Log of the President's Trip to the Berlin Conference (July 6, 1945 to August 7, 1945)," *StudyLib* <https://studylib.net/doc/8414894/log-of-the-president-s-trip-tothe-berlin-conference> (accessed 1 May 2020).

Robbins, Robert M., "Eddie Allen and the B-29," in Chester Marshall (ed.), *The Global Twentieth Vol. III* (Tennessee: Global Press, 1988).

Rooney, Bill, "Bill Rooney remembers: A Catholic chaplain named Adler," *40th Bomb Group* <www.40thbombgroup.org/memories/Memories38.pdf> (accessed 14 August 2014).

Roosevelt, Eleanor, "Women In Defense, Office For Emergency Management, 1941," *National Archives and Records Administration* <https://archive.org/details/gov.archives.arc.38686> (accessed 14 July 2019).

Roosevelt, Franklin D., "Document for February 19th: Executive Order 9066: Resulting in the Relocation of Japanese," *National Archives* <www.archives.gov/historical-docs/todaysdoc/?dod-date=219> (accessed 24 April 2020).

Roosevelt, Franklin D., "Fireside Chat, 9 December 1941," *The American Presidency Project* <www.presidency.ucsb.edu/documents/fireside-chat-12> (accessed 11 February 2019).

Roosevelt, Franklin D., "Fireside Chat, 23 February 1942," *The American Presidency Project* <www.presidency.ucsb.edu/documents/fireside-chat-6> (accessed 18 February 2019).

Roosevelt, Franklin D., "Fireside Chat, 28 April 1942," *The American Presidency Project* <www.presidency.ucsb.edu/documents/fireside-chat-5> (accessed 18 February 2019).

Roosevelt, Franklin D., "Message to Congress on Appropriations for National Defense, 16 May 1940," *The American Presidency Project* <http://www.presidency.ucsb.edu/ws/index.php?pid=15954> (accessed 29 January 2019).

Ross, Bill D., *Iwo Jima: Legacy of Valor* (New York: Vintage Books, 1986).

Roth, Morton, "Going Overseas, Part 1," *40th Bomb Group* <www.40thbombgroup.org/memories/Memories22.pdf> (accessed 14 August 2014).

Sakaida, Henry, *Imperial Japanese Navy Aces 1937–45* (London: Osprey Publishing, 1998).

Sakurai, Tokuzo, "A B-29 Was Shot Down," *Shisui Hometown Research Society Newsletter*, No. 98 (1 October 2000).

San Francisco News, "Japan Bombed," *The San Francisco News*, Vol. 42, No. 142 (15 June 1944).

Schoettler, Carl, "U-boat skipper recalls good hunting off East Coast," *The Baltimore Sun* <www.baltimoresun.com/news/bs-xpm-1992-11-02-1992307117-story.html> (accessed 17 February 2019).

Scott, James M., *Target Tokyo: Jimmy Doolittle and the Raid That Avenged Pearl Harbor* (New York: W.W. Norton & Company, 2015).

Selden, Kyoko and Selden, Mark, *The Atomic Bomb: Voices from Hiroshima and Nagasaki* (New York: M.E. Sharpe, 1989).

Sherrod, Robert, "Saipan: Eyewitness Tells of Island Fight," *Life Magazine*, Vol. 17, No. 9 (28 August 1944).

Sherrod, Robert, "The First Three Days," *Life Magazine*, Vol. 18, No. 10 (5 March 1945).

Sherrod, Robert, "The Nature of the Enemy," *Time Magazine*, Vol. 44, No. 6 (7 August 1944).

Shumway, Raymond E., "Letter to his family, 8 August 1945," in Martha Sue Stroud (ed.), *For Love of Country: The Price of Freedom* (Texas: Nortex Press, 2000).

Shumway, Raymond E., "Letter to Lloyd Hale, 8 August 1945" (Sam Kidd, Jr., collection).

Siegel, Adam B., "Wartime Diversion of U.S. Navy Forces in Response to Public Demands for Augmented Coastal Defense," *Naval History and Heritage Command* <www.history.navy. mil/research/library/online-reading-room/title-list-alphabetically/w/wartime-diversionus-navy-forces-response-public-demands-augmented-coastal-defense-cna.html> (accessed 21 February 2019).

Sinclair, Boyd, "Running On Time In a Timeless Land," *CBI Order of Battle* <www.cbi-history. com/part_vi_ba_railway2.html> (accessed 19 August 2019).

Smith, Hibbard A., "Going Overseas, Part II," *40th Bomb Group* <www.40thbombgroup.org/memories/Memories24.pdf> (accessed 14 August 2014).

Smith, Holland M. and Finch, Percy, *Coral and Brass* (Washington, D.C.: Zenger, 1979).

Sons of the American Legion, "Manual of Ceremony and Prayer," *The American Legion* <www.legion.org/sons/filelib/BroPrayerMn12.pdf> (accessed 26 September 2017).

Speer, Bob, "Pappy's Boys Report: The Jap is Good," *AAFPOA Brief*, Vol. 2, No. 13 (27 February 1945).

Speer, Robert, "Five Star Report', *AAFPOA Brief*, Vol. 2, No. 32 (10 July 1945).

Speer, Bob, "Official Photographers of Japan," *USASTAF Brief*, Vol. 2, No. 36 (7 August 1945).

Speer, Bob, "The Last Mission," *USASTAF Brief*, Vol. 2, No. 40 (V-J Day Issue).

Spitzer, Abe, "Abe Spitzer's Diary," *Atomic Heritage Foundation* <www.atomicheritage.org/sites/default/files/resources/Abe%20Spitzer%20Diary.pdf> (accessed 2 July 2020).

Spitzer, Abe and Miller, Merle, *We Dropped the A-Bomb* (New York: Thomas Y. Crowell, 1946).

Standard Oil Company, *M-69 … The Fire Bomb That Falls on Japan* (New York: Standard Oil Company, 1945).

Statistical Control, 73rd Bombardment Wing, *73rd Bombardment Wing Summary of Operations: Nov. 1943 Thru Aug. 1945* (Saipan: 73rd Bombardment Wing, 1945).

Stewart, Carroll, *The Most Honorable Son: Ben Kuroki* (Nebraska: Nebraska Printing Center, 2010).

Stoumen, Lou, "Superbases," *Yank*, Vol. 3, No. 5 (21 July 1944).

Stoumen, Lou, "B-29 Raid on Japan," *Yank*, Vol. 3, No. 5 (21 July 1944).

Stout, Wesley W., *Great Engines and Great Planes* (Michigan: Chrysler, 1947).

Sutherland, John H., *The Hundred Missions: The History of the 73rd Bomb Wing, Volume I* (Saipan: 73rd Bomb Wing, 1945).

Takaki, Koji and Sakaida, Henry, *B-29 Hunters of the JAAF* (Oxford: Osprey, 2001).

Tanner, Dean, Olson, Mrs. George, Cooney, Wilbur and Ponder, J.D., "George Olson and the Blown Blister Accident over Texas," *40th Bomb Group* <www.40thbombgroup.org/memories/Memories55.pdf> (accessed 14 August 2014).

The Fighting AAF, "Fighting AAF Radio Shows: Fighting AAF, B-29 Mission Over Japan," *Japan Air Raids.org* <www.japanairraids.org/?page_id=20> (accessed 11 January 2011).

Thomas, Gordon and Witts, Max Morgan, *Ruin from the Air: The Enola Gay's Atomic Mission to Hiroshima* (Michigan: Scarborough House, 1990).

Tibbets, Paul W. Jr., Stebbins, Clair and Franken, Harry, *The Tibbets Story* (New York: Stein and Day, 1978).

Tillitse, Lars, "When Bombs Rained on Us in Tokyo," *Saturday Evening Post*, Vol. 218, No. 28 (12 January 1946).

Togo, Shigenori, *The Cause of Japan* (New York: Simon & Schuster, 1956).

Truman, Harry S., "Letter from Harry S. Truman to Bess W. Truman, July 18, 1945," *Harry S. Truman Presidential Library and Museum* <www.trumanlibrary.gov/library/truman-papers/ correspond-ence-harry-s-truman-bess-wallace-truman-1921 1959/july-18-1945> (accessed 13 May 2020).

Truman, Harry S., *Memoirs by Harry S. Truman: Volume One: Year of Decisions* (New York: Doubleday, 1955).

Truman, Harry S., "Radio Report to the American People on the Potsdam Conference," *Harry S. Truman Library and Museum* <www.trumanlibrary.gov/soundrecording-records/sr61-37radio-report-american-people-potsdam-conference> (accessed 26 July 2020).

United States Department of Defense, *The Entry of the Soviet Union into the War Against Japan: Military Plans, 1941–1945* (Washington, D.C.: United States Department of Defense, 1955).

United States Department of the Interior, War Relocation Authority, *Nisei in Uniform* (Washington, D.C.: US Government Printing Office, 1944).

United States Strategic Bombing Survey, *Effects of Incendiary Bomb Attacks on Japan: A Report on Eight Cities* (Washington, D.C.: United States Strategic Bombing Survey, 1947).

United States Strategic Bombing Survey, *Japanese Air Power* (Washington, D.C.: Military Analysis Division, 1946).

United States Strategic Bombing Survey, *Japanese Air Weapons and Tactics* (Washington, D.C.: Military Analysis Division, 1947).

United States War Production Board, Conservation Division, "Get In The Scrap: A Plan for the Organization of the School Children of America in the National Salvage Program, 1 September 1942," *Southern Methodist University Library* <http://digitalcollections.smu.edu/ cdm/ref/collection/hgp/id/524> (accessed 16 March 2019).

UNT Digital Library, "Back the Attack! War Bond Poster," *University of North Texas Digital Library* <https://digital.library.unt.edu/ark:/67531/metadc196/> (accessed 20 June 2019).

UNT Digital Library, "For Freedom's Sake War Bond Poster," *University of North Texas Digital Library* <https://digital.library.unt.edu/ark:/67531/metadc600/> (accessed 20 June 2019).

UNT Digital Library, "I gave a man! War Bond Poster," *University of North Texas Digital Library* <https://digital.library.unt.edu/ark:/67531/metadc462/> (accessed 20 June 2019).

U.S. Air Force, "General Emmett O'Donnell Jr.," *U.S. Air Force* <www.af.mil/About-Us/Biographies/ Display/Article/106016/general-emmett-odonnell-Jr./> (accessed 6 September 2019).

U.S. Air Force, "The Air Force Story: Chapter 24: Air War Against Japan," *YouTube* <www. youtube. com/watch?v=m7JgXOxOAeQ> (accessed 5 September 2012).

U.S. Army, "WWII U.S. Army Enlistment Records," *WWII U.S. Army Enlistment Records* <www. wwii-enlistment.com> (accessed 22 September 2017).

U.S. Army Air Forces, *Erection and Maintenance Instructions for Army Model B-29 Airplane, T.O. 01-20EJ-2* (Illinois: U.S. Army Air Forces, 1944).

U.S. Army Air Forces, "Missing Air Crew Report 11221," *National Archives Catalog* <https:// catalog. archives.gov/id/91106509> (accessed 15 September 2019).

U.S. Army Air Forces, "Missing Air Crew Report 14232," *National Archives Catalog* <https:// catalog. archives.gov/id/91151849> (accessed 18 March 2020).

U.S. Army Air Forces, "Missing Air Crew Report 14593," *National Archives Catalog* <https:// catalog. archives.gov/id/91156180> (accessed 15 September 2019).

U.S. Army Air Forces, Office of Flying Safety, *How Not To Fly The B-29* (Illinois: U.S. Army Air Forces, 1945).

U.S. Army Air Forces, Office of Statistical Control, *Army Air Forces Statistical Digest, World War II* (Washington, D.C.: Office of Statistical Control, 1945).

U.S. Naval Academy Virtual Memorial Hall, "CHARLES H. SAWERS, LCDR, USN," *U.S. Naval Academy Virtual Memorial Hall* <https://usnamemorialhall.org/index.php/ CHARLES_H._ SAWERS,_LCDR,_USN> (accessed 21 June 2018).

U.S. Naval Academy Virtual Memorial Hall, "PORTER W. MAXWELL, CDR, USN," *U.S. Naval Academy Virtual Memorial Hall* <https://usnamemorialhall.org/index.php/ PORTER_W._ MAXWELL,_CDR,_USN> (accessed 21 June 2018).

U.S. Navy, "SS-239, USS WHALE Submarine War Patrol Report," *Issuu* <https://issuu.com/ hnsa/ docs/ss-239_whale> (accessed 10 October 2017).

U.S. Navy, "U.S. Navy Casualties, Bureau of Personnel Entries by Date – 1945," *Naval-History. net* <www.naval-history.net/WW2UScasaaDB-USNBPbyDate1945.htm> (accessed 20 June 2018).

U.S. Navy, VF-31, "Original US WWII USN Pilot Distinguished Flying Cross KIA Named Grouping: Aircraft Action Report No. VF31-13, 24 July 1945," *International Military Antiques* <www.ima-usa.com/products/original-u-s-wwii-usn-pilot-distinguished-flying-cross-kian-amed-grouping?variant=26171563205> (accessed 21 June 2018).

U.S. Office of War Information, *Japanese Propaganda* (California: U.S. Office of War Information, 1945).

U.S. Treasury Department, War Finance Division, "Handy Reference Guide to 4th War Loan, 15 January 1944," *U.S. National Archives and Records Administration* <https://www.archives.gov/ education/lessons/war-bonds.html> (accessed 23 June 2019).

Vander Meulen, Jacob, *Building the B-29* (Washington: Smithsonian Institution Press, 1995).

Veth, K.L., "Shootout at Palembang," *American Aviation Historical Society Journal*, Vol. 25, No. 1 (spring 1980).

War Department, Office of the Assistant Chief of Staff, G-2, "MAGIC – Diplomatic Summary No. 1233, 10 August 1945," *National Security Archive* <https://nsarchive.gwu.edu/documents/ atomic-bomb-end-world-war-ii/077a.pdf> (accessed 1 September 2020).

War Department, Office of the Assistant Chief of Staff, G-2, "MAGIC – Far East Summary No. 507, 9 August 1945," *National Security Archive* <https://nsarchive.gwu.edu/documents/ atomic-bomb-end-world-war-ii/074.pdf> (accessed 4 August 2020).

War Department, Office of the Assistant Chief of Staff, G-2, "MAGIC – Far East Summary No. 515, 18 August 1945," *National Security Archive* <https://nsarchive.gwu.edu/documents/ atomic-bomb-end-world-war-ii/090.pdf> (accessed 4 August 2020).

War Finance Division, U.S. Treasury Department, *Straight Talk about the 7th War Loan* (U.S. Government Printing Office, 1945).

Warnock, A. Timothy, "The U.S. Army Air Forces in World War II: Air Power Versus U-boats: Confronting Hitler's Submarine Menace in the European Theater," *Internet Archive* <https:// archive.org/details/AirPowerVersusUboats> (accessed 17 February 2019).

Welty, G.D., "Magnesium Alloys in Aircraft-Engine Construction," *SAE Transactions*, Vol. 27, 1932, *JSTOR* <www.jstor.org/stable/44436648> (accessed 10 January 2021).

Werrell, Kenneth P., *Blankets of Fire: US Bombers over Japan during World War II* (Washington: Smithsonian Institution Press, 1996).

Whitman, Howard, "U.S. Based Bombers Blast Ten Nazi Subs: Daily News, 28 August 1943," *Newspapers.com* <https://www.newspapers.com/newspage/435674188/> (accessed 12 March 2019).

Wolfe, Kenneth B., "The Men of the B-29s," *Air Force Magazine*, Vol. 27, No. 9 (September 1944).

Wolk, Herman S., *Cataclysm: General Hap Arnold and the Defeat of Japan* (Texas: University of North Texas Press, 2010).

Wood, F.G. Jr., "40th Bomb Group History Report, January 1944," *40th Bomb Group* <www.40thbombgroup.org/Archives/40thBG_Files/40th_Jan44.pdf> (accessed 14 August 2014).

Wood, F.G. Jr., "40th Bomb Group History Report, March 1944," *40th Bomb Group* <www.40thbombgroup.org/Archives/40thBG_Files/40thBG_Mar44.pdf> (accessed 14 August 2014).

Wood, F.G. Jr., "40th Bomb Group History Report, April 1944," *40th Bomb Group* <www.40thbombgroup.org/Archives/40thBG_Files/40thBG_Apr44.pdf> (accessed 14 August 2014).

Wood, F.G. Jr., "40th Bomb Group History Report, May 1944," *40th Bomb Group* <www.40thbomb group.org/Archives/40thBG_Files/40th_May44.pdf> (accessed 14 August 2014).

Wright Aeronautical Corporation, *Wright Cyclone 18 Aircraft Engine* (New Jersey: Wright, 1942).

Wright Aeronautical Division, Curtis-Wright Corporation, "Historical Engine Summary," *Aircraft Engine Historical Society* <www.enginehistory.org/Piston/Wright/C-WSpecsAfter1930.pdf> (accessed 3 January 2021).

Wright, Wiley R., *Aircraft Accident Classification Committee Report on Boeing Aircraft Company Model XB-29, Serial No. 41-003, February 18, 1943* (Washington: U.S. Army Air Forces, 1943).

XXI Bomber Command, "Attention Japanese People," *Air Intelligence Report*, Vol. 1, No. 22 (4 August 1945).

XXI Bomber Command, *Combat Crew Manual* (location unknown: XXI Bomber Command, 1945).

XXI Bomber Command, "Effects of Incendiary Attacks," *Air Intelligence Report*, Vol. 1, No. 4 (29 March 1945).

XXI Bomber Command, *Flight Engineer's Information File* (location unknown: XXI Bomber Command, 1945).

XXI Bomber Command, "Jap Instructions On Fighting B-29s," *Air Intelligence Report*, Vol. 1, No. 3 (22 March 1945).

XXI Bomber Command, A-2 Section, Tactical Mission Reports: *Mission No. 26* (4 February 1945); *Mission No. 29* (10 February 1945); *Mission No. 34* (15 February 1945); *Mission No. 37* (19 February 1945); *Mission No. 38* (25 February 1945); *Mission No. 40* (10 March 1945); *Mission No. 41* (12 March 1945); *Mission No. 42* (14 March 1945); *Mission No. 43* (16 March 1945); *Mission No. 44* (20 March 1945); *Mission No. 47* (27 March 1945); *Mission No. 50* (31 March 1945).

Yank, "Building the Base," *Yank*, Vol. 3, No. 28 (29 December 1944).

Zamperini, Louis and Rensin, David, *Devil at my Heels: A Heroic Olympian's Astonishing Story of Survival as a Japanese POW in World War II* (New York: Harper, 2011).

Index

Adler, Bartholomew, 72-73.
Africa, 21, 23, 66-67, 126, 192, 198, 250, 253.
Afrika Korps, 23.
Agather, Victor, 63.
Agiworld, 26.
Aioi Bridge, 258.
Air-Sea Rescue, 206, 252.
Air War Plans Division, 24, 29.
Albury, Charles, 291.
Allen, Edmund "Eddie," 22, 38-40, 42-47, 51-52, 67.
Allied powers, 227, 285, 287.
Aluminum Trail, 71.
Alvarez, Luis, 272.
America's Junior Army, 33.
American Maid, 111-114, 116-117.
Anami, Korechika, 280, 282-284, 286-290,
    292-293, 295.
Angell, Robert, 113-114, 116.
Appignani, George, 74-76.
Arents, LeRoy, 79-80.
Arnold, Henry "Hap," 61, 291, 325.
    20th Air Force, 69, 162, 164, 239-240.
    58th Bomb Wing, 56, 62, 158.
    AAC/AAF strengthening, 18-19, 21, 24.
    AAF strength and operations, 59, 239-240.
    B-29 engines, 47, 67-68.
    B-29 *Gen. H.H. Arnold Special*, 62, 78.
    B-29 in England, 67.
    B-29 operations, 69, 162, 165, 230, 234,
        239-240, 286.
    B-29 project and production, 21, 47-48, 53, 62.
    background, 18.
    Battle of Kansas, 62-64.
    bombing Germany, 231-232.
    bombing Japan, 162, 164-166, 230-231, 286.
    briefing from LeMay to end war, 231-232.
    command changes, 158, 240.
    defending the U.S., 29.
    ending the war, 231-232, 234, 237, 286.
    heart attacks, 158, 164.
    incendiary attacks, 164-166.
    MacArthur meeting, 234.

    Operation Downfall, 234.
    XB-29 crash, 47.
Ashby, Yearby, 209, 217, 225.
Ashworth, Frederick, 275-276.
Asia, 22, 25, 161, 201, 235, 282, 305.
Atanis, Jack, 209, 217, 225.
Arisue, Seizo, 270.
Atomic bombs
    arrival on Tinian, 242, 246-247, 274-275.
    arming, 255, 257, 274.
    assembly, 245, 247, 271-272, 292.
    B-29 modifications to carry, 256, 300.
    blast effects, 226, 251-252, 261-262, 265-266,
        268-271, 268-272, 276-277, 286.
    blast instruments, 272.
    bomb commander, 252, 275, 277.
    bombing tactics, 250, 258.
    briefings, 170, 250-254, 273.
    casualties and damages from, 265-266,
        268-271, 304.
    detonation, 226, 229-230, 251-252, 259-262,
        265-266, 276-277.
    decision to use, 243, 304.
    defense and countermeasures against, 271, 286,
        294.
    design and development, 18, 226-227, 246-247,
        250.
    development costs, 226-227, 247.
    drop maneuver, 258, 261, 276.
    ending the war, 228-229.
    German development, 17-18, 243, 267.
    gimmick, 249, 251-252, 268, 271.
    Hiroshima strike, 258-264.
    historical debate, 304-306.
    Japanese damage reports, 265-266, 270-271.
    Japanese development, 270, 295.
    Japanese military reactions, 268-270.
    loading, 256, 264, 271.
    messages about, 227-228, 263-264.
    morality, 304-306.
    Nagasaki strike, 276-278.
    plutonium cores, 226, 291.

power of, 250-253, 264.
preparations, 229.
propaganda leaflets, 262, 266.
Pumpkin bombs, 258, 291, 294.
shipments, 229-230, 242, 247.
shockwaves, 259-261, 276.
statements, Japan, 268-269.
statements, United States, 264, 266-268.
strike force, 250.
surrender debate, 280, 282-283, 297.
targets, 251, 258, 273, 286, 291.
testing, 226-227, 271.
third bomb, 284, 291-292.
uranium, 17, 245-247, 269.
warnings, 242, 247, 264, 266-267, 272.
weaponeer, 252, 255.
see also Little Boy; Fat Man; Manhattan Project
Attu Island, 30, 101, 138, 142.
AWPD-1, 24.
Axis powers, xi, 22, 27, 32-34, 59, 191.

B-17 bomber, 19-20, 23-24, 35, 37-38, 43, 47-49,
   52, 57-59, 65, 67, 80, 103, 107, 119, 159, 253,
   314, 325.
B-24 bomber, 59, 61, 67, 71, 105, 166, 182-183,
   191-193, 210, 315.
B-29 '728, 85-88.
B-29 bomber
   aerodynamics, 23-24, 38, 40, 42, 49.
   Battle of Kansas, 64, 66-67, 80.
   CFC gunnery system, 23, 79-81.
   contracts, 21-23, 27, 36, 43.
   data plates, xiv, 105-106, 119, 121-124, 129,
      188, 301-302.
   design, 21-24.
   design changes, 52, 63.
   engine cooling problems, 48-49, 64, 67-69.
   engine failures, 41-44, 50-51, 56, 58-59, 66-67,
      69, 73, 88, 107, 157, 163, 166, 202.
   engine fires, 42-44, 46, 49-52, 68-69, 76, 83,
      85, 116, 202.
   first flight, 38.
   flight test program, 39-40, 42-43, 46, 52.
   Japanese fighter tactics against, 119-120.
   Japanese ramming attacks, 119-121, 123-127,
      187-188, 313.
   losses and casualties, 302.
   maintenance, 56, 58-59, 68, 71, 160, 181.
   manuals, 56-57, 71, 314.
   Model 345, 20-21, 41.
   modifications, 57-59, 63-64, 67-68, 248, 256.
   pathfinders, 165, 167-168.
   production, 23, 34-38, 43, 47-48, 52, 55-57, 59,
      62-64, 67, 78, 80, 240.

precision bombing, 160, 162, 165.
prototype crash, 43-45.
prototype crash investigation, 47, 49-52.
relics, 119, 122-124, 188.
retirement, 301.
Silverplate, 248, 250, 256, 271, 274, 291,
   300-302.
special project, 47-48.
training, 47-48, 57-59, 63, 66, 71, 79-80, 84,
   107, 160, 195-196, 203, 216, 240, 248-250,
   258, 302, 319.
transporting fuel and supplies, 70-71.
see also Incendiary attacks; XB-29
B-29er, xi, xiv, 71, 77, 88, 104, 116-117, 128, 132,
   144, 146, 150, 155-156, 158, 160-162, 179,
   183, 212-213, 215-216, 223, 248, 286, 298,
   300-302, 306, 313-314, 316, 322, 324-325.
B-29 Liaison Committee, 47.
B-29 school, 57.
B-29 Special Project, 48.
Bainbridge, Kenneth, 226.
Baker, Addison, 193.
Balloon bombs, 162.
Bangkok, 71, 73.
Banzai charges, 99, 138, 142, 148.
Barnes, Philip, 275, 277.
Barr, Julius, 47.
Bartlett, John, 113-114, 116.
Bartlett, Warren, 208-209.
Bataan, 27, 29, 103, 178, 194-195, 312.
Bataan Death March, 178, 194.
Battle of Britain, 22.
Battle of France, 21-22.
Battle of Hong Kong, 137.
Battle of Kansas, 64, 66-67, 80.
Battle of Leyte Gulf, 99.
Battle of Los Angeles, 28-29.
Battle of Midway, 30.
Battle of Okinawa, 229, 244-245.
Battle of Saipan, 99, 102, 234.
Battle of Tarawa, 99.
Battle of the Coral Sea, 30.
Battle of the Philippine Sea, 99.
Beahan, Kermit, 250, 258-259, 268, 275-276, 294.
Beall, Wellwood, 22, 24, 38.
Beecroft, Larry, 108, 116-117, 306.
Baldwin, Burton, 79, 83-84, 86, 90, 92, 97, 223.
Bell Aircraft, 35, 38.
Bell Bomber Plant, 55.
Bena, Joseph, 134.
Berlin, 17, 22, 107, 126, 227, 241, 266.
Big Stink, 273, 275.
Big Three Allied powers, 227.
Bismarck Sea, 147.

Bitter, Gustav, 169, 177.
Black Sunday, 192.
Black Tom Island, 30.
Blackett, Frank, 209, 225.
Blaine, Charles, 44.
Bock, Frederick, 272.
Bockscar, 271-276, 278, 298, 300-302.
Boeing Aircraft Company 20, 46.
    prototype crashes, 46-47.
Boeing Field, 38, 42, 44, 46, 51, 53.
Boeing Flight Test and Aerodynamics, 22, 39-40.
Boeing Flying Fortress School, 57.
Boeing Plant 1, 23.
Boeing-Renton, 35, 38, 62.
Boeing-Wichita, 35, 39, 53, 62, 64, 67, 78, 256.
Bomb commander, 275.
Bombing of Oregon, 30.
Bonne, Gerald "Jerry," xii-xv, 212, 318-323.
Brechtbill, James, 208-209.
Brennan, Harold, 317-318.
Brief magazine, 87, 112, 160-161.
Britain, 18-19, 21-22, 24, 241, 281, 285.
British Army, 20.
British Expeditionary Force, 20.
Brokaw, Tom, xi.
Brookings, Oregon, 30.
Brown, Harold, 183-184, 187, 189, 200, 321.
Buckley, Edward, 259, 268, 270-271, 273, 276, 278, 291.
Bungo Channel, 207, 221.
Burchinal, David, 237.
Burger, Knox, 108, 112, 116, 164.
Burma, 25, 68, 158.
Byrnes, James, 284-285.

Cairo Declaration, 242.
Campbell, James, 134.
Cape Mendocino, 26.
Carde, Freeland, 206-207, 218.
Caron, George, 256-257, 261-262.
Carpenter, Larry, 132, 325.
Carpenter, Vere, 130-134.
CBI Theater (China-Burma-India), 68, 181.
CFC gunner, 80, 88, 97, 111, 116, 145, 208, 313, 317.
CFC gunnery system, 79-81.
Chakulia, 67, 72.
Chauncey, Charles, 300.
Chengtu, 61.
Chennault, Claire, 70.
China, 25, 29, 60-61, 68, 70-74, 76, 79, 82-83, 85, 88, 96, 104, 137, 139, 149, 158, 241, 279-280, 285, 305.
Chubu Army District, 118.

Churchill, Winston, 20-21, 165, 227-228.
Civil Air Patrol, 29.
Clifford, Howard, 121.
Clinkscales, Robert, 120.
Cobb County Army Airfield, 55.
Coggins, Herb, 76.
Cold War, 24, 229, 301.
Collison, Thomas, 46.
COMSUBPAC (Commander, Submarine Force, U.S. Pacific Fleet), 207-208.
Commonwealth Club, 194-196.
Concentration camps, 183.
Connell, John, 134.
Costello, Edward, 274-275.
Cook, Dick, 113.
Cook, Frank, 67.
Couch, Howard, 57, 71.
Courageous Battle Vows, 138.
Cox, James, 144.
Cox, Leonard, 108, 112, 116.
Cozzens, James, 232-233.
Crane, Frank, 108, 116.
Crim, James "Jimmy," 319-321.
Crim, Silver, 319-323.
Crosby, Bing, 187.
Crowe, Frank (Pilot), 113-116.
Crowe, Frank (Marine), 145.
Crowcroft, Frank, 183-184, 186-187, 312.
Crowcroft, Viva, 186.
Curtis, Carl, 197.
Cyanide capsules, 253.

Daily Target, 239.
Davis-Monthan Air Force Base, 122.
Dansfield, Bob, 44-45.
Darwin, 25.
Data Plate, xiv, 105-106, 119, 121-124, 129, 188, 301-302.
Dauntless Dotty, 107, 109, 125, 172.
D-Day, xi, 155, 183.
DeCory, L.N., 79.
Defense POW/MIA Accounting Agency, 321-323.
Dehart, Pappy, 257, 259-260, 268, 271, 275-276.
Denton, Guy, 113.
Devesci, Frances, 186.
DeWitt, John, 26.
Ding Hao, 70.
Ding How, xiv.
Distinguished Flying Cross, 103, 108, 121, 124, 315-318.
Distinguished Service Cross, 108.
Dixson, Elmer, 106.
Domei News Agency, 239, 269, 284.

Doolittle, Jimmy, 29, 104, 109, 230, 240.
Doolittle Raid, 29, 104, 108-109, 169, 230, 304.
Douglas Aircraft, 28.
Downey, John, 274.
Downey, William, 253.
Dragon Slayer, 125-126.
   see also Ki-45
Dresden, 165.
Dunkirk, 20.
Dutch Harbor, 30.
Duzenbury, Wyatt, 254.

Eaker, Ira, 234.
eBay, xiii-xiv, 78-79, 83, 86-92, 94, 97-98,
   102-106, 119, 122-124, 127-129, 150, 155,
   210-212, 214-215, 217, 225, 298-299, 301,
   307-309, 314-318, 320-321.
Echols, Oliver, 48.
Edmundson, James, 66.
Ehrenberg, Jack, 109.
8th Air Force, 102, 107, 159, 240.
Einstein, Albert, 17-18.
Einstein-Szilard letter, 17-18.
Eisenhower, Dwight, 234.
Eldorado, 141.
Ellwood Oil Field, 27-28.
Elsner, Burt, 73.
Emidio, 26.
Engine fires
   see R-3350 engine
England, 22, 40, 66-67, 102, 109, 159, 169,
   191-192, 241.
English Channel, 20-22.
Enola Gay, 247, 254-258, 261-262, 273-275, 304.
Epting, Jake, 192.
Erskine, Graves, 148.
Europe, 18-22, 24, 26, 40, 59, 66, 107, 109,
   125-126, 161-163, 192, 196, 198, 227, 229, 231,
   235, 237, 240-241, 250, 253, 266, 305.

F6F Hellcat, 220-222, 224.
F-13, 105.
Fat Man atomic bomb, 245-247, 258, 264, 271,
   274, 292, 300-302.
FBI, 197.
Ferebee, Thomas, 253, 258, 261-262.
Fermi, Enrico, 17.
Farrell, Thomas, 229, 255.
Ferraro, Anthony, 317, 325.
Fifth Amphibious Corps, 141.
Fifth Fleet, 140.
Fifth Marine Division, 154.
58th Bomb Wing, 55-59, 62-64, 66, 68-71, 73,
   78-80, 82-85, 95-96, 104, 158.

Fighting AAF, 183, 200, 321.
Fighting Squadron 27, 224.
Fighting Squadron 31, 222.
Firebomb attacks
   see incendiary attacks
1st Anti-Submarine Squadron, 315.
1st Combat Radio Team, 183.
First Motion Picture Unit, 57.
1st Ordnance Squadron, 245.
First World War, 18-19, 22-23, 30, 39, 169, 227,
   247.
504th Bomb Group, 201.
505th Bomb Group, 197.
509th Composite Group, 248-250, 252-253, 256,
   258, 274, 294, 301-302.
Flak, German, 159, 162.
Flak, Japanese, 75-76, 80-81, 88, 103, 105,
   107-109, 111, 121, 126, 144, 156-157, 161-163,
   165, 169-170, 173, 181, 183-184, 192-194, 207,
   213, 257-259, 261, 264, 275-277, 294, 302, 307,
   311, 321.
Forrestal, James, 143.
40th Bomb Group, 59, 61, 64, 66-67, 71, 73-74,
   325.
47th Sentai, 105.
Fourth Marine Division, 141, 147, 149.
4th Sentai, 119.
442nd Infantry Regiment, 196.
444th Bomb Group, 58.
462nd Bomb Group, 58, 79, 82, 87-88.
497th Bomb Group, 108, 111, 120, 125-127.
499th Bomb Group, 123.
France, xi, 17, 19-22, 27, 59, 159.
French Frigate Shoals, 29.
Frigidaire Refrigerator Company, 36.
Frye Meat Packing Plant, 45.
Fujimoto, Kenji, 120.
Fujioka, Hideo, 117-118.
Fujita, Nobuo, 30.
Fukubayashi, Toru, 133, 152, 325.
Funabashi, Japan, 126.
Futaba School, 174, 177-178.

G4M "Betty" bomber, 136.
Gallagher, Raymond, 259, 270-271, 273, 285,
   291, 295.
Garland, Judy, 19.
General Motors, 36, 47.
Gen. H.H. Arnold Special, 62, 78.
Gestapo, 21.
Giles, Barney, 162.
Gimmick (atomic bomb), 249, 251-252, 268, 271.
   see also atomic bombs
Gisburne, Edward, 75-76.

Germany, 17-22, 24-26, 30, 59, 102, 165, 169, 182, 192-193, 199, 227-228, 231-232, 237, 240-241, 244, 247, 266.
Glenn L. Martin Company, 35, 248.
Goad, Lloyd, 132.
Goin' Jessie, 300.
Golden, G., 79.
Goldstein, Henry, 209, 217, 225.
Great Britain, 18-19, 21-22, 24, 241, 281, 285.
Great Depression, 81, 190.
Great Marianas Turkey Shoot, 99.
Greatest Generation, xi, 14, 81, 128, 303, 320, 324.
Greene, Melvin, 186-187, 312.
Griffith, Mel, 109.
Ground Observer Corps, 29.
Groves, Leslie, 227-229, 246, 254, 291.
Guadalcanal, 30.
Guam, 25, 99, 101, 158, 166, 170, 180, 216, 230-232, 237, 240, 316, 320-321.
Guillain, Robert, 169.
Gulfamerica, 27.

Haddow, James, 76.
Haley's Comet, 124-125, 127-128, 130, 132-134, 152, 188, 313, 315-316, 325.
Hall, William, 221.
Halloran, Raymond "Hap," 168, 173, 179.
Handy, Thomas, 235.
Hansell, Haywood, Jr., 102-104, 106-107, 119, 136, 157-158, 160, 164, 325.
Hansen, Al, 109.
Hardegen, Reinhard, 26-27.
Hardy, Graydon, 134.
Harman, Leonard "Jake," 47-48, 53, 55, 66-67, 70, 73.
Harmon, Millard, 160.
Harrison, George, 227.
Hart, Alvin, 111-117.
Hart, Charles, 104-105.
Harte, Ronald, 74, 76-77.
Harvey, Alva, 58.
Hassell, Cecil, 134.
Hata, Shunroku, 286.
Haynes, George "Bill," 150-152, 154-156.
Haynes, Robert, 126, 160, 168-169.
Hawaii, 24, 114, 118, 154, 160, 198, 232, 274-275, 312.
Heart Mountain War Relocation Center, 196.
Hellbirds, 79, 82-83.
Hellbird War Book, 87, 89.
Hellcat, 220-222, 224.
Hemingway, Ernest, 27.
Henderson, Charlie, 184, 186-188.

Hepburn, Katherine, 35.
Hill, Allan, 145-146, 313-314.
Himalayas, 61, 70, 85.
Hiranuma, Kiichiro, 282.
Hirohito, Emperor, 106-107, 110, 138-139, 147, 168, 172-173, 246, 256, 266, 280-293, 295, 311.
   coup attempt, 294-295.
   decision to surrender, 281-283, 292-293.
   Imperial Rescript, 293.
   surrender broadcast, 295.
Hiroshima, 273, 276, 280, 294.
   atomic strike, 258-264.
   blast instruments, 272.
   casualties and damages, 265-266, 270-271, 286, 304-305.
   controversy, 304-306.
   strike messages, 263-264.
   strike reactions, Japanese, 268-270.
   strike recording, 262.
   strike reports, Japanese, 265-266, 268-271.
   strike statements, American, 264, 266-268.
   target selection, 251, 257-258.
Hitachi Training Air Division, 125.
Hitler, Adolf, 17-24, 192, 243.
Hodgen, F.G., 75.
Hokkaido, 242, 290.
Hollywood, 33, 35, 39, 57, 172, 192, 194, 254, 273.
Honorable Discharge Emblem, 213.
Honolulu Star-Bulletin, 110.
Honshu, 104, 163, 202, 233-234, 237, 242.
Hoover, Herbert, 235.
Hornet, 29.
Hsingching, 73.
Hughes, Howard, 192.
Huie, William Bradford, 143.
Hump (Himalaya mountains), 61, 70-71, 82, 84-86, 88.

Ibuki, Yukako, 152.
Icenhower, Kirk, 208-209.
Imperial Conference, 281-283, 289, 291-293.
Imperial General Headquarters, 147.
Imperial Iron and Steel Works, 73.
Imperial Japanese Army, 137, 178, 279.
Imperial Japanese Navy, 24, 207.
Imperial Palace, 106, 280-281, 287-288, 292, 295.
Imperial Rescript, 293, 295.
Incendiary attacks, 145-146, 164, 181, 231.
   blitz, 181.
   bomb specifications, 163-164, 166-167.
   bomb tests, 164.
   cities attacked, 181, 296.
   damage and casualties, 164, 180-181, 296-297, 305.

description of falling bombs, 168-171.
Dresden, 165.
Japanese incendiary attacks, 37, 162.
Meetinghouse 2, 166.
moral questions, 165, 305.
planning, 163-167.
test attacks, 164.
Tokyo attacks, 164, 168-175.
Incendiary bombs, 30, 110, 162, 164-165, 167-172, 175, 181, 231.
India, 60-64, 66-70, 72-73, 80, 82, 84-85, 87-88, 93, 95-96, 104, 158-159, 170.
Inland Sea, 201-201, 207, 221.
Internment camps, 194.
Invasion of Japan
see Operation Downfall
Isley Field, 136.
Iwo Jima
air attacks from, 136.
airfields, 135-136, 139, 143-145.
atomic strike missions, 251, 257, 273, 276.
B-29 emergency landings, 143-145, 155-156, 202, 313.
battle of, 138, 140-143, 146-148, 240, 244.
casualties, 141-143, 145, 148.
cemetery, 148-149.
flag raising, 142-143.
fortifications and defenses, 138-141.
invasion, 140-142.
invasion planning, 140-141.
Japanese defense of, 138, 147.
Japanese final attack, 147-148.
Japanese final surrender, 148.
letters from, 173, 151, 153.
Medal of Honor, 148.
militaria, 150-151, 155.
Mount Suribachi, 139, 141-145, 150-151.
sand, 141, 143.
strategic importance, 135-136.
topography, 135-136, 139.
see also Tadamichi Kuribayashi

Jacobs, Raymond, 143.
Japan
air raid casualties and destruction, 304-305.
cities destroyed, 296.
empire of, 25, 55, 76, 103, 105-106, 110, 147, 161, 231, 235, 240-241, 245-246, 277.
homeland military strength, 235, 244-245.
last-ditch weapons, 245.
military conquests, 25, 30.
national polity, 280, 282, 284, 287-288, 292-293.
People's Volunteer Corps, 244.

Prisoners of War, 105, 127, 130, 132, 169, 178-179, 310-311, 314.
Prisoner of War camps, 105, 127, 130, 132, 169, 178-179, 311.
Soviet Declaration of War, 278-279.
Tripartite Pact, 22.
war crimes, 118, 312-313.
weather, 110, 157, 160-166, 184, 247, 251, 257, 272-273, 275, 285, 302.
see also atomic bombs; Hirohito, Emperor; incendiary attacks; Ketsu-Go Operation; Operation Downfall; surrender of Japan
Japan Air Raids.org, 183, 325.
Japanese Americans
see Nisei
Japanese diplomatic code, 247.
Japanese Empire, 25, 55, 76, 103, 105-106, 110, 147, 161, 231, 235, 240-241, 245-246, 277.
Japanese fighter aircraft, 81-82, 84, 103, 105, 109, 111-114, 119-121, 124-128, 136, 161, 181-186, 204, 221, 248, 256, 258, 275-276, 313.
Japanese fighter ramming attacks, 119-121, 123-127, 187-188, 313.
Jenkins, James, 197-198.
Jeppson, Morris, 255, 257.
Jerstad, John, 193.
Jet stream, 161.
Johnson, Dale, 74.
Johnson, E.K., 75.
Johnson, Robert, 314.
Joint Chiefs of Staff, 69-70, 158, 228, 232-237.
Joltin' Josie, The Pacific Pioneer, 102-103, 161.
Jorgenson, Gordy, 197.

Kaiten manned suicide torpedo, 221.
Kamikaze, 120, 147, 229, 244, 290.
see also Special Attack Units
Kanto plain, 233.
Kato, Masuo, 239.
Kato, Tadao, 297.
Kawabe, Torashiro, 269, 279-281, 283.
Kawanishi H8K, 29.
Kawasaki (city), 12, 145, 321-322.
Kawasaki (manufacturer), 113, 125, 160.
Kazuyo, Funato, 168, 170-171, 176-177, 179-180.
Kazuyo, Hiroko, 171, 176-177, 179-180.
Kazuyo, Koichi, 176.
Kazuyo, Teruko, 168, 179.
Kazuyo, Yoshiaki, 176.
Keller, John, 72-73.
Kelso, Bill, 28-29.
Kempeitai, 88-89, 117-118, 146, 168, 173, 179, 289, 309-313.
Kempeitai prison, Tokyo, 168, 173, 179.

Ketsu-Go Operation, 244.
Ki-44 fighter, 105.
Ki-45 fighter, 124-125, 127, 134, 187-188, 313.
Ki-61 fighter, 111, 113.
Kidd, Sam, 203-206, 209-211, 213-220, 222-223, 225.
Kidd, Sam Jr., 215-217, 222-223, 325.
Kido, Koichi, 287-291.
Kilner Board, 18.
Kilner, Walter, 18.
Kimura, Sadamitsu, 119.
King, Ernest, 236-237.
Kiska, 30.
Kitty Hawk, 23.
Knudsen, William, 47, 57, 71.
Kobayashi, Yuichi, 125-127, 134.
Kobe, 88, 181, 231.
Koibuchi, Natsuo, 125, 127.
Kokura, 251, 273, 275-276, 304.
Koyo, Ishikawa, 171.
Krantz, Jim, 111-116, 118.
Krantz, Mildred, 115-116.
K-rations, 82.
Kubota, Shigenori, 178.
Kuharek, John, 259, 268, 271, 273, 276, 278.
Kujukuri Beach, 283, 302.
Kumeji, Komoto, 139.
Kure, 153, 207, 221-222, 266.
Kuribayashi, Tadamichi, 137-142, 147-148.
    background, 137-138.
    final attack and death, 147-148.
    final message, 147.
    Iwo Jima strategy, 138.
    thoughts about America, 137.
    see also Iwo Jima
Kuribayashi, Takako, 137.
Kuroki, Ben
    Arrival on Tinian, 198.
    B-24 crew assignment, 192.
    B-29 training, 197.
    background, 190-191.
    capture and escape, 192.
    Commonwealth Club speech, 194-195.
    death, 190.
    exemption to fight, 197.
    internment camps, 194, 196.
    legacy, 199.
    lucky ears, 199.
    New York Herald Tribune Forum speech, 199.
    nightmares, 198.
    Ploesti mission, 192-193.
    racism, 191-192, 194, 197, 199.
    stabbing, 198-199.
Kuroki, Fred, 190-191.

Kwajalein, 141, 160.
Kyoto, 243.
Kyushu, 182, 202, 233-237, 242, 244, 273, 313.
Kyushu University, 314.

Ladd, Jack, 69.
Laggin' Dragon, 273-275, 301-302.
Larson, Les, 50.
Laundry number, 213.
Lawrence, J.P., 319.
Leahy, William, 233, 236, 284-285.
Lee, Knute, 210, 215.
Lee, Robert, 56.
LeMay, Curtis
    305th bomb group, 159, 162.
    background, 158-159.
    B-29 losses, 162, 166, 181.
    Bell's palsy, 158.
    bombing problems, 160-162.
    calling his shots, 238-239.
    chat with McKelway, 170.
    command changes, 158, 240.
    ending the war by bombing, 231-232, 237, 304.
    European operations, 159.
    German flak defenses, 159, 162.
    incendiary attack blitz, 181.
    incendiary attack morality, 165.
    incendiary attack planning, 165-167.
    incendiary attack strategy, 162-165.
    Japanese flak defenses, 162-163.
    leadership style, 159-160, 166.
    Meetinghouse 2 briefing, 166.
    Meetinghouse 2 strike results, 180-181.
    meeting with Arnold, 231-232.
    meeting with Joint Chiefs, 237.
    meetings with Norstad, 162, 166, 234.
    promotions to general, 159.
    promotion, USASTAF, 240.
    promotion, XXI Bomber Command, 158-159.
    propaganda leaflets, 238-239, 241.
    reputation, 158-159.
    weather over Japan, 160-162.
Lewis, Robert, 254, 257.
Lifeguard submarines, 207, 222.
Life magazine, 33-34, 87, 101, 142.
Life raft, 203-209, 216, 275.
Lindbergh, Charles, 18.
Little Boy atomic bomb, 245-247, 255, 257, 261, 274, 278.
Little Gem, 109.
Lodovici, Olinto, 130.
Lomas, George, 208-209.
Long Beach, 28-29.
Long Island, 26, 30.

Longstreet, Helen, 56.
London, 22, 107, 192.
Los Alamos weapons laboratory, 227, 245, 247, 291-292.
Los Angeles, 25, 28-29, 186.
Love, Edmund, 100.
Lowman, Clarence, 71.
L.P. St. Clair, 25.
Lucas, George, 58.
Lucas, Jacklyn, 148.
Lucky Lynn, 108, 112, 116.
Luder, M.F., 28-29.
Luke the Spook, 301.
Luftwaffe, 18-20, 22, 24, 231.
Luxembourg, 20.
Luzon, 235-236.
Lyon, Ben, 192.

M-69 incendiary bomb, 163-164, 166-169.
   see also Incendiary attacks
MacArthur, Douglas, 140, 162, 234-236, 286.
Mackey, Bill, 62.
Mae West life vest, 74, 203, 207-208.
Magic, 107.
Magnesium alloy, 48-49.
Magnesium fires, 49, 51, 69.
   see also Wright R-3350
Makasan railway shops, 71.
Malmedy massacre, 83.
Malo, Raymond, 144-146, 156, 313, 315.
Manchuria, 25, 82, 84, 153, 228-229, 279, 285, 290, 305.
Manhattan Project, 18, 227-230, 245, 247, 305.
Mariana Islands, 85, 99, 102-104, 135-136, 144, 156-159, 161, 167, 175, 181, 186, 216, 239, 242, 248-249, 262, 286, 297.
Marianas Turkey Shoot, 99.
Marietta, 35, 38, 55, 62.
Marshall, George, 24, 48, 70, 197, 199, 232-237, 285-286, 291.
Marshall Islands, 29, 59.
Mathers, Ira, 64.
Martindale, Robert, 105.
Martin-Omaha, 35, 248.
Matsumura, Shutsu, 167.
Matulis, Algernon, 75.
Maxwell, Porter, 221.
McDonell, Walter, 134, 315-316.
McKelway, St. Clair, 170.
McNeley, David, 88-89, 95, 117, 313.
McVay, Charles, 229-230.
Medal of Honor, 100, 148, 193.
Meetinghouse 2, 166.
Memphis Belle, 107, 109.

Merrian, Mickey, 209, 217.
Meyers, Bennett, 64.
Midway Atoll, 25, 30.
Military police, 88, 250.
Millennium Falcon, 58.
Miller, Betty, 317-318.
Miller, Mark, 325.
Mine, aerial, 82-83, 201-202, 297.
   see also Operation Starvation
Mine, naval, 206.
Miracle of Dunkirk, 20.
Mitchell, Billy, 19, 22, 69-70.
Mitchell, John, 56.
Mito Airfield, 125.
Mitsubishi, 136.
Mitsubishi aircraft engine factory (Nagoya), 120.
Missing In Action, xii, xv, 71, 130, 205, 209, 221, 313, 320, 323.
Meiji, Emperor, 293.
Mockler, Don, 145, 325.
Mockler, Edwin, 144-146, 315.
Model 299, 47.
Model 345, 20-21, 41.
Moesi River, 82.
Mohn, Fritz, 44.
Monroe, Marilyn, 36.
Monterey Bay, 26.
Morgan, Robert, 107, 109, 125-126, 172, 181.
Morone, Serafino, 309-313.
Morris, Lester, 309, 311-312, 317-318.
Motoyama Airfield No. 1, 143.
Moscow, 24, 227, 246.
Mount Fuji, 109, 172.
Mount Suribachi, 139, 141-145, 150-151.
Mukden, Manchuria, 84, 96.

Nagasaki, 280, 291, 294, 300-302.
   atomic strike, 276-278.
   target selection, 251, 273, 275-276.
Nagoya, 111-113, 115-116, 120, 160, 181, 187, 211, 231.
Nakajima Musashino aircraft plant, 107, 110, 160, 162, 166.
Nanking, 304.
Napalm, 163-165, 168, 171.
National Museum of the United States Air Force, 298.
Naval Construction Battalions, 142.
Nazis, 17, 241.
Nazi Germany, 17-18, 20, 26.
Nebraska, 35, 190-191, 194-197, 199.
Necessary Evil, 257.
New England Air Museum, 96-97.

New York, 26, 30, 74, 79, 97, 128, 186, 199, 204, 248.
New York Harbor, 30.
Neyer, Kenneth, 221.
Nimitz, Chester, 140, 146-147, 152, 162, 232, 236, 240.
9th Bomb Group, 144, 145, 298, 303.
9th Bomb Group Association, 145, 298-300, 303.
Nisei, 191, 194, 196, 198.
Nishina, Yoshio, 270.
Nishino, Kozo, 26-28.
Nobe, Shigeo, 120.
Nobel Prize, 243.
Nobuyoshi, Sadaoka, 138.
Norden bombsight, 161.
Norness, 26.
Norquist, Ernest, 178.
Norstad, Lauris, 158, 162, 164, 166, 180, 232, 234, 285, 291.
North Africa, 23, 126, 192, 198, 250, 253.
North Field, 255.
Northern Ireland, 24.

Oahu, 24-25, 29.
O'Donnell, Emmett, 103, 107.
O'Keefe, James, 67, 82.
Okido, Sanji, 289.
Okinawa, 140, 184, 229, 233, 236, 239-240, 244-245, 276, 278, 301.
Okumura, C.S., 188.
Old-Bitch-U-Airy Bess, 80-87, 89-91, 95-98.
    bail out, 79, 83.
    battle damage, 84.
    engine fire, 83.
    scrapping, 84.
    see also Charles Trabold
Oliver, Philip, 58, 66, 68.
Olivi, Fred, 277-278.
Olsen, Blaine, 218.
Olsen, Russell, 199.
Olson, Abram, 56.
Olson, George, 60.
Omaha, 35, 62, 194, 248.
Omaha Beach, 155, 183.
O'Malley, William, 70.
Omori Prisoner of War Camp, 105, 127, 132, 178-179, 311-312.
Omura Naval Air Station, 184.
Onishi, Takijiro, 281, 290.
105th Infantry Regiment, 99.
Operation Barbarossa, 24.
Operation Coronet, 236-237, 302.
Operation Downfall, 236-237.
    invasion casualties, 228, 233-236, 243-244.

Operation K, 29.
Operation Matterhorn, 60-63, 70-71.
Operation Olympic, 236.
Operation Starvation, 201.
Operation Tidal Wave, 192.
Oppenheimer, Robert, 226-227, 229.
Oregon, 26, 30, 75, 162.
Osaka, 88, 116-118, 181, 230-231, 313.
Ostfriesland, 19.

P-51 fighter, 37, 147.
Pacific, 26, 30, 59, 78, 87, 99, 103, 140-142, 160, 162, 195-199, 203-205, 207, 212, 217, 221, 228, 235, 240-241, 263-264, 282, 286, 312.
Pacific Union, 116.
Paine, Thomas, 32.
Palembang, 82.
Paris, 21.
Parsons, William "Deak," 230, 247, 251-253, 255, 257-258, 261-262, 264, 271.
Pathfinder B-29s, 165, 167-168.
Pearl Harbor, xii, 25, 29-30, 35, 59, 72, 77, 103, 106, 110, 136, 154, 159, 190, 192, 194, 230, 239, 267.
Pentagon, 232.
People's Handbook of Resistance Combat, 245.
People's Volunteer Corps, 244-245.
Phelps, Raleigh, 126, 160-161.
Philippines, 25, 27, 29, 103, 119, 140, 178, 199, 222, 234.
Phillips, Charles, 173-174.
Phillips, Lyman, 103.
Pleus, William, 134.
Plevan, Vaughan, 83-84, 95, 97.
Ploesti, 166, 192-193.
Plutonium, 226, 246-247, 271, 274, 291.
Plutonium-239, 246.
    see also Fat Man atomic bomb
Point Arguello, 26.
Poland, 19.
Pollock, Russell, 124.
Ponte Vedra Beach, 30.
Potsdam, 227-228, 229, 263.
Potsdam Conference, 227-229, 246, 266.
Potsdam Declaration, 241-243, 246-247, 280-285, 288-290, 292, 297.
Power, Thomas, 166, 181.
Pratt, 57, 59, 60-61, 63.
Precision bombing, 160, 162, 165.
Preisser, Albert, 128, 130, 134, 313.
Price, James, 117.
Price, William, 187.
Prisoner of War, 105, 127, 130, 132, 169, 178-179, 310-311, 314.

special prisoners, 132.
Prisoner of War camps, 105, 127, 130, 132, 169, 178-179, 311.
Project Alberta, 245, 247, 258, 272, 292.
Propaganda
    American, 123, 239, 269, 290.
    German, 165.
    Japanese, 102.
Pumpkin bomb, 258, 291, 294.
Purnell, William, 229.
Purple Heart, xii, 198, 212-213, 302, 308-309, 312, 315-316, 318.
Putt, Donald, 38, 47, 52, 63.
Pyote, 84.

Quonset hut, 115, 216, 248, 250, 268.

R-1820 engine, 48-49.
R-3350 engine
    backfires, 50-51.
    cooling problems, 48-49, 64, 67-69.
    changes and improvements, 42, 47, 50, 54, 64, 68.
    design and development, 41, 48-49, 54.
    failures, 41-44, 50-51, 56, 58-59, 66-67, 69, 73, 88, 107, 157, 163, 166, 202.
    fires, 42-44, 46, 49-52, 68-69, 76, 83, 85, 116, 202.
    swallowed valve, 68.
    XB-29 crash investigation, 47, 49-52.
Radar, 22-23, 28-29, 58, 64, 71, 73, 79, 81, 83, 114, 116, 123-124, 130, 136, 160-161, 166, 173, 202-204, 206-207, 209, 217, 241, 268, 276, 301.
Radar observer, 23, 81, 83, 116, 123, 130, 160, 173, 203-204, 209, 217, 268.
Ralston, Harry, 44.
Ramming attacks, 119-121, 123-127, 187-188, 313.
Rationing, 33.
Ration stamps, 33.
Reagan, Ronald, 57.
Red Army, 19.
Reed, Al, 47.
Relocation camps
    see internment camps
Reye, Heather, 28-29.
Renton, 35, 38, 44, 62.
Rockwell, Norman, 36.
Rommel, Erwin, 23.
Roosevelt, Eleanor, 35.
Roosevelt, Franklin, xii, 17, 19-21, 24-25, 27, 32, 34-35, 61-62, 142, 194, 233.
Rosenthal, Joe, 143.

Rosie the Riveter, 36.
Roth, Morton, 62.
Royal Air Force, 22, 165.
Runaway propeller, 42, 112, 121, 202, 223.
Russia, 78, 228-229, 278, 287, 290.
Ruptured Duck, 213.

Sachs, Alexander, 17.
Sacred Decision (Seidan), 282-283.
Sagane, Ryokichi, 272.
Saipan, 69, 104, 106-107, 111-112, 115-116, 119-1221, 123-124, 127, 130-131, 136, 141-142, 158, 161, 166, 172, 179, 234, 239.
    air base construction, 99, 103-104.
    Banzai charge, 99-100.
    battle of, 99-100.
    civilian casualties and suicides, 100-102.
    first B-29 arrival, 102-103.
    Japanese air attacks, 136.
Saipan ratio, 234.
Saito, Yoshitsugu, 99.
Sallade, Thurman, 77, 80, 89-97.
Salm, Henry, 316-317.
Salomon, Ben, 99-100.
Samoa, 26.
Samurai, 137-138.
Sanadayama Military Cemetery, 117.
Sandhofer, Seymour, 80.
San Antonio 1, 106.
San Francisco, 25, 108, 186, 194, 217, 230, 249, 269, 305.
Santa Barbara, 26.
Santa Monica, 28, 194.
Sato, Naotake, 246.
Saunders, LaVerne, 70, 72.
Saving Private Ryan, 183.
Sawers, Charles, 221.
Schairer, George, 22, 24, 38.
Schmidt, Harry, 141.
Scrapbooks, 12-13, 127-132, 212, 313, 318-322.
Scrap drives, 33.
Seabees, 142-143, 150.
Sea of Japan, 201-202.
Second Army, 258, 286.
2nd Air Force, 195.
2nd Armored Division, 227.
2nd Imperial Guards Division, 137.
2nd Ranger Battalion, 183.
Secretary of the Navy, 29, 143, 285.
Seattle, xi-xii, 20-21, 23-25, 34, 36, 38, 43, 44, 47, 49, 57, 97.
7th War Loan (Bond) Drive, 240.
73rd Bomb Wing, 103-104, 125-127, 239, 325.
Shady Lady, 127, 134.

Sharks, 204-205.
Shaver, Manila, 168.
Sheffield, W.W., 79.
Sherrod, Robert, 101-102, 142.
Shimizu, Jun, 105.
Shimonoseki Strait, 201-202.
Shinkai Bridge, 171, 176.
Shinodayama military training grounds, 117.
Shisui, 127.
Shockley, William, 243.
Shumate, James, 307-309, 311-312, 315-318.
Shumway, Raymond, 201-212, 214-217, 220, 223, 225, 309.
Siegel, Leroy, 186-187, 312.
Siegel, Sarah, 186.
Siemes, John, 305-306.
Silverplate B-29, 248, 250, 256, 271, 274, 291, 300-302.
Silver Star, 152.
Simms, Ginny, 194.
Singapore, 25, 80-81, 96.
6th Bomb Squadron, 316.
Smith, Fred, 233.
Smith, Hibbard, 66.
Smith, Holland, 140, 143.
Smith, Robert, 186-187.
Smoky Hill, 56-57.
Soldier's Medal, 215, 223, 225.
Solomon Islands, 25, 30, 59, 197.
Sophia Catholic University, 169, 177, 295, 305.
Soviet Union, 19, 24, 78, 228-229, 235, 246, 279-280, 282, 285, 305.
Spaatz, Carl, 240, 263, 285-286, 291.
Special Attack Units, 120, 244-245, 290.
    see also Kamikaze
Special prisoners, 132.
Spitzer, Abe
    509th Composite Group, 248-250, 258, 294.
    atomic bomb thoughts, 251, 262-263, 274.
    atomic strike briefings, 249-254, 273.
    atomic strike report, 277-278.
    atomic bomb test drops, 268, 271.
    background, 248-249.
    death, 301.
    diary, 251, 301.
    end of war, 295.
    Hiroshima strike, 258-261.
    Japanese surrender, 268, 270.
    Nagasaki strike, 276-278.
    Pumpkin bomb missions, 258, 285-286, 291, 294.
    takeoff for Nagasaki, 274, 301.
    weather reports, 257, 275.
Spruance, Raymond, 140.

Stalin, Joseph, 227-229, 243, 246.
Stambaugh, Claude, 105.
Star Wars, 58.
Stealing the Superfortress, 78.
Steenberg, Bill, 220, 222, 224-225, 307, 314.
Steinhardt, Herbert, 149.
Steinhardt, Robert, 149.
Stimson, Henry, 24, 29, 197, 227-229, 235, 243, 247, 284-285.
Stoumen, Lou, 74-76.
Stovall, Bill, 108-109.
Straight Flush, 291.
Strategic Air Command, 24.
Strategic bombing, 22, 24, 60, 70, 102, 160, 231-232.
Steakley, Ralph, 104.
Strong, Russell, 114, 116-117.
Submarine, American, 202, 206-209, 215-218, 220, 222, 237.
Submarine, German, 26-27, 30, 315-316.
Submarine, Japanese, 25-30, 147, 244, 256.
Super Dumbo, 206-209.
Supreme Council for the Direction of the War, 279-283, 287, 289-290.
Surrender of Japan
    acceptance, 293, 295.
    aftermath, 295.
    American calls to surrender, 241-242, 266-267, 272.
    American debate, 284-285.
    announcement, 284, 295.
    atomic bomb influence, 283, 293, 297, 306.
    B-29's impact on decision to surrender, 297.
    coup attempt, 292-295.
    Imperial Conference, 281-283, 289, 291-293.
    Imperial Rescript, 293, 295.
    Japanese debate, 280-282, 287-293.
    overtures to Russia, 246-247.
    Potsdam Declaration, 241-243, 246-247, 280-285, 288-290, 292, 297.
    sacred decision, 283.
    surrender leaflets, 262, 266, 286-287, 290-291.
    terms, 285, 288-289, 293.
Suzuki, Kantaro, 244-246, 280-283, 288-290, 292, 297.
Sweeney, Charles, 257, 259-260, 268, 273-278.
Szilard, Leo, 17-18.

Tachikawa Kempeitai, 309.
Taisho, Emperor, 137.
Target 357, 160.
    see also Nakajima Musashino aircraft plant
Tarawa, 59, 99, 101, 142.
Tashiro, Toshio, 146.

Task Force 58, 99.
TBM torpedo bomber, 207, 219-220.
Teller, Edward, 18.
Terror bombing, 165.
Terry and the Pirates, 119.
The City of Muncie, 183, 186-189.
The City of Phoenix, 309, 312.
The Dragon Lady, 119-124, 129, 188.
The Great Artiste, 250, 257-258, 262, 268,
   272-273, 275, 291.
Third Marine Division, 147-149.
Third Fleet, 207, 221.
Third Front, 33.
3rd Photo Reconnaissance Squadron, 104, 106.
Thompson, K.D., 83.
Three-billion-dollar gamble, 18, 41, 61.
305th Bomb Group, 159, 162.
314th Bomb Wing, 166, 181.
315th Bomb Wing, 321.
330th Air Service Group, 103.
Thumper, 126-127, 160.
Tibbets, Paul, 249-258, 261-263, 271-273, 304.
Tillitse, Lars, 168.
Time magazine, 72, 102, 194, 316.
Tinian, 85-86, 99-100, 142, 144, 158, 166,
   198, 201, 203-204, 216-218, 223, 230, 242,
   245-248, 254-256, 263, 270-271, 273-278, 286,
   291-292, 294-295, 298, 301-302.
Togo, Shigenori, 246-247, 280-283, 287-288,
   290.
Tojo, Hideki, 138.
Tokyo, 74, 77, 103, 112, 122-123, 125-127, 130,
   133, 137-139, 144, 147, 156, 166-167, 199, 247,
   265, 269-270, 272, 279, 285, 287, 290, 292,
   294-295, 305, 307, 310, 314, 321-323.
   air defenses, 105, 125-126, 165, 181.
   air raid casualties and damages, 110, 160, 162,
      164, 180-181, 231.
   Doolittle raid, 29, 108-109, 230.
   first B-29 raid, 106-110, 116, 119, 169, 306.
   flak, 105, 165, 181.
   household industries, 163-165.
   incendiary attacks, 146, 164, 168-175, 180-181,
      313.
   industries and targets, 99, 160, 163-165, 180,
      231.
   invasion defenses, 244, 283.
   invasion plans, 233-234, 236-237.
   January 27, 1945, raid, 123-127.
   Kempeitai prison, 168, 179.
   Prisoner of War camp, 105, 127, 130, 132-133,
      178.
   propaganda leaflets, 238-239, 241, 286-287,
      290.
   reconnaissance of, 104-106, 120, 136, 152.
   targets, 104, 106-107, 110, 163-165, 180, 286.
   target for atomic bomb, 243, 286, 291.
   Tokyo military prison, 146, 313.
   war production, 163-165.
   weather, 157, 160.
Tokyo Bay, 105, 133, 145-146, 178, 201, 313,
   321-323.
Tokyo Kempeitai, 146, 168, 173, 179.
Tokyo Military Prison, 146.
Tokyo plain, 234, 237, 244.
Tokyo Rose (radio propagandist), 105.
Tokyo Rose F-13, 105-106, 122, 152.
Tone, 222.
Torpedo Squadron 34, 219.
Towers, Les, 47.
Toyoda, Soemu, 290, 292.
Trabold, Charles
   background, 79.
   best friend, David McNeley, 88-89, 117.
   bombardier items on eBay, 89-96.
   combat, 79-84, 223.
   crew photo, 87, 89, 97.
   death, 322.
   eBay items, 78-79, 84, 86-96.
   fate, 92, 95, 97, 188.
   flak, 80-81.
   friendship with author, 98, 322.
   food, 81-82.
   gunnery, 79-81, 84.
   introduction to author, 79.
   naming their B-29, 80.
   near crash, 85-86.
   parachute, 78-79, 83-84.
   shooting down fighters, 81.
   telephone poles, 86, 88.
   training, 79.
   woodworking, 97.
   YB-29, 80.
Treaty of Versailles, 18.
Trinity test site, 226, 229.
Tripartite Pact, 22.
Triple Intervention, 293.
Truman, Harry
   Allied reply to Japan, 284-285.
   atomic bomb decision to use, 243, 304.
   atomic bomb messages, 227-229, 263-264.
   atomic bomb private thoughts, 243, 264.
   atomic bomb test, 227-228.
   atomic bomb statements, 264, 266-268, 270,
      272.
   diary entries, 227, 243.
   ending the war without Russia, 229.
   invasion casualties, 228, 233-236, 243-244.

invasion strategy, 233-237.
meeting with Hoover, 235.
meeting with Joint Chiefs of Staff, 233-237.
meetings with Stalin, 228-229, 246.
Operation Downfall, 236-237.
Potsdam Conference, 227-229, 247.
Potsdam Declaration, 241-242, 266-267.
R-3350 engine investigation, 47.
strategy to defeat Japan, 232-237.
surrender negotiations, 246, 284-285.
tour of Berlin, 227.
Tsuchikura, Hidezo, 174-175, 177-178.
Tsukakoshi, Hisashi, 172-173.
Tu-4 bomber, 78.
12th Air Division, 265.
20th Air Force, 69-70, 86, 102, 107, 158, 162, 166, 212, 239-240, 258, 285, 302, 316.
23rd Marine Regiment, 141.
25th Marine Regiment, 141.
27th Marine Regiment, 141.
28th Marine Regiment, 141-142, 151.
29th Bomb Group, 187.
Twining, Nathan, 240.

U-boats, 26-27, 30, 315-316.
Ueno Zoo, 179.
Ugaki, Matome, 269.
Ultra, 107.
Umezu, Yoshijiro, 282, 287, 290, 292.
Unbroken, 105.
United States Strategic Air Forces in the Pacific, 240.
Uranium, 17, 245-247, 269.
Uranium-235, 245-246.
U.S. Congress, 19-21.
U.S. Army, 18, 24, 99, 127, 137, 148, 152, 159, 164, 178, 190, 196-197, 213, 215, 234, 237, 285, 312, 314.
U.S. Army Air Corps, 18-22, 41, 47, 158-159, 191, 212, 285.
U.S. Army Air Forces, ix, xii, 27, 35-36, 38, 47, 56-57, 62, 64, 87, 105, 140, 143, 160, 183, 191, 231, 245, 300.
  Air War Plans Division, 24, 29.
  atomic strike force, 249-250.
  B-29 orders, 23, 27, 36.
  blockade and bombardment of Japan, 233, 237.
  defending the United States, 29.
  establishment, 24.
  Japanese post-war interrogations, 297.
  overseas operations, 59, 239-240.
  strength, 29, 59, 239-240.
  training accidents, 58-59.
  XB-29 crash report, 49-52.

U.S. Marines, 30, 59, 101-102, 106, 138-143, 145-146, 148-150, 155-156, 230, 256.
U.S. Navy, xii, 19, 30, 70, 99, 101, 104, 162, 207-208, 220, 237.
U.S. Pacific Fleet, 25, 207.
USS Augusta, 263.
USS Blackfish, 216.
USS Independence, 224.
USS Indianapolis, 229-230, 242, 246, 256.
USS Monterey, 220.
USS Underhill, 221.
USS Whale, 206-211, 215-220, 222-225, 307.
USS Winged Arrow, 217.

VII Fighter Command, 147.
Van Kirk, Theodore, 253, 258.
Vivisections, 314.
Vladivostok, 78.

Wake Island, 25.
Walker, 57-58.
War bonds, 34.
War crimes, 118, 312-313.
War Department, xii-xiii, 19, 23, 130, 197, 243.
War production, 30, 33-34, 163, 232.
Washington, D.C., 17, 38, 48, 61, 69, 104, 137, 158, 166, 197, 227-228, 232, 237, 240, 254, 263-264, 285, 294-295.
Washington, George, 32.
Watkins, Marvin, 313.
Watson, Edwin, 17.
Weaponeer, 252, 255.
Wells, Edward, 22.
Wells. H.G., 261.
Wendover, 249, 274.
Werewolf, 127.
Wersebe, Ed, 45, 52.
Western Defense Area, 26.
White House, 17, 142, 232-235, 247, 266, 284.
White, Theodore, 72.
Wichita, 35, 39, 53, 62, 64, 67, 78, 256.
Wigner, Eugene, 18.
Williams, David, 134.
Williams, Warren, 195, 197.
Wilson, Donald, 112-114.
Windberg, Harold, 208.
Wittee, Harrison, 114-116.
Wizard of Oz, 19.
Wolfe, Kenneth, 47-48, 53, 56-57, 60-61, 67-68, 70, 73, 76, 158, 160.
Women Airforce Service Pilots (WASPs), 35.
Women in Defense, 35.
World War II Veterans, xi, xiv, 182, 218, 303.
Wright Aeronautical Corporation, 41, 48.

Wright Brothers, 18, 23, 48.
Wright Field, 47, 56, 64.
Wright, George, 108.

XB-29
    aerodynamics, 23-24, 38, 40, 42, 49.
    Allen's concerns, 43.
    arrival in Kansas, 53.
    construction, 22-23, 34-36.
    contracts, 21-22.
    crash, 43-45.
    crash causes, 51-52.
    crash investigation, 47, 49-52.
    crash statement, 46.
    design, 21-24.
    design changes, 52, 63.
    engine failures, 41-45.
    engine fires, 42-44.
    first flight, 38.
    flight test program, 39-40, 42-43, 46, 52.
    model 345, 20-21, 41.
    project, 21-22.

second prototype first flight, 42.
special project, 47-48.
third prototype near crash, 52-53.
wing design, 23.
XB-35, 24.
XB-36, 24.
XX Bomber Command, 70-71, 158-159.
XXI Bomber Command, 102-104, 106, 155,
    157-160, 162, 164, 170, 201, 230, 234, 237,
    239-240.

Yalta conference, 228.
Yank magazine, 74, 108, 164.
Yawata, 55, 73, 75, 77, 99, 107, 110, 120, 158, 230.
YB-29, 59, 67, 80.
Yokohama, 231, 237.
Young, Donald, 252-253.

Zachary Taylor National Cemetery, 127.
Zamperini, Louis, 105.
Zero (fighter), 57, 109.
Zimmerman, Robert, 221-222, 224, 307, 313.